RURAL ROOTS OF REFORM BEFORE CHINA'S CONSERVATIVE CHANGE

China's economic and military rise dominates discussions of the world's most populous country. Resilient authoritarian government is credited with great successes, but this book expands the discourse to include governance by village heads – who often ignored central politicians. Chinese reforms for prosperity started circa 1970 under rural and suburban leaders. They could act autonomously then because of unexpected political and technological opportunities. Their localization of power eroded socialist controls. Since 1990, central leaders have tried to reverse reforms made by resilient local bosses.

New findings, especially from the Yangzi delta around Shanghai, challenge the top-down approach to thinking about governance. As Deng Xiaoping admitted, the nation's spurt of prosperity began in local communities rather than Beijing. Reforms for triple cropping and rural industrialization started long before Mao's death (not in 1978, the date most writers cite). Country factories competed with state industries for materials and markets. Shortages by the 1980s led to inflation, government deficits, unofficial credit, unenforceable planning, illegal migrations, then international exports – and severe political tensions. After 1990, Party leaders sought policies to build a Leninist regime that is mostly post-socialist. These reactionary changes have lasted into the era of Xi Jinping. China's reforms and subsequent changes can be understood as results of unintended situations not just ideas, and local not just central politics.

This book will interest students and scholars of Chinese, as well as any readers who wonder about comparative development.

Lynn T. White III is an emeritus professor and senior research scholar in the Woodrow Wilson School, Politics Department, and East Asian Studies Program of Princeton University.

RURAL ROOTS OF REFORM BEFORE CHINA'S CONSERVATIVE CHANGE

Lynn T. White III

LONDON AND NEW YORK

First published 2018
by Routledge
2 Park Square, Milton Park, Abingdon, Oxon OX14 4RN

and by Routledge
711 Third Avenue, New York, NY 10017

Routledge is an imprint of the Taylor & Francis Group, an informa business

© 2018 Lynn T. White III

The right of Lynn T. White III to be identified as author of this work
has been asserted by him in accordance with sections 77 and 78 of the
Copyright, Designs and Patents Act 1988.

All rights reserved. No part of this book may be reprinted or reproduced or
utilized in any form or by any electronic, mechanical, or other means, now
known or hereafter invented, including photocopying and recording, or in
any information storage or retrieval system, without permission in writing
from the publishers.

Trademark notice: Product or corporate names may be trademarks or
registered trademarks, and are used only for identification and explanation
without intent to infringe.

British Library Cataloguing-in-Publication Data
A catalogue record for this book is available from the British Library

Library of Congress Cataloging-in-Publication Data
Names: White, Lynn T., III, 1941– author.
Title: Rural roots of reform before China's conservative change / by Lynn
    T. White III.
Description: Abingdon, Oxon ; New York, NY : Routledge, 2018. |
    Includes bibliographical references and index.
Identifiers: LCCN 2017060133 | ISBN 9780815371045 (hbk) |
    ISBN 9780815371052 (pbk) | ISBN 9781351247696 (ebk)
Subjects: LCSH: Decentralization in government—China. |
    Central-local government relations—China. | Local government—
    China. | Agriculture and state—China. | Economic
    development—China. | China—Politics and government—
    1976–2002. | China—Politics and government—2002–
Classification: LCC JQ1509.5.D42 W47 2018 | DDC 320.80951—dc23
LC record available at https://lccn.loc.gov/2017060133

ISBN: 978-0-8153-7104-5 (hbk)
ISBN: 978-0-8153-7105-2 (pbk)
ISBN: 978-1-351-24769-6 (ebk)

Typeset in Bembo
by Apex CoVantage, LLC

for
my teachers and
my students, from whom I have learned much

CONTENTS

List of tables	*ix*
Acknowledgements	*xi*
Abbreviations and acronyms	*xiv*
Romanization	*xvi*
Prologue: Local-political growth, behavioral periodization, and policy reactions	*xviii*
1 Farmers start the end of the centralist revolution	1
2 Ex-peasant industrialists end most socialist planning	38
3 Varied managers reform China's power structure	57
4 Countryside businesspeople modernize China's markets	81
5 Rural leaders beat urban planners	91
6 Tax collectors and subsidizers shape central-local relations	125
7 Budgeteers face the 1980s crisis	158
8 Owners manage urban corruption and companies	174
9 Bankers arrange credit, savings, and depreciation	219

viii Contents

10	Technicians innovate to sell quality products	253
11	Long-distance traders and Jiangnan regionalists create new markets	267
12	Service providers rule collective and private enterprises	314
13	Migrants staff China's reform economy	333
	Epilogue: local and medial powers, not just central powers; situations, not just ideas	364
	Index	*371*

TABLES

1.1	Indices of reported official state procurement prices for grains and industrial crops	17
1.2	Reported industrial portions of total output, Chuansha County, Shanghai	20
1.3	Songjiang County, Shanghai, 1965–1987, population and output	22
1.4	Development in Qingpu County, Shanghai, 1970–1987	24
2.1	Industrial percentages of total product at Tangjiacun	40
2.2	Tangqiao rural industrialization, Suzhou Prefecture, 1967–1985, and rural industrialization in all of Jiangsu, 1970–1985	42
2.3	Reported industrial percentages of gross output values	51
3.1	Rural industry or rural agriculture: a partial trade-off	61
3.2	Percentages of gross value in PRC industrial output by ownership type	62
5.1	Percentage of raw materials for Shanghai steelmaking allocated by state plans	98
5.2	Reported shortages of materials in Shanghai, 1985	98
5.3	Sources of reported Shanghai income	98
6.1	State extraction, by province	126
6.2	Shanghai's relative non-use of budgeting	134
6.3	Major cities' budgetary revenues over budgetary expenditures and budgetary revenues minus expenditures per person in Shanghai, Jiangsu, and Zhejiang	135
6.4	Shanghai's budgetary expenditures and revenues through early reforms	140
6.5	Shanghai revenues, 1952–1990, with comparisons	141
6.6	Provincial revenue retention and subsidy norms, 1980–1983	145

x Tables

7.1	Profits and taxes realized from local state-owned industries per 100 yuan of capital	161
7.2	Income and realized profits and taxes per 100 yuan of capital in the cities that govern all Jiangnan rural counties, 1985	163
7.3	Shanghai revenues decline, 1980–1987	165
8.1	Shanghai and other provinces' industrial output portions by ownership type, 1980 and 1990	184
8.2	Percentages of GDP by ownership sector in Shanghai, 1978–1989	185
8.3	Quick rise of the production responsibility system, 1979–1982, in Shanghai industries	195
8.4	Declining vertical and rising horizontal integration in PRC urban economies	211
9.1	State investment in Shanghai	224
9.2	Interest rates on different Shanghai bank loans	226
9.3	Ownership composition of fixed capital investment	227
9.4	Loans and production, East China province units, first half of 1986 only	233
9.5	Interest offered to different Shanghai bank depositors	235
9.6	Consumption and disposable income, by province	236
9.7	Shanghai residents' private deposits in banks	237
10.1	Declining Shanghai share of China's exports	259
11.1	1983 Economic indices for provinces in the expanded Shanghai Economic Zone	291
11.2	Yangzi delta growth rates, in national perspective	301
12.1	Labor productivity in Shanghai services and manufacturing	315
12.2	The fall and rise of Shanghai's service sector, 1952–1992	317
12.3	Street factories in Shanghai, 1977, by product	322
13.1	Registered migration to and from Shanghai	334
13.2	Migration to and from Yangzi delta cities: Shaoxing and Xiashi	338
13.3	Reported transient populations of PRC cities during reforms	353

ACKNOWLEDGEMENTS

I could never have done this research without the loving encouragement of my wife, Barbara-Sue White, who has published books about Hong Kong and shared my own experiences there and in Shanghai. The book is dedicated to my teachers. It is likewise dedicated to a younger generation of scholars: my graduate and undergraduate students, including many who are now tenured in our common field. I have learned a great deal from them. The lives of these friends will be affected, for better or worse, by China's political development. This book about the roots of Chinese reform, and then its change in reaction to them, should interest many readers.

Warm thanks go to all my helpers, some anonymous and many in a list below, who have read parts of this manuscript or have in various ways improved it. I am especially thankful to Hong Kong University's Centre for Asian Studies, which is now part of the HKU Institute of Humanities and Social Sciences, and to its successive heads Edward Chen, Wong Siu-lun, and Angela Leung. The cover picture was taken near Suzhou in the 1980s. Generous logistical help also came from Priscilla Roberts in Hong Kong. Generous logistical help also came from Priscilla Roberts in Hong Kong. Jimmy Wang, a computer guru in Princeton's Woodrow Wilson School, has provided invaluable support over decades for all my projects including this book. My main formal affiliation has been with Princeton, but informally I am still connected to UC Berkeley's Center for Chinese Studies, where long ago I was a graduate student.

Further thanks go to Douglas Merwin, to referees 'blind' and seeing, to Routledge editors Stephanie Rogers, Georgina Bishop, and Luke Allen, as well as copy editor Rodney Williams and project manager Tina Cottone. I am also grateful to Routledge for permission to use material from my 1998 book *Unstately Power: Local Causes of China's Economic Reforms*, which won the Association for Asian Studies prize, named for my former teacher Joseph Levenson, as the best book of its

xii Acknowledgements

year concerning twentieth-century China. From this later viewpoint of 2018, it is clear that much of China's politics in the new century has been a centralist reaction to the partial localization of power that book described. The dynamics of this change now call for some revision of the nearly existential tendency to treat politics as central in China (*Zhongguo*). I hope that Chinese and Western readers who have used that normal discourse are not so offended by my expansion of it that they think I am rejecting it wholly. I appreciate their work too and am only suggesting more attention to local politics that has sometimes been very powerful because large numbers of local Chinese leaders faced similar unintended contexts and acted in parallel with each other.

I also thank many wonderful colleagues who recently or long ago provided pointers to literature, to people I consulted, or to other ways for improving this book: Michael Agelasto, David Bachman, Joseph Bosco, John P. Burns, Chai Ling, Chan Kam-wing, Chan Man-hung, Chen Dingyue, Chen Haowen, Chen Jing, Chen Shenshen, Chen Yuqun, Chen Xiaoping, Cheng Chaoze, Joseph Cheng, Cheng Kaiming, Cheng Xiaonong, Chiao Chien, Gregory Chow and Paula Chow, Tom Christensen, Donald Clarke, Roger Cliff, Alison Conner, Frank Dikötter, Anthony Diller, John Dolfin, Audrey Donnithorne, Joshua Eisenman, Fu Qiangguo, Mary Gallagher, Rick Glofcheski, Julia Gramer, Gu Mingyuan, Guo Xiaolin, Carol Hamrin, Chad Hansen, Norma Harris, Nancy Hearst, He Deyu, Claire Hollingworth, Marlowe Hood, Huan Guocang, Philip C. C. Huang, Hung Shufen, John Kamm, London Kirkendall, Kuah Khun Eng, Y.Y. Kueh, Erik Martínez Kuhonta, H. K. Kwan, Reginald Y. W. Kwok, Lee Chin-chuan, Elida Lee, Lee Ying-fen, Beatrice Leung, C. K. Leung, Li Cheng, Li Wuwei, Li Xiaodong, Li Xuecheng, Liao Nien-fu and Chen Lu-ning, Lin Hao, Lin Lu, Lin Quanshui, Liu Ching-chih, Lu Feiyun, Lü Zheng, Ma Da, Neysun Mahboubi, Meng Hongwei, Alice L. Miller, Erik Mobrand, Tom Moore, John Norris, Pei Minxin, Peng Dajin, Peng Wen-shien, Judith Polumbaum, Qin Jianxun, Stanley Rosen, Sigrid Schmalzer, David Shambaugh, Shi Qingkai, Shi Qingsheng, Shih Hsiao-yen, Shu Hanfeng, Shu Renqiu, Sia Yin-ching, Ronald Skeldon, Song Jun, Su Chi, Su Songxing, Antony Tatlow, Wang Chongfang, Wang Gungwu, Wang Shaoyun, Xia Jinxiong, Wang Juan, Wang Xu, Philip Wickeri, Adam Williams, Linda Wong, Wong Siu-lun, Wu An-chia, Wu Guoguang, Yang Bucai, Yang Dali, Yang Meirong, Yang Sizheng, Yao Liang, Yao Tinggang, John Yasuda, Yen Chengzhong, Yu Shutong, Zhang Jian, Zhang Linlan, Zheng Yongnian, Zhang Yongwei, Zhang Yue, Zhou Ji, Zhou Jianping, Zhou Ruijin, Zhu Xingqing, Zhuang Ming, Zou Fanyang, and several PRC citizens who prefer not to be listed. Special thanks go to Julie Yuwen Chen of the University of Helsinki, who in 2016 invited me to present an earlier version of this text – and to two of my former co-authors on other projects, Kate Xiao Zhou and Cheng Li.

The author's debts to further institutions are heavy: to the Academy of Social Sciences in Shanghai, the Institute of International Relations at National Chengchi University and the Academia Sinica on Taiwan, Universities Service Centre at the Chinese University of Hong Kong – and for financial help, the Harry Frank Guggenheim Foundation, the Chiang Ching-kuo Foundation, and Princeton University.

I remain solely guilty as the perpetrator. This book contains strongly stated views. The paradigms and definitions used here are different from those employed by many other scholars. My hope is that they will become interested in these as supplements to their previous principles. I am also in debt to the many researchers who are cited in footnotes, from whose varied and wonderful works I continue to learn.

Lynn T. White III
Princeton and Berkeley

ABBREVIATIONS AND ACRONYMS

BR	*Beijing Review*
CCP	Chinese Communist Party
CD	*China Daily*, Beijing
CNA	*China News Analysis*, Hong Kong
CPSU	Communist Party of the Soviet Union
CR	Cultural Revolution
CYL	Communist Youth League
EE	*Eastern Express*, Hong Kong
FBIS	*Foreign Broadcast Information Service*, Washington
FEER	*Far Eastern Economic Review*, Hong Kong
GMRB	*Guangming ribao* (Bright Daily), Beijing
IT	information technology
JFRB	*Jiefang ribao* (Liberation Daily), Shanghai
Jiangnan	Wu-dialect rich flatland south of the Yangzi River (esp. Sunan and Zhebei)
JJRB	*Jingji ribao* (Economic Daily), Beijing
JJYJ	*Jingji yanjiu* (Economic Research), Beijing
KMT	Kuomintang (Nationalist Party; a.k.a. Guomindang)
LDB	*Laodong bao* (Labor News), Shanghai or Beijing
LW	*Liaowang* (Outlook), Beijing
NCNA	*New China News Agency*, Shanghai unless noted
NPC	National People's Congress
PLA	People's Liberation Army
Post	*South China Morning Post*, Hong Kong
PRC	People's Republic of China
QNB	*Qingnian bao* (Youth News), Shanghai and Beijing
RMRB	*Renmin ribao* (People's Daily), Beijing

SF	*Shanghai Focus* (*China Daily* weekly supplement), Shanghai
SHGYJJB	*Shanghai gongye jingji bao* (Shanghai Industrial Economy)
SHJJ	*Shanghai jingji* (Shanghai Economy)
SHJJDB	*Shanghai jingji daobao* (Shanghai Economic Herald)
SHJJNJ##	*Shanghai jingji nianjian, ##* (Shanghai Economic Yearbook, year number)
SHJJYJ	*Shanghai jingji yanjiu* (Shanghai Economic Research)
SHTJNJ##	*Shanghai tongji nianjian, ##* (Shanghai Statistical Yearbook, year number)
SJJJDB	*Shijie jingji daobao* (World Economic Herald), Shanghai
SME	small and medium enterprise
Sunan	Southern Jiangsu Province, originally including Shanghai
WHB	*Wenhui bao* (Wenhui News), Shanghai [or Hong Kong, if noted]
XDRB	*Xingdao ribao* (Singapore Daily), Hong Kong
XMWB	*Xinmin wanbao* (Xinmin Evening News), Shanghai
XWB	*Xinwen bao* (News Report), Shanghai
XWRB	*Xinwen ribao* (News Daily), Shanghai
ZGQNB	*Zhongguo qingnian bao* (China Youth News), Beijing
ZGTJNJ##	*Zhongguo tongji nianjian, ##* (Chinese Statistical Yearbook, year number)
Zhebei	North Zhejiang Province (esp. as distinct from Wenzhou, further south)
ZW	*Zhanwang* (Prospect), Beijing

ROMANIZATION

The *pinyin* romanization system may at first seem extremely odd to English speakers, because it uses frequent *c*'s, *q*'s, *x*'s, *z*'s, and *zh*'s with unexpected sounds. It is even more counterintuitive than the Wade-Giles system, an older alternative that was developed by British diplomats and missionaries. But *pinyin* has become standard in the People's Republic of China and in most publications. It has also replaced traditional "post office" spellings (Peking is now Beijing, Amoy is Xiamen, even Hongkong is occasionally Xianggang). A brief table can help people gain confidence about saying words in *pinyin*. The system needs a bit of study because of the five consonants listed above and below. But these can easily be learned.

The basic unit of Chinese is the syllable (which is always written with a single character). When you see a romanization, it is usually either one or two syllables long. If it is two, the division should be obvious in the lettering. Pronounce each syllable as a unity. Try not to extend diphthongs (elided vowels) so that they sound like two syllables.

Chinese, like any other language, has a distinctive sound system. So exact equivalences to English are hard to reproduce on a printed list. Tones (that change or hold pitches within syllables) are not covered by most romanization systems, including pinyin. The aim here is only to give people who know other languages enough accuracy to be brave when referring to Chinese words. Below are nine signs for sounds that most differ from what English speakers expect. The first five are consonants always at the beginnings of syllables. After these, four syllable endings are also listed. A reader who follows this table – and says all other *pinyin* as if it were English – can feel optimistic that the pronunciation will be in the ballpark.

five sounds to start syllables:

c- = TS- (a hard, plosive *ts*- sound)
q- = CH- (also plosive, as in "*ch*ime")
x- = SH- (soft "sh-," tongue flat not rounded)
z- = DZ- (consonant as in "a*dz*e," but initial)
zh- = J- (a hard j-, as in "*j*am"; tongue rounded)

four sounds to end syllables:

– ian = -IEN (have a "*yen*" for this)
– ong = -UNG ("Acht*ung*!" as in German)
– ui = -WAY (as in "s*way*")
– i = -EE usually (but occasionally like "-R," or "-UH")[1]

Pronounce all other letters as in usual English. (So most vowels are long, as in Latin.) Assume that most romanized words have two syllables. The odd symbol in this system is *-i*. A policy for many English speakers is to ignore its irregularities, which are detailed in a note below.

Note

1   Here is a footnote on the *-i* in *pinyin*, and it can be skipped by most speakers of English unless they are interested. This vowel symbol is pronounced in no fewer than three variant vocalizations and stands for the English sounds (in capitals below):

1. "-EE" after *b-, m-, p-* (labials) (the vowel is intuitive and long); *bi, mi,* and *pi* are easy [like bee, mee, pee]
    and *d-, l-, n-, t-* (dental stops and liquids); this is easy, *di, li, ni, ti* [say dee, lee, nee, tee]
    and *j-, q-, x-* (palitals) (pinyin *qi* as "chee," *xi* "she," *ji* as "jee"). BUT rules 2 and 3:
2. "-R" after *ch-, r-, sh-, zh-* (retroflexes) (like the vowel in "shirt"), try: *chi* [say chr], *ri* [rr], *shi* [shr], *zhi* [jr]
3. deep "-UH" after *c-, s-, z-* (dental sibilants) (short "uh" in "uh huh"), try saying *ci* [tsuh], *si* [sz], *zi* [dzuh].

Pinyin without diacriticals does not indicate tones, which are as integral to Chinese syllables as are consonants or vowels. But *-i* is another technical flaw. The *-i* is a case in which the printed symbol does not map uniquely to a single sound. Because *pinyin* is praised for its distinction between palitals and retroflexes (*j-* vs. *zh-*; *q-* vs. *ch-*; *x-* vs. *sh-*), such blitheness about the *-i* is weird.

However, English readers who do not know Chinese can be confident enough if they will only take the trouble to memorize the table above for the *c-, q-, x-, z-,* and *zh-* initials, and (less important) the three syllable ends *– ian, -ong,* and *-ui.* Then they can neglect further problems, including this *– i,* on which Beijing's linguistic advisors erred by allowing too many ambiguities.

PROLOGUE

Local-political growth, behavioral periodization, and policy reactions

> Generally speaking, our rural reforms have proceeded very fast, and farmers have been enthusiastic. *What took us by surprise completely was the development of township and village industries. . . . This is not the achievement of our central government.* Every year, township and village industries achieved 20 percent growth. . . . This was not something I had thought about. Nor had the other comrades. This surprised us.
>
> — *Deng Xiaoping*[1]

Most people think of China's reforms as generally economic and centrally led – but in practice, they began in new local politics. Increased wealth generated change, and the causes of China's rise are political in "grassroots" rather than Beijing politics. Most writers describe the leadership of prosperity as almost entirely central, ignoring that it started with new rural agronomies and factories. A quasi-official mantra holds that reform began in 1978, when Deng Xiaoping became pre-eminent. Deng himself was more honest than to make this claim, as he says clearly in the quotation presented above. He and his "other comrades" were of some importance, especially when they blinked at changes initiated by local leaders; but they did not start China's reforms and rise, contrary to the usual discourse, which as centralist is existentially Chinese but is also adopted by foreign officials and most journalists and academics.

Data on rural factories' production, presented in this book, prove that growth accelerated during the early 1970s, long before 1978, in the places where most Chinese then lived. Its initiators were mostly officials in rural production teams and brigades, nominally under communes. These local leaders transformed many peasants into workers in 1970s and 1980s. After 1989, "reform" (*gaige*) localizations were changed to centralizations, as Beijing reacted with policies attempting to restore its authority. Effective "governance" of crises that threatened Party-state "resilience" became the main issue for officials, journalists, and academics alike. Chinese changes after 1990 were unlike the reforms of 1970–1989.

Evidence in this book shows that:

- China's "rise" began about 1970–1971, earlier than the periodization that dates it from 1978.
- Political actors (local entrepreneurs especially, not just central leaders) were crucial for it.
- It began as new machines facilitated more triple cropping, grain taxes, and rural autonomy.
- China's "green revolution" then legitimated machine repair shops and new rural industries.
- Country factories used capital and materials, causing factor inflation for urban state plants.
- By the mid-1980s, China had to end socialist planning for most industrial inputs and credit.
- Jiangsu or Zhejiang places thrived greatly, linked by kin to Shanghai manager-technicians.
- State and private migrations enlarged mid-sized cities. Families influenced migrations too.
- Few economists predicted China's rise; most theories disregard local leader-entrepreneurs.
- Growth in Taiwan 1950s–1973, Thailand 1985–1997, and Philippine stagnancy were localist too.
- Price inflation worsened 1989 political unrest. Zhu Rongji's 1990s policies stabilized rule.
- State revenue decreases that cut 1980s budgets were selectively reversed in later decades.
- Corruption among Chinese probably aided growth, even if it alarmed foreign investors.
- Resilience in China's polities of any one size mainly meant less of it in those of other sizes.
- Authoritarianism is a trait of organizations of all sizes in many countries, including China.
- Post-1970 "reform" bred post-1989 reactionary "change." The two eras must be contrasted.
- Later top leaders (Hu, Xi) fought localism; the book concerns roots and results of reforms.[2]

To define reforms as led mainly by famous politicians is to ignore too many facts. China's high leaders in Beijing have a clear interest in providing information that justifies this top-down view, because the economic results of reforms have been hugely popular. Reform politics localized previously central powers. In the 1990s, and with increased intensity after 2009 and 2013, the government intensified efforts to restore the "central state." This term is at least a connotation of the country's very name, *Zhongguo*. Beijing unsurprisingly advertises centralism as the most existential, patriotic, basic "Chinese characteristic."

"Rise" and resistance to foreign oppression are the main themes of China's national anthem ('*Qilai!*'), which is of great symbolic importance to the Chinese Communist Party (CCP), which seldom differentiates itself from China as a nation. The official view of the origins of China's "rise" excludes, on an *a priori* basis, the aspects of reforms that are caused by entrepreneurship and political leadership in local Chinese units – notably small and medium enterprises in villages that are not formal parts of the 'state.' In rural China during Mao's years, in places where most Chinese people resided, these units were communal production teams and brigades. They began the process of bringing new prosperity – and new problems – to millions of people. By the mid-1980s, their factories caused price inflation, forcing an end to most central and medial planning of light industries. The CCP remained Leninist in organization; but during reforms, China's resources went increasingly into local networks, as extensive data presented later in this book will show. Changes by the 1990s and later decades became reactionary. The central government reacted to its loss with restorative measures. The "Law on Agriculture in 1993, new Petition Regulations in 1995, and the Budget Law in 1995 [for example] reflected efforts to redress local misbehaving," but these decrees were sometimes counter-effective.[3] Rural protests rose, after links between central and local leaders frayed during the halcyon reform years of 1970s growth and 1980s inflation.

Governance occurs in power networks of many sizes and types.[4] Unofficial "social" or "civil" networks become political when they issue mandates that determine resource use, for example. They have local policies. They often hide information from "higher" authorities – which are then not most powerful, not really higher.[5] State elites are constrained because they rely on local leaders to provide growth and employment.[6] China's "rise" has rural roots, and it has improved the livelihoods of hundreds of millions. It began in local polities during 1969–1976, a period usually conceived as the second stage in the Cultural Revolution. Many intellectuals and officials were hurt then; so they are sure nothing good could have happened during those years. But industrial-commercial prosperity for most Chinese began then. So did central government losses of wealth and power, and these outflows to localities were torrential from 1970 to 1990.

While Mao's communism declined as a basis for CCP legitimacy after his 1976 death, the Party increasingly depended on economic successes and nationalism as major claims to popular support. Quick growth produces losers as well as gainers. Modernization often creates political disequilibria.[7] The most obvious economic loser during China's reforms was the state budget – for reasons that no part of the country illustrates better than Shanghai and its environs. Documentation here focuses on this largest Chinese city, and especially on the larger Yangzi Delta and

"Jiangnan" rural regions surrounding Shanghai.[8] Nationwide data are also offered to show how the reform syndrome soon spread throughout China, although it appeared initially in Jiangnan and in just a few other traditionally rich parts of the country such as the Pearl River Delta.

The central government over many years has repeatedly stressed Shanghai's importance as a base for China's modernization. But the state relied so heavily on Shanghai revenue that growth there was usually slower than in other Chinese cities. Smaller settlements on the Jiangnan flatland boomed heartily throughout the 1970s – largely because their products displaced products from Shanghai urban factories on markets throughout China (and later abroad). Although this pattern created problems for the big-city economic hub, it hardly discomfited the many Shanghai families and very local leaders who readily identify *both* with the metropolis *and* with other parts of East China where they have kin. The other 'hometowns' (*guxiang*) of local Shanghai leaders and technicians prospered throughout the 1970s and 1980s, the era that this book documents as China's reforms.

Continuity from 1950s state consolidations to 1970s-1980s reforms, then 1990s+ changes

Light industry dominated Shanghai's economy before China's revolutionary state was formed in 1949. That is the historical explanation for this largest Chinese city's later high-tax, restrained-growth syndrome. Industries producing consumer products were tools to garner government revenues. As planners gained coercive control of markets throughout China during the 1950s, the state could decree factory input prices low and consumer prices high. They used police powers to fix these rates. The difference, in profits mostly from large urban light industries, went to the state. As those industries were nationalized, they became the major source of funds for the government.

Consolidation of the socialist state in the early 1950s had brought sharp violence against suspected counterrevolutionaries. The Korean War gave the government of "New China" an opportunity to recruit urban youth from bourgeois families on patriotic bases to the Communist cause. Party leaders trusted former guerrilla soldiers better than capitalists; so by 1956, these relatively uneducated cadres, leading a "Transition to Socialism," were put in charge of China's complex urban economy. Many proved to be incompetent managers. So when Mao invited appraisals of CCP administration in the "Hundred Flowers" campaign of 1957, local elites who had been displaced by former guerrillas found much to criticize. Schoolteachers, scientists, businesspeople, deputy mayors, publishers, car wreckers, funeral home directors, professors, doctors, humorists, women's cadres, and some workers and Party members all "bloomed" with particular or general, polite or impolite statements about the incompetence of new socialist managers – who were told to attend meetings and hear these criticisms.[9] Later, in reversals at the same meetings, the critics were accused as anti-revolutionary "rightists." A movie actor then claimed, "Only lies are safe."[10] So the ambitious 1956 "Transition to Socialism" led directly to the 1957 "Hundred Flowers" mutual embarrassment of CCP cadres and their critics – and the job transfers of many members of both those groups to offices in small cities, whence they could boss peasants.

The Great Leap Forward of 1958 grew out of the Hundred Flowers, because its "decentralization to middle levels" was staffed by these two mutually embarrassed groups: The ex-guerrillas who knew that 1957 criticisms of their ineptitude had been accurate, and their critics who finally realized they had been naïve to chastise a coercive regime. Many from both groups were moved from big cities to offices in middle-sized towns. Especially in provinces such as Anhui and Henan, the Leap's "decentralization to middle levels" was so agreeable to some empowered medial leaders, put in charge of millions of new clients, that they followed Maoist central policies avidly.[11]

Later, the Great Leap Forward orders sent from Beijing through them to rural leaders became disastrous. In populous provinces such as Sichuan and Shandong, famine caused many deaths in 1959, but local leaders saw a need for their clients to have enough food; by 1960, they reversed many policies. Household plots, free markets, and cottage industries were partly relegitimated by pronouncements such as the "Sixty Articles" that were drafted by Peng Zhen and Deng Xiaoping in March 1961. Local administrators in some places failed, for their own reasons, to follow the 1960s central government signals for quiet retrenchment – with the result that famine varied geographically. In provinces such as Jiangsu, Zhejiang, and the Shanghai province-level municipality, where rural administrators moderated excesses of the Leap, the Party retained somewhat more widespread legitimacy over the next three decades than it did in places like Anhui and Henan, which suffered holocausts of hunger.[12] Even in places where fewer people died, local peasant leaders knew about the disasters and learned reasons to doubt the omniscience of high Party leaders.

Then the Cultural Revolution of 1966–69 and the "long 1970s" were eras of transformation in China's international as well as domestic politics. After the Sino-Soviet split became public, and with the Kissinger and Nixon visits to China in 1971–1972, China's global policies altered in ways that many other researchers have covered well.[13] Changes of China's cultural life in the 1970s are also fascinating, e.g., in the field of painting; but the present book focuses on political economy.[14]

A decline of government monitoring capacity became acute by the late 1960s and 1970s. Shanghai's most important product, from Beijing's viewpoint, had always been money. Reform policies came not mainly from liberal epiphanies among national leaders such as Deng Xiaoping. Instead, they came from the rise of cooperative quasi-private factories in rural areas whose local leaders the state could not fully control after the Leap and Cultural Revolution. Planners were decreasingly able to deliver rural inputs to urban Shanghai light industries, or to sell urban factories' products in competition with harder-to-monitor self-financed countryside factories.

The slowly growing unavailability of materials and markets hindered urban Shanghai production by the 1980s. That largest city was practically the only

Chinese province-level unit to have a *lower* yearly growth rate in 1979–1939, after "reforms" were officially announced, than in the long earlier time-span of 1953–1978.[15] Official decrees about reforms in 1978 (which were actually hesitant then, as later pages will show) did not reduce central impost rates in Shanghai nearly as much as in other places. More important, the continuing depreciation of Shanghai's capital stock was left basically uncompensated until after the 1980s. High taxes and continuing controls are reasons for Shanghai's relatively poor 1979–1989 performance. The neighboring provinces of Jiangsu and Zhejiang grew at an average annual rate of 5.6 percent in the long 1953–1978 era – but then respectively at 11.0 and 12.8 percent during the following decade, 1979–1989. But Shanghai grew at 8.7 percent in the earlier period; and its rate fell to 7.6 percent in 1979–1989, which was a golden time for most other Chinese places. These results are particularly striking because agriculture (normally a slow-growth sector despite its importance) was a smaller contributor to Shanghai's product than services and industries.

The main problem was not just that fiscal extraction from Shanghai remained high in real terms after 1978. The problem was that the impost rate did not decline after the city's capital infrastructure had already been milked dry. Shanghai industry was not permitted to recuperate from depreciation until the 1990s. Shanghai had much the highest annual growth rate of local fiscal extraction in 1953–1978 (rising 17.5 percent annually on average, compounding over time). In 1979–1989, it was the only province-level unit to record a negative rate of fiscal growth (−0.1 percent).[16] With so little capital investment over previous decades, the city's tax base had not been sustained. Factories had been dilapidated and lost abilities to produce more taxes or good products.

From rural areas, the People's Republic of China (PRC) state during its revolutionary heyday had mainly taxed in grain. But during reforms this national in-kind tax became less effective – partly because grain imposts could no longer be levied in customary annual amounts from an industrializing countryside, and partly because the urban population that the grain tax fed was expanding quickly despite official efforts to maintain residence controls (*hukou*). If 1953 and 1978 are compared directly, the state's net grain tax amount rose only 19 percent over that long quarter century; but the number of urban people depending on this food rose 120 percent.[17] As the technology to grow grain improved, countryside people could avoid famine despite their own increasing numbers. More important, local networks under leaders of former tillers established factories and directed more labor into higher-profit activities in factories and stores.

Rural leaders' memories of the post–Great Leap famine, together with the Cultural Revolution's decimation of town- and city-based cadres who had earlier controlled rural areas, hindered the state's control of most of China's people by the 1970s.[18] A majority of the population was then still working on the land at least part-time. A detailed political ethnography of a Henan village makes clear that many state cadres, during the Leap and early 1960s, were mandated to do cruel things to peasants; so officials came into conflict with China's strongest polities, i.e., families.[19] When top levels of the Party lost control of the countryside because of

xxiv Prologue

early-1960s famine and late-1960s violence against monitors, peasant leaders went their own way. They did so on the basis of no coherent leadership or ideology, but they acted in parallel with each other because they faced similar situations.[20] The state had more capacity to control people before 1970, when cities did not become larger than the available food supply could sustain, and when rural peasants had to stay in agriculture and out of industry so that big state factories prospered. But by the 1970s, neither of these conditions still applied. The result, mostly unintended, was later called reform.

This book follows, through most periods of PRC history, the types of actors mentioned in the thirteen chapter titles: farmers, rural cadres, nonstate managers, country traders, planners, tax collectors, budgeteers, urban executives, bankers, technicians, long-distance traders, service providers, and migrants. The treatments begin chronologically, to trace developments of China's reforms from their roots in late 1960s and then early 1970s agriculture, through the consequent growth of rural industries, then the rise of state factory input shortages that led to 1980s inflation, and the political reactions after 1989.[21]

Premier Zhu Rongji, together with his boss President Jiang Zemin, created 1990s policies to bring more order to China, so that Party dominance would not be threatened by forces that had become obvious in the 1980s. This rebuilding of "the Chinese Leviathan" took time.[22] As Zheng Yongnian writes, "large-scale systematic privatization," which had emerged in practice if not policy from the 1960s and 1970s, was renounced in rhetoric after 1989. So "China's SOE [state-owned enterprise] sector was strengthened rather than weakened" by Zhu's and Jiang's policies of the late 1990s.[23] But these centralizing changes were unlike earlier localist "reforms" that are misleadingly given the same name. Huang Yasheng recognizes that China's new entrepreneurship emerged largely from rural areas (although he does not find its start in the late 1960s and early 1970s). Huang sees that state-controlled urban firms competed sharply with rural ones. Mainly citing central policy directives, he does not stress the local interests of rural leaders; but he sees that a reversal occurred in the 1990s.[24] Yuen Ang argues that the state led development indirectly, through "enabling reforms." With most other researchers, she sees reforms starting later than they actually did. She writes of "franchised decentralization" and "directed improvisation," without seeing that the leaders of localization were themselves local, as they reduced poverty.[25] Daniel Mattingly shows that, after 1990, rural organizations – traditional lineages, temples, churches, and clubs – allowed local elites to confiscate villagers' land and tax the rural poor.[26] Many other authors argue that economic reform preceded political reform – but they miss too much whenever they neglect *local-political* reform, imagining that the economic change could have occurred without indigenous leadership. Jiang Zemin's and Hu Jintao's centralist clamp-downs reversed pre-1990 localizations. By 2013, under Xi Jinping, conservative change became reactionary as the Party increasingly used methods of centralized coercion to restore power it had lost during the reform era of the 1970s and 1980s.[27] Local leaders then had fewer incentives to try policy experiments.[28]

Xi's period is decisively post-reform, although only some analysts yet stress the empirical basis for seeing it as an era of reactionary conservatism against the earlier reforms.[29] It might not remain so. Xi is a 'princeling,' but his father Xi Zhongxun (d. 2002) arguably became the least illiberal major leader in the first CCP generation, after suffering in Party jails both during a 1935 rectification movement and during the Cultural Revolution.

However the younger Xi's rule turns out, many recent books by Western academics show that economic "rise" has increased demands on China's government. Scarcities of natural resources and civic values leave these demands unsatisfied. They could worsen a "Thucydides trap" danger of Sino-American war if handled badly, and this would greatly delay any possible evolution of fair diversity in China.[30] Even more books by journalists and academics concern domestic development. Dozens of recent publications – a truly astounding number – moot the effective or ineffective "governance" of "crises" in fields as diverse as leadership succession, medicine, environment, or growth. They focus on whether the "China model" will increase or reduce the Party-state's longevity or "resilience."[31] They have been supported by a comparative politics literature on resilient authoritarianisms and "hybrid regimes."[32] A few have related resilience to "democracy." But that liberal concept is no more than a hope of struggle for popular semi-sovereignty anywhere.[33] And it has taken many forms in China: mass populism in revolutionary decades, village elections as prosperity spread in the 1980s, "intra-Party" democracy after 1990, "consultative" democracy now. Recent scholarship mainly moots an ontological "China model" and its ability or inability to sustain the Party-state. Essays in English have appeared particularly from China-born scholars who have raised the quality of research in this field during recent decades and have differing views on this question of regime resilience.[34] Hung Ho-fung finds a "postmiracle China that will grow increasingly assertive in attitude, while remaining constrained in capability."[35] François Godemont sees a "new normal" in China that differs in fundamental ways from the early reform decades.[36]

In this book, which primarily concerns the roots of reform, the main approach is thematic. The first word or phrase of each chapter title refers to a type of Chinese actor who aided reforms. Such an analysis requires historical flashbacks. Each kind of functional actor remained important throughout the two reform decades, 1970–1990, and thereafter. The first focus here is on the start of China's phenomenal "rise" and on the power of local politics and policies that explain China's reforms after 1970 – which led to reactive changes after 1990.[37] This text does not start with an ontological "model," making deductions from that. It starts with behavioral evidence (usually of measurable reforms) and then induces generalizations about local, medial, and central powers. There is no reason here to give priority to either intentions or unintended situations, because they both impelled actors to do what they did.

Notes

1 *Renmin ribao* (People's Daily) [hereafter *RMRB*], 13 June 1987. Emphasis added.
2 Some of these ideas and data, without references to recent debates about authoritarian resilience, were offered in Lynn White, *Unstately Power: Local Causes of China's Economic Reforms* (Armonk: M.E. Sharpe, 1998). That book did not include most of the

xxvi Prologue

propositions listed above, especially about China's changes after 1989. See also Lynn White and Kate Xiao Zhou, "Quiet Politics and Rural Enterprise in Reform China," *Journal of the Developing Areas* 29 (July 1995), 461–90.

3   Juan Wang, *The Sinews of State Power: The Rise and Demise of the Cohesive Local State in Rural China* (New York: Oxford University Press, 2017), 81–82.

4   Fads about "governance" are discussed and evaluated in Lynn White, "Temporal, Spatial, and Functional Governance of China's Reform Stability," *Journal of Contemporary China* 22: 83 (May 2013), 791–811, which is partly inspired by E. E. Schattschneider, *The Semi-Sovereign People* (Hinsdale, IL: Dreyden Press, 1975).

5   Susan L. Shirk, *The Political Logic of Economic Reform in China* (Berkeley: University of California Press, 1993), especially chapter 9, uses a rational-actionist approach to define a political culture in China of local "consensus" decision making. This habit hides information from "higher" (actually less powerful, so behaviorally 'lower') authorities. A language of "levels" in politics can obscure what actually happens. Shirk would prefer the term "political logic" to the word "culture."

6   See Charles Lindblom, *Democracy and Market System* (Oslo: Norwegian University Press, 1988); and Mark Granovetter, "Economic Action and Social Structure: The Problem of Embeddedness," *American Journal of Sociology* 91 (November 1985), 481–510.

7   Mancur Olson, Jr., "Rapid Growth as a Destabilizing Force," *Journal of Economic History* 23:4 (December 1963), 529–52; or Samuel Huntington, *Political Order in Changing Societies* (New Haven: Yale University Press, 1968).

8   Shanghai was once part of southern Jiangsu (a.k.a. Sunan). The term Jiangnan includes all the nearby flatland, including northern Zhejiang from which about a quarter of Shanghai families historically hailed.

9   Lynn White, "Leadership in Shanghai, 1955–1969," in *Elites in the People's Republic of China*, Robert Scalapino, ed. (Seattle: University of Washington Press, 1972), 317–27.

10 *Xinwen ribao* (News Daily), November 28, 1957.

11 On "decentralization to middle levels," see Franz Schurmann, *Ideology and Organization in Communist China* (Berkeley: University of California Press, 1966).

12 Dali Yang, "Making Reform: Leadership, Societal Initiative, and Institutional Change in China" (Princeton University, Politics Dept. Ph.D. thesis, 1992), later *Calamity and Reform in China: State, Rural Society, and Institutional Change Since the Great Leap Famine* (Stanford: Stanford University Press, 1996), op. cit., chapter 3.

13 Works by Odd Arne Westad, Priscilla Roberts, and their co-authors, e.g., O. A. Westad, "The Great Transformation: China in the Long 1970s," in *The Shock of the Global: The 1970s in Perspective* Niall Ferguson, Charles S. Maier, Erez Manela, and Daniel J. Sargent, eds. (Cambridge: Harvard University Press, 2010), 65–79.

14 For more, see works such as Ellen Johnston Laing, *The Winking Owl: Art in the People's Republic of China* (Berkeley: University of California Press, 1989), and Lynn White, *Unstately Power: Local Causes of China's Intellectual, Legal, and Governmental Reforms* (Armonk: M.E. Sharpe, 1999).

15 The only province with a lower rate of "national income" growth was arid Qinghai. See *Quanguo ge sheng zizhi qu zhixia shi lishi tongji ziliao huibian, 1949–1989* (Historical Statistics Collection on Provinces, Autonomous Regions, and Municipalities Throughout the Country, 1949–1989), (Beijing: Zhongguo Tongji Chuban She, 1990), 47.

16 Ibid., 51.

17 Daniel Kelliher, *Peasant Power: The Era of Rural Reform, 1979–1989* (New Haven: Yale University Press, 1993), 51. A relevant argument is Kate Xiao Zhou, *How the Farmers Changed China: Power of the People* (Boulder: Westview, 1996), originally a Princeton University Politics Dept. Ph.D. dissertation. I have learned much from my previous "students."

18 About determinative effects of the famine on decollectivization, analyzed over few-decades intermediate periods of time, (such as most social scientists and most historians for opposite reasons both tend to miss), Dali Yang, *Calamity and Reform in China*. For another

approach, see Frank Dikötter, *Mao's Great Famine: The History of China's Most Devastating Catastrophe, 1958–62* (London: Walker, 2010).

19 Ralph Thaxton, *Catastrophe and Contention in Rural China: Mao's Great Leap Forward Famine and the Origins of Righteous Resistance in Da Fo Village* (New York: Cambridge University Press, 2008).

20 For comparison, Frances Fox Piven, and Richard A. Cloward, *Poor People's Movements: Why They Succeed, How They Fail* (New York: Vintage, 1979).

21 Barry Naughton, *Growing Out of the Plan: Chinese Economic Reform, 1978–1993* (New York: Cambridge University Press, 1995) – although data presented in chapters below show that the analysis can go back further than 1978.

22 Dali L. Yang, *Remaking the Chinese Leviathan: Market Transition and the Politics of Governance in China* (Stanford: Stanford University Press, 2006).

23 Yongnian Zheng (with Yanjie Huang), *Market in State: The Political Economy of Domination in China* (forthcoming), manuscript p. 2.

24 Yasheng Huang, *Capitalism with Chinese Characteristics: Entrepreneurship and the State* (New York: Cambridge University Press, 2008).

25 Yuen Yuen Ang, *How China Escaped the Poverty Trap* (Ithaca: Cornell University Press, 2016).

26 Daniel Mattingly, *The Art of Authoritarian Control: Institutions and Development in Rural China* (forthcoming), and Mattingly, "Elite Capture: How Decentralization and Informal Institutions Weaken Property Rights in Rural China," *World Politics* 68:3 (2016), 383–412.

27 Amy Freedman, "The State of Democracy in Asia," chapter 29, *Routledge Handbook of Politics in Asia*, Shiping Hua, ed. (Abingdon: Routledge, 2018).

28 Jessica Teets, Reza Hesmath, and Orion Lewis, "The Incentive to Innovate? Behavior of Local Policymakers in China," *Journal of Chinese Political Science* 22:4 (December 2017), 505–17.

29 See Carl Minzner and Jeremy Wallace [who do not wholly agree with each other], "Is China's Reform Era Over?" *FP* <foreignpolicy.com/2015/07/28/china-reform-era-xi-joinping-new-normal>, July 28, 2015.

30 Examples of recently published books that relate China's domestic problems to international strategies include: Damien Ma and William Adams, *In Line Behind a Billion People: How Scarcity Will Define China's Ascent in the Next Decade* (Indianapolis: Pearson FT Press, 2013); Regina Abrami, William Kirby, and Warren McFarlan, *Can China Lead? Reaching the Limits of Power and Growth* (Cambridge: Harvard Business Review Press, 2014); Thomas Christensen, *The China Challenge: Shaping the Choices of a Rising Power* (New York: Norton, 2015); Jacques deLisle and Avery Goldstein (eds.), *China's Challenges* (Philadelphia: University of Pennsylvania Press, 2015); Joshua Eisenman and Eric Heginbotham (eds.), *China Steps Out: Beijing's Major Power Engagement with the Developing World* (New York: Routledge, 2018); Jonathan Fenby, *Will China Dominate the 21st Century?* (New York: Polity Press, 2014); Jeremy Haft, *Unmade in China: The Hidden Truth About China's Economic Miracle* (New York: Polity Press, 2015); Mel Gurtov, *Will This Be China's Century? A Skeptic's View* (Boulder: Lynne Rienner, 2013); Martin Jacques, *When China Rules the World: The End of the Western World and the Birth of a New Global Order* (New York: Penguin, 2012); John Mearscheimer, *The Tragedy of Great Power Politics* [that China's rise cannot be peaceful] (New York: Norton, 2014); Li Minqi, *China and the Twenty-First-Century Crisis* (New York: Pluto Press, 2015); James Steinberg and Michael O'Hanlon, *Strategic Reassurance and Resolve: US-China Relations in the Twenty-First Century* (Princeton: Princeton University Press, 2014); Edward Steinfeld, *Playing Our Game: Why China's Rise Doesn't Threaten the West* (New York: Oxford University Press, 2010); an historical summary in Fei-ling Wang, *The China Order: Centralia, World Empire, and the Nature of Chinese Power* (Albany: SUNY Press, 2017); and from a cultural anthropologist, John Osborg, *Anxious Wealth: Money and Morality Among China's New Rich* (Stanford: Stanford University Press, 2013). A fascinating and somewhat less doubtful perspective is

xxviii Prologue

Wang Hui, *The End of the Revolution: China and the Limits of Modernity* (New York: Verso, 2011). A PRC quasi-official view, contrasting with all the above and finding a new era already, is Col. Liu Mingfu, *The China Dream: Great Power Thinking and Strategic Posture in the Post-American Era* (New York: CN Times, 2015).

31 An absolutely startling number of major recent books in English concerns Chinese governance and regime longevity. Their main arguments, showing PRC strengths and weaknesses, are often similar even when their conclusions about China's net success or failure differ. A recent example is Hongyi Lai, *China's Governance Model: Flexibility and Durability of Pragmatic Authoritarianism* (London: Routledge, 2016). Here are more, in order by the authors' surnames: Daniel A. Bell, *The China Model: Political Meritocracy and the Limits of Democracy* (Princeton: Princeton University Press, 2015); William Callahan, *China Dreams: 20 Visions of the Future* (New York: Oxford University Press, 2013); Jing Chen, *Useful Complaints: How Petitions Assist Decentralized Authoritarianism in China* (Lanham: Lexington Books, 2016); Xi Chen, *Social Protest and Contentious Authoritarianism in China* (New York: Cambridge University Press, 2012); Jae Ho Chung (ed.), *Charting China's Future: Political, Social, and International Dimensions* (Lanham: Rowman and Littlefield, 2006); Bruce Dickson, *The Dictator's Dilemma: The Chinese Communist Party's Strategy for Survival* (New York: Oxford University Press, 2016); Lowell Dittmer and Guoli Liu (eds.), *China's Deep Reform: Domestic Politics in Transition* (Lanham: Rowman & Littlefield, 2006); James Fallows, *Postcards from Tomorrow Square: Reports from China* (New York: Vintage, 2009); Xingyuan Feng, Christer Ljungwall, and Sujian Guo, *The Political Economy of China's Great Transformation* (Abingdon: Routledge, 2016); Baogang He and Stig Thøgersen, "Giving the People a Voice? Experiments with Consultative Authoritarian Institutions in China," *Journal of Contemporary China* 19:66 (2010), 675–89; Sebastian Heilman and Elizabeth Perry, *Mao's Invisible Hand: The Political Foundations of Adaptive Governance in China* (Cambridge: Harvard University Fairbank Center, 2011); Pierre Landry, *Decentralized Authoritarianism in China: The Communist Party's Control of Local Elites in the Post-Mao Era* (New York: Cambridge University Press, 2008); Nicholas Lardy, *Sustaining China's Economic Growth After the Global Financial Crisis* (Washington, DC: Peterson Institute, 2012); Cheng Li, *Chinese Politics in the Xi Jinping Era: Reassessing Collective Leadership* (Washington, DC: Brookings, 2016); Perry Link, Richard Madsen, and Paul Pickowicz (eds.), *Restless China* (London: Rowman & Littlefield, 2013); Daniel Lynch, *China's Futures: PRC Elites Debate Economics, Politics, and Foreign Policy* (Stanford: Stanford University Press, 2015); John Naisbitt and Doris Naisbitt, *China's Megatrends: The 8 Pillars of a New Society* (New York: Harper, 2010); Barry Naughton and Kellee Tsai, *State Capitalism, Institutional Adaptation, and the Chinese Miracle* (New York: Oxford University Press, 2015); Jean Oi, Scott Rozelle, and Xueguang Zhou (eds.), *Growing Pains: Tensions and Opportunity in China's Transformation* (Stanford: Asia-Pacific Research Center, 2010); Henry Paulson, *Dealing with China: An Insider Unmasks the New Economic Superpower* (New York: Twelve, 2015); Randall Peerenboom, *China Modernizes: Threat to the West or Model for the Rest?* (New York: Oxford University Press, 2008); Minxin Pei, *China's Trapped Transition: The Limits of Developmental Autocracy* (Cambridge: Harvard University Press, 2008); Minxin Pei (ed.), *China's Crony Capitalism: The Dynamics of Regime Decay* (Cambridge: Harvard University Press, 2016); Stein Ringen, *The Perfect Dictatorship: China in the 21st Century* (Hong Kong: Hong Kong University Press, 2016); David Shambaugh, *China's Future* (Cambridge: Polity Press, 2016); Shambaugh, *China's Communist Party: Atrophy & Adaptation* (Berkeley: University of California Press, 2008); Susan L. Shirk, *China: Fragile Superpower* (New York: Oxford University Press, 2007); Huisheng Shou, *Globalization and Welfare Restructuring in China: The Authoritarianism That Listens?* (Abington: Routledge, 2016); Jonathan Stromseth, Edmund Malesky, and Dimitar Gueorguiev, *China's Governance Puzzle: Enabling Transparency and Participation in a Single-Party State* (New York: Cambridge University Press, 2017); Zixue Tai, *The Internet in China: Cyberspace and Civil Society* (London: Routledge, 2006); Jessica Teets, *Civil Society Under Authoritarianism: The China Model* (New York: Cambridge University Press, 2014); Rory

Truex, *Making Autocracy Work: Representation and Responsiveness in Modern China* (New York: Cambridge University Press, 2016); Kellee Tsai, *Capitalism Without Democracy: The Private Sector in Contemporary China* (Ithaca: Cornell University Press, 2007); Martin King Whyte (ed.), *One Country, Two Societies: Rural-Urban Inequality* (Cambridge: Harvard University Press, 2010); John Wong and Zhiyu Bo, *China's Reform in Global Perspective* (Singapore: World Scientific, 2010); Teresa Wright, *Accepting Authoritarianism: State-Society Relations in China's Reform Era* (Stanford: Stanford University Press, 2010); Xi Jinping, *The Governance of China* (Beijing: Foreign Languages Press, 2014); Guobin Yang, *The Power of the Internet in China* (New York: Columbia University Press, 2009); Guobin Yang (ed.), *China's Contested Internet* (Copenhagen: NIAS Press, 2015); Li Zhang, *In Search of Paradise* (Ithaca: Cornell University Press, 2010); Yongnian Zheng, *Technological Empowerment: The Internet, State, and Society in China* (Stanford: Stanford University Press, 2007). The authoritarian governance success or failure topic varies somewhat less than the titles imply. Many more are in Chinese. See also items in adjacent notes.

32 Just a few examples are: Steven Levitsky and Lucan Way, *Competitive Authoritarianism: Hybrid Regimes After the Cold War* (New York: Cambridge University Press, 2010); Jason Brownlee, *Authoritarianism in an Age of Democratization* (New York: Cambridge University Press, 2007); Larry Diamond, "Thinking About Hybrid Regimes," *Journal of Democracy* 13:2 (2002), 21–35; Paul Brooker, *Non-Democratic Regimes: Theory, Government and Politics* (New York: St. Martin's, 2000); Andreas Schedler, "The Logic of Electoral Authoritarianism," in *Electoral Authoritarianism: The Dynamics of Unfree Competition*, Andreas Schedler, ed. (Boulder: Lynne Rienner, 2006), 1–23; and Jennifer Gandhi and Ellen Lust-Okar, "Elections Under Authoritarianism," *Annual Review of Political Science* 12 (2009), 403–22.

33 E. E. Schattschneider, *The Semi-Sovereign People*, op.cit.

34 The *Journal of Contemporary China*, founded by Zhao Suisheng, has often published relevant research, e.g., January 2017 (26:103). The lead article by Zhao, "Whither the China Model: Revisiting the Debate," 1–17, relates China's export-led growth to reforms, whose bases are the topic of this book. Many now wonder whether economic slowing mean that reforms have ended. On PRC-born scholars' contributions to what we know, Lynn White, "Chinese Political Studies: Overview of the State of the Field," *Journal of Chinese Political Science* 14:3 (2009), 229–51.

35 Hung Ho-fung, *The China Boom: Why China Will Not Rule the World* (New York: Columbia University Press, 2015). I do not take a stance on the proposition in Hung's subtitle. I study comparative politics more than international relations, and no modern country can prosper without both market efficiencies and a regulatory state. Karl Polanyi, *The Great Transformation* (New York: Rinehart, 1944).

36 François Godemont, *Contemporary China: Between Mao and Market* (Lanham: Rowman & Littlefield, 2016).

37 See Christian Göbel, "Regime Building After Tian'anmen: Fine-tuning Indoctrination, Cooptation, and Repression," in *Ideocracies in Comparison*, Uwe Backes and Steffen Kailitz, eds. (London: Routledge, 2015), 198–220.

1

FARMERS START THE END OF THE CENTRALIST REVOLUTION

Could mere tillers, under their local leaders in Maoist communes, conceivably have reformed China? A rhetorical tendency, among most Chinese and among most foreign sinologists too, is to answer such a question in the negative mainly on the basis of traditional ways of talking about power. Farmers are distant from the center of China's state.

Centralism is linked to nationalism in official discourse. *Zhongguo* is often translated in English as "the middle kingdom," but this standard Chinese name for the country has multiple connotations. According to the traditional Confucian view of a legitimate political order, an exemplary emperor's virtue is the natural basis of communal strength. His merit is supposed to inspire his ministers to act morally, and they in turn motivate the heads of families, who influence more local or peripheral others.[1] This concentric image of a righteous state admits no final external boundaries. It is not Westfalian in "international" terms. Instead, everybody's eyes are supposed to look toward a single focus.

China, when conceived this way, gives primacy to the central state. Correct analysis, according to this view, tends to discount evidence that beneficial change in civilization, politics, or prosperity could emerge from peripheral actors such as tillers, who are far from that center. Yet such evidence, when it exists, is fully Chinese. No culture is homogeneous.[2] Facts of a localist sort tend to confirm an understanding of communal change that is officially suppressed. These data tense against the dominant discourse. Understandably, this main centralist way of thinking also affects foreigners who write about China, including overseas officials, journalists, and academics.

This orthodoxy also tends to prioritize ideas, "models," "thoughts," and norms above unintended factors that concurrently affect what actually happens. The standard discourse may have some "Chinese characteristics," but it is not behavioral – and does not cover most Chinese. This nation has the oldest continuous polity on

2 Farmers & the centralist revolution

the face of our planet. "Sons and daughters of the dragon" are understandably proud of that fact. A reason for the country's multi-millennia-long resilience (much longer than the mere centuries or decades of any dynasty or republic) is the coordination of governance that was sustained by academic examinations, tests on ideas, to qualify state bureaucrats. If all effective politics is presumed to be within the state – rather than also in other polities such as villages, local or medium-sized businesses, sects, brotherhoods, or families – then all important causes may lie in ideas and intellectuals. Evidences of causes that are not based in official norms are, according to this paradigm, bits of fact that can be ignored.

This way of thinking has normally been applied to Chinese "reforms since 1978"; but it is demonstrably incomplete. Reform politics started in medium-sized and small organizations. This pattern is not unique in developing countries. Sizes of collectivity naturally relate to each other; and in most countries, small and middle-sized ones are crucial. As Robert Bates points out, "Governments in Africa subsidize fertilizers, seeds, mechanical equipment, and credit" for substantial farmers – with the ostensible aim of increasing food production, but with the additional result of bolstering well-established, modern farmers rather than newcomers, small-scale, and traditional farmers.[3] The same thing happened in China, but the government there too could not control all the networks whose support nonetheless helped it stay in power. It had to accommodate far more policies from leaders of small and middling units than it liked to admit.

In Mao's time, near-elimination of the price of land was the most important subsidy to local cadres. Fields during that period were supplied to rural teams on the basis of institutions that evolved out of 1950s land reforms. Nothing was paid for using plots. Local leases were rent-free, simply allocated. In exchange, cadres (*ganbu*) organized farmers to sell products cheaply. In China, even more than in most other parts of the developing world, such as Africa, local organizations were traditionally well developed, just as the central state is. Chinese rural leaders tend to be proud of their links to the state; but objectively, they also had conflicts of interest with that center. The most obvious such tension by 1970 was whether they could garner more profits from processing rural materials. By that year, country notables were better placed to make gains in this tug-of-war over profits from manufacturing because they also led more triple cropping, which gave the regime (at its many sizes-of-zoom) more grain tax.

"Agriculture is the root" was a Maoist slogan that emphasized the importance to the revolutionary state of peasant support for the traditional grain tax. On the Yangzi delta, even before the early 1970s, two new conditions appeared: First, *the productivity of rural labor rose*, because field work was mechanized quickly. Second, *the state could not take its previous high rake-off* from profits of industry, because it lost much of its monitoring ability through Cultural Revolution abuse of its own bureaucrats in the late 1960s. It also lost much legitimacy among peasant leaders who had followed its orders that had led to the post-1958 famine. Urban state leaders slowly found that they could not prevent the rise of new rural competition.

Field mechanization and a rise of triple cropping in the late 1960s and early 1970s used technologies that freed large amounts of labor from land near Shanghai. Some local leaders established country factories at this time, using raw materials that had previously gone to state industries, which were the central government's main sources of revenue. This was the seed of China's reform, and for a time it weakened the central revolutionary regime that had been run in crucial respects from Beijing. This "green revolution" of the late 1960s and early 1970s came from many kinds of agricultural extension: walking tractors and rice transplanting machines, new seeds for grains that used the sun's energy to yield more edible calories rather than long stalks. "Miracle" rice required more fertilizer (increasingly inorganic) and more reliable water, as supplied by canals during dry spells and tube wells in soggy seasons. Shanghai's rural suburbs in 1965, for example, were only 17 percent machine tilled. By 1972, this portion was already 76 percent – and at 89 percent by 1984.[4] That was explosive growth.

What did the ex-peasants, displaced from fields by these machines, do for incomes? Some – not all – local leaders set up factories, often in team or brigade collectives (rather than larger communes), at first using local labor. Producing cement, bricks, pumps, bootlegged cigarettes, and other easily salable products did not require great amounts of capital or high technology. So in the early 1970s, quick rural industrialization – not planned by the national government and disserving its eventual interests – meant that state enterprises could no longer commandeer all the materials to which they had become accustomed at prices the state companies were budgeted to pay. Later, an export boom, inflation, bribes for procurement agents, government budget deficits, a drop of state control over migrants, and other aspects of China's reforms followed this agricultural mechanization and its most important economic results, rural factories.

Countryside leaders' tacit autonomy: its technological and political bases

Technical extension in agriculture would not alone have guaranteed that local leaders in peasant communities might found factories. Some could respond this way, especially by 1970–1971, because urban offices that the central government had assigned to control the countryside were decimated in the Cultural Revolution. Violence in that movement meant that cadres in cities and towns, who usually monitored rural affairs, no longer were politically self-confident. So brigade and village leaders were liberated, and power localized. Similar localizations had occurred historically in China (notably after the Taiping Rebellion) and in other countries after major spates of revolutionary violence.[5]

Also, many urban cadres, though normally respected by rural leaders for their governmental status, had given earlier advice to farmers that had led to hunger. After the state's partial "penetration" of villages in the 1950s, the famine of 1959–1961 encouraged local peasant leaders at least tacitly to make more decisions by themselves, for their clients not just their official "superiors."[6] Brigades and teams

4 Farmers & the centralist revolution

were added to the commune structure in 1959–1960. The post-Leap famine was statistically the largest human disaster of the twentieth century except for World War II. Estimates of above-normal mortality in China during the famine range from 17 to 30 million.[7] For most Chinese, it was a more important occurrence than the Cultural Revolution – though few publications stress this difference. Scholars have written more often about the liberation of 1949, the ideals and violence of 1965–1969, or economic modernization from 1978 onward. These events all involved changes of ideas at the top of the political system, where intellectuals tend to concentrate their attention. We can ask what we do not understand about history because intellectuals write it.[8]

The famine of 1959–1961 (like the rise of early reforms after 1970) deeply affected peasants. It had multiple causes, important among which was that grain-distribution networks imposed during the Leap were about three times larger than low-waste, efficient units would have been.[9] The famine tended to delegitimate the Party in areas where local CCP leaders had followed orders from their official superiors, and the urban Cultural Revolution amplified that effect. A rural Shaanxi woman, when asked about the Cultural Revolution, replied that "we simply did not take part."[10]

Rural leaders sought both new technologies and new systems for compensating agricultural labor. "Responsibility fields" (*zeren tian*) were introduced extensively as early as the post-Leap retrenchments of the early 1960s, legitimated by the "Sixty Articles" of 1961. Household contracting was maintained in secret at many places through the Cultural Revolution, until it was re-legitimated publicly in the late 1970s.[11]

Hesitant central policies gave political cover for many local leaders to do as they wished – and agricultural extension programs provided material backing. Three kinds of equipment, especially, saved agricultural labor. First, machines to pluck rice seedlings from nursery fields (*bayang ji*) became widely used on the Yangzi and coastal deltas farther south from the late 1960s, and fairly soon thereafter in other rice-producing parts of China. A second major technology involved machines that transplanted these seedlings into larger paddies (*chayang ji*). Third, the same period also saw an increase of hand tractors (*shoufu tuola ji*), which could be used in both nursery and large fields to aerate soil or to pull a plowshare (*li*) or reaper (*shouge ji*). The engines of these light "walking tractors" could be hitched to pumps. With other attachments, they could haul trailers carrying crops (or anything else) to markets.[12]

Energy for some of these machines came from greater supplies of gasoline. Small rural units needed money to buy petrol, a commodity that remained under planning longer than most because capital and control of oilfields was relatively easy for the state to monitor. Electricity was also increasingly used for machines, rural lighting, and wired loudspeaker networks that praised Maoist values. Propaganda discouraged moral hazards inherent in communal organization, such as free-riding, absconding to other places, and shirking work.[13] The total wattage of all agricultural machinery in Shanghai's rural areas rose 19 percent *annually* between 1965 and 1978 – a very high rate, compounded for a long period.[14] From 1979 to 1989, years that most writers describe as the initial period of China's reforms, the annual increase was far lower – less than 3 percent.[15]

This halcyon 1965–1978 increase of electricity use on the extensive fields of suburban Shanghai saved a great deal of labor. In 1965, few or no mechanical planters or harvesters were evident in Shanghai's green "suburbs," which reached far beyond the built-up city. But by 1974, the number of planting machines was almost 9,000 (up from zero a decade earlier). By 1976, it was 27,000. This area in 1974 also had over 1,000 large harvesters, and almost 8,000 by 1976.[16] This sharp increase of agricultural machinery in the Yangzi delta during the late 1960s and early 1970s was a basis for rural industrialization that became the driver of reforms. These machines freed labor. More important in political terms, they gave more local leaders means to seek new wealth and power. Policies for agricultural extension brought technological opportunities – and a higher portion of China's wealth – to rural power networks that later policies could not reverse, regardless of the effects of these reforms on the state. No such basic set of technological innovations had occurred on Yangzi paddies since the Song, when new "Champa" *indica* rice arrived there.[17]

Over time, the 1960s–1970s mechanization of agriculture spread to other parts of China, starting with irrigation. The horsepower of all China's pumps and water-moving machines doubled in the decade before 1973.[18] From 1971 to 1975, local authorities completed 4.5 million small water conservancy projects.[19] Throughout the whole country, the number of machines in 1978 stood at the following percentages of those in 1970: pumps, 246 percent; motorized transplanting machines, 262 percent; large and middle-size tractors, 355 percent; walking tractors, 631 percent; and agricultural pick-up trucks, 914 percent.[20] This growth of mechanization caused new prosperity and "reform" for most Chinese. The flat Jiangnan area around Shanghai was notable only because the rise there was quick and early. In 1970, the machine-cultivated portion of all China's planted land was 12 percent; but by 1978 this portion was over 35 percent. The horsepower of all of China's agricultural machinery was about six times greater in 1979 than in 1970.[21]

In Sichuan, far inland, Zhao Ziyang was Party Secretary from 1975 – and within this reformer's first three years there (before late 1978), Sichuan industrial output rose by 81 percent, and agricultural product by 25 percent.[22] Agricultural mechanization was supported by new technical facilities in rich parts of China, but the most important support, which was political, came from farmers' leaders.

By the mid-1970s, each of China's provinces had a research institute to study new seeds and new uses for agricultural machines. Shanghai and South China provinces set up programs to adapt machinery to water-covered paddies.[23] Shanghai's Chongming County Agricultural Machines Research Institute began in 1971; and by 1974, it was involved in 29 such projects. In the winter of 1975–1976, Chongming's institute worked on new designs of machines to take seedlings from nursery fields. The best aspects of seven different models were combined in a device ready for the spring harvest of 1976.[24] After such improvements raised grain output, local

6 Farmers & the centralist revolution

leaders with support from some central leaders (not including socialist-conservative 'radicals,' the 'Gang of Four' who disliked local power that threatened socialist planning) spread these techniques widely throughout China. But because one result was more grain tax, the radical politicians grumbled more than they acted.

In 1975, more than half (51 percent) of all "means of production" in Shanghai's rural counties belonged to the lowest-level units, the production teams. Only 15 percent belonged to brigades, and 34 percent were commune property. Radical quasi-mayor Zhang Chunqiao, head of the Shanghai Revolutionary Committee, thought the communes' portion was too low and the team (village) portion far too high.[25] But Zhang's views were not shared by most farmer leaders, over whom he just apparently ruled. He fulminated that independent rural factories would eventually weaken the state. He was right (in both futurist accuracy and socialist conservatism), but rural leaders continued to make money and raise local resources. Because they paid increasing taxes, there was little that Zhang or his "Gang of Four" accomplices could do to restrain them.

There are many reasons why agricultural reforms raised output. In the crop cycle, there are diseconomies of scale for labor use, except during "rush" periods such as transplanting and sowing when almost all hands have traditionally helped in the fields.[26] State cadres' attempts to organize the rural economy led to agricultural extension of seed-types, fertilizers, and irrigation that proved fruitful. But they also led to campaigns that ignored what local leaders knew about local clients and local land. After the famine, and especially after 1965, directives from "the center" could often be ignored if grassroots leaders wished to resist them. If the compensation system for peasants depressed labor incentives, a person who worked hard would not necessarily earn much. But after the benefits of agricultural extension were spread, growth in rural China depended on localization.[27] Eventually, many tillers and their leaders benefited.

Reforms for local decision making meant that the green revolution had political results, even though few then or since have talked about them as such. By the late 1960s and early 1970s, localities' power rose. First it did so in rich rural places, such as Jiangnan outside metropolitan tax bases. Within a few years, this tide swept the nation. To some extent, Maoists (sometimes including the shifty Chairman) endorsed it through rhetorical calls to reduce rural taxes and apply policies "according to local conditions" (*yindi zhiyi*). Agrarian conditions for more wealth and power in medium-sized rural units had been growing for some time, but by 1970 more political conditions were also present, although only some local leaders chose to act on them.

Reforms also began during the early 1970s in other fields – ranging from foreign policy and military budgets to media technology and much else. By 1973, Deng Xiaoping reappeared in politics. Deng was First Vice-Premier in 1974–1975, in effect running China's government for Premier Zhou Enlai, who had cancer. It is no longer adequate to assert that "the reforms" began in 1978, or that their usual supporter Deng was influential for the first time in that year.

Also, it would hide far too much to claim that the Cultural Revolution concluded in 1976, rather than 1969.[28] Mao himself declared at the 1969 Party Congress that the CR had "ended" in victory. Consistency was never the Chairman's forte. The most important reform – more grassroots control over resources – began in the early 1970s. This localization was largely an unintended effect of earlier state measures for agricultural extension. It is properly called a localization of power, not a "decentralization." This existentially centralist state, *Zhongguo*, seldom seriously decentralized power. Reforms were political, not just economic, and local leaders for political and technological reasons gained power.

New demographics: ex–field hands whom local leaders could gratify

The green revolution freed a rising number of tillers from hard work in fields. The population rose at the same time, because of anti–infectious-disease service and a lack of birth control under Mao's pro-natalism. Field area per farmer became smaller in absolute terms, because there were more people and because land encroachments from cities and factories were greater than reclamations. There was less area for each farmer to till. Arable land per head nationwide was 11.6 Chinese "acres" (*mu*) in 1952, but it was 6.3 *mu* by 1983.[29]

Pre-reform years gave China more babies; but from 1970 to 1980, China's total fertility rate plummeted by three-fifths, from 5.8 to 2.3.[30] Mortality decline occurred while per capita income was lower than in other countries, as modern medicine lowered death rates. The government did not plan for the long-term effects of these changes, which largely predated 1978. The lower birth and death rates did not impede the reform economy between 1970 and 1990; but as demographic cohorts aged in later years, China's demographic transition strained against economic growth.

Such changes are gradual, and pressure on China's workers was compounded by other factors. Mechanization increasingly replaced manual farming. All of China's 1952 agriculture used 250,000 horsepower, but by 1983 that mechanical muscle was up to 2.5 billion horsepower – a growth of machine energy, over three decades, of 35 percent annually (compounding). Per field hand, this meant 0.14 horsepower in 1952, but 1.5 horsepower three decades later (8 percent annual growth).[31] This change was exponential, although some inland provinces did not see it strongly until the 1980s.

In Jiangnan, population pressure on land became severe early. For example in Zhejiang, the officially categorized "agricultural" (actually rural) population rose from 18 million in 1949 to 34 million in 1982. While the rural labor force almost doubled over this long time, arable land decreased. There were 30 million *mu* of tillable land in 1952; but this figure dropped in absolute terms (to 28 million *mu*) in rural Zhejiang over the next three decades. Per person arable there between 1952 and 1982 dropped from 3.8 to 1.6 *mu*. "As a result, a huge amount of surplus labor power appeared."[32]

8 Farmers & the centralist revolution

The whole wide Yangzi delta by the late 1980s contained over 800 people per square kilometer. This was somewhat lower than the density in rural parts of Shanghai Municipality, but it was still high over such a large area. An economist rued: "As industries and cities develop – big and middle-sized cities as well as small towns – they occupy more and more land. Arable land is decreasing." Near the delta's Lake Tai, tillable land per capita by the late 1980s was 1.2 *mu*, down from 2.2 *mu* in the 1950s.[33] Despite variations in levels of crowding, green regions had ever more people on ever less tillable land.

Improvements in field technology nevertheless caused food production to rise in rich areas. Rural surpluses became larger. Typical farmers (not including rural factory workers, except insofar as they were part-time tillers) after maintaining themselves, by 1974 in Suzhou for example, produced enough grain for one other person, edible oil for two, meat for three, and cotton for eight.[34] An interesting aspect of these estimates is that the largest non-grain crop (cotton) was the main item in surplus. What Suzhou farmers did was to provide inputs for rural workshops that provided jobs for their newly industrialized local kin, or for themselves in slack agricultural seasons. They made more money as factory workers.

In rural Shanghai, population densities were high: roughly one person per *mu* of arable land. The Yangzi delta, in good years on good land, could produce high levels of output: for example, 18 tons of grain per hectare of paddy in one crop of early rice, one crop of late rice, and perhaps another of winter barley or wheat (if enough fertilizer were used and fields were not left fallow). By the mid-1970s, these rates had already been achieved. In 1971, just a few years earlier, the average per hectare production for the municipality had been only 7.5 tons.[35]

So population was up, production was up faster, and some agricultural labor was redundant. As Fei Xiaotong roughly estimated, "If every laborer can manage four *mu* of land, one third of the population was [agricultural] surplus labor in the early 1970s."[36] What were they to do with themselves? Local leaders solved the problem by finding money in multifarious ways, including 'back-alley banks' and traditional rotating loans.[37] They invested in repair shops and then manufacturing plants that hired their clients and could provide extra incomes for themselves.

Triple cropping and the state's implicit contract with farmers

Radicals in the central state and provinces had a totally different solution: just more rice in triple-crop areas, and more pressure on peasants to work in fields only. This plan would have raised output per land unit, facilitated grain tax deliveries, used labor extravagantly, and discouraged rural competition against state industries. Especially in areas with sandy soil, where cotton tended to be the monoculture, growing much more rice was unfeasible, and the traditional tax was usually collected in cotton. But central state cadres mandated the planting of grain wherever they could. Many leaders of farmers saw problems (harder work, higher taxes, and lower returns) in these "radical" mandates to avoid setting up factories.

"Agricultural involution" is a long-term phenomenon, occurring when each unit of land can grow more only with increasingly intensive labor.[38] The marginal return to rural labor then approaches zero. Such a situation can persist for centuries; and state elites can be content with it, especially if the crop is easy to measure and tax. This is the pattern that, after more gradual changes earlier, was broken on the Yangzi delta by the early 1970s, when many local leaders rejected yet more intensive agricultural involution in favor of rural industrialization.

Throughout Jiangnan, output growth had preceded this period. Historians studying rural change in the Yangzi delta as far back as the Ming have not found a long-term rise in productivity per person, despite increases of product per unit of land. Returns to the state, which claims its share as the ultimate rentier, rose over time. Returns to tillers did not.[39] Commerce and traditional industry flourished, so that even in the mid-1950s, some PRC historians claimed Jiangnan was not just "feudal" but had long showed "incipient capitalism" because of technological changes and wage labor.[40] During the 1980s, these ideas came in for stringent criticism from other historians – not on grounds that the delta's economic structure was unchanging, but because of doubts about calling the direction of change "capitalist."

PRC government policies furthered a process of agricultural intensification and "involution" that had lasted for centuries. But agricultural extension policies led to local cadres starting factories. Many scholars, overly impressed by centralist rhetoric, failed to see that capital for new industries was kept by local cadres from more central tax collectors. The green revolution let farmers' leaders pay normal dues to officials while also committing resources to rural enterprises, from which they benefited more.

The state encouraged multiple cropping regardless of labor efficiency, and peasants only sometimes complied. As late as 1959 in Suzhou Prefecture, for example, many fields were still single-cropped annually. But double cropping is an old practice. In rural Shanghai, triple cropping had been reported as a rare novelty in 1956, when a small part of Songjiang County managed to harvest two crops of rice and one of wheat. By 1965, still only 2 percent of arable land in Shanghai was triple cropped. The next years saw pell-mell change; and by 1971, three-quarters of all land in Suzhou Prefecture were triple cropped. Most grain fields in the Shanghai suburbs were also triple cropped by 1971. By 1974, of the two-thirds of Shanghai land used for grain, 83 percent produced three harvests.[41]

Triple cropping nonetheless entails measurable problems for farmers who do it. If grain is harvested three rather than two times a year, total output value near Shanghai rises about 40 percent (rather than by 50 percent as the 3-to-2 ratio might imply). Shorter crop seasons and technical problems lower yields. But triple cropping raises incomes to farmers by an average of only 16 percent – even though much more than 16 percent additional labor is required.[42] Three harvests also increase the need for expensive fertilizers. Rice is practically never attempted for all three seasons on a plot; but it can be planted for two. Rice-rice-wheat is a common pattern, if in some years a field can be fallow or in legumes.

10 Farmers & the centralist revolution

"Miracle" grain varieties have short stalks, putting more of the energy that the plant gets from the sun into making the fruit, the seeds that people can eat. In one- or two-crop regimes, longer stalks were left on the fields to rot and refertilize. The demands of three crops can reduce soil quality. In the three-season pattern, there is less time to grow clover, which can be fed to pigs for another means to enrich the fields.[43] Chemical fertilizers cost money, and the frequent regulation of water level that short-stalk rice requires is tedious. The yield is higher from three crops, but the work is hard – and an increasing portion of it was done by women.[44]

Men shifted from farm work into factories at first more than women did. State pressure on rural areas to feed cities, together with new opportunities for rural families to get income from industries, meant more female paddy workers. "Assisted by children and parents, a Taixian woman can on average manage 0.3 hectares of farm land. . . . But the question, 'Who should be growing crops,' is far less worrisome than the fact that men are not willing to do it."[45] The state harassed local peasants to grow grain. Men largely got their wives and daughters to grow enough so that local leaders would not receive criticism from their bureaucratic superiors.

As Sigrid Schmalzer's 2016 book shows, use of local talents (*xiangcun tiancai*) and of labor increased together with exploitation of the newly available agronomies.[46] "Mass science," applied to agriculture, created more massive prosperity. Han Dongping presents a leftist account of progress in a Shandong village during the officially designated Cultural Revolution years.[47] The total amount of fertilizer used throughout China rose fivefold from 1968 to 1980 (from 100 to 500 kilos per hectare). Mao's "one pig per *mu*" (*yimu yizhu*) was combined with a greater availability of petroleum-based agricultural chemicals.

Seed changes affected output, too. About 12 percent of China's total paddy was planted with high-yield dwarf varieties in 1965, but that portion soared to 80 percent throughout the country by 1977.[48] Adding another crop raises state revenues. It also can increase peasants' dissatisfaction with officials, unless the processes of planting, transplantation, fertilizer spreading, and harvesting are mechanized quickly. The specifics of this situation were not aired in public until long after triple cropping had spread. Frank Leeming found that "Shanghai and Suzhou . . . originated the powerful current of criticism of triple cropping which appeared in the winter of 1978–79."[49] The trouble, from farmer leaders' viewpoints, was that maintaining the fecundity of triple-crop fields required great amounts of inorganic fertilizer, which costs money. These local leaders relayed to tax collectors field workers' complaints that triple cropping led to overwork and illness. Triple-crop agriculture was better for the state than for land fertility or farmers' incomes – unless more tillers could move into factories at least part-time. So for paying the tax, local leaders could drive an implicit bargain with the state to develop manufacturing too. This was a new social contract for rural China.

Triple cropping, if mechanized, provided local leaders with more grain with which to cement their own connections to state cadres and to their local constituents. Three harvests were scarcely feasible without machines and without the active consent and participation of farmers, who in this process became more specialized

Farmers & the centralist revolution **11**

and less like traditional peasants. The only way for the government to get such consent, and the additional grain from the third crop, was to let rural leaders develop machine shops, factories, and sales networks.

"Radical" socialist statists in Mao's time, notably Zhang Chunqiao, were as conservative as Mencius on the need to have full public granaries. For them, this was essential to socialism, and Mao himself decreed slogans about storing grain. To raise production, Mao called for the "complete mechanization" of all agricultural processes. But the unintended effect of such modernist passion, given the technological possibilities of Chinese agriculture, was the need to mobilize more work from field hands. This required allowances for more rural activities that eventually weakened the state sector. Ex-peasants in this situation concentrated not just on the possibility of more income through industry, but also on the fear of more work through triple cropping. Their attitudes have been informally reported in a rural saying: "Better a little factory than a ton of grain to the *mu*."

Mechanization-industrialization became politically more feasible than agricultural mobilization alone. By the start of the 1970s, rural industries were legitimated in localities before all the central authorities unconditionally approved. This development was propelled by technological opportunities and potentials for labor in small communities, not by central government intentions or long-term planning. Many tillers moved out of agriculture. The ones who stayed on the land used more operating capital and equipment, becoming agricultural workers, farmers in more autonomous polities, no longer peasants.[50] Their economic diversification weakened the state, of which they still spoke well. It benefited local power networks more than the central one.

Decollectivization

Most rural communities were still officially supposed, in the Maoist state's ideal, to be "one crop producers" (*danyi shengchan zhe*). Monoculture had downsides for tillers and their leaders, not just because it aided tax assessments but also for other reasons: Single crops were subject to plant epidemics. The opposite habit, mixing species, can be advantageous when the roots of some crops (e.g., beans) foster bacteria that fix nitrogen in soil that other crops (e.g., rice) can use. Mixing species in the same field lets different plants' roots take water and nutrients from different levels of the soil. This practice is also beneficial if the intertwined roots of species help prevent erosion. But collectivized agriculture was mainly plantation monoculture, forgoing those benefits for the sake of easier marketing and taxation. China's reforms for two decades brought a greater range of crops, planted after increasingly independent local decisions.

The commune system was modified before it was abolished. Some local cadres "lent" (*jie*) land to farmers during the early 1970s, lest they face political criticism for "contracting" (*bao*). They continued to underreport actual crop yields, so as to leave a surplus for local distribution. Private plots were expanded without clear authorization from "higher levels." Collectively owned trucks were used to haul

12 Farmers & the centralist revolution

individual households' goods to free markets. Brigade workshops repaired privately appropriated tools. Public storehouses protected households' grain. Peasants spent more time, especially in main agricultural seasons, on their own plots – and local leaders did not dock their work points in collectives. Families used their most active members in private work; they often sent older or less energetic members to be symbolic representatives of the household in communal work projects.[51]

Many parts of Jiangsu adopted "quota management" (*ding'e guanli*) for grain long before 1978.[52] Communes formally lasted, in a few areas as late as the fall of 1983, but they had ceased to have their previous functions before that. Many communes became large townships, and production teams reverted to became villages. Since most were officially "one-crop producers" of rice, an index of reportable decollectivization is the portion of other crops.

Jiangnan was not the only region that saw such change. In Sichuan, too, the process of rural reform began on the Chengdu plain in the early 1970s – before 1975, when Zhao Ziyang became the provincial First Secretary of that huge inland province, which was then China's most populous. As Chris Bramall wrote, Sichuan's "decollectivization was driven from below – and occurred early – but was not ratified by local government until much later."[53] Much of wheat-growing North China was poorer and more conservative, but both agricultural mechanization and Maoist communalism were boosted by the Northern Districts Agricultural Conference, held at Dazhai, Shanxi, in 1970. "Radicals" are often mislabeled as "leftists" in China, but they were rightist conservatives wanting to preserve socialist planning rather than reform it. They were hesitant throughout the country to allow freedom for rural leaders.

As late as December 1978, the Third Plenum of the Eleventh Party Congress passed a resolution specifying that "contracting to households" was illegal.[54] If 1978 is taken as the crucial watershed toward reforms, this was a very odd way to begin them. That part of the resolution was apparently a political sop to conservatives. More reform-minded leaders may have known that such "leftist" (reactionary-socialist) policies would be unenforceable anyway.

Yet the resolution's ambiguous wording had reformist aspects too: It raised the authority of local work teams and suggested that agricultural commodity prices should rise by 25 percent. It encouraged more sideline production and proposed opening more local markets. The Plenum showed political divisions; so local leaders could follow whatever mandates they liked, ignoring the ones they disliked. It would be difficult to prove their activities were much affected by this broadly worded compromise document, despite its prestigious source and frequent citations of it. The same evolution might well have happened on the ground regardless of the Plenum. In fact, it had already happened, begun earlier. Local magnates who wanted agricultural reform had already initiated it. Leaders at various sizes of polity who did not want it were still slow to start it. If any behavior was demonstrably affected by this stately decree, it is mainly to be found in changes in the ways people spoke, not in what they did.

In the spring of 1979, as Daniel Kelliher points out, "The top leadership in Beijing was against the experiment in family farming."[55] That did not stop the trend. High leaders had much to lose from it in the long run; but they probably sensed that if they tried to end it, they would face local disregard. Friedman, Pickowicz, and Selden, writing about a place in North China quite different from the Shanghai delta, report[56]:

> Villagers were not pawns permitting socialist kings to push them around. Local leaders tried to woo and win the resources controlled by higher-ups. Villagers and their allies and patrons among officials also tried, as they had for many generations under various regimes, to dodge, deflect, and blunt the impact of demands detrimental to local interests and values. Those negative impacts gradually eroded the new state's popular legitimacy.

Sometimes centralist directives were unambiguous and stronger. What were the conditions for the power of peasants' leaders? Kelliher proposes that tillers in reform China have exercised power under three conditions. First, they did so if their own preferences were compatible with the state's main announced program at the time, which was economic modernization. Second, many had to act in parallel, even though any attempt to form permanent interest groups or policy factions remained taboo. Third, the Party-state elite had to perceive that allowing local demands to be met would not threaten its secure tenure – at least not immediately. The gradual shift to recognize family farming met all these criteria.[57]

The state in the reform era sometimes won conflicts even with large numbers of people. Over the long haul, however, it did not effectively constrain local power: The top elite's main program was subject to many interpretations; many different kinds of demands could be phrased in terms of "modernization." Also, the CCP's surveys of mass views affected state policy through mechanisms that open documents do not show. Even when protests or petitions, seldom reported in the press, were minor, they often confirmed confidential surveys and caused local leaders to collude against being controlled.[58] Local cadres might tacitly lead petitioners against the state. They can fight what Mao called a protracted war. They are all over the map. If they lose ground on an issue, they come back again later.[59] The state sometimes wins, but centrists are outnumbered. Government strength can emerge from conflicts between reformers and conservatives in localities when they disagree. But if enough local leaders, for their own reasons, keep acting together for a long time, even with scant articulation or coherent ideology, their power tends to prevail.[60]

A crucial local freedom concerned decisions to plant crops from which rural units and their leaders, rather than tax collectors and price planners, could extract money. China's vertical (*tiaotiao*) hierarchies for rural areas were mostly organized to tax and purchase (at low prices) traditional main commodities, especially grain. Therefore local agricultural entrepreneurs obtained better profits by growing almost anything other than the officially designated main produce of the area. Institutional

14 Farmers & the centralist revolution

habits of taxing or requisitioning any year's increase in the main product gave an incentive to use land, instead, for novel crops. A national paper admitted, "As to new industries such as edible mushrooms, flowers, and plants, export of labor services, and so forth, it has thus far not been known which [planning/bossing/'mother-in-law'/'*popo*'] department should take charge of them as their 'anchor.'"[61] Local leaderships – small "area" or "piece" (*kuaikuai*) leaderships[62] – acquired an interest in planting new crops for which state bosses did not exist or were impotent.

So "subsidiary" crops, carrying low or no taxes, had gross real values that nearly doubled (up 91 percent) in the Shanghai suburbs during the short period from 1978 to 1980. Main crops' total value dropped during the same years more than a fifth (down 21 percent). In these two years alone, the value of reported high-tax crops shifted from being 74 percent more than that of subsidiary crops to being 28 percent less.[63] Data on earlier years are hard to find, because subsidiary crops were then below the state's radar. They were grown but not reported. Shanghai suburban farmers changed what they did, aiming to maximize profits.

Innovations in crops or accounting systems met political resistance. Cadres in different villages or towns had different propensities to accede to the wishes of either their Party-state monitors or their local clients, when these wishes were inconsistent. Public, as distinct from tacit, decollectivization generally began in 1978, with the guarantee (*chengbao*) system, under which the state made formal contracts with the moribund communes, and the communes did so with brigades. This process often began early in jurisdictions that had poor land, most of which in Shanghai is near the seacoast.

To the east and south of the metropolis, where the soil is somewhat sandy and cotton was the main crop, the advent of artificial fibers (together with new ways of growing competitive cotton in North China) caused many farmers to switch into raising fish. Others moved into growing vegetables or other activities, not all agricultural. Local leaders, in areas without much tax potential that was obvious to the state, could experiment with decollectivization long before Beijing mooted reforms. Contracts between peasant households and fish-farming brigades existed in East China, according to a report from a poor inland place, as early as 1969. These exchanges did not just presage reforms; they were early reforms. They often violated official policies during the Cultural Revolution. They flourished, despite the radical politicians of that time, and often they could be kept secret.[64]

Nationally, grain production in China during the 1950s was four-fifths of total agricultural output. It was almost the same portion in the 1960s – but gradually it dropped to three-fifths by the mid-1980s.[65] The role of grain in total agricultural output value for later years trended downward: in 1985, 63 percent; 1986, 62 percent; 1987, 61; 1988, 56; 1989, 56; 1990, 58; and 1991, 57.[66] A reason was that farmers, and especially their leaders, preferred to grow non-grain crops that were less taxable – or to manage factory work.

When peasant leaders obeyed the state, as many did, they could fail as synaptic "hinge leaders," serving their formal bosses but not serving their local constituents well.[67] Some Sunan (South Jiangsu) counties in the 1970s increased their grain outputs almost 100 percent.[68] But the costs of new techniques that enabled so much more taxable rice rose 250 percent.[69] If the state kept its low, fixed grain prices, the increment of production was financially unsustainable for tillers, because the costs of inputs for new rice seeds were high. Similar problems affected other crops. When forty workers as late as 1980 harvested vegetables for a whole afternoon and sold the produce at fixed prices to Baoshan County, they received only 30 yuan – less than they had paid for fertilizer alone. The state's price for these vegetables was so low, the head of a brigade said he "had no way of settling accounts" with his farmers.[70]

Some officials' opposition to household contracts, family farms, and grain markets

Household contracting was a traditional option in the 1970s, because families had been the agricultural accounting units before 1949. Households were the basic participants in "mutual assistance teams" that were established in 1953, the "lower-level agricultural producers' cooperatives" of 1954–1956, and even the "higher-level APCs" in 1956–1957. The Great Leap Forward broke this pattern temporarily. The proto-reformist "Sixty Articles" have been traced to 1960 rules in Wuxi (Jiangsu), written by four middling officials and then espoused in central councils by Tian Jiaying.[71] By 1961 at least, the need for grain during the famine caused local cadres to let households work together. The "Sixty Articles" that authorized this have often been attributed to Deng Xiaoping (or Liu Shaoqi), although further scholarship suggests that the ever-inconsistent Chairman Mao may at least have blinked at this much rural privatization – and locally, none of these famous people were in charge. Tillers' immediate leaders made most decisions. In more than half of all work teams, separate families often had particular duties. So the much-publicized contracting by households after 1978 had earlier precedents, but the main conclusion is that villages and local leaders were always important.

Rural land contracting rose not smoothly but in surges, and differently under different local cadres. Decollectivization was a top-down policy in many parts of China during the four years before 1982. As David Zweig writes, Chinese peasants throughout the 1970s had scant sympathy with agrarian radicals' ideas about how they should organize farming.[72] But local leaders were never in full agreement with each other, to judge from their actions. Articulations of policies on family farms came from high state officials, but decollectivization was sometimes opposed by local officials.[73] Many cadres loved the collectives, and their reasons could lie both in their own future career prospects (where Leninist appointment systems that overly dominate academic discussions were important) – but also in their commitments to communalist ideology along with other interests of their local clients. Chinese had for decades been experimenting with both markets and planning.[74] Results were what mattered, and quasi-capitalist forms brought growth along with inequality.

16 Farmers & the centralist revolution

When leaders opposed decollectivization, more of their followers stayed on fields in low-benefit work rather than moving to occupations that provided more gains for themselves and their immediate clients or families. But when local leaders and followers noticed that other places prospered, they tended over time to follow policies that had raised wealth. Locally led decollectivization was a major example of "contagious capitalism."[75]

After the "responsibility system" was announced in 1978, peasants' enthusiasm to contract plots was high, and this freed previous tillers for factory work. Keenness for this combined agricultural-and-industrial reform was so great that "[a]nything decided at night would be acted upon by midnight." Decollectivization was not an idea from Beijing, where factions were divided. The decisive impetus for it came from local farmers' leaders.[76] No less an authority than Deng Xiaoping attested to his astonishment at this crucial reform. He was surprised by the cadre-entrepreneurs, and he described them in a classical phrase: "a strange army appeared from nowhere" (*yijun tujing*).[77] His honesty on this point is shown by his statement quoted on the first page above: "What took us by surprise completely was the development of township and village industries. . . . This is not the achievement of our central government. . . . This was not something I had thought about. Nor had the other comrades. This surprised us."[78] Although most writers still attribute the start of reforms mainly to his leadership, Deng did not make this claim – and he was in a position to know.

By 1980, China's top politicians were unwilling or unable to countermand tens of thousands of local decisions for agricultural contracting and rural industrialization. These political choices were made by some (not all) local leaders, starting in rich Chinese provinces and soon thereafter in poorer ones. Household contracts in Anhui, for example, by 1980 already covered 40 percent of production teams, 50 percent of Guizhou teams, and 60 percent of Gansu teams.[79] Although many foreign and Chinese writers have ascribed rural decollectivization solely to norms from Beijing, that is not the main way reforms happened. Some local leaders thought, not without some reasons, that communalistic socialism might remain beneficial to their followers, and others guessed that conservative Party monitors would influence their future careers more than their clients could. These leaders prevented "sprouts of capitalism" in their areas. Those who guessed oppositely engaged in the quasi-capitalism that became "contagious" among localities.

As township enterprises boomed and cadres realized they could allocate labor more profitably to factories than fields, many leased plots were later abandoned. Enthusiasm for them rose or fell depending on market demands for agricultural products. After the mid-1980s, when markets for meat and other sideline products boomed, "Peasants again showed a renewed passion for land." In Zhejiang, 1.1 million *mu* opened for new fruit orchards and fish breeding in 1986. There was also more specialization between different rural areas. Zhejiang's Hezhou Prefecture, for example, grew more tangerines to supply its two new citrus-processing factories. Zhoushan Prefecture raised more shrimps, fish, and shellfish than before. In classic market style, "all products for which the prices were liberalized [i.e., could not be prevented from rising] were developed relatively early, at a quicker pace, and in greater varieties."[80]

State procurement price changes for grains and industrial crops are a rough index of the relative powers of peasant and central networks. Local leaders often expressed discontent with prices they deemed too low by defaulting on deliveries. Official prices of rural factors for urban plants were almost flat in 1966–1978. State agencies naturally liked to keep their money, and they had ideological arguments against the "economism" of giving peasants more for their work. Yet at the same time, the increasingly sophisticated technology of Chinese agriculture (more machines, more fertilizer, and more irrigation required by better seeds that allowed more grain taxes) raised production costs, especially in triple-crop areas. To the extent that free, illegal, or nonstate markets could be repressed, this combination of policies grew some grain, but with official prices that remained stagnant. So peasants went into factories instead, becoming workers.[81]

A minority of ex-farmers went into commerce rather than manufacturing. During the early 1970s, individual peasants wanting to sell food had to do so themselves. Wholesale food transactions broke the law unless the state conducted them. Peasants could not legally sell to a retailer. This reduced their incentives to grow and trade supplementary foods such as vegetables, even though many were able in practice to make these sales, evading police. In 1979 the law was changed, and the revival of retail agents made food markets more efficient.[82]

The official state procurement price for grain was, for seventeen years after the famine, fairly flat. There were slight increases in 1961, 1966, and 1978 – but in size, these were overwhelmed by the 1985 increase, in which the grain price doubled. The *combined total* increases over the thirty-three years from 1951 to 1984 were only about two-thirds of the single-year 1984–1985 increase. Table 1.1 does

TABLE 1.1 Indices of reported official state procurement prices for grains and industrial crops (1950 = 100)

	Grains	*Industrial Crops*		*Grains*	*Industrial Crops*
1951	118.3	118.4	1973	222.2	164.9
52	121.4	113.0	74	222.4	165.1
53	137.1	112.9	75	222.8	165.1
54	137.1	119.3	76	222.8	165.1
55	137.3	120.0	77	222.8	165.8
56	139.9	122.6	78	224.4	174.0
57	141.4	126.4	79	271.3	200.4
58	145.1	127.9	80	271.8	210.8
59	147.0	129.9	81	283.5	215.0
60	151.7	133.8	82	283.5	215.2
61	191.9	140.6	83	283.5	215.4

(Continued)

18 Farmers & the centralist revolution

TABLE 1.1 Continued

| | Industrial | | | Industrial |
	Grains	Crops		Grains	Crops
62	192.4	145.0	84	282.4	212.8
63	190.9	152.9	85	522.2	277.3
64	189.2	152.6	86	573.9	287.3
65	190.9	152.8	87	619.8	296.8
66	220.8	152.8	88	710.3	330.3
67	221.1	154.9	89	901.4	385.5
68	221.1	154.9	90	840.1	431.4
69	221.1	154.9	91	788.0	438.3
70	221.1	154.9	92	829.8	423.0
71	222.0	161.4	93	968.4	476.2
72	222.2	164.2	94	1419.5	687.7

Source: *Zhongguo tongji nianjian, 1991* (China Statistical Yearbook, 1993), State Statistical Bureau, ed. (Beijing: Zhongguo Tongji Chuban She, 1980–1992), 257; and the 1992 edition, 263; and calculated from the 1995 edition, 247. Shifts of accounting methods may have occurred in 1990–1991. The 1984–1990 era (and the mid-1990s, but by that time the state contracted to buy less than before) showed quick increases.

not report real scarcities or unofficial prices. These rose faster in many periods of reform, including the early 1970s, than the state procurement prices. But the table shows the delayed effect of scarcities on plans, especially the striking rise of rates that the state needed to pay for grain from 1984 to 1989, as well as the slight ebbing in 1990 but sharp rise thereafter, until Premier Zhu Ronji's mid-1990s policies finally began to restrain this inflation.

State control over grain prices faltered slightly in 1979 and collapsed by 1985. Another change, however, came much earlier: In 1971–1972, state procurement prices for economic crops rose somewhat, after a long period of stability since the end of the post-Leap depression. Rural factories were already competing with the state sector for industrial crops. Mandated purchases of some inputs, notably cotton, were still the order of the day in communes devoted to that as the main product. But especially for subsidiary industrial crops, there was price inflation. By 1978–1979, delivery shortages to the state by rural industries made the state boost non-grain factor prices again.

To what extent did localities actually sell commodities at the state-set prices? This question is difficult to answer in any particular year, although later years' plan prices suggest the reality. It is likely that the *reported* official prices did not apply to all sales. Urban cadres, to keep their factories running, reportedly sometimes contributed side-payments to rural cadres.

For grain, decollectivization led to higher harvests, but demand for food soared even faster. The state doggedly tried to retain its "unified purchasing policy," which in Mao's time had allowed huge extractions from the countryside for urban industrial development. When the state price was good, peasants willingly sold; but the state had to use more and more price incentives to get grain for its urban employees to eat. During reforms prices generally rose, as Table 1.1 shows. Yet this quickly upended official budgeting. Government granaries sometimes could not hold all they had contracted to buy, and high inventories might restrain price increases, but just temporarily. Agricultural planning had been easier for the state when it could rely on rural cadres more, and on price incentives less, to obtain rice for urban tables.

This problem extended to other foods, too. Peasants had one million more chickens than state purchasing agents had budget to buy, during 1983 in Jiangsu's Hai'an County. So the farmers strung many of these million chickens on bicycles and took them off to sell in Nanjing.[83] Most local leaders in such situations almost surely deemed themselves loyal socialists. But they needed free markets. State procurement requires state money. When production soared beyond officially planned amounts, state cadres lacked enough funds to implement the plans. This was not a question of ideology; it was a question of payment.

When cadres could not meet their obligations to the chiefs of farming networks, the latter were relieved of the need to reciprocate. Party and government leaders of townships (*xiang*, often having populations of a few thousand people) are the lowest cadres in China's administrative structure. Town leaders were supposed to meet goals that the state lists in order to retain their posts – although enforcement of such norms has been spotty when local. Chiefs of villages (*cun*, often a few hundred people) are now supposed to be elected; and in earlier times too, village chiefs were not formal parts of the state's structure. These relatively autonomous village chiefs are generally older than township leaders, who sometimes are youths wanting promotions – and thus may be mindful of their monitors, as are heads of counties, the next level up the bureaucratic ladder.[84]

The state is conceived as a hierarchy. Practically no one ever speaks of it otherwise. What the "higher" leaders in this system needed from rural areas during the reform years was grain. But "lower" leaders had decreasing interests in providing it. So for example, peasants planted rapeseed on nearly half their land in a large region of Zhejiang in 1983. The profits were enough to buy grain for their required deliveries to the state. But this meant less rice for China overall. So a law decreed that each team should put grain on four-fifths of the fields.[85] Laws of this sort pleased socialist leaders in Beijing, who knew that urban state workers expected their usual rations in politically important cities. But in practice, despite such laws, state leaders soon had to pay more if they wished to get grain.

By the mid-1980s, when purchases at higher fixed prices worsened the state budget deficit, the government had to change its previous policy of purchasing mandatory grain amounts to a more flexible system of contracts. These contracts often contained clauses about floods or droughts that would reduce peasants' obligations – and clauses about state obligations, especially amounts to be paid if official warehouses were too full to take grain on the agreed dates.[86] Prices and amounts changed so fast, the previous entitlements to the state were replaced by entitlements to peasants, which the government could no longer fully afford. By the same token, the State Planning Commission in 1985 had to give up its previous hope of restraining either grain or industrial crop prices. Reforms continued after 1985, but effective state price-setting for most commodities had already stopped. This book's next chapter contains more data on the mid-1980s end of most planning.

Local leaders of China's main labor force (part-time farmers) responded to this situation with gusto. In the short period from 1984 to 1986, one-eighth of all China's proletariat reportedly quit farming to "engage in industry and service trades in towns and urban areas."[87] Rural incomes rose sharply during those years – and over 80 percent of the new wages came from commercial businesses and services. Coastal areas led central and western parts of China in this growth. Development of the densely populated "green city" in Shanghai's suburbs was especially fast.[88]

From fields to factories in the "green city"

The Shanghai province-level unit included two rural parts: relatively fertile inland areas that garnered heavy harvests of rice, and less fertile cotton areas near the sea. Chuansha, a cotton-growing suburban county with sandy soil, had long-standing links to urban textile mills; but the industrial portion of its own output rose quickly in the first half of the 1970s. The name of this large county meant "River Sand." Chuansha County is now Pudong. It is highly atypical of rural China, but its main product had been agricultural for decades. Chuansha had especially strong traditions of nonstate political organization, including secret societies, religious sects (ranging from animist to Christian), and serious trade unions. Shanghai's Green Gang crime leader of the Republican period, Du Yuesheng, was a Chuansha native. Evidence of shamanism remained strong there as late as the mid-1980s. Chuansha farmers included many Roman Catholics. When this county during reforms was renamed Pudong New District (a 'xinqu,' absorbing former Nanhui County too), local construction teams and the nonstate gangs behind them made sure they received many of the new construction jobs. The CCP was not alone in its ability to mobilize Chuansha people.[89] Table 1.2 shows a rather flat curve of the industrial

TABLE 1.2 Reported industrial portions of total output, Chuansha County, Shanghai

1949	46%	1970	54%
52	53%	75	74%
62	52%	78	75%
65	51%	80	85%
		85	91%

Source: *Chuansha xian zhi* (Chuansha County Gazetteer), Zhu Hongbo, ed. (Shanghai: Shanghai Renmin Chuban She, 1990), 251, is unusual because it gives a bit of information for the early 1970s. The table includes all years for which these data were published. Similar gazetteers were scanned for Shanghai's Baoshan, Chongming, Fengxian, Jiading, Jinshan, Qingpu, and Songjiang counties; but except as reported elsewhere in this current book, they offer sparse data or comments on the early 1970s. Academic attention to those years has mainly concerned tragedies of the Cultural Revolution.

portion of Chuansha product during the height of revolutionary centralization through the 1960s.

The county leaders were still responding then to municipal and central instructions to grow their main taxable product (cotton), because the Leninist appointment system remained strong until the mid-1960s, and capital funds and technical means to industrialize in Chuansha became available gradually.

Local hinge leaders increasingly had the option of responding more to their networks' local opportunities than to mandates from the bureaucracy. In 1970–1975, as Table 1.2 shows, industrial activity accelerated sharply. The portion of output from Chuansha factories rose by 20 percentage points in that half decade. This rate may have been exceeded only in the two years after 1978 – when previously hidden industrial production was easier for local leaders to report, and when further reforms of the economic structure carried forward the momentum that had started much earlier in the decade.

The CCP's Leninist appointment system attracts attention among political scientists because it looks effective on an organization chart. But in China from 1970 to 1990, its norms became somewhat less efficient except at high administrative levels, because of situational resource changes. An intellectual history of Soviet studies would show that Leninist structures there were overrated by many academics and journalists until the late great USSR collapsed. Admittedly China is not the USSR (whose ethnic structure was different), and PRC Leninism may last for some time. But Charlotte Lee shows that the rise of markets in China's mixed capitalist-socialist economy has affected CCP ideology, along with cadres' training and promotion norms.[90] The market changed the Party, even if socialist conservatives resisted that trend. Centralist appointment systems are important, but early reforms challenged them. Rational leaders think about their benefits from clients, not just from monitors.

Chuansha comparisons with some other Shanghai counties show contrasts. Chuansha industry contributed 54 percent of product value in 1970, up by two deciles in the next five years to 74 percent. But Songjiang County, a carbon-soil, traditionally rice-growing area of Shanghai, provides data shown on Table 1.3, suggesting that Songjiang local cadres obeyed government instructions to stress agriculture more faithfully than did their Chuansha peers. By 1970, even though Songjiang was richer (the county seat was larger, and more of the area was built up), just 46 percent (rather than Chuansha's 54 percent) of its total output was industrial. By 1975, the Songjiang figure was up to 61 percent; this was a fast increase, but not to Chuansha's 74 percent by the same year. Local leaders determined this difference, and variations of local cultures and agricultures concurrently help account for it. Rural leaders responded diversely to the state's demand to tax the main crop – and in effect, for either slower or faster local development.

Even in relatively conservative rice-growing counties with large settlements, such as Songjiang, the early 1970s rate of industrial growth was unprecedented. From 1970 to 1975, the average rate of industrial growth in all of Songjiang was 21 percent (and for rural industry alone, 37 percent). But starting from 1978 over

22 Farmers & the centralist revolution

TABLE 1.3 Songjiang County, Shanghai, 1965–1987 population (in thousands), gross outputs of industry, agriculture, and rural industry (in m. yuan) budgetary fiscal revenues (in m. yuan), and changes in these (notice especially changes of data from the early 1970s)

Year	Pop.	Change	Indu	Change	Agricu.	Change	Ru. Ind.	Change	Budget Fiscal	Change
65	380	5.3%	72	26.3%	75	−20.2%				
66	395	3.9%	49	−31.9%	87	16.0%				
67	396	0.3%	65	32.7%	89	2.3%			25	25.0%
68	407	2.8%	66	1.5%	98	10.1%			29	16.0%
69	415	2.0%	67	1.5%	114	16.3%	13		25	−13.8%
70	421	1.4%	86	28.4%	106	−7.0%	17	30.8%	23	−8.0%
71	424	0.7%	115	33.7%	118	11.3%	35	105.9%	31	34.8%
72	425	0.2%	136	18.3%	133	12.7%	35	0.0%	36	16.1%
73	430	1.2%	157	15.4%	136	2.3%	45	28.6%	44	22.2%
74	435	1.2%	183	16.6%	149	9.6%	53	17.8%	51	15.9%
75	439	0.9%	208	13.7%	134	−10.1%	75	41.5%	56	9.8%
76	443	0.9%	226	8.7%	139	3.7%	83	10.7%	55	−1.8%
77	450	1.6%	248	9.7%	123	−11.5%	98	18.1%	57	3.6%
78	454	0.9%	272	9.7%	145	17.9%	115	17.3%	59	3.5%
79	462	1.8%	333	22.4%	155	6.9%	150	30.4%	62	5.1%
80	464	0.4%	382	14.7%	148	−4.5%	195	30.0%	79	27.4%
81	473	1.9%	453	18.6%	215	45.3%	271	39.0%	80	1.3%
82	479	1.3%	524	15.7%	260	20.9%	316	16.6%	83	3.8%
83	481	0.4%	640	22.1%	225	−13.5%	384	21.5%	88	6.0%
84	482	0.2%	730	14.1%	256	13.8%	443	15.4%	97	10.2%
85	483	0.2%	1004	37.5%	229	−10.5%	636	43.6%	111	14.4%
86	486	0.6%	1215	21.0%	259	13.1%	844	32.7%	133	19.8%
87	492	1.2%	1664	37.0%	303	17.0%	1202	42.4%	162	21.8%

Source: Songjiang xian xianqing: Xiandai hua jincheng diaocai (The Current Situation in Songjiang County: An Investigation of the Modernization Process), Yao Xitang, ed., vol. II (Shanghai: no publisher but probably the Shanghai Academy of Social Sciences, n.d.) between 6 and 4; a misprint caused two pages each to be labeled 4, 5, and 6. The outputs are gross values of production. "Rural Industry" is *xiangzhen gongye*. "Budget fiscal revenue" is *caizheng shouru*. Percentages were calculated with help from research assistant Peng Dajin. The last column shows changes that are difficult to interpret partly because they omit Songjiang extra budgets, and mainly because 'radical' politics of reporting almost surely affected the figures. The irregular pattern is: high but decreasing rates of reported revenues in 1971–1976; then low rates until c. 1983, but with one very high year (perhaps because of a reporting campaign); then moderate and slowly increasing rates of extraction to 1987. Songjiang is not an officially neglected place; it contains many state and other industries. It is an important tax base, and the available data may show as much about reporting as about comprehensive realities.

the same number of years, factory growth was lower, at 17 percent (for rural industry, 26 percent) – and then only 14 percent during the next year, 1984.

These reforms showed a pattern that was common in many places: a boom in the early 1970s, a period of less change after 1976, then some resurgence after 1978, another reported slowing in 1984–1985, another push in the late 1980s (and later, another deceleration under the reversal of reforms in 1989–1990, followed by some growth and centralizing changes thereafter). No aspect of this pattern after 1978 (until 1990) was lacking earlier in the 1970s.

Among the 25,000 production teams in all of rural Shanghai during the last year when these teams were still formally mandated by the government (1978), the average distribution to rural workers was 230 yuan. Only about 1.2 percent of the teams handed out more than 300 yuan. At the low end, about 6 percent distributed 120 yuan or less. A focused study of ten rich and ten poor Shanghai rural production brigades (*shengchan dadui*, larger than teams) found that, by 1978, there was a 71 percent difference in their per capita incomes, and a 91 percent difference in their average fixed investment per worker.

Why did the state's revenue collectors allow the ten prosperous brigades to become rich? The answer seems evident in those localities' ability to pay off state cadres by delivering more grain – either by growing it, or more often by using collective industrial profits to buy it. Earlier, the wealth difference between these rich and poor brigades was not great; as late as 1966, the surveyed brigades that later enjoyed higher incomes delivered only a bit less grain than the ones which later remained relatively poor: 556 *jin* per worker, rather than 580 *jin*.[91] But by 1978, per capita deliveries from the ten rich brigades in the survey had risen by more than three-quarters (to 980 *jin*), while the poor ones' deliveries had fallen by almost one-quarter (to 472 *jin*).[92] In heavily taxed Shanghai, no local leaders got their economic autonomy free of charge. But by 1978, their factories let some of them pay for it.

Zooming to polities of brigade or village sizes shows disparate early reform results

Rural leaders' practical attitudes toward "higher" administrative levels differed by both place and personality. Variance among local leaders goes far toward explaining different localities' economic stagnancy or growth during the early 1970s. Along Shanghai's coasts, on soil near the Yangzi or toward Hangzhou Bay, sedimentation created land above sea level only over the last millennium or so. (Future dangers to Shanghai because of rising sea levels are severe.) Agriculture near these shores produces less than do fields further inland, because coastal soil contains sand and salts. It has a tendency to cake. Ploughing and irrigation are relatively difficult there. But coastal areas had advantages in a period of quickly localizing industrial growth. Cotton, rather than rice, was the main crop; and demand for fiber remained strong in Jiangnan mills. Especially when coastal collectives could avoid selling cotton through state channels, they made good profits.

Dengyi and Shanhuang brigades, both in Chuansha, had almost identical net incomes in 1966. But by 1978, Dengyi's income had doubled – while Shanhuang's had risen more than ten times. The ecological, resource, and market conditions facing the two brigades were similar. So the question becomes: Why did Shanhuang's cadres start subsidiary industries despite the late-1960s and early-1970s political risks to themselves of nurturing "sprouts of capitalism," while Dengyi's leaders feared this risk? The more liberal leadership also encouraged peasants on their own

24 Farmers & the centralist revolution

time to raise more pigs, chickens, and milk cows. They supported harvesting grass from coastal commons and founding cottage industries, especially in embroideries. When situational factors gave similar opportunities to different leaders, they did not always react in the same way. The main answer may well lie in their personalities as leaders.

In another inland county of Shanghai, which had richer agricultural soil, a similar contrast has been documented between Xinlong and Yenong brigades. In the 1960s, these two places were broadly similar; but near the start of the 1970s, they were contrastive. Surplus agricultural workers in Xinlong were encouraged by brigade leaders to raise ducks, chickens, pigs, fish, and mushrooms, and to truck these goods to markets in central Shanghai. Yenong did none of these things extensively – with the result that by 1978, its workers produced 75 percent less value than those of Xinlong.[93]

Data are also available from Qingpu County, another carbon-soil and relatively conservative place adjacent to Songjiang. The published numbers suggest effects of politics on reporting especially of registered population. Some people apparently moved to larger settlements, including central Shanghai, as the Cultural Revolution weakened monitoring offices in the early 1970s. Economic data on Table 1.4 suggest just a slightly lower rate of industrial growth in Qingpu, compared with

TABLE 1.4 Development in Qingpu County, Shanghai, 1970–1987 (growth percentages for sectors and population)

Year	Industry	Grain	Trade	Pop.
1970		−1	−2	1.9
71	17	7	4	1.0
72		9	18	1.0
73	25	5	13	1.5
74		3	8	0.5
75	19	−6	9	0.5
76	7	13	8	1.2
77	11	−19	−6	1.7
78	24	34	16	0.7
79	23	9	23	1.0
80	19	−22	17	0.5
81	17	−1	4	1.4
82	14	22	1	1.4
83	19	−2	10	0.5
84	23	9	20	0.2
85	41	−23	26	0.2
86	18	6	15	0.9
87	36	−5	22	0.9

Source: Calculated from *Qingpu xianzhi* (Qingpu County Gazeteer), Feng Xuewen et al., eds. (Shanghai: Shanghai Renmin Chuban She, 1990), grain, 206; gross value of industrial output, 271; retail trade, 360; population, 148.

nearby counties, during the early 1970s, followed by the common deceleration in 1976–1977, and then again an increase after 1978, with considerable fluctuations in the rate continuing later. Qingpu reports on grain are interesting, because that traditionally rice-growing county's production of the staple was low in the early 1970s and then decreased in many later years (despite a few when the cadres filed very high numbers). The Qingpu County Gazeteer's fluctuating statistics may reflect political campaigns that influenced records, not just the behaviors they purport to describe. Recurrent exhortations from various high leaders that every county should grow more grain had no clear long-term effect. Weather naturally makes annual crops vary,[94] but a broader pattern is not hard to find. The 1987 tonnage of Qingpu rice was scarcely greater than that of a decade and a half earlier in the early 1970s. The long-term trend for Shanghai suburban grain production was unsurprisingly stagnant and then negative.

Further outside Shanghai on the delta, the rampant exodus of workers from fields to factories was impressive. Between 1983 and 1987, one third of the peasants in Taixian County, Jiangsu, quit farming. They earned less money if they stayed on the fields. In the urbanized county seat, the average 1983 personal income was 645 yuan – but the average Taixian farmer got less than half as much, 287 yuan. By 1987, wages for both categories had approximately doubled, but the difference between them was greater. Some farmers who had tilled rice specialized then in animal husbandry or fish-raising. Many set up stores or found jobs in township "collective" (proto-private) industries. Others "became workers in small firms, often affiliated with larger enterprises in towns and cities."[95] The agricultural labor force of Wuxi County also declined sharply, at an annual rate of 13 percent between 1978 and 1985.[96]

Many ex-farmers went into construction, living at rural homes but going for day labor to building sites in more urban areas. This pattern was encouraged by Shanghai's city administrators, who could not easily stop the incoming flood of labor and wanted new infrastructure: "Experience shows that it is easier to cope with the inflow of rural people if they are involved in short-term projects. All in all, construction workers are easier to manage than those who open grocery stores or restaurants and stay on indefinitely."[97]

Agricultural-industrial contracts that local leaders made with households

Some agricultural households contracted with local governments to produce set quotas of crops. They became farming "specialists." Others worked in factories. Dongfang Township, near Wuxi, from the fall of 1983 allocated 70 percent of its large tracts of agricultural "responsibility land" to just 85 families, a small minority in that town. Leaders of Yongnan village, Yuqi Township, in 1984 consolidated the land previously tilled by 327 families, re-allocating it to merely 10 households. "This greatly raised agricultural efficiency."[98]

The laborers of Changjiao village, Changshu (also in Jiangsu), were 80 percent "industrial" by 1984. But somebody had to till the land – or supervise migrant

26 Farmers & the centralist revolution

workers from poorer parts of China who tilled it. Local cadres contracted farming. They were still organized under units that had names to accord with the statist terminology of the PRC. Sometimes new plantations could change their unit designations from agricultural to industrial, even though both were often administered together by village elites. As Fei Xiaotong wrote,[99]

> Local leaders carried out a uniform management of agriculture and rural industry. Under this system, those who engaged in agricultural activity actually became members of rural industries. [Local 'industrial' offices] organized agriculture, rural factories, and sideline production too. In Wuxi County, 7,000 responsibility-land families were managed by rural enterprises. There was an agricultural department in rural industrial offices. Peasants who wanted to do agricultural work had to apply for land from this department. They submitted the income from the land for which they took responsibility, but they could get wages from rural industry.

These new rural farmers, if they were not migrants, had better social security than their predecessor peasants. The tightness of organization in these areas would have pleased the ancestors of some cadres, who could come from old leading lineages there.

In agricultural contracts, the legal parties on one side were often cooperatives. The other side was usually a household rather than an individual. The text of an agricultural contract from the early 1980s specified that the local cooperative (*she*) should provide land, water, seeds, fertilizer, and machines or animals. The family nominally agreed "to arrange the contracting household's production tasks according to state plans." The household (*hu*) in theory could "not without permission buy and sell, transfer, or leave uncultivated, build houses, place graves, or plant bamboos or trees on contracted land." The household at least formally undertook to "accept cadres' correct leadership and overall arrangement." The contracting family also promised "to have children according to birth plans," as well as "to ensure timely completion of the sales task for agricultural products."[100] "Economic punishments" were prescribed for contract violation. Such provisions echoed Mao-era rural arrangements, but these contract provisions replaced plan commands. Enforcement became more local and variable.

A major benefit of contracting to households was that the family could sell surplus from the land, above the agreed "sales task." The rhetorical language of planning permeated contracts even after the socialist substance had weakened. As was typical of China's reforms generally, new practices were rephrased in old terms even when previous norms were not followed. Transactions costs of sudden changes in household sales patterns meant that the new system resembled the old one more than most economists discovered.[101] But rural incentives to produce rose, as dependent peasants became more independent farmers. Collective localization (often mistaken for 'decentralization') was the trend, even if the result was far from "free" capitalism.

Agricultural yields were maintained in many East China areas, although most peasants left agriculture. Specialized farming families in a rural Zhejiang township by the mid-1980s were only 10 percent of the entire workforce; nine-tenths of all laborers there were in factories.[102] Family farms flourished, and plots that could not be tilled by "farmers preferring to work in township enterprises" were re-contracted to households specialized in agriculture. In one Zhejiang county, only 3 percent of the rural families delivered one-third of the grain needed to meet the county's state quota.[103] A reason for sharp local rises of labor productivity in the 1980s was increased use of field machinery. Rural industrialization provided unprecedented amounts of capital in the countryside, and this affected not just factories but also agriculture.

Ten Sunan townships in Wuxi, Changshu, and Wuxian counties set up "agricultural experiment zones" in 1988, to test possibilities for greater mechanization and to "consolidate land holdings and attract more investment."[104] The remaining farmers were a smaller part of the population, and pre-industrial rural politics ended – but agriculture was still important, as its methods mechanized.

Not all peasant families on the Shanghai delta liked household contracting. In international perspective, this is unsurprising. Even in highly industrialized countries (France, Japan, and others), nostalgia for old-style farming has been slow to disappear and has affected politics. In China, groups of all sizes became more active because of industrialization. These included cooperating sets of about ten households, production teams of about one hundred families, natural villages that were larger, and marketing communities that contained as many as 2,000 households. The units that lost most from reforms were bigger than those whose leaders flew below the effective purview of the central state. "Top-down" discourses about Chinese politics rely on a premise that the nation's governance traditions have been mostly autocratic.[105] That premise is generally true – but autocracies can be local as well as national.

Post-1984 efforts to revive state agriculture

Suzhou peasants had a slogan: "Better to plant cotton than rice, better melons than cotton, better sugar than melons; but best of all is to start a factory."[106] China's top planners' interests opposed the interests of a rural majority, and the peasants prevailed. Local networks on the Shanghai delta planted less rice and increasingly sold their cotton, melons, and sugar for processing in their own collective factories.

The budget crisis by 1985 made the state restructure agricultural procurement. Bureaucrats still tried to force peasants to plant unprofitable grain. These official efforts were in some cases temporarily effective, but they proved too expensive to sustain. Such changes were touted at the time as "reforms," but they were reversals of previous reforms run by farmers' leaders. Agriculture sagged in Shanghai's suburban counties during the 1980s for many reasons. A peak in the number of small and hand-guided tractors was reached by 1984; but five years later, in 1989, the suburbs used 17 percent fewer of them. Larger tractors increased in number slightly, but the

28 Farmers & the centralist revolution

reduction of arable land and the transfer of labor into industries reduced the number of "walking tractors."[107] These were used mostly for rice, and by the mid-1980s revenue collectors liked them more than rural leaders did.

State decrees exhorted peasants to grow more grain, but this had scant relevance to what happened. Grain output in Shanghai over the long 1987–1992 era varied no more than 6 percent between the high and low years. The last year was the lowest.[108] Grain production fluctuates with weather; but except for this variance, the curve was essentially flat, avoiding declines because of administrative pressure on production (or pressure to over report production). When buying new equipment, village leaders chose not to replace old tractors; they put their capital to other uses.

East China peasants enjoyed a "double liberation" of both work and ownership. On one hand, they could shift from fields to factories, stores, or construction teams (*jianzhu dui*). On the other, they accumulated property in trucks, tractors, and houses. Long-term rental contracts in the 1980s raised confidence that they acquired *de facto* ownership rights in land – even though, legally, they only leased agricultural land.[109]

Government bureaus seldom received full data on what farmers were actually doing. City-based officials were reluctant to spend much time in rural areas, especially poor places. For example, farmers in one part of Anhui diversified their economy during the early 1980s by developing freshwater oyster beds, but they were almost never visited by the commercial offices that were supposed to monitor them. Local tax bureau cadres sometimes came, but revenue collectors (as in other countries) seldom found it easy to obtain complete data on production.[110]

Rural leaders in both fields and factories were somewhat constrained by promises they conventionally promised to keep. Farmers and rural entrepreneurs seldom wrote the contracts they were supposed to follow.[111] They did not advertise to visiting researchers (Chinese or foreign) the extent to which they sidestepped cadres' orders. Local leaders had no interest in publicizing the extent to which they kept contract enforcement local. Sometimes the government decreed peasant freedoms (e.g., to choose which crops to grow, or to sell surpluses-over-quota on open markets), while local leaders forced peasants to plant other crops or sell in markets the leaders preferred. Local corporatism reduced state power.

Under the headline "Farmers Ignore Administrative Orders and Do Their Own Thing," the *China Daily* reported that a village in Zhejiang's Yuhang County evaded extensive official plans to grow jute for state-owned mills. Commands to plant jute were formally conveyed to peasants by township officials, but the farmers had strong economic disincentives to comply. The annual monetary yield per hectare of jute was 900 yuan, but the same land planted in fruit or mulberry trees rendered 15,000 yuan. The peasants therefore grew jute on less than one-twentieth of the acreage where they were officially bidden to grow it. As a farmer said, "Now that we have the decision-making power over production, the township government has no power to order us about. If the jute price is raised high enough, we'll be willing to plant it."[112]

A town in Tongxiang County, Zhejiang, became "the kingdom of ducks" because the local environment was ideal for breeding these fowl. The leader, who sponsored more duck-raising, earned 30,000 yuan a year by the late 1980s ("nearly ten times the income of the Zhejiang provincial governor," a PRC paper noted). His fellow villagers all soon bred ducks too. Most families in that town during 1989 earned more than 10,000 yuan a year. The boom also led to industrial diversification, because the village founded a factory producing duck feed. As a local tycoon put it, "Believe me, we've really become masters of production. . . . That government officials have become our servants is a great change, brought about by reform."

Another local farmer-turned-duck-breeder suggested that alterations in the terms of trade between agriculture and industry had long been overdue. She expressed resentment at the expense of consumer durables, which in her view had become exorbitant in rural areas: "Farmers are not demanding higher prices for farm products. What we demand is a rational price parity between manufactured goods and farm products. . . . We would not be happy if the government raised the prices of manufactured goods only, but not the prices of farm products. I am sure the [unofficial] price reform, which is enlisting the support of 800 million rural residents, will succeed."[113]

The most important manufactured good that China's new agronomy required was inorganic fertilizer. The petrochemical industry provided much of this, but its production required large capital investments, as well as inputs from limited places that state conservatives (often associated with the army) could still control. Petroleum-based products were not among the commodities for which planning ended in the mid-1980s. Burgeoning nonstate agriculture benefited state oil bureaucracies. Farm input prices, paid largely for fertilizers derived from crude oil, doubled in just two years from 1986 to 1988.[114] This made growing rice unprofitable, farmers claimed. When state planners did not restrain the inflation of fertilizer prices, peasants cited this as a reason to grow less grain. New agricultural technology, sponsored by the state, in some ways reduced the state's ability to extract grain levies. Green revolution threatened what was left of the red one by the mid-1980s.

Central bureaucrats wanted to wrest higher rural profits, taking rents that could compensate the state's losses to flourishing nonstate networks during late reforms. Sales taxes on non-grain agricultural products were therefore hit with increments of 10 to 30 percent in 1989.[115] Many such sales could be hidden, however. Because the government could not reliably monitor rural production, the main effect of the new impost was apparently to increase incentives to conceal grain sales and shipment means (e.g., by 'boat people' who had tugs or barges and were ethno-religious minorities).

Mechanized and chemicalized agriculture freed labor; but after triple cropping brought higher outputs, available technologies could not easily further raise grain harvests. As Philip Huang has written, partly on the basis of data from Songjiang County, Shanghai, "To put it bluntly, marketized farming in the 1980s did no better in crop production than it did in the six centuries between 1350 and 1950, or than collective agriculture did in the preceding three decades." Total rural production had sharply grown – but the big increase was industrial, not agricultural. It "came not from 'private' crop production and petty commerce that were given so much press, but rather from rural industry and new sidelines."[116] According to a 1993 sample, the odds that a laborer would have at least some nonfarm work was 30:1 in the area around Zhangjiagang, Jiangsu.[117] Nonfarm jobs paid much more than work in paddies.

Unintended effects of local industrialization

China's central leadership was broadly supportive of the idea of rural prosperity. Top elites had mostly favored agricultural mechanization, hoping that both the rural and urban effects would be beneficial to the state. But major effects of agricultural extension had not been clearly foreseen in Beijing – especially the deleterious unintended consequences for state industries and budgets.

This phenomenon is not just Chinese. A study comparing adoptions of agricultural technology in two parts of Indonesia concluded that Javanese adopted green revolution farming more easily than Ambonese – largely because the Javanese were more statist. They followed advice from Jakarta, which was based on new agronomy; and their crop yields rose. Central Java peasants trusted their local leaders better than did those on the island of Ambon in the Moluccas, and local leaders in Java also trusted the state better.[118] Such an attitude was present throughout much of the Yangzi delta too, but under socialism it led eventually to an ironic result: Government-supported agricultural programs later raised problems for government.

How did Chinese peasant leaders make reforms when their lineages and independent organizations had been repressed in the 1950s and 1960s? Part of the answer is that many rural leaders shaped state campaigns to benefit themselves and new locals whom they recruited as partners, without openly challenging government advertisements of official effectiveness. Daniel Kelliher noted the operation of inarticulate power: "Peasants with no plan, no communication, and often no knowledge of each other's action behaved as if acting in concert. Unanimity of action came from the sameness of circumstance."[119]

This influence was not random. It was not like Brownian motion, because it usually emerged as a reaction to technological opportunities or to official measures that had been used earlier to mobilize and save resources for the state.[120] Local means and norms changed in parallel, responding to new economic possibilities and old administrative policies. Such changes can make powerful politics, even when the local strategies they imply are "weak," mute, without any articulation in "civil society."[121] China's ex-agriculturalists were able to make massive reforms because many of their first initiatives were situational, not normative. The Chinese central elite included "meritocratic" intellectuals, who proudly presumed that ideas must shape situations more than vice-versa.[122] Ex-peasant leaders could find in this assumption a beneficial bluff: They could retain good faith and credit with state hierarchs (and could maintain their own local hierarchies) by accepting the definition of politics as mainly a matter of ideas – all the while taking concrete resources that had previously been the state's. To make money, they readily ceded or adapted symbols.

The liberation of agricultural labor in the early 1970s conjured reforms more surely than did 1978 pronouncements by CCP politicians in Beijing. If most high PRC leaders had been interested in Marxism as a means of political analysis, rather than merely a language to legitimate their rule, they could have been interested in this transformation of rural China. Here is a case where Marx's ideas on the technological causes of political shifts apply well (as arguably they do not in some other cases).[123] Alterations of "substructural" technology constrained China's government. They gave material wherewithal to local political networks that were partly beyond the state's reach. New rural technologies freed people (or at least local leaders) in a classic Marxist way, although the Marxist state did not applaud its own withering.

The beneficiaries had been mere peasants. Statist intellectuals noticed the process but did not soon take it seriously. A Communist reactionary, writing a book that became well known among PRC intellectuals in 1994, eulogized "the basic correctness of Mao's strategy of keeping peasants bound in poverty to the land [because of] the threat peasants have increasingly posed to China's social stability."[124] This conservative writer excoriated a reformist "provincial party secretary" (Wan Li, though the book did not identify him) for maintaining that "China's peasants are simple and dutiful; their only demand is to eat their fill and have the freedom to farm." But according to this socialist hardliner, "once the peasants have filled their stomachs, they most certainly will continuously raise other demands. And these demands are no longer demands for a low level of existence. They have the desire to develop." They migrate to cities, violating laws and becoming a "powder keg," a "living volcano" that threatens national stability and Party rule.[125] Most data about reforms can be organized by such an analysis. But this Marxist/nationalist writer was unwilling to favor China's majority, who wanted to better their own lives, over a political elite that was (and is) determined to stay in power.

Agricultural extension policies were not originally intended to stymie the revolution. In practice, they made China's localities more industrial and autonomous. These rural roots of reform weakened the central state from about 1970 to 1990.

Notes

1 *The Works of Mencius*, James Legge, tr. (New York: Dover Books, 1970), and many later translations of this most influential Confucian writer, including Wm. Thedore deBary and Irene Bloom, *The Sources of Chinese Tradition*, vol. 1 (New York: Columbia University Press, 1999), 114–58.

2 Clifford Geertz, "Deep Play: Notes on the Balinese Cockfight," in *The Interpretation of Cultures* (New York: Basic Books, 1973), 412–42, shows that traditions as diametrically different as cockfights and Brahmana ordinations are both "like Bali."

3 Robert Bates, *Markets and States in Tropical Africa: The Political Basis of Agricultural Policies* (Berkeley: University of California Press, 1981), 50.

4 *Chûgoku no toshika to nôson kensetsu* (Chinese Urbanization and Rural Construction), Kojima Reeitsu, ed. (Tokyo: Ryûkei Shosha, 1978), 293–94 and 299.

5 Stanley Spector, *Li Hung-chang and the Huai Army: A Study in Nineteenth-century Chinese Regionalism* (Seattle: University of Washington Press, 1964); and Franz H. Michael,

32 Farmers & the centralist revolution

Regionalism in Nineteenth Century China (Seattle: University of Washington Press, 1964); works of Zhang Zhongli and Hsiao Kung-chuan are relevant, as is the less Chinese-domestic discourse of John King Fairbank in *Trade and Diplomacy on the China Coast* (Cambridge: Harvard University Press, 1953).

6 Helen Siu, *Agents and Victims in South China: Accomplices in Rural Revolution* (New Haven: Yale University Press, 1989); Franz Schurmann, *Ideology and Organization,* explores the personnel aspects of state penetration of village politics.

7 For these estimates, see J. Dreze and A. Sen, *Hunger and Public Action* (Oxford: Clarendon Press, 1989), Table 11.2.

8 This paraphrases a final exam question that I recall from my previous teacher Joseph Levenson, an intellectual historian.

9 G. William Skinner, "Marketing and Social Structure in Rural China," *Journal of Asian Studies* 24:1–3 (November 1964–May 1965), 3–43, 195–228, 363–399.

10 Jacob Eyferth, "Liberation from the Loom? Rural Women, Textile Work and Revolution in North China," in *Maoism at the Grassroots: Everyday Life in China's Era of High Socialism,* Jeremy Brown and Matthew D. Johnson, eds. (Cambridge: Harvard University Press, 2015), 151.

11 Some specific evidence comes from Anhui. Dali Yang, "Making Reform," 185, cites Ou Yuanfang, *Anhui baogan daohu yanjiu* (A Study of Anhui Household Contracting) (Hefei: Anhui Renmin Chuban She, 1982).

12 The introduction of hand tractors was important not just in the rice-growing south, but also in North China that during most seasons grows wheat, alternating with peanuts, rice, and other crops. *Wenhui bao*, Shanghai [hereafter *WHB*], December 19, 1977.

13 Joshua Eisenman writes about propaganda's role trying to reduce moral hazards. His book, *Red China's Green Revolution: Technological Innovation, Institutional Change, and Economic Development under the Commune* (New York: Columbia University Press, 2017) was originally a 2012 UCLA Political Science dissertation that he sent me before publication. He compares the "church of Mao" in China's communes with other communalistic endeavours by Pietists, Shakers, kibbutz members, and Owenites. Communes face organizational problems that a religion can reduce.

14 The source, like too many others published in China, faithfully avoids offering statistics for any years between 1966 and 1976, as if that period did not exist. The 19 percent annual increase is calculated from *Shanghai shi nongye jixie hua fazhan zhanlue yanjiu* (Studies on Strategy for Developing Agricultural Mechanization in Shanghai Municipality), Xie Zifen, ed. (Shanghai: Shanghai Kexue Puji Chuban She, 1991), 104.

15 Marion J. Levy, *Modernization and the Structure of Societies* (Princeton: Princeton University Press, 1966) symbolized modernization in a ratio of animal to machine power. Scholars who dislike the idea of modernization (I join most Chinese in finding it organizes evidence) might still be interested in the dramatic increase of mechanical power after 1965.

16 Also, markets in agricultural products boomed during this time. The marketed tonnage of pork from Shanghai's suburbs, for example, rose 84 percent between 1965 and 1973. See a book by the most distinguished non-Chinese team working on such issues: *Chûgoku no toshika*, 293–94 and 299.

17 Higher-yield cotton seeds were also found then; the increase of Song rice and cotton made better food and clothing. Stephen Morgan, "City-Town Enterprises in the Lower Changjiang (Yangtze) River Basin" (M.A. dissertation, Asian Studies, University of Hong Kong, 1987), 22–23; Philip Huang, *The Peasant Family and Rural Development in the Yangzi Delta, 1350–1988* (Stanford: Stanford University Press, 1990). For more on Shanghai's "green" suburbs before 1965, Lynn White, "Shanghai-Suburb Relations, 1949–1966," in *Shanghai: Revolution and Development in an Asian Metropolis,* Christopher Howe, ed. (Cambridge: Cambridge University Press, 1981), 241–68.

18 Xiao Zhenmei, *Xian jieduan zhi dalu nongjing biange* (The Transformation of the Mainland's Rural Economy at the Present Stage) (Taibei: Juliu Tushu Gongsi, 1988), 126.

19 Bo Fengcheng, *Zhonggong nongye xiandai hua zhengce zhi fenxi* (An Analysis of CCP Rural Modernization Policy) (Taipei: National Chengchi University M.A. Thesis, 1978, supervisd by Agricultural Economics Prof. Lee Teng-hui, later ROC president), 30.

20 Calculated from absolute numbers of these machines, reported in *Dangdai Zhongguo de nongye jixie hua* (Agricultural Mechanization in Contemporary China), Wu Shaowen, ed. (Beijing: Zhongguo Shehui Kexue Yuan, 1991), 53.

21 Joshua Eisenman, *Red China's Green*, manuscript graphics 3.13 and 3.14, based on Ministry of Agriculture statistical handbooks.

22 "Obituary: Zhao Ziyang," *BBC*, January 17, 2005, http://news.bbc.co.uk/2/hi/asia-pacific/2989335.stm.

23 *WHB*, June 10, 1976.

24 *WHB*, December 19, 1977. The spring harvest was then called the "three-snatch" (*sanchiang*). For more on the politics of the rice cycle, see Lynn White, "Agricultural and Industrial Values in China," in *Value Change in Chinese Society*, R. Wilson, S. Greenblatt, and A. Wilson, eds. (New York: Praeger, 1979), 141–54. After Taiwan and Hainan, Chongming in the mouth of the Yangzi is China's third largest island; it is a largely rural county of Shanghai Municipality.

25 Zhang Chunqiao in *Hongqi* (Red Flag), No. 4 (April), 1975, 3–12, cited in Domes, *Socialism*, 84.

26 See Lynn White, "Agricultural and Industrial Valuees in China,"

27 See Nicholas R. Lardy, *Agriculture in China's Modern Economic Development* (Cambridge: Cambridge University Press, 1983), and Peter Nolan and Suzanne Paine, "Towards an Appraisal of the Impact of Rural Reform in China, 1978–1985," in *The Re-emergence of the Chinese Peasantry: Aspects of Rural Decollectivization*, Ashwani Saith, ed. (London: Croom Helm, 1987), 82–83.

28 This 1969 end for the Cultural Revolution makes most sense to me. But another concluding date could be 1971, with Lin Biao's fall. The late-reform political uses, for the Chinese government, of a 1976 ending date are discussed in Anita Chan, "Dispelling Misconceptions About the Red Guard Movement: The Necessity to Re-Examine Cultural Revolution Factionalism and Periodization," *Journal of Contemporary China* 1:1 (1992), 61–85. Another essay, highly compatible with the argument here, is Sebastian Heilmann, *Turning Away from the Cultural Revolution: Political Grass-Roots Activism in the Mid-Seventies* (Stockholm: Center for Pacific Asia Studies Occasional Paper 28, September 1996).

29 The Chinese land unit, *mu* (sometimes spelled *mou*), is about one-sixth of a Western acre.

30 Feng Wang, "China's Population Destiny: The Looming Crisis," www.brookings.edu/articles/chinas-population-destiny-the-looming-crisis/.

31 *Zhongguo renkou qianyi* (Population Shifts in China), Tian Fang and Ling Fatong, eds. (Beijing: Zhishi Chuban She, 1987), 23–32; and as mentioned earlier, Marion J. Levy, *Modernization and the Structure of Societies*.

32 *Zhongguo renkou*, 248–259.

33 Yao Shihuang, *Jin sanjiao de tansuo* (Search for the Golden Delta) (Chongqing: Chongqing Chuban She, 1988), 10–12.

34 *RMRB*, September 17, 1975, quoted in Frank Leeming, *Rural China Today* (London: Longman, 1985), 106.

35 Frank Leeming, *Rural China*, 104–06.

36 Fei Xiaotong and Luo Yanxian, *Xiangzhen jingji bijiao moshi* (Comparative Models of the Village and Town Economy) (Chongqing: Chongqing Chuban She, 1988), 40–45.

37 Kellee Tsai, *Back-Alley Banking: Private Entrepreneurs in China* (Ithaca, NY: Cornell University Press, 2002) describes this in later years. PRC private finance is comparable with local (not state) support for small and medium enterprises (SMEs) in Taiwan's years of fastest development.

38 The classic is Clifford Geertz, *Agricultural Involution: The Processes of Ecological Change in Indonesia* (Berkeley: University of California Press, 1963).

39 Philip C. C. Huang, "The Paradigmatic Crisis in Chinese Studies: Paradoxes in Social and Economic History," *Modern China* 17:3 (July 1991), 311.

34 Farmers & the centralist revolution

40 Li Bozhong explored cropping patterns and fertilizers, and Wu Chengming found Ming "sprouts of capitalism" near Shanghai. Li's title suggests the story, "'Mulberries Take Over Rice Fields':The Intensification of Agricultural Production in Jiangnan during the Ming and Qing," cited in Philip Huang, "The Paradigmatic Crisis," 301.

41 This calculation did not try to estimate the price effects of the marketed third-crop grain. Materials compiled by the Shanghai Revolutionary Committee, reported in Frank Leeming, *Rural China*, 110–12.

42 Leeming, ibid., 110–13.

43 Lynn White, "Agricultural and Industrial Values in China," 141–54, on the social effects of crop cycles.

44 Compare Jacob Eyferth, "Liberation from the Loom?" 131–53, about communes' role in exploiting female labor growing cotton in Shaanxi – but there was similar change in grain-growing places. This was not a monotonic "liberation" for women.

45 *China Daily* [hereafter CD], January 24, 1989.

46 Sigrid Schmalzer, *Red Revolution, Green Revolution: Scientific Farming in Socialist China* (Chicago: University of Chicago Press, 2016). See also Sigrid Schmalzer, "Youth and the 'Great Revolutionary Movement' of Scientific Experiment in 1960s-1970s Rural China," in *Maoism at the Grassroots*, 154–78. Schmalzer is pathbreaking on "native knowledge" (*xiangtu zhishi*) in Maoist agronomy. Her work complements this book's coverage of materialist causes that also affected China's reforms. Eisenman in *Red China's Green* extends this by showing the national extent of change (not just in places like Jiangnan or Hebei) and showing how Maoism tried to fix moral hazards inherent in collectivism.

47 Dongping Han, *The Unknown Cultural Revolution: Life and Change in a Chinese Village* (New York: Monthly Review Press, 2008).

48 Joshua Eisenman, *Red China's Green*, graphics 3.4 and 3.6, based on Ministry of Agriculture statistics.

49 Frank Leeming, *Rural China*, 112–13.

50 Kate Xiao Zhou, *How the Farmers Changed China*; and Ph.D. dissertation, Politics Department, Princeton University, 1994.

51 From Domes, *Socialism*, 91–92.

52 Dali Yang, "Making Reform," 185, cites *RMRB*, June 24, 1978. There are similar reports from other provinces, ranging from Guangdong to Gansu.

53 Chris Bramall, "Origins of the Agricultural 'Miracle': Some Evidence from Sichuan," *China Quarterly* 143 (September 1995), 732 and 753.

54 "Contracting to households" is *baochan dao hu*. Kate Xiao Zhou notes the text of this resolution in Yang Jianwen, et al., *Dangdai Zhongguo jingji sixiang* (Economic Thought in Contemporary China) (Shanghai: Sanlian Shudian, 1991), 395–412.

55 Daniel Kelliher, *Peasant Power*, 63.

56 Edward Friedman, Paul G. Pickowicz and Mark Selden, *Chinese Village, Socialist State* (New Haven: Yale University Press, 1991), xv.

57 Adapted and slightly altered from Daniel Kelliher, *Peasant Power*, Chapter 6.

58 Jing Chen, *Useful Complaints* and Juan Wang, *Sinews*, 140. Also Rory Truex, "Consultative Authoritarianism and Its Limits," *Comparative Political Studies* (June 2014), 1, notes that "Respondents randomly exposed to the National People's Congress' (NPC) new online participation portals show greater satisfaction with the regime and feelings of government responsiveness, but these effects are limited to less educated, politically excluded citizens." On another limit, see Juan Wang, "Shifting Boundaries Between the State and Society: Village Cadres as New Activists in Collective Petitions," *China Quarterly* 211 (September 2012), 697–717.

59 Sidney Tarrow, *Power in Movement: Social Movements and Contentious Politics*, 3rd ed. (New York: Cambridge University Press, 2011). Also Scott Boorman, *The Protracted Game: A Wei-ch'i Interpretation of Maoist Revolutionary Strategy* (New York: Oxford University Press, 1969), showing protraction in terms of a real (Chinese) game, not just a theory.

60 Frances Fox Piven and Richard A. Cloward, *Poor People's Movements*.

61 *FBIS*, December 1, 1987, 17, quoting *RMRB* of November 24.

62 For a classic account of the old distinction between "vertical" or "string" (*tiaotiao*) and "horizontal" or "piece" (*kuaikuai*) leaderships, see Franz Schurmann, *Ideology and Organization*. This sociologist adapts an idea from Durkheim (which he calls 'human' vs.'technical' organization) to typify the traditional social bonds that hold "piece" areas together.

63 Calculated from output figures, in 1970 prices, from *Shanghai shi nongye*, 102.

64 *Gaige mianlin zhidu chuangxin* (Reforms Face System Innovation), Development Research Institute, ed. (Shanghai: Sanlian Shudian, 1988), 285.

65 The portion of grain in all agricultural output was 80 percent in the 1950s, 75 to 80 percent in the 1960s, but just slightly more than 60 percent in the 1980s, according *Zhongguo renkou*, 23–32.

66 *Zhongguo tongji nianjian, 1992* [*ZGTJNJ92*], 329.

67 Synaptic leadership is an idea developed by anthropologists: Grant Evans, *Laos: The Land in Between* (London: Allen and Unwin, 2003); also Helen Siu, *Agents and Victims* – and especially G. William Skinner, "Overseas Chinese Leadership: Paradigm for a Paradox," in *Leadership and Authority: A Symposium*, Gehan Wijeyewardene, ed. (Singapore: University of Malaya Press, 1968), 191–203.

68 "Sunan" is used here for counties that by the mid-1980s were under the jurisdictions of Changzhou, Wuxi, Suzhou, and Nantong cities, i.e. Wu-dialect (Shanghainese) Jiangsu. The term "Jiangnan" also includes other parts of the Shanghai Economic Zone in its small version, proposed in April 1983, i.e., the counties under the Zhejiang cities of Jiaxing, Huzhou, Hangzhou, Shaoxing, Ningbo, and Zhoushan Prefecture (an archipelago), and Shanghai Municipality.

69 Daniel Kelliher, *Peasant Power*, 120.

70 *Jiefang ribao* (Liberation Daily, hereafter *JFRB*), September 6, 1980.

71 Dali Yang, "Surviving the Great Leap Famine the Struggle over Rural Policy 1958–1962," in *New Perspectives on State Socialism in China* Timothy Cheek and Tony Saich, eds. (London: Routledge, 2016 [orig. 1997]), 296, notes 103 and 104, show that the previous centralist attribution of post-Leap change needs revisiting.

72 David Zweig, *Agrarian Radicalism in China, 1968–81* (Cambridge: Harvard University Press, 1989).

73 The irony that the policy was supposed to be "applied in accord with local conditions" (*yindi zhiyi*) is noted by Sigrid Schmalzer, *Red Revolution, Green Revolution*, and in Jonathan Unger, "The Decollectivization of the Chinese Countryside: A Survey of Twenty-eight Villages," *Pacific Affairs* 58:4 (Winter 1985–86), 585–606.

74 Lin Chun, *The Transformation of Chinese Socialism* (Durham: Duke University Press, 2006) offers fine background.

75 Mary Elizabeth Gallagher, *Contagious Capitalism: Globalization and the Politics of Labor in China* (Princeton: Princeton University Press, 2005; orig. Ph.D. dissertation, Politics Department, Princeton University, 2001).

76 Kate Xiao Zhou, *How the Farmers Changed China*, passim.

77 See also Ezra F. Vogel, *Deng Xiaoping and the Transformation of China* (Cambridge: Harvard University Press, 2011), 445. Deng's remark could refer to 1974–75, when was acting premier, and to years after 1978 when he was supreme leader.

78 *RMRB*, June 13, 1987.

79 Solomon M. Karmel, "The Neo-Authoritarian Contradiction: Trials of Developmentalist Dictatorships and the Retreat of the State in Mainland China" (Princeton University Politics Department Ph.D. dissertation, 1995), 25, quoting a speech of Gu Zhong, published by the Beijing Economics Association.

80 *FBIS*, December 1, 1987, 17–18, quoting *RMRB* of November 24.

81 See Dali Yang, "Making Reform," chapter 4.

82 *WHB*, December 21, 1979.

83 *RMRB*, January 5, 1984.

84 On the current autonomy of village chiefs (and perhaps county heads), as compared to township leaders, I learned from Zhe Ren's talk at Berkeley on Feb. 29, 2017. On much earlier rural structures, see Hsien-Chin Hu, *The Common Descent Group in China*

36 Farmers & the centralist revolution

and Its Functions (New York: Viking Press, 1948). The quality of the post-1989 elections of village chiefs stirs debates. This book does not interpret local politics as 'democratic'; politics in most places is locally authoritarian.

85 Jean C. Oi, *State and Peasant in Contemporary China* (Berkeley: University of California, 1989), 211.

86 Ibid., 174.

87 *FBIS*, December 29, 1987, 41, radio of December 28.

88 For more, Lynn White, "Shanghai-Suburb Relations," 240–68.

89 More on variation of local county cultures, notably Chuansha particularism, is in chapters about religion and about foreign trade in Lynn White, *Unstately Power: Local Causes of China's Intellectual, Legal, and Governmental Reforms* (Armonk, NY: M.E. Sharpe, 1999).

90 Charlotte Lee, *Training the Party: Party Adaptation and Elite Training in Reform-Era China* (New York: Cambridge University Press, 2015).

91 One *jin* (or *shijin*) is about one-half kilogram.

92 Frank Leeming, *Rural China*, 108.

93 Materials compiled by the Shanghai Revolutionary Committee, reported in Frank Leeming, *Rural China*, 109.

94 Comparisons of agricultural data from different Shanghai counties generally show increases or decreases of output in synchronization among them for most years – but not for all (e.g., 1981 or 1987).

95 This one-third was surveyed at 32 percent. *China Daily*, Beijing [hereafter *CD*], January 24, 1989.

96 *China's Rural Industry: Structure, Development, and Reform,* William Byrd and Lin Qingsong, eds. (Washington: World Bank, 1990), 395.

97 *CD*, January 24, 1989. Construction workers are sometimes derogatorily called "coolies"; this word is etymologically from Indian languages through Thai/Pali, rather than from Chinese *kuli*, 'bitter strength.'

98 Fei Xiaotong and Luo Yanxian, *Xiangzhen jingji*, 67.

99 Ibid., 67–74. For an historical collection of Fei's essays during long-term researches on another Sunan village, Kaixiangong, see Fei Hsiao-tung [older romanization on titlepage], *Rural Development in China: Prospect and Retrospect*, foreword by Tang Tsou (Chicago: University of Chicago Press, 1989).

100 A sample contract text is in Peter Nolan and Suzanne Paine, "Towards an Appraisal," 99–101.

101 A nice exception is Chris Bramall, *China's Economic Development* (Abingdon: Routledge, 2008). A parallel argument for industry can be found in Dorothy J. Solinger, "Urban Reform and Relational Contracting in Post-Mao China," in *Reform and Reaction in Post-Mao China: The Road to Tiananmen*, Richard Baum, ed. (New York: Routledge, 1991), 104–23.

102 Yao Shihuang, *Jin sanjiao*, 140–44.

103 *FBIS*, March 11, 1988, 36, radio of March 10.

104 *FBIS*, February 2, 1988, 36, radio of January 31.

105 This assertion is consistent with Elizabeth J. Perry, "Chinese Conceptions of 'Rights' from Mencius to Mao – and Now," *Perspectives on Politics* 6:1 (March 2008), 37–47.

106 Quoted in Frank Leeming, *Rural China*, 119.

107 The 1984 number was reported (too) exactly at 32,972; but in 1989, only 27,473 tractors. *Shanghai shi nongye*, 104.

108 Calculated from *ZGTJNJ* (in years noted below), finding a low in 1992 and a high in 1991 by inspecting the following pages, always in the edition of the next year: for 1987, 250; 1988, 202; 1989, 367; 1990, 350; 1991, 362; and 1992, 368.

109 *Gaige mianlin*, 4.

110 Ibid., 250.

111 Philip Huang, *Peasant Family*, 206–07, 233–34.

112 *CD*, January 16, 1989.

113 Ibid.

114 Guilhem Fabre, "The Chinese Mirror of Transition," *Communist Economies and Economic Transformation* 4:2 (1992), 262–63.

115 *CD*, April 12, 1989.

116 Philip Huang, *Peasant Family*, 17–18.

117 The survey covered ten counties in as many provinces, and the chances of nonfarm work in this S. Jiangsu place was higher than in any of the other locations. See William L. Parish, Xiaoye Zhe, and Fang Li, "Nonfarm Work and Marketization of the Chinese Countryside," *China Quarterly* 143 (September 1995), 718.

118 Jacques Bertrand, "Compliance, Resistance, and Trust: Peasants and the State in Indonesia" (Princeton University Politics Department Ph.D. dissertation, 1995), chapter 5.

119 Daniel Kelliher, *Peasant Power*, 30–31.

120 Lynn White, *Policies of Chaos: The Organizational Causes of Violence in China's Cultural Revolution* (Princeton: Princeton University Press, 1989) describes three organizational policies, linked to Weber's three forms of authority: charismatic campaigns, patronist monitoring, and categorical labeling. These helped cadres know whom to serve and whom to ignore during state consolidations of the 1950s and early 1960s. By 1965–69, the same policies were used by people who had been disserved by earlier policies to scare, control, and label. A summary is Lynn White, "The Cultural Revolution as an Unintended Result of Administrative Policies," in *New Perspectives on the Cultural Revolution*, W. Josephs, C. Wong, and D. Zweig, eds. (Cambridge: Harvard University Press, 1991), 83–104.

121 See both James C. Scott, *Weapons of the Weak: Everyday Forms of Peasant Protest* (New Haven: Yale University Press, 1985), and Frances Fox Piven and Richard A. Cloward, *Poor People's Movements*.

122 Daniel A. Bell, *The China Model*.

123 Karl Marx, "The German Ideology," in *Literary Theory: An Anthology*, 2nd ed. (Oxford: Blackwell, 1998), 653–658.

124 This book is reviewed by Joseph Fewsmith, quoting a pseudonymous "Leninger," *Disan zhi yanjing kan Zhongguo* (Looking at China Through a Third Eye), tr. Wang Shan [this must also be a pseudonym, because the book needed no translator] (Taiyuan: Shansi Publishing House, 1994), in *Journal of Contemporary China* 7 (Fall 1994), 101.

125 Ibid. Dostoyevsky's Grand Inquisitor, like Leninger, claims most people "will marvel at us and worship us like gods because, by becoming their masters, we have accepted the burden of freedom they were too frightened to face," Fyodor Dostoevsky, *The Brothers Karamazov*, Andrew MacAndrew, tr. (New York: Bantam Books, 2003; orig. 1880), 338. But not all data confirm such claims.

2

EX-PEASANT INDUSTRIALISTS END MOST SOCIALIST PLANNING

Processing raw materials is almost always more profitable than extracting them. Exceptions are resources such as petroleum, whose extraction requires large amounts of capital – and these few commodities remained under socialist planning after the mid-1980s. But rural manufacturing have historic traditions on the lower Yangzi. Silk-weaving, ceramics, handicrafts and household industries prospered there for centuries. Electricity and internal combustion engines as early as the 1930s provided more power for local factories, and old canals offered easy transport for factors and products. East China villages could make and sell goods so long as competition from Shanghai did not drive their consumer products off the market.[1] When they could mechanize their industrial production, their business capital grew.

In the first two decades of PRC planning, the state stressed industrial growth in large inland cities rather than coastal cities. Shanghai, southern Jiangsu, and northern Zhejiang were taxed more heavily than most of China. Many of these revenues went into state coffers managed in Beijing, and then from there to western and inland areas where returns on capital were slower than in Jiangnan.[2] This investment strategy, pursued for two decades, ignored advantageous economic "externalities" along the coast that could have expanded capital more quickly than in the places where the money was sent. Taxes collected on rural industries were lower than on urban factories in Mao's time, but planners in the 1950s and 1960s could still prevent the quick expansion of countryside factories. They thwarted competition against products from urban state plants, which provided most of China's budget.

So in the early 1950s, rural industrial enterprises were founded only sporadically in East China. Chances to start such factories became available during the Great Leap Forward of 1958, but rural capital was scarce before the "green revolution," which arrived a decade later. In Jiangsu, the provincial government in the Leap announced that every commune should open 15 to 25 small factories "within three to five years" – although the Leap's agricultural failure soon obviated many of these plans, as local money was diverted to buy food. The economic depression of the early 1960s led to retrenchment, during which the government closed about half of the rural plants (over 5,000 of them during 1961 in Jiangsu, for example). Not all such factories were shuttered, although many surviving firms remained small, hidden, and underreported. Even when particular local industries did not outlast the post-Leap depression, peasant leaders remembered their ability to run them.[3]

The quick growth of Yangzi delta agriculture in the late 1960s, and of rural industries in the 1970s, came partly from old local manufacturing and trading habits that resurfaced as the Cultural Revolution weakened state monitors. As soon as village managers in rural parts of the delta had the chance to diversify their production after 1970, because of new inputs or few controllers, they did so. When they could retain money, they invested it in ways that kept profits local. So the output of Jiangsu rural industries rose in terms of gross output by more than three times between 1970 and 1975. The rise in rural industrial product reported from Jiangsu commune-run factories during these years was higher (262 percent) than from brigade-run factories (172 percent), although local brigade industries probably reported less fully than did communes in this era when "radical" politicians such as Zhang Chunqiao criticized rural industrialization.[4] Industry's portion of rural Jiangsu's total output value was 7 percent in 1965, 13 percent in 1970 – and up to 40 percent by 1976.[5]

Zhejiang's growth rates also accelerated early. The gross value of that province's industrial output rose each year, in the half decade before 1974, at almost the 17 percent annual rate achieved in the half decade following 1978. These early data are difficult to interpret, both because severe late-1960s political disruptions may have depressed industries in Zhejiang more than in other provinces that were so large, and especially because statistics on rural industrial output in the early 1970s was almost surely underreported. In any case, there was some sag in the middle 1970s; Zhejiang gross industrial output in both 1974 and 1975 was reported as lower than in 1973. It bounced up to a new high in 1977, and then expanded into the 1980s.[6]

The factories responsible for most rural-industrial growth on the delta were not private; they were originally collective. Cooperatives run by villages and brigades had grown during the Great Leap Forward of 1958, even though they had been curbed during much of the 1960s.[7] The biggest economic change in the early 1970s was the rise of team, brigade, and commune enterprises. Such firms, which later were run by towns or villages and then often private entrepreneurs, were not just precursors of China's reform. They were its beginning.

Types of workers and industries that rural cadres managed in the early 1970s

Provincial data from very large areas such as Jiangsu or Zhejiang give an overview of reform in an extensive region of China where reforms were early. But information from other provinces shows that Jiangnan was not unique.[8] Statistics from more local booming places on the Shanghai delta tell the tale more dramatically.

40 Ex-peasant industrialists

Industry's portion of gross output value in rural Tangjiacun, in Qingcun Commune, Fengxian County, Shanghai, was only 7 percent in 1970. Already by 1971 it was 11 percent, then up sharply to 22 percent in 1972, 44 percent in 1973, and a startling 59 percent in 1974. These figures on rural industry's contribution come from a place that a foreign (Japanese) anthropologist deemed reasonably typical of the area.[9] The percentages on Tangjiacun industrial growth in Table 2.1 show that the early 1970s acceleration was not only steep but also constant until 1975 (when Zhang Chunqiao's last spurt of radical politics in Shanghai apparently forced underreporting), sagging until 1981, before a further rise slower than in 1970–1974.

By the same token, the portion of gross output value from agriculture in Tangjiacun plummeted from 80 percent in 1970 to 16 percent in 1987. Industrial performance in this rural place started reforms there.

Tangjiacun was only a village; but by 1970 it had a metalworking factory with 25 employees – a number that became ten times larger by 1980. By the latter year, after a decade of *de facto* reforms, this place also had further plants. By 1985, it employed 500 local industrial workers.[10] In later years, especially by the 1990s presuming this village was similar to others in Shanghai's suburbs, new laborers were immigrants from inland provinces.

Reforms had begun in many locations with the founding of a particular industry or a single factory. In 1972, a plastics plant and a silk filature were started at the Shanghai rural commune that has been best documented, Qingcun in Fengxian County. These were the first sizable local industries there; and they produced for sale elsewhere, rather than creating products such as fertilizer or household goods for use just within the local community. Although Qingcun Commune's enterprises employed about 400 workers in 1966, the number by 1971 was over 800, by 1972 over 1,000, and by 1978 over 1,700.[11]

The same pattern can be found throughout the delta. At Tangqiao Commune (Suzhou Prefecture, Jiangsu) the early 1970s was likewise a period of quick expansion. Some of Tangqiao's firms had been founded in the Great Leap Forward, but most were started in the first half of the 1970s. Tangqiao's agriculture reportedly reached limits of likely productivity under current technologies of that time. So the only way for peasant leaders to raise their followers' incomes was to set up factories making new kinds of products. Brigade-run enterprises of 1958 in Tangqiao

TABLE 2.1 Industrial percentages of total product at Tangjiacun

1970	7	1975	57	1980	57	1985	79
71	11	76	52	81	69	86	81
72	22	77	48	82	65	87	80
73	44	78	35	83	74		
74	59	79	39	84	78		

Source: Ishida Hiroshi, *Chûgoku nôson keizai no kiso kôzô: Shanhai kinkô nôson no kôgyôka to kindaika no ayumi* (Rural China in Transition: Experiences of Rural Shanghai toward Industrialization and Modernization) (Kyôto: Kôyô Shobô, 1991), 149.

Commune were formally reported to have closed in 1962, but this may have just been political correctness; in any case, some of them resumed in 1970.[12] Because these businesses did not accord with the then-current policy of "learning from Dazhai," which stressed that rural places should "take grain as the key link" (*yi liang wei gang*), local Tangqiao authorities supporting such factories ignored some Party directives.[13]

Leading radicals, later identified with the "Gang of Four," opposed rural industries as peasant capitalism. Various central and provincial politicians disagreed among themselves about the appropriate kinds and extent of rural industrialization. Radical "policy winds" were recurrent, fiercely opposing tillers' entrepreneurship – especially in East China, where Shanghai head Zhang Chunqiao was the main administrator. "Moderate" winds also blew then. In 1971, Tangqiao set up its first power plant, along with a cardboard box factory, several metal shops, and an animal feed processing factory. In the next year, one of its rural production brigades set up a brick factory that proved to be very profitable. By 1973, the value of that brigade's industrial product (240,000 yuan, with profits that were perhaps underreported at 25,000 yuan) quickly made it the richest village in the commune.

Word of such success spreads quickly in a farming society. By 1974, Tangqiao leaders set up an industrial office; and later analysts said the commune cadres "ran a certain political risk (*mao yiding zhengzhi fengxian*)."[14] At first, many new plants in this commune were formally under the umbrella of a "comprehensive factory" (*zonghe chang*). By the end of 1976, this pretense of planning was no longer needed, and the plants split under separate managements. By the next year, many villages in the commune found that the more they invested in agricultural production, the less total profit they made. Despite continuing campaigns under Hua Guofeng for agriculture to "study Dazhai," industrialization continued in many Jiangnan places. State leaders did not bring this change; village and town leaders did. The reported number of factories at Tangqiao doubled in just two years from 1976 to 1978.[15]

By the end of the decade, numerous rural plants had younger managers. Village leaders who had established or reopened factories in the first part of the decade recruited new, more technically adept cadres in a classic circulation of elites (in this case, a local one). Persons from families that had been rich before the revolution were often active in such plants, and now they could reassume greater roles.[16] The new leaders sought much wider markets for local products. By the beginning of 1982, Tangqiao factories sent a "comprehensive sales team" to tour about a dozen provinces in search of buyers. The township also established 90 long-lasting "sales points" in various Chinese cities, including some that were not served by producers of competing products.[17] This was not yet private capitalism, but it showed collectives' abilities to seek markets. Tangqiao entrepreneurs raised the standards of their management and the quality of their products.

Nearly half of the Tangqiao plants that remained at the end of 1985 had been founded before the Third Plenum of 1978. Of those, one-third were established in the years 1970–1972; and most of the others were Great Leap Forward plants that had reopened before 1978.[18] By the mid-1980s, more than half of the workers in

42 Ex-peasant industrialists

these factories were women. Practically no employees in village-run (*cunban*) factories had urban residence permits for the relevant city (Suzhou), and only 4 percent did so in plants that were township run (*xiangban*). Many workers in rural industry were by 1985 migrants from outside the township: 22 percent in the village-run factories, and relatively fewer (14 percent) in the ones run at higher rural levels.[19]

Tangqiao can represent the overall pattern, along with more comprehensive figures from Jiangsu as a whole. Reporting problems were reduced when data were published by careful Shanghai social scientists who obtained information directly from Tangqiao sources after incentives either to show production or to avoid taxes had lessened. Information from both the province and the commune are presented in Table 2.2. The less regular pattern for all of Jiangsu may be a less accurate index of behavior than the steadier one for the single township that has been studied more closely. Reporting may have been less constant than economic behavior. Tangqiao enjoyed a quantum leap of industrial growth in 1971, followed by maintenance of quick growth throughout the later reform years.

TABLE 2.2 Tangqiao rural industrialization, Suzhou Prefecture, 1967–1985, and rural industrialization in all of Jiangsu, 1970–1985 (gross value of industrial product in thousand yuan, percentage growths; rural industrial product in total Jiangsu gross output, with percentage growths of that ratio)

	Tangqiao Commune (Township)		Jiangsu Province	
	r.i. thou. yuan	*% change*	*% rur. ind. / total prod.*	*% change*
1967	146			
68	169	16		
69	210	24		
70	391	81	7	
71	1038	165	8	14
72	1611	155	9	13
73	2380	148	10	11
74	2910	122	12	20
75	3736	128	16	33
76	5299	142	21	31
77	10031	189	31	48
78	17025	170	31	0
79	24788	146	33	6
80	42727	172	43	30
81	61099	143	44	2
82	66100	108	42	−5
83	91916	139	46	10
84	129630	141	49	7
85	204270	156	58	18

Sources: Rounded to nearest percentage point from figures in Xu Yuanming and Ye Ding, *Tangqiao gongye hua zhi lu* (The Way to Industrialization in Tangqiao) (Shanghai: Shanghai Shehui Kexue Yuan Chuban She, 1987), 61, and *Jiangsu xiangzhen gongye fazhan shi* (History of the Development of Jiangsu Rural Industry), Mo Yuanren, ed. (Nanjing: Nanjing Gongxue Yuan Chuban She, 1987), 321–22 and 402.

In Shanghai's extensive green suburbs, the pattern resembled Tangqiao's – even though radical administrators in the mid-1970s city center discouraged rural industries and probably dampened rural reporting. Proximity to the metropolis spurred quick diversification in previously agricultural areas. The family origins of many urban cadres and technicians provided economic benefits for nearby rural places. At Qingpu County, Shanghai, from 1969 to 1973, the annual rate of gross industrial growth was 21 percent, whereas from 1979 to 1985, it was just one point higher (22 percent). New ventures were founded readily: The number of factories in this large suburban county rose 2.1 times from 1969 to 1973, but just 1.3 times over a later equal period, from 1978 to 1982.[20] Many of these firms were formally or informally connected to urban plants. Some factories had failed and/or had deregistered to avoid controls during the relatively brief hiatus of reforms in 1976.

Zooming "down" to a more local level in rural Shanghai County, Shenzhuang Commune's "household subsidiary production" by 1974 accounted for 40 percent of the value of all output. Private plots, fish breeding, handicrafts, and short-distance transport all flourished, as did rural industry. "Radicals" criticized such growth not just because it was (as they rightly said) proto-capitalist, and not just because it diverted resources and took markets from state-owned enterprises, but also because it threatened the supply of low-cost grain to workers in urban state factories. Communes on the delta raised staple food output in the mid-1970s, but their main prosperity came from small firms that shifted the interests of laborers away from rice paddies.

An unidentified "average" county in Suzhou Prefecture in 1974 already had 46 percent of its rural workforce in industry (perhaps some on a part-time basis). In Shanghai's Jinshan County by 1974, only half of all rural workers were reported to be agriculturalists. Less than half spent most of their work hours in paddies, although there was political pressure to report as many tillers as possible. In the "East is Red Production Brigade," despite its name, "Some cadres interested themselves more in production for cash than in the political line, encouraging diversification and economic crops at the expense of grain production; and some prosperous peasants neglected collective production in favor of private plots and free markets."[21]

Data on the shift from state-owned to collective production also show the same change. Nonstate output as a portion of total product from rural communes, brigades, and teams in Jiangsu's Wuxi County rose sharply: It was just 23 percent in 1970; but by 1977, it was 64 percent.[22] State-managed companies' portion of output value fell. These figures may underreport the change, because the state tended to fix high prices for products from its own factories, and because some collective-made goods were probably hidden to avoid taxes. This 1970–1977 shift predated the official 1978 onset of reforms. Most early rural plants, when registered at all, were licensed in brigades, and to a lesser extent in communes. The ownership type that boomed early was collective, not state – or private (yet). The change was based on specifically new institutions: During the single year 1974 in Wuxi County, 1,212 new rural factories were founded (among a reported total of 1,600 rural factories). Some were re-registered Leap plants. Privatization of ownership was not relevant in this era. Autonomous local management of collectives was the main change.

44 Ex-peasant industrialists

Brigades ran or authorized – the word *ban* has either meaning – nearly four-fifths of Wuxi County's 1,600 rural factories in 1974. The output of these firms by 1977 exceeded that of the burgeoning industries in Wuxi City (a prefecture city, *diji shi*), even though capital investment in rural Wuxi places was much lower. The founding dates for most such companies were reportedly in the early 1970s. Wuxi County established many then, but it shared the widespread slowing (or hiding) of reforms in 1975–1976, so that the number reported to a Western economist in 1978 was only 16 percent higher than in 1974.[23]

The portions of industrial employment at the most local village (*cun*) level, as distinct from that at the "higher" township/commune level, changed sharply during reforms at Tangjiacun, Fengxian County, Shanghai. The village-run factories' portion of local industrial workers was not linear but hump-shaped over the whole reform era, rising and then falling: 34 percent were hired by the village 1971, up to 65 percent in 1979, then down to 43 percent by 1988. Non-local immigrants by late reforms replaced locals in difficult and low-paying jobs at village plants. Officially "private" (*siying*) hiring in all three years was minimal, respectively rounding to 4, 0, and 5 percent.[24]

Illegal factories: reformers vs. radicals

As sociologist Fei Xiaotong has written, at least some the factories were secret:

> In the later stages of the Cultural Revolution [this refers to the early 1970s], many small enterprises emerged in Sunan. These enterprises, established by local cadres, were illegal [*sic*] at that time. They were "underground." Because of the Cultural Revolution, higher level cadres had no time to deal with such things; so more and more enterprises emerged. Peasants did not mind what the nature of ownership was. The only thing they did mind was to keep up their livelihood. . . . Capital came from collective accumulation; communes used a portion of their funds to develop [industrial] production after the income distribution. . . . The government did not give money or invest. . . . But this was the only way for peasants to make their living at that time.[25]

The North China Agricultural Conference and relative moderates in Beijing during the early 1970s condoned locally owned rural cooperative industries, while radicals simultaneously tried to enforce restrictions against them. Such ambiguity was typical of reforms – not just in the 1970s. Serious socialists saw that rural factories' competition with state plants would threaten the Party's ability to plan the economy and finance the central budget. Many such factories were therefore clandestine; but they were actively sponsored by local "state" cadres who undermined at least some of the mandates sent to them from "high levels" of the state. They did not advertise their insubordination, of course, and they could usually cite opposite mandates more to their liking. Splits between conservatives and reformers at the top allowed local cadres to keep low profiles, making profits and employing local clients (and later migrants). As Fei says, "At the very beginning of these enterprises, they were not called village and town industries (*xiangzhen gongye*) but commune and production term enterprises (*shedui qiye*). . . . Actually, every commune and every village was an economic enterprise. . . . Big collectives were still managed by local governments, and for a long time there was no separation between enterprises and [local] governments."

At this time, there were also "small collectives," which were "established by individuals."[26] These businesses were an early-1970s form of enterprises that in later years were often called "dependent firms" (*guahu*), because they relied for protection on local "state cadres" who were actually rather separate from more central parts of "the state."[27] Local officials acquired positive interests in these enterprises, even when they did not manage them. Economic expansion in their jurisdictions gave them more bargaining chips with which to deal with monitors "above" them in the bureaucracy.[28] The new profits became important for politics. Local cadres had more wherewithal to grease palms at higher administrative levels, and these fresh resources raised local cadres' power. Their legitimacy from holding low-level "state" offices surely helped them too; but access to goods, ranging from fertilizer to factory capital, was increasingly important. As entrepreneurs without official status gained more assets, top bureaucrats could no longer "capriciously order farmers around."[29] This was not a matter of "democracy," since the local polities were largely autocratic. It did, however, mean more freedom for most of China's leaders, who did not live in Beijing.

The CCP government was not quickly and obviously weakened by rural industrialization. Its response was reactive, sporadically acknowledging what had happened for the sake of eking some taxes out of situations it could not control. Top leaders found in the 1970s that important parts of rural China had "five small industries" (*wu xiao gongye*), producing steel, machines, chemical fertilizers, coal, and cement; so some officials encouraged these. But country factories inevitably vied with state firms selling the same commodities and needing similar materials to make them. The state plants produced more efficiently than the small ones, often because they had better economies of scale. But there is nothing inherently "small" about steel, machines, chemicals, coal, or cement.[30] Local companies appeared in all these fields – but they often hid their activities to avoid monitoring, imposts, and restrictions. They were officially supposed to stress rural producer goods, but soon they made consumer goods too.

An American delegation visiting rural Chinese industries in 1975 concluded, "Much decision making in China has been decentralized to lower levels; and scientific and technical personnel from Peking, even if they were so inclined, cannot usually order factory and county revolutionary committees to divulge information that these revolutionary committees themselves, for whatever reason, are reluctant to give out."[31] This delegation visited several small plants on the Yangzi delta (in three Wuxi communes and Shanghai's towns of Jiading and Malu). Their report found that "[t]he prime motive force for this extensive development lies within the counties and communes themselves. Provincial and central government planners

46 Ex-peasant industrialists

sometimes provide financial aid and more frequently technical assistance, but it is the interest of the localities that drives the program forward."[32]

It may be unimportant whether top state leaders in the early 1970s were unified or divided as they faced this independent industrial development. Some were clearly willing to wink at it. All high state cadres, including radicals, knew about this new manufacturing, because China's leaders had access to many kinds of information, sampled from locations and summarized in limited-circulation reports. They could not have missed such a major trend. Radicals noted that it weakened the "dictatorship of the proletariat," as embodied in their state. But top leaders at that time apparently had no unified will to prevent local power networks from expanding factories, and they were in any case unable to stop such an endemic development. In the mid-1970s, when famous radicals had greater effective control at the center (and when at Mao's moribund court, personal factors such as Deng Xiaoping's temporary eclipse and Zhou Enlai's cancer were important), the radicals' main effects were to chastise the rate of rural factory growth and reduce the rate at which it was reported. About 1975, when these socialist-conservatives who most wanted to reverse nonstate industrialization had a temporary political resurgence, the trend was slowed – but did not stop. A weakening of China's centralized revolution was evident in the 1970s, and it lasted until the 1990s.

Xu Jiatun was a top administrator in Jiangsu during the 1970s (becoming the provincial governor in 1977). He was also the highest Party leader to leave China after June 4, 1989, and the memoirs that he later wrote abroad were frank. Xu's language remained statist, the standard dialect that most leaders and intellectuals use. But from the safety of a Buddhist monastery in California, Xu reminisced about his time in Jiangsu's capital, Nanjing, and he expressed pride at the province's economic progress: "I tell you, we took a different road from the rest of the country. 'The planned economy was crucial, and the market economy was a supplement.' We had openly to support this, but in fact we had gone beyond it."[33]

Some central leaders were willing to condone local initiatives, Xu says, even when they were unwilling to be activists for rural enterprise. There is scant contemporary evidence that province-level cadres went beyond the ambiguity Xu expressed. Some were plainly against rural industrialization and agricultural decollectivization. After the Jiangsu Party committee ordered lower CCP branches in 1975 to "oppose capitalist tendencies more energetically," peasants reacted by slaughtering team- and brigade-owned livestock and by diverting water to their own plots. In Jiangsu's Nanchang County and Zhejiang's Shaoxing County, there was "widespread sabotage."[34] Behavior varied among county leaders and more locally. Unified decisions about rural industrialization were difficult, then, to enforce in an area as large as a province. Opportunities for local networks differed among parts of China, but the whole Wu-dialect flatland provided a fertile context for new industries, no matter what high politicians wanted. Xu observes that markets overtook plans early in Sunan. Xu and his colleagues had few effective bureaucratic helpers in the early 1970s, after the Cultural Revolution had cowed so many. He simply blinked at the change, seeing it from his Nanjing office.

Shanghai's most powerful politician at that time, Zhang Chunqiao (one of the Gang of Four), was not willing to blink. Zhang fulminated about "sprouts of capitalism (*zibenzhuyi de mengya*) in the countryside." His shrill complaints were widely deemed in the West at the time to be a mere mantra, representing what any devoted leftist would have said reflexively, with or without evidence. Now it should be clear that Zhang knew exactly what he was talking about. Partly because of the power of Shanghai's radicals, the city's suburbs did not develop as quickly as Sunan. Leaders of the Star Brigade in Chengbei Commune, Songjiang County, Shanghai, for example, were excoriated by radicals for having grown the least grain of any brigade in that commune during the decade before 1975. The fault reportedly lay in "capitalist" tendencies among local cadres who started industries that took labor from paddies. Brigade officials were particularly criticized for claiming they had a shortage of workers.[35] In the radicals' view, they were assigning their workers to the wrong tasks: to factories rather than fields.

Administrative superiors did not always know what their nominal subordinates were doing. Steven Butler shows that the basis of rural autonomy was an avoidance of monitors. The main issue was "at which level decision-making is made feasible by the nature of the problem at hand."[36] Away from Shanghai, in hilly regions at the edge of the delta and beyond ('Ningbo more far' as outdated Pidgin poetically put it), there is evidence of great autonomy at this time. In 1975, Changqi Commune in Zhejiang "suffered from the capitalist faction's influence among the leading comrades." Workers left planned production in favor of "sideline" occupations (which included factories), and this pattern was said to be widespread throughout Zhejiang. A county of inland Anhui was reported to be suffering from capitalist "corruption of alarming proportions."[37] Wenzhou, in southern Zhejiang, took the trend to extremes – and did so earlier than public discussion of the singular "Wenzhou model" that later became the archetype for risky reform. Private enterprise in that city and its isolated delta, which had been flourishing on illegal bases for years before the spring of 1977, was the target of attacks in a government campaign that year against "capitalist forces." This hassle merely forced private firms underground on a temporary basis.[38] Wenzhou, despite being a major city with a large population and many locally initiated (not centrally initiated) commercial connections to other parts of China, was not linked to the national railroad network until 1998. It was richer than it reported, but it had never been a major source of collectable state revenue.

Scant official support was available for most Jiangnan plants in the 1970s, even at locations on the Yangzi delta much closer to Shanghai. Team or brigade factories, and most commune plants, were treated by high cadres as crucially different from the state enterprises under planning. As one report put it, "Rural industry had no registration among the state's industrial departments, and no place in the state plan." So the government's economic committees, central or provincial, normally refused to guarantee provisions of credit, materials, machines, energy, or markets. On the other hand, these nonstate firms "had relatively complete freedom to do their business. . . . [T]hey could adapt to suit changing circumstances and could survive." In contrast to most state firms, they were highly competitive traders.[39]

48 Ex-peasant industrialists

Rural enterprises in the early 1970s were started outside the designated "five small industries." Entrepreneurs established factories in many sectors, illegally if necessary.[40] In Jiangsu during 1970, a polyester fiber workshop created a large mill and developed new equipment for it.[41] Many parts of the China coast saw a "second economy" developing in this period.[42] The state budget was disserved by the emergence of all these new firms. They flourished not because of production efficiency, but because they could operate more flexibly in both upstream and downstream markets, seeking opportunistic benefits in either the socialist or proto-capitalist contexts. Beijing's policies were mixed, trying to contain new firms by encouraging that they be formed under middle levels of administration, rather than under local units where state control was even more tenuous. As early as August 1971, central decrees condoned the founding of some factories under prefectures or counties. At these middling-high levels of bureaucracy, larger imposts on economic activity could be expected than if the factories were mainly established under communes, brigades, or teams. But for rural firms, the State Council had already provided in 1971 that "60 percent of the profits made by newly established local industries at the county level could be kept at the county level."[43] The central state's problems were accurately to count those profits, collect the other 40 percent, and prevent major startups in smaller localities.

Slogans acclimatized high cadres to rural industries. Cultural Revolution mantras that had been originally designed for urban purposes (to legitimize contract labor, or to send city youths to the countryside) could be adapted to justify rural industries. Such factories were alleged to create all-purpose proletarians who were "at once workers and peasants" (*yigong yinong*). The new plants hastened "integration of farm and factory" (*nonggong yiti hua*). Also, they discouraged the influx to cities by allowing laxly employed rural people to "leave the soil but not the countryside" (*li tu buli xiang*). These were a national "reservoir" of surplus farm labor – but actually, rural factory workers had scant interest in returning to drudgery in paddies. Old slogans put a patina of official legitimacy on a trend that was out of the state's control. Mere words could not make the pattern serve the central government.

Collective firms were numerous in Shanghai's rural suburbs during the early 1970s, and they paid low taxes and relatively few workers' benefits in comparison with state companies. They supplied less medical care, less housing, less time off, and lower wages – but still, they paid enough to attract labor. Many youths who had been rusticated in the late 1960s returned to Shanghai in the next decade (especially in its latter half) and could become politically restive if given nothing to do. The state had annoyed many of these youths by sending them to the boondocks in 1968; so it had built the barrel over which it now found itself.

A survey showed that "permanent" emigration from Shanghai over a long term had been more than six times more usual to cities with over a million inhabitants than to smaller cities with more than half a million – and was also about six times more frequent to smaller settlements of less than 500,000.[44] Not all these changes of household registration to small places actually remained permanent. "Rusticated" people came back to cities. By 1971, the state sacrificed some control over local materials and product markets, in order to keep unemployed youths (euphemistically called "social youths," *shehui qingnian*) off the streets of Shanghai by allowing collectives to hire them in the central city, or more often in the suburbs. By 1979, the "substitution" (*dingti*) program meant that some youths could take urban work in a state or collective firm after a parent was supposed to retire from the same job. Not all such "substitutions," however, really involved parental retirements.

The annual operating budget that collectives allocated per job was closer to a subsistence rate of pay than traditions in the state sector would allow. An economic historian wrote:

> Urban and town collective enterprises . . . operated during the Cultural Revolution. At that time, there were a lot of intellectual young people who could not find jobs in state firms. Collectives became an important place for them to work. . . . According to statistics of the Shanghai Handicraft Bureau, its collectives on average needed 2,278 yuan to arrange a job, but state firms took 10,049 yuan to do the same thing. . . . Street enterprises played an important role. Street firms had to collect financial resources and materials by themselves. They had to take charge of their own marketing. They also had independent accounts. They were not subordinate to any level of government or to a trade system. They were established totally to resolve the employment problem for young people. After 1970, state enterprises, schools, and universities also established small enterprises in order to arrange employment for the family members of their workers. . . . Small collectives got opportunities to survive and develop. Actually, they carried out a portion of the state ownership enterprises' functions. Shanghai street enterprises had an industrial output value more than 1 billion yuan. The figure was nearly three times that of 1966. . . . From 1971 to 1976, the average annual growth rate of state output was 5 percent, but that of collectives was 13 percent. . . . According to 1975 statistics, the profit rate per hundred yuan in state firms was 15 percent, but in collective enterprises, 44 percent.[45]

Collectives hired many "social youths" and solved a short-term political problem for the state – while weakening state control of markets and worsening fiscal difficulties for officials later.

Even when high-placed radicals opposed rural industries' prosperity, arguing for more planning of production, many local leaders' support for nonstate factories did not waiver. Since rural industries were booming anyway, flexible Marxists gave it an ideological gloss. Marx himself had called for the release of productive forces that "slumber in the lap of social labor."[46] No credible advocate for the proletariat could long argue that China's countryside should remain poor. No Chinese could long claim to be patriotic while standing foursquare against most compatriots, tillers who increased resources that arguably strengthened the nation as a whole. But radicals like Zhang Chunqiao saw that the rural trends threatened state planning and Party elites. One reason why the PRC state of the early 1970s began to lose

50 Ex-peasant industrialists

control of rural China is that its leaders' goals were mixed. If the top politicians had been more united on any rural policy, the long-term result would almost surely have been the same. Hopes among the national leaders were sufficiently diverse that local factories were not easily repressed.

China's leaders were divided collectively or within individuals. They split between "leftist" conservatives and nascent reformists. "Radical" socialists preferred portfolios in cultural and urban affairs rather than economic and rural fields. Shanghai Mayor Ke Qingshi in the early and middle 1960s separated cultural czars like Yao Wenyuan and Zhang Chunqiao from economic czars like Cao Diqiu and Chen Peixian.[47] An irony of the reform period, already evident in its early beginnings, was that rural prosperity created by local industrialists helped legitimize the CCP after its traumas in the post-Leap famine and the 1960s Cultural Revolution. Local entrepreneurs might evade the government's imposts, hide data from tax collectors, and castigate uncooperative cadres. If rural people had not made themselves richer by foisting reforms on the Party-state in the 1970s, the CCP would have enjoyed less "performance legitimacy."

Different rates of reform in different parts of China

Reforms came earlier to the Yangzi delta than to most parts of the country. But recent evidence suggests that similar patterns also occurred in many regions.[48] Reforms were not immediate on a nationwide basis, but they were more prevalent than official sources reported. Jiangnan development of rural industry was faster than parallel changes in the country as a whole, but inland boondocks areas held down the average for any index by which reform might be measured. For example, by 1976 Huayang Commune/Township, Songjiang, Shanghai, had an industrial portion of total output already at 43 percent – a figure that rural China on average reached a decade later, in 1986. Industrial growth in commune factories, and later in township and village plants, was uneven over both time and place. In Huayang, large increases in the portion of total output value from industry came in 1971–1975 (and in the single year 1980, when reporting may have become more complete). The periods 1975–1979 and 1981–1983 at that place showed somewhat less change (see Table 2.3).

The flatland around Shanghai has strong traditions of rural entrepreneurship. A dense network of canals is only the most obvious physical manifestation of a commercial culture the region has nurtured for centuries. The Yangzi delta's physical plant to support medium-distance traders who lack much capital is unexcelled anywhere. For state planners, this infrastructure for autonomy has created problems of control since the 1950s. Cadres had tried to respond by subsidizing canal tugboats, behind which long trains of otherwise freelance freight barges (each with a family aboard) might be cheaply pulled – and thus monitored. But "boat people" sometimes dropped the tether. If, despite poverty, they could get their own engines and avoid harassment from the water police (*shuijing*), they could increasingly fend off, making money on their own.

This created tensions between ethnic groups and cowed bureaucrats. Boat people, some of whom in Shanghai's Qingpu and Chuansha counties have been Roman

TABLE 2.3 Reported industrial percentages of gross output values

	Huayang	Rural China
1971	27%	7%
72	31	8
73	35	9
74	35	10
75	41	12
76	43	17
77	46	21
78	47	23
79	46	24
80	58	27
81	61	22
82	61	22
83	64	24
84		28
85		37
86		43

Source: Rounded percentages, from Philip C. C. Huang, *The Peasant Family and Rural Development in the Yangzi Delta, 1350-1988* (Stanford: Stanford University Press, 1990), 355.

Catholic for generations, saw themselves as separate from the generally richer farmers in their areas.[49] Some reported visions of Saint Mary. A Shanghai Social Sciences Academy writer reported that "[in] March, 1980, . . . Qingpu Catholics heard the rumor that the 'Blessed Mother' would show her power and presence by appearing on Sheshan hill [where a pre-1949 basilica to Mary is still in use]." They "shouted reactionary slogans" and "abused the government" until the state's Qingpu Catholic Patriotic Association ordained a priest for them. Marian visions have occurred in many countries (France, Mexico, Philippines, and others), but the Party apparently did not expect one in Shanghai. The CCP's secular papers, such as *Wenhui bao* and *Jiefang ribao*, reported it. Believers took this as confirmation it had happened. From 1984 to 1987, fifteen hundred Catholics were baptized in Qingpu. "Subethnic-Han" boat people could make money in haulage – and could diversify into new trades. The "Baihe Aquatic Brigade" in Qingpu set up a shoe factory and a box factory.[50] It was difficult for the regime to plan Jiangnan markets, because canals and autonomous traders dispersed commerce away from central oversight.

Different East China towns have for centuries been somewhat specialized in manufactures, or marketing, or administration, or transport, or simply residence.[51] This traditional diversification became a basis of local initiatives during reforms – even though the particular institutions that new leaders used were not like pre-1949 structures. Private and individual trade was politically prohibited or discouraged in 1971–1978, but the collective and commune economies developed

52 Ex-peasant industrialists

quickly. Jiangnan made early distinctions between "private" (*siying*) enterprises that could hire outside workers, "individual" (*geti*) units that relied on one household, and "joint" (*lianhu*) firms that combined several households. These types were contrasted with collective (*jiti*) and state-run (*guoying*) firms. The collective sector by the early 1970s was the largest fast-growth one. But so many collectives were so plainly under the leadership of one or a few cadres, they were operationally (not legally) private.[52] This pattern also applied in other regions that experienced relatively early reforms. The highly efficient water transport system of southern Jiangsu and northern Zhejiang was unexcelled in China, but similar reforms followed in reform-prone smaller deltas and plains (e.g., near Guangzhou or Chengdu) that have comparable infrastructures. These inherited situational contexts combined with local leadership choices to determine the intensity of reforms.

Sunan did better in expanding rural industries than historically poorer and economically less diversified regions such as Subei (northern Jiangsu). By 1982, the gross product of rural industries per person in Wuxi, Sunan, was 714 yuan, the highest level in the province; and in the premodern Sunan administrative center of Suzhou, it was 537 yuan. But in north Jiangsu's major city of Xuzhou in 1982, this per capita product was only 74 yuan; in Lianyungang, 68 yuan; and in Huaiyang, just 40 yuan. Even the provincial capital of Nanjing, which usually tended to have conservative leaders, recorded a level of just 143 yuan, lower than Zhenjiang, Changzhou, or any other large city in Sunan further south of the Yangzi.[53]

If legally provincial units are used for this comparison, Shanghai Municipality's high taxes and multitude of large state-run heavy industries prevented it from excelling. In mid-reforms from 1982 to 1986, Jiangsu and Zhejiang grew much faster than Shanghai – having 17 and 21 percent annual industrial output increases, respectively, in comparison with Shanghai's 7.5 percent. Although Shanghai in 1982 still had 26 percent more total industrial yield by nominal value than Jiangsu (with state-fixed prices), that large province overtook the metropolis as China's largest industrial producer by mid-1985. Stagnancy in central Shanghai's state sector was responsible for this difference. In 1982, factory output value from government firms predominated in all three places: 58 percent in Zhejiang, 60 percent in Jiangsu, and 87 percent in Shanghai (at prices set for different commodities by markets or state planners). By the mid-1980s, however, state enterprises created less than half of all industrial product in both Jiangsu and Zhejiang – but still over 80 percent in Shanghai.[54]

From 1978 to 1984, the average annual growth rate of *rural* enterprise output in Suzhou, Wuxi, and Changzhou (all in southern Jiangsu) was reported at 30 percent.[55] In the single year between 1984 and 1985 alone, the amount of product made by rural industries under these Sunan jurisdictions reportedly rose by half. Factories contributed 70 percent of the value of all rural production in those places, and already countryside plants delivered one-third of fiscal revenues.[56] These three prefectures by 1988 were producing 43 percent of the industrial output of Jiangsu – by then, the highest among China's province-level units.[57] Rural industrialization hurt the central state's ability to get money. So many top leaders actively tried, without much success, to close 1980s country markets and factories that operated with few plans or low taxes and profit-remittances.[58] The rural boom localized the resource base for Chinese politics.

Different regions in China prospered at different rates – as is entirely normal in the economic evolution of any large nation. It is now clear that during the early 1970s more entrepreneurship and prosperity developed in more parts of the country than official records of that time suggested. Chinese development after 1970 was quick. By the 1990s and 2000s, however, cadres from the Maoist period retired. The central government's 1993 Law on Agriculture and the 1995 Petition Regulations and Budget Law were central efforts to reduce "local misbehaving" and local power. County administrations came under more central control, but links to towns and especially villages frayed.[59] The state tried to monitor villages, but power there had grown along with output.

Notes

1 Debates long raged among R. H. Tawney, John Lossing Buck, Fei Xiaotong, Jack Potter, Ramon Myers, and others on whether China's urban growth helped or hurt peasants. Fei's book *Xiangtu chongjian* (Rural Reconstruction) (Shanghai: Guanchashe, 1949) shows electricity and internal combustion engines enabled some localization of industrial production.
2 A debate about taxes between economists Nicholas Lardy and Audrey Donnithorne is assessed in Chapter 6, concluding that Mao's state sent extensive resources inland but official reports failed to cover Shanghai's income or capital.
3 *Dangdai Zhongguo de Jiangsu* (Jiangsu in Today's China), Liu Dinghan, ed. (Beijing: Zhongguo Shehui Kexue Chuban She, 1989), 106.
4 *Jiangsu xiangzhen gongye fazhan shi* (History of the Development of Jiangsu Rural Industry), Mo Yuanren, ed. (Nanjing: Nanjing Gongxue Yuan Chuban She, 1987), 140.
5 This early-1970s increase was overwhelmingly in southern Jiangsu. See *Xin Zhongguo gongye jingji shi* (A History of New China's Industrial Economy), Wang Haibo, ed. (Jingji Guanli Chuban She 1986), 364.
6 The pattern in Zhejiang is broadly similar to Sunan's, though it was affected by floods in some years, notably 1975. Tensions between native Zhejiang and originally non-local cadres (many of whom arrived from Shandong with Chen Yi's army) help account for variations in the extent to which outputs were reported. Data are in *Zhejiang tongji nianjian, 1989* (Zhejiang Statistical Yearbook, 1989) (Beijing: China Statistics Press, 1989), 22.
7 Xu Yuanming and Ye Ding, *Tangqiao gongye hua zhi lu* (The Way to Industrialization in Tangqiao) (Shanghai: Shanghai Shehui Kexue Yuan Chuban She, 1987), 38, offers numbers for Tangqiao teams, gross outputs, and profits.
8 Joshua Eisenman, *Red China's Green*, passim, gathers new data on this point.
9 Ishida Hiroshi, *Chûgoku nôson keizai no kiso kôzô: Shanhai kinkô nôson no kôgyôka to kindaika no ayumi* (Rural China in Transition: Experiences of Rural Shanghai toward Industrialization and Modernization) (Kyôto: Kôyô Shobô, 1991), 149, does not stress this interpretation, but his data suggest it. See also Chris Bramall, *The Industrialization of Rural China* (Oxford: Oxford University Press, 2007).
10 After that, Tangjiacun's carpentry and barrel industries failed for financial reasons; so the *reported* number of employees in its village factories by 1987 decreased to 425. Ibid., 138–39, provides information about just a single place, but the wealth of circumstantial evidence in Ishida's book raises confidence that Tangjiacun is not a "Potemkin" village. I realize that not all readers are dying to know exactly how many barrel makers Tangjiacun had in 1987. But the issue is larger: Local reporting from this independent source

54 Ex-peasant industrialists

(a Japanese anthropologist) provides more accurate suggestions, even about large situations, than ostensibly comprehensive reporting from sources that have official interests. Ishida offers a useful check on bias, because he could monitor 'on the spot' the consistency of many different kinds of data.

11 Ishida Hiroshi, *Chûgoku nôson*, 121 and 132.

12 Xu Yuanming and Ye Ding, *Tangqiao gongye*, 10, says that Party members at Tangqiao took the initiative to spur the development of these new and reopened factories.

13 David Zweig, *Agrarian Radicalism*. See also Xu Yuanming and Ye Ding, *Tangqiao gongye*, 10–13.

14 Xu Yuanming and Ye Ding, *Tangqiao gongye*, 13.

15 For more, see Xu Yuanming and Ye Ding, *Tangqiao gongye*, 15–17.

16 Ibid. This phenomenon is also noted for poorer areas and for agriculture by Jonathan Unger, "'Rich Man, Poor Man': The Making of New Classes in the Countryside," in *China's Quiet Revolution: New Interactions Between State and Society*, David Goodman and Beverley Hooper, eds. (New York: St. Martin's Press, 1994), 43–63.

17 The references to this *zonghe tuixiao duiwu* team and the *xiaoshou dian* sales points are at ibid., 25.

18 Based on calculations from a complete list of Tangqiao factories in Xu Yuanming and Ye Ding, *Tangqiao gongye*, 139–43. These pages include information on each plant's number of employees, fixed capital, liquid capital, and 1985 production.

19 Calculated from figures in ibid., 68. These may be underestimates, however, neglecting temporary and contract workers including migrants.

20 The number of factories is large enough for a credible sample: 1969–1983, 346 to 732 factories; 1978–1982, 598 to 796. *Qingpu xianzhi* (Qingpu County Gazetteer), Feng Xuewen, ed. (Shanghai: Shanghai Renmin Chuban She, 1990), 270–71.

21 Frank Leeming, *Rural China*, 104–05.

22 Ibid., 115.

23 For the data, see ibid.

24 The township (*xiang*; earlier, commune) accounted for 62 percent of reported industrial employment in 1970, a low of 35 percent in 1978, and then back up to 45 percent in 1988. Ishida Hiroshi, *Chûgoku nôson*, 151.

25 Fei Xiaotong and Luo Yanxian, *Xiangzhen jingji*, 5–9.

26 Ibid., 1–4.

27 For more on *guahu*, Lynn White and Kate Xiao Zhou, "Quiet Politics and Rural Enterprise in Reform China," *Journal of the Developing Areas* 29 (July 1995), 461–90.

28 David Zweig, "Urbanizing Rural China: Bureaucratic Authority and Local Autonomy," in *Bureaucracy, Politics, and Decision Making in Post-Mao China*, Kenneth G. Lieberthal and David M. Lampton, eds. (Berkeley: University of California Press, 1992), 334–59.

29 Scott Rozelle, "Decision-Making in China's Rural Economy: The Linkages between Village Leaders and Farm Households," *China Quarterly* 137 (March 1994), 123–24. The author thanks Joanne Ramos for referring him to this source.

30 Christine Wong, Thomas Rawski, and other economists have assessed the comparative efficiency of various kinds of plants. Small plants – even economically successful ones – often turn out to be technically inefficient. Like the socialist enterprises they tend to replace, they mobilize resources better than they coordinate resources. A major advantage of the state sector in the 1970s and beyond was its ability to acquire capital openly. See a comparison, by product type rather than ownership, showing this advantage in Rawski's *Economic Growth and Employment in China* (New York: Oxford University Press, 1979), 47 and passim.

31 *Rural Small-Scale Industry in the People's Republic of China*, Dwight Perkins, ed. (Berkeley: University of California Press, 1977), 2.

32 Ibid., 252.

33 Xu Jiatun in *Shijie ribao* (World Daily), May 6, 1993.

34 Jiangxi Provincial Broadcasting Station, November 25, 1975, and Zhejiang Provincial Broadcasting Station, November 16, 1975; Jürgen Domes, *Socialism in the Chinese*

Countryside Rural Societal Policies in the People's Republic of China, 1949–1979, tr. Margritta Wendling (London: C. Hurst, 1980), 90.

35 *WHB*, December 4, 1975.

36 Steven Butler, *Agricultural Mechanization in China: The Administrative Impact* (New York: East Asian Institute, Columbia University, 1978), 45.

37 *Zhejiang ribao*, October 8, 1975, Anhui Provincial Broadcasting Station, August 23, 1975, and Zhejiang Provincial Broadcasting Station, October 6, 1975; Jürgen Domes, *Socialism in the Chinese*, 88.

38 Zheng Yongnian reports this from a Government of Wenzhou document, *Wenzhou shiqu geti gongshang yehu qingkuang diaocha* (Investigation of Private Industrial and Commercial Firms in Wenzhou, 1984). Wenzhou's autonomy is bolstered by the local dialect, sometimes called the "devil's language," distantly related to Shanghainese but not mutually comprehensible even with other tongues of the Shanghainese "Wu" group – and not understood outside the delta of the Ou River.

39 *Xin Zhongguo gongye*, 361–63.

40 Samuel Ho, *Rural China in Transition: Non-Agricultural Development in Rural Jiangsu, 1978–90* (New York: Oxford University Press, 1994), 18.

41 Audrey Donnithorne, "China's Cellular Economy: Some Trends Since the Cultural Revolution," *China Quarterly* 52 (October–December 1972), 607.

42 John Burns, "Rural Guangdong's Second Economy," *China Quarterly* 88 (December 1981), 629–44.

43 Prefectures (*diqu*) are areas comprising several counties (*xian*). *Xin Zhongguo gongye*, 356–58.

44 *Zhongguo 1986 nian 74 chengzhen renjou qianyi chouxiang diaocha ziliao* (Sample Survey Materials on 1986 Chinese Migration in 74 Cities and Towns), *Chinese Demography* Editorial Group, ed. (Beijing: *Zhongguo renkou kexue* bianji bu, 1988), 24.

45 *Xin Zhongguo gongye jingji shi* [*XZGGYJJS*], 359–61.

46 Karl Marx and Frederick Engels, *Manifesto of the Communist Party* (Beijing: Foreign Languages Press, 1970), 37.

47 Lynn White, "Leadership in Shanghai, 1955–69," op cit., 346, or Lynn White, *Policies of Chaos*, 224.

48 The most important recent evidence is in Joshua Eisenman, *Red China's Green*. Future research might compare local, statist, or globalist causes of reform in deltas of the following rivers: the Min (Fuzhou), Jiulong (Xiamen and other cities), Han (Shantou and Chaozhou), and the Zhu (Guangzhou and other cities near Hong Kong). Comparisons can be made rich parts of Shandong and the Chengdu plain far inland. Several scholars have done relevant work, including Ezra Vogel on Guangdong, where reforms were quick, and Dorothy Solinger on Hubei, where they were slower.

49 Zhufeng Luo, *Religion Under Socialism in China*, tr. Donald E. MacInnes and Zheng Xi'an (Armonk: M.E. Sharpe, 1991), 210–14 are all about Qingpu Catholic boat people. Catholic Mary and Buddhist Guanyin have similarities.

50 Donald E. MacInnes, *Religion in China Today: Policy and Practice* (Maryknoll, NY: Orbis, 1989), 278, 280–81.

51 Fei Xiaotong, *Small Towns in China: Functions, Problems, and Prospects* (Beijing: New World Press, 1986).

52 An economist, interviewed in the Chinese Academy of Social Sciences, 1988.

53 *Jiangsu xiangzhen*, 448.

54 *Far Eastern Economic Review* [hereafter *FEER*], December 11, 1986, 82–83.

55 Some of this increase almost surely represents more complete reporting from rural factories that before 1978 had to hide their output – or even their existence – both for political reasons and to avoid central imposts. But see Fei Xiaotong and Luo Yanxian, *Xiangzhen jingji*, 46–48.

56 Part of the increase may result from more complete reporting. But these industries grew very quickly at this time. *Hengxiang jinji lianhe de xin fazhan* (The New Development of

56 Ex-peasant industrialists

Horizontal Economic Links), Shanghai Economics Association, ed. (Shanghai: Shanghai Shehui Kexue Yuan Chuban She, 1987), 96.

57 *South China Morning Post* [hereafter *Post*], August 29, 1988.

58 David Zweig, "Rural Industry: Constraining the Leading Growth Sector in China's Economy," in *China's Economic Dilemmas in the 1990s: The Problems of Reforms, Modernization, and Interdependence*, Joint Economic Committee, ed. (Washington, DC: Government Printing Office, 1991), 418–36.

59 Juan Wang, *Sinews*, 66, 81.

3

VARIED MANAGERS REFORM CHINA'S POWER STRUCTURE

Local chiefs authorized new factories – but what kinds of grassroots managers most helped specific types of industrial development? Were Party or state cadres differently involved at different degrees of zoom in this huge country? Was prosperity led by mostly unofficial entrepreneurs, who may or may not have been in the same family lineages as local cadres? Do accurate answers to such questions tend to vary over separate periods of reforms, different sizes of networks, or specific places?

Some new factory managers on the Yangzi delta in the 1970s had worked in commune or brigade governments, in local Party or Communist Youth League committees, or in local units of the military. Others, who were of sharply rising importance during the 1980s, had previous careers as technicians or traders. Even when their backgrounds were originally local-political or lineage-related rather than technical, market incentives increasingly tended to make them business specialists rather than political generalists.

Peasant cadres and brigade Party secretaries composed the first reform generation of Sunan leaders in rural industries. Many during the early 1970s were old and lacked much education. Village leaders in China were not on state salaries; they were (and are) not civil servants. Even in the era of communes, relatively few rural leaders were so – and these were usually imposed on localities from higher administrative levels. If village cadres tried to use outmoded methods of agricultural management to run modern firms, they ran into problems. Some admitted they were not up to the job. Dealing in new markets, and selling products that were less standard than grain, created a need for younger, educated rural leaders. Many who took such roles after 1976 were ex-urban "intellectual youths"; these created another generation of local leaders who had lived at least for a few years in the rural places where they established new firms. Later, a third generation of still-better-educated youths ran many Sunan rural companies. "In Maojiao Township, Zhangjiagang [Jiangsu], fourteen old leaders who were not good at enterprise management in rural enterprises were forced to retire in 1984, and nineteen young leaders were appointed as managers. Among them, twelve were technicians." These were said to have "great authority (*da quan*) to distribute profits, hire workers, and award or punish them."[1]

The most telling contrast was with urban executives, who adapted their management to the premise that state cadres at higher "levels" would be able to aid their concrete operations: "Compared to managers in cities, rural executives are more powerful and independent. Town leaders only involve themselves with rural businesses indirectly and in economic terms. The government never interferes with the daily affairs of enterprises." For this autonomy, higher-"level" government leaders exacted a price that entrepreneurs gladly paid[2]:

> Many managers must have several thousand *yuan* as a mortgage before they can be appointed or can apply to be managers. In Zhanjiang and Wuxi [Sunan cities], plant directors must pay 10 percent of the planned enterprise profit before they can become formal managers. . . . If managers cannot complete their quotas, they have to pay for this incapability. On the other hand, the local governments give high awards to managers who show good performance. If they fulfill their plans, they may earn salaries one to three times above the average wage of the workers.

Parvenu rural entrepreneurs in Shanghai's suburban Jiading reportedly tended to be young, partly educated, and well connected with local leaders. Some had been cadres in town government, although toward the end of reforms they openly expressed fears and resentments about potential conservative changes in state policies. They liked the status quo in which they prospered.[3] Three keys to success, as these entrepreneurs identified them, might be summarized in alliterative English: "capital, courage, and connections."

A major reason why Sunan enterprise managers usually preferred remaining in the collective sector, instead of founding private firms, is that they liked to deal with town leaders – who were often friends or kin – rather than with tax cadres from higher administrative levels. If their firms remained legally collective or 'dependent' (*guahu*), rather than becoming private, they had better official cover against demands from more centralist government agents. Even if bribes and imposts on an enterprise remained just as great under collective as under state ownership, the funds taken from collectives tended to remain local. Rural factory heads stood a greater chance of influencing the later use of such money, when more of it remained in town. Collective managers maintained good relations with leaders in local governments.

Collectives flourished much better than formally private firms. For example in Jiangyin, near Wuxi, a private entrepreneur named Ren in the early 1980s opened an ironworks. Within two years, he was able to repay the 35,000 yuan loan with which he had started. Such prosperity, creating a new local leader, depended on community support; so the private entrepreneur voluntarily paid the electricity, water, and ploughing bills of a hundred local households. But such prosperity – especially in a firm that had no socialist cover – also bred envy and costs: The town government approached this entrepreneur to pay a land-use tax he had not expected. Then a fisherman, who claimed that the ironworks scared fish away from a nearby river, organized a gang of sixty boat people to smash windows and equipment in the smelter. "Even though Mr. Ren had thousands of yuan, he could not get any help, because his factory was privately owned."[4] The entrepreneur, no longer able to do business, gave his whole plant to the local production team as a collective, retaining his position as manager. This allayed his problems with immediate neighbors, but his troubles were not ended. When bureaucrats in a higher-level Wuxi company learned that he had given away his profitable plant, they were angry that he had offered it to the local team rather than to their own office. So they sent tax collectors to inspect his books. Then they sued him – without success, because he had broken no laws. The court upheld his right to continue in business, as manager of a collective.

It was often crucial for profitability that local firms remain nominally collective, but the authority of their managers was usually as full as that of any private tycoon. During the late 1970s, small rural industries might be leased to their former directors or to ex-agricultural cadres. In order to maintain local budgets, cadres insisted that earlier state profits from such firms be replaced by other kinds of rents and taxes. Former managers or experienced team leaders were the main bidders for such leases. In some cases, local magnates found ways practically to give the factories to themselves. But as Jean Oi has written, "For the most part, team leaders had to exit the historical stage. . . . The post-1978 reforms robbed team leaders of most of their power, leaving them either as team leaders or as newly designated village small group leaders, with few duties."[5] Many resisted these changes, while others prospered in the new era if they had technical skills.

Scattered PRC evidence suggests that most rural industrialists by the 1980s had not been cadres. Local ex-officials often joined new businesses – but they usually did so if their former posts had been at very low administrative levels. Many ex-commune or brigade cadres assisted the new economy without taking entrepreneurial risks, while ex-team leaders more often participated in it directly. Inland areas reported more former high officials in new managements than coastal areas usually had. A large survey in an inland county found that 43 percent of the "specialized households" were headed by former team cadres, but a similar survey in coastal Fujian yielded a portion well below 5 percent.[6] The power of township or higher cadres was seldom so great that they could permanently scuttle peasant entrepreneurship. Many former officials lost influence. Some opposed new developments, while most accommodated it and extracted resources from it for themselves and their communities. A minority of cadres, especially those who had technical training, became entrepreneurs themselves.

This evolution of local leaders, occurring early in Jiangnan, was later replicated elsewhere. In areas of North Jiangsu where the salt gabelle had traditionally made government the main entrepreneur, new rural industries ran into problems because local bureaucrats habitually stifled businesses they could not control. They tried to enforce the norm that "officials supervise, while traders manage" (*guandu shangban*). But cadres

60 Varied managers & China's power structure

in July 1986 founded a conglomerate operating in rural areas around Xuzhou, making products for export. This company had branches in many towns and was thus called a "multi-village enterprise" (*duozhen qiye*).[7] "New" companies of this sort were apparently efforts by bureaucrats to restrict profitable cooperatives that had sprung up more locally in the early reform period. These might be ordered to amalgamate, when high- and mid-level administrators wanted to maximize the revenues remitted to their own control.

This sprawling joint company near Xuzhou suffered "multi-faceted interventions" (*duofang chashou*) from higher officials. They wanted to appoint their own friends to top jobs in the regional corporation that had nominal charge of local collectives. This management form was familiar, derived from "mother-in-law" corporations that had supervised factories in Mao's time. Higher bureaucrats in this Xuzhou combine were accused of taking money for personal loans from the corporate till. To counteract such tendencies – which finally bankrupted the joint company – the prefectural government established three regulations: that factory managers should not suffer interference from the outside, that leaders should not hire their relatives, and that such a company could not borrow money without high-level authorization. This reportedly changed policy from "an interference mode to a service mode" (*ganyu xing wei fuwu xing*). The original leaders of the local plants remained in place and could operate under new rules that facilitated credit and technical improvements.

Yet a 1990s survey of rural businesses found that a great majority still called on relatives for capital loans. Most enterprises in this survey also hired kin from single local lineages in managerial posts. As an interviewee put it, "Relatives are reliable; one can relax with them." Another manager revealed his liking for hiring kinfolk: "That way, what I say goes." Over four-fifths of top staff, and nearly three-fifths of contractors, in a sample of thirty-four rural firms were "relatives or close contacts."[8]

Capital was an obvious need for rural firms, and new managers could often obtain money. According to an estimate for China as a whole, the total amount of wealth that peasants had – in houses, tractors, animals, trucks, stored grains, monetary savings, and other assets – increased almost ten times by value between 1978 and 1985. The total in 1978 was calculated at about eighty billion yuan; and in 1985, seven hundred billion.[9] Some of the increase may have come from better reporting in later years, as the central state's ability to levy taxes decreased. In any case, rural entrepreneurs decreasingly needed state banks to raise seed money. "White slips" (*baitiaozi*) were paper IOUs given by local cadres as payment for commodities they purchased on behalf of the state.[10] They diverted procurement funds to finance the township and village enterprises (TVEs) they managed – and practically owned.

Rural factories entail new rural leadership, as industry displaces agriculture

The reform boom was industrial, and local notables who would not switch from their traditional roles in agriculture tended to lose power. The nationwide swell of rural industries was quick, and rise of this growth created an inverse mirror-image in the ups and downs of agricultural output.[11] When rural industry rose fastest in these years, agriculture often declined or rose slowly, as Table 3.1 shows. Hikes of official grain purchase prices were required, in effect, to buy peasant labor from rural factories for use in paddies. If grain prices had not gone up, state grain procurement would surely have deteriorated faster (and city people would have had less to eat). The central government paid more, and went more deeply into debt, in hopes of keeping both its rural and urban constituencies content.

The rise of rural industry took resources and personnel from agriculture. When rural factories' output growth accelerated, agriculture's output decelerated. For the great majority of reform years especially from 1972 to 1985, either rural industry or else agriculture did better than in the previous year – but not both. Also, in years when rural industry grew fastest on a nationwide basis (1974–1976, 1984–1985), agriculture did less well. But by the mid-1980s, the rates of growth in rural industry

TABLE 3.1 Rural industry or rural agriculture: a partial trade-off (China's national growth rate percentages, 1972–1986, faster [f] or slower [s] than previous year)

	Agricultural growth	*Industrial growth*	*Faster ag. or slower ind. since previous*	
1972	−0.2	29.8		
73	8.4	9.8	f	s
74	4.5	18.5	s	f
75	3.1	32.8	s	f
76	2.5	44.8	s	f
77	1.7	23.2	s	s
78	8.1	15.4	f	s
79	7.5	16.4	s	f
80	1.4	21.3	s	f
81	5.8	7.5	f	f
82	11.3	9.7	f	f
83	7.8	23.3	s	f
84	12.3	53.0	f	f
85	3.4	67.1	s	f
86	3.4	33.3		s
87	16.4	38.0	f	f
88	25.5	45.6	f	f
89	11.3	23.1	s	s
90	17.3	14.2	f	s
91	6.5	23.0	s	f
92	11.4	53.8	f	f

Source: Figures to 1986 were calculated from *Zhongguo tongji nianjian, 1987* (China Statistical Yearbook, 1987), State Statistical Bureau, ed. (Beijing: Zhongguo Tongji Chuban She, 1987), 352; and from 1987, ibid., 1993 edition, 333. The highest figure on the table (67 percent for rural industry in 1985) probably arises not just from high real growth that year but also from an accounting change: Some growth of "agricultural" units' output in previous years came from industries licensed by low-level agricultural offices; but by 1985 and later, the administrations in charge of rural output were more accurately described. In a few of the years for which the comparison can be made, the output change from the previous year was unidirectional in both industry and agriculture (although very high inflation in 1987–1988 was a cause of synchrony in those years). In most years, the directions of growth in the two sectors were opposite.

62 Varied managers & China's power structure

were so high (and were reported fairly high even in years such as 1989–1990, when central leaders were doing all they could to get more grain), this trade-off ceased. The industrial sector already dominated the rural economy by the end of reforms.

Few rural enterprises were directly run by villages or townships, even though these units in the mid-1980s licensed most of them. Companies mainly had contracts with these administrative units. Some reform managers were supposed to be appointed for fixed terms – and this was an apparent change from Mao's time, when managers' tenures had no usual limit. Contracts were regularly renewable; they existed largely as symbolic ciphers for defunct personnel planning – and no manager of a profitable rural firm was likely to be denied renewal, particularly if appropriate local benefits were distributed. Workers in rural enterprises, especially those licensed at the village level or below, were apparently never unionized. If they were local, many employees (and managers) received much of their compensation in the form of bonuses, so that the low wage scales of previous plans ceased to restrict salaries.[12] Table 3.2 shows that collective and "other" firms expanded much faster than state-owned companies.

TABLE 3.2 Percentages of gross value in PRC industrial output by ownership type

	Collective	*State-owned*	*Other*
1965	10	90	0
70	12	88	0
78	22	78	0
79	22	78	0
80	24	76	1
81	25	75	1
82	25	74	1
83	26	73	1
84	30	69	1
85	32	65	3
86	34	62	4
87	35	60	6
88	36	57	7
89	36	56	8
90	36	55	10
91	36	53	11
92	38	48	14
93	38	43	19
94	41	34	25

Source: The figures are rounded and approximate, and their meaning is not entirely consistent from one firm to the next, in part because there are many kinds of management within each of the three main categories: collective, state, and "other." The "other" category refers to private firms (49 percent of the total, including a few remaining from 1949), but also to "joint" state-private ones, and to both joint jurisdiction and private firms from the mid-1980s and thereafter. See *Zhongguo tongji nianjian, 1991* (China Statistical Yearbook, 1991), State Statistical Bureau, ed. (Beijing: Zhongguo Tongji Chuban She, 1991), 396; but somewhat different figures lower for the collective and private sectors are in ibid., 1986, 273, ibid., 1988, 318 (see also 311), ibid., 1990, 413, and ibid., 1991, 391. Figures for 1991 come from ibid., 408; and for 1992–1994 from calculations based on ibid., 1995, 377. The definitions and reporting apparently improved over time.

These changes gave local leaders in the countryside more power, while mid- and high-level rural bureaucrats became less influential. A very rough way to judge the changing clout of different kinds of leaders is to look at the ownership categories. The proportion of output from collectives in China rose sharply before 1978. Many data in this book are from Jiangnan, but Table 3.2 offers nationwide figures. These may understate the rise of local units – and the fastest rise of the most local firms – because leaders on the spot had at least as much chance to hide rural production before 1978 than later. The Yangzi delta experience, showing very quick growth of small rural industries then, gives an early picture of what happened in other rich rural areas, and thereafter in poorer places. The trend in Jiangnan was very fast, but its direction was reflected in national averages even during the early 1970s.

A difficulty in interpreting such data is that the term "collective" covers a wide variety of firms. The core problem is to judge the relative weight of collectives legitimated by towns and counties ("big collectives" as Fei Xiaotong calls them) compared with *de facto* private "small collectives," which were nominally under village governments. This weighting changed over time. Township and village enterprises – which need not be conflated as generic 'TVEs' – each accounted for about half of the nonstate rural industrial output. A 1985 Wuxi County report put the higher-level township and lower-level village licensees each at 48 percent of product.[13] Villages (*cun*) may have low rank, but together they licensed about half of China's rural industry by output. Both large and small collectives were important, perhaps about equally so. Growth of both types outpaced central, provincial, and prefectural state factories.

Rural youths move to cities

The Party became a decreasing presence in China's rural areas by late reforms. Many active young people, of the kinds that rural Party branches near Shanghai had employed for decades, could come at least to medium-sized cities even during the early 1970s. Immigration rose sharply then to cities having between 500,000 and 1,000,000 people, though not yet to larger cities. To these sizable but not gigantic places, gross immigration *trebled* from 1969 to 1972. Many youths who had been sent out of Shanghai after 1968, for example, were able to return to medium-sized Yangzi cities in the early 1970s (before they flowed back to the metropolis after 1978). Many rural young people who had been born in the countryside also joined this immigration to mid-sized cities.[14]

Demographic changes tended to reduce rural recruitment to the Party. Total CCP membership reached 49 million by the end of 1990, when most members were apparently still in the countryside. But the absolute number of rural members was decreasing by mid-reforms. Government media complained of "a tendency toward senility in rural Party organizations."[15]

Talented ex-peasants and rural youths could make better careers during pre-1990 reforms by staying out of the Party than by submitting themselves to its rules. The remaining tillers were increasingly independent farmers, and they too wanted less regulation from above. Party members in the country became less useful than

64 Varied managers & China's power structure

in the past. Top CCP leaders had not planned this apathy to be part of reforms – even reformers among them spoke against it – but the distance between the Party and the peasants had grown. The Leninist organization became even more urban than before. In cities too it lost some influence to other networks before 1990. The meaning of membership changed for many Communists. The CCP as a disciplined organization was increasingly separate from rural industry, the most dynamic part of China's economy.

National periodization based on behavioral turning points

A critic might suggest that the data above, showing quick nonstate rural growth since the early 1970s, cannot prove much because these began from a "low base." Production from rural industries (as distinct from agriculture) had indeed been less impressive in 1965–1970 than later. But the fast industrial-commercial change after that suggests a need for better periodization of "reform" and for more analysis of the Cultural Revolution's effects on governance. Many data in this book's tables show patterns of localization and growth after 1970, at least to the middle of the decade, that are similar to those in most year spans after 1978. Often the series show temporary decelerations in 1975. Many also show some slowing in the early 1980s, and again in 1989–1990. A large change to nearly opposite, centralizing types of change followed 1989 – so the word "reform" becomes less applicable after 1990.

National published data for total industrial growth show that the gross value of reported Chinese industrial output grew at an average annual rate of 12 percent from 1965 to 1970, dropping to 8 percent in 1970–1976 – and rising again to 14 percent in 1976–1978.[16] Heavy industry and state prices accounted for most of this change, which at first might seem to show that the early 1970s was a period of recession, not a beginning of reform boom. But such data, reported mostly from state-owned firms in a highly politicized era, hide the experiences of most Chinese. Locally, in the Yangzi delta and soon far beyond, finer-grained surveys in later reports show that rural industry was growing fast but was not yet having to report fully. The early 1970s was a period when many collective factories accelerated their production but had unusually strong incentives to hide it; so rates of change were hidden. The capture of production materials by low-tax and underreporting firms caused severe shortages in the state sector – whose problems became a correlate of reform prosperity, not a counterindication of it.

The logical problems of discounting the significance of the early reforms after 1970, despite the initial low base of production from which many rural industries began, would be several: How low is "low"? When the level in a time series is practically zero, as for some of these it was near the start of the 1970s, then a clear rise is something to be explained. It marks a watershed. If a higher initial value were required before any change could be deemed notable, then how much higher should it be? If that reasoning were tried for many of the time series, then figures from 1984–1985 (in some fields where change had slowed temporarily in the previous few years) would be as convincing a start for reforms as 1978 could be. But to say that China's reforms began in 1985 would neglect too many changes before then. In any case, the official 1978 watershed does not hold up, for many *local* behavioral time series taken together, as a more fundamental transition than 1970–1971.

The main reason for the usual emphasis on 1978 clearly relates to interests of (and in) famous Beijing leaders. The standard periodization presumes reforms started from the wisdom of central seers, notably Deng Xiaoping. Not only does this view deny him credit for his reform activities in 1974–1975, when as First Vice-Premier of China (when Zhou Enlai was expiring of cancer), Deng ran the government. It ignores Deng's own honesty (expressed in his statement at the start of this book) that the fastest-growth part of China's economy was initiated by local leaders and "took us by surprise completely." Deng's elite for two decades had interests in dating the end of the Cultural Revolution no earlier than the year of Mao's death, 1976, or better, the year of Hua Guofeng's replacement by Deng, 1978. They criticized Mao's responsibility for 1958–1961 and 1966–1969 disasters – though not so much that Mao's mantle became too tattered to be worth inheriting.[17] The standard periodization overstates the power of the central Party as China's socialist revolution was winding down.

A 1981 Central Committee resolution found the root of Cultural Revolution chaos in "a grave 'Left' error" that "does indeed lie with Comrade Mao Zedong. But after all, it was the error of a great proletarian revolutionary. . . . Comrade Mao Zedong's prestige reached a peak, and he began to get arrogant."[18] The common 1966–1976 account of the Cultural Revolution prejudges an answer to an empirical question: Can crucial roots of reform be found outside Beijing during that decade? The official periodization hides too much not only about reforms, but also about the Cultural Revolution. It suggests that campaign was a fairly homogeneous decade of turmoil. Then after a brief hiatus under Hua, reforms are said to have begun under Deng in 1978. That view overwhelmingly structures scholarship, in the West and China too, and even among researchers who realize that 1966–1976 was not, actually, a whole decade of uniform politics or policies. It makes no sense of many behavioral trends that are clearly relevant to reform – not just in rural industry, but also in other fields.

This is not to claim, however, that the Cultural Revolution ended (or that reforms began) in all spheres of Chinese life simultaneously.[19] Change came later and less surely for many intellectuals than for most others, notably peasants-becoming-workers. In normative fields of culture and political rhetoric, reform was slower and less decisive than in situational fields such as rural industry or international trade.[20] Researchers have tended to neglect early 1970s changes in arts and ideology.[21] Most intellectuals faced a somewhat different situation after 1970 than before. After that year, there was less chaos on the streets than in 1966–68, and there was less extensively organized coercion among most urban people than in the Cleaning Class Ranks Campaign of 1968–1970, which was largely run by the army. Intellectuals are very important in any society, but it is time to begin writing about Chinese politics as if governmental and dissident intellectuals, despite their status, were not the only participants.

No periodization can ever be perfect; yet in writing political history, the time eras chosen for analysis tend to frame whatever else is said. A periodization is only an idea, an analytic frame that does not exclude other patterns in which real evidence might be understood. Whether China's sputtering reforms "really" began in 1971 rather than 1978, the proposal that they did so serves as a scope for seeing many aspects of Chinese politics that have often been obscured. It is hard to imagine more benefit that could come from a concept.

Inefficiencies of rural and suburban factories

Putting rural factories at the start of an account of reforms from the 1970s to 1989, followed by a new period of governance to restore regime resilience from 1990 for the next three decades at least, explains much about the early era's trends of localization, inflation, corruption, and prosperity. An economist can nonetheless rue village industries, despite their fast growth, because of their inefficiencies.[22] Tax avoidances and beneficial prices, accorded by local regimes to local firms, could make small factories profitable – even if available technologies and factor distributions made economies of scale better in larger plants.

On the other hand, central planning of resources can also lead to waste. This was evident in the Cultural Revolution official investment policies of 1964–1971, which favored gigantic state industries inland, the "Great Third Front" (*da san xian*).[23] Inefficiencies of megaprojects later became more evident, notably in the Three Gorges Dam scheme. Local leaders are not by definition efficient users of capital – but neither is the central state. Only evidence can measure efficiency.

Jiangsu industry's "total factor productivity" has been reported according to the official periodization of reforms. From 1953 to 1978, this index showed a 2.1 percent annual decline; but in the next decade, it reportedly grew 4.4 percent yearly. Yet if shorter time periods are considered, the most startling results are a very sharp decline during the post–Great Leap depression, some rebound from this low-productivity era that continued into the Cultural Revolution, a rise in the early 1970s, a temporary reported decline that began by 1975 for a couple of years, and then a re-ignition of total factor productivity in industry after 1977.[24]

State industries may be compared with collectives, during reforms, to assess their efficiencies in using all factor inputs. The results are revealing: The localization of the Yangzi delta economy increased the efficiency of trade (and also of all sectors taken together on the delta). Non-commercial sectors were less efficient. The economic rise of local, autonomous authoritarian managers meant that quasi-private industries relentlessly exploited cheap factors, especially labor. New rural industries mobilized resources, sometimes in a coercive manner rather than in a civil way. They increased the economy's inputs even more than they increased the outputs; so most industrial sectors as economic machines were wasteful of the inputs they recruited well. Sunan collective firms did not use resources with greater efficiency than state firms.[25]

Quasi-capitalist local economic leaders, running Sunan collectives, mobilized factors to raise production and make profits. Available evidence nonetheless suggests that their new factories' input/output ratios were probably even worse, on average, than those in the state sector. "Total factor productivity" in rural industries rose, but it did so slowly. Most rural leaders were no longer Maoists; but now in local networks, they had communitarian resources and a great deal of exploitative power. They took the same growth mechanism that planners had used (and continued to use in industries requiring high capitalization). They merely miniaturized it. They were local economic supply-side Stalinists – entrepreneurial petty tyrants, more than productivity maximizers.

Their firms nonetheless excelled at filling market demands. Rural industries' products were generally priced lower than similar-quality items from the state sector, and the types of goods they made were nimbly chosen. About half of China's cement and two-fifths of the nitrogenous fertilizer, both fast-expanding sectors, came from rural industries in the early 1970s.[26] Central authorities sometimes tried to close local factories that were objectively less efficient than state plants, but local authorities were usually able to prevent such closures.[27]

PRC state pricing traditionally overvalued manufactures and undervalued the products of agriculture. So rural leaders had strong incentives to process the crops or ores their own areas could produce. Most had less incentive to develop bulk transport between jurisdictions, even though canal haulage had earlier been a major growth sector in East China (including the Yangzi delta before 1949). This pattern changed slowly in the reform era, as more rural factories opened and more bulk products were transported by increasingly independent barge managers. By 1982, four-fifths of the wood merchandise supplied to Shanghai came in finished or semi-finished form (according to a source that was supposed to remain confidential).[28] More of the processing fees went to the countryside. Cities, including the big metropolis, were redistribution points, not just processing points.

High-skilled and low-skilled migrant labor exploitation in rural factories, 1970s and 1980s

Managers in the countryside during reforms could exploit labor. They could avoid high tax-and-profit extractions – or at least could make sure revenues were kept local, more likely to be used in their own interests. Such businesses also hired more executive and technical personnel. The number of rural managers per laborer rose. One source improbably suggests that in 1982, there were as many rural factory managers as workers. This would have made the employee/employer ratio 1.0, but then it reportedly soared to 3.4 by 1989.[29] These figures understate the ratio by omitting contract and temporary laborers, especially immigrants who were not fully registered in the places where they had jobs. However this may be, many rural managers worked hard, while others had sinecures.

Their staffs were greater than they reported. The signal success of rural industries during this period, powered partly by a rise in the laborer per manager ratio, is one

68 Varied managers & China's power structure

measure of efficiency in rural plants. The state factories with which the country-side factories competed successfully were also inefficient users of labor and other factors. Tyrannical local leaders were able to exploit unregistered labor thoroughly. This proto-capitalist growth raised China's wealth, but it does not present a wholly rosy picture.

Local potentates could put more of their friends into good jobs as these trends continued into the 1990s and later. The influx of migrant contract laborers, of whom half or more were unregistered and uncounted, expanded to provide factory infantries for the new rural-industrial generals. An advantage of countryside manufacturing that competed with the urban state sector was low wages. In 1982, for example, rural firms admitted hiring 35 percent of China's whole industrial workforce, while they admitted making only 12 percent of the country's industrial product (by taxable value).[30] Part of this difference might lie in high planned prices for state-sector goods, but it is also consistent with low wages and low labor productivity, with high profits, in rural factories. These industries employed a great many ex-farm workers, who would not have gotten the jobs if the managers had to pay more. This was a situation of "growth with unlimited supplies of labor."[31]

Migration and census data reflect this reform, and they are the main topic of Chapter 13. The reported part of Shanghai's population in the suburbs expanded from 41 percent in 1965 to 49 percent in 1978 – even though urban district boundaries were expanded by fiat at the expense of suburban counties.[32] Low rural wages were supported by the premodern tradition of residence controls, which reduced the markets on which peasants could offer their services, and by higher birth rates among commune members than among city people.

The revolutionary regime through the 1960s was so solicitous of unionized urban proletarians, its policies created a situation in which its own state factories were easily underpriced by countryside labor. Revived rural organizations in the early 1970s used this person power in areas where old entrepreneurial traditions still existed. The Cultural Revolution in cities and towns disabled the offices that might have prevented such a revival. The revolutionary regime was a necessary if insufficient cause of its own demise.

Labor in Shanghai County, a green suburb southwest of the main city, switched into local industry with extraordinary speed; and apparently none of these workers were unionized. By 1978, fully 24 percent of all non-urban workers there were already listed as employees of factories organized by either villages/*cun* or townships/*xiang*, which are smaller than counties/*xian*. Just two years later in 1980, this portion (which by then may have been more fully reported) was up to 39 percent.[33]

Suburban township factories grew far more quickly than city counterparts. So Shanghai urban "laborers were not reluctant to work there [in suburbs], even if they did not move their families to the suburbs. The state had to spend a lot of money to subsidize workers' transport costs." Their daily commutes were opposite of normal for modern societies: out of Shanghai in mornings, returning in evenings. Rural factories not only used materials that formerly had gone into the more centrally planned sector; they also gave jobs to former state-factory workers whom the rural boom had put out of business. This created odd daily commutes for workers who kept their household registrations in the big city but found jobs in nearby rural towns. A Shanghai reporter went one afternoon to visit a large suburban factory and found that "[at] 4 p.m., there were already ten big buses along the road in front of the plant. Workers stood in line, waiting to go back into Shanghai city." The daily trip required one and a half hours each way, and this factory could afford to spend 400,000 yuan per year in wage supplements for transport (public bus fares were subsidized and low, but those vehicles were very crowded).[34] Rural factory managers could pay the expense by avoiding production in the more regulated higher-tax central city, and by higher returns from Shanghai urban workers for technical or exacting tasks.

Many inland Yangzi delta localities started new industrial centers from scratch, inviting outside labor of either low-pay or high-skill types to do the work. Bixi, Changshu, in Sunan, began the 1980s as "a small village of twenty families." Then Bixi somehow acquired the status of a township – on speculation, because previously it had been just a village with "a very narrow street and low houses." Four bridges were built across its canal, and beside them rose commercial buildings and twenty factories. By 1986, this small village-become-township had "attracted more than 5,000 people to come work." Most, in this case, were apparently migrants from farther inland. The new township had spent more than 7 million yuan, of which rural industries used 6 million.[35] A rich business group from Bixi had apparently made money elsewhere and decided to invest it back home, where the communal rewards were good and the state could less easily monitor profits.

Rural industry thus transformed the occupational structure of Jiangnan, as local and then migrant peasants became workers. At Shazhou, in Suzhou Prefecture, processing factories and field machine repair shops by the mid-1970s already employed thousands. This place was a truly green, rural area at the time, and few migrants had yet come there. More than 95 percent of Shazhou adults still spent at least some time in field work. By 1978, however, the area had 314 rural enterprises, mostly factories under nominally "agricultural" units, in which 10 percent of the laborers officially registered as tillers working full time, and a larger number part time. Change continued quickly in the next five years. By 1982 Shazhou rural factories almost trebled in number, as industrial workers became 39 percent of the local rural labor force.

In Wujing County, Changzhou Prefecture, non–field hands flocked to the booming house construction trade, as well as to transport and factory jobs, so that the nonagricultural portion of the labor force by 1982 was 38 percent. In Wujing, there was one rural house-builder or transport worker for each two laborers in factories. Fei Xiaotong concluded that by the early 1980s, "About one-third of the labor power in Sunan had turned to industry from agriculture within five years."[36] Even this conclusion, showing abrupt change, may be based on figures that underreported part-time employment in rural industries during the mid-1970s. Sociologist Fei may have had scarcely more comprehensive data than officials had. The change to factories was by any account sharp for millions of Jiangnan people.

In 1985, three-quarters of the 16,600 workers in Tangqiao, Suzhou, were involved full-time in rural industry.[37] By then in Nantong County, Jiangsu, more than one-third of the whole proletariat for both fields and factories was either working in collective firms or away from home, some in the nearby metropolis of Shanghai.[38] The Nantong dialect is difficult for either Shanghainese or Mandarin-speakers to follow, and a very Chinese joke is that it is 'nantong' ('hard to communicate'). After the mid-1980s, such factories would have had to stop expanding if they had hired fewer outsiders. Supplies of local labor had become limited, but the supply of migrants willing to take rural factories' pay was still ample.

"Collective" firms made seven of every eight new hires for regular jobs in Shanghai suburban towns during the 1980s. Full-time jobs were allegedly 56 percent of all hires in these places. "Informal" temporary, contract, and seasonal jobs accounted for the remaining 44 percent – but this minority may be understated. Of the impermanent jobs that managers reported, seven-tenths were registered as temporary, and three-tenths as contract. "Seasonal" employment was a separate category, whose omission from most accounts suggests a further underreport of informal hiring.

In Shanghai suburban towns from 1980 to 1986, the official count of regular employment rose just 45 percent. Academic surveyors ventured a guess, however, that during this time the number of informal jobs actually rose at least 500 percent.[39] This situation evokes a principle like Heisenberg's: To gather accurate information, some coercive (police, prosecutor, court, union, or tax) authority would be involved – but it was precisely to keep data from such agencies that local managers were secretive. Gathering facts affected their content. Many social scientists are likewise so eager to crunch numbers that they do not consider motives creating biases when the numbers are compiled. Not all data sets are problematic, but all statisticians who want to ignore this issue are naïve.

For each new regular long-term job in rural Jiangnan industry, there were perhaps five new non-permanent places. Such an estimate is admittedly difficult to prove – but the rate of informal, unregistered hiring by local collectives was reportedly very high. State factory managers in the suburbs had financial incentives to hire temporary labor, since the national wage scales for unionized employees were fairly generous. Private entrepreneurs in the early 1980s were fewer than they later became, but they had little to lose by living up to their official reputations and exploiting labor. Even then, they could usually reclassify their firms as collectives. Managers in all ownership sectors increasingly hired contract workers. Nonstate bosses, in particular, could employ temporary labor.

Maoist controls in earlier years had prevented workers, as well as managers, from moving freely. State employees could find switching jobs difficult, because the security bureau in the unit the worker was leaving was supposed to acquiesce by sending to the new firm a secret file (dang'an) that gave the Party's evaluation of the person. Rural small firms could often ignore the norm to require such a file. Their business was more exclusively business; so these documents, as well as household registrations and other certificates, were decreasingly needed for employment.

Less than half of mid-1980s Shanghai suburban workers in small industries had their households permanently registered in Shanghai. Four towns, varying in size and together credibly typical of the suburbs, provided evidence showing this. About one-third of the suburban workers there (31 percent) labored daily in built-up areas but lived elsewhere nearby, often under ex-peasant landlords. One-fifth (21 percent) of this surveyed group lived in the Shanghai suburbs without any legal household registrations, practically all for more than a year. Just 48 percent were registered as permanent.[40]

Exploitation of workers in some rural factories was brutal. A May 1989 survey found that two-thirds of the workers sampled in one Shanghai suburb were recruited from a distance. Factory heads and labor bosses drove them mercilessly, sometimes using open coercion – just as earlier in the century labor contractors and secret society leaders had done.[41] Local long-time suburban residents, by contrast, could go to downtown Shanghai to do menial work. Fields were tended largely by the elderly, if at all. Many rural industries in this sample produced garments. Their "collective" managers, closely connected with local officials not under effective state control, seemed mainly interested in making money.[42]

Reports of more egregious exploitation came from East China areas further inland. Cangnan County, Zhejiang, surveyed 284 rural factories and found sweatshops containing about 500 child laborers between 10 and 16 years of age (with an average age of 13.6 years). Girls comprised 83 percent of the total, and almost all in the 1980s came from nearby villages. Just one-fifth of these children had finished second grade in primary school. About one-third were illiterate. They worked from eight to eleven hours, on piece rates, earning 1.2 to 3 yuan per day. A report of abuses stressed the effects of toxic chemicals on the health and mental development of the children, especially those in unventilated plastics shops using xylene, cycloketone, and banana oil solvents. Similar scandals were said to exist in many other rural factories that were not surveyed.[43] Labor exploitation by local managers is a major aspect of the reforms, and many sources show a strong correlation between the informality of hiring and the formal lowliness of the administrative level that licensed the employer.

Adult workers also voted with their feet to be exploited. They moved to rural factories, away from fields, and came great distances to make new livings. Their industrial wages were pittances, but the amounts were still generally higher than compensation for work in paddies. Migrants to a locality did not immediately demand to be treated as well as locals. As Fei has reported, "Some rural enterprises employed more outside workers than local workers, but rural firms give low pay to outside workers. Not only the local laborers, but also the outside workers, do not think this is wrong or unreasonable."[44]

Rural factories' technology, taxes, and credit

Top state leaders alternated between two opposite policies toward rural industry. Conservative lions favored repression of nonstate enterprises, while reformist

72 Varied managers & China's power structure

foxes tended to favor benign neglect that allowed some local change. "Lions" who strengthen elites' cohesion alternate with "foxes" who strengthen elites by making them adapt.[45] Both the conservative and reformist threads of policy can be traced in China from the early 1970s at least. The contradiction between them – and the fact that official decrees about rural factories alternated in basic intent – rendered each of the two strains no more than partly potent. Central politicians' attitudes toward rural industry would warrant more attention if they were more clearly responsible for any consistent result.

A crucial question was the extent to which managers could take risks with money. How much capital, embodying either new or old technology, could factory managers either keep within their firms, or else reap for local officials whom they could influence? Many means for syphoning credit to firms were available: bank loans, tax holidays certified by various administrative levels, acquiescence to traditional rotating loan schemes or local equity sales, contributions of various kinds, direct allocations of public money to new firms, infrastructural investment to make companies profitable, and other subsidies. In the opposite direction, money flowed through bribes, taxes, and remittances from profits. The main difference between central and local firms was not among these means, nor was it just in the monetary totals. It was between the different extents to which credit went for risky but potentially rewarding ventures – or, instead, only for safe business as usual. Money regenerated itself quickly when put to uses that met demands. State corporate executives set an abysmal track record in this race, if they are compared with rural entrepreneurs. They had scant incentives to take risks.

Some rural firms boosted production quickly, even while their reported capital rose slowly. From 1978 to 1983, while Wuxi rural enterprises increased output by 24 percent per year, their net assets were said to rise annually by only 7 percent. Sales revenues were used mainly to buy more inputs. Rural places began with scant industry; but they boomed despite a lack of capital. Informal local policies may also have discouraged full reporting of assets.

Rural industrial output value in Wutang Township, Changzhou, Jiangsu, was 88 million yuan in 1976 and reached 2.5 billion in 1982, a 75 percent *annual* growth, compounded over those six years.[46] Rural industry's share of gross output value in Sunan by 1985 was at least one-third of all industrial output value there. The portion in Wuxi was 34 percent; in Suzhou, also 34 percent; Changzhou, 22 percent; and Nantong, 30 percent – and these figures include township but not village-run factories, which by then were expanding fastest in less built-up flat parts of the delta. Urban factories also flourished. By 1985, industry accounted for about 90 percent of all income in Sunan.

Most local leaders who took risks and cut red tape to achieve this result were ostensibly part of the state, often at its county (*xian*) or township (*xiang*) levels. As most writing about contemporary China overemphasizes, they had reasons to claim they were proud, loyal "state cadres" (*guojia ganbu*). Their decisions for collectives nonetheless undermined the state sector. Local leaders in Suqian County, Jiangsu, helped peasants leave rice paddies by offering credit, materials, training, and licenses for work as tailors, carpenters, blacksmiths, nursery-school operators, small factory managers, and shopkeepers. Specialized ex-peasants were increasingly given permission to move from rural places into towns.[47]

Provincial (*sheng*) and prefectural (*di*) leaders, and even magnates in ministries, were forced to recognize this situation. They wanted to take credit for the increased production and flourishing markets. In Shanghai, however, huge revenues and state industries meant that high-level acquiescence to local industries was delayed about half a decade behind Jiangsu and Zhejiang. This delay was less serious for small plants licensed by villages than for larger firms – but it caused resentments among Shanghai rural entrepreneurs who saw their peers across provincial borders facing an easier regime. Taxes on Jiangsu collectives were reduced in 1979, apparently to stimulate their development and to improve reporting. The province government in Nanjing later announced that some new rural collective enterprises would be exempt from taxes for three years. Those contracted in 1981 would be tax-free for two years; and those that had already opened, for at least one year.[48] These allowances gave county and township officials leeway to extend the exemptions. So the economic boom just across Shanghai's boundary was meteoric. Total gross 1985 production in Kunshan County, in Jiangsu but bordering Shanghai, rose 51 percent in a single year.[49]

High reformers publicized some of the most successful plants in Jiangnan, despite high conservatives' worry about their competition with state factories. The Haiyan Shirt Factory group was endorsed by the Zhejiang CCP Committee in March 1983, and plans were made to stop "controlling" collectively owned enterprises in favor of "assisting" them. These Zhejiang firms produced 23 percent more gross output in the first ten months of 1984 than in the same period of the previous year, and 22 percent more profit.[50]

Collective firms by the mid-1980s practically eliminated state firms in some of Shanghai's suburbs. In the Chongming County seat, fully 99 percent of all new hires in the mid-1980s went into collectives. But at Jinshanwei, an otherwise comparable town, collectives then offered only 15 percent of the new jobs, and the state sector still made up 85 percent. Local variation depended largely on different decisions by local leaders.[51]

Entrepreneurs often had to pay for medium-level bureaucratic support. Their rising resources could finance this. Jiangsu in 1985 produced more than one-fifth of gross output in all of China's rural industries. Zhejiang accounted for almost another tenth. Shanghai produced only 4 percent of China's rural industrial output (and its sister municipalities, Beijing and Tianjin, made just 2 percent each).[52] This meant, however, that Jiangsu, Zhejiang, and Shanghai rural factories together comprised one-third of the country's. In terms of tax receipts from these industries, the three contiguous East China provinces contributed 44 percent of the nation's total. This fiscal portion was far more than their 33 percent of the national output. The proportional difference between their rural industries' output and extraction, however, was less than for the same provinces' state sector.

Shanghai's role in the boom was not just slower and more hidden, but also more technical. Jiangnan is an economic unity, regardless of province boundaries by

74 Varied managers & China's power structure

which Jiangsu, Zhejiang, and Shanghai are divided. Reasons for this unity will be covered extensively in later chapters on urban management and "horizontal relations." Places near the municipality's borders, whence many of its residents' families had come, benefited enormously from a combination of technology from Shanghai but lower taxes elsewhere. Fei Xiaotong wrote that[53]

> most rural industry in the four prefectures [of Jiangsu nearest Shanghai] developed economic and technical cooperation with Shanghai. . . . [T]he economic development of Shanghai had a great impact on the rural industries and the whole surrounding area, playing the part of an economic center. Among the more than 2,000 rural factories in Wuxi, 709 were linked with major plants in large and medium-sized cities such as Shanghai. . . . [This was] a new pattern of industrialization in China, where "big fish help small fish and small fish help shrimps."

By the mid-1980s, however, Fei's "big fish" were becoming less official, and the "shrimps" were nominal cooperatives – while their managers were acting like private entrepreneurs, and the stately shark got less food.

Within Shanghai, the main aim of centrally appointed municipal politicians had for decades been to raise money for the state budget. Rural enterprises in Shanghai's suburban counties were caught in a bind, because they faced increasing competition from similar firms elsewhere, while they also faced province-level administrators whose careers depended on upward fiscal remittances. Small Shanghai firms reportedly "worried" that high taxes were reducing their profits, especially in comparison with nearby Jiangsu companies. Detailed examples of the troubles of specific small businesses in Shanghai's Chuansha, Jiading, and Songjiang Counties were adduced to show that costs other than labor and materials – especially for "administration" and taxes – were higher than in neighboring Suzhou and Wuxi. A newspaper article suggested that Shanghai tax policies might be reformed to allow suburban industries quicker development, so as to provide a larger tax base in the future. Such policies, the newspaper argued, had been followed successfully in Guangdong, Zhejiang, and Jiangsu.[54]

"Fake statistics" were inevitable in this situation. Localities of many sizes underreported their production, labor force, factor use, assets, profits, and other data. Quantitative lying was an embarrassment to the government, and not just for symbolic reasons. "Fake figures" were a problem that a State Statistics Bureau leader much later could admit. "Under-reporting of profits and tax revenues" was publicly confessed, by the 1990s, as a major kind of "negative, corrupt behavior." As a Statistics Bureau cadre said, "Local officials know that others will judge the achievements of their political careers based on statistics." These reporting problems were "worst from coastal areas and township enterprises."[55]

This was all illegal, of course. It was a situation in which "nothing is allowed, but everything is possible" – and by 1996 after reforms had changed, it led to temporary government decrees against the publication of many kinds of economic data.[56]

Notes

1 *Liaowang* 2, January 1988, 26.

2 Ibid., 27.

3 Lu Feiyun, "*Zhuanye chengbao zhe – Yige xin jieceng de quqi*" (Specialized Contractors – The Origins of a New Stratum), *Shehui* (Society), 3, Shanghai, 1990, 30–31.

4 *Post*, February 11, 1989.

5 Jean C. Oi, *State and Peasant*, 185.

6 Victor Nee, "Peasant Entrepreneurship and the Politics of Regulation in China," in *Remaking the Economic Institutions of China and Eastern Europe*, V. Nee and D. Stark, eds. (Stanford: Stanford University Press, 1991), 185–86.

7 *Jingji xinwen bao*, January 26, 1989.

8 Solomon Karmel, *The Neo-Authoritarian Contradiction: Trials of Developmentalist Dictatorships and the Retreat of the State in Mainland China* (Princeton University Politics Department Ph.D. Dissertation, 1995), 72–74, quoting 1992 work by Wang Manchuan.

9 *Gaige mianlin*, 4 and 9. Inflation before 1985 contributed greatly to these results – but price rises were even faster in the late 1980s.

10 Juan Wang, *Sinews*, 79.

11 Yang Dali, "Making Reform," 156.

12 Peter Nolan, "Petty Commodity Production in a Socialist Economy: Chinese Rural Development Post-Mao," *Market Forces in China*, 12.

13 The small remainder of the recorded total – which may be less than the real total – was divided between production team enterprises, partnerships, and private enterprises that might also underreport. Wuxi has many large companies. The chance that the portion of village-run industry there would be overreported is low. *China's Rural*, William Byrd and Lin Qingsong, eds., 68. Among the four counties surveyed by the World Bank, the ownership structure in Jieshou, Jiangxi, was most different from that of Wuxi, Jiangsu. This relatively poor Jiangxi county borders Fujian, and demonstration effects are suggested because private enterprise contributed about one-third of the nonstate output there.

14 *Zhongguo 1986 nian 74 chengzhen renkou qianyi chouxiang diaocha ziliao* (Sample Survey Materials on 1986 Chinese Migration in 74 Cities and Towns), *Chinese Demography* Editorial Group (Beijing: *Zhongguo renkou kexue* Bianji Bu, 1988), 340. For a Taiwan comparison, which shows youths leaving the countryside for Taipei and Kaohsiung, see Bernard Gallin, *Hsin Hsing, Taiwan: A Chinese Village in Change* (Berkeley: University of California Press, 1966).

15 *CD*, October 10, 1990.

16 Peter Nolan and Robert F. Ash, "China's Economy of the Eve of Reforms," *China Quarterly* 144 (December 1995), 981–82.

17 Anita Chan, "Dispelling Misconceptions," and next note.

18 *Resolution on CPC History, 1949–81* (Beijing: Foreign Languages Press, 1981), 41 and 46. But 1965–1969 violence arose when the Party's methods to consolidate the post-1949 revolution (campaigning, monitoring, and labelling) were adopted by others, notably people who had been repressed in that 1950–1965 process; Lynn White, *Policies of Chaos*.

19 For a more general retrospective that highlights issues not covered in the present book or my other publications, see Lynn White, "Introduction: Explanations for China's Revolution at its Peak," *Beyond a Purge and a Holocaust: The Cultural Revolution Reconsidered*, Kam-yee Law, ed. (Basingstoke: Palgrave Macmillan, 2003), 1–22.

20 These terms "normative" and "situational" are used in Talcott Parsons, *The Structure of Social Action* (New York: McGraw-Hill, 1937). Parsons is abstract, no longer faddish, and content with a style in English that is nearly unintelligible – but his ideas have wide application.

21 But see Lynn White, *Unstately Power: Local Causes of China's Intellectual, Legal, and Governmental Reforms*, 9–39 and 141–214 (including plates of paintings), or Ellen Johnston Laing, *The Winking Owl*, and other art histories of the PRC.

78 Varied managers & China's power structure

22 Christine Wong, "Fiscal Reform and Local Industrialization," *Modern China* 18:2 (April 1992), 197–227.

23 Barry Naughton, "Industrial Policy During the Cultural Revolution," in *New Perspectives on the Cultural Revolution*, op. cit., 153–81, provides investment data from state construction budgets that could justify both an earlier starting date (1964) and an earlier ending date (c. 1970) than are usual in descriptions of the Cultural Revolution.

24 This and the next two paragraphs interpret material found by Penelope Prime, "Industry's Response to Market Liberalization in China: Evidence from Jiangsu," *Economic Development and Cultural Change* 1992, 37–40.

25 The calculation is complex for reasons involving intermediate inputs. By one accounting, state industries raise factor productivity more than collective industries; using another test, the opposite is true. The conclusions are drawn from data in Penelope Prime, ibid.

26 Peter Nolan, "Petty Commodity," 11.

27 Christine Wong, "The Economics of Shortage and Problems of Reform in Chinese Industry," *Journal of Comparative Economics* (1986), 363–87.

28 *Shanghai jingji, neibu ben: 1949–1982* (Shanghai Economy, Internal Volume: 1949–1982), Shanghai Academy of Social Sciences, ed. (Shanghai: Shanghai Shehui Kexue Yuan Chuban She, 1984), 683.

29 Sources cited in Yang Dali, "Making Reform," 258.

30 This 12 percent by value is probably underreported, but the qualitative point still stands. Y. Y. Kueh, *Economic Planning and Local Mobilization in Post-Mao China*, (London: SOAS Contemporary China Institute, 1985), 56.

31 W. Arthur Lewis, "Economic Development with Unlimited Supplies of Labour," *The Manchester School of Economic and Social Studies* (1954), 139–91. "Unlimited" supplies refer to workers willing to toil at slightly more than subsistence wages. They do not last forever.

32 Calculated from figures in *Shanghai tongji nianjian 1988*, Shanghai Statistical Yearbook 1988 [hereafter, with adaptation for various years, *SHTJNJ88*] (Beijing: Zhongguo Tongji Chuban She, 1989), 77. This offers numbers without noting changes of boundaries that affect the data. A jurisdictional change occurred in 1983. (Earlier boundary changes, e.g. in 1959, predate the comparison made here.)

33 *Xian de jingji yu jiaoyu de diaocha* (Survey of County Economies and Education), Task Force for Research on China's Rural Education, ed. (Beijing: Jiaoyu Kexue Chuban She, 1989), 127.

34 Yao Shihuang, *Jin sanjiao*, 105–132.

35 Ibid.

36 Fei Xiaotong and Luo Yanxian, *Xiangzhen jiangji*, 48–50.

37 Xu Yuanming and Ye Ding, *Tangqiao gongye*, 5.

38 Stephan Feuchtwang, "Basic Social Security in the Countryside," in *The Re-emergence of the Chinese Peasantry: Aspects of Rural Decollectivization,* Ashwani Saith, ed. (London: Croom Helm, 1987), 192. For background on Nantong, Shao Qin, *Culturing Modernity: The Nantong Model, 1890–1930* (Stanford: Stanford University Press, 2003). Like Yangzhou, Nantong is a north-of-the-Yangzi city with Jiangnan culture.

39 *Fei zhengshi zhigong* includes *linshi gong, hetong gong*, and *jijie gong*. Sometimes texts also mention workers who are part-time or periodic (*zhouqi*). But no statistics at all were found on seasonal or part-time informal labor – even by an expert team of Fudan and East China Normal University surveyors – apparently because local managers would not tell academics about these. On regular workers, more is known. The portion of them hired by suburban collectives was reportedly 78 percent; with only 13 percent employed by state plants, and 10 percent by private firms, in this 1986 survey of four Shanghai *zhen*. *Zhongguo yanhai diqu xiao chengzhen fazhan yu renkou qianyi* (Migration and the Development of Small Cities and Towns on the China Coast) Liu Zheng ed. (Beijing: Zhongguo Caizheng Jingji Chuban She, 1989), 187.

Varied managers & China's power structure **79**

40 The towns (*zhen*) in this fascinating study were Jinshanwei, a designated "satellite city" (*weixing cheng*) of Shanghai in Jinshan County (near Hangzhou Bay, and south of the county seat, Zhujing); Chengqiao, the county seat and largest town on Chongming Island; and Luodian, a *zhen* under Baoshan County, whose c. 10,000 population in the mid-1980s was one-third the size of Chengqiao and one-fifth that of Jinshanwei, and three times that of the smallest *zhen* studied: Zhuiqiao, in southern Shanghai County about halfway between the metropolis and its major suburb Minhang. *Zhongguo yanhai diqu xiao chengzhen fazhan yu renkou qianyi* (Migration and the Development of Small Cities and Towns on the China Coast), Liu Zheng, et al., ed. (Beijing: Zhongguo Caizheng Jingji Chuban She, 1989), 178–81.

41 Jean Chesneaux, *The Chinese Labor Movement, 1919–1927*, tr. Hope Wright (Stanford: Stanford University Press, 1968), and *Popular Movements and Secret Societies in China, 1840–1950*, Jean Chesneaux, ed. (Stanford: Stanford University Press, 1972).

42 This report on exploitation is Hua Daming, "*Xiangban chang dui nonggong de guofen bodu ying yinqi zhuyi*" (The Overexploitation of Workers by Township-run Factories Calls for Attention), *Shehui* 2 (Society), Shanghai, 1990, 12–13.

43 Victor Nee, "Peasant Entrepreneurship," 198–99.

44 Fei Xiaotong and Luo Yanxian, *Xiangzhen jingji*, 77–81.

45 Vilfredo Pareto, *The Rise and Fall of Elites*, intro. by Hans Zetterberg (New York: Arno Press, 1979), uses concepts from earlier Italian and Roman writers.

46 Village industries often grew faster than township ones, though reported data on this lower "level" are less reliable. Fei Xiaotong and Luo Yanxian, *Xiangzhen jingji*, 40–45.

47 Sidney Goldstein and Alice Goldstein, "Population Movement, Labor Force Absorption, and Urbanization in China," *Annals of the American Academy of Political and Social Science* 476 (1984), 99–100.

48 *Dangdai Zhongguo*, Liu Dinghan, ed., 605. Thanks goes to Zheng Yongnian for this reference.

49 *Hengxiang jingji*, 143.

50 *FBIS*, December 21, 1984, 5, radio of December 17.

51 *Zhongguo yanhai diqu xiao chengzhen*, 1.

52 The need to hide rural output to evade Shanghai's high taxes may make this 4 percent an underestimate. This book avoids tenths of percents, which are usually scientistic but unscientific. I describe uncertain portions as rough fractions, when data collection offers no accuracy. See *China's Rural*, William Byrd and Lin Qingsong, eds., 256. Hebei produced 10 percent; Shandong, 9 percent; and Guangdong (if figures are complete) a low 7 percent. Each other province had a lower figure.

53 Fei wrote this in 1986. Also Chris Bramall, "The Wenzhou 'Miracle': An Assessment," *Market Forces in China: Competition & Small Business, The Wenzhou Debate*, Peter Nolan and Dong Fureng, eds. (London: Zed Books, 1990), 54–55.

54 *Shanghai gongye jingji bao* (Shanghai Industry Report) [hereafter *SHGYJJB*], February 15, 1988.

55 *Eastern Express*, March 2, 1994.

56 *New York Times*, January 21, 1996, 4–4.

57 Yao Shihuang, *Jin sanjiao*, 105–132.

58 See Jane Kaufman Winn and Tang-Chi Yeh, "Relational Practices and the Marginalization of Law: Informal Financial Practices of Small Businesses in Taiwan," *Law and Society Review* 28:2 (1994), 193–232.

59 Susan Greenhalgh, "Families and Networks in Taiwan's Economic Development," in *Contending Approaches to the Political Economy of Taiwan*, Edwin A. Winckler and Susan Greenhalgh, eds. (Armonk: Sharpe, 1988), 242.

60 Shieh Gwo-shyong, *"Boss" Island: The Subcontracting Network and Microentrepreneurship in Taiwan's Development* (New York: Lang, 1992), 35–39, suggest comparisons with the mainland.

61 Thomas Piketty, *Capital in the Twenty-First Century* (Cambridge: Harvard University Press, 2014), 13–15, shows the "Kuznets curve" is a fantasy – and how it reveals the political fears and hopes of its era (as do most social theories).

62 Evan Osnos, *Age of Ambition: Chasing Fortune, Truth, and Faith in the New China* (New York: Farrar, Straus and Giroux, 2015).

63 Danny Unger, *Building Social Capital in Thailand: Fibers, Finance, and Infrastructure* (Cambridge: Cambridge University Press, 1998), 1.

64 Kellee Tsai, *Back-Alley Banking*.

65 *China's Rural*, William Byrd and Lin Qingsong, eds., 223.

66 *CD*, November 9, 1990.

4

COUNTRYSIDE BUSINESSPEOPLE MODERNIZE CHINA'S MARKETS

In the PRC's two revolutionary decades, the 1950s and 1960s, the state not only became the main producer. State planners also structured the main markets. During reforms, rural enterprises decreasingly depended on sales to government companies. Already by 1970, manufacturing firms in Zhangjiagang, Jiangsu, sent only 15 percent of their products through state commerce departments, 35 percent through other contracts, and 51 percent to free markets. By 1978, the state purchased only 8 percent of these firms' production; and by 1988, only 3 percent. In that last year, 11 percent of rural production was already exported abroad, while 86 percent was sold under contracts to cooperatives or on domestic free markets.[1]

The state's planning organizations lost clout as buyers. Markets were still made by power institutions, but no longer just by relatively centralist ones.[2] As early as 1971, trade fairs were active around Shanghai, offering local manufactures for sale nationally. In October of that year, industry in suburban Qingpu County was growing quickly, and "twelve products from seven factories" were on sale to buyers who visited the county's Exhibition Hall. In the previous year, the county's CCP had been "restored at all levels" as the Cultural Revolution receded, and the Fourth Qingpu County Party Congress was held in May 1971. But legal and police organs took longer to revive. By January 1974, the Qingpu County Court was "restored." Centralized "military control was cancelled" in the same month at the local public security bureau; and this is important, because marketing often requires police protection. By the spring of 1976, Qingpu's "agricultural" (by then largely industrial) brigades all did their own accounting.[3] Restored local governments, after the Cultural Revolution ebbed, often became the protectors of nonstate industries.

Consumption, as well as production, became more rural during reforms. This reversed the trend of the 1950s and 1960s, which had been toward relatively more consumption in cities. From 1952 to 1978, a quarter-century-long period for which data are available, urban consumption rose at a rate above 5 percent annually,

82 Countryside businesspeople

while the rural figure crept up just 2 percent per year. By contrast, during the half decade after 1978, consumption rose 3 percent annually in cities, but 9 percent per year in the countryside.[4]

Housing booms herald consumption. In 1975, fully 99 percent of residential buildings in the best-surveyed Shanghai suburban village were just one-story – but by 1987, the single-floor portion of homes in the same place plummeted to 31 percent; the remaining seven-tenths had at least two levels.[5] When families have more rooms in their homes, they buy things to put there. Residential construction in the PRC (as in Taiwan during its fastest economic growth) was a major spur to the economy, especially in the countryside where peasants often interpreted long-term lease contracts for paddy land as a convenient way to find building space. Their local leaders only sometimes balked.

Village and township cadres, whose autonomy largely arose from abilities to monitor land use, generally encouraged new trade. Commerce in China's countryside was sometimes restricted by county-level bureaucrats – but not when they could tax it. Reforms increased rather than reduced *local* imposts on rural commerce. County militia and trade bureaus reportedly kept out products against which nearby factories did not want to compete. County regimes' inspection cars ('*guan ka*') patrolled rural roads, demanding local tolls from trucks.[6] Commercial drivers did not resist these tolls; they paid, received receipts, and were later reimbursed by their units. Their own property was seldom at risk; so they did not protest the levies – or point out the formal illegality. Imposts by local and central coercive powers differed, even though both kinds of regime were greedy. Traders could sometimes circumnavigate the local governments that were most covetous, in favor of those that maximized revenues by charging lower rates.

Many rural industries still dealt with their previous socialist upstream suppliers and downstream markets.[7] Many farmers still coordinated their field production in habitual ways.[8] But over time, more autonomous agents in rural China had options to switch to other methods or traders. Inertia and transaction costs disinclined people to bargain with new partners, and market contracts often echoed previous plans. The option to change partners affected economic relationships, even when that choice was not taken. The move toward more liberal markets was slower than most publicists and economists supposed; but over time, it was a trend.

"Models" and Wenzhou as an excuse

Proto-capitalist modes were thought by government and dissident intellectuals to require a patina of theory. So new economic "models" (*moshi*) emerged during reforms in East China. Most striking was the "Wenzhou model," identified with that large but isolated city on the Zhejiang coast. Wenzhou, despite its urban population of over half a million then, was safely sequestered from the rest of China and was thus a place that could host economic experiments. Wenzhou had never been a major tax base. It was not linked to the national rail network until 1998, and during early reforms there was no regularly scheduled air service.

Wenzhou is south of the Jiangnan delta, in Zhejiang, whose main northern cities are culturally and linguistically part of that delta. The Wenzhou 'dialect' of Wu/Shanghainese is a different language.[9] Many links between the delta flatland and Wenzhou have been substantive. When Jiangnan traders could not do their business on their own turf at sufficiently low rates of official extraction, they sometimes made the trip to do it in Wenzhou. Private Wenzhou banks loaned much credit. Partly because of illicit contacts between Wenzhou boats and those from Taiwan, but most especially because of the city's isolation, this was a pardonable place for daring local tests of PRC capitalism. The 1980s saw a spate of books by reformist intellectuals about Wenzhou.[10] About 80 percent of all Wenzhou capital was by the late 1980s private, rather than state or collective. Over 100,000 Wenzhou salespeople, scattered throughout China, launched strenuous marketing efforts on behalf of traders from that quasi-independent prefecture. Here was a highly distinctive, exploitative, entrepreneurial kind of PRC economy.

Other models also proliferated. Closer to Shanghai, the "Sunan model" of South Jiangsu was mainly distinguished by small collective enterprises.[11] Aside from the Sunan, Wenzhou, and Gengche (in poorer North Jiangsu) models in East China, the south advertised a Zhujiang (Pearl River) model around Guangzhou and Hong Kong. Others were the Minquan model of Fuzhou and the Baoji model in Shaanxi. Planning commissions were partly replaced by local slogans, even in lower-income regions; theorists put forward a "Langfang model" of the north, a "Tianshui model" of the west, and a "Fuyang model" in the central part of the country. These were all named after the counties or prefectures in which various experiments were mooted.[12] Details of differences between them are less important than intellectuals' charming premise that recent ex-peasants would have reasons to adopt whatever terms wiser men decided were best for them. The rural actors were not making models, however. They were making money.

Modeling changed after 1989. Chinese economists emphasized by the early 1990s that northern Zhejiang and southern Jiangsu used somewhat different models. In Sunan, industrial returns from collective enterprises were in that post-1989 era not accelerating at the previous brisk pace, reportedly because local governments gave wrong incentives to management, labor, and capital, just as the previous system of state corporations had done. In North Zhejiang, on the other hand, local governments often limited themselves to protecting, rather than managing, collective enterprises. The result was more efficiency, according to this analysis. The post-socialist Wenzhou model, in the southern part of the province, had legitimated higher levels of freedom in villages and towns throughout Zhejiang.

Wenzhou's influence slowly spread northward into Sunan and Shanghai, although that largest city always had a reputation (and practice) of being more obedient to centralist directives. Differences between the collective Sunan model and the private Wenzhou model have been overblown in both Chinese and Western sources. The main distinction relates to ownership form, but bosses of collectives were often at least as tyrannical, or exploitative of others on behalf of their own clients, as were private owners. Autonomous practical managers, irrespective of ownership

84 Countryside businesspeople

type, were more interested in low state imposts than were the government cadres they replaced during reforms. In Sunan, most new firms were not state owned. Collectives there were supposed to be linked to the state system more closely than private firms. Party bureaucrats could neither run the government without money from the Yangzi delta nor prevent the rise of new industries; so they gradually found themselves agreeing to Sunan reforms.[13]

In Wenzhou, which was smaller, then poorer, and geographically isolated, more firms could become private. Wenzhou had an unpromising tax base, and high politicians had larger fish to fry. As a Chinese economist put it, referring to the lower taxes in this secluded city, "The financial advantages of the Wenzhou model go a long way towards explaining the extremely lively state of manufacturing and commercial activity in many villages in the municipality."[14] But actually, the same difference was widespread; collectives on the Shanghai delta also paid a much lower portion of their earnings in central imposts than old state industries there did. The Sunan and Wenzhou models had a practical similarity: More money remained local.

Chinese writers stressed distinctions between these models because Wenzhou presented an obvious ideological problem – and opportunity. Reformers needed to defend the emerging pattern there against the (accurate) claim that it was not socialist. Market economists could argue that in a marginal area like Wenzhou, testing new economic forms served a national purpose without endangering the national budget. But this merely decorated the broader fact that local leaders in many coastal areas could now be more solicitous of their own budgets. The Sunan version of the model was adapted to a relatively high-tax environment, whereas the Wenzhou version was adapted to an area from which Beijing never expected much in taxes. The basic thrust of both the Wenzhou and Sunan models was more local autonomy, both managerial and financial.

Some entrepreneurs on the flatland openly envied Wenzhou's loose regulations. Zhejiang Governor Ge Hongsheng proudly asserted that his whole province (he did not distinguish Wenzhou from the northern part) could be different from others. As a reporter wrote, "While the whole country is going all out to increase the efficiency of large state-owned enterprises, Zhejiang is studying how to increase the production and management level of its small and rural enterprises."[15]

An issue was whether tax-and-profit imposts could be reduced for large collectives. "Big labor-hiring households" with about fifty workers each in rural Wenzhou during 1985 were very profitable; just one in twenty lost money. One-tenth of these private firms reported between 100,000 and 150,000 yuan of profits that year, and nearly half made between 30,000 and 100,000 yuan. The average private enterprise income, reported in this survey, was about 50,000 yuan on an output value of about 500,000 yuan – a reported profit rate of 10 percent. Party members were prominent in running these private firms, but non-Party people also partook. About two-thirds of these large firms had capital pooled among several households, although the remaining third were one-family shops.[16] Wenzhou's penetration of far-flung markets was based on cheap labor and materials prices; but as a Chinese economist confessed,[17]

The tax burden is light. This is mainly because the small, scattered, and independent nature of household industries makes it difficult for tax collection agencies to devise suitable methods of taxation. The majority of families engaged in household industries have not registered for tax purposes; and of those who have registered, many do not keep accounts; and even those that do, fail to keep them accurately. . . . According to statistics collected by the departments concerned, tax revenue of 1.26 million yuan should have been levied on household industries weaving plastics located in Rui'an County's Shencheng District [Wenzhou prefecture] on the basis of the value of production and marketing in 1984; but in fact, the value of taxation was only 0.6 million yuan [*just 48 percent of the taxes legally due*]. In Xianjiang Township, household industries producing shoes made of plastic and artificial leather should have paid taxes of 3.5 million yuan over a period of six years according to the value of its production, but only 0.26 [*7 percent of taxes due*] was received.

The main effect of the Wenzhou model was to make conservative reform leaders on the larger, wealthier, nearby Jiangnan delta seem staid, naïvely loyal, almost antireformist. Wenzhou as a symbol, outlying but legitimated, justified lessening the state burden in the most taxed part of China.

Sunan growth and exports as local powers and reforms altered

Rural industries were supposed to "go to the locality for three things" (*san jiu di*). Procurement, processing, and sales were all supposed to occur only in a collective's immediate vicinity. For processing, this norm was enforceable because it met local interests. But once rural factories were established, they in practice obtained factors and sold products wherever they could profitably do so. The state's control of trade gradually eroded.[18]

This discomfited planners, who tried to reverse the trend when the economic strain on state factories became high. But in all of South Jiangsu's townships, production grew about 25 percent in the single year 1988. The state's bankers ordered that credit to rural industries in 1989 should drop to less than half the 1988 amount (from 14.7 billion yuan to 7.1 billion). The People's Bank raised interest on savings deposits from February 1, 1989, in an attempt to capture money that would otherwise go into rural loans that the state could not control.[19] The effectiveness of such measures is difficult to prove, because violators could hide their actions.

After the Tiananmen crackdown, reports suggested the annual growth rate in Sunan was down to 5 percent (although township enterprises still created about two-thirds of all industrial output there). Hardliners by August 1989 vowed to close 10 percent of China's registered rural factories. But most workers in rural industries would not go back and till fields. A spokesman for the Ministry of Agriculture's Rural Enterprise Bureau claimed, "The amount of land is limited; there is no land to which they can return."[20] The modesty of 10 percent as a target for closures suggests scant confidence among socialist conservatives that they could shut rural industries. The number of formerly registered but still operational firms probably rose in 1989, despite the change of more pressure against reforms. The official credit crunch against rural industries in that year may have decelerated rural growth then, even as underaccounting affected published figures. The Ministry of Agriculture reportedly opposed the hardline policy, which was just slightly softened the next year as inflation dropped somewhat.[21]

Centralists lost their rural agents to industrialization during the 1980s, and Leninist controls on them were not well restored until the following decade. "Basic level cadres" decreased in number nationwide, by one-half from 1978 to 1984, and this was just the start of a hollowing of government and Party offices throughout rural China. Although township officials during this period rose slightly, former brigade-level cadres were down by 13 percent – and the number of village/production team or small group cadres plummeted 69 percent.[22] By the mid-1980s, there was "no assured source of funds" to pay rural cadres. "Some village cadres have not received pay for many years." At least one-tenth of Zhejiang villages had "nobody to take responsibility for the work."[23]

The portion of inactive local governments rose further in later years. A 1992 State Council report suggested that three-tenths of the Party's previous rural organizations were defunct, and another six-tenths were "weak" or "disorganized," leaving only one-tenth strong. A 1994 survey suggested that three-quarters of the Party's organizations were in "a state of collapse." Three-tenths of village government offices by this time had no resources with which to function.[24] Almost four-fifths of village leaders surveyed in a Jiangsu study admitted openly that a reason for their support of rural industry was to become more independent of higher state authorities.[25]

In the 1990s, the state tried to reverse this situation. A reason for some high-level support of rural industries, even during the post-Tiananmen conservative change, was that these factories brought hard currency. Central politicians were not of one mind, however. Bureaucrats favoring rural industries still fought hardliners who wanted to close them. The prowess of rural factories earning foreign exchange gave them national attention as well as local power. A Zhejiang shoe manufacturer, the Seagull Foreign Trade Industry United Corporation, in late 1988 had been "by far the biggest foreign exchange earner" among all rural Chinese enterprises. Its general manager waxed lyrical about the company, calling it "a little blade of grass that has grown out from between the stones" of overbearing rules. This factory made shoes largely from parts produced in household workshops. It sold shares and paid dividends, and it created seven-tenths of its whole rich township's total production value.[26]

The Township Enterprise Administration of the Ministry of Agriculture in September 1989 hosted a national export fair. During the first half of that year, China's township firms exported 41 percent more than in the same period of the previous year; and their foreign earnings were already US$3.8 billion. They employed at least

24 percent of the rural labor force nationwide (on the brave assumption that the published statistics were complete). Their gross industrial output value was reported at 21 percent of China's total in the first half of 1989.[27]

The technological sophistication of rural industries was also rising sharply. In southern Jiangsu, a computer factory run by "peasants" was advanced enough to make components for missile-launching systems.[28] Software writing was a localized experimental activity in many countries; and Jiangnan bred some competent nerds by the 1980s. The functional equivalents of their "garages" were usually suburban. Technical flexibility and high standards justified official support for firms that otherwise might have been closed because they competed with state companies. Some sold equipment to Army units that protected them.

The reported annual growth rate of Jiangsu rural companies in the last months of 1989 (after Tiananmen) was only 2.4 percent; but by August 1990, it jumped back up to 8 percent.[29] This bumpy progress could be continued because rural industries were increasingly able to get support from higher levels of the state administration that their advocates could penetrate. The Ministry of Agriculture had strayed into industry and industrial finance, because ex-peasants did. It recognized in 1990 the existence of rural stock markets – and the need to begin regulating them – with a set of "Temporary Provisions on Farmers' Cooperative Enterprises Held in Shares." These rules insisted that rural firms selling equities to the public must be called "collectives." The shareholders could resell their interests at will; so from a financial viewpoint, collectives' situation was like that of a private company raising new capital on an open market. The law imposed "administrative fees" and requirements that firms should pay normal taxes as well as retirement and welfare benefits. The main restrictive provision was that not more than 20 percent of net profits could be distributed as dividends, and 60 percent had to be reinvested. But local managers could find ways to redescribe their budgets and lessen such strictures.[30] The regulation of capital markets for rural industries barely stabilized share prices. To the extent that it required new ventures to register, it created opportunities for bureaucrats to use the regulations corruptly. In any case, ministerial agents began monitoring these markets more closely in 1990.

Fei Xiaotong wrote that "Sunan's today will be other places' tomorrow."[31] This was happening nationally by the 1990s, even as Beijing pressed for recentralization and post-reform changed "reforms." An estimated 1,600,000 farmers in 1991 alone were "newly released from the land this year, as a result of continued growth in the country's rural enterprises." They could expect jobs, as rural industries continued in the early 1990s to grow at rates that approached one-fifth or more annually. Rural manufacturing was by that time not only the fastest-growing sector, it was already very large in absolute terms. By the end of 1990, rural industries accounted for 25 percent of China's total GDP and 60 percent of all rural production value. Ninety million people were registered as employed in rural industries, and the real number may have been much higher.[32] Two years later, at the start of 1993, the number of rural employees was reported at over 105 million.[33] The 1990 figure implies that rural industries employed 87 percent as many people as state industries. The 1993 figure implies these two sectors were about equal in employment.[34]

Rural industrial markets as a spur of 1970s–1980s reforms that the 1990s regulated

Incentives from new markets, which often involved traders who had earlier particularistic bonds, do not solely account for the spectacular long-term industrial growth rates that approached 20 percent annually during reforms. Nor do they alone explain the respectable growth of agriculture that often exceeded 5 percent or the whole economy's rate that topped 10 percent during reforms. Local entrepreneurialism is arguably the basic cause of booms in both commerce and industry.[35] This factor operated in markets and factories; and it is local and political, more than it is economic.

Rural industries and liberated commerce were the most presentable outcomes of local-political entrepreneurialism. Their new resources created new power. They sprang from a green revolution and quietly changed China's political structure. The new firms were often inefficient, and their decision structures were undemocratic. Most were exploitative and uncivil. But many flourished, and they outstripped the state sector because they were relatively free of bureaucratic control and taxation.

Local cadres' loss of face during the post-Leap famine and then the Cultural Revolution was largely redeemed when these bosses could lead prosperity in their places. The reform syndrome was generally foisted on China's most famous central leaders by myriad ex-farmer chiefs whose names are unknown. When "the great and the good" lack enough resources to maintain their elite, as Pareto suggested, new powers replace them.[36] This happened in China, as the centralist revolutionaries finished doing all they could do for the country.

Notes

1 Zhangjiagang Bureau of Rural Industries, *Zhangjiagang shi xiangzhen gongye zhi* (Gazetteer of Zhangjiagang Rural Industries) (Shanghai: Shanghai Renmin Chuban She, 1990), 80, referred to me by Zheng Yongnian.
2 Police and fiscal centralization has always accompanied modern transformation, which power networks outside the state also induce. Historical examples of centralizations, including China's after 1949, often postdate revolutionary violence. Attending only to central governments would nonetheless ignore the cumulative power of local networks. Karl Polanyi, *The Great Transformation*; E. E. Schattschneider, *The Semi-Sovereign People*.
3 *Qingpu xianzhi*, 42–45.
4 Urban purchases rose four times, 1952–1978, but in the countryside just 58 percent. But in 1978–1983, the locations reversed: up 17 percent in cities – and 51 percent in rural areas. I calculated annual rates from *Zhongguo renkou*, 23–32.
5 These data are from Tangjiacun, Fengxian County, Shanghai – a place whose typicality has been checked by a non-official academic. See Ishida Hiroshi, *Chûgoku nôson*, 192.
6 Similarities to the local "likin" (*lijin*) taxes of imperial times are evident. Neither localism nor centralism is new in China.
7 An analogous situation for large state companies is described with reference to Oliver Williamson's theory in Dorothy Solinger, "Urban Reform," 104–123.
8 Thomas Gold, "Still on the Collective Road: Limited Reform in a North China Village," in *Chinese Economic Policy: Economic Reform at Midstream*, Bruce Reynolds, ed. (New York: Paragon House, 1988), 41–68.

9 Linguists name "Wu" languages (Shanghainese and Wenzhouese) after the ancient state of Wu, dating from the Western Zhou (after 1000 BCE). Wu dialects in mountains draining tributaries of Zhejiang's Ou River are like Wenzhouese – but cannot readily be understood even by people from that city. Few others stand any chance of understanding them.

10 A sampling: Yuan Enzhen et al., *Wenzhou moshi yu fuyu zhi lu* (The Wenzhou Model and Way to Affluence) (Shanghai: Shanghai Shehui Kexue Yuan Chuban She, 1987); *Wenzhou qiye dachuan, 1986* (Compendium of Wenzhou Enterprises, 1986), Wang Wence, ed. (Wenzhou: Wenzhou Shi Qiye Guanli Xiehui and Wenzhou Shi Gongye Pucha Bangong Shi, 1986); *Wenzhou moshi de lilun tansuo* (Theoretical Exploration of the Wenzhou Model), Lin Bai, ed. (Nanning: Guangxi Renmin Chuban She, 1987); and *Wenzhou shiyan qu* (The Wenzhou Experimental Zone), Pan Shangeng, ed. (Beijing: Nengyuan Chuban She, 1988).

11 Xu Yuanming and Ye Ding, *Tangqiao gongye*, 3, describes the Wenzhou and Sunan models, as well as a Gengche model – about which it offers no detail – for less-developed North Jiangsu (Subei, an area that many in Jiangnan denigrate).

12 *FBIS*, December 21, 1987, 21, reporting *RMRB* of December 5.

13 This echoes Chinese politics in the "Nanking decade" of 1927–37, when the centralizing militarist Kuomintang (led by Chiang Kai-shek) was in tension with its Shanghai capitalist constituency. See Parks M. Coble, Jr., *The Shanghai Capitalist Class and the Nationalist Government, 1927–37* (Cambridge: Harvard University Press, 1986).

14 Dong Fureng, "The Wenzhou Model for Developing the Rural Commodity Economy," in *Market Forces in China: Competition & Small Business, The Wenzhou Debate*, Peter Nolan and Dong Fureng, eds. (London: Zed Books, 1990), 84.

15 *CD*, June 22, 1991.

16 Calculated from Chen Ruiming, "A Preliminary Analysis of the 'Big Labor-Hiring Households' in Rural Wenzhou," *Market Forces in China*, op. cit., 141.

17 Li Shi, "The Growth of Household Industry in Rural Wenzhou," *Market Forces in China: Competition & Small Business, The Wenzhou Debate*, Peter Nolan and Dong Fureng, eds. (London: Zed Books, 1990), 115–16. In the original, county is *xian*, district is *qu*, and township is *xiang*.

18 Compare Louis Putterman, "Institutional Boundaries, Structural Change, and Economic Reform in China," *Modern China* 18:1 (January 1992), 3–13.

19 *Asian Wall Street Journal*, January 23, 1989.

20 *Post*, August 11, 1989.

21 Interview with an officer at the US Consulate-General in Shanghai, June 1991.

22 Chen Kaiguo, *Zhongguo nongcun da qushi* (*Trends in Rural China*) (Hefei: Anhui Renmin Chuban She, 1989), referred by my friend Wang Xu, who after finishing a Princeton Ph.D. returned to work for the Chinese government on village politics – but then very sadly died of cancer.

23 Quoted from a Zhejiang deputy governor by Tyrene White, "Political Reform and Rural Government," in *Chinese Society on the Eve of Tiananmen: The Impact of Reform*, Deborah Davis and Ezra Vogel, eds. (Cambridge: Harvard University Press, 1990), 49.

24 This all-China report is based on information from Pei Minxin in a paper, "Creeping Democratization in China?" kindly sent by the author.

25 Wang Xu referred me to this in Scott Rozelle and Richard Boisvert, "Quantifying Chinese Village Leaders' Multiple Objectives," *Journal of Comparative Economics* 18 (1994), 25–45.

26 *CD*, March 10, 1988.

27 *CD*, August 2, 1989.

28 *FBIS*, December 21, 1987, 21, reporting *RMRB* of December 5.

29 *CD*, September 26, 1990.

30 Edward Epstein, "China's Legal Reforms," in *China Review*, Kuan Hsin-chi and Maurice Brosseau, eds. (Hong Kong: Chinese University Press, 1991), 9.8.

90 Countryside businesspeople

31 Fei Xiaotong and Luo Yanxian, *Xiangzhen jingji*, 1–4.
32 *CD*, April 12, 1991.
33 *ZGTJNJ93*, 395.
34 For 1990 the data are better; see *ZGTJNJ91*, 201, for the denominator.
35 For more suggestions along this line, but in the production of a commodity that requires more capital, see Roger Cliff, "Technical Progress and the Development of China's Steel Industry Under Mao," MS paper kindly sent by the author.
36 The classic on "circulation" of conservative and adaptive members of healthy elites comes from a brilliant reactionary: (Count) Vilfredo Pareto, *The Rise and Fall of Elites*, or *The Other Pareto*, Placido Bucolo and Gillian Bucolo, tr. and eds. (New York: St. Martin's Press, 1980).

5

RURAL LEADERS BEAT
URBAN PLANNERS

Chapters above, concerning farms, rural factories, and markets, show that the roots of China's reforms can be found in local industrial results of early agricultural extension and triple cropping. In large cities, where the state had greater fiscal interests than it had in paddies, the situation was more complex. Part of the rural-urban difference was motivational: Campaigns from the 1950s to the 1970s had discouraged morale among entrepreneurs in major cities. China's urban industrial reforms cannot be ascribed wholly to causes that were concrete, because some factors for change were based in feelings about personal statuses that these intensive political campaigns affected.

Another set of reasons, treated in this chapter, was situational and external to people, rather than intended and attitudinal. It can be summarized in inflation. The rural boom created an unanticipated context for urban state industries' markets. State managers in the 1970s and 1980s found it harder both to buy factors and to sell products. Shortages, and then rising prices, became mechanisms of reform. Inflation is a sensitive topic, and published data on it are difficult to interpret because state and market prices influenced each other. The 1980s were highly inflationary. Prices by the end of that decade rose at rates unprecedented for the PRC; some observers recalled the 1940s. After Zhu Rongji's measures to control inflation in the post-reform 1990s, rates of growth exceeded rates of inflation. This was a change.

Shortages of materials for state industries emerged in the 1970s before prices rose sharply. Labor unrest and management difficulties were already rife by 1975, when a State Planning Commission document declared its managers "in chaos because of raw materials shortages, low productivity, and rising costs."[1] These problems cumulated for a decade at least, and by the mid-1980s they forced major structural changes and an end of socialist planning for most products.

"Three breakouts" in hiring, wages, and grain procurements

"In the beginning of the 1970s," as a PRC publication explains, "the country's economic life had 'three breakouts' [*sange tupo*]." The reported number of workers in state units reached 50 million, wage expenses for them became more than 30 billion yuan, and the state's grain purchase volume was 80 billion kilos. Each of these "breakouts" was unintended, each can be dated from the early 1970s, and each caused problems for planners – while also aiding China's economic boom. Conservatives for socialism regarded the hiring, wages, and procurements "breakouts" as dangerous to the Party-state.

Only three million workers were supposed to be added to the labor force in 1970 and 1971 according to official plans; but in practice, ten million were hired. Even in these years, top planners' efforts to allocate the most crucial input of production (labor) were already constrained by local leaders acting in response to common situations. Under the state budget, total wage expenses in 1971 were supposed to be 29.6 billion yuan, but 30.2 billion were said to be paid, and this was almost surely an underreport. Grain sales volume was supposed to be only 79 billion kilos, but the actual volume was 86 billion, and the state was the buyer of last resort at prices that it was politically loath to reduce, no matter whether it had spare funds. Bureaucrats needed to incentivize farmers to harvest enough grain for urban people who otherwise might become politically restless.

Budget crunches and unintended results of previous rural policies, rather than any liking for free markets among most communist leaders, combined by 1971; and officials tried to respond to these problems. Many aspects of the early 1970s pattern strongly resembled the state's difficulties during the 1980s. At least six of the ten million unauthorized hirings in 1970–1971 were of workers "from the countryside." These were peasants who became temporary workers and youths who refused to stay in rustication. "On one hand, agricultural labor decreased quickly because so many people left rural areas, hindering rural economic development; on the other, crop supply tension rose quickly because so many urban workers were hired in such a short time." There was, in most areas then, no major grain shortage; but the "crop supply tension" resulted from a lack of official money to buy food from peasants for workers, causing resentment in both groups.[2]

Beijing tried at that time (and for years later) to solve its problems by leaders' decrees: "Premier Zhou Enlai discovered the 'three breakouts' problem first." At a national economic planning conference from November 16, 1971, to February 12, 1972, Zhou pointed out dangers to the state's budget that were implicit in these trends. "However, his ideas could not be implemented" for reasons of state weakness that the official explanation dared not explain. So the "three breakouts" continued, strengthening local power networks at the state's expense. Through the end of 1972, the number of workers reached 56 million (over the plan by another two million, assuming all hires were reported). The state wage bill was then 34 billion yuan, up four billion from 1971. Crop sales volume reached 93 billion kilos, up more than

Rural leaders beat urban planners **93**

4 billion over 1971 – although the 1972 grain that the state could or did purchase was only 79 billion kilos.[3]

The patterns of later reforms were already obvious: The Party launched sporadic efforts to strengthen control of urban hires, while trying to spur grain production and pay as little as possible for procurement so that its proletarian constituency in politically important cities might remain satisfied without wage increases. Local power networks acted in precisely opposite directions: hiring more cheap workers in both rural and urban areas, compensating efficient technical or managerial employees, and refusing to produce rural grain until the state was willing to pay more for hard work in fields. This last problem was particularly acute in the early 1970s, when new rice technologies, which allowed greater total yields through triple cropping, pressed the marginal benefit to peasants of producing rice lower than before.[4]

Neither side in this prolonged tension between centralist planners and local leaders could obtain total victory. The government had some successes. But local power networks' autonomy over their hires, wages, and procurement budgets became stronger, on an upward ratchet-like zigzag trajectory rather than a smooth one. This was the pattern from 1970 for many years until the early 1990s. It was then reversed in the post-reform centralist era, for the next quarter century at least. The post-1990 pattern echoed an earlier centralizing trend during the 1950s, in which the state in its period of revolutionary consolidation had penetrated many urban and rural networks.[5]

The start of the input factors crisis

China's largest metropolis prospers on manufacturing and trade, not extraction. Shanghai has the dubious distinction of being practically the only province-level unit in China never to have produced any coal.[6] As many places in East Asia have shown, local primary production is not a prerequisite for economic success – so long as raw materials can be bought and brought from elsewhere.

Before 1949, Shanghai industrialists were famed for their sharpness in trade and finance as well as management. But the Transition to Socialism of the 1950s retired old businesspeople, who were replaced by new cadres, including many demobilized Red Army soldiers. The functions of managers changed, and revenues became as important as profits in their claims to their posts. Bureaucrats administered government plans in offices that often became more physically distant from factories or shops. Cadres in central, provincial, city, and county or district departments that oversaw factories were responsible for obtaining raw materials, getting capital credit, marketing products, and maximizing fiscal revenues.

Economic planning required political control. The mobility of factors in China fell under state plans that were supposed to allocate both commodities and people. Later, by the 1970s, reforms in practice meant inconsistent or weak central limits on land use, rural work point systems, and loans as well as less strict criteria for business licenses, urban household registrations and rations of food, housing, education, and jobs — even marriage and birth certificates. These reforms together allowed economic factors, as well as people, to seek more profitable uses.

Shanghai factory input prices were kept low in Mao's years, as were prices for rent and food. This situation led economists to call the city a "price basin" (*jiage pendi*). Officially, prices were of three kinds: fixed (*dingjia*), negotiated (*yijia*), and floating (*fujia*). The legal prices of commodities that could be controlled were usually set on a "cost plus" basis. Expenses and taxes at a major producing location for any good would be added to other outlays (e.g., for transport). As reforms progressed, especially in the 1980s, price competition raised business efficiency, and cost-plus calculations to fix prices became less enforceable. But for early reforms or where socialist norms continued, the price of a commodity at a single place, usually the largest center of production, remained the baseline. Shanghai was for many items the largest producer. Transport and other costs within the city were cheaper than they would have been without state subsidies. This became an accounting rationale for an essentially political policy: low prices in Shanghai.

Cheap prices, however, hindered the stream of goods into the metropolis. As a newspaper pointed out, "Water flows to a low place, but commodities go to a high [price] place."[7] Shanghai materials purchasing departments by the 1980s were said to be "poor" and lack cash. Actually, they were poor because Shanghai suffered China's highest extraction rate, while flourishing rural industrialists could then pay more for inputs that otherwise would come (and previously had come) to the city.

Shanghai's *urban* industry grew more slowly in the early 1970s than in the late 1960s. From 1966 to 1970, Shanghai's "national income" (*guomin shouru*) grew 14.0 percent annually — not radically below the 18.0 percent 1963–1965 growth during recovery from the post-Leap depression. Political disruptions of businesses at the peak of violence during the Cultural Revolution, in 1966–1970, did not slow Shanghai's growth as much as might have been expected. But from 1971 to 1975, the municipality's annual growth of *urban* industry was only 6.3 percent.[8] Other data, reported somewhat differently but on a basis that was officially supposed to be confidential (*neibu*), may be more honest. These indicate that Shanghai's income from 1966 to 1978 increased by an annual rate of 10.2 percent. But in the years from 1979 to 1982, its growth decelerated to 7.0 percent. In particular, heavy industrial production in the central city decelerated from 10.0 percent annually in 1966–1978 to 2.6 percent in 1979–1982.[9]

The reasons for the slowdown were almost surely multiple. Fiscal imposts on urban factories rose during the early 1970s. Capital for Army-related projects, of which Shanghai's high politicians in the "Gang of Four" founded many in the city during the late 1960s, decreased by the 1970s. Perhaps the mid-1960s high tide of the Cultural Revolution inspired some workers' enthusiasm that later atrophied.[10] But the main reason for the 1970s urban slowdown was that Shanghai's state factories were struck with a raw materials shortage. Booming rural industries elsewhere in East China had money to buy factors that planners could no longer commandeer with either police or budgets. The 1970s reforms meant faster economic expansion for most of China, but not for central Shanghai.

State control lasted longer over goods that are physically bulky per unit of value. Planning was also somewhat robust for materials that could be extracted only at specific locations, or that could be made only with capital-intensive technologies from bulk materials (e.g., coal at major seams, inorganic fertilizers from petrochemical factories). Official control over *de facto* nonstate managers was hard to maintain for small but valuable goods, those extracted in many places, and those that can be made with little capital,.

Central politicians tended to encourage production they could tax. Hua's Guofeng's economic program of 1978 echoed slogans from the Great Leap calling for support from central planners, heavy industries, and the Army. Hua saw the habit of continuing to honor Mao's policies as a source of stability for continued imposts that supported these networks. But by 1978, Hua lost politically. Hua and many of his followers had not suffered during the Cultural Revolution. These conservative lions were able to mobilize less support in the Party than did Deng Xiaoping's diverse, still cautious coalition of foxes.[11]

Locally, practical problems accumulated to confirm the view that China needed new, expert managers to replace the demobilized generalists who had dominated the urban economy for a quarter century. Before 1979, the Shanghai Production Materials Service Company already could not "freely manage" its trade. So it established new markets for inputs (as well as some for finished goods).[12] By the end of that year, over 1,000 sellers and buyers from many provinces exchanged commodities worth more than 300,000 yuan *each day* at this company's main market. Yet a socialist notion had been that such markets, where prices for major commodities were bargained rather than decreed, should have been unnecessary.

The Shanghai Handicrafts Bureau, desperate for inputs, had to negotiate long-term "compensation trade" (barter) contracts in 1979. In that year and the next, it signed ten such agreements with trading enterprises in Jiangsu, Zhejiang, Jiangxi, Hunan, and Guangxi. Its first treaties, which set the pattern, were with the Hangzhou Light Industrial Bureau and with Jiangsu's Zhenjiang Prefecture Building Materials Bureau. Under a large group of such contracts, Shanghai's "handicrafts" bureau bartered 9.8 million yuan of machinery in exchange for raw materials. The inland areas promised to send Shanghai (within periods of years that the contracts specified) 6,000 metric tons of thin paper, 1,000 tons of thick paper, 100 tons of glue, 6,000 tons of cement, and 1,000 sets of wooden furniture.[13]

Already by 1980, allocation through normal city plans could provide only 30 percent of the local demand for most construction materials – roof beams, bricks, steel rods, and glass.[14] Inland leaders did not always deliver the inputs they had promised. Between 1980 and 1982, the total value of goods available on Shanghai's raw materials markets fell by 60 percent.[15]

Firms producing consumer goods did better than Shanghai's heavy industry in the late 1970s and 1980s. But their performance was still not as good as in previous years, relative to that of domestic competitors. Light industrial production was stressed, and its rate of expansion, at 7.0 percent annually in 1966–1978, rose only to 8.5 percent in 1978–1982. The latter period saw a clear decline in Shanghai's

96 Rural leaders beat urban planners

capital-intensive industries and an expansion of businesses that gathered revenues for Beijing coffers. After 1982, when inputs became scarce, the city's light industries suffered too.

"Wars" for raw materials

Input shortages for state factories cumulated in the 1970s, and traditionally high inventories delayed their effects. For example, tea-growing cooperatives in East China began to process local leaves rather than delivering them to state plants; so a "tea war" raged by 1980. Government economists still wrote plans for practically all commodities, but rural managers did not follow them. A business cycle, which was locally linked to Pareto's "circulation" between reformers and hardliners, emerged in cities because rural reforms affected urban plants.

Shanghai's light industrial production increased 10 percent yearly from 1979 to 1981, and this was the main reason for the concurrent annual rise of 2.3 percent in the city's industrial profits and taxes. But in the first ten months of 1982, the rate of growth in urban light industry halved. Textiles were especially hard-hit, and cloth production in that year decreased by 3 percent. Profits and taxes from urban textile plants went down by more than 10 percent. Other parts of the country had "caught up" with Shanghai.[16] They had caught on that the state could not easily punish rural places for violations of materials delivery plans.

The official explanation for this problem in Shanghai was different, putting a positive spin on the facts. It noted that technical improvements in other provinces had created the basis for sharp competition with Shanghai products. Although the city won 49 percent of the first prizes in product fairs during 1980, in the next year it won 41 percent, and in 1982, thirty-seven percent. The inland infrastructure for improved manufactures had been accumulating for many years. The good news for many people was that the partial collapse of central delivery plans inspired diversification – and Shanghai technology transfers – to other parts of Jiangnan.

The bad news was that Shanghai's urban economy could no longer obtain its habitual supply of inputs. The number of Shanghai products under mandatory production quotas had to be officially allowed to drop in the mid-1980s, from 150 kinds of commodities in 1984 to 37 types in 1987.[17] Over the same years, the number of products for which city agencies could require mandatory sales also went down, from 53 to 23. The number of raw materials that were distributed under the city's plans likewise decreased, from 19 to 13. Even then, not all mandates were fulfilled. Socialist planners largely went out of business in the mid-1980s.

"Developing the commodity economy without commodities is a major vexation for many enterprises in Shanghai."[18] The gallows humor of two irreverent journalists, who wrote this, was justified by facts. A 1985 survey of a large number of major Shanghai manufactures showed that state plans could supply all the needed materials for only 27 percent of them. The firms making this quarter of previously produced items could "still" garner "a certain profit." For another 18 percent, however, rising input costs meant profits much lower than plans foresaw, as well as "difficulties" in obtaining inputs. For fully 55 percent of the surveyed products, factories could no longer pay rising costs of inputs without losing money.[19]

Raw materials prices before the 1980s were often low even when there were shortages. Unintended reforms made them high and volatile. The portion of all Shanghai factory inputs allocated by plan plummeted, from about 70 to about 20 percent, in the mid-1980s crisis. Planners did not wish this drop, but they could not deliver the goods.[20]

Shanghai factories reported having to fight "big wars" to get rabbit hair, wool, ramie, silk cocoons, and cotton ('*tumao dazhan, yangmao dazhan, zhuma dazhan, canjian dazhan*, and *mianhua dazhan*').[21] The whole of Jiangnan in 1986–1987 delivered fewer silk cocoons to Shanghai than before, because Jiangsu and Zhejiang local leaders had set up more of their own local mills. Planners were unable to maintain quality standards, even when inputs were delivered. When mulberry areas supplied cocoons at this time, rural managers sent many that had not been inspected, in which the worms were still alive. The water content of such cocoons was higher; so they were heavier – and the quota was by weight. But the worms were still spinning inside, and these cocoons contained less silk. Jiangsu and Zhejiang cocoon sellers in the mid-1980s paid more attention to batches sent to factories in their own provinces, perhaps because these plants were better situated to complain when deliveries were bad.

Silk is a quintessential Jiangnan product, but the government's centralized companies paid farmers little for cocoons or woven silk, while charging high prices to foreign buyers. Peasants in East China found ways around this and engaged in "wild and erratic price rises by illegal silk traders, especially in Jiangsu and Zhejiang."[22] Although export demand for Chinese silk reportedly remained higher than supply, government policies to control and extract money from this market affected the flow of goods. China's total raw silk production by 1988 could meet only 70 percent of all new and old factories' total needs.[23]

Xinjiang and Mongolia did not deliver as much wool or hides to Shanghai as they had previously done. Mainly in an effort to assure wool supplies, Mayor Jiang Zemin himself in April 1986 led a Shanghai trade group to Inner Mongolia. A return delegation came to Shanghai in late 1987, visiting several firms, including the Shanghai Leather Shoes Factory, which uses Mongolian hides, and discussing "several projects to develop raw and semi-finished materials industries."[24] But in the mid-1980s, when the prices of many goods were allowed to float, the habit of markets by political arrangement tended to weaken.

The central government's ability to supply Shanghai with raw materials decreased, when the prices of more inputs were allowed to float and more inland local "guaranteed delivery contracts" emerged. Of all the resources for steelmaking distributed under the state plan in various years in the 1980s, the percentage Shanghai obtained from state plans dropped dramatically. There were especially sharp decreases in 1985 and 1987, as Tables 5.1 and 5.2 show.

TABLE 5.1 Percentage of raw materials for Shanghai steelmaking allocated by state plans

Year	Percent
1981	86
82	78
83	73
84	75
85	58
86	54
87	34

Source: *Shanghai jingji nianjian, 1988* (Shanghai Economic Yearbook, 1988), Xiao Jun et al., eds. (Shanghai: Shanghai Renmin Chuban She, 1988), 84. "Raw materials for steelmaking" are *gangcai ziyuan*, measured here by value.

TABLE 5.2 Reported shortages of materials in Shanghai, 1985

	Requirements (m. metric tons)	Planned allocation (%)	Shortage (%)
Cement	3.5	51	49
Steel	2.43	60	40
Lumber	1.5	60	40
Ferrous metals	0.21	69	31
Chemical inputs	3.04	76	24

Source: The cement allocation includes both central and local planned deliveries; apparently the other materials were all centrally regulated. Tabulated from narrative material in *Shanghai jingji* (Shanghai Economy), January 1985, 3; the percentages are calculated.

TABLE 5.3 Sources of reported Shanghai income

	(percentages)	
	1980	*1986*
Government (city & local)	76	58
Firms (esp. collective)	9	18
Individuals & private firms	16	24
Totals	c. 100	100

Source: Xu Zhenliang, "*Shanghai caizheng shouru 'huapo' de xiankuang, chengyin ji qi duice*" (The "Slide" of Shanghai's Financial Income: Situation, Reasons, and Countermeasures), in *Caijing yanjiu* (Finance and Economics), March 1988, 18–23. "Firms" are *qiye*. "Shanghai national income" (*guomin shouru*) does not include a very few large plants that are in the city but are wholly managed by central ministries.

During the first half of 1986, as one analysis put it, this "Shanghai disease (*Shanghai bing*)" of input shortage brought a depression to local processing industries. The growth of the city's production during that time was lower than during the same period of 1985, and much lower than all of China's. In industry, the national growth rate during the first five months of 1986 was 4.8 percent; but in Shanghai, only 1.8 percent. That low increment was mainly attributable to large factories in suburban Baoshan and Jinshan counties. During some of these months, Shanghai's total industrial growth was negative.[25]

Shanghai domestic sales of industrial products showed a further drop in 1986. Clothing sales went down 3 to 4 percentage points.[26] Also, the portion of industrial income in the municipal government's budget plunged. This recession affected collective industries even more than state-owned ones, if the reporting is believable. The causes of such disasters were many, and they could be phrased in reformist terms even though reforms were the short-term cause of most of them.

Fulfillment of delivery obligations under the "responsibility system" had been massively "impeded." The quality of products in sixty-one companies was declared substandard, and twenty-seven of these were given "red light" warnings.[27] In a survey of many industrial finished products, 36 percent were substandard. But the biggest change from the previous pattern in Shanghai was the shortfall of materials deliveries.

Shanghai factories had to find more of their own materials, especially if their profits-and-taxes contributions were relatively unimportant to the government. Plants under the city's Handicrafts Bureau by 1983 already had to garner 43 percent of their nonferrous metals by themselves, and 60 percent of their steel.[28]

Both people and local enterprises increased their share of Shanghai's income, at the expense of government, during the 1980–1986 period. Shanghai's state industries were particularly hard-hit. Profits and taxes for each hundred yuan of fixed capital in them declined from 81 to 45 yuan.[29] Price-adjusted costs, for each yuan of state sector product, rose by 8.1 percent in 1986 alone.

Managers' lives in Shanghai became more difficult. No longer did external bureaucracies "distribute" materials and financial credit to them. They had to pay new attention to whether their products were actually sold. The costs to careers of negotiating with superiors had, in earlier eras, been lower than the costs of fending independently – but by 1985, the purported superiors had little help to offer. The hard world of upstream and downstream markets appealed to economists, reforming politicians, and intellectuals cheering from the sidelines. For Shanghai managers, calling for efficiency was less important than providing raw materials. The Party had allowed other provinces to have more gradual adjustments to markets. Shanghai still had high tax burdens, and few sizable private enterprises or large new collective firms could operate openly in the central part of the metropolis even as late as 1988.

The cost per hundred yuan of industrial output that Shanghai had to pay in 1987 was high, at 76 yuan for all factors.[30] Centrally mandated prices, which had been enforced earlier by police power, had mostly ended.[31] These mandates had required state coercion to be effective, and their defeat must be traced to similarly coercive networks that were local. As Fei Xiaotong admitted, "Managers in rural enterprises use some unsuitable methods to get what they need." He offered a reason: "This may be necessary, because we have not yet established a market from which they can meet demand."[32]

An estimated 590 million yuan of additional funds were required in Shanghai's main fifteen municipal bureaus for materials, industry, and commerce during 1986, because of inflation for inputs within that year.[33] This twelve-month increment of costs for inflation alone was about ten percent of total expenditures in Shanghai in 1986.[34] Official banks made more loans.

By 1988, state and market prices for factors diverged so much that, for example, a metric ton of aluminum officially cost 4,800 yuan, but the market price (at which a ton of aluminum could actually be obtained) was 12,000 yuan. Timber planks of a standard width per square meter at the state price theoretically cost 90 yuan, but the actual market price was 500 yuan. A ton of coal was planned to cost 50 yuan, but the ton could not be had for less than 110 yuan.[35]

Local jurisdictions outside Shanghai sometimes required "export licenses" for their materials. Authorities in Inner Mongolia held on to their cashmere wool for local weaving: "Unless you sack us, you can't have it!" A Zhejiang local planning committee attempted to prevent Jiangsu mills from buying raw silk, so that it would be processed in Zhejiang where those worms were. Jurisdictions also inhibited imports of manufactured goods. Shanghai bicycles could sometimes be wholesaled only on the condition, imposed by inland authorities, that the seller also buy a quantity of local goods. Tractors from Changzhou, in Jiangsu, were popular among Chinese tillers (and were exported), but they could not be registered for licenses in some places, where gasoline could thus not legally be bought for them.[36] Managers had to find informal means to deal with bossy localists, whether or not such agreements served the interests of the state that was rapidly becoming less socialist.

Economists claim a commodity at one time and place can have two efficient prices

By the mid-1980s, an "army" of rural factory managers oversaw nimble, exploitative, profitable firms that could afford to buy inputs at prices the budgets of state companies could no longer afford. So the government legalized former black markets. It let state factories sell items at 20 percent above the planned prices (*jihua jia*) after those firms claimed to have fulfilled their production quotas. This marked-up rate was euphemized as a "state-guided price" (*guojia zhidao jia*). But the two-price policy was, at first, unintended and unwanted by planners. It was praised as wise not just by governments, but also by many economists. For example, three of them in the West wrote:

> The dual pricing system allowed state-owned enterprises to sell unused input quota at market prices to township and village enterprises (TVEs) that were

outside the command economy. Such exchanges not only protected the original privileges of higher ranking entitlements, but also presented TVEs with opportunities to access industrial inputs via market channels and to participate in the market economy. In other words, the dual pricing system provided a functional pricing mechanism for rent-sharing through both hierarchical and market systems.[37]

This may be interesting as abstract theory. But as evidence in this book shows, the units that needed more access to industrial inputs were not TVEs but were state enterprises.

Most economists usually say that a commodity of a standard quality at a single time in a single place has just one rational price. If it does not, efficient allocation is unlikely to occur. But in the 1980s when China was booming, the most distinguished international non-profit banks (like international businesses) were very eager to get into China and into the good graces of its government. These economic scholars forgot a normal principle of their profession: At any time, supply and demand for a commodity in a market would generate just one price for optimum allocation. The other kind of rationality, protecting "the original privileges of higher ranking entitlements," was political rather than economic.

A 2017 book by Julian Gerwitz argues that Westerners such as Nobel prize economist James Tobin influenced China's national policies from the late 1970s.[38] That may be true for large state-owned enterprises. But China's local leaders had policies too, and notes about tête-à-tête conferences among famous foreign economists and Chinese politicians need not displace information about the major effects of local entrepreneurs and technological changes that affected most Chinese people. As Gerwitz says, open discussion of macroeconomic ideas was reduced after 1989, when macropolitical worries within the CCP elite became intense.

Shanghai investment inland

There is nothing unusual about cosmopolitan centers in developing economies financing raw materials extraction for their own industries. At the height of China's revolution in the mid-1950s, this practice was nationalized. The central government largely paid for major projects, including industries that started production about 1958. Then military managers took charge of "Great Third Front" inland investments of 1964–1971. Vertical integration in urban Shanghai companies during the mid-1970s remained extensive, especially in heavy industries.

Of all firms managed in the city under the First Ministry of Machine Building during 1976 above the district level, 80 percent ran subsidiaries that extracted their raw materials. Some were praised for being "large and complete" (*da er chuan*). Others were medium-sized or small – but just as "complete" in terms of vertical integration. A ministry survey found that two-thirds of these companies made the capital goods they used. In Mao's time, Shanghai managers developed a habit of trying to maximize the predictability of their supplies.[39] The rise of markets with

102 Rural leaders beat urban planners

chancy fluctuations knocked this comfortable but inefficient system into the brave new world of competition.

Shanghai investments inland were expensive. Materials shortages might have caused more of them during the 1970s, but they cost money and the city's top politicians (appointed from Beijing) were committed to keeping Shanghai's central remittances high. Fiscal "slippages," which were delayed in Shanghai until the 1980s, partly reflected planners' realization that the metropolitan economy needed new supply sources. By 1982–1983, Shanghai invested heavily in extractive industries of Sichuan, Shanxi, Shaanxi, and Anhui. Municipal planners had long wanted to do this; but central planners had earlier vetoed such initiatives in favor of investing directly through ministries. A reason why Shanghai could make such investments by the 1980s was that the center could not, because of its general budget deficit.[40]

One agency for garnering raw materials from other parts of China was the Shanghai Joint Development Corporation (Shanghai Lianhe Fazhan Gongsi), established in 1984. Within the following three years, it set up twenty-seven "materials production enterprises" in other provinces. Investments were made in places as far afield as Qinghai and Ningxia to bring materials like aluminum construction materials to Shanghai. Connections with inland areas were run through state corporations, which became more autonomous in bargaining as mandates alone no longer delivered supplies.

By the end of 1985, Shanghai's textile industries established 1,100 joint projects in the municipality's ten suburban counties. Only 5 percent were "joint enterprises," but 50 percent were "cooperative processing points."[41] These were like traditional companies for out-contracting (*waibao*). Together they contributed just 8 percent of Shanghai's textile output, but they dispersed technology to counties while giving urban plants more assured supplies of cotton.

Inland investment in factories whose products came through the city consumed over a billion yuan of Shanghai capital in 1987 alone. Metropolitan companies in many fields had no alternative to investing elsewhere.[42] A 1988 report said that Shanghai had forty "production materials trade centers" in other provinces.[43] Many cities competed for materials from rural networks, which were decreasingly willing to part with them at low prices without side benefits. When a thermal power plant was needed in Nanjing, local banks successfully issued bonds to finance it, but only on condition that the stockholders would enjoy priority in buying the plant's electricity after it was built.[44] Vertical ties remained almost as strong as in the planned economy, for commodities the state could still allocate; but during reforms, more of them were arranged directly between localities, and fewer benefited the central state.

Shanghai Municipality in the single year 1987 started eighty-eight major projects in other provinces to obtain raw materials. The number of subsidiaries for this purpose was reported at 667, and Shanghai investment for such firms was more than a billion yuan. Under the contracts, Shanghai was scheduled to obtain sixty-eight kinds of raw materials with a total value of 3.5 billion yuan.[45] These estimates assumed prices could be fixed into the future. When they went up, the rural places benefited most.

Sometimes inland jurisdictions took money from Shanghai firms to produce raw materials – but later kept the inputs to process themselves. The central state was unable to prevent this even in its most profitable of all industries, cigarettes. The Shanghai Cigarette Company helped finance production in a Henan tobacco-growing area that was supposed to send its entire crop to the metropolis. The quality of shipments turned out to be low. When the leaves were graded, assessors deemed one-quarter of them unfit to use. So the Shanghai company refused to buy the bad leaves. But during reforms, input markets were sellers' markets. The Henan suppliers, apparently threatening to send their whole crop to new cigarette companies elsewhere, succeeded in raising the price the Shanghai company had to pay for good leaves, to cover their losses from the non-sale of bad ones.[46]

A Shanghai metal processing company in 1986 similarly invested 6.7 million yuan in a far western Qinghai company, which signed a contract guaranteeing the Shanghai investing firm 7.8 percent of its bauxite production at a set price as part of its dividend. By 1988, however, this Shanghai-Qinghai scheme failed. The inland mine delivered only three-fifths of the agreed amount, and the Shanghai buyer had to pay a higher price.[47] A 1988 journal reported that Shanghai had put 920 million yuan into 599 materials-supply projects in other provinces, in hopes of obtaining various inputs.[48] Many such ventures succeeded, but others did not.

The paper crunch as an example

Before 1987, one ton of newsprint paper in Shanghai had cost 900 yuan; but by late 1988, it cost 3,400 yuan. At least one supplementary publication of the *Liberation Daily* (*Jiefang ribao*, official organ of the Shanghai CCP) was temporarily suspended in November 1988 solely because there was no paper on which to print it.[49] The famous and important newspaper *Wenhui News* (*Wenhui bao*) in early 1987 had a supply of paper on hand that would last seven months; but by the worst period of 1988, this had been reduced to a supply for just two days.

Editors were very willing to editorialize that the situation was "tense" (*jinzhang*). Distinguished journalists, in high Party posts, were not just worried about the paper shortage. They were apoplectic about it. They faced a real possibility that their media would fail to appear, merely for lack of paper. Journalists are normally an articulate lot, and this situation sent them through the roof; so no shortage has been better reported in Shanghai than the lack of newsprint. In May 1988, a metric ton of paper was supposed to cost 1,550 yuan at the state-fixed price. But local paper mills in southern China were then charging 200 yuan more than that to their wholesalers. For Shanghai journals, newsprint was unavailable below 2,500 yuan per ton.[50] The market was volatile because paper in different places had very different prices. Northern paper (mostly from the Northeast) cost 1,550 yuan; in the South (where the main producers were Guangdong, Fujian, and Jiangxi), it cost 1,750 yuan; and the market price in Shanghai and other Jiangnan cities was 2,500 yuan.

104 Rural leaders beat urban planners

A paper supplier in Fujian Province demanded foreign exchange for providing newsprint – which came from Chinese, not foreign, trees. Under state plans, convertible currency was supposed to be used, normally under close supervision, only to purchase imports. But this Fujian paper company got what it asked.[51] Nonetheless, most of the price increases were not just results of the paper mills' cupidity. Wood and labor costs had risen sharply, especially in South China. The price there of a ton of timber for paper in early 1988 was about 400 yuan – between two and three times the 1985 price. Even at the 1988 prices for newsprint, mills made low profits. Absorption of labor in more lucrative industries, combined with a very long-term ecological decline in supplies of wood and sharp rises in prices for paper-processing chemicals, were inflationary. The only reason why paper prices had remained low until the mid-1980s was that planners had been able to commandeer factors, essentially by police methods, without serious attention to scarcity values.[52] One side of the coin was higher prices; the other was lower coercive and monitoring capacity in the central state compared with local networks.

During the first third of 1988, all of China produced 28 percent less newsprint than in the same period of the previous year. Yields in Guangdong, Fujian, and Jiangxi were all down, and mills closed for lack of wood. The estimated 1988 demand for paper nationwide was 600,000 metric tons, but the rate of production was only 450,000 (one-quarter less).[53] China's average per capita consumption of newsprint at this time was only 0.48 kilos (compared with a world average then of 6 kilos, including an average of about 20 kilos in developed countries). None of China's public newspapers, and reportedly few of the limited-circulation media, bear any resemblance to the heft of the *New York Times*. So Shanghai editors opined they were not demanding too much when asking for budgets to finance newsprint.

Some Chinese industries are spendthrift with resources, but others, including journalism, are abstemious. Aside from the Shanghai Party's *Liberation Daily*, only three other eight-page newspapers were published in China during the late 1980s: *People's Daily*, *Bright Daily*, and *Tianjin Daily*. Circulation of *Liberation Daily* reached a peak in the early 1980s, standing at 9.3 million in 1984. But by 1987, this figure dropped to 8.5 million; and to 8 million by the next year. Part of the reason was a price increase to buy enough newsprint.

The main official response to the paper shortage was a plea for recycling. The Shanghai Paper Company in 1989 "had to buy 140,000 tons of pulp from China and abroad . . . and also made use of 230,000 tons of waste paper as raw material for pulp." In a recent previous year, the company had obtained 83,000 tons of pulp from the state, but by 1989 this amount was down to 17,000 tons.[54] Waste paper became the main source of raw material for these Shanghai factories. An apologist claimed that buyers from outside the city "stole" scraps before these could reach the city's mills[55]:

> Paper factories are waiting for materials, and many have to close. Most paper recycling stations in Shanghai were established by educated youths, private households, welfare organizations, or street offices. But recently,

paper businessmen from Jiangsu and Zhejiang came to Shanghai with huge amounts of money to buy waste from these paper recycling units. They pay in cash at a high price. Their business is very smooth. They collect waste paper during the day but transport it out of Shanghai at night for sale to local paper factories in Jiangsu or Zhejiang.

The chief editor of *Wenhui News* in 1988 told me his journal should really be eight pages, not just four. The only reason for its size was a lack of paper. Importing from sources like Canada or Alaska, which sold to Japanese publishers, for example, was out of the question. *Wenhui bao* was one of China's most distinguished newspapers, read by educated people in many cities throughout the country; but it earned practically no foreign exchange. The chief editor, a distinguished Communist, frankly hoped that Chinese relations with Russia (then still Soviet) might improve, but his reason had nothing at all to do with international relations or socialism.[56] He was interested in any means to get paper. He had to find a way around PRC foreign exchange controls. Barter was possible from the largest forests on the horizon, which were in Siberia.

In-kind exchanges: meeting shortages without the politics of inflation

"Compensation trade" (*buchang maoyi*) was the elegant official name for bartering. This method was extensively used in interprovincial trade of scarce goods. For example, by the mid-1980s, Shanghai was sending bicycles and washing machines to Jilin in China's Northeast, exchanging them for paper pulp.[57] Barter arose because factories needed raw materials that the plan no longer supplied, but it also arose for a second reason: Consumer durables in the 1980s were priced by state regulations at amounts lower than they could actually fetch from consumers. Buyers now included many rich peasants and rural industrialists. The price fixers did not keep up with the boom, but they feared unrest among urban state employees if they let the retail costs of consumer durables soar because of demand from nouveaux riches in rural areas.

When factories traded manufactures in kind directly for inputs, they could stay in operation. Urban inflation was the main political danger, but with barter there were no monetary prices. The breakdown of planning encouraged economic expansion through barter. This exchange method in the 1980s further postponed the effects of shortages on prices, even after coercive means to restrain prices failed. So the government developed an official interest in legitimating barter trade. Some cadres thought this method of exchange was very socialist, a way to avoid the cash nexus.

Exchanges in kind rather than money were also given cachet by their use in international trade. They obviated the need to obtain official approvals to spend hard currency. But "compensation trade" mainly grew within China when buyers needed goods and had the physical wherewithal to obtain them. The system seemed familiar, because ration quotas (along with money) had long been required to obtain goods. It seemed necessary, after allocations by fiat were no longer effective to get inputs delivered.

Barter arrangements became so common that state agencies published rates of exchange for them – even though few barter trades were written into plans. For example, one metric ton of steel was supposed to be exchanged for 16 to 25 tons of cement, or 2 to 5 cubic meters of lumber, or 2 to 3 tons of pig iron, or 1.6 to 3 tons of iron salvage, or one-quarter to one-third of a ton of copper, depending on quality.[58] Similar barter exchange rates were also officially published for aluminum, rubber, fertilizers, "East Wind" trucks, jeeps, and cars produced by China's joint enterprise with Volkswagen. These rates were indicative only; they left margins for further bargaining. Each province regularly published lists of materials that it had for exchange, as well as lists of materials it needed. "Adjustment meetings" (*tiaoji hui*) were convened to circulate the lists and conclude barter deals.

A difficulty of this system is that the bits of information necessary to make it work multiply geometrically, as the number, variety, and quality of products expand to resemble those in the real world. In 1987, the State Statistical Bureau at the central level published a matrix of non-monetary prices to be used for barter. This valued just ten industrial goods in terms of just twenty-one agricultural products. Even if issues of product quality, season, and transport are ignored, the exercise already implied an array of 210 barter "prices" (compared with 31 prices that would be needed if money had been used).[59] The amount of information to be processed soars, if barter is the mode of trade.

Money as an institution has drawbacks. But the spectacle of a modern government trying to run parts of a diversified economy without it soon suggests that on the whole, money is not a bad idea.[60] The value of this invention is that it concisely summarizes a complex situation. A price is the most classic example of an unintended, "situational" social fact. The buyer wants it lower, while the seller wants it higher. Yet when people do not give goods to each other (as they often do), they can trade in the context of each other. There is no reason to privilege either situational or normative evidence of motives to action – or to prioritize large, medium, or small actors except on empirical grounds. Compensation trade became especially unwieldy when it involved the transfer of non-tangible assets, such as technology or services. Shanghai was relatively rich in these.

The city's main items for barter were consumer durables, and during late reforms it used in-kind trade extensively. By 1987, about 15 million yuan worth of bicycles, refrigerators, and cars that Shanghai sent to various inland places paid part of the bill for 330 million yuan worth of raw materials. Municipal leaders wanted to reduce prices of rural inputs that came from areas they could not control, while keeping the prices of processed goods from state factories high, so that they could serve their careers by maintaining Shanghai's fiscal remittances to the state.

Industry-agriculture terms of trade moved during reforms in a direction more favorable to agriculture. Such terms can be quantified by choosing a single year (e.g., 1987) and then showing the higher rate of inflation from various earlier years of agricultural than of industrial goods. Specifically, the 1987 purchase prices of agricultural subsidiary products were 130 percent above those of 1965; 122 percent above 1970; 99 percent above 1978; 52 percent above 1980; and 19 percent above 1985. On the other hand, 1987 rural retail prices of industrial products were only 12 percent over those of 1965; 18 percent over 1970; 20 percent over 1978; 19 percent over 1980; and just 8 percent over the 1985 levels.[61] So since each earlier year, the price rise by 1987 had been greater for agricultural than for industrial goods.

Shanghai in each of these years was at the extreme low end, among all provinces, for the cheapness of the agricultural raw materials it was planned to buy.[62] Continuing state subsidies kept the prices low – not to benefit the city, but to maximize the government's fiscal revenue that depended on Shanghai's imports of inexpensive materials.

Shanghai in each of these years also had the highest provincial ratio for the planned value of the industrial goods it produced divided by the value of the agricultural goods it purchased. Terms of trade were such that the real 1987 value of agricultural raw materials in 1965 prices that Shanghai bought per 100 yuan of its industrial sales in 1965 prices was only 0.65 yuan; and for 1970 prices, 0.69 yuan; for 1978, 0.76; for 1980, 0.95 yuan; and for 1985 prices, 1.19 yuan. So by the mid-1980s the terms of trade turned against Shanghai state-owned industries – and when they did so, the change was sharp. Planners could no longer use the city's light industries to provide so much of the state budget.

Beijing and Tianjin, the other two province-level units most similar to Shanghai, were near the national average (usually below it) for all these years in the value of agricultural raw materials that they bought per unit of industrial product. But Shanghai was always highest in the country, until the mid-1980s inflation forced more localization of trade.

Imports and new sales channels

A *Liberation Daily* columnist, writing for socialist conservatives in the CCP newspaper, suggested in 1988 that Shanghai's economic troubles could not be blamed solely on a lack of materials. If the city could raise the prices of its products, it would have had enough money to buy inputs. Or if the city could dispose of its own products by barter, the problem might also be solved.[63] But national plans constrained retail product prices, which were relatively easy to monitor, better than it constrained factor prices, which were harder to check accurately when suppliers charged high unplanned rates.

Protectionism limited factor imports from abroad. During Shanghai's long-gone period of fastest growth ending in 1937, its producers had brought inputs from any place in the world where the price and quality were best. This was a distant memory for socialist planners, whose patriotism was merchantilist; but by the 1980s, rural industrialization reduced their sources of supply within China. So in 1984 and 1985, shortages were so great that Shanghai spent about half of its foreign exchange reserves to import raw materials rather than new technologies.

108 Rural leaders beat urban planners

Bankers had a proposal to relieve the hemorrhaging of reserves: More credit for Shanghai loans could have let factories pay for domestic materials, so that fewer raw imports would be needed.[64] But this would require major subsidies from Beijing. The central government was more in the habit of taking money from Shanghai than giving to it. When raw materials became unavailable to Shanghai firms from previous domestic sources at sufficiently low prices, many searched abroad; but the rules mandating firms to balance foreign exchange inflows and outflows militated against foreign purchases.

Regulations against buying abroad bent under pressure from the mid-1980s factors crisis. Ninety-four percent of Shanghai's 1986 foreign imports were "means of production," including many raw materials. In 1987, this figure rose to 98 percent. That year, the total cost was US$1.79 billion, of which $1.75 billion went for "physical materials." Over nine-tenths of the total went to raw inputs, not to capital that might embody new technology. Only $85 million went to capital – just 5 percent of the city's total foreign exchange cost.[65] Progress in using foreign exchange to develop new Shanghai industries was less than it would have been if the need for raw materials had been less urgent.

Shortages also led to new institutions, especially brokerage firms, that sought buyers, markets, and "stable sources of materials" around the globe and throughout China. By early 1988, Shanghai's Taicang Road was one of many streets where middlemen traded.[66] The central city's most reliable suppliers were its closest ones, in Jiangnan where urban managers often had family connections. In August 1987, the Shanghai Materials Bureau organized "development companies" that served as brokers or intermediaries for finding inputs.[67] It also set up "materials trade centers," as well as a market for foreign sellers of industrial materials. The bureau's Party school established training courses for managers in suburban counties, helping them establish companies that could provide more agricultural products to the city. Shanghai's ten counties supplied about one quarter more, by value, in 1987 as in the previous year.

During the late 1980s, "exchange fairs" offered another way for Shanghai firms to seek raw materials. In 1987, for example, one such market drew "production materials service companies" from practically all of China's other provinces. In a span of three days, the value of trade was more than one billion yuan.[68] Still, the Shanghai Electric Cable Factory in mid-1988 was daily losing 400,000 yuan because of a shortage of copper. Part of the staff was laid off for three months. The average cut in their bonuses and "floating wages" was 30 percent.[69] Inflation and rising tastes for consumption, however, meant that the factory's employees were "unwilling" to become unemployed. Of this factory's total estimated copper requirement for the second half of 1988, the state plan was scheduled to provide only 22 percent – and the planners could not "guarantee" even half this small portion. Shanghai factory managers often overestimated their needs as a bargaining ploy; and by mid-1988, they carried this ruse far. During the previous year, the price of copper had risen 86 percent. It was more profitable to hold copper in inventory than to process it.[70]

Profit for the Electric Cable Factory managers came from laying off workers, while staying in business to hoard copper without producing wire.

The chief cadre of this factory offered large bonuses for any of his employees who could line up purchases of more copper. The profits and taxes that the cable plant was able to remit, in 1986 and 1987, amounted to 200 million yuan; but the value of the factory's total product in the first half of 1988 was 178 million. The manager of the cable plant raised questions in public about whether it should not be possible to expand the powers of large and medium enterprises that lacked raw materials, so that at least some of them might become parts of a "special factory system" (*techang zhi*), authorized to import raw materials so they could "struggle to have rice to eat" (*zheng fan chi*).

In light industries' spending, more than four-fifths of the inflation at this time came from rising materials costs.[71] In thirty-one light industrial firms by the middle of 1988, production costs went up 14 percent over costs a year earlier. In some product lines, 1988 inflation was over 50 percent. Labor costs were relatively stable, although expenditures to subsidize workers' food rose. Managers openly admitted that public discussion of future "housing reforms" (involving higher rents) scared them. Whatever the merits of this idea, they had no spare money to pay for it.

The main flow of factors was out of Shanghai, because prices remained low there for items that could still be bought. The factory that made prize-winning "White Cat" washing powder, mostly sold in Shanghai, began to lose money in the mid-1980s. Raw materials costs were up, but the manager could not raise the product price. The right to approve any inflation, even of a detergent's price, was in Beijing not Shanghai. Fully ten months of intensive negotiations and frequent northward trips were needed, in order to get a small price rise of 0.40 yuan per box.[72] Buying agents from other areas quickly discovered they could send delegations to Shanghai to purchase the city's products at low cost. Low-price rules, enforced in Shanghai to prevent wage inflation for heavily taxed state firms there, were ignored elsewhere.

Sales were fueled by official attempts to keep Shanghai's consumer prices lower than those in other places. This trade had several aspects: It tended to boost the volume of goods that Shanghai could report sending inland. Between 1986 and 1987, the outflow of all products from Shanghai to other provinces increased 64 percent. Shipments to Guangdong (especially Shenzhen) and Fujian were great, because prices were high there. For example, Shanghai's Phoenix and Everlasting bicycles could be sold in Shenzhen for 350 yuan – double the Shanghai retail price. Garment prices were also several times higher in Guangdong.

Trade between Shanghai and other parts of the PRC flourished during reforms. The combination of relatively high Shanghai wages (at least among employees in state firms) and profits in shops selling goods imported from elsewhere meant that the portion sold in Shanghai but produced elsewhere rose sharply. Much of this increase was caused by state-fixed price differences in various parts of China.

A second aspect of the trade increase was that outflows of goods from Shanghai created shortages in the city's markets. Speculative profits from price differentials

110 Rural leaders beat urban planners

were enormous. If goods could be bought at official low prices in the city but then sold in eager free markets elsewhere, a trader could become rich without adding any economic value. To slow the loss of goods so that Shanghai's demand could be met, the municipality set up inspection stations at its borders, trying to prevent "exports."

Domestic bulk exports from Shanghai of grain, cigarettes, pork, and sugar were illegal unless planned. These items were all supposed to be kept less expensive in the city. On one road leading out of the city, a truck in 1988 would have to pass through seventeen inspection stations, but incentives to smuggle were great. For example, during April of that year, the price of rice was 0.15 yuan per Chinese pound (*jin*) in Shanghai; but in Jiangsu, it was twice as much. Admitting they could no longer effectively control prices, officials authorized some Shanghai price hikes in 1988. During the first three months of the year, prices of more than 300 products in the city were "adjusted," all upward, on average more than 20 percent. Some rose by half. Included were the prices of soap, salt, shoes, raincoats, thermoses, and many other staples and items for daily use.[73]

Basic consumer goods (especially foods, housing, and transport) were the main items still legally under state pricing. Capital and raw materials exchanges, where enterprises had to deal, became freer than markets where ordinary urban residents traded. State prices in 1978 had applied to 188 agricultural products – but by 1988, the number was reduced to just 3. Among consumer durables, 392 were subject to fixed prices in 1978 – but a decade later, only 46 were controlled. By 1988, among capital goods, 80 percent of their total value was priced by free markets.[74] The reason for continuing price controls on food, housing, and transport was political: The government wanted to avoid wage increases and urban unrest.

Shortages of non-staple consumer goods and inputs rose. A city leader averred that Shanghai people often "heard about raising production but did not see much buying." The mayor complained that "Shanghai people can't buy Shanghai products." A 1988 newspaper admitted that planned prices for Shanghai goods outside the city were at least 15 percent higher than in the city – and for illegal exports, the difference was greater. This was true of consumer products, especially "industrial enterprise commodities," whose exports from Shanghai rose 60 percent between 1986 and 1987 alone.[75] Rules mandating low prices in the city gave companies incentives to sell elsewhere.

Shanghai, which trades widely throughout the nation, has many east-west streets named after Chinese cities and north-south streets with names of provinces. A 1988 article, alluding to this pattern, which is not unique to Shanghai, said it was particularly appropriate there because the metropolis was still economically central to China as a whole.[76] Four-fifths of Shanghai's raw materials in the mid-1980s came from other provinces, and Shanghai was a "locomotive" and "processing factory" for the whole country.[77] The article claimed that for every ten yuan of production in Shanghai, the state in 1988 still received 8 yuan in profits and taxes. One-sixth of the total revenue of the Chinese government came from Shanghai. Local people could well argue that their city was loyally Chinese, not separate from the rest of the country.[78]

Non-Shanghai interests among Shanghai managers

When Shanghai firms did not receive inland materials for which they had contracted, this was not always a personal worry for managers. Many Shanghai businesspeople had kinship links to inland places that benefited from cooperative arrangements with companies in the metropolis. If the state bureaucracy cared for Shanghai firms only as revenue sources, managers might have little compunction about taking a similarly narrow view. By the middle and late 1980s, they could get permission from procurement officials in municipal bureaus to sign almost any deal with inland places that promised markets or materials – whether or not that locality would actually deliver. When these bargains in practice only worked to the advantage of other Jiangnan places where the managers had family ties, these cadres might willingly bear the problems for their plants back in the city. Under planning norms, they were not supposed to be ultimately responsible for lining up their factory inputs anyway.

This situation did not, when it arose, solve Shanghai's problems. Also, some executives in the city were not closely associated with other places in Jiangnan (or with other places that might help them, or that they could help). No effective legal means compelled authorities outside Shanghai to send "compensating" materials on time. None compelled managers to insist on deliveries. Contracts specified delivery dates, but there was no real sanction against defaulters who failed to meet these schedules. In the suburbs, five Shanghai counties had signed compensation trade contracts outside the municipality for 400,000 tons of cement by June 1986, but only 36,000 tons actually came – less than one-tenth of the total due. Three counties had signed "compensation trade" agreements for steel, but they received only 14 percent of the metal for which they paid.[79] Inland suppliers usually claimed this was merely delay, not default; but actually they elsewhere found buyers able to pay higher prices. They could put off fulfillment of contracts indefinitely, and this was hard to distinguish from not fulfilling them at all. If top Shanghai politicians had career interests in Beijing, as evidence about their trajectories suggests they did, then local Shanghai factory managers who served places elsewhere in Jiangnan might similarly let their personal interests affect their actions.

Beyond shortages: the mid-1980s watershed for socialism and plans

By the second quarter of 1984, deliveries to Shanghai of inland iron, lumber, fuel, ferrous metals, coal, water, and chemicals suffered sharp drops – by at least 30 percent below plan for each of these major materials, and for some of them by 50 percent below plan. Industrial energy shortages were severe and halted some factories' production in a startling, unintended way. Shanghai paid 545 million yuan for industrial fuels in 1984. But by 1985, the city's energy costs rose "wildly" to about one billion yuan. At least 30 percent less was supplied, despite this near-doubling of payments for energy in a single year. Especially in fields where finished product prices were unelastic, the losses from higher outlays for major inputs in 1985, compared with the previous year, were enormous. They were estimated at 730 million yuan of lost profits in the steel industry alone.[80]

Shanghai managers less often got extensive free credit, and this was at least an excuse for any consequent issue. Urban factory executives could only sometimes solve the mid-1980s input shortages by their previous usual method, which was to arrange loans and offer higher payment for materials. Thus they tended (politely, so as not to discomfit their suppliers with accusations) to describe much of the problem in terms of a restricted money supply. For "lack of funds" to buy inputs, the Shanghai Dyeing Factory unexpectedly had to stop producing during twenty-five days in 1986. Textile factories in all of Shanghai together suffered losses that were apparently too severe to publish. The government could arrange some new money ('printing it') on an inflationary basis, as was necessary so that inputs could be bought.

Bureaucratic companies had become unused to completing jobs quickly. Hoarding of materials and late deliveries had been established as lubricant habits in the economy for decades – so managers' reactions to sustained large shortages were delayed. Cadres during reforms suffered few sanctions for being slow. But later, in the 1990s, when more materials were delivered to construction companies, for example, Shanghai businesspeople recovered their flair for speed, and the result was legendary. Buildings sprang up like mushrooms. Wags said Shanghai's municipal bird was the crane. Construction activity in the mid-1980s and 1990s disrupted firms adjacent to building sites. But Shanghai demand for more space was urgent, and units registered at relatively low administrative levels could supply it by using workers with temporary or no licenses to be in the city. Because of construction, and because of unreliable coal supplies, whole districts of Shanghai periodically suffered "stopped electricity, stopped water, and stopped gas." In the first quarter of 1986 alone, losses for this reason in the metropolis were estimated at 71,560,000 yuan.[81] The economy nonetheless boomed.

Real wages declined on average, despite Party leaders' hopes to keep compensation for workers stable. In state-run units, incentives for labor productivity dropped along with pay, which was not quickly price adjusted. Cadres in old state businesses lacked new money to give their employees, especially in contrast to the paymasters of collectives. Slogans, medals, and administrative orders no longer served passably to replace hard cash. Year-end bonuses (*nianzhong jiang*) and material incentives of 1985 were less in Shanghai than in other cities – and labor productivity statistics at the beginning of 1986 showed a decrease.[82] These were probably based on underreports.

State managers' economic environment left them few ways to do their jobs well. Many simply resigned, taking more technical or limited-liability posts that offered more chance of success – sometimes in smaller or private firms at lower-tax Jiangnan places whence their families had hailed. Some of these "guerrilla warriors" could switch posts nimbly. They deemed it foolhardy to take blame for enterprise failures they knew they had no means of correcting. Managers of state companies in urban Shanghai, as distinct from more specialized experts, could not in this era easily recruit successors. Propaganda about the need to increase the authority of managers, even exhortations about the need to decrease the power of Party generalists, could not compensate for a lack of money, energy, and raw materials. Reforms by the mid-1980s, when both fixed and free prices were used on various markets, could not reverse the decline of Shanghai's entrepreneurial culture that Maoists had begun in the mid-1950s. Reforms ironically worsened the slippage of authority among urban managers of state firms.

Officials blamed each other for structural faults caused by the high tax regime and counter-effective national plans. Scapegoats were needed for production losses. Discipline inspectors and tax collectors tended to chastise the managers of state firms. If a factory head had successfully reformed a plant so that its production rose, its input shortages became more severe than would have occurred under lackadaisical management that needed fewer materials. A diligent director could thus become a target of criticism. As a commentator pointed out, infighting severely harmed the "activism" of factory managers.

From the viewpoint of most local actors, the practical content of socialism was oversight by a supervising corporation. Especially as reforms weakened the role of planning, these increasingly resembled holding companies. Urban ministries were colloquially given the derogatory name "mothers-in-law" (*popo*, traditional tyrants of new wives in Chinese families). Factory managers had the uneasy status of new brides, married into the socialist clan but with low status. For most firms, the "mother-in-law" was a municipal bureau, formally in charge of many dispersed factories or stores. This overbearing relative was usually in a head office geographically separate from the component firms. Managers were notoriously hemmed in by these "supervising agencies" (*zhuguan* was the official non-pejorative term for *popo*).

This structure, which had been imposed after the state controlled more markets in the 1950s, provided a kind of relief to Shanghai managers decades later, when planning largely collapsed because new rural entrepreneurs outbid them for materials. The task of finding inputs and markets was supposed in theory to be the job of the supervising corporations. Shanghai's cadres in local stores or factories could forswear responsibility for these tasks. Their "popo" bosses were often in sufficiently secure political posts to withstand criticism. This structure paid taxes, employed some lucky workers, and preserved bureaucratic jobs with good salaries and perks. It did little to advance Shanghai's economy.

Because Shanghai was an "important economic center," notably for revenue, central leaders' ideas about it were mostly conservative. Although suggestions had often been made to cut costs by reducing the number of supervising "administrative companies," there had been practically no action on this.[83] A reformist article, listing relevant problems, raised suggestions to solve them. First, it recommended a

114 Rural leaders beat urban planners

"management responsibility system," under which factory CCP committees would defer to managers on most decisions. Second, it advocated that firms should be "accountable," assuming "economic responsibility" for profits and losses on which "there is no roof above and no floor below."[84] Third, it recommended policies to avoid restricting enterprises that could be profitable but lost money only because of state pricing. "One-knife-cuts-all" uniform guidelines in state banks could be replaced by different policies for loans to factories that faced different external prices, despite the special pleadings for money that would follow such flexibility. Fourth, the article called for serious "rearrangement" of governmental supervising organs, loosening controls over subordinate firms, not just reshuffling personnel into offices with new names but old styles, just "changing the soup but not the medicine."[85] Fifth, hiring and personnel could be put under factory managers, even though that change would reduce the powers of Party committees.

A 1985 draft of a new Enterprise Law, which got as far as the NPC Standing Committee, mentioned no role at all for Party committees within firms. Legislators argued it was "not advisable" for government laws to define the role of the CCP, and this draft law did not confirm local trade unions' (or Party) leadership of workers' congresses. But it was not passed.[86] Conservative laws were later adopted in the 1990s, but this draft shows reformers wanted to restructure labor relations and management more than CCP conservatives would allow.

Many related policies were likewise mooted but not adopted: Sales of more shares in companies might have been allowed. Workers might have moved between jobs more easily. Salaries and retirements might involve more incentives. The habit of discussing many measures – but then shelving them for possible later action only – became common. An article listing all these proposals averred that Jiangsu and Zhejiang had adopted more reform policies than Shanghai. Their prosperity had accordingly progressed faster. Cures for the "Shanghai sickness" – which was a governance sickness – could involve expanding the responsibility of factory managers, increasing firms' freedom to hire contract labor, and lowering the power over factories of Party generalists and non-productive supervisory bureaus.[87] Yet such policies threatened to reduce the power of established cadres. Some were later adopted, but this happened slowly because of political resistance from CCP lions.

Hepatitis as a spur to reform in 1988

Random external shocks often help stimulate institutional change. A major outbreak of hepatitis afflicted Shanghai at the beginning of 1988. Hepatitis A is a viral liver disease caused by eating infected food or drinking septic water, and it can spread among ill people who contact each other. The reformers in this case were a batch of contaminated clams. They were effective because the malady spread very quickly, with big effects on industry and revenues. Shanghai's total production was 17 percent less in February than in January 1988.[88]

It had been clear to central politicians for some time that the city's function as their most reliable tax base had suffered "slippage" (*huapo*). The hepatitis epidemic solved no problems; but by exacerbating them, it led to lower tax remittances and more public discussion of Shanghai's future. At about the time of this event, the State Council (China's cabinet) mooted a new approach to raw materials shortages. Rather than trying to restore whole plans, it set priorities. In effect, the plan was to be followed for those priorities, many of which involved activities that remitted profits to Beijing. For other activities, the plan could in practice miss fulfillment.

First, "key factories" were identified, as were the main materials they lacked – and the State Council proclaimed the official plan should be enforced as regards these particular factories and supplies. Second, special priority was to be given to all electrical products. Third, the Council issued a norm that materials departments ought to stress coordinating rationed supplies for the production of specialized products. Fourth, the Council advocated free trade for other products. The most basic inputs (27 of them) fell under "mandatory planned management (*zhiling xing jihua guanli*)."[89] Another much larger set (496 products) were under "indicative planning (*zhidao xing jihua*)," which actually did not involve much planning at all. The "indications" merely legitimated free trade, dubiously enforceable purchase contracts, or markets that supposedly could be entered by designated traders only.

The state cabinet's policy was clear in that it distinguished different classes of commodities which were, or were not, subject to free trade. But it was difficult to enforce, partly because products on the two different lists were often used together as factors of production. Also, many of the twenty-seven materials that were supposed to be fully planned were inputs for making downstream products that were less controlled. When inland authorities set up factories to produce goods that had off-plan prices using planned materials with prices that were decreed low, authorities could not ensure supplies of those inputs. Factors tended to be processed in the districts that extracted them. By creating varied rules for different groups of products, the State Council in practice gave traders greater leeway to do as they wished.

Bureaucrats in the corporations that "supervised" factories often pressed plant managers to take charge of chancy purchasing and selling. Central officials managed to shift some risk to city ones, but local urban factory managers had good reasons not to take such responsibility until they were given the financial freedom to pay market prices. By 1988, thirty to forty percent of all Shanghai's industrial materials in many fields were still planned to come through government, often through municipal bureaus (*ju*) or large state holding companies (*gongsi*). These "higher level" (*shangji*) offices often had to scramble on free markets for inputs that other jurisdictions failed to deliver.[90] When remittances of funds to Beijing decreased, as happened temporarily because of hepatitis in 1988, managers could buy more factors.

At the high tide of planning in Shanghai's urban economy, at least 70 percent by value of all raw materials for the city's industries had been allocated through the state. Already by 1988, the portions had been reversed from their levels a decade earlier: Shanghai local agents then had to find 70 percent of all inputs themselves. This problem affected not only main materials such as steel and lumber, but also miscellaneous items like dried potatoes, industrial salt, and leather.[91]

In the second half of 1988, partly because of shortages and hepatitis problems during the first half, planners mustered more raw materials for Shanghai. The city's economy responded smartly, with a better growth rate than in most Chinese provinces. Partly for this reason, and because many revenues had been "hidden" in Shanghai budgets below the province level, the city fathers slightly overfulfilled their revenue quota in 1988, to make up for the bad first half.[92]

Factory closures, industry subsidies, and bankruptcies

The hepatitis epidemic temporarily brought a standstill at some factories, and it raised the politically sensitive question of whether long-term difficulties should bring plant closures. But almost no state factories were shut down. Managers' autonomy and factory independence are not necessarily salutary, unless bad management carries a threat of bankruptcy. If cadres' failure merely leads to state bailouts and subsidies – and increased taxes to pay for them – that is not evidence of reform. Much insolvency in particular firms was not caused by faulty managers, but by changes in prices of inputs or products. By the late 1980s, the state tried to accomplish on reform markets what it had failed to do by planning. Larger subsidies went to support factor prices for whole nationalized industries-in-trouble than to bail out individual plants. State enterprises lost about 20 b. yuan before the 1990 changes, but the government's price-support subsidies were perhaps five times that amount.[93] This policy fostered inflation, and it would have worked much better if the state had been able to afford it.

Bankruptcy laws in China began largely as an ideological critique by reformers against inefficient management in state enterprises. Almost everyone agreed there was much maladministration in these firms. But the stress on bankruptcy laws for individual companies (even though these laws were opposed by political conservatives) missed a larger point: The state no longer had its previous capacity to maintain both its political and fiscal bases in big cities. The centralist system as a whole teetered on bankruptcy by 1989. Its supplies and markets were increasingly dominated by many smaller political networks. State leaders lacked the resources to do things they deemed essential.

An Enterprise Bankruptcy Law had been adopted in 1986 "for trial use" only. It had in 1987 still "not been extensively implemented." It was not supposed to be "enforced" until November 1988.[94] When enterprise deficits arose, firms took "full responsibility for their profits but cannot assume full responsibility for their losses. Rather than going bankrupt, they demand loans from banks through the government. . . . Even when these enterprises are fined and ordered to repay the bank loans they have borrowed at a higher interest rate, they will still ask for more bank loans, because they know that they will not suffer losses themselves."[95] Local laws were adopted with different definitions of bankruptcy and with varying provisions about the types of firms to which it might apply. Bankruptcy laws were not written to constrain state firms effectively.

Private and collective companies likewise often fell on hard times because of rampant inflation. Such firms were not line items on any official budget, and high officials had not given wage assurances to their workers; so they could go bankrupt. They were not part of the regime's system; no government credit was available to save them. Visiting economists were not told that bankruptcy laws were implemented in ways that protected state firms particularly.

Outside the planned system, some companies did go bankrupt. The Shanghai Collective Enterprises Administration held an auction in 1988 to sell collapsed firms to the highest bidder. "Individuals" (private companies) were not allowed to bid; only collectives, state enterprises, and joint ventures could do so. The director of the Administration promised that successful bidders could make all decisions on both production and management in their newly acquired companies.[96] Newspapers duly heralded that Shanghai had procedures for bankruptcy. They did not herald that debt-heavy state corporations were effectively exempt.

Amalgamation of sick firms with healthy ones was permitted in low-tax jurisdictions – but not in Shanghai, lest remittances to Beijing be reduced under autonomous managers. Profitable state enterprises in 1988 freely bought money-losing ones in some Chinese cities, including Beijing and Shenyang, but not Shanghai.[97] Buy-out mergers encouraged investment in insolvent subsidiaries, to put them back in the black. But this practice reduced total profits – and fiscal revenues – at least over the short or medium term. The greatest virtue of spreading losses among firms was local-political: Managers and workers could keep their jobs. Structural changes aiming at better management occurred elsewhere, but not in the metropolis, whose long-term prosperity Beijing politicians considered less important than its current remittances.

State enterprises resisted many reforms. Their managers' incentives were not much changed by shifts in the main target quotas (taxes, profits, or output) they were supposed to deliver. Shortages of materials and capital, scarce means of solving these, "soft budget constraints," a lack of quality and design standardization, and widespread reliance on collective rather than individual responsibility for performance – all these factors remained substantially unchanged in large state plants through the 1980s.[98] The lack of serious management reform, despite high politicians' speeches calling for it, was especially striking in some cities (such as Wuhan and the region around it). Where change was greatest, in smaller southern cities, the dependence of managers' careers on their economic performances still remained weak in the state sector. Shanghai and its delta was a middling case, with more serious management reform than in the area around Wuhan but less than in the delta around Guangzhou. Promotions of better-educated company heads began to alter this pattern, but structural changes in the incentives they faced came slowly. Often the economically rational solution (bankruptcy) seemed politically dangerous.

Literal power, not just the political kind, began to falter; by the late 1980s, fast growth and insufficient investment strained Shanghai's electricity supplies. The voltage was often not up to par, and a shortage of lines caused overloading.[99] Low

118 Rural leaders beat urban planners

voltage affected 352 factories for over a quarter of the days in the first six months of 1988, and overloading boded fire hazards. By the end of the year, the city's electricity supply was publicly reported to be at 94 percent of the planned amount.[100] Shanghai sent coal buying teams to Shanxi, Inner Mongolia, Henan, and other mining provinces. Energy-consuming factories had to lessen their work hours. The city "moved step by step to a five-day week" – even though plans did not yet call for that modernization.

Coal, the main energy source, is a bulk resource that the government could control somewhat. The state had a monopoly of the rail system, and it had a near-monopoly of excavating major seams, although many smaller coal mines also existed. Rural industries outside the state system were hard-hit by coal shortages, although many could trade or bribe their way to finding supplies. Countryside firms often had money for purchases, and they usually had strong local political support to get any nearby supplies that might be available.

Energy shortages idled "about 15 percent" of Shanghai's production in the early part of 1989, when "many factories [were] running only four or five days a week because of the power shortage."[101] A local economist pointed out that services and light industries consumed less energy than heavy industries. Energy-expensive plants had been imposed on Shanghai at Baoshan and Wujing, whose large steel and chemical complexes were under direct central management and taxation. The coal shortage was obvious to residents, since it affected people both at work and at home. Other materials shortfalls in the late 1980s had more delayed consequences.

Factories using chemicals in Shanghai suffered such severe shortages of inputs by the end of the decade, their managers and workers cooperated in unprecedented ways to keep the plants in operation. Wujing Chemical Factory, Chenyuan Chemical Factory, Pudong Chemical Factory, and other large plants were by some reports in danger of closing. Because these factories provided downstream supplies to textile, drug, and other light industrial companies, the danger to Shanghai's economy was great. For example, chemical factories needing industrial salt to make alkalis in January 1989 had been promised 38,000 metric tons for that month. Apparently they had expected to purchase more on the open market, up to their total requirement then of about 50,000 tons. But a newspaper reported on its front page that "not a single ton has reached Shanghai."[102] The central government said factories could use reserve warehoused salt – but little was available.

Shanghai's Chemical Industries Bureau sent buyers urgently "like sparks" to salt-producing areas of Tianjin, Shandong, and Jiangsu. They met problems at each of these places. In Shandong, a cold spell was said to have frozen canals, so that barge transport of salt had stopped. In northern Jiangsu, the port facilities were claimed to be inadequate. In Tianjin, a structural reform of the relevant company had divided it into two parts; so salt would no longer be provided from there as in the past. The most important problem, however, was that inland places had established their own chemical factories that used all their salt.

The Shanghai Solvents Factory had only three days' supply of industrial alcohol and other materials that it claimed as needed. Because of a nationwide shortage of kerosene, which is used to make urea, the Wujing Chemical Factory (apparently Shanghai's largest producer of fertilizer) was forced wholly to suspend its production in early 1989. Shanghai factories had no funds to move into new products. They simply closed old lines. The upshot was that the city government was "urgently asking for help" from central departments – whose budgets were still addicted to their accustomed fixes of Shanghai profits and taxes, but whose resources to keep Shanghai factories in the black had vanished.

Nonstate plants' closure was the central hardliners' policy solution. A late-1989 campaign against nonstate industries was advertised as an effort against inflation – and indeed, rural factories' ability to pay higher prices for inputs created issues for state industries. But until the 1990s, the regime failed to redirect material flows back into the government sector. By October 1989, Shanghai's industrial production was down 6 percent below the same month in the previous year. Light industries' output was down 8 percent (and heavy industry by 4 percent, a loss only half as much for a sector facing less nonstate competition). Declines were blamed on a "slack market."[103] But the market for nonstate industries' products was not slack. As a cadre of the Shanghai First Commerce Bureau said, "We must find a way out." The city government vowed "immediate measures to salvage some of the major enterprises in trouble." This proposal was expensive, and the underlying problems were long-term rather than temporary.

Rural companies, which were supposed to trade with the Shanghai state sector only under plans, could avoid doing so by the end of the 1980s. They made more money by trading with each other. In its fight against them, the conservative government had to blink first. Until the 1990s, it lacked power to enforce its policy of partial economic recentralization, and the costs of that policy were high. Rural entrepreneurs, using their own resources and power networks, for some time (and in some fields permanently) outlasted the state.

The political lions' roar nonetheless reached parts of the countryside. When police investigated restaurants in a Jiangsu county, they found that over three-quarters of small state-owned eateries exceeded their planned profits. For this success, they were fined.[104] They had reportedly paid their taxes, but local conservative leaders did not like the disruption that growth brought. Surplus production and remittances could elicit praise from reformers, but the surplus profit weakened plans.

The *Economic Daily* at the end of October 1988 reported that China had "thirty million workers with nothing to do. . . . More than 400,000 enterprises across the country are operating at a loss, and three-quarters of them should be closed." This PRC newspaper estimated that the government would have to spend half its industrial profits, or about 40 b. yuan, "to subsidize ailing state-owned enterprises this year."[105] It was clear this situation could not last long; but the nation's political cycle by late 1989 headed into a deeply conservative mood, and most state factories continued to limp along.

Non-intellectual rural entrepreneurs made no appearance at Tiananmen. But they were the regime's most relentless and dangerous opponents. By 1990, Shanghai Municipality was spending over half of its municipal budget on price subsidies.[106]

120 Rural leaders beat urban planners

The regime had to pay a larger portion of its resources to support its political-economic system, which separated urban workers from potentially or actually dissident intellectuals. The Ministry of Materials and Equipment by the end of 1990 "decided" to change from being "the official distributor of supplies" into being merely a "market broker."[107] Such a makeover had in fact already occurred, without benefit of state blessing. The ministry in effect announced that it would do only what it still had the capacity to do. Reality was declared official.

Further changes brought disruptions of old industries. Chinese cotton production dropped from 6.5 million tons in 1991 to just 4 million in 1993. This was awful news for the Shanghai industry employing more workers than any other. The cotton price had been too low, and people in cotton-producing areas had never been controlled as tightly as those in areas growing grain; they had more readily used their land and labor for industry. So the price of cotton more than doubled in the mid-1990s, and old cloth factories closed. One cadre claimed by 1994 that "[a]bout 90 percent of the textile factories in Shanghai have recently shut down." Many textile workers – overwhelmingly women – lost their jobs or were "sent down from posts" (*xiagang*), receiving only a fraction of their former salaries as a kind of delayed severance pay.[108]

Half of China's state enterprises by the mid-1990s were running deficits, and another third would have been in the red except for hidden subsidies.[109] Urban inflation remained rampant, "as high as 40 percent" in unofficial reports. Industrial strikes rose, because state firms had no money to pay millions of their workers. Shanghai was the last test of Chen Yun's "birdcage" hopes for market socialism. Chen, who for decades had been a major CCP economic guru, espoused a policy of using the market and command economies together.[110] Since all developed industrial nations have both strong markets and much regulation, his idea had theoretical appeal to all but the truest believers in either capitalism or socialism. Chen thought market socialism would work in China if limits on free trade allowed state cadres to set the prices of major commodities. So he likened the free market to a bird, which could be kept in a cage large enough that it could live, but small enough that it would not fly out of control.

Shanghai had been Chen's best cage. The 'planned market' economy worked passably in big cities – but only so long as the state was strong enough to keep free traders from amassing major wealth. The question then became political, not economic: Could the state, as the revolution wound down, continue to direct behavior among local leaders? During the 1980s, that question was answered in the negative. By 1990, and up to the present, the state reacted with efforts to centralize an economy that reforms had localized.

Notes

1 Roderick MacFarquhar, *The Politics of China, 1949–1989* (Cambridge: Cambridge University Press, 1993), 293–94.
2 *Xin Zhongguo gongye jingji shi*; quotations and figures are from 337–338. In late 1970, the total number of state workers was 53.18 million.
3 Ibid.

4 Other Asian governments sometimes introduced new technologies that made rice an unprofitable crop for tillers. Ferdinand Marcos' "Masagana-99" reforms forced farmers to plant short-stalk high-yield rice that grew well in some years but created total crop failures after major typhoons or droughts (netting overall losses for tillers). Lynn White, *Philippine Politics: Possibilities and Problems in a Localist Democracy* (Abingdon: Routledge, 2015), 100–17, cites work by Brian Fegan, David Wurfel, Umehara Hiromitsu, James Boyce, Ernest Feder, and Frank Lynch. Marcos made rice an unprofitable crop.

5 Most comprehensive is Ezra Vogel, *Canton under Communism: Programs and Politics in a Provincial Capital, 1949–1968* (Cambridge: Harvard University Press, 1969).

6 *Zhongguo gongye de fazhan, 1949–1984* (China's Industrial Development, 1949–1984), Guojia Tongji Ju, Gongye Jiaotong Wuzi Tongji Si, ed. (Beijing: Zhongguo Tongji Chuban She, 1985), 53; the only other such unit may be Tianjin.

7 "*Shui wang dichu liu, huo wang kaochu zou,*" *JFRB*, May 15, 1988.

8 Shanghai's 1966–1975 average annual growth of income, at 10.2 percent, was faster than its 1976–1985 growth at 8.4 percent. Shanghai's income growth was reported for 1976–1980 and again for 1981–1985 at 8.4 percent in both periods. *SHTJNJ88*, 52.

9 *Shanghai jingji, neibu ben: 1949–1982*, 991.

10 G. William Skinner and Edwin Winckler, "Compliance Succession in Rural Communist China: A Cyclical Theory," in *Complex Organizations*, Amitai Etzioni, ed. (New York: Holt, 1969), 411ff.

11 This interpretation (minus the stress on late-1970s hesitancy) follows Richard Baum, *Burying Mao: Chinese Politics in the Age of Deng Xiaoping* (Princeton: Princeton University Press, 1996), extended by his student Joshua Eisenman, *Red China's Green*.

12 *WHB*, December 20, 1979.

13 *WHB*, June 11, 1980.

14 *JFRB*, September 6, 1980.

15 *Dangdai Zhongguo de jingji tizhi gaige* (Reform of the Economic System in Modern China), Zhou Taihe, ed. (Beijing: Zhongguo Shehui Kexue Chuban She, 1984), 559.

16 *Jingji shichang yanjiu* (Economic Market Research), January 1983, 1.

17 *Shanghai jingji nianjian, 1988* (Shanghai Economic Yearbook, 1988), Xiao Jun, ed., (Shanghai: Shanghai Renmin Chuban She, 1988), 90.

18 *FBIS*, November 26, 1986, 3, radio of November 20.

19 *Shanghai jingji* (Shanhgai Economy), [hereafter *SHJJ*], January 1985.

20 The time period was not specified; it was probably 1984–1987. *JFRB*, May 15, 1988.

21 *RMRB*, August 16, 1988, also reported losses in the silk industry and inferior-quality cocoon deliveries.

22 *CD*, November 2, 1988.

23 *RMRB*, August 16, 1988.

24 *FBIS*, December 7, 1987, 39, radio of December 4.

25 Although the article claimed this was low tide in a cycle and that Shanghai had recently been more "stable" (*pingwen*) than other places, those others were progressing much faster. *SHJJYJ*, January 1987, 60.

26 Ibid.

27 This meaning of "*hong deng*" contrasted with an enthusiasm the phrase was once supposed to elicit, e.g., in Jiang Qing's model opera "The Red Lantern" (*Hong deng ji*). *SHJJYJ*, January 1987, 60.

28 *SHJJ*, January 1985, 3.

29 See the same source as for the table. Valuation of fixed capital presents problems that have kept some of my calculations out of the book. But the change reported here is so sharp that it is significant if understood as a trend.

30 Comparable figures in a group of cities were: Shanghai, 76 yuan; Chongqing, 68; Xi'an, 67; Shenyang, 66; Haerbin, 63; Tianjin, 62; Beijing, 59; Nanjing, 56; Guangzhou, 53; Dalian, 53; Qingdao, 49; and Wuxi, 32. Figures were not available for smaller or rural places (where they would have been lower) or Wuxi or Suzhou, even though those Sunan cities were generally included in the survey. *SHGYJJB*, August 19, 1988.

122 Rural leaders beat urban planners

31 The next chapter tries to calculate the monetary value of coercive mandates for low input and high output prices in Shanghai.

32 Fei Xiaotong and Luo Yanxian, *Xiangzhen jingji*, 51–55.

33 Although *SHJJ*, January 1987, 24, is not explicit on how this 590 m. yuan was calculated, it may have been the additional money spent in 1986 because of materials cost inflation.

34 *SHTJNJ93*, 55, where total local expenditures of the state in 1986 are recorded at almost exactly ten times this 590 million.

35 These figures were supplied by Kate Xiao Zhou, on the basis of work by Hu Heli, "The Estimation of Rent-Seeking in China, 1988," *Journal of Comparative Economic and Social Systems* 5 (1989), 10–15.

36 The particular Zhejiang local effort failed. These examples are in Huang Weixin, *Economic Integration as a Development Device: The Case of the EC and China* (Saarbrücken: Nijmegen Studies in Development, Breitenbach Verlag, 1992), 53–54. Changzhou could export its fine tractors abroad; I saw many of them in Nepal.

37 Derek Headey, Ravi Kanbur, and Xiaobo Zhang, "China's Growth Strategies," 9, www. arts.cornell.edu/poverty/kanbur/China'sGrowthStrategies.pdf.

38 Julian Gerwitz, *Unlikely Partners: Chinese Reformers, Western Economists, and the Making of Global China* (Cambridge: Harvard University Press, 2017).

39 Cao Linzhang, Gu Guangqing and Li Jianhua, *Shanghai shengchan ziliao suoyu zhi jiegou yanjiu* (Studies of Shanghai Production and Ownership Structure) (Shanghai: Shanghai Shehui Kexue Yuan Chuban She, 1987), 146.

40 Interview with a Shanghai economist.

41 There were only 84 *lianban qiye*, but 861 *xiezuo jiagong dian: Hengxiang jingji lianhe de xin fazhan* (The New Development of Horizontal Economic Links), Shanghai Economics Association, ed., (Shanghai: Shanghai Shehui Kexue Yuan Chuban She, 1987), 132.

42 *Shanghai jingji nianjian, 1988* [hereafter *SHJJNJ88*], 140–41.

43 These were (*shengchan wuzi maoyi zhongxin*); *Liaowang* 47 (1988), 12.

44 *FBIS*, November 14, 1986, 1, radio of November 11.

45 *SHJJNJ88*, 139.

46 *Shanghai qiye* (Shanghai Enterprise), February 1985, 43.

47 Linda Li, "Central-Provincial Relations in the People's Republic of China, Nature and Configurations" (SOAS Ph.D. dissertation, 1994), ch. 7, 8, quotes Tu Jimo in *Shanghai jihua jingji tansuo* (Discussions on Shanghai's Planned Economy) 1 (1990), 29.

48 *Liaowang* 47 (1988), 12.

49 This was the *Shanghai yebao*; interview by the author at the *Liberation Daily* office one week after the suspension occurred. It was then unclear when or whether this publication could resume, and apparently it did not.

50 *JFRB*, May 25, 1988.

51 This and related data come from the author's 1988 interviews.

52 For information on similar cases, see Lynn White, *Shanghai Shanghaied? Uneven Taxes in Reform China* (Hong Kong: Centre of Asian Studies, University of Hong Kong, 1989).

53 The amount was 88,000 tons in the first quarter of 1988 alone.

54 *Shanghai Focus* [weekly local supplement to *China Daily*; hereafter *SF*], March 19, 1990.

55 *Xinmin wanbao* (Xinmin Evening News) [hereafter *XMWB*], April 2, 1989. *XMWB*, an evening "social" paper bought by its readers rather than offices, was the best source of local-political information in Shanghai. For some reform years, it was the highest-circulation newspaper in China.

56 Author's interview with *Wenhui bao* Chief Editor Ma Da.

57 *Liaowang*, no. 47 (1988), 12.

58 *JFRB*, April 13, 1988.

59 The full matrix would be printed here, and would be instructive for readers in capitalist countries who are not used to contemplating the implications of trying to run a diversified economy without the aid of money – but I respect the patience of the typesetter. Did you really want to know that in 1987 (still neglecting season, location, quality, or

more subtle considerations such as the greed or personal connections of traders) 100 kilograms of Chinese tung oil should trade for 595.74 bars of soap or 1096.08 packs of matches? For this and much more, see a table in *Zhongguo wujia tongji nianjian, 1988* (Statistical Yearbook of Chinese Prices, 1988), Urban Society and Economy Survey Group, ed., (Beijing: Zhongguo Tongji Chuban She, 1988), 114–5.

60 Money in China was first evidenced in the Shang, conventionally 1760 to 1050 BCE.

61 These estimates are based on prices of the base year. See *Zhongguo wujia*, 108–112.

62 This index does not include grain and other foods, which, however, were also subsidized to mesh with low wage costs in Shanghai's state-owned enterprises. The figures are in ibid.

63 *JFRB*, May 30, 1988.

64 The amount spent was the equivalent of US$6 million. *SHJJ*, January 1987, 24, was written by a staff member of the Hongkou Branch of the Industrial and Commercial Bank of China.

65 *SHJJNJ88*, 121.

66 *CD*, February 29, 1988.

67 These development companies, designed for trading rather than extraction, were *kaifa gongsi*; brokers were *jingji ren*; and intermediaries, *zhongjie*. The trading centers were called *wuzi maoyi zhongxin*. *SHJJ*, February, 1988, 21.

68 The exchange fairs were *jiaoyi hui*, and the service companies were *shengchan ziliao fuwu gongsi*. *SHJJNJ88*, 33.

69 Floating wages were called *fudong gongzi*, though most Chinese socialists advocate fixed basic wages for unionized employees. *SHGYJJB*, July 28, 1988.

70 Calculated from *SHGYJJB*, July 28, 1988, which gives raw figures.

71 *SHGYJJB*, July 25, 1988.

72 *JFRB*, April 18, 1988.

73 A comparison was made with the "Oil Crisis," in *JFRB*, April 18, 1988.

74 *Shanghai jingji daobao* (Shanghai Economic Report) [hereafter *SHJJDB*], August 22, 1988.

75 These commodities were called *gongye qiye shangpin*. *Jingji ribao* (Economic Daily) [hereafter *JJRB*], January 18, 1988.

76 This pattern largely predated 1949; but after Liberation, as streets that had foreign names were given Chinese ones, the habit continued. Bubbling Well Road became Nanjing Road W.; Avenue Joffre, Huaihai Road C.; Avenue Edward VII, Yan'an Road S.; Route des Soeurs, Ruijin Road 1; Rue du Consulat, Jinling Road E.; Route Cardinal Mercier, Maoming Road S.; Avenue Pétain, Hengshan Road; and Lincoln Avenue, Tianshan Road. Shanghai, the "other China," is linked more than nominally to the rest of the country.

77 *Zhongguo qingnian bao* (China Youth News) [hereafter *ZGQNB*], September 20, 1988.

78 Compare Marie-Claire Bergère, "'The Other China': Shanghai from 1919 to 1949," in *Shanghai: Revolution and Development in an Asian Metropolis*, Christopher Howe, ed. (Cambridge: Cambridge University Press, 1981), 1–34.

79 It is unclear whether the contracts provided for damages in case of late delivery or default. The five counties needing cement were Baoshan, Fengxian, Jinshan, Qingpu, and Songjiang; and the three needing steel were Baoshan, Fengxian, and Songjiang. *Hengxiang jingji*, 207–08.

80 *Shanghai jingji yanjiu* (Shanghai Economic Research) [hereafter *SHJJYJ*], January 1987, 60; this apparently included large state steel plants, notably at Baoshan.

81 *Ting dian, ting shui, ting qi*. Ibid. for the data here and in the earlier paragraph. My wife and I, staying at the hostel of the Shanghai Social Sciences Academy in 1988, experienced electricity stoppages.

82 Ibid. The source also claimed high bases of productivity in the early 1980s.

83 These *popo* companies were also called *xingzheng xing gongsi*. The list of proposals is in *SHJJYJ*, January 1987, 60.

84 *Shang bu feng ding, xia bu bao di*. Ibid.

124 Rural leaders beat urban planners

85 *Huan tang, bu huan yao.* Ibid.
86 Murray Scot Tanner, *The Politics of Lawmaking in Post-Mao China: Institutions, Processes, and Democratic Prospects* (Oxford: Clarendon Press, 1999) (seen in MS).
87 Ibid.
88 *FBIS*, March 7, 1988, 76, radio of March 4.
89 The materials departments were called *wuzhi bu*, and the most important of these was the municipal one, the Wuzhi Ju. *SHGYJJB*, July 21, 1988.
90 Interview with an economist at the Shanghai Academy of Social Sciences.
91 These percentages are of value. Various sources estimate the portion the state delivered in 1988 differently, but always between one-fifth and one-third. See *JFRB*, May 15, 1988; *ZGQNB*, September 20, 1988; and *Liaowang*, no. 47 (1988), 12.
92 This information comes from interviews with a highly knowledgeable source in Hong Kong. A few relevant statistical data are available on a limited-circulation basis, and I was (unusually) asked not to quote them; but *SHTJNJ93*, 55, shows a 1988 increase in Shanghai fiscal revenues, after decreases during the previous two years.
93 See *FEER*, March 21, 1991.
94 The first city allowing a bankruptcy was Shenzhen. See Edward Epstein, "China's Legal Reforms," 9.24–25.
95 *FBIS*, December 29, 1987, 45, reporting *RMRB*, December 15.
96 *CD*, March 11, 1988.
97 *CD*, February 29, 1988.
98 The best description of the problem is in Dorothy J. Solinger, *China's Transition from Socialism: Statist Legacies and Market Reforms, 1980–1990* (Armonk: Sharpe, 1993), Chapters 4 and 5.
99 *SHGYJJB*, July 25, 1988.
100 Calculated from *XMWB*, December 8, 1988.
101 *CD*, March 13, 1989.
102 The phrasing was harsh: "*dan yidun ye meiyou di Hu*," *SHGYJJB*, February 2, 1989.
103 *SF*, November 13, 1989.
104 *Jiangsu fazhi bao*, January 21, 1989.
105 *CD*, October 31, 1988.
106 The portion was 53 percent. Another report suggests that 16 percent of municipal revenue was spent on subsidies in 1985, but this may be for food alone. See Linda Li, ch. 6, 19.
107 *CD*, December 4, 1990.
108 This is based on *Cankao xiaoxi* (Reference Information), May 27, 1994, and on reports from a good friend of the author.
109 This report came from the PRC-run Hong Kong New China News Agency, reproduced in *Post*, April 23, 1994.
110 Many works refer to Chen Yun, including *Chen Yün's Strategy for China's Development: A Non-Maoist Alternative*, Nicholas R. Lardy and Kenneth Lieberthal, eds. (Armonk, NY: M.E. Sharpe, 1983).

6

TAX COLLECTORS AND SUBSIDIZERS SHAPE CENTRAL-LOCAL RELATIONS

Financial extraction from Shanghai was traditionally heavy, and this situation continued through the 1980s at least. Erosion of the socialist tax base by rural industries made the central bureaucracy try to take more profits and taxes from firms about which it had more information, notably in Shanghai. This seemed natural, because the city produced so much. Throughout China there has long been fiscal unevenness among different sectors and jurisdictions. Some bear high rates of tax; others are subsidized.[1] This pattern gives lightly taxed jurisdictions incentives to separate themselves from places that bear heavy imposts. Most local leaders hide their funds and act independently when possible. Extraction and subsidy rates have been high, subject to changing officials' promises. During reforms they were not uniform. The extraordinary importance of Shanghai for China's finances, at least through the mid-1980s, is apparent from Table 6.1.

Not all of Shanghai's revenue has gone to the central government. But the portion of the city's total revenues that went to Beijing during the whole long period from 1949 to 1984 was 87 percent, with only 13 percent remaining in local tills.[2] During Mao's time, from 1950 to 1976, Shanghai sent thirteen times more revenue to the central government than the amount it received for the municipal budget. Nearly a decade later, in 1984, it still had to give more than 85 percent of its revenue to Beijing.[3]

Hesitant central announcements of reform did not change the center's need for Shanghai money. From 1980 to 1984, after reforms were officially proclaimed, Shanghai still kept only 12 percent of its revenues to cover local spending. In Guangdong, the comparable figure over the same period was 82 percent.[4] Not only were amounts of extraction from Shanghai very much higher than in any other province-level unit on a per-person basis – even much higher than from Tianjin, the most similar municipality in China – the lack of spending per unit of revenue and the portion of revenues sent to the central treasury were also much higher.

TABLE 6.1 State extraction, by province: ratios of state expenditures over revenues (percentages) and state revenues minus expenditures per person (yuan), counting both budgetary and extrabudgetary reported funds

	Spending/revenues %				(Revenues minus spending ¥)/pop			
	1982	1983	1984	1983	1982	1983	1984	1985
Shanghai	**23**	**27**	**36**	**39**	**1349**	**1218**	**1142**	**1253**
Tianjin	68	70	67	71	234	215	265	288
Beijing	54	69	74	74	375	237	232	264
Liaoning	62	69	72	79	134	100	107	98
Jiangsu	**60**	**61**	**68**	**70**	**66**	**72**	**67**	**71**
Zhejiang	**66**	**65**	**72**	**71**	**51**	**58**	**52**	**68**
Shandong	79	79	84	82	21	25	20	28
WHOLE PRC	**79**	**82**	**89**	**90**	**29**	**25**	**18**	**20**
Hubei	79	79	84	89	25	27	23	18
Hebei	86	83	92	93	15	21	11	11
Guangdong	101	103	98	95	−2	−3	3	10
Hunan	86	88	93	99	13	11	7	2
Henan	102	89	95	101	−1	8	4	−1
Sichuan	91	95	98	102	6	4	2	−2
Anhui	83	89	98	104	12	8	2	−4
Jiangxi	113	112	124	115	−9	−9	−21	−17
Fujian	104	128	113	112	−4	−27	−15	−19
Guangxi	111	114	128	120	−8	−11	−21	−21
Yunnan	106	114	122	113	−6	−15	−27	−21
Guizhou	138	144	150	126	−21	−23	−35	−23
Heilong'g	127	114	121	111	−34	−21	−36	−24
Shaanxi	117	121	133	122	−13	−20	−35	−27
Shanxi	100	98	102	115	0	4	−4	−31
Gansu	109	118	132	123	−11	−20	−41	−35
Jilin	117	109	117	121	−22	−13	−31	−47
In. Mong.	178	171	200	170	−76	−77	−124	−109
Ningxia	180	200	200	200	−76	−97	−141	−135
Xinjiang	192	173	183	211	−36	−59	−101	−142
Qinghai	225	200	217	200	−170	−80	−144	−207
Tibet	4600	2800	5900	1800	−520	−610	−560	−520

Notes and sources: The table is in order by 1985 revenues minus expenditures per person. The relative positions of provinces (especially Shanghai) are more certain than the exactitude of the numbers. Note especially the Shanghai, Jiangsu, and Zhejiang levels, the subsidies for western provinces, esp. Tibet, and the "whole PRC" line. Computed from raw data in *Zhongguo caizheng tongji*, 1950–1985 (Chinese Fiscal Statistics, 1950–1985), Comprehensive Planning Office of the PRC Ministry of Finance, ed. (Beijing: Zhongguo Caizheng Jingji Chuban She, 1987), 54 and 144 for the budgetary and extra revenues, and 92 and 145 for the budgetary and extra expenditures. Many, perhaps not all, subsidies for raw materials are included in statistics for spending. A complete list of the line items which make up the spending categories is not public − even though interviewed Chinese economists said the government keeps unpublished figures on the reasons why it ran large deficits, and subsidies rank high among these reasons.

How great were subsidies to Shanghai because of fixed prices for inputs and products?

This analysis cannot be deemed complete, even through the reform period in Table 6.1, because Shanghai industrial materials prices have for many years been kept low – as have prices of rent and food (though not of some consumer durables). There is no full budgetary record of these implicit subsidies to cities, including Shanghai. How large were they? Did they compensate Shanghai for its extraordinarily high taxation?

Many low prices for factors and high prices for products were matters of law, not markets. Police enforcement of plans *as* law – i.e., state coercion – was the bulwark of this structure. Full statistics have not been found on the actual or implicit state subsidies for cheap raw materials delivered to Shanghai, or on high Shanghai product prices, because the bulk of such subsidies never appear on budgets. They were based in non-monetary coercion and Leninist promotion norms.

Is it possible to make an estimate of the value of non-monetized subsidies? Perhaps some subsidies are included in the numbers for extrabudgetary spending; and to the extent they are, the analysis has covered them. A complete list of the items which make up the expenditure categories is not public. In an effort to track the reasons for its budget deficits, the state reportedly tried to keep statistics on these amounts. But it would be brave to assume that all, or even most, such subsidies are in the published budgetary and extrabudgetary spending data.

What was the difference between actual prices charged to Shanghai for factors and to other places for Shanghai products, on one hand, and their theoretical scarcity prices on the other? According to Ministry of Agriculture estimates (referring specifically to 1978, but stated broadly enough to apply in many reform years), the prices of retail sales in rural areas throughout the country averaged 15 to 20 percent above their scarcity values, on a weighted basis. But the official prices of all products coming from rural areas averaged 25 to 30 percent less than their values.[5]

On this basis, it is possible to make a rough estimate of the effect of state-mandated prices in subsidizing Shanghai by lowering the cost of its factors and raising the cost of its products. This amount may then be compared with the city's high tax and profit burdens, to see how much it compensated for them. At least two assumptions are needed: First, the calculation cannot be considered exact; the aim here is only to gather a broad sense of economic realities as a prerequisite for political analysis. Second, it is realistic to assume that Shanghai did not immediately suffer higher consumer prices when the state raised rural procurement prices, because the extra money to farmers came from the central government budget rather than from Shanghai. It is possible, for the sake of this crude estimation, to say that Shanghai faced a price structure in 1983 not entirely unlike that in 1978, even though this structure became problematic for the city in 1984, when many prices floated upward very quickly.

The calculation is as follows: Shanghai's net 1983 purchases of rural subsidiary products from other Chinese areas were 2.4 b. yuan, and their scarcity-price value

128 Tax collectors and subsidizers

can be estimated at 3.3 b. The difference (the implicit 1983 subsidy to Shanghai from cheap factors) was thus about 0.9 billion.[6] In the downstream direction, Shanghai's net domestic sales of high-price manufactures in 1983 was worth 10.0 b. yuan nominally, or 8.5 billion at scarcity prices, for an implicit subsidy to Shanghai of 1.5 b. yuan from sales.[7] The sum of these subsidies for factors and sales was thus about 2.4 billion yuan (or a bit below that, using more decimals than any of this figuring justifies). This is not a trivial amount, but it is *very* much less than the 1983 revenue burden on Shanghai, counting both budgetary and extrabudgetary sources, of 19.9 billion.[8] So the implicit subsidy lessened the direct burden by one-tenth or a bit more – in any case, not by an overwhelming amount.

In other words, benefits to Shanghai through state pricing scarcely began to counterbalance the direct central extractions. The main fact here is not that the subsidies were low, but that the exactions were enormous. These "taxes" were so great, credible reports suggest not only that Shanghai managers had more incentives to hide money than did cadres anywhere else in China, but also that they actually did so in great amounts, which government collectors have on a confidential basis reportedly tried to estimate.[9]

The policy of hiding accurate books "under the rice bin" and of concocting false ones for tax collectors is no novelty among East Asian entrepreneurs. Linda Chelan Li's attempt to compute the excess of actual Shanghai investment over the amounts reported in official budgets estimates hidden surplus capital at 195 percent of plan in 1988; 135 percent in 1991; and 145 percent in 1992.[10] Also, Shanghai's high portion of "improper accounts" for tax collection was second among all China's provinces in the early 1990s (Guangdong took gold, quite literally, in this unofficial race).[11] Despite Shanghai's possible distinction as the foremost center of fake, misleading, and incomplete accounts in China, this city has also been the site of major extraction. Shanghai economists call their city China's "pocket" (*koudai*), because the government always reaches into it for money.

This odd honor grew out of Shanghai's history. It was China's foremost light industrial center for many decades before the middle of the twentieth century. By Mao's time, urban Shanghai state-owned industries bought raw materials at low state-mandated prices, processed them at fairly low wages, and sold consumer products at high state-fixed prices. The profits redounded largely to Beijing coffers. The metropolis acted like a sponge, soaking up largely non-urban resources for the national budget.[12]

Rural industries after 1970 changed this pattern, and Shanghai's profits ebbed during the 1980s inflation as country factories competed for inputs. Extractions revived somewhat during Zhu Rongji's post-reforms of the 1990s, and they continued to fluctuate as Hu Jintao and then Xi Jinping tried to balance enterprise and regulation, economic development and political stability. Deng Xiaoping had said, "Development is the hard truth," but also "Stability is of overriding importance." Deng's two propositions are in tension. Economic development sometimes aids political stability, but it also creates politically disruptive pressures when people's selves, environs, and work earnings are threatened, as they were by 1990.[13]

The case of the missing money: a clue in Shanghai's capital-output ratio

Much debate about the extent of extraction turns on the completeness of reported budgets. Nicholas Lardy argued in Mao's time that Shanghai paid very high taxes. This pattern continued through the early 1980s, stumbling later before it changed somewhat in the 1990s. Without claiming that the published data are complete, it is possible to stress with Lardy that available figures showed high taxation and central state power for some time. Other scholars, following Audrey Donnithorne, stressed that China's compartmentalized economy gave many incentives to hide money, so that the official figures were incomplete. Actually, these two viewpoints, though published as different and competing, are compatible with each other in both logic and practice, as will be shown here.

These two economists ignited one of the most fruitful debates among sinologues. They mooted the extent to which China has been fiscally centralized or fragmented, integrated or compartmentalized. Donnithorne's classic on *China's Economic System* showed how "cellular" the PRC economy has been. But Lardy responded with provincial budget data seeming to have an opposite implication: China's coastal areas were taxed heavily, by a centralized bureaucracy in Beijing, to support inland provinces.[14] After these two published, many other scholars refined the terms of their debate. Two contributors told sequels: Thomas Lyons stressed the importance of Donnithorne's insight that China's economy was surprisingly unintegrated.[15] Barry Naughton, a former student of Lardy's, found that over the whole 1965–1971 period, the central government spent fully *two-thirds* of its industrial investment budget in inland "Third Front" projects – which were extremely slow to return all the capital they absorbed.[16] Much of this money came from Shanghai (in practice it was mostly wasted), but it had been collected.

This debate among economists was the most precise genre of a broader academic literature, which had begun earlier, during the 1960s, in efforts to explain the Great Leap Forward. Schurmann, Townsend, and Skinner conceived the Leap not just in terms of its ideology, but as an attempt at organization.[17] Its egalitarian and activist norms could then be analyzed in terms of their functions, not as abstract philosophies or dogmas. Such studies of the Leap affected – and improved – research on China in later years. The economists were exploring the linked fiscal and investment aspects of this organizational view of China. Their arguments were quantitative, but the conclusions were about central and local organization – and they seemed to contradict one another. Shanghai, as the pre-eminent taxpayer, was at the center of the economists' discussion. Another new look at the situation here suggests, however, that it is possible simultaneously to find that the published budgets were grossly incomplete, that Shanghai was very heavily taxed, that the economy remained cellular, and that much of the relevant politics was between central and local leaders in the city and with its rural suppliers.

Is Shanghai's growth consistent with its scant capitalization in published budgets? Do the reported investment figures imply a capital-output ratio for the city's

130 Tax collectors and subsidizers

industry that is credible, or instead one that is too low to sustain the reports of its industrial product, which might be more complete? The argument that follows tries to test, at least broadly, for omissions from the budget data. The conclusion will be that Shanghai's industrial growth over the long term must have used far more capital than the published budgets show.

Field, Lardy, and Emerson estimated that Shanghai's gross value of industrial output (GVIO) near the start of the era of full planning, in 1957 after the 1956 "Transition to Socialism," was 11,402 million yuan.[18] The 1957 investment in the city was 372 million, of which an estimate of 250 million were industrial.[19] If so, the 1957 ratio of industrial investment over gross industrial product in Shanghai must have been very roughly 0.02. Of course this does not include old investment, nor was all of the capital immediately productive; but if we consider a much longer time – say, twenty years – the problems of old capital and time lags become insignificant. Over that time, a rough but safely overestimated 1949–1973 ratio of industrial capital to gross industrial output may be obtained after dividing the 0.02 investment rate by the pace of industrial expansion in Shanghai over this long period.[20] What was that latter rate? According to one calculation, the ratio of capital to gross output in Shanghai's industry over this long time was below 0.2.[21]

Gross output, however, double-counts values added whenever they are exchanged in semi-finished goods between firms. A standard estimate of the extent of such double counting would put the sum of industrial values added (industrial GDP) at about 40 percent of gross industrial output. This adjustment raises the 0.2, above, to 0.5 – still far too low to believe, as a capital-output ratio in a large industrial economy.

Arthur Lewis notes a "remarkable agreement" among economists: "first, that in the industrial countries the ratio of the value of capital to the value of output seems to be pretty constant at the margin, when capital-intensive and capital-sparse industries are taken together; and second, that this marginal ratio lies between 3 to 1 and 4 to 1, when the value of land and other natural resources is excluded from capital, and the value of external assets from both capital and income."[22]

A ratio for industry might go somewhat below 3.0. But 0.5 – or two or three times that figure, as the case in Shanghai perhaps was – would be remarkable to the point of impossible, for a very big industrial city over a period of decades. Arguments using numerical evidence in this book are offered only when shifts of quantities are dramatic. This is an example.

So the published data about capital seem to be radically incomplete. All the economists whose estimates are used here agree that the available investment data, especially if they exclude extrabudgetary investment, have been at least somewhat partial. Enterprises illegally diverted working capital to fixed investment. Shanghai's managers used their pools of skilled labor and some ability to acquire extra raw materials to produce capital goods within their own repair facilities and workshops. Also, increased productivity with nearly constant average wages in Shanghai raised state industry profits, and thus state revenue, faster than output. In addition, some allowance could be made for variations in capital-output ratios among different places and sectors. China as a whole may have a modestly smaller ratio than do most countries, and Shanghai almost surely had the lowest ratio in the country (if anybody possessed fully accurate figures to calculate it, which is unlikely because revealed money became taxed money). It is likely that much of the reason for the big shortfall in reported capital for Shanghai was the hiding of money by local managers there.[23] Even Shanghai's industry was not efficient enough to reproduce resources as fast as the published budgets imply.

How much should Shanghai pay?

Was such a high tax on Shanghai justifiable in terms of economic growth? The reasoning here, and the picture of heavy exaction that it paints with wide margins for uncertainties, would still not be enough to prove that Shanghai's burden was excessive for purposes of growth (even though this kind of reasoning is already adequate to raise political questions). Economically, the rub in the high tax policy is this: Extraction from areas like Shanghai, in which companies' external economies can regenerate capital more quickly than other places, may become so severe that the country's overall development – even the long-term growth of poor areas to which short-term money is sent – became slower than it would have been if a less draconian tax had been imposed on coastal areas. An economic model, offered below, might tell how much tax Shanghai should have paid, assuming an aim of maximum long-term growth. It is hard to adapt for testing the national efficiency of the actual tax, but it suggests the Chinese government had a patriotic case to answer when imposing such uneven extractions.

Shanghai's relatively good transport location, skilled labor force, wide variety of pre-existing industries, and other advantages allow many new investments there to return capital more quickly than equal investments elsewhere in China can do. On the other hand, scattering resources all over the country could widen the range of places where future investments can prosper. A pro-inland policy may provide "external economies" for future investments in poor places. Such dispersal encourages the training of modern labor in the boondocks, and it provides more semi-finished products and transport for later ventures there. This varies by industry; but in general, for most lines of work, Shanghai's advantages are more favorable than in most PRC locations. A policy of dispersed investments, such as China used before the 1980s more than other developing countries did, might slow GDP growth in the short term – but could allow faster growth later, because of spreading infrastructure, trained labor, and dispersed markets. The danger is that such a communitarian long-term policy could drain rich areas so much, the benefit for inland places could be overwhelmed by the costs of not recouping capital quickly.

So what is the best balance between Chinese coastal investment, which generally leads to spurts of growth soon, and inland investment to have more widespread growth later? Some neoclassical Western economists use a "turnpike" metaphor to

132 Tax collectors and subsidizers

describe a growth-efficient way to put capital in sectors (which in this China case are geographic)[24]:

> Take *any* initial capital structure [a matrix with sectoral dimensions, e.g., by place and industry] and *any* desired terminal structure. . . . The corresponding optimal capital program will be describable as follows: The system first invests so as to alter its capital structure toward [growth-efficient] proportions. . . . When it has come close to these proportions, it spends most of the program-ming period performing steady growth at the maximal rate. . . . Then it bends away . . . and invests in such a way as to alter the capital structure to the desired terminal proportions. . . . It is like a turnpike paralleled by a network of minor roads. There is a fastest route between any two points. . . . The best intermediate capital configuration is one which will grow most rapidly; even if it is not the desired one, it is temporarily optimal.

This model shows, in abstract, the problem faced by planners who wanted to tax Shanghai for the sake of developing other places. Even if this set of allocative values was right in some moral sense, too much burden on Shanghai could slow long-term growth nationally (even inland alone) by forgoing too many profits from coastal areas that regenerate money quickly if temporary unideal allocation was allowed. This point required a change in CCP thinking about Shanghai. It was outside the mentality of Mayor Chen Yi, when in the 1950s he plainly said, "We must evacuate the population of the city systematically and transfer factories to the interior whenever possible."[25] During Chen's mayoralty in the mid-1950s, some Shanghai factories were actually moved, with their staffs, to inland places such as Shaanxi.

During reforms, and occasionally before then, state leaders showed some under-standing that extremely high taxation of productive places could hurt the country by slowing overall growth. An example was Mao Zedong's 1956 speech on "Ten Great Relationships."[26] But evidence shows they did not act on this perception. To serve other values and inland political constituencies, Chinese leaders have seldom stressed growth efficiency. Shanghai paid a great deal under this policy, and a more important question is how much China as a whole paid in lost growth. Huge investments went for disastrously unprofitable industries in the "Great Third Front." This was mostly a policy of the 1960s, although it did not entirely cease when China's reforms began. By 1988, the program was still run by a State Council organ called the "Third Front Enterprises Management Office" (Sanxian Qiye Guanli Bangong Shi). Many projects were associated with the People's Liberation Army, and politicians had reasons not to end them. Not until the 1990s was it possible for President Jiang Zemin (with Zhu Rongji) to order the PLA to give up control of these and other businesses.[27] At the same time, Jiang invited capitalists into the CCP, recruiting their support for China's still-authoritarian political economy.[28] Xi Jinping has backtracked on that policy only slightly.

Not all national tax revenues over these decades went to poor inland places. Coastal Liaoning, Guangdong, and Shandong were also important recipients by the early 1980s. Provincial capitals as a group, prominently including Shanghai, Zhejiang's capital Hangzhou, and Guangzhou in the far south, had higher remittance rates per person than did other large cities in the same provinces, such as Zhejiang's Ningbo or Guangdong's Foshan, which are not capitals.

Beijing was in a special category, and published data understated the difference between Shanghai's and Beijing's fiscal treatments. A higher portion of spending in Beijing never appears in geographically organized budgets or extrabudgetary reports, but instead is in the national accounts of ministries and other functional units. These built a great deal of infrastructure, e.g., housing, that is nominally not Beijing's even though it is located in that city. As late as 1984, Shanghai delivered profits and taxes of 16 billion yuan, compared with Beijing's 4.56 billion. But Shanghai's reported expenditures that year were 2.77 billion yuan, compared with Beijing's of 2.71 billion (98 percent as much).[29] These figures underreport the difference. The national "capital" deserves the pun as its name. Two decades before Shanghai's construction boom in the 1990s, Beijing already had many new streets and buildings, a subway system, and better urban maintenance. After 1990, that pattern changed.

Most expenditure in Shanghai during reforms went toward keeping up its role as a tax base. Light industries renovation was reported as extensive by 1979. This was overdue, because rural markets for Shanghai consumer products flourished throughout the 1970s and capital was needed to make them. The stress on light industries was also consistent with more localization of fiscal powers to the city. At first, this was a derogation of power to top Shanghai municipal officers (appointed by the central state and fully part of it), not to Jiangnan managers at the factory level who led the new prosperity. So Shanghai participated in the national wave of "management by dividing fiscal levels." An announced aim was to change a situation in which Shanghai had been "unified too much and administered to death."[30]

The high tax-and-profit extraction rate affected all aspects of Shanghai's politics and economy. Central politicians included the major satraps sent to head the municipal government. Some of the mayors, notably Jiang Zemin and Zhu Rongji, later led the nation. Provincial wealth correlated with high taxes, high status for the province head, low rates of expenditure through official budgets, and high rates of hiding capital. Shanghai is not unique in having depended to a great extent on non-plan spending. But it is the extreme example of such places, which prominently included nearby Jiangsu and Zhejiang. High extraction from rich places gave local leaders strong reasons for extrabudgetary and hidden accounting.

Province-level units such as Shanghai that reported light reliance on extrabudgetary revenues nonetheless reported extensive non-plan spending. Bank accounts are easier to conceal than construction sites. After rich places paid high regular taxes and profits, they could extract less by other means. Having proportionately little to spend in the regular plans, Shanghai more often ran into unexpected, less fully authorized costs. Shanghai's reliance on non-budget spending did not, however, mean that it had more to spend on a per capita, per product, or any other standard basis; in any of these terms, the metropolis still had least.

TABLE 6.2 Shanghai's relative non-use of budgeting: budgetary over reported extrabudgetary revenues and budgetary over reported extrabudgetary expenditures

	(percentage ratios)								*index*
	Budget/extra revenues				*Budget/extra spending*				*(sum*
	1982	*1983*	*1984*	*1985*	*1982*	*1983*	*1984*	*1985*	*%s)*
Shanghai	**25**	**29**	**33**	**37**	**66**	**54**	**57**	**75**	**376**
Jiangsu	**46**	**51**	**64**	**63**	**74**	**86**	**81**	**102**	**567**
Liaoning	58	74	79	101	67	71	65	73	588
Beijing	57	75	83	88	74	71	77	83	608
Tianjin	44	46	50	63	138	100	91	96	628
Shandong	50	75	78	78	97	84	93	106	661
Zhejiang	**57**	**55**	**60**	**60**	**100**	**110**	**116**	**128**	**686**
WHOLE PRC	62	70	74	76	111	113	116	129	751
Hubei	58	58	60	70	125	127	123	138	759
Hebei	78	81	82	84	113	108	124	120	790
Hunan	70	76	76	82	110	125	125	133	797
Guangdong	76	89	74	66	100	119	130	156	810
Sichuan	76	83	89	95	119	109	123	121	815
Anhui	64	73	79	80	131	143	133	155	858
Henan	45	53	56	55	158	158	176	185	886
Shanxi	95	104	115	116	117	100	103	138	888
Shaanxi	64	87	100	85	170	127	135	165	933
Fujian	93	108	88	72	133	129	140	182	945
Heilong'g	141	132	111	97	117	115	109	125	947
Jiangxi	100	86	93	95	125	142	157	165	963
Gansu	92	100	92	94	108	160	175	171	992
Yunnan	100	106	105	93	127	150	163	168	1012
Jilin	142	150	173	141	100	100	92	121	1019
Guangxi	108	100	107	100	131	146	164	167	1023
Guizhou	129	78	82	80	175	229	233	240	1246
In. Mongol	260	200	188	173	167	177	207	200	1572
Xinjiang	200	150	157	138	188	271	230	264	1598
Ningxia	150	150	200	133	200	233	300	250	1616
Qinghai	300	150	200	250	200	233	225	250	1808

Notes and sources: This table roughly measures the extent to which different provinces rely on budgets to manage state revenues and expenditures, compared with extrabudgetary funds and expenditures. The (calculated) sums in the right-hand column serve as a coarse index of differences between provinces. Budgetary subsidies to border areas are evident near the bottom of the chart (though the available figures for Tibet, where the government and Army spend freely to ensure control, are excluded as especially incomparable with the other statistics). Provincial wealth correlates with nonreliance on budgets, and this is affected by the central bureaucracy's eagerness to subsidize prices in important tax bases. Computed from raw data in *Zhongguo caizheng tongji, 1950-1985* (Chinese Fiscal Statistics, 1950–1985), Comprehensive Planning Office of the PRC Ministry of Finance, ed. (Beijing: Zhongguo Caizheng Jingji Chuban She, 1987), 54 and 144 for the budgetary and extra revenues, and 92 and 145 for the two types of expenditures.

Comparisons with other cities

More than two-thirds of Shanghai's population (or Tianjin's or Beijing's) is urban, and comparisons with China's poorer provinces can mislead. But Shanghai's fiscal situation can be compared with those of other cities in East China. Statistics are available; and they are revealing, although they do not cover the part of revenues and expenditures that is extrabudgetary.

Shanghai was not the only city on the delta to have a high official extraction rate. Compared with other parts of the country, extraction minus expenditure in Shanghai's adjacent provinces and cities was generally heavy. But from 1981 to 1985, as Table 6.3 shows, the ratio of revenues over spending in those places dropped – and somewhat converged. The cause was local Chinese power, especially in rural factories.

Commodities produced in Shanghai also reaped sales taxes throughout China, not just in the city. During the mid-1980s, the average sales tax on Shanghai goods

TABLE 6.3 Major cities' budgetary revenues over budgetary expenditures and budgetary revenues minus expenditures per person in Shanghai, Jiangsu, and Zhejiang

	(revenues/spending percentages)					*1984 revs-exps*
	1981	*1982*	*1983*	*1984*	*1985*	*(yuan/person)*
Shanghai	1054	880	808	582	432	11073
w'ted av.	*936*	*803*	*558*	*470*	*370*	*363*
Hangzhou	536	563	470	n/a	323	322
Wuxi	1058	840	569	505	523	282
Suzhou	930	585	420	363	391	212
Changzhou	1085	810	436	372	404	193
Nanjing	515	510	366	312	296	171
Ningbo	845	1016	428	360	264	137
Huzhou	552	561	342	244	277	67
Nantong	1068	752	279	241	273	56
Yangzhou	517	351	161	155	175	20
Liany'g'g	340	309	165	124	146	13
Wenzhou	n/a	n/a	138	109	126	4

Notes and sources: The second row is a weighted average for all these cities, and its decrease shows a lessening of collectable extraction in the mid-1980s, when planning for most consumer products ended because of competition from rural factories. Note decreases for Shanghai among the first five columns. Note some convergence among cities by 1985, when reforms increased the role of local (versus high) politics in extractions. Shanghai and Sunan cities, and provincial capital Hangzhou, were taxed more heavily than Nanjing (which like Yangzhou and Lianyungang was long run by cadres from northern Jiangsu). Southern Zhejiang's Wenzhou was nearly exempted. The order of the table is by 1984 budgetary revenues minus expenditures per capita. Computed from raw figures in *Zhongguo caizheng tongji, 1950-1985* (Chinese Fiscal Statistics, 1950–1985), Comprehensive Planning Office of the PRC Ministry of Finance, ed. (Beijing: Zhongguo Caizheng Jingji Chuban She, 1987), 57, and *Zhongguo chengshi tongji nianjian, 1985* (Statistical Yearbook of Chinese Cities, 1985), State Statistical Bureau, ed. (Beijing: Zhongguo Tongji Xinxi Zixun Fuwu Zhongxin & Xin Shijie Chuban She, 1985), 37.

136 Tax collectors and subsidizers

was 21 percent, higher than sales imposts on goods from nearby Jiangnan cities (for Wuxi and Suzhou, they were only 13 and 12 percent).[31]

A progressive profits tax introduced in 1984 varied rates by taxable amount, industry, and location. A gist of the change was that Shanghai ended up paying one-quarter of the whole country's money that was produced by the progressive aspect of the tax. This could have resulted from several factors (larger plants in Shanghai, better management, or less ability to hide profits from tax collectors). Of the 1,411 Shanghai enterprises that had to turn in taxes on profits above the minimum bracket, 72 percent remitted one-fifth of their profits or more, and 39 percent had to remit three-tenths or more.[32]

National comparisons also show how Shanghai budgetary extraction compares with cities outside the East China area. Since Tang times (618–19907 CE), the Yangzi delta has been a center of production, whereas official consumption and top politics were often elsewhere, especially in the north. In the modern era, including republican times, Shanghai capitalists were in tension with military politicians, whose main tie to them was taxation.[33] This pattern did not change for many years, even during China's reforms.

Exactions other than money, and the rise of post-entrepreneurialism

The tax regime under Mao's centralized state affected Shanghai in non-monetary ways too. The metropolis not only put more funds into the PRC budget than did other places. It also exported more technicians, had fewer nonstate institutions relative to its size (including collective and private enterprises), and operated under famously tighter rules. Most important, the heavy tax regime drained the spirit of enterprise. As a local editor put it, "Shanghai was the 'golden milk-cow' of the planned economy. As long as the state fed and protected it, Shanghai continued to give the most milk. But . . . the city learned to rely on the state and lost its ability to organize its own markets and sources of raw materials."[34] This loss of managerial will arguably was a long-term cost for China, not just Shanghai, but it is difficult to quantify. Non-monetary extractions from the city are hard to separate from direct imposts.

Technical talent and machines were systematically removed from Shanghai, just as funds were.[35] This became a pattern soon after the PRC's establishment. When the Northeast needed skilled laborers in its electrical, chemical, rubber, and machine industries, a Technical Recruiting Team got them from Shanghai.[36] When a new automobile factory was established in North China, over 10,000 Shanghai engineers and workers went there to build it.[37] In the first decade of the revolutionary regime, a campaign forced many Shanghai firms to leave the city entirely – though many went to nearby places. Sixteen newly "joint state-private" stencil factories were ordered to shift from Shanghai to Hangzhou.[38] Other firms went further, to Lanzhou, Urumqi, or Xining.[39] All told, 196 factories and 168 stores left the city for twenty different provinces in the 1956 "Transition to Socialism" year alone.[40] This pattern continued in the later 1950s, and it removed institutions and physical plant as well as personnel.[41]

Private enterprises in Shanghai were thus nationalized long before reforms. Private firms, when they revived in the 1980s, had to pay an 84 percent "accumulation tax" (*leijin shui*).[42] In Jiangsu, the rates included a 20 percent income tax (*suode shui*) and 5 percent business tax (*yingye shui*) on profits. Shanghai private entrepreneurs could finally ask by 1988 that the municipal government pass a law to protect them. Taxes and license fees were, they complained, more onerous than in other places. The relatively great difficulty of renting space meant that urban Shanghai's reforms outside the state sector were as constrained as were reforms in state-owned factories. Private and collective sectors in Shanghai remained small by any measure as a portion of the economy, and they remained so later than in other places. The manager of a metal-punching factory in Shanghai's Jiading County figured that if he could move his plant just a few kilometers across the border into Jiangsu, his profits would rise by 50,000 to 60,000 yuan each year.[43]

Shanghai private managers reported that taxes they faced were "heavy and diverse," preventing their development. The Coral Knitting Factory in the first quarter of 1988 had gross revenue of 317,000 yuan, and it had profits of 36,000 yuan; but the private manager reported that this firm, after taxes, could retain only 4,000 yuan. So his effective tax rate was 89 percent.[44] Levies this high suggest many books must have been cooked – as almost surely they were. Otherwise, a business under such conditions would have scant incentive to exist. Pressure to hide money amounted to a control, because it threatened managers with being found illegally hiding assets. The main unevenness was that Shanghai businesses were less in charge of their fates than were firms in other places.

Competition for Shanghai from cities nearby and inland

Shanghai was compared to a "big boat" (*da chuan*) – not liable to rock, but also difficult to turn. This pattern was hard to hide from some foreign investors. Throughout China, including Shanghai, overseas businesses were supposed to enjoy a choice among "three capital" (*san zi*) arrangements: foreign investment and management, joint investment with Chinese management, or joint investment with joint management. But in Shanghai, interpretations of these rules were more restrictive than elsewhere.[45]

The Chinese government announced industrial innovations that encouraged companies to explore new products and management forms. But Shanghai, because its main product was revenue, only occasionally benefited from allowances for experiment. For example, during early 1988, sixteen cities, including Changzhou, Guangzhou, Nanjing, and Ningbo – but not Shanghai – were chosen to "trailblaze" new PRC urban reforms. Among the many areas to be explored was "experimentation in the reduction of tax rates [and] creating an external environment of fair competition for various types of enterprises."[46] In these cities outside Shanghai, stock shares could be sold by factories to encourage more efficiency among large state enterprises – even though paying dividends directly reduced state revenues. Local bankruptcy laws in these cities were not just passed; some were implemented, allowing strong managements to buy out weak ones. More short-term money markets were approved, and "the wage system of enterprises was to be separated from the wage system of [state] institutions." Such reforms would have benefited Shanghai too. Open discussion of them, even if implementation was ragged, allowed more flexibility in the ossified economic structures of many cities. But the central budget makers and their satraps in Shanghai forced any such changes to be clandestine in the large industries that provided their most important tax base.

The metropolis acquired a reputation as a "house that follows the law" (*shoufa hu*). Mayor Zhu Rongji said in September 1988 that Shanghai people are very "law abiding" (*guiju*).[47] He surely meant this as a compliment, not a snicker, but some locals rued their costly allegiance. A disgruntled columnist said Shanghai was always overly "law abiding, following the straight and narrow" (*xungui daoju*). The only things that could be done were those which appeared on official documents with red letterheads (*hongtou wenjian*).[48]

Shanghai economists have often argued that big cities in general, and their own city in particular, have been heavily "controlled."[49] Reins that bridled the city included particularly strenuous birth and household controls, restrictions on land use, rations on non-industrial energy consumption, and other restraints. High tax-and-profit extraction was the most obvious example of economic control – but it was integrally related to others. What the tax regime showed was not injustice to Shanghai, and certainly not ordinary poverty there, but an uneven pattern of control that worked against the city more sharply than politicians who enforced it wished to make public.

Shanghai's imposts were high, and the first major reason for them was the city's history as a light industrial center, making consumer goods that provided a means for the government to tap resources in China's largest market, which was rural. Second, Shanghai was a base for radical national politicians during the whole decade of the 1960s (not just 1966–1970), and at later times too. Third, political reasons for partiality against Jiangnan and Shanghai were based in subethnic tensions between northern Jiangsu (Subei) people in government and the urban majority, whose ancestors hailed mostly from southern Jiangsu or northern Zhejiang. All three factors affected periodic negotiations with the central government about provincial tax rates.[50]

Conditions for politically easy-to-tax consumption-oriented industries

Shanghai's traditional forte, light industry, meant that the city's economy came under more stringent planners' control than that of any other province-level unit. During the 1950s, the Chinese government raised money mainly because of two overlapping "scissors gaps" (*jiandao cha*, a term adopted from Soviet 1920s debates).

(a) An urban/rural gap: The state set product prices from urban state factories high and agricultural product prices low. It owned the factories and reaped revenues on the price difference sales to most Chinese, who were then still rural.

(b) A heavy-industry/light-industry gap: The state also tended to set light industrial prices high, but heavy industrial prices low — because the former sell mainly to consumers, whereas the latter sell largely to other state-owned units. In pre-reform years, the government budget benefited, and all Chinese people paid.

Shanghai had a great deal of light industry in the 1950s and developed its consumer goods sector further during the next decade. So the government was then able to process many low-priced agricultural inputs and sell the products dearly.

Especially in the Great Leap Forward of 1958, Shanghai developed more heavy industries. Despite their capital expense and inability to absorb much labor, heavy industries might have strengthened the city's overall fiscal autonomy if those big factories had been locally run. But the largest remained central fiefdoms, owned and run entirely by ministries in Beijing. They did not hire nearly so many workers as light industries, but they fostered a conservative, unionized, male workforce in Shanghai that provided support for top municipal leaders. The latter were appointed by Beijing to ensure the flow of taxes, which came especially from light industries that employed more women.

For three decades after the mid-1950s, this urban structure was consolidated. When the state could no longer hide its inability to provide low-priced inputs for light industries, their costs rose and the "scissors gap" between light and heavy industries brought less revenue. So a long-term basis was created for more potential ability in the city to reinvest profits, although in the short term Shanghai factories' costs kept on increasing. The metropolis faced competition from rich but lower-tax areas of China. Its efficiency declined, as measured by ratios of total product over costs. Taxability was important in Shanghai's historical evolution as a center mainly for revenues in the 1950s; but by the end of reforms after 1989, materials price inflation had drastically cut the state's profits from this way of using the metropolis.

Bureaucratic inertia and political habits in both Beijing and Shanghai tended to slow the fall of the city's extraction rates. Not until the economic inflation of the middle 1980s and the 1990s political change did central cadres begin to alter their norms on intended taxation. The tax base for many quick-growth industries, selling to a newly wealthy rural population, had already left Shanghai. Light-industrial reasons for the historically high extraction applied less strongly by the 1990s. The state could no longer benefit from "scissors gaps."

Did resentment of Shanghai's role in the Cultural Revolution bring higher taxes?

To what extent did Shanghai's history, during rule by the "Gang of Four" (and relatively radical mayors Chen Yi and Ke Qingshi in the 1950s and 1960s), create

140 Tax collectors and subsidizers

norms that maintained its tax burden? Especially in the late 1960s, many other provinces' production of consumer goods suffered more than Shanghai's.[51] In 1969, for example, the metropolis's growth rate was relatively fast. This was an era in which "the whole country protected Shanghai," at least for the purpose of trying to ensure materials supplies.[52]

Over the long 1953–1982 period, Shanghai's budgetary revenues rose at the phenomenal rate of 17.4 percent annually, as Table 6.4 shows. Expenditures also rose each year, but at a much lower rate of 7.6 percent. The only era, among the few periods covered by this "confidential" source, when the annual increase of expenditures was greater than that of revenues was 1966–1978. The increase of discrimination against local units in Shanghai slowed during the early 1970s, but spending always remained far less than revenues. Money from Shanghai has been greater than money spent there in all periods of PRC history.

Shanghai's infrastructural investment was three times higher in 1977–1982 than in 1966–1976, but this mainly reflects a need to remedy earlier depreciation.[53] "Gang of Four" rule in Shanghai poured money into military and heavy industrial plants, not into infrastructure, urban services, or startups of industries with new technologies. Shanghai's history of fiscal treatment in the late 1960s was somewhat less extractive than in some other years, but the expenditure pattern was similar to that since 1949. The city was allowed to spend relatively little (on a reported basis at least), and money went mainly to projects that benefited central interests. Gang of Four member and *de facto* mayor Zhang Chunqiao influenced this result, but so did other leaders.

During the time that Shanghai radical politicians held power, taxes rose quickly. So did the percentage of local revenue from local taxes toward the end of that time, about 1975. Table 6.5 shows the reported numbers. Radicals put some money into Shanghai, but they extracted fast-increasing amounts also for national politics that benefited them (as non-radical Shanghai top leaders in other eras also did). Although Shanghai expenditures as a portion of local revenues rose notably, they likewise did in the Chinese municipality most like Shanghai (Tianjin) – albeit the larger city had a higher base level. The partial lessening of pressure on Shanghai's finances in these years cannot be taken as a peculiarity of radical rule, since it applies elsewhere too.

TABLE 6.4 Shanghai's budgetary expenditures and revenues through early reforms (average annual percentage increases)

	1953–1957	*1958–1965*	*1966–1978*	*1979–1982*	*1953–1982*
Local revenue	24	41	7.9	−0.3	17.4
Local expenditure	4.8	12.3	10.4	−6.2	7.6

Source: Shanghai jingji, neibu ben: 1949–1982 (Shanghai Economy, Internal Volume: 1949–1982), Shanghai Academy of Social Sciences, ed. (Shanghai: Shanghai Shehui Kexue Yuan Chuban She, 1984), 993. Separate figures for years in the early 1970s were, unfortunately, not offered in the source, nor were extrabudgetary numbers.

Tax collectors and subsidizers 141

TABLE 6.5 Shanghai revenues, 1952–1990, with comparisons (first column in billion yuan; then percentages) (then contrasts with Tianjin, Guangdong, and Guangzhou)

	Revenue	Revenue Sources			Shanghai | Tianjin		Guangd | Guangz	
	bil yuan	Central units' %	Sh. unts' %	Loans & bonds %	Spending as % Sh. revenue	Spending as % of T. rev.	S/R %	S/R %
1952	2	87	7	6	11	28	46	
57	5	90	9	1	8	20	45	
62	6	28	71	1	6	25	46	
65	8	24	74	1	9	26	47	
70	11	12	86	1	11	23	52	
75	15	7	91	1	18	27	50	
78	19	11	88	1	14	37	70	
79	19	10	88	1	14	40	81	
80	20	12	87	1	10	36	73	
81	20	15	84	1	9	35	69	
82	20	16	82	1	10	53	76	
83	20	23	75	1	11	52	81	
84	22	24	75	1	14	47	97	
85	26	30	69	1	17	56	96	
86	26	30	68	1	23	64	109	51
87	24	30	68	2	22	56	97	49
88	26	38	60	2	25	78	107	47
89	30	44	55	1	25	84	103	53
90	28	40	58	1	27	90	115	66

Source: *Shanghai tongji nianjian, 1988* (Shanghai Statistical Yearbook, 1988), Li Mouhuan, ed. (Shanghai: Shanghai Shi Tongji Ju, 1988) [SHTNNJ88], 65, and SHTNNJ91, 53, from which the yuan figures are rounded to the nearest billion and most percentages are calculated. Another table, in *Shanghai Statistical Yearbook: 1988 Concise Edition*, Municipal Statistical Bureau of Shanghai, ed. (Beijing: China Statistical Publishing House, 1988), 25, provides the basis for calculating the last Shanghai column, on the ratio of total budgetary expenditure in total revenue. High Tianjin expenditure/revenue ratios may relate to Beijing ministries' units there; *Tianjin tongji nianjian, 1986* (Tianjin Statistical Yearbook, 1986), Tianjin Statistical Bureau, ed. (Beijing: Zhongguo Tongji Chuban She, 1986) [TJTJNJ86], 333-34; TJTJNJ88, 237; and TJTJNJ91, 267. For raw data that were the basis for Guangdong calculations, *Guangdong sheng tongji nianjian, 1986* (Guangzhou: Guangdong Province Statistical Yearbook, 1986), Guangdong Province Statistical Bureau, ed. (Beijing: Zhongguo Tongji Chuban She, 1986) [GDTJNJ86], 299, GDTJNJ87, 367, and GDTJNJ91, 340. See also *Guangzhou tongji nianjian, 1991* (Guangzhou Statistical Yearbook, 1991) (Guangzhou: Guangdong Province Statistical Yearbook, 1991), 24–25. Some percentage columns may not add to 100 because of rounding.

Under the radicals' tax regime, the Shanghai city government was given a great many firms to run without even nominal supervision from cadres in Beijing. The rise of extraction (especially for an era in which prices were stable) was very sharp at this time. After 1976, the acceleration of total taxes did not reverse; on the contrary, it continued at least through 1978.

142 Tax collectors and subsidizers

Reforms of less tightly controlled places, especially those in Jiangnan outside central Shanghai, reduced those areas' contributions to the central budget. So after 1975, until the 1990s, a lower portion of the central funds were spent for infrastructure in the metropolis. The ratio of Shanghai local spending to revenue began a period of decline that lasted at least until 1981, flattening but then increasing as the 1980s inflation hit. (These changes are presented in the sixth column of Table 6.5, along with comparative figures from Tianjin, Guangzhou, and Guangdong that show much higher ratios of local spending to local revenue for all periods in those cities – and in the Tianjin case, a 1975–1981 pattern that contrasts sharply with that in Shanghai.) Only later, by 1984–1985, when the state planning system collapsed, did the spending/revenues ratio begin to rise in Shanghai. The reason was not just that the city's factories desperately needed capital after many years of uncompensated depreciation. Evidence from behavior and reasonable premises about interests also suggest the central state could then no longer effectively prevent them from keeping more funds.

A corollary, presented in a column of Table 6.5, was that the government in the 1980s had to rely increasingly for Shanghai revenue from units that were wholly under the central state. From 1975 to 1990, this portion rose from 7 to 40 percent. The fourth column shows that units under Shanghai control paid heavily from 1970 to 1984. Then they paid less during the inflation until 1990. Total extraction rose later, although prices affected all these numbers.

Shanghai had sent 88 percent of its fiscal income to the central government in 1970. In 1971, a new revenue system was introduced, and this early localizing reform followed the slogan "fixed receipts and fixed expenditures, with both receipts and expenditures guaranteed."[54] Fiscal powers were "sent down," as the managements of enterprises localized. A principle of the Fourth Five-Year Plan (1971–1975) was that "upward remittances would be guaranteed, and the surplus would be retained, as determined each year."[55] These early 1970s national rules are like those in post-1978 reforms. These procedures for setting Shanghai's rates still meant high taxes on flows that could not be hidden.

Shanghai's 1971 fiscal target of 10.882 billion yuan was overfulfilled slightly. The local expenditure target was only 9 percent the size of the revenue quota for that year.[56] It was underspent by 5 percent. Such high taxation and low spending meant that all of Shanghai for 1971 had a paltry 426 million yuan to keep – at least, only that much was reported. This was less than 4 percent of actual revenues. The low retention (some of which was later contributed to the national budget), when supplemented with the central government's actual total expenditure in Shanghai, totaled just one-eighth as much as the city's intake of all official money. 'Radical' Gang of Four member Zhang Chunqiao chaired the Shanghai Revolutionary Committee (government) from 1967 to 1976.

In 1972, tax plans were changed in a way that further disadvantaged Shanghai: Each province-level unit, including the metropolis, was required to send half of any collected surplus over a set amount (a standard 100 million yuan) to the central government – regardless of the province's economic size or its politically normalized expectation of usual remittance. The 1972 fiscal target set for Shanghai was 11.893 billion yuan; and in that year, the actual collections were 57 million above that. But in 1973, the target went up to 12.404 billion, and excess collections were 369 million (of which most was sent to Beijing). From 1971 to 1973, the money that Shanghai could retain was reportedly less than 12 percent of what it forwarded to the national government.[57]

For 1974 and 1975, the announced extraction rules became yet more severe. Central authorities declared that Shanghai could retain only 1.1 percent of its targeted fiscal revenues, plus 30 percent of collections above that. The combined quota for these years was 27.332 billion yuan, and actual collections were 3 percent less than that. The city thus could retain less than 300 million yuan – far less than in 1973. This pressure on Shanghai during 1974–1975 was exercised through raising the city's fiscal target (agreed by Zhang Chunqiao) beyond what was collectable. Shanghai's expenditures had to come from a set, small percentage of that amount. Post-1978 reform tax policies for the metropolis bear a stronger resemblance to those of 1970–1971 than to the temporary super-draconian policies of 1975.

In 1976, the tax system was changed yet again, in a way whose only clarity was its reflection of conflicting top policies. The new formulae for figuring taxes were complex enough to incorporate all the diverse extractive principles of various earlier years. Local receipts and expenditures were supposed to be fixed, but also "linked." Shanghai's economic performance was anemic during that year, notably in heavy industries.[58] State profits went down. In 1976, Shanghai's fiscal quota was lowered to 13.840 billion yuan, of which only 95 percent was collected. At the same time, the central government reduced Shanghai's authorization to spend as much as had been originally planned.[59] The habit of each province's leader bargaining for its tax rate, with no national standard portion all places should pay, had become normal.

Did Jiangnan's disdain of Subei politicians cause state extraction unevenness?

Simple political discrimination against Shanghai is, among the hypothesized reasons for the high taxes, one of the most plausible and understandable – but all the evidence for it is circumstantial. An outline of East China's political economy must take account of the continuing power of politicians associated with Gen. Chen Yi's Third Field Army, which "liberated" Jiangnan in 1949 and established all major administrations there. Cadres from relatively poor parts of East China were very important in the new government, and many from Shandong and northern Jiangsu had scant reason for fondness toward Jiangnan. Shanghai people often openly disdained them, and it is unsurprising that they resented this opinion.[60]

Jiangnan people were not dominant at the top of Shanghai politics (or in Jiangsu or Zhejiang) after 1949, even though they staffed most managerial posts, had deputy positions, and remained a large majority of the population. Leaders from less

144 Tax collectors and subsidizers

well-to-do parts of the country dominated two activities in Shanghai: leading the city's Party, and picking the city's garbage.

Jiangnan people in Shanghai sometimes freely report that they scorn habits of the approximately one-quarter of their city's population that hails from Subei, northern Jiangsu. Bigotry is not a uniquely Chinese trait (it is evident in India or America, for example), but China is not immune to it. Subei people are disproportionately employed in lowly occupations such as sanitary maintenance, stevedoring, and construction. They are said to wear garish clothes, eat too much garlic, and have bumpkin culture. Discrimination has given the local government, often led at the top by Communists from north of the Yangzi who were educated in Shanghai, an interest in affirmative action. Top city leaders have had a non-local view of Shanghai's proper role in China's whole polity and economy. Analysts often assume these cadres mainly wanted promotions to Beijing and agreed to high Shanghai taxes for that reason. But resentment of Jiangnan had multiple sources.

Among later mayors, the most important 1980s politician was Jiang Zemin (mayor, 1985–1988; Shanghai CCP Secretary, 1987–1989). Jiang was originally from Yangzhou, an elegant city that he seemed to consider Subei, although it is culturally medial. Surprisingly many Shanghai local people openly reported disliking Jiang, despite his suaveness and high political position (General Secretary of the whole CCP, 1989–2002). Jiang was seen by some interviewees in Shanghai as essentially a tax collector. During his earlier period as Minister of Electronic Industries (1983–1985), Shanghai was often on the short list of places for approval of investments in computers – just the sort of industry the metropolis then needed. Jiang presided over a series of decisions that sent high-tech projects to Beijing and elsewhere, rather than Shanghai. In May 1989, Jiang personally ordered the closing of the most important reformist newspaper in the city, the *World Economic Herald* (*Shijie jingji daobao*). When he was elevated to the CCP General Secretaryship the next month, he acquired a high-profile role in a national government whose most obvious traits were its willingness to use coercion and run budget deficits. Interviewees in the metropolis, referring to their top local leaders over several decades, claimed such politicians "speak Beijingese but not Shanghainese."

Subei cadres have also been crucial in another administration of importance to Shanghai: the top of the Jiangsu Party. That large next-door province (of which Shanghai historically was part) usually had lower tax rates, especially in its north. Subei leaders in the provincial capital, Nanjing, sought to control the parts of Jiangsu that produce money most quickly, Sunan south of the river. They were content to see Shanghai taxed, since factories in that biggest city competed with many Jiangsu industries. Most Shanghai people identified with Jiangnan, not with Subei or conservatives in Nanjing. The metropolis was Jiangsu's main economic rival – and partner. Some saw Shanghai as a place that needed to live down its history as a "parasitic consumption city."

Sunan leaders speaking Wu dialect (Shanghainese) in Jiangsu's booming southern cities such as Suzhou and Wuxi have had extensive personal links to Shanghai. They sometimes enjoyed a relatively favorable economic climate Nanjing arranged for them – in fact, they were the biggest beneficiaries of this situation. Shanghai businesspeople often had kin in Jiangnan. They could find personal (local-political) rewards in the larger political structure that emerged, even if it slowed Shanghai's growth.

Tax negotiations

In a pathbreaking move of 1979, the state decided to "divide the stoves from which people eat" (*fenzao chifan*), so that the center disclaimed a right it was slowly losing anyway: It was no longer supposed to take funds arbitrarily from provinces without their leaders' approval.[61] Supervising offices, above the factory or store level where production or services take place, in theory became responsible for losses in units bureaucratically below them – and for subsidizing them when they could not break even.

An annual economic conference in Beijing, which became a regular institution in the 1980s, included the leaders of all provinces, along with representatives of central ministries that wanted money. The centrally appointed leaders of Shanghai attended – and were duly honored for the great sums they volunteered, or 'voluntold,' their city to pay. Even Shanghai people who thought Shanghai's tax from this process was too large could be proud it made a great contribution to China. During this period, the central budget began to develop big deficits, largely because farmers had to be paid real money to supply food for the state's urban workers. Beijing was compelled in some cases explicitly to "borrow" from provincial governments, especially Shanghai. These funds were never returned.

In February 1980, a "financial guarantee system" was mooted in the State Council for all parts of the country.[62] To maintain some predictability in central government revenues, this system was not implemented nationwide on an immediate basis – and when it was implemented, the rate for each place was negotiated separately. What happened, over the next several years, can be schematized in a chart that shows the kind of system that determined each province's revenue retention or subsidy, as well as the coefficients involved. Table 6.6, presenting this information for

TABLE 6.6 Provincial revenue retention and subsidy norms, 1980-1983 (summary of kinds of central government agreements with each locality) (percentages and millions of yuan)

	1980			1981			1982			1983		
	Way %		Subsidy	Way %		Subsidy	Way %		Subsidy	Way %		Subsidy
	(1)	(2)	(3)	(1)	(2)	(3)	(1)	(2)	(3)	(1)	(2)	(3)
Shanghai	Z	8.6%f		Z	8.46%		Z	10.51%		Z	n/a	
Tianjin	Z	30.6%f		Z	31.07%		Z	34.92%		Z	n/a	
Beijing	Z	28.1%f		Z	26.95%		Z	35.49%		Z	n/a	
Liaoning	B	30.1%		B	30.0%		B	30.0%		B	34.2%	

(*Continued*)

TABLE 6.6 Continued

	1980			1981			1982			1983		
	Way %		Subsidy	Way %		Subsidy	Way %		Subsidy	Way %		Subsidy
	(1)	(2)	(3)	(1)	(2)	(3)	(1)	(2)	(3)	(1)	(2)	(3)
Jiangsu	B	39.0%		B	37.0%		B	38.0%		B	35.7%	
Shandong	H	10.0%s		B	48.9%		B	48.9%		B	51.5%	
Zhejiang	H	13.0%s		H	13.0%		B	56.0%		B	51.8%	
Hebei	H	27.2%s		H	27.2%		B	67.5%		B	63.5%	
Hubei	H	44.7%s		H	44.7%		B	69.0%		G	63.8%	
Hunan	H	42.0%s		H	42.0%		B	75.0%		G	70.3%	
Anhui	H	58.1%s		H	58.1%		B	77.0%		B	76.15%	
Henan	H	75.4%s		H	75.4%		B	82.0%		G	77.8%	
Sichuan	H	72.0%s		H	72.0%		B	85.0%		B	83.7%	
Shaanxi	H	88.1%s		H	88.1%		B	100%		B	100%	
Shanxi	H	57.9%s		H	57.9%		H	75.4%		G	82.6%	
Guangdong	D			D			D			D		
Fujian	D		150	D		150	D		150	D		63
Jiangxi	H		138	H		138	H		138	H		150
Gansu	H	53.2%s		H	53.2%		B	80.0%		H		169
Jilin	H		300	H		300	H		300	H		234
Guangxi	H		297	H		327	H		359	H		308
Ningxia	H		300	H		330	H		363	H		355
Qinghai	H		402	H		442	H		486	H		452
Yunnan	H		330	H		477	H		525	H		448
Tibet	H		496	H		546	H		601	H		581
Guizhou	H		526	H		578	H		636	H		597
Heilong'g	H		887	H		887	H		887	H		900
Xinjiang	H		895	H		984	H		1083	H		1121
In. Mong.	H		1168	H		1285	H		1414	H		1387
Total Subsidies			5889			6444			6941			6765

Notes and abbreviations: Blank cells indicate no transfer of money; numbers indicate provincial governments' funds, coming either from retention on the specified bases or from central subsidies. The table has been put in approximate declining order of extraction, based on a revision of the other table on extraction by province; the list in the source is regional. Each tax regime involves three elements:

(1) "Way" or method (*banfa*) of figuring local retention,

Z = zong'e fencheng, percentage part of total revenues is retained by the local government, to be renegotiated each year (in these years, for the then-three "directly ruled cities" only, with Shanghai having much the lowest retention rate)
H = huafen shouzhi, % or amount of specific line items of state revenues and budget is retained by the locality, to be renegotiated each year
B = bili baogan, guarantee to locality of a variable % of local tax revenues only, for several years running
D = da baogan, a "big" guarantee that the province is free of central taxes, for several years running (in these years, only for Guangdong and for Fujian with a subsidy also)
G = guding bili zong'e fencheng, a fixed % of total revenues goes to the locality, for several years running

(2) "Division ratios" (*fencheng bili*),

f = fencheng bili, the locally retained percentage of all local revenues, or
s = gongshang shuiliu, the locally retained percentage of industrial and commercial taxes

(3) "Fixed amounts of subsidy" (*butie ding'e*), for some places.

Source: Tian Yinong, Zhu Fulin, and Xiang Huaicheng, *Zhongguo caizheng guanli tizhi de gaige* (The Structural Reform of Chinese Fiscal Management) (Beijing: Jingji Kexue Chuban She, 1985), 88–1989.

all of China's provinces in the early 1980s, is arranged in approximate descending order by the extraction that each tax regime implied. The rates of impost decreased in later years, but the types of arrangement remained similar. The pattern is motley, and only in the early 1990s did some leaders such as Zhu Rongji seriously propose a uniform tax law to replace it.

Shanghai has been subject to several different fiscal rules, of which the most important lasted from 1976 until the mid-1980s materials crisis. Under the 1976 system, the center set both a revenue target and a local spending target for Shanghai. All other tax collections went to Beijing up to the mandatory revenue target – as well as 70 percent of any above that target, though a close analyst of this situation has claimed, "in practice the target was so high that it was very difficult to overachieve."[63]

By 1985, "slippage" in earlier years showed the structure had to be changed. So the 1976 fiscal reform was reformed yet again. Shanghai was promised 23.2 percent of its "local revenue" that year, apparently not including any from the central state sector in the city. This portion was scheduled to continue for the next six years, although in fact it did not. This percentage was still low, but the center did not budget it in detail. The 1985 total remittances were 77 percent of Shanghai revenue, rather than 88 percent as in 1980–1984. This was still far too high to keep most factories open, as events soon showed. There is an uncharitable way to put this: Either the Beijing-appointed Shanghai municipal leaders in 1985 made faulty economic predictions, or else they acted more on the basis of their own partialities and careers (which depended on central remittances) rather than the interests of the city.

Yet a third fiscal reform was needed already by 1988 because of the hepatitis epidemic and low collections over the previous two years. There had been yet more "slippage." So the tinkering continued: from a low percentage of retention back to a low absolute amount of retention (as in 1976). The weight of net tax, figured either way, was the main issue; but a discourse on methods obfuscated it with some success. The city fathers agreed to a "contract," committing Shanghai to remit 10.5 b. each year from 1988 to 1990, retaining the rest. This was better than the previous tax regime, but still much the heaviest for any Chinese province. The "slippages" of 1981–1983 and 1986–1988 were the main generators of fiscal reform in Shanghai.

Although Shanghai came out worse than any other province in terms of each set of extraction rules, the municipality claimed to extend a more uniform system over its own subordinate areas. By 1985, the portion of urban districts' revenue they could keep was raised; they retained almost a quarter (23 percent on average) of the profits from district-managed firms. District and county governments signed five-year remittance contracts with the city in 1988. Budgeting for local governments was not zero-base; it explicitly started from "the basic figures for last year's receipts and expenditures."[64] But receipts rose, and local expenditures were largely off budgets.

Sometimes, when the central state was strapped for funds, it solved the problem by neglecting to pay its bills rather than by trying to raise more money. The most public example during the early and mid-1980s came in the form of unexpected

148 Tax collectors and subsidizers

deductions from the salary checks of state workers. Mandatory payroll deduction schemes were instituted by 1983–1984 for involuntary purchases of state bonds.[65] The rates of this confiscation were not high (about 20 yuan per year for people with normal incomes, and more for anyone who was affluent). Such bonds had five-year maturities, with no option of early redemption. By 1986, speculators in Shanghai purchased the bonds at discounts of about 20 percent. So shortly thereafter, the People's Bank of China began redeeming them at face value. This did involve the state's "face" and may have been necessary to keep a Ponzi scheme credible, although investment information on these bonds was scanty.[66] It was difficult for bond holders to get their funds, partly because bank hours were restricted. The wage-based bonds made clear, however, that state imposts could be placed in an unexpected way on individuals directly (even if, for practical reasons, they were administered through banks). Reforms did not eliminate direct extractions of this sort.

By 1987, the fiscal guarantee system was extended to districts by the city (just as the central government extended it then to Shanghai as a whole). The slogans governing this fiscal localization were nearly the same between districts and municipality as they were between provinces and Beijing: "definite amounts of payment, linking income to expenditures, sharing the total sum, and fixing the system for three years" (*ziding jishu, shouzhi guagou, zong'e fencheng*, and *yiding sannian*).[67]

Localization at lower administrative levels brought more practical autonomy than localization to the province-municipality did, because the top rungs of provinces were generally staffed by loyal centrists on Leninist appointment escalators. The Latinate abstract " -tion" ending of a word like "localization" may suggest that any such change was passive. It was not a "decentralization" policy of Beijing. Mostly it was a policy of many local leaders, reacting in parallel to similar unintended circumstances. The relation of Shanghai's top leadership to the center was different from the relation of more local chiefs to them. Further "down" this large formal system, the heads of scattered offices had increasing independence. Span-of-control issues in China's lanky bureaucracy were endemic, especially for control of small-size units that were run by little dictators. This slowly became more true of urban, not just rural, localities.

By 1988 in the hepatitis epidemic, Shanghai relaxed rules by which tax receipts would be divided between the city and its urban districts or counties. An expenditure base was set for each district or county, which could keep that amount. Revenues above that were divided. Districts and counties were "guaranteed" 70 percent, giving the city 30 percent for two years; and for the next three, the division was supposed to be equal. Macroeconomic five-year planning was a fantasy after reforms, and more local units hid parts of the tax base. This plan was called "guarantee the base, divide the increment, and set [this plan] for five years" (*jishu baogan, zengshou fencheng, yiding wunian*).[68]

A report covered the seven county-level jurisdictions, nationwide in China, that during 1988 paid the highest state revenues. *All* these counties turned out to be in Jiangnan (three near Wuxi, one near Hangzhou, plus three counties of Shanghai).[69]

Such statistics might suggest that the Yangzi delta was the only rich part of China, though it was not. Guangdong benefited from being peripheral – and invested by Hong Kong tycoons, who despise taxes. Chengdu benefited from being far to the west. There are other rich Chinese places. Jiangnan was the rich part that paid the highest extraction rates. No explanation separate from central political habit is obvious to this author, but perhaps other researchers can find one.

The basic productive units in any economy are enterprises; and an even more local look at these shows big differences between firms in the same fields but different places. They compete with each other for both inputs and markets. Variation in their tax treatment directly affects their ability to survive. Many local industrial yearbooks published in China during reforms offer detailed data, institutional as well as statistical, about particular plants. In 1983 for example, the Shanghai Flour Factory had production per unit of capital at about the same rate as was reported from a similar "keypoint" flour factory in Guangzhou. But the Shanghai mill paid about half again as much state profits and taxes per unit of capital. In another case, data for the Shanghai Cigarette Factory, when compared with those from all other "keypoint" cigarette factories (in Changde, Kunming, Qingdao, and Wuhan) show that while the 1983 return of profits and taxes per yuan of fixed capital averaged 60 percent higher in Shanghai, and of operating capital a sharp 288 percent higher, the Shanghai return per yuan of sales revenue after taxes was 11 percent lower.[70]

Shanghai managers thus customarily hid more funds (especially liquid non-fixed capital) than did managers elsewhere, because they customarily had to pay higher rates of tax and profit extraction. These greater rates of impost gave Shanghai cadres greater incentives to obfuscate the ways they handled their factories' money. What firms (or provinces or other jurisdictions) do is determined by a highly political combination of secrecy and bargaining. Premises about standard procedures cannot explain the observable pattern. Every tax in China, at least until the 1990s, has been a particular arrangement.

Summary results of heavy taxes

Shanghai investment was reportedly only 2 percent of the national total over the first three decades of the PRC.[71] So the city's capital stock was very old by the end of this period. It had scarcely changed half a dozen years later, in the mid-1980s. The city's industrial equipment became antiquated, and sectors that paid higher imposts did not all receive higher reimbursements for depreciation. From 1949 to 1978, investment in Shanghai's light industry was only 4.3 percent of the city's total industrial investment. Even this small amount could not be used freely by factory managers; it came in the form of funds assigned for particular purposes, and these line items were not easily fungible.[72]

Shanghai's cotton textile industry, in particular, was a "tree for shaking off money."[73] Profits from Shanghai cloth production accounted for 30 percent of the national total from that industry in 1979 – and textiles provided 39 percent of the city's total industrial profits. But in the three decades after 1949, the state invested

150 Tax collectors and subsidizers

only 500 m. yuan in Shanghai textile plants. Eighty percent of the cloth factory premises in 1980 dated from before the anti-Japanese War.[74]

Even by 1987, one-third of the machines under the Shanghai Textile Bureau had been built in the 1930s or 1940s – slightly less than in other light industries, because the relative ease of state control over bulk cotton inputs made cloth an especially lucrative source of remittances. In the woolen industry, however, the portion of pre-1950 machines was even higher, four-fifths.[75] Differences of this sort, as interviewees confirm, correlated with varying degrees of freedom given to plant managers. High-tax-yield production was more monitored and supported by the state, whose personnel resources did not allow the same intensity of control over low-tax-yield industries.[76]

Equipment in the country as a whole was newer than in Shanghai. By 1985, one-third of the machines used nationally in large and medium plants had been made during that decade; and 77 percent had been produced in the 1970s or 1980s. Less than one-quarter predated 1970.[77] These portions show reluctance by PRC planners to retire old machines anywhere, but Shanghai was forced to make do with ancient capital much longer than other cities.

The capital Shanghai received was often of most use to Beijing bureaucracies. Huge amounts were poured into a few large blueprints for centrally owned plants. The most famous example was the Baoshan Steel Mill, in Wusong on the Yangzi shore north of the main city. Local and national debate raged during the late 1970s on this financially and ecologically dubious project. In June 1979, the State Finance and Economic Commission discussed the Baoshan Steel Mill, and mistakes of planning were admitted. But "because construction had already been decided," there were calls for the whole Party to unify behind the project.[78] Baoshan confirmed an ex-Stalinist investment strategy for China's biggest city.[79]

High-technology development in the metropolis was seen by socialist conservatives as a threat to tax collection. Local housing maintenance costs were another threat to total extraction (when the government had paid some of them). The central bureaucracy's abstemious attitude toward Shanghai hurt not only the productive infrastructure, but also the livelihoods of people. Fiscal imposts affect lives, not just bureaucratic budgets, and good housing was most obvious among the shortages caused by high taxation. Various parts of Shanghai and different specific families varied considerably in the amount of space they had. Suburban peasants naturally had much more room in which to live than did dwellers of the built-up city – and farmers near the edge of the metropolis leased living space to immigrants without legal household registrations, often at high rents.

The severe, long-term deficit in Shanghai housing was inseparable from a similar deficit in public transport. Most new housing was far away from workplaces in the city. Planners resisted the idea that people should live where they wished, instead of in satellite towns. General spending for maintenance of the city was budgeted abstemiously, at 3 percent of government expenditure from 1957 to 1965, up to 6.3 percent in 1981 because by then the need for upkeep had become acute.[80] This was evident in all kinds of urban infrastructure. Compared with the other sixteen largest PRC cities, Shanghai on a per capita basis in 1985 had fewer hospital beds, university places, or consumer service units.[81]

Only 50 percent of telephone calls got through to their recipients in mid-1980s Shanghai, even with redialing. It was commonly known that, during business hours, numbers with some exchange prefixes were effectively unavailable; the caller would hear signals indicating that the system was more or less permanently busy until evening after offices closed. Of switchboards, lines, and other telephone equipment, three-tenths were thirty or more years old.[82] This situation improved toward the end of the decade, because the government correctly sensed that business investors would not come if they could not make phone calls. But in 1987, Beijing had 7.0 telephones for each hundred people in the urban districts, while Shanghai had 4.8 phones.[83] Later, by the 1990s and 2000s, the arthritic state-run landlines were almost completely displaced by cell phones.

The 1986–1990 Five-Year Plan was mostly earmarked for big projects such as Shanghai's port expansion, sewage plants, and (because the need was so obvious) some new housing. Parks and schools had lower priority.[84] Reforms, in other words, did not lessen the pressure of taxes on people's daily lives. A city official claimed: "The average Shanghainese is not happy. He works hard to contribute one out of every six yuan the country spends, but he cannot even get a decent place to live."[85]

National patterns of funding altered sharply by the mid-1980s – and this is made clearest if the situation of that period is compared with earlier decades. The documented portion of all China's government budgets spent by central ministries decreased from about 70 percent in the 1950s, down to 60 percent in the 1960s, and further down to an average of about 50 percent in the first seven years of the 1980s. From 1981 to 1985, the portion of the state budget transferred to individuals, especially as wages and bonuses, exceeded three-fifths. Also, the portion of national income in the hands of local governments, enterprises, functional agencies, and service units – but outside their budgets – increased from 14 percent in 1979 to 21 percent in 1986.[86] Even though the extrabudgetary income of these nominally subordinate units was reported only half as large as the state budget, the increments in absolute values by the mid-1980s were similar, as between the PRC budget and reported extrabudgets.

Shanghai in late reforms badly needed general infrastructure, but central conservatives still wanted to keep money for firms that produced the greatest tax revenues. The response of Shanghai local leaders, more independent by the 1990s, was to invest in infrastructure with large loans, whose repayment would require putting money later into factories. As the Director of the Shanghai Planning Commission explained, "The [investment limit] 'cage' was really too small. . . . Now that infrastructural projects were already in progress, we could only cut the industrial projects. But in this way, we would have cut our ability to pay back the loans for infrastructural projects."[87]

In 1990, when China's President Yang Shangkun visited Shanghai, some local people "complained to him about the plight of Shanghai and mocked that they wondered whether it was the center's policy to see the decline of Shanghai." Yang reassured Shanghai leaders that "the center was determined to assist Shanghai," and he claimed that Deng Xiaoping (also then in town) had the same view.[88] They were grateful for the city's relative quiescence in 1989, under then-Mayor and Premier-to-be Zhu Rongji.

So Beijing leaders gradually rethought the national economic structure. April 1990 and March 1992 saw new central concessions of powers to the city. These surely aided urban Shanghai's change in the early 1990s, and a political view of the situation is that Beijing at this time had no other option. Safety for the regime lay, more clearly than before, in lower rates of extraction from this metropolis. During later years, from the 1990s under Presidents Jiang Zemin, Hu Jintao, and Xi Jinping, Shanghai infrastructure projects for highways, bridges, and mass transit were lavishly supported. After decades of neglect, China's largest metropolis built modern infrastructure. A recent book reports a Chinese saying: "If you want wealth, first fix the road" (*yao zhifu, xian xiulu*).[89] Money for this was more forthcoming after 1990.

Cellular bargaining vs. overall planning: Jiangsu, Zhejiang, Shanghai and "Beijing"

The extractive *and* cellular pattern during reforms meant that decisions were made variously at different times to maximize taxes or to maintain local exemptions. Jiangsu was often more successful in political negotiating than was Shanghai, partly because the newness and geographical dispersion of Sunan rural industries made extraction more difficult for high officials, and partly because norms that constrained growth have been ignored more readily in that province – and in Zhejiang. Jiangsu overtook Shanghai in the mid-1980s as China's most productive province.

Less than a month after the Gang of Four was arrested in 1976, Jiangsu was designated an "experimental province" for fiscal reforms. Beijing set a yearly portion of Jiangsu revenues that would be handed over to the central budget. In 1977, this amount was 58 percent of the local fiscal intake (and from 1978 to 1980, it was 57 percent). Under a four-year guarantee, Jiangsu could keep the remainder.[90] Like Guangdong or Fujian – but unlike neighboring Shanghai – Jiangsu was officially allowed to prosper. But no standard for uniform treatment guided decisions in China as a whole. The cellular structure meant that each compartment had an individualized regime. Taxes were haggled, year by year and place by place.

Some payments, even after reforms, have been traditional and in kind, not in money. At least twenty provinces agreed to give the central government first claim on negotiated amounts of specific classes of produce. In the case of Shanghai, light industrial products as a group are among those which central ministries supposedly had options to buy. These were "appropriated commodities" (*diaobo shangpin*). They were not purchased by the central government ('Beijing'), but were simply transferred to its offices, much as tribute in imperial times had been shipped on the Grand Canal to the northern capital.

Shanghai's tributes included many consumer durables, such as refrigerators and color TV sets. Money for the budget in Beijing was always the most important contribution from the Yangzi metropolis, but in the 1980s years of barter trade, goods were often paid too. A Shanghai economist averred that the process for determining this structure of taxes, prices, profits, and production has been guided not by economic principles but by political ones. He sarcastically chided the State Planning Commission for being, in practice though not in name, just a "State Bargaining Commission" ('*guojia tanpan weiyuan hui*' was his memorable, mocking phrase).[91]

Similar negotiations took place periodically in Beijing at national conferences setting provinces' share of central revenues and disbursements. Shanghai's top leaders were often deemed to have their jobs because they made big promises of remittances, while representatives of poorer inland provinces could offer much less. Bureaucrats in the central government supported the idea that Shanghai should make large contributions, since it had always done so. But this history of haggling ended with centralizing changes after localizing reforms in the wake of Tiananmen, 1989. Shanghai was restored as a major financial center, though its overall output was overtaken by other Chinese places with which it had close links, especially in Jiangnan. In rural areas, counties were more tightly integrated under state supervision. Counties became fiscal "leviathans" over towns, although links to village cadres frayed.[92]

In later centralizing years, Shanghai dipped down among China's top dozen province-level units by output value. The top four in order eventually became Guangdong, Jiangsu, Shandong, and Zhejiang.[93] In 1994, Zhu Rongji's efforts to counteract the political and economic effects of the 1980s inflation had brought serious controls; so the reported share of central revenues among all extractions jumped above 55 percent (and local revenues dropped to less than 45 percent).[94] Just a year earlier, in 1993, the center had collected less than a quarter of total taxes; so the reported central portion doubled in a single year. Zhu surely led a "reform," but it was not like the reforms of 1970–1990. This change differed from the localizing reforms of the previous three decades. In later years up to the present, the central and local portions of revenue remained within five percentage points of an equal division between them.

Notes

1 "Tax" is different from "profit" – but in China, profits from state-owned industries mostly go to governments. Later pages include a discussion of the reform policy of "replacing profits with taxes." This slogan does not illegitimate treatment of their aggregate, which at least until the mid-1980s was largely *de facto* tax administered in many complex ways.
2 *Shanghai caizheng yanjiu* (Shanghai Financial Research), February 1985, 10.
3 *Far Eastern Economic Review*, Hong Kong, December 12, 1985, 28.
4 Linda Li, using the statistical yearbooks, ch. 4, 24.
5 This estimate, based on official sources, must reflect the conclusions of limited-circulation (unavailable) reports. "Scarcity value" is a term that could have several definitions, but we can trust that the renowned economist Ma Hong used a viable one. The amount of retail products sold in rural areas was 81 b. yuan, and all rural products garnered 46 b. that year. The government's total 1978 revenue from police effects on prices might therefore have been *very* roughly 25 b. yuan, or about one-fifth of the value of all these exchanges (127 b. yuan). Calculated from *Zhongguo jingji jiegou wenti yanjiu* (Studies on

154 Tax collectors and subsidizers

Issues of Chinese Economic Structure), Ma Hong and Sun Shangqing, eds. (Beijing: Renmin Chuban She, 1981), 126–27.

6 The agricultural subsidiary products sold to Shanghai were worth 2.776 billion, but this should be reduced by the 0.408 b. such goods that left the city. The real price is found as the quotient of that difference divided by 0.725 (unity minus the average of 25 and 30 percent). Ibid. and Tao Yongkuan, *Dali fazhan disan chanye* (Vigorously Develop Tertiary Industry) (Shanghai: Shanghai Shehui Kexue Yuan Chuban She, 1986), 72.

7 The numbers are: 11.979 b. yuan total 1983 Shanghai industrial domestic exports, minus 2.008 b. similar imports, making a net of 9.971 b., divided by 1.175 (unity plus the average of 15 and 20 percent), to render a real value of 8.486 b., which exceeds the nominal value by 1.485 b. yuan, viz. the implicit subsidy. *Zhongguo jingji jiegou wenti yanjiu*, 126–27; and Tao Yongkuan, *Dali fazhan disan chanye*, 72.

8 The main point in this calculation does not depend on the precise figures (which can also be made using 1978, 1980, and 1984 figures in the sources). By no means did the revenues from implicit subsidies all stay in Shanghai; they were included in profits, largely from state-owned industries, and the bulk of them were remitted into the central budget in any case. The 1983 revenue figure is a sum of 15.4 b. budgetary and 4.5 b. yuan extrabudgetary monies; see *Zhongguo caizheng tongji, 1950–1985* (Chinese Fiscal Statistics, 1950–1985), Comprehensive Planning Office of the PRC Ministry of Finance, ed. (Beijing: Zhongguo Caizheng Jingji Chuban She, 1987), 54 and 144.

9 From a discussion with a very well-informed economist, not in Shanghai, who referred to reports on this subject that he could not safely show me.

10 Linda Chelan Li, "Provincial Discretion and National Power: Investment Policy in Guangdong and Shanghai, 1978–1993" (manuscript of May 1996), 7.

11 Ibid., ch. 6, 35.

12 Economist Audrey Donnithorne has used this metaphor of the sponge.

13 This is indebted to a talk by Yang Dali on "China's Illiberal Regulatory State," Princeton University on April 25, 2016. On bodies, environs, and earnings, see Karl Polanyi, *The Great Transformation*). Also Samuel Huntington, *Political Order in Changing Societies*.

14 See Audrey Donnithorne, "Comment: Centralization and Decentralization in China's Fiscal Management," *China Quarterly* 66 (June 1976), 328–39, and Nicholas Lardy's immediately following "Comment." Donnithorne's previous works, "China's Cellular Economy," 605–12, and *China's Economic System* (New York: Praeger, 1967) were background. Lardy later published *Economic Growth and Distribution in China* (Cambridge: Cambridge University Press, 1978).

15 See Thomas P. Lyons, *Economic Integration and Planning in Maoist China* (New York: Columbia University Press, 1987).

16 See Barry Naughton, "The Third Front: Defence Industrialization in the Chinese Interior," *China Quarterly* 115 (September 1988), 351–86.

17 Franz Schurmann, *Ideology and Organization in Communist China*, James R. Townsend, *Political Participation in Communist China* (Berkeley and Los Angeles: University of California Press, 1967), and G. William Skinner, "Marketing and Social Structure,"

18 Robert Michael Field, Nicholas R. Lardy, and John Philip Emerson, *Provincial Industrial Output in the People's Republic of China: 1949–75* (Washington, DC: U.S. Department of Commerce, Bureau of Economic Analysis, 1976), 11, 20–30, also U.S. National Foreign Assessment Center, *China: Gross Value of Industrial Output, 1965–77* (Washington, DC: National Foreign Assessment Center, 1978), 5. For an earlier estimate in different prices, see *A Reconstruction of the Gross Value of Industrial Output by Province in the People's Republic of China: 1949–73* (Washington, DC: U.S. Department of Commerce, 1975), Table 2, 9. The much later Chinese *SHTJNJ86*, 44, says the 1957 industrial output figure was 11,851 million yuan – so the 1975 estimate published in Washington is not very far away from the 1987 one published in China. Considering the climate of scarce data in which Field, Lardy, and Emerson then worked, that was an accomplishment.

19 Not all investment went to industry – housing, roads, and agriculture claimed shares – but most of it was industrial. Counting all of it as industrial would not much alter the

conclusions below. See Lardy, "Centralization . . . ," 40. In a personal communication, Nick Lardy agreed that the 250 million rough estimate might be reasonable.

20 This 1957 rate of investment does not generally underestimate Shanghai's industrial investment for the whole Maoist period. Within the First Five-Year Plan, 1957 was almost surely the highest year for Shanghai investment; and 1953–1957 capitalization in Shanghai was reportedly a greater portion at least of local revenue (0.0725) than in the whole 1949–1973 period (0.067). See Lardy, "Economic Planning . . . ," 112.

21 Statistics from Field, Lardy, and Emerson, *Reconstruction*. . ., loc. cit., imply that Shanghai's portion of China's total GVIO declined only slightly over about two decades (from 19 percent in 1952 to 16.5 percent in 1971). Michael Field, "Civilian Industrial Production in the PRC: 1949–74," in *China: A Reassessment* . . ., 149, reports China's industrial economy was, over this term, expanding at about 13 percent per annum; so Shanghai's industry must have grown almost as fast, since its portion of the country's total was fairly stable. More recent information could be used for this estimate; but the data previously published are as appropriate for the argument, are substantially the same, and show the ability of outside economists to make credible estimates even with figures from the late Mao period.

22 W. Arthur Lewis, *The Theory of Economic Growth* (Homewood: Irwin, 1955), 201.

23 Some ideas in this paragraph are from Nicholas Lardy, who generously commented in a personal communication on an earlier version of this argument. Audrey Donnithorne has also offered ideas on it, and I am grateful to both. Lardy's stress on coastal taxation and Donnithorne's stress on "cellularity" are both accurate – and entirely compatible with each other.

24 Robert Dorfman, Paul A. Samuelson, and Robert Solow, *Linear Programming and Economic Analysis* (New York: McGraw-Hill, 1958), 330–31 and generally chap. 12. Economists ordinarily use this "turnpike model" to analyze sectors defined by savings and consumption – but its beauty is that it can apply to any sectoralization.

25 Quoted in Rhoads Murphey, *Shanghai: Key to Modern China* (Cambridge: Harvard University Press, 1953), 27–28. See also Janet Salaff, "The Urban Communes and Anti-City Experiment in Communist China," *China Quarterly* (January-March 1967), esp. 83–84.

26 *Chairman Mao Talks to the People*, Stuart R. Schram, ed. (New York: Pantheon, 1974), 61–83.

27 Henry Chu, "Beijing Orders Army to Give Up Its Businesses," *Los Angeles Times*, July 23, 1998.

28 Teresa Wright, *Accepting Authoritarianism*.

29 Calculated from *FEER*, December 11, 1986, 82.

30 "*Tong de tai duo, guande tai si,*" The new fiscal system was called "*caizheng guanli fenji,*" Jiang Zemin et al., *Shanghai dangzheng jigou yange* (The Transformation of Shanghai's Party and Administration) (Shanghai: Shanghai Renmin Chuban She, 1988), 143.

31 I divided figures on sales-tax creation per worker by figures on revenue production per worker in *Shanghai gongye jingji bao* (Shanghai Industrial Economy), August 19, 1988. Approximate rates were: Beijing, 22 percent; Shanghai and Wuhan, 21 percent; Dalian, 20 percent; Tianjin, 19 percent; Guangzhou, 18 percent; Qingdao, 17 percent; Chongqing, 15 percent; Haerbin and Xi'an, 14 percent; Wuxi, 13 percent; and Suzhou, 12 percent. Interviewees said sales taxes were incompletely paid in places where goods were produced.

32 Cao Linzhang, Gu Guangqing, and Li Jianhua, *Shanghai shengchan*, 222; for some additional information, see also *Shuiwu gongzuo shouce* (Tax Work Handbook), Zou Yunfang, ed. (Beijing: Nengyuan Chuban She, 1987), 119 and other pages.

33 Parks Coble, *Shanghai Capitalists*.

34 Zhu Xingqing, an editor at the quasi-dissident *World Economic Herald* with whom I also conversed, is quoted in *FEER*, December 11, 1986, 83.

35 See Nicholas R. Lardy, "Comment," *China Quarterly* 66 (June 1976), 349.

36 *LDB*, April 26, 1950.

37 *New China News Agency*, Shanghai, August 31, 1953.

156 Tax collectors and subsidizers

38 *NCNA*, January 14, 1956.

39 *NCNA*, February 15 and May 30, 1956; *JFRB*, June 4, 1956.

40 *XWRB*, January 19, 1957, implies that the modal ejected factory moved thirty employees, and the average moved store had eleven; but many were larger.

41 See Lynn White, "The Road to Urumqi: Approved Institutions in Search of Attainable Goals in Pre-1968 Rustication from Shanghai," *China Quarterly* 79 (October 1979), 481–510.

42 This "accumulation tax" would, if enforced, reduce private capital sharply. *SHJJ*, April 1988, 26.

43 Based on an interview in Shanghai, also sources in adjacent footnotes.

44 *SJJDB*, August 29, 1988.

45 See Lynn White, "Joint Ventures in a New Shanghai at Pudong," in *Advances in Chinese Industrial Studies: Joint Ventures in the PRC*, Sally Stewart, ed. (Greenwich, CT: JAI Press, 1995), 75–120.

46 *FBIS*, February 1, 1988, 35–36, radio of January 18.

47 This word could also be translated as "Obedient," *ZGQNB*, September 20, 1988.

48 This kind of company is called a *taozhai gongsi. JFRB*, May 9, 1988.

49 The extent of this "*kongzhi*" is stressed in *Zhongguo shehui zhuyi chengshi jingji xue* (Chinese Socialist Urban Economics), Zhu Linxing, ed. (Shanghai: Shanghai Shehui Kexue Chuban She, 1986), 41.

50 For more about these negotiations, see Michel Oksenberg and James Tong, "The Evolution of Central-Provincial Fiscal Relations in China, 1971–1984: The Formal System," *China Quarterly* 125 (March 1991), 1–32.

51 Jiangsu, however, did notably well in this period. See Penelope B. Prime, "The Paradox of Industrial Take-off in Jiangsu Province During the Cultural Revolution," paper presented at Harvard University in May, 1987.

52 Interview with a Shanghai economist, who used the phrase "*quanguo baohu Shanghai*,"

53 *Shanghai jingji, neibu ben: 1949–1982*, 798.

54 "*Dingshou dingzhi, shouzhi baogan*" sounds strikingly like slogans of the mid-1980s, although it comes from 1970 (in a plan first implemented the next year). So does the next sentence's "*xiafang caiquan*," *SHJJNBB49–82*, 891.

55 Ibid., "*baozheng shangjiao, jieyu liuyong, yinian yiding*."

56 Ibid. quotes the expenditure target at 961 billion yuan. The rate of overfulfillment of the 1971 revenue target was 3 percent. Even this limited-circulation source does not give such detailed figures on reform years – maybe because the Shanghai economists who wrote it were especially upset by the exorbitant tax rates during the early 1970s proto-reforms.

57 Ibid.

58 *Shanghai jingji, neibu ben: 1949–1982*, 30, presents graphs that suggest this.

59 Small fees on real estate, licenses, and other items were introduced after 1977 to raise more local revenues. Most state revenues continued to come from profits and taxes on state companies. *Shanghai jingji, neibu ben*, 892.

60 Emily Honig, *Creating Chinese Ethnicity: Subei People in Shanghai, 1850–1980* (New Haven: Yale University Press, 1992).

61 *SHJJDB*, July 25, 1988. The difficulty of keeping stoves together, for a household, is a full symbol of modernization in Margery Wolf, *The House of Lim* (Boston: Beacon, 1972).

62 *Zhonghua renmin gonghe guo jingji dashi ji, 1949–1980* (Chronicle of Economic Events in the PRC, 1949–1980), Fang Weizhong, ed. (Beijing: Zhongguo Kexue Chuban She, 1984), 645.

63 See Linda Chelan Li, ch. 4, 23. For facts in the next paragraph, see 25–27.

64 *JFRB*, April 1, 1988.

65 This material comes mainly from interviews in Shanghai.

66 Charles Ponzi, a Bostonian, in 1919 paid back old investors with "interest" money he received from new ones. Ponzi schemes work, without any productive investment, so long as public credibility in them continues to escalate. Then they can collapse spectacularly.

67 *SHJJNJ88*, 100–02.
68 *JFRB*, February 4, 1988. Planning ended during reforms, except for some large capital projects.
69 In order by amount of payment: Wuxi County (Jiangsu), Chuansha (Shanghai), Jiading (Shanghai), Changshu [county-level] City (Jiangsu), Xiaoshan City (Zhejiang), Jiangyang City (Jiangsu), and Nanhui County (Shanghai). *XMWB*, January 24, 1989. China at this time had more than 2,000 counties, plus 200 odd county-level cities. The seven that paid most taxes were all in Jiangnan.
70 Calculated from tables in *Zhongguo gongye de fazhan, 1949–1984*, 160 and 163 (where an average is taken of rates from the four non-Shanghai cigarette plants). The Chinese and international politics of nicotine addiction is a sadly reliable supplier of revenues. *The Political Mapping of China's Tobacco Industry and Anti-Smoking Campaign* (Washington, DC: Brookings Institution, 2012) is one of many pioneering researches by Cheng Li (orig. Li Cheng).
71 *Zhongguo shehui zhuyi chengshi jingji xue*, 89.
72 *WHB*, December 4, 1979.
73 "*Yao qian shu*," *WHB*, August 10, 1980.
74 *WHB*, August 10, 1980.
75 *Hengxiang jingji*, 131.
76 For general treatment of the political importance of CCP personnel scarcity, Lynn White, *Policies of Chaos*, which explains the Cultural Revolution policies of "rebels" largely as echoes of 1950s and early-1960s policies by which the new state saved resources by scaring, bossing, and labeling people in administratively handy categories.
77 *CD*, February 1, 1988.
78 *Zhonghua Renmin Gonghe Guo jingji dashi ji*, 625.
79 The city's second-largest capital construction project was the Shanghai Shidong No. 2 Power Plant (like Baoshan also in Wusong). It was built with funds raised by the Huaneng International Power Development Company and the Shanghai government. *FBIS*, February 2, 1988, 36, radio of January 30.
80 *Shanghai jingji, neibu ben*, 913.
81 Reginald Yin-wang Kwok, "Metropolitan Development in China: A Struggle Between Contradictions," *Habitat International* 12:4 (1988), 201–02.
82 Tao Yongkuan, *Dali fazhan*, 59.
83 Calculated from *Zhongguo chengshi tongji nianjian, 1988* (Statistical Yearbook of Chinese Cities, 1988), State Statistical Bureau, ed. (Beijing: Zhongguo Tongji Xinxi Zixun Fuwu Zhongxin and Xin Shijie Chuban She, 1988), 23–25 for the population figures and 239–41 for the telephones.
84 See *FEER*, December 12, 1985, 30.
85 Ibid., 28.
86 This statistic is called the "*difang, bumen, qiye he shiye danwei zhangwo de yusuan wai zijin*." Ibid., 14, also says its average rate of increase from 1979 to 1985 was 22.4 percent.
87 Chen Xianglin's speech to a 1989 NPC meeting is quoted in Linda Li, ch. 6, 27.
88 Quoted from interviews by Linda Li, ch. 6, 11.
89 Hongyi Lai, *China's Governance Model*, 44, offers this nice slogan while translating it more abstractly.
90 *Zhonghua renmin gonghe guo jingji dashi ji*, 571.
91 Interview in Shanghai, November 1988. This economist thereafter departed from China.
92 Juan Wang, *Sinews*, 125.
93 By 2014, Shanghai was twelfth (on a purchasing power parity basis), according to the International Monetary Fund's *World Economic Outlook Database*, www.imf.org/external/ns/cs.aspx?id=28 – but it is relevant that the municipality's closest-linked provinces, Jiangsu and Zhejiang, remained among the wealthiest four.
94 Figure 7.1 in Yongnian Zheng (with Yanjie Huang), *Market in State*, based on National Bureau of Statistics data. See also Yongnian Zheng, *De Facto Federalism in China: Reforms and Dynamics of Central-Local Relations* (Singapore: World Scientific, 2007).

7

BUDGETEERS FACE THE 1980S CRISIS

China's government budget deficit rose by 50 billion yuan from 1979 to 1986.[1] Shortages of public funds at many sizes of administration did not appear suddenly. Attention to Shanghai, which provided the highest rate of revenue, reveals some reasons for the national problem. Revenues remitted in 1979 from the city's state enterprises were 9.5 percent higher than in 1978, but their incomes were only up 1.8 percent. In the next year, Shanghai state firm profits rose only 2.9 percent – but their incomes decreased 1.9 percent. By 1981, because of rules allowing more profit retention and lower product prices, total revenues remitted from state enterprises were down 4.7 percent. So 1981–1983 saw Shanghai's first "fiscal slippage" (*caizheng huapo*), a term that came into official discourse only in the middle 1980s, especially during the second slippage after 1986. Competition from other provinces that paid lower rates had caused reductions of state profit remittances from Shanghai.[2]

This aspect of reforms becomes clearest when contrasted with the very different post-Tiananmen 1990s, when tax collectors garnered more for the state. They revived fiscal authoritarianism in local polities, at least down to the size of counties, not just the national bureaucracy. Cadres at medium bureaucratic levels extracted more from tillers – and this change along with local leaders' private predations caused national ministries to fear that farmers would become restive against the Party-state. A recent book by Hiroki Takeuchi shows that the authoritarian central regime cared more about political threats than about failures of governments to provide public goods, even as the supply of private goods rose.[3] Beijing claimed to "reform" taxes by the new century, but these changes were mainly aimed at recentralizing domination after small localities had become stronger. Fiscal effects of 1970–1990 reforms brought reactive policies later.

After reform deficits became too obvious to hide by the late 1970s, "fiscal slippage" worsened quickly from the viewpoint of the state. In 1981, realized profits and taxes for each unit of fixed capital in Shanghai was 3.4 times the national average; but by 1983, they dropped to 3.1 times the national average. If the same comparison is made to include working capital, the decrease is from 3.1 times to 2.8 times.[4]

Technical improvements in nearby provinces created sharp competition for Shanghai. Whereas the city had won 49 percent of the first prizes in product fairs during 1980, it won only 41 percent by 1981, and 37 percent in 1982. Shanghai could still sell many manufactures; but its relative inability to reinvest profits, rather than sending them to the central treasury, was one of the factors that eroded its old claim to make China's best goods.

Rural prosperity created much bigger domestic markets. This benefited Shanghai firms as well as their competitors. By the early 1980s, even though Shanghai's total shipments of industrial goods did not rise quickly, the city sent out larger quantities of consumer durables. Washing machine sales in 1982, for example, went up by 116 percent; bicycles rose 36 percent; tape recorders, 33 percent; and sewing machines, 26 percent.[5] These figures for selected goods, combined with stagnant total sales values for all goods, imply that domestic exports within China of other major commodities (apparently including textiles and tractors, and perhaps machines generally) decreased from Shanghai in the early 1980s. Other Chinese places now sold more textiles and tractors.

In 1983, Shanghai made 13 percent of China's light industrial products – a portion that had gradually declined from over 20 percent in the 1950s – but it was still generating 18 percent of the China's taxes and profits. The city sent most products (more than three-fifths) to other provinces, and a further portion went abroad.[6] This had been the city's strength for most of a century, but reforms gave Shanghai competitors in old fields. Because the state plan still required very high taxes and remittances from the city, it could not easily move into new fields.

Budget effects of inland competition in old rather than high-tech industries

Economists at the Shanghai Academy of Social Sciences tried to calculate the extent to which the decline of revenues (profits and taxes) in Shanghai state industries can be attributed to rising raw materials prices in 1985–1987. They estimated this effect by a ratio: The numerator was the change of actually remitted taxes and profits. The denominator was factories' income change because of materials price increases. If high, this ratio would show the effect on remittances for each change of Shanghai enterprise income due to rising factor prices. It was an index of the government's ability to control prices on Shanghai's ability to pay taxes and profits. Putting actual figures into the model showed that 75 percent of the reduction in Shanghai state industry's capacity to remit money, during 1986 and 1987 compared with 1985, was linked to factor price changes.[7]

The same calculation can also be performed sectorally, to show that materials price rises accounted for 97 percent of the revenues "lost" in metals other than steel, as well as 77 percent in steel, 73 percent in ordinary machines, 69 percent in rubber, 40 percent in plastics, 14 percent in electronics and telecommunications, and

160 Budgeteers face the 1980s crisis

11 percent in precision machinery.[8] So Shanghai's high-tech industries, in which the crucial input was skilled labor, fared better in mid-1980s inflation than did the state's old tax producers.

In other words, the materials crisis ironically forced a new structure in the city's economy that the bureaucracy did not plan. This reform was unintended. Perhaps Beijing's state bureaucrats were not especially interested in having Shanghai as an important center for silicon electronics. Many of their specific decisions on IT and other investments in the 1980s suggest their greater interest in Beijing or Xi'an. Wuxi also found capital for its computer industry, albeit not mostly from the state. The materials crisis meant that Shanghai went into this sector that used educated talent but did not require rural inputs – and electronics emerged as a taxpaying industry. The collapse of inefficient state businesses, and the rise of new firms, was beneficial in terms of jobs, but this reform was often unintended.

State profits: comparisons of cities, sectors, and years

Inland competition also forced management reorganization. It might at first seem odd that the reported profits of Shanghai's centrally managed state firms rose after 1980, while those of locally managed state firms declined. These effects are accounting mirages, at least as regards industry; and the reasons are two: After 1980, the central government took over several large factories that had previously been run by the municipality (notably the Jinshan Chemical Plant and several Shanghai shipyards). The first part of the 1980s also saw the establishment of several new central corporations, including national companies for chemicals and ships. Ministries assumed control of such industries and absorbed their profits.

The second reason concerns profits from banks. Many of these, notably the People's Bank, were central enterprises. Like other central firms, they remitted profits directly through their ministry. But before reforms ignited the economy, bank profits were low; so banks sent little profit into the central treasury. As interest rates on loans rose, banks in Shanghai supplied more to Beijing.

Most "state-owned" industries are managed and accounted locally rather than centrally. Table 7.1 shows how they fared in the eight largest Chinese municipalities, as well as in all of the officially designated cities, *shi*, numbering about three hundred in this period. The position of Shanghai becomes evident on this table, as does the sharpness of change in the mid-1980s.

Shanghai until 1984 realized profits and taxes at a much higher rate than any other large city in China – but then a sharp decline began in the mid-1980s. Shanghai also paid a greater portion of this realized money to governments at both central and local levels.[9] Technical problems implicit in proper interpretation of the published figures on Table 7.1 are many, and there would be no excuse to report these data if there were not a very sharp gradient of difference in Shanghai over just a few years in the mid-1980s, or if there were not an even sharper gradient between Shanghai and the other big cities.

These figures require notes, and interviews with Shanghai auditors engaged in mid-1980s state extraction give a less incomplete picture. Methods of evaluating fixed

TABLE 7.1 Profits and taxes realized from local state-owned industries per 100 yuan of capital (in yuan; for urban districts only, and with subordinate counties for the largest 1984 cities)

	1983	1984	1985	1986	1987
Shanghai urban districts		73	63	42	34
w/rural suburbs		63			
Beijing urban districts		36	36	31	29
w/rural suburbs		35			
Tianjin urban districts		33	35	32	29
w/rural suburbs		33			
Shenyang urban districts		22	23	22	19
w/rural suburbs		27			
Wuhan urban districts		21	26	23	26
w/rural suburbs		21			
Guangzhou urban districts		37	39	32	31
w/rural suburbs		35			
Haerbin urban districts		16	17	15	15
w/rural suburbs		16			
Chongqing urban districts		22	24	16	18
Averages for urban districts only:					
the 8 largest cities ('84 pop. >2 m.)	39	38	39	31	28
Next largest cities (1->2 million pop.)	25	28	30	26	24
Next largest (500,000->1 m.)	34	27	25	21	21
Next largest (200,000->500,000)	22	19	19	18	18
Next largest (c.100,000->200,000)	18	20	20	18	17
All c. 300 cities	26	27	27	23	22
All China	21				

Sources: See notes in the main text for caveats about this table, which should be read not for exact quantities but for the dramatic gradients it shows among cities and years in the mid-1980s. Such slopes may be reliable, even when some numbers have been manipulated for local-political purposes. Some figures, rounded here, are in *Zhongguo chengshi tongji nianjian, 1985* (Statistical Yearbook of Chinese Cities, 1985), State Statistical Bureau, ed. (Beijing: Zhongguo Tongji Xinxi Zixun Fuwu Zhongxin & Xin Shijie Chuban She, 1985), 146–52, and *Zhongguo tongji nianjian, 1985* (China Statistical Yearbook, 1985), State Statistical Bureau, ed. (Beijing: Zhongguo Tongji Chuban She, 1985), 53–77, for 1984; *China: Urban Statistics, 1986*, State Statistical Bureau, PRC, compiler (Hong Kong: Longman, 1987), 290–293 and almost identical figures for a slightly different indicator in *Zhongguo chengshi jingji shehui nianjian, 1986* (Economic and Social Yearbook of China's Cities, 1986), Zhongguo Chengshi Jingji Shehui Nianjian Lishi Hui, ed. (Beijing: Zhongguo Chengshi Jingji Shehui Chuban She, 1986), 44–51 for 1985; *Zhongguo chengshi tongji nianjian, 1987* (as above), 155–62, for 1986; and *Zhongguo chengshi tongji nianjian, 1988* (as above), 185–93, for 1987. Additional relevant sources (but reporting the situation somewhat differently) are *Zhongguo gongye jingji tongji ziliao, 1987* (Statistical Materials on China's Industrial Economy, 1987), Guojia Tongji Ju, Gongye Jiaotong Wuzi Tongji Si, eds. (Beijing: Zhongguo Tongji Chuban She, 1987), 129, on 1985–86; and *Shanghai tongji nianjian, 1988* (Shanghai Statistical Yearbook, 1988), Li Mouhuan, ed. (Shanghai: Shanghai Shi Tongji Ju, 1988), 66, on 1987. The 1983 figures are available for the indicated lines in *Zhongguo shehui zhuyi chengshi jingji xue* (Chinese Socialist Urban Economics), Zhu Linxing, ed. (Shanghai: Shanghai Shehui Kexue Chuban She, 1986), 41. Readers may notice that, although this book relies on many quantities, regression models are never attempted in it. Political reporting biases can affect the results of sensitive regressions of various types. Conclusions are claimed only when gradients in "uncrunched" data series over time or space are notably sharp.

162 Budgeteers face the 1980s crisis

assets and of handling extrabudgetary funds sometimes changed. It is unclear how much of the gradient over time in the Shanghai figures, and of differences between Shanghai and other places, resulted from altered reporting practices. Consider the denominator underlying Table 7.1. "Capital" (*zijin*) includes fixed and circulating capital, is calculated at year's end, and has two parts: quota circulating capital (*ding'e liudong zijin*, administered by banks) and fixed capital net value (*guding zichan jingzhi*, based on original prices minus yearly depreciation).[10] "Circulating capital" comprises five elements: reserve capital (*chubei zijin*, the value of materials yet to be processed), production capital (*shengchan zijin*, materials being processed), finished product capital (*chengpin zijin*, items yet to be sold), overstocked materials (*chaochu jiya wuzi*, in warehouses and not necessarily ever sold – often a large item!), and losses on assets to be junked (*dai chuli liudong zichan sunshi*).[11] Before 1985 in Shanghai, and before 1978 in all of China, the central government could claim 100 percent of local industrial taxes (though some might flow back to the paying province as subsidies or investments).[12] The numerator term "profits and taxes" (*lishui*) is also hard to translate concisely, because "profits" include items that are incentives to labor: welfare funds (*fuli jin*), bonus funds (*jiang jin*), and production development funds (*shengchan fazhan jin* – also often used not for investment, but for incidental administrative and sales costs, since much investment came from administrative allocations or state bank loans).

In 1984 and previous years, Shanghai paid much of its collected "profits and taxes" into Beijing coffers. For the next three years, fewer profits and taxes were realized. Inflation made the rates of payment from these funds into all government budgets decline.[13] This reduction of Shanghai's tax burden, however, was offset because the government could no longer so fully guarantee Shanghai factories raw material supplies or enough budget to buy them. This policy, putting more factory inputs on the market, aimed to raise economic efficiency – and eventually it would do so – but the transition period was inevitably painful for Shanghai.

The reduction of this city's extraordinary remittances by 1987, when the state did far less to guarantee factor prices, is clear in these figures. Capital per unit of product value in Shanghai was less than elsewhere, while extraction remained heavy though decreasing. These statistics, based on both fixed and circulating capital, may be more useful than comparative statistics based on gross value of output, because the latter index includes double-counted products, and the degree of vertical integration has been relatively high in Shanghai.

The term "profits and taxes" refers to money that goes into a considerable variety of uses: remittances to the central budget (for units that are centrally managed) and to the municipal budget (though much of that 'local' money is later also remitted to Beijing). Welfare funds and "production development funds," as well as other portions of income retained in factories, are included; but such legally retained monies remained fairly small in Shanghai before the 1990s.

Shanghai had more profitable industries in its counties than many other Chinese cities did in their built-up areas. Suburbs had lower remittance rates per unit of capital, but Shanghai's nonetheless realized revenues effectively, if the available figures are accurate. The main overall conclusion, however, is that the biggest city's profitability to the state plummeted in the mid-1980s.

The unexpectedly low tax/profit payments of the cities between one and two million population in Table 7.1 (eleven cities in 1984) arises from the fact that most are provincial capitals: Nanjing, Xi'an, Chengdu, Changchun, Taiyuan, Lanzhou, and Jinan are all in this group.[14] The next largest cities, with populations between 500,000 and a million (thirty-one of them in 1984, and a few more in later years because of population rises), tended to be industrial and to pay more heavily than province capitals. Variations in the rates of realized profits and taxes in years such as 1985, according to interviewees, came largely from mixed patterns of borrowing by different cities to pay their tax burdens. Many such loans were repaid irregularly, or later than scheduled. The main collateral seems to have been the symbolic prestige of local politicians, on which banks could not easily foreclose.

The rate rose sharply at which Shanghai local-run state factories could retain profits. It was 34 percent by 1987 (up from just 5 percent in 1979, then 16 percent in 1984).[15] This would have been more meaningful, if there had been less inflation in the 1980s. The price rises affected norms of politics. The state treasury learned it could not expect so much as in the past from locally managed government firms from which supervisory corporations had defected.

Another aspect of this table (or any other report that deals comprehensively with all of China or any other developing country) is great variance over the nation's geography. In 1985, the product per person in counties of the Yangzi delta was 1,174 yuan – more than twice the all-China average of 529 yuan. Realized remittances of profits and taxes per 100 yuan from all industrial enterprises on the delta was 50 yuan in 1985, compared with just 21 yuan for the whole country. Table 7.1 shows differences between localities nationally, while Table 7.2 focuses on Jiangnan.

TABLE 7.2 Income and realized profits and taxes per 100 yuan of capital in the cities that govern all Jiangnan rural counties, 1985 (in yuan; in order by state profits and taxes)

	local income / 100¥ cap.	profits and taxes / 100¥ cap.
Shanghai	2539	63★
Huzhou	622	50★
Hangzhou	905	46★
Ningbo	788	38★
Wuxi	1094	36
Jiaxing	706	34★
Shaoxing	510	33★
Changzhou	888	32
Suzhou	883	32
Nantong	520	28

* Shanghai and Zhejiang cities are asterisked; Jiangsu cities are not.
Source: *Shanghai jingji qu fazhan zhanlue chutan* (Preliminary Research on the Development Strategy of the Shanghai Economic Zone), World Economic Herald and Shanghai Economic Zone Research Society, ed. (Shanghai: Wuxi Branch of Shanghai Eighth People's Printers, 1986), 30–31. "Local" income means "local national income" from the city.

164 Budgeteers face the 1980s crisis

Shanghai's value added per unit of capital was almost five times that of the least-taxed places in the delta. Nantong and Shaoxing were the only prefectures in this area that reported being below the national average of output per unit of capital. (Some reasons lie in probable underreporting; others lie in Nantong's exceptionally outdated textile equipment, which was not renovated because of lack of funds during earlier years, and in the numerous traditional handicraft industries of Shaoxing, which despite their fame were low on planners' priority lists.) Jiangsu was more successful than Zhejiang or Shanghai at avoiding taxes on production.

Many light industrial centers remitted big dollops of money. A deputy director of the Hangzhou Planning Commission, for example, complained in 1985 that his city could keep too little of what it earned. Jiangnan's burden increased during the early 1980s, when Guangdong, Fujian, and other places were more lightly taxed. In 1984, Hangzhou paid 38 percent more than in 1980. The portion of Hangzhou extraction sent to central budgets was nearly the same in 1980 and 1984 (at 86 percent). By 1985, Hangzhou could keep even less of what it collected.[16] This provincial capital of Zhejiang paid dearly.

From 1982 to 1986, both Jiangsu and Zhejiang grew much faster than Shanghai – with 17 and 21 percent annual industrial output increases, respectively, compared with Shanghai's 7.5 percent. In 1982, Shanghai still had 26 percent more industrial yield than Jiangsu; but the province overtook the city as China's largest industrial producer by mid-1985. The stagnancy of the state sector, more prominent in Shanghai because of that city's role in China's fiscal system, was mostly responsible for this 1980s difference between Shanghai and Jiangsu.

In 1982, the state-owned sector had dominated all three provinces in terms of output value: 58 percent in Zhejiang, 60 percent in Jiangsu, up to 87 percent in Shanghai. But by the mid-1980s, state-owned enterprises generated less than half the industrial product of both Jiangsu and Zhejiang, though still over 80 percent in Shanghai.[17] More analysis by ownership sectors can be made, but the relative rise of nonstate firms in the adjacent provinces had major revenue effects on the comparison with Shanghai, whose economy was still largely in state firms.

Tax collection in other parts of East China, by early 1989, involved less direct participation by tax offices than during previous years. In one Subei city, for example, an earlier policy of active inspections, "going to doors to receive taxes," was replaced by a stress on propaganda, "paying imposts by going to the [tax office] door."[18] This meant that inspectors visited business premises less often. Education of company managers was supposed to raise compliance. Tax evasion was still, of course, illegal. Within one week after a sporadic campaign to publicize punishments that had been meted out to a hundred private firms that evaded taxes, the tax office received a windfall of payments. But the number of rural China's firms and the difficult-to-monitor independence of their managers had increased.

Furthering of "slippage" in the 1980s

The decline of Shanghai local revenues per yuan of gross product, from 1978 to 1987, was more than 40 percent.[19] *Three-quarters of this decline came in 1984–1987,*

Budgeteers face the 1980s crisis **165**

the years when Shanghai profits and taxes were plummeting even faster than those of the nation as a whole.[20] The rate of the dive accelerated in the single year 1987 particularly: Shanghai's fiscal revenues fell by 550 million yuan in 1986, but then by another 1,110 million in 1987.[21] This caused consternation among the military, industrial, educational, and other state bureaucrats whose budgets it affected.

During the 1980s, Shanghai's government revenues – both those collected for the local budget and those forwarded to Beijing – dropped sharply because Shanghai businesses could not keep up with nearby rural competitors. Table 7.3 shows the extent of these changes during the years when they were sharpest. Groups smaller than the national or municipal bureaucracies controlled more resources than in previous years. But some large state factories that were owned and managed completely from Beijing, such as the Baoshan Steel Plant and Jinshan Chemical Factory, were not included in the table's figures. Because of these plants, which used bulk inputs that planners could still allocate, state revenues from Shanghai on average still increased 2.3 percent per year from 1980 to 1986. The greater freedom from tax of Shanghai's medium and small enterprises was nonetheless a major change: enough to create rising government deficits throughout the 1980s.

By 1987, the "slippage" of fiscal revenues in Shanghai industry was partly attributed to poor management. But it was too facile for top bureaucrats to blame factory managers in this case; the main cause lay in rural markets, which prospered more than planned "markets." New trading fairs that served factories in the countryside tended like vortex whirlwinds to draw in primary produce, because they offered higher prices. Factory raw materials accounted for 80 percent of all industrial costs in Shanghai's low-capital environment. Input price rises took the decisive toll on factory profits.[22]

But when Shanghai revenue was "lost" to planners, it was not lost to everybody. Wealth did not disappear just because centralist organizations failed to collect it.

TABLE 7.3 Shanghai revenues decline, 1980–1987

	Shanghai local govt revenues (m. yuan)	All Sh R's as Part of Nat'l (percent)	All Sh R's as Part of Sh Nat'l Income (percent)	Sh Local R's as Part of Sh Nat'l Income (percent)
1980	17.5	18.3	70.4	61.9
1981	17.4	18.8	70.3	60.0
1982	16.8	17.9	68.0	56.9
1983	15.6	16.4	67.3	51.5
1984	16.4	15.1	63.2	48.1
1985	18.4	14.4	64.4	45.0
1986	17.9	12.0	60.6	42.2
1987	16.5			

Source: "National income" (*guomin shouru*) just means income, rather than all income that is produced nationally. (This standard English translation might mislead.) See several tables in Xu Zhenliang, "*Shanghai caizheng shouru 'huapo' de xiankuang, chengyin ji qi duice*" (The 'Slippage' of Shanghai's Financial Income: Situation, Reasons, and Countermeasures), in *Caijing yanjiu* (Financial and Economic Studies), March 1988, 18–19.

Most of it went to other parties inside and outside the metropolis. Of the reduction in Shanghai revenues during 1987, calculations show that 57 percent was "shifted" from Shanghai elsewhere, often to leaders of smaller collectivities, as the city "reduced and adjusted" taxes and raised depreciation allowances. The Shanghai Finance Bureau calculated that 37 percent of the total revenues lost to local state offices was kept by enterprises within the city. Reportedly 57 percent went to other provinces and the center. Yet another 7 percent went to active and retired workers. This accounts for all of the "loss."[23] The center and other provinces still got nearly three-fifths, but revenue slippage shocked high officials, who wanted their usual money. Others, including many in Jiangnan, received it through various channels. In terms of overall economic efficiency, the change was almost surely positive, albeit unintended by the Party-state.

Taxes under "moderate" and "hardline" politicians

All planners agreed that Shanghai had to move into new fields, but the bureaucracy was slow to finance technological change. Conservatives thought that urban reformers were in danger of "killing the chicken that lays the egg" (*sha ji qu luan*). But consciousness of policy effects proved to be less important than institutional habits. Shanghai's electronic equipment industry, for example, progressed slowly. One local economist overstated the case, saying that "nothing has happened" and that Beijing politicians and their local satraps wanted only to maximize Shanghai as a source of revenue. He said the government was willing to gamble with Shanghai's money to the last penny.[24]

Central government budgeteers had become so addicted to Shanghai money, they got themselves into the position of trying to control all important economic initiatives in the city, whether they really preferred that policy or not. Institutionalized tax habits set the municipality's economic course well into the 1980s, at least as much as any particular national leaders did. As it became increasingly clear that Shanghai could not fulfill its earlier role in China's fiscal system, top cadres in Beijing were impelled by the inflationary squeeze to conclude that Shanghai must change. High politicians of different stripes did this, even when they disagreed over what the change should be. In late 1987, reformist Party head Zhao Ziyang and conservative Vice-Premier Yao Yilin made a joint inspection tour to Shanghai, apparently to find out what could be done about maintaining the city's declining contribution to Beijing.

The weeks after that visit were a turning point in official rhetoric about Shanghai, although the sequel was shaped by circumstances irrespective of words. The State Council in December approved a "Report on Deepening Reform, Opening Wider to the Outside World, and Accelerating the Development of an Export-Oriented Economy in Shanghai." This called for an "all-encompassing financial contract system," more exports to raise foreign exchange for the purchase of better technology and needed materials, and fixed-amount fiscal contributions from Shanghai for five years.[25]

Zhao Ziyang stressed that Shanghai's contribution to China should be measured in terms of its physical production, implying that he no longer saw the city's tax-and-profit remittance as the main aim. He said, "Shanghai's position is such that if Shanghai doesn't progress, then the whole country will have difficulty progressing." Zhao was also in favor of putting rural areas under the administrative guidance of their central market cities; and for Shanghai, the largest metropolis in China, that could have meant a large hinterland. It was easy to see how such notions would be appealing in Shanghai. But Zhao was not the only kind of politician in China, as June 1989 made very clear.

Conservatives, seeking to modernize rather than destroy the Party patronage system that still ruled most areas, were represented in Shanghai by the municipal government – even though the cosmopolitan styles of many city fathers concealed that relationship. Jiang Zemin's plan for the Shanghai economy, expressed in an early 1988 speech, was a study in flexible contradictions. On one hand, he said Shanghai should "learn humbly from the advanced experience of Guangdong Province in deepening reform."[26] On the other, "being the largest economic center in our country, Shanghai most prominently reflects the planned economy."[27] The answer, according to Jiang, was contracts: "fixing basic quotas, guaranteeing fulfillment of these quotas, sharing surpluses, and making up for shortages." To prevent the case-by-case, year-by-year habit from obviating these incentives, the contracts "once signed, should remain unchanged for five years." And they should allow institutions to raise money from "their own operations to support themselves." Reformers liked these policies, conservatives were wary, and Jiang hedged. To the extent liberties were allowed, they temporarily meant less central revenue. Hesitant reforms were inspired by inflation more than by liberal epiphanies among Beijing leaders.

Continued high-tax regimes, illegalities, and quiet politics

When traders are independent of the state, then government action on markets nonetheless involves them in politics. For example in France, where *dirigisime* got its name, state rules have often politicized private firms.[28] But Shanghai managers in firms of any size have been so tied to the state for so long, even entrepreneurs in middle-sized and small firms by the end of the 1980s were affected by officials. Their reaction to state intervention would often be to avoid bureaucrats, rather than to participate in politics hoping for better public rules. Like "weak" individual actors in other contexts, they used secrecy as a major political weapon. They were collectively strong enough to be, in effect, public.[29]

The Party often discouraged the voicing of managers' views in Shanghai, and cadres responded to China's periods of political thaw more slowly than did other actors.[30] In the 1980s, however, urban factory heads faced rural suppliers who had more localist collective ethics. The power of China's planners became weaker, as the power of China's rural managers became stronger.

Leaders of small and medium enterprises in Shanghai by the end of the decade had reasons to be more active, if seldom more articulate. Transfers of industrial raw

168 Budgeteers face the 1980s crisis

materials soared throughout the country. When these transactions were still illegal, some of the arrested criminals had previously worked in the factories from which they hijacked materials. They were familiar with ways to obtain these, and undoubtedly some of them had been managers. Others were identified as buyers from rural industries. In either case, their business boomed: "The more they steal, the more bold they become."[31] Bosses and workers in Shanghai were eager to cooperate with such traders when the alternative was to close shop. Factory or store heads might face a choice between breaking the law and firing their employees, and it is unsurprising that in the interest of their local political clients, such leaders often thought the illegal ex-statist option best.

Attempts to recentralize control of funds and taxes

Under the national guarantee (*baogan*) system that was announced in 1988, Shanghai planned to send 10.3 billion yuan annually into central government accounts during the three years 1988–1990. But these public plans about province-level actions were no more stable than were local contracts after earlier case-by-case bargaining. Because of factory input and hepatitis problems, central authorities tried to muster more raw materials for Shanghai in 1988, and the city's industrial economy responded with a better growth rate in that year. So the "guarantee" was upped, as Beijing's revenue demand rose again. Shanghai's actual 1988 remittances were 10.5 billion yuan (200 million more than had been projected). Jiang Zemin, as the chief local politician, apparently gained credit for this overfulfillment. The difference between Shanghai and other provinces remained huge; Guangdong, for example, in 1988 remitted much less than the southern province's production would have warranted if treatment had been uniform: only 0.42 billion.[32]

China's leaders agonized about the central government deficit. Official economists claimed that the fiscal reform policy of "dividing the stove to eat," despite its benefits for local budgets, meant the central state had less money. As a Beijing writer pointed out, China's budgetary revenue fell below the portion that was seen in some (smaller) Western countries where national governments get 60 to 70 percent of all taxes. Workers' wages, new money in local cooperatives or private firms, and extrabudgetary money by the late 1980s comprised three-quarters of China's income – up from two-thirds only a few years before. One writer suggested that Beijing should collect more money, even if it also established a "system of dividing taxes" under which centrally collected funds would be sent to local governments.[33]

The Beijing viewpoint, whatever it was, meant less in the late 1980s than it earlier had. Top PRC leaders kept sending down dicta, many of which were received but merely filed by cadres in dynamic sectors of China's economy. For example, the State Council (cabinet) approved rules restricting the size and use of managers' discretionary funds. It decreed that these funds should be reduced 20 percent in 1988 below 1987 levels – but during the first seven months of 1988, expenditures from such funds actually rose 20 percent instead.[34] This was not a minor line item. The total of discretionary funds for these months was greater than the sum of money for all urban construction and education, almost 37 billion yuan throughout the country.

Debates about imposts

In the tense multi-norm period of 1988–1989, writers close to the central government also raised questions about Shanghai's tax treatment. Two reporters for a Beijing journal criticized Shanghai people's view that a "cosmic imbalance" was at the heart of the city's problems. They said Shanghai's people too often felt the state should "protect" that city because it paid so much in taxes. This attitude led to laziness, they claimed; and it meant Shanghai firms became like flowers in a hothouse, unable to withstand the winds of competition.[35] Such views might be expected in Beijing, but other writers responded that central policies had built this hothouse by imposing an environment of heavy taxes and rules, so that Shanghai's once-famous entrepreneurialism had at least temporarily disappeared. The conclusion from planning's collapse became explicit: Shanghai leaders should "break out of the circle of 'not asking anyone for anything.'"[36]

During the thaw that ended at Tiananmen in June 1989, published articles could raise questions about whether Shanghai was receiving a fair deal under reforms. The city had often been praised officially as the "elder brother" among Chinese localities because of its contribution to central coffers: "Shanghai is the big brother; he cares for the family before himself." Eldest brothers in Chinese tradition have special responsibility to care for parents – and a favorite metaphor likens the government to parents. The state (*guojia*) is called a kind of family (*jia*), borrowing prestige from China's smallest and strongest power institutions. The elder brother (*gege*) is specifically obliged to provide resources first, and these may later be divided among the younger brothers (*didi*, other provinces). But now, as a 1988 article said, reforms had altered this pattern by creating enormous growth throughout China's inland areas.[37]

This article opined that if the policies accorded to Guangdong (allowance for easier importing and exporting, and low-tax 'responsibility contracts' at all levels) were also applied to Shanghai, the East China metropolis could catch up with Guangdong in about three years. But the author who made the estimate also said the bias implicit in Shanghai's high taxes was inevitable. If China's biggest city were allowed to participate fully in international markets, and if it failed in the fierce competition there, the effects on national revenue would be too disastrous for China. Therefore experimental policies for importing, exporting, leasing, financing, and personnel reforms – such as were variously allowed in other places (Guangdong, Chongqing, Wuhan, and Shenyang were all cited) – could not be implemented in Shanghai until they were sure to work. Cities with smaller taxpaying roles could be in some futuristic China. But for patriotic reasons, Shanghai could not.[38]

Shanghai's reformist *World Economic Herald* carried detailed descriptions of generous rules allowed for Guangdong, but not for Shanghai, during the 1980s. These policies allowed fixed and predictable tax levies; they let local cadres take charge

170 Budgeteers face the 1980s crisis

of balancing the local budget over long periods, without running local deficits by sending high remittances to Beijing. Some rules informally extended the loose norms of Shenzhen and Guangdong's other special zones throughout that whole southern province.[39] The newspaper scarcely needed to mention the contrast with Shanghai to make its localist point.

Shanghai's own Party newspaper, the *Liberation Daily*, was also not too reticent to report in mid-1988 that the city could retain only one-third as much money in absolute terms as Beijing (and half as much as Tianjin) – despite its greater production.[40] Official sources recognized "differences between the southern coastal regions adjacent to Hong Kong and Macau, on one hand, and the northern coastal regions, on the other; between old industrial bases and newly arising cities."[41] To broach this issue, even in defense of the central government's uneven taxes, was to answer questions about justice that were on Shanghai people's minds.

Economic growth and perceived fairness

Albert Hirschman presents a model of conditions under which groups may postpone their frustration when they see other groups advancing more quickly. He refers mainly to classes, as in Brazil, that long remained poor even as the country prospered. He likens their situation to that of drivers stopped in a two-lane tunnel. When the other lane (e.g., a 'middle class') begins to move, poor groups may be happy even if they remain stuck. The advance of the others could forebode motion for themselves.[42] This "tunnel effect" may illustrate why Shanghai people were slow to become irate about their taxes, even as they knew that other places enjoyed much lower rates. They may have deemed this a good omen for their own futures as next in line for prosperity. The 1990s showed they would have been somewhat justified in thinking so; but by June 1989, the central government's resource in patience from them had been stretched thin. Hirschman's scheme broadly predicted what happened in Shanghai: The state reacted by taking less from the city. The reasons were partly economic; but more crucially, they were political. The hardline regime after June 1989 could not afford to lose its wavering constituencies in Shanghai; so it finally had to supply them.

Just a month after Tiananmen, Finance Minister Wang Bingqian said that Beijing's program of "austerity" to cut government expenditures was not working: "Not only has there been a failure of bringing down outlays which were supposed to have been cut . . . rather, those expenditures have been increased from last year." In the first five months of 1989, "taxes paid by state firms" were 38 percent less than in the same months of the previous year. Administrative expenses in the first five months of 1989 had been scheduled to rise only 2.5 percent; but in fact, they rose 24 percent. Government spending as a whole had gone up 16 percent; but revenues, only 8 percent.[43]

This Finance Minister did not suggest any dramatic solutions, but an *Economic Daily* editorial proposed more money should be put into coal, oil, and steel – industries the state could most easily monitor because of the heavy capitalization and bulky materials they use. But this recommendation could not accomplish what mid-1989 socialist conservatives wanted. They were reluctantly forced to update and downscale their planning system, which had been deeply eroded in the mid-1980s. Conservative change, even if still called "reform," could not destroy the dynamic new firms that had given China much of its recent growth and most of its new jobs. Incomes had become more equal in the 1970s and 1980s, because more rural wealth had been created in local units, including families (as had happened in Taiwan during its period of fastest nonstate growth after Chiang Kai-shek's land reform). But in post-reform PRC years after 1990, inequality rose.

China's national Gini in 1981, affected already by early 1970s reforms, had been a low 0.288, showing much equality by international standards. A lower Gini means more equality. But in 1998, it was up to 0.403, and by 2001 to 0.439 (close to the US figure at that time).[44] China's income inequality rose to a peak of 0.491 in 2009 and lessened only a bit thereafter, to 0.462 (still far above the UN's inequality 'warning' level of 0.4).[45]

Fair conclusions about Shanghai taxes can be several, despite the complexity of the situation and practical or moral uncertainties that arise from it. In economic terms over many years, extraction from the metropolis was almost surely too high for China's maximum long-term growth. In patriotic terms, the economic result in Shanghai and in places where most of the extracted money went (as compared with those the government neglected) may be an indictment of past state mismanagement. China is not the only country with such problems. The Chinese leaders who were responsible will never be held accountable, especially for money that was wasted on inland or political client networks. Many who created the fiscal structure that lasted through the 1980s soon retired. State allowances for Shanghai development in the early 1990s were the regime's necessary reaction to its economic-political quandary. Counties and towns nationwide were supposed to balance budgets, without borrowing, under China's first Budget Law of 1995. This was not observed.[46] Local government debts rose, but the trend in the 2000s was change toward a tighter fiscal regime.

Notes

1 *Caijing yanjiu* (Financial and Economic Research), May 1988, 15.
2 *Shanghai jingji, neibu ben*, 889.
3 See Hiroki Takeuchi, *Tax Reform in Rural China: Revenue, Resistance, and Authoritarian Rule* (New York: Cambridge University Press, 2014).
4 These figures also show that Shanghai was relatively rich, but their meaning in terms of people's lives is less easy to determine. *Shanghai shehui xiankuang he qushi, 1980–1983* (Situations and Trends in Shanghai Society, 1980–1983), Zheng Gongliang, ed. (Shanghai: Huadong Shifan Daxue Chuban She, 1988), 203.
5 *Shanghai jingji, neibu ben*, 562.
6 *Shijie xin jishu geming yu Shanghai de duice* (The Global Revolution in New Technology and Shanghai's Policies in Response), Shanghai Economic Research Center and Shanghai Science and Technology Committee, ed. (Shanghai: Shanghai Shehui Kexue Yuan Chuban She, 1986), 194.

172 Budgeteers face the 1980s crisis

7 The economists who computed this ratio (not identified by name) would not have put the issue in this fashion, at least not in print. I was at the Shanghai Social Sciences Academy shortly after they published. Several intellectuals there spoke this way about the effects of factor prices. Some premises in this model can be questioned. A topic that deserves more exploration is the loss of remittances caused by cases in which Shanghai industries had to close because they could not buy materials at all. Non-price effects on profitability (including inadequate management) could also affect remittances. *SHJJ*, April 1988, 26–27.

8 Ordinary machines are *yiban jixie*, while precision machines are *jingmi jixie*. *SHJJ*, April 1988, 28.

9 A group of administrative centers with relatively high rates of payment from realized profits and taxes shown on this table is the group of cities (thirty-one of them in 1984) between 500,000 and 1,000,000 population. That group, including many provincial capitals, remitted about 85 percent of its realized income, whereas the other three types of cities (below the largest) could retain 5 or 6 percentage points more, e.g., in 1984. This may have been a transient phenomenon, because reform was sometimes (before 1989) better supported both at the top level and in hard-to-control small places than at middle levels.

10 *Tianjin tongji nianjian, 1987* (Tianjin Statistical Yearbook, 1987), Tianjin Statistical Bureau, ed. (Beijing: Zhongguo Tongji Chuban She, 1987), 120 and 352, for clear definitions.

11 *Shanghai shi 1985 nian gongye pucha ziliao* (Materials from the 1985 Industrial Survey of Shanghai), Gu Delun, ed. (Shanghai: Zhongguo Tongji Chuban She, 1988), 723–24.

12 Interview with a Chinese economist, 1988.

13 Interviews confirm this, as does Xu Zhenliang, "*Shanghai caizheng shouru "huapo" de xiankuang, chengyin ji qi duice*" (The "Slide" of Shanghai's Financial Income: Situation, Reasons, and Countermeasures), in *Caijing yanjiu* (Finance and Economics), March 1988, 18–23.

14 The very low burden of one capital reported on the table, Haerbin, may reflect that the oil center of Daqing is in the same province, Heilongjiang. Local officials could pay from oil revenues and may have had military backing to keep their taxes low.

15 *Shanghai: Gaige, kaifang, yu fazhan, 1979–87* (Shanghai: Reforms, Opening, and Development, 1979–87), Shanghai Statistical Bureau, ed. (Shanghai: Sanlian Shudian, 1988), 44.

16 Calculated from *Shanghai jingji qu fazhan zhanlue chutan* (Preliminary Research on the Development Strategy of the Shanghai Economic Zone), *World Economic Herald* and Shanghai Economic Zone Research Society, eds. (Shanghai: Wuxi Branch of Shanghai Eighth People's Printers, 1986), 266.

17 *FEER*, December 11, 1986, 82–83.

18 *Shangmen shoushui* was thus replaced by *nashui shangmen*. See *Jiangsu fazhi bao* (Jiangsu Legal System Report), January 21, 1989.

19 *SHJJ*, February 1988, 5.

20 In 1984, Shanghai had 30 yuan of realized profits and taxes per 100 yuan of capital, but in 1987 this was down to 21 yuan. The estimate in the text is calculated from *Zhongguo chengshi tongji nianjian, 1985* (Statistical Yearbook of Chinese Cities, 1985), State Statistical Bureau, ed. (Beijing: Zhongguo Tongji Xinxi Zixun Fuwu Zhongxin & Xin Shijie Chuban She, 1985), 146–52, and ibid. for 1988, 185–93.

21 *JJRB*, August 15, 1988.

22 *SHJJNJ88*, 23.

23 The rounded percentages (I usually avoid decimals as unscientific) add to 101. *SHJJ*, February 1988, 5.

24 This was expressed in Chinese form, on analogy to an old saying, "if you don't go to the Yellow River, you can't die yet" ("*bu dao Huanghe xing, busi*"); and for the government, "if it doesn't take the last fen. . ." (*bu ba zuihou yifen qian. . .*)

25 *FBIS*, March 4, 1988, 9, radio of the same day.

26 Learning from Guangdong's experience was not totally easy for Shanghai, in part because more Hong Kong money went there. For quotations here and the previous paragraph, see *Shanghai jingji qu*, 14.

27 *FBIS*, February 1, 1988, 40–41, radio of January 23.
28 Ezra N. Suleiman, *Private Power and Centralization in France: The Notaires and the State* (Princeton: Princeton University Press, 1987).
29 For comparative perspectives on this phenomenon, see James C. Scott, *Weapons of the Weak*; and an application to large-scale Chinese politics, Lynn White, *Policies of Chaos*, 308.
30 For more, see Lynn White, "Leadership and Participation: The Case of Shanghai's Managers," in *Citizens and Groups in the People's Republic of China*, Victor Falkenheim, ed. (Ann Arbor: University of Michigan Press, 1986), 189–211.
31 *Yue tou, yue dan da.* Ibid.
32 Based on conversations with Shanghai economists.
33 This proposed system was a "*fenshui zhi*," *Caizheng* (Finance), March 1988, 36.
34 *JFRB*, August 19, 1988.
35 *Liaowang*, no. 47 (1988), 12.
36 Ibid.
37 "*Shanghai shi da ge, xian gu jia, hou gu ji*," "*Jiao gei fumu, zai fen gei xiongdi*," according to *Zhongguo qingnian bao*, September 20, 1988.
38 *ZGQNB*, September 20, 1988. This article was by a Wang An – but apparently not the Shanghainese-Massachusetts computer magnate.
39 *SHJJDB*, August 22, 1988.
40 *JFRB*, May 15, 1988.
41 *FBIS*, March 11, 1988, 33, reporting *RMRB* of March 9.
42 Albert Hirschman, "Changing Tolerance for Income Inequality in the Course of Economic Development," *World Development* 1:12 (1973), 24–36. Hirschman, who lived in Princeton and helped teach my seminars, was seen at the opera in New York. To get there, he passed through Lincoln Tunnel near rush hour. The "tunnel effect" is an intriguing theory that, unlike many of Hirschman's other contributions, may still require broader empirical confirmation.
43 *Post*, July 8, 1989, for this and the next paragraph.
44 Hongyi Lai, *China's Governance Model*, 48.
45 www.statista.com/statistics/250400/inequality-of-income-distribution-in-china-based-on-the-gini-index/. Hongyi Lai, *China's Governance Model*, 121, lists ten Central Committee policy documents that were designed to reduce the income gap between urban and rural areas. Rises in the Gini suggest decrees' effectiveness was not great.
46 Juan Wang, *Sinews*, 87.

8

OWNERS MANAGE URBAN CORRUPTION AND COMPANIES

For urban industry, the main content of the Chinese revolution was an attempt to extend socialist management. In the 1950s, the change toward planning was bumpy but broad. Businesspeople were targets as well as actors in this drama, which was wholly political. It involved patriotism, unpredictable spasms of violence, and introspection by individuals on how they should use their lives. Most Chinese were proud to hail the formation of a strong government in 1949, after foreign occupations of their country.

Quick official violence in the 1950s Suppression of Counterrevolutionaries campaign scared more people than it assaulted directly. The Korean War provided occasions for formerly bourgeois youths to prove their nationalism. Many urbanites wondered how they could mix their own cultural, religious, and personal habits with the official new collectivism. Concepts of corruption changed and tightened. Masses were mobilized to clean streets, swat flies, kill snails infected with schistosomiasis, get inoculations, report embezzlers, and speak better Mandarin.[1] The Party in the first half decade of the 1950s created a psychological climate in which its opponents lost clout – but its adherents were at first too few or undereducated to fill local power vacuums, especially in modern businesses. The Party lacked enough personnel to ensure its control, especially in cities that had industrial economies as complex as Shanghai's. But as the new order was established in the early 1950s, it reached a climax with the "Transition to Socialism" of 1956. The pecking order of companies by ownership status became more than an official mantra: "first the state, later the collective, last the private" (*xian guojia, hou jiti, zai geren*). Private businesses mostly closed. China's reforms, two and three decades later, reversed this order in practice.

Origins of "mother-in-law" supervising corporations

Political leaders have long been deemed generally superior to business leaders in China. The classic *Yantie lun* (Discourses on Salt and Iron), compiled by Huan Kuan during the reign of Emperor Wu of the Han dynasty (r. 141–87 BCE), shows that Chinese debate about the state's role in economic management is ancient.[2] So do earlier works called the *Guanzi* (named for Guan Zhong, d. 645 BCE).[3] Much later, relying on the premise of central glory in some of these traditions, the late-Qing statesman Li Hongzhang advocated that "officials supervise and commercial people manage" (*guandu shangban*).[4] Li knew that government support was often needed to set up new industries, and he liked to link firms to the state regardless of legal property arrangements. Li adapted tradition, claiming mandarins have rights to structure a modern economy.

By the mid-1950s, state corporations, each of which grouped many firms in the same trade, were put under Shanghai's municipal bureaus. The Party at that time had enough power among workers and patriots to force nationalization on capitalists. Businesspeople who cooperated and put their firms under socialist supervision did not have to close shop. On the contrary, their expertise was needed. But there were not enough Communist managers to replace the capitalists. So in the 1950s the CCP distributed its few trusted accountants (and many demobilized soldiers wanting urban sinecures) into corporations that "supervised" factories but were often located in offices physically far away from production sites or stores.

Within each whole industry, Shanghai's structure was divided in two: "government business management departments" (*zhengfu hangye guanli bumen*) and "civilian business associations" (*minjian hangye xiehui*).[5] The government organs were charged to take care of middle- and long-term plans, including investment, credit, product quality, and technical improvement. Local firms and civilian associations were supposed only to "assist and consult with" their supervisory agencies, rather than making plans. This structure lasted many years through campaigns in 1956, 1958, and the early 1960s. But with the Cultural Revolution and 1970s lapses of materials deliveries, the supervisors were weakened.

This top-heavy management system needed reform. In Shanghai, it changed slowly because of taxes; but reforms affected the system's parts differently. A few major offices reported directly to the mayor, with responsibility for large sectors such as commerce, light industry, agriculture, or finance. A second administrative layer consisted of municipal bureaus in more specific areas such as grain or textiles. At the third level of firms, managers were supposed to meet quotas. In industry, large corporations managed many subordinate factories. In commerce, there was commonly an intervening layer of urban district corporations (*qu gongsi*) or central stores (*zhongxin dian*). Reforming economists wished to amalgamate the submayoral offices and the municipal bureaus. They wanted to extend authority to match accountability farther down in the system.

Ownership can imply several different types of rights that are mutually dependent. They are a function of law as it is actually enforced, not just as it is written. The state – or whatever other coercive network is effective – affects marketed commodities, since it tries to set rules for selling or out-contracting assets. The right of regulating markets is not ordinarily conceived as a matter of ownership, but it can limit what happens to commodities in a way that is indistinguishable from ownership rights. A second kind of ownership is the right to foreswear control of an asset, to sell it; this kind of right is usually conceived as the main one. A third category of ownership allows decisions on how "owned" resources are used. A fourth category is the right to income from property. There is priority among these ownership rights, because some (e.g., the right to sell) foreclose others. Theorized linkages between the different kinds – especially those typified by selling, managing, and receiving income – inform debates about the efficiency or justice of various ownership regimes. China's top leaders, as regards property "owned by the whole people," became unable during reforms to prevent alienation of many state ownership rights. Administrative levels of the Chinese government often conflicted on ways to arrange the management of businesses.

In 1965 nationally, over 10,000 large firms making 47 percent of all (officially priced) state-factory output were supposed to be run directly by central ministries. This situation did not last long, even on a nominal basis. So in the early 1970s, many nonmilitary central enterprises were switched to provincial control. They were still "state firms" – provinces, prefectures, and counties in China were (and are) formally agencies of this unitary state. So were communes at that time. They were still "owned by the whole people," but run in different respects by a mixture of administrative levels. Already by 1971, only 142 firms producing just 8 percent of China's output were designated as wholly central.[6] One result was that depreciation funds from large factories were then, in most areas, sent to local governments. China's state industries by the early 1970s were already more localized.

Reforms at that stage were changes of management, not of legal ownership. For years, formal sales of urban "state property" were prohibited. Top leaders hoped that functional or local bureaucrats could manage assets to ensure good income flows into central coffers. Because of the continuing normative importance of state institutions for local Chinese leaders, these hopes were fulfilled, especially in Shanghai, until the effective planning context for them mostly collapsed. During reforms, the development of collective and private property came mostly through economic growth, rather than through sales from the state.

Entrepreneurs and radicals alter ownership norms, notwithstanding intentions

Because the Cultural Revolution incapacitated most central ministries, localization of control over property during the early 1970s occurred largely by default. The climate of mixed fear and enthusiasm in the 1950s had cowed businesspeople and centralized socialism – and the Cultural Revolution in the 1960s operated by the same mechanism, except that the politically cowed people on that occasion were socialist cadres and the result was localization. All the industrial ministries, the People's Bank, and the Ministry of Finance were decimated. The State Planning Commission (SPC) expired by 1969, and Premier Zhou Enlai set up a temporary group to fill the void – but skilled administrators were so demoralized that few plans were strictly enforceable. A "Little State Planning Commission" of fifty people tried to do the job of the previous SPC with its thousand experts.[7] In view of China's size

Owners manage urban corruption & companies   **177**

and the political chaos of the time, this was a mere gesture at socialism. Planning largely capsized, without planners.

Central coordination nonetheless remained more important for urban Shanghai than for most of China. Beijing depended on its top appointees in each province, who were part of the unified state even though they could assume some advocacy roles for their regions. By the early 1970s, their conferences replaced the pretense of planning that had been fashionable until the mid-1960s. Central ministries had important roles in industries that depended on heavy inputs or heavy capitalization; but their Beijing offices became mostly secretarial, following the decisions of conclaves of top politicians in Party meetings.

In every year of the 1970s and 1980s at least, there was an economic meeting in Beijing among provincial leaders. The agenda included figuring out how the central government's budget would be met. Poor inland provinces with strong guerrilla heritages, along with defense and heavy-industry offices that needed money, tended to dominate these gatherings during early reforms. The meetings were reportedly cordial, and everyone regularly agreed that Shanghai was making a large contribution to China. But until the mid-1980s, it was not the task of the Shanghai representatives to lower their city's assessment. Instead, their main job was to promise the maximum amount the city might pay.

Planning was increasingly difficult. Similar firms, using similar materials to make similar goods, were often coordinated neither by single-price markets nor by unified management. Machine-building enterprises, for example, were fragmented in Shanghai among more than ten municipal bureaus by the mid-1980s. Food processing companies were distributed among more than eight bureaus. Construction and metallurgy were split among another eight (also owing obedience to five districts and nine counties). Packaging businesses were led by twenty-two "systems."[8] "Property rights" (*chanquan*) were periodically devolved during reforms from supervising companies to subordinate units. But in many cases, this meant that no unit became clearly responsible for assets or companies. Special policies (*teshu zhengce*) sustained inefficient firms. One Shanghai economist recommended that badly managed enterprises should be allowed to go bankrupt. Then they could be put up for public auctions where any government agency, social organization, corporation, or (later) individual that had money to buy them might do so.[9]

"Managers' responsibility" was a two-edged sword. A reformist party secretary in one East China plant put the problem neatly: He said the traditional style of "separating authority from responsibility" meant that CCP policymakers could not be blamed for their mistakes – and factory managers (who were often blamed for bad results) could not make policy. The real deciders had no responsibility, and the managers who had "responsibility" could not make policy. This was not the kind of power businesspeople craved.

So mid-1980s reformers advocated a new "managers' responsibility system."[10] In 1984, as inflation soared, one of them called a meeting of all his plant's employees to announce that henceforth the manager (rather than the Party secretary) should have full authority over five major areas: policies, production, administration, guidance,

178 Owners manage urban corruption & companies

and even personnel. But such a situation, in this case for a joint venture, was rare. This case was mainly an example of how the "opening" to foreign investment provided demonstration effects for domestic Chinese companies. In most of the latter, "managers' responsibility" was at least partly a matter of maintaining companies' Party cadres' ability to keep their links to clients safe from political danger in a time of volatile budgets and spiraling prices. Ambiguities in implementing the slogan "managers' responsibility system" (*lingli fuze zhi*) reflects tensions that are typical of reforms.

Ironic equilibrium: efficient managers' incentives to desist from managing

The degrees of freedom that factory heads could exercise varied sharply by sector. In light industries and handicrafts – except textiles – 60 percent of the managers by the mid-1980s had free rein to "adjust" their planned quotas. But in heavy metallurgy, inputs were also tight but the consumers were often powerful bureaucracies, and planners could still prevent plant managers from making such "adjustments." In machines and construction, only 15 percent of business heads could alter their quotas; in chemicals, 17 percent; and in instruments, one-quarter. Cloth was the sector whose managers remained most constrained, because it was most important for central revenues. Only 11 percent of textile factory managers could "adjust" their quotas. Textiles plants were like heavy industries, not like other light industries. High rates of executive freedom correlated by industry with low tax rates.[11]

Plans did not die; they just faded away. Factory managers complained that the rules distinguishing "mandatory" from "indicative" plans were increasingly vague and changeable. Plans could be enforceable (*zhiling xing*) or merely directive (*zhidao xing*) – and a single company might have both types simultaneously for different aspects of its operations. If a manager were successful in making more than the promised quota of products, in the next year the surplus would often be included in the mandatory amount. An "indicative plan" was really not a plan at all, but a fishing license for materials purchases in hopes of over-quota production. As the director of the Shanghai Third Steel Mill said, his mandatory planned quota was already so high, any flexibility to produce surpluses on the "indicative plan" was "empty talk."[12] His factory usually ran at full capacity. His supervising bureau raised the mandatory amount whenever there was a chance they could get more product within the fixed plan. This steel mill had a right to sell above-quota products, but the "mother-in-law" adjusted the mandate-plan to make sure there never were any. The incentive to hide production was great.

Although state quotas were usually mandatory, upstream units' targets for raw materials deliveries were often just indicative. Mixing the two kinds of plan meant no effective plan. Factor costs increased fast, and inputs became scarce during the 1980s; so basic quotas were hard to produce. A complaint from factory managers was that mandatory plans quickly changed to include any products that the market temporarily made profitable. But if supplies were plenty, e.g., if finished goods were hard to sell, the supervising agencies would classify them as part of the "indicative plan."[13]

The grant to managers of powers to sell above-quota products was therefore a recipe for endemic local conflict between them and supervisors who had long handled their procurement and merchandising. If a factory made marketable "hot products" (*rexiao shangpin*), the "mothers-in-law" would confiscate them by declaring them within the mandatory quota. During the 1980s, large corporations increasingly needed "hot products" to barter for scarce raw materials. Managers' rights to sell over-quota surpluses became inconsequential, unless they had political cover to misreport their situations.

Well-known Shanghai brands, including many that became "hot products," tended to be made in companies that were increasingly controlled as shortages worsened. The more enterprising a factory manager was − the more innovative, stylish, marketable, and profitable the products became − the less benefit that same manager would generally be allowed to keep.

This ironic equilibrium, under which the success of internal reforms in efficient units brought greater remittance pressures, was surprisingly widespread in Shanghai's economy during the 1980s. The head of a plant that made one of the city's famous brands of toothpaste said that he had been driven to advertise his lesser known lines, rather than his more profitable wares, so as to keep some of his managerial powers. This syndrome, brought on by reforms in a context of ever-less-successful state efforts to restore fiscal control, was the opposite of a profit incentive. As another Shanghai factory manager put it, "A gold brand or a silver brand is nothing, compared to a so-so brand of freedom (*jinpai, yinpai bu ru zapai ziyou*)."[14]

Macroeconomic management with multiple pricing

The government had its problems, too. Party leaders wanted to placate potentially restless urban workers while also keeping wage budgets low in state firms. The most sensitive places in Chinese politics were cities. Since the state-fixed prices of basic urban goods (food, housing, energy, transport) floated upward to approach levels that reflected scarcity, these commodities were subsidized. Party conservatives saw problems of political management whose solutions were often in tension with the issues faced by factory managers.

Conservatives' favored solution was to try to arrange low prices for crucial constituencies, notably urban workers. In practice, they often set up systems that profited relatively few people. For example, the Shanghai Blanket Factory in 1985 could legally sell its blankets in Shanghai's "price basin" for only 72 yuan each (making a mere 3 yuan profit). The price of similar blankets from Yinchuan in Ningxia was not effectively controlled, however, and these blankets fetched 120 yuan on free markets nationwide, establishing a normal price. So illegal private traders smuggled blankets out of Shanghai to other provinces. As the manager of the Shanghai Blanket Factory sarcastically put it, "This is the state giving a cash subsidy, so that the [smuggling] private entrepreneurs get rich."[15] Multiple pricing that attempted political management did not work.

180 Owners manage urban corruption & companies

Other unintended effects from centralized management arose because of a shift of the way factories got new credit. Under the pre-reform system of "unified receipts and unified expenditures" (*tongshou, tongzhi*) practically all the money a company made was sent to higher levels of the state. Any money a factory needed was appropriated from there.[16] By the mid-1980s, however, hand-outs were usually replaced by repayable loans, because central agencies otherwise would run short of money. Factory managers realized that any new profitable production they undertook on the basis of borrowed funds would become part of their "mandatory" quotas. They had no incentive to take out these loans, even if the capital were needed to implement good money-making ideas, because they would later be unable to repay. Shanghai's equipment was obsolescent in many industries. Even some conservative politicians saw that Shanghai should move into new industries that would require massive infusions of capital for higher technology. But the inertia of bureaucratic interests – built into the structural separation of supervising and operating managements and their differing abilities to control income flows from "state" property – distorted policies for urban growth.

Obsolete equipment, holding back long-term productivity, could not be replaced in many industries because of short-term efforts to control inflation. The Yangzi Lumber Mill in Shanghai, for example, had many pre-1937 machines. Its manager looked into the possibility of new investment. Even using a depreciation period of 26 years, he figured that his total annual "development fund" (renovation money) was just one-third of what would have been necessary to pay the interest on the capital improvements his factory needed. His proposal would only have replaced worn-out equipment; if he opted to go further, bringing in new technology, the bill would have been higher. This manager therefore did not take out a loan to counterbalance depreciation. He thought his supervisors, in offices away from the factory, would over time keep the development fund low, whether or not his production improved.[17]

Managers' costs during reforms were also raised by expenses for social responsibility (*shehui fudan*) to their employees. Some of these might have been borne by the municipal budget, if less money were remitted upward to ministries in Beijing. Costs rose in the 1980s for housing construction, pensions for retired workers, child care (*zaofang zijin, tuixiu gongren tuixiu jin, zhurou jiage butie,* and *yingyou er tuofei*), and other items.[18] Factories had increasing difficulty to find money for all this. It is debatable whether these costs should have been municipal or corporate. They were underfunded, especially as the city's budget maintained its central remittances while its revenues were slipping. But some managers used their scarce "production development funds" for welfare or bonuses. Since money for major technological improvements would bring more exactions, demands, and interference from supervisors, managers preferred to keep low profiles and build up personal support among subordinate clients instead. A way for Shanghai executives to serve business efficiency and their own constituencies at the same time was to use money for "joint enterprises" in other parts of the delta, where taxes were lower and "mother-in-law" agencies were farther away.

Supervisory companies could demand "autonomy" as easily as basic-level factories could. The meanings of autonomy in these two contexts were opposite. Powers 'lost,' devolved, or localized from relatively central authorities are not 'lost' to China; on the contrary, they are seized by other Chinese. Powers that are centralized are lost to localities but not to Chinese. Local authorities may use them best for people's benefit, or more central authorities may; that is an empirical question. Some local factory heads claimed that profit-collecting supervisors were mainly interested in seeing their subordinate firms debilitated. With dramatic flourish, a Shanghai factory executive used bitter metaphors: "The method by which supervising agencies control firms now is that 'live fish eat dead fish,' 'only be afraid of a live business, not of a dead one,' 'only be afraid of a rich enterprise, not a poor one.'"[19]

Official chops were still needed from "mother-in-law" agencies for many decisions at the factory level. The "vetos" (*foujue quan*) that these chops represented were, one factory manager said, increasing rather than decreasing in the 1980s as more market regulations replaced plans. Much-publicized intentions among top reformers to reduce them were said to be ineffective. The "factory manager's responsibility system" was supposed largely to have replaced Party cadres' authority, but in practice many firms did not follow this norm. "If factory managers make a decision, but if the Party committee disagrees, it cannot be carried out."[20] The pattern was implicitly compared with the feudal custom by which a weak emperor would "hang a curtain and listen to policy" from advisers behind it (*chuilian tingzheng*).[21]

Obstacles to efficient localization of Shanghai management were many. Clear laws protecting factories and their cadres were still absent in the late 1980s. Restructuring was often opposed by interests in politically powerful supervising corporations. The management culture that state policies had sponsored for years discouraged get-up-and-go within the urban state sector, which was reformed or replaced mostly because of competition elsewhere, especially among newer firms in rural and suburban areas.

Three types of "ownership," but one type of politics at many sizes

China officially has three ownership systems – by the state (theoretically representing "all the people," called the *chuanmin suoyou zhi*), by collectives (*jiti suoyou zhi*), and by private persons (*geti suoyou zhi*). These can also be used, in any combination, to create a diverse fourth "joint" (*lianhe*) category. But dissenters joke that in fact China has just one major ownership system: by supervising "departments" (one reformer called this the *bumen suoyou zhi*, using a very unofficial name for it).

The Chinese state slowly had to accept, in the course of reforms until the 1990s, that it could not fully control many low-level units of its administrative hierarchy. Many "state" cadres were not solely beholden to the state. Official definitions of ownership categories nearly acknowledged this situation. Government offices reported statistics from four types of owners, of which three require little

182 Owners manage urban corruption & companies

explanation here. The issue of "state cadres" acting outside the official apparatus arises most often in the large and important third category, the collectives.

1) State-owned enterprises are fully "nationalized," though often managed by provincial or other jurisdictions.[22]
2) Private enterprises are fully owned and operated by individuals.
3) Collective enterprises are diverse. They are first officially subdivided into two types, urban or rural. Each of these contains three subtypes: Within the urban category, some collectives are controlled as satellites by state enterprises; these are often locally designed to minimize remittance imposts and hire more staff than the personnel rosters of state enterprises allow. A second type of urban collective is supposed to be controlled by local governments at the city, district, or street levels (*shi, qu,* or *jiedao*). But ownership is not vested in the state, since these are collectives. It is socialist at the local level, monitored by local leaders who can have concurrent official posts but somehow should avoid using government powers unduly to help their firms corruptly. A third type covers "true" collectives, formed by individuals cooperating with each other who find they can succeed best by not formally designating their businesses "private." Rural collectives also come in three types. First are firms authorized by local governments that are not state enterprises; companies in this category created the "Sunan model" that provided dynamism for reform near Shanghai and is the most important category on this list. A second type is founded by local community organizations that are not technically part of the state but have official status, such as "united front" groups. A third sort comprises rural collectives run by groups of ordinary citizens.[23]
4) A residual "other" category includes all kinds of firms that are joint (state-with-collective, collective-with-private, state-with-foreign, collective-with-foreign, and so forth). Among such firms, the degree of coordination by high state bureaucrats varies greatly, from considerable planning to very occasional visits.

These categories make clear that "the state" has no clear boundary vis-à-vis local power networks in business. Furthermore, executives' actual practices are seldom set by legal ownership categories. Some local managers wield less influence than the state suggests they might, while others by circumstance, personality, or political links (*guanxi*) wield more.

Reform meant a rise of collective ownership, not mainly private ownership. In central Shanghai, this change came later than in rural areas. It often began covertly in urban lanes, because conservatives' control of zoning prevented new businesses from acquiring quarters on main streets. Collective firms grew nonetheless, partly because the quality of service in the state sector was uneven. In Shanghai, consumers took particular pride in their consciousness about quality.[24] To sum up: Ownership change in central Shanghai was slow. It was mostly toward the collective, not the private, form before the 1990s. It arose first in market niches and in geographical corners that the state had neglected.

Collectives' dominance over ownership change in Shanghai

Collective industries on average paid lower wages than state-owned industries. In urban Shanghai they were subject to almost as much official planning. Theoretically, workers in collectives were supposed to have some rights to make production decisions; but in practice, their managers did this. Pensions in collective industries were usually less generous, although bonuses were sometimes better. The average size of these companies, as measured either by output or employees, was relatively small. Conservative Party officials felt collectives were scarcely legitimate, not advanced historically, merely a transitional form of ownership, to be replaced later by state plants.

By 1980, the existence of discrimination against collective industries was, in effect, admitted officially – yet they were declared essential.[25] Planners laid stress on the need to have more specialized collectives, and explicit calls were published to oppose discrimination against these. Reformers declared collectives to be, in Marxist terms, historically as legitimate and prospectively as long-lasting as state industries (and they duly noted that Marx foresaw the withering away of the state). Although workers' administrative rights over purchasing and marketing decisions were usually fantasies, the theory underlying them was published.

Shanghai collectives became especially important in retailing perishable goods, which required more care than state units reliably mustered. Collectives in the early 1980s sold 63 percent of subsidiary food products by value, and 35 percent of other non-grain foods – but only 4 percent of staple grains (which were usually rationed). State-owned shops at this time still controlled over 90 percent of reported sales in clothing, stationery, and department stores – and state shops had higher portions of these markets in Shanghai than in most Chinese cities. In any service that required particular care, collectives could thrive in competition with state firms. Among restaurants and other eateries in Shanghai, 84 percent of the firms by 1983, and already 51 percent of the sales volume, were collective.[26] Urban industry remained overwhelmingly state owned, and private firms were mostly unregistered and small.

State industry remained far more important in Shanghai than in nearby and comparable places, even well into the reform era. The growth rate of both collective and state industry in Shanghai, as Table 8.1 suggests, was slower than in other rich provinces.

As seen in Table 8.2, of Shanghai's reported GDP in 1978, the state sector produced 84 percent; in 1985, 72 percent; and in 1989, 63 percent. Similar calculations for Guangzhou, a provincial capital, indicate a 1989 public sector share of GDP almost identical to that in Shanghai. But a much lower share, 36 percent, was state-sector in the large Guangdong non-capital (and more lightly taxed) city of Foshan.

184 Owners manage urban corruption & companies

TABLE 8.1 Shanghai and other provinces' industrial output portions by ownership type, 1980 and 1990 (percentages of gross value, and increase percentages)

	1980		1990	
	State-owned	*Collective*	*State-owned*	*Collective*
SHANGHAI portion %	87	12	64	21
1980–1990 % increase			41	247
JIANGSU portion	57	33	34	40
1980–1990 % increase			129	440
ZHEJIANG portion	56	43	31	60
1980–1990 % increase			212	690
GUANGDONG portion	63	28	35	27
1980–1990 % increase			237	494
ALL CHINA portion	76	24	55	36
1980–1990 % increase			136	396

Sources: See *Quanguo ge sheng zizhi qu zhixia shi lishi tongji ziliao huibian, 1949–1989* (Historical Statistics Collection on Provinces, Autonomous Regions, and *Municipalities Throughout the Country, 1949–1989*) (Beijing: Zhongguo Tongji Chuban She, 1990), 387; *Zhejiang tongji nianjian, 1991* (Zhejiang Provincial Yearbook, 1991), Zhejiang Statistics Bureau, ed. (Beijing: Zhongguo Tongji Chuban She, 1991), 155–56; *Jiangsu tongji nianjian 1991* (Jiangsu Statistical Yearbook, 1991), Jiangsu Statistical Bureau, ed. (Nanjing: Zhongguo Tongji Chuban She, 1991), 122 and 124; *Zhongguo tongji nianjian, 1991* (China Statistical Yearbook, 1991), State Statistical Bureau, ed. (Beijing: Zhongguo Tongji Chuban She, 1991), 396; *Shanghai tongji nianjian, 1991* (Shanghai Statistical Yearbook, 1991), Li Mouhuan et al., eds. (Shanghai: Shanghai Shi Tongji Ju, 1991), 153; *Guangdong tongji nianjian, 1991* (Guangdong Statistical Yearbook, 1991), Guangdong Province Statistics Bureau, ed. (Beijing: Zhongguo Tongji Chubanshe, 1991), 96–97; and the *Far Eastern Economic Review*, December 18, 1986, 107.

By the same criteria, the 1989 state share of product in Suzhou was 31 percent; and in Ningbo, 30 percent; these are not provincial capitals.[27] Between the first two years of the 1990s, when the portion of gross output in state plants decreased in Zhejiang from 31 to 29 percent, in Jiangsu from 34 to 33, and in China as a whole from 55 to 53 percent, the portion of state production rose in Shanghai by a slight amount, to 65 percent. The Tiananmen shock may quickly have affected economic decisions.[28]

During the reform years until 1989, China's state-owned sector did not everywhere give way to the private sector; it gave way to collectives. This fact did not fit some Western preconceptions of reforms. Journalists and economists, who were joined by PRC planners wanting to hoodwink foreign investors to raise more capital and technology from them, fostered the impression that urban China was privatizing. That largely happened after 1990, unless collectives be deemed *de facto* private. Table 8.2 shows that although the reported state share of China's GDP decreased in Shanghai (and for comparison, in Tianjin) between 1978 and 1989, the private sector remained small. The table aims to include all sectors, not just industry. More private ownership arose later; but in large cities, the relative decline of state firms was mainly accompanied by a growth not of private enterprises, but of collectives.

Owners manage urban corruption & companies **185**

TABLE 8.2 Percentages of GDP by ownership sector in Shanghai, 1978–1989 [Cheng Xiaonong's estimates for Shanghai in brackets] (Tianjin data in parentheses)

	State-owned (guoying)		Collective (jiti)		Other (private & joint/mixed)	
1978	[84] 87	(76)	12	(22)	1	(2)
79	86		13		1	
80	85	(75)	14	(23)	2	(2)
81	83		14		3	
82	81	(72)	16	(26)	3	(3)
83	80	(71)	17	(26)	3	(3)
84	78	(70)	19	(23)	3	(7)
85	[72]	(68)		(26)		(6)
86		(65)		(22)		(13)
89	[63]					

Sources: This became, especially after the mid-1980s, a topic for which the interpretation of statistics was difficult. Some technical problems are reviewed in Cheng Xiaonong, "The Structure of Economic Growth in China: An Approach to Measuring the Contribution of the Public and Non-Public Sectors, and Some Estimations" (unpublished paper, Princeton University, 1993); and Cao Linzhang, Gu Guangqing, and Li Jianhua, *Shanghai shengchan ziliao suoyu zhi jiegou yanjiu* (Studies of Shanghai Production and Ownership Structure) (Shanghai: Shanghai Shehui Kexue Yuan Chuban She, 1987), rounded from 214. This is based on national income (*guomin shouru*), including all goods and services. The Tianjin figures come from *Tianjin tongji nianjian, 1986* (Tianjin Statistical Yearbook, 1986), Tianjin Statistical Bureau, ed. (Beijing: Zhongguo Tongji Chuban She, 1986), 89. Guangdong statistical yearbooks for 1986 and 1987 do not seem to offer data analyzed by ownership sector. More appropriate comparisons would be with other cities, but many urban yearbooks also do not emphasize this topic. Some of the data are from *Tianjin tongji nianjian* (Tianjin Statistical Yearbook), Tianjin Statistical Bureau and Liang Zhaoxin, ed. (Beijing: Zhongguo Tongji Chuban She), for 1984, 4; 1985, 5; and 1987, 49.

These changes in the largest cities, which are important for the central budget, differed from reforms elsewhere. In most of China, especially outside cities, the collective, quasi-private, local-state-licensed and local-controlled sector grew sharply. Regular state firms in 1978 still made more than three-quarters of China's industrial product; but by 1992, their reported share of manufactures had dropped to about half the country's total. If agriculture and services are counted along with industry in China as a whole, about one-quarter of the economy's 1992 output value was in the state sector.[29]

Wenzhou is an East China city that contrasts with Shanghai, because in that exceptional Zhejiang place by 1986, only 17 percent of gross industrial output came from state factories, 53 percent from collectives, and 30 percent (reported) from private factories. In commerce, the state and private sectors' lag behind collectives was less than in manufacturing: 28 percent of goods were sold in 1986 through Wenzhou state-owned stores, 35 percent through collectives or cooperatives, and 37 percent reportedly through private shops.[30] But this city is an extreme case; an exception testing the rule.

186 Owners manage urban corruption & companies

Shanghai's position was at the other end of the tax-and-control spectrum. It was not completely off the charts, because other large cities' industries were about three-quarters nationalized. But in those other cities, the portion from the collective sector averaged about twice Shanghai's. In all of China's officially designated "cities," 77 percent of factory output by value in 1988 was state, 21 percent was collective, and the private sector was still (reported as) a minor residual at 2 percent.[31]

Only 2 percent of Shanghai's industrial output by the late 1980s came from collective and private industries together, much less than in most Chinese cities. Collective enterprises there, more than in other places, have also been more tightly restricted as regards the authority of managers. Some urban Shanghai collectives were hard to distinguish from state firms, mainly because their extraction regimes were similar. In Guangdong under reforms, the term "cadre" (*ganbu*) has generally referred to state officials only. But in urban Shanghai, collectives' leaders were also called "cadres." They paid enough taxes to earn the title.

Shuffling nameplates and merger mania

The mid-1950s Transition to Socialism is relevant to 1980s ownership reforms, because it is what they practically reversed. Early PRC planning, in factories and especially in stores, had been largely a matter of putting new nameplates on previously private enterprises, calling them branches of state corporations. In industries such as textiles, the centralizing regime could induce capitalist owners to part with their factories, because the new revolutionary state could influence materials flows and mobilize ex-bourgeois on patriotic grounds. This process of the mid-1950s created a nationalized monopolistic structure, in which the government made manufacturing profits.

Many commercial firms, especially family-run shops, also accommodated their new status as branches of large socialist wholesaling and retailing corporations. Their prices and supplies were partly fixed by the state; but the regime had too few personnel to monitor them all. But relatively centralist leaders tried to take over any activities that made profits.

In later years, they tried to externalize, turning over to lower administrations any activities that led losses. Higher bureaucrats often assumed control of factories that had earlier been managed locally, or else sloughed off others that had been managed more centrally, depending on profitability. The tradition of tinkering with nameplates became well established in China and lasted after the 1950s. It involved a stress on functions and factories from which the state (at any level) could make money, because it could control inputs or because large amounts of capital were required. Except for military industries, high state planners often ignored markets where production and sales, to the extent these could be monitored, did not allow high extraction of profits and taxes.

When the central state took over plants "owned by all the people" that had previously been administered locally, spending by the jurisdiction whose revenues had been raided did not necessarily fall. In budget negotiations, the loss was often made up by political fiat, reallocating funds.[32] Central conservatives (whose army and heavy industrial ministries needed money) tended to argue against such reallocations, demanding further shifts of functions among administrative levels.

Socialist conservatives argued for large centrally managed plants, thinking these would be sure successes because of high-placed political support. Shanghai's output growth in 1980–1988 was far below the national average, and conservatives explained this by blaming the 1986 abolition of 68 large corporations. "According to this answer, all Shanghai needs is to return to the large-scale [state corporation] economy."[33] Most economists, however, knew that the roots of the industrial problem lay in factor markets and in the long-term depreciation of Shanghai's capital stock, which local companies could not correct without retaining more profits. Reshuffling nameplates on major factories would not reverse the deterioration. National politicians tended to propose organizational fiddling, and local reformers tended to suggest lower taxes.[34]

The statist tradition was that Beijing should treat "the country as a single chessboard" (*quanguo yipan qi*), maximizing revenues wherever possible.[35] The Seventh Five-Year Plan allowed the Ministry of Electronics Industries, for example, to retain profits from its companies. But most money was not retained in the places where it originated. When chronic inefficiencies became impossible to hide in the managements of state-owned firms, a common response of high bureaucrats outside the fiscal system was to approve enterprise mergers (*qiye jianping*).

Basically different kinds of leaders might together agree on managerial mergers, even if they disagreed about much else. The Army and heavy industrial ministries had long managed large firms. Party conservatives could point out that Cultural Revolution radicals had criticized Liuist "trusts," which therefore after 1976 had to be deemed good. Marxist reformers, too, could see how *zaibatsu-* or *chaebol-*like coordination had raised the international competitiveness of Japan or South Korea. So politically different leaders might agree on the value of mergers while putting off knottier questions of what kinds of mergers they meant. By August 1988, new marriages of more than 400 state-owned firms were officially blessed in about half of China's provinces. High reformers sponsored the idea that "the best win and the weak are defeated," i.e., merged.[36] They spoke in favor of the survival of the fittest. But their criteria for fitness were odd, because profits were seldom based on scarcity prices and unfit managers often just joined larger enterprises. Such mergers spread losses while saving cadres' jobs.

The acquiring companies assumed control of their new subsidiaries, in exchange for assuming their debts. An alternative option was that an acquiring company could pay a higher administrative level for the assets of a failed business. A third method was called "first guarantee, then merge," which meant that the buying company would assume contractual obligations to meet product, profit, tax, and other quotas of the bankrupt company, also paying its debts. Or high state decisions could simply mandate "uncompensated transfers." Late 1988 sources claimed that this last, coerced kind of transfer could meet the "mutual interests" of all parties; financial payments might prevent firing staff. In theory all state enterprises were

188 Owners manage urban corruption & companies

property of "the whole people." Many were deemed "too big to fail," and high politicians were like owners.

Fourteen Shanghai towel factories were merged "with compensation" in the mid-1980s under the Shanghai Dalei Clothing Factory. Within ten months, the total budget for wages went up by half, because some women employees who had apparently been laid off could resume their jobs after the merger.[37] Machiavellian-Paretan conservative lions in China had a goal that matched their distaste for elite circulation: They wanted to retain their own jobs. This was different from the principle of maximizing profit, but it served political stability and maintained "face" among bureaucrats even when their companies were failing.

A debate has flourished between scholars who stress that corporatist leaders stymie the market's ability to allocate resources and income, and other scholars who say the market allocates well.[38] Those who stress local corporatism and those who prefer market incentives are both able to find valid data for their opposing policies by looking at different Chinese places or periods. One reason is that labor demand varied. The nationwide economic boom eroded planners' power and encouraged migrants into urban areas, including Yangzi delta cities where local labor could not fill all the new job opportunities. Companies there followed the pattern the Party used in large cities during Mao's time: Favored local workers got plum posts, and temporary migrant workers received less good jobs at lower wages. Units wanting completely to exclude outsiders tended to lose market share and disappear or be merged.

Contracts, particularist management, and local entrepreneurs' incentives against reform

The contract system for state-owned industries implied that the government would become like a stockholder – originally with 100 percent of the shares. So supervisors and factory managers needed to justify their and their clients' jobs. For creating sinecures, contracts served as well as plans had. Some kinds of reform challenged institutional and career interests, but others avoided upsetting bureaucracies. Proposals for "decentralization" that allowed cadres in localities and offices to maintain their vested interests were easy to adopt. These can be called "particularistic contracting."[39] But "standardization reforms," redistributing rights or money, drew bureaucratic fire from agencies they disadvantaged. Even when such reforms were advocated by high politicians, they were not necessarily implemented.

A random survey of 100 Shanghai state factories in 1985 showed that 77 percent still lacked the authority to "adjust" their plans. The idea behind contracts was that local managers should agree to their conditions of doing business. Prior to the mid-1980s reforms, sixth-tenths of the surveyed factories lacked any right to sell their own products. Nearly three-quarters could not set their prices – even for products over planned quotas. Four-fifths still did not purchase their own materials.[40] All the surveyed companies also lacked rights to set their employees' wages (although this was less important, because they could set bonuses). In other words, most managers' *external* powers, involving the firms' relations with markets, had been legally authorized but were still unrealized. Such reforms were supposed to be major new industrial policies proclaimed from Beijing, but medial anti-reformers slowed them. Market pressures were the strongest reformers.

Managers understandably avoided many tasks in fast-changing materials markets. Their rights to adjust *internal* aspects of their firms expanded more quickly. For example, 66 percent of surveyed firms could freely allocate their own liquid capital, and three-quarters could decide how to use any excess fixed capital. Also, 73 percent could set their own internal organization charts without consulting higher levels. Almost two-thirds assumed the authority to decide issues concerning their workers (except for basic wage rates, which they could supplement with other emoluments). In addition, practically all the managements (98 percent) had rights to promote at least some of their employees.

With respect to one kind of external power – the right to set up joint projects with other jurisdictions or offices – 81 percent of the managers said they could act on their own. This was the main external authority that many local leaders wanted, considering the net pressures on them, because most others in the mid-1980s implied more costs than benefits. So Shanghai companies became generally free to associate with each other and with firms in other places.[41] Because partners elsewhere usually had less restrictive rules on market operations, "horizontal" connections were a crucial aspect of reform as it was actually implemented.

All this still fell short of the visions of central reformers in the mid-1980s, whose initiatives were stymied not just by central conservatives but also *collectively* by more powerful sets of medial urban managers. These business cadres did not need to articulate their position or organize in public. All they needed to do was to act on their interests in parallel with each other, choosing selectively from central mandates without any call openly to oppose anything from on "high." Not all the conservatives were central, nor all the reformers local.

Adopting the contract system without adopting ownership reform meant that a "mother-in-law" supervising agency or corporation could sign a contract on behalf of its subsidiary factory. Contracts could tightly bind factories to socialist trusts. When contracts first replaced plans, they often temporarily strengthened ex-planners. But oversight agencies often had little sense of what was possible and what was not in production operations. Also, some factories or stores had more than one supervising "mother-in-law." If its different "higher-level" agencies signed contradictory contracts on its behalf, the manager was still supposed to deliver.[42] Without much enforcement or sanction, such contracts meant little. In the long term, managers' authority nonetheless rose.

"Because contracting gave every organization the opportunity to retain its privileges through bargaining, it was easier for contracting to win a consensus of bureaucratic support than for inherently redistributive policies such as tax or price reform to do so."[43] Sometimes the bargains resulted in terms that were good for the leaders of small firms; this was usually the case in rural areas. But contracts could also have the opposite result. Enterprise freedom could shift risks previously borne

190 Owners manage urban corruption & companies

by bureau-level planners to factory directors instead. As a Shanghai manager complained, "When supply becomes short on the market, all products are purchased [by the supervising bureau] and plants are not permitted to sell by themselves. When the market slumps, plants are ordered to sell their products by themselves."[44]

Supervision sometimes tightened during reforms, and leaders of local networks were at a disadvantage if leaders of larger networks had accurate information about local activities. This was more important than whether such power was exercised through plans or contracts. Before 1986, for example, the Shanghai No. 10 Iron and Steel Corporation could use its own scrap steel and leftovers – so it "organized surplus labor" to make more washers. These were "warmly welcomed in the United States and Canada. However [in 1986], these scraps were allocated in a unified way by the higher-level units. The equipment which produces washers has had to suspend operations and wait for the arrival of scrap." If the mother-in-law office had never heard about the scrap or the washers, the factory could have earned more foreign exchange.

Plans were often used for quota production – but contracts for surplus. This combination could be devastating for any urban manager who did not underreport surplus. "Production plans show the quota is raised at each level. While the ministry draws up its plan, the municipality and bureau have drawn up their own plans to increase production. As a result, enterprises have no products in excess of production targets and, accordingly, nothing to sell."[45]

Contract terms

In late 1986, only 18 percent of Shanghai's total output value was reportedly still under the mandatory plan. But almost 100 percent of the "main products" in crucial industries, including metals and textiles, were subject to plans at least of the "indicative," "guidance," "advisory" type. "In some departments, even products in excess of production targets are also incorporated into the 'mandatory plan.'" When the plan did not suit them, bureau-level cadres could in practice neglect it. Factory managers at "Shanghai's cotton textile plants all complain that, although the State Council has plainly stipulated that cotton yarn is a product under the 'guidance plan,' the departments concerned simply deprive them of the right given by the State Council to sell products in excess of production targets."[46] Bureau cadres were more obliged to deliver profits and products upward than to deliver raw materials with which the goods could be made. As a bureau cadre said, "We have had to lay down 'hard and fast rules' for yarn-producing enterprises. Otherwise, who is going to shoulder the responsibility to fulfill the output value plans issued by Shanghai Municipality and the Ministry of Textile Industries?"[47]

This tightening of control reversed grants of discretion that had been made earlier. As the director of the No. 19 Factory of the Shanghai Cotton Textile Corporation put it,[48]

> Over the past two years [1985–1986], our plant has used the right to establish horizontal relations with fraternal provinces and cities. We have helped

supply each others' needs and invigorated our enterprise. Now that the [Textile] Bureau has taken this minor right away, how can we supply each others' needs and maintain horizontal relations? If a commodity [cotton] is in great demand, then it is more important to give enterprises the power of decision to handle this commodity, to encourage them to raise production by establishing more domestic ties.

The best revenge of local managers, faced with pressures from leaders in their supervising corporations, was to try to hold the "mothers-in-law" responsible for finding inputs and selling products. Few state plant managers wanted to deal in reform markets they were not used to commandeering. If the costs of inputs were high, or if the materials were simply unavailable, that was not supposed to be the plant managers' problem. The officials to whom they could refer such issues were at a sufficiently high political level to keep their jobs without really performing them. This system (like others in many countries) was built to preserve careers, rather than for any purpose more fit to discuss.

As one economist said of Shanghai corporation managers in the 1980s, "They can't break with the higher level (*libukai shangji*)."[49] They had strong disincentives to cut this tie; it was a bond of conflict but also of dependence. "Guaranteed management contracts (*chengbao jingying hetong*)" in early 1988 still governed relations between 92 percent of Shanghai's state-owned firms and their supervising corporations.[50] Guarantees by the basic-level factories and stores were of three sorts: to remit an amount of profits, to protect technical quality, and (for some firms) to guarantee specified amounts of foreign exchange from export sales. The first guarantee – to remit money upward – was the most onerous, applying to all state firms.

Different kinds of contracts were required of different companies, despite this main contract proviso about remittances. Many (38 percent of the enterprises) guaranteed a basic quota of profits to higher levels, as well as a fraction of any profits above that. Another 37 percent signed contracts that guaranteed a fixed remittance only – but it was often high. A further 25 percent were asked to contract a set remittance during the first year (perhaps not very high, in view of materials shortages), but then increasing amounts for several years afterward.[51] An official fantasy was that the materials shortages would cease. Time periods of contracts varied, but many were for three or five years. These reform contracts in the state sector were like previous plans, because their frequent violations punctuated their repeated renegotiations.

Incentives of managers or owners

When plans or contracts existed, state-appointed managers did not necessarily follow them. As one executive said, "We have just two principles. One is satisfying demand. The other is making money."[52] In an attitude survey of enterprise cadres in the early 1980s, barely half the respondents (52 percent) claimed to put the state plan above other considerations when making decisions. Fully 27 percent admitted they would put their own firms' interests above those of the state plan. Another

192 Owners manage urban corruption & companies

21 percent said they would pay prime attention to their customers' needs. Attitude polls are difficult to relate to behavior. But 46 percent of these managers expressed frank willingness to violate plans.[53]

In this same group of businessmen, 60 percent had been appointed solely by higher level cadres, and 31 percent had received their posts only after a period of "fermentation" and discussion at basic levels. (The other 9 percent got their jobs by other methods, including elections.)[54] Once they were in their posts, no matter how they had been chosen, half admitted putting the interests of their local networks foremost.

Managers could often adapt plans to serve those interests. When the "guarantee system" (*chengbao zhi*) was studied in October 1987 among Shanghai firms, 78 percent of respondents reported they had a one-man management system or leased their factories to a single boss. The person who took responsibility for production, in 85 percent of these cases, had been a member of the previous "leading group" in the factory. Only 10 percent of new managers came from outside. From the viewpoint of executives, an advantage of the contract system was that their own salaries in most cases doubled.[55]

Contract systems were supposed to be implemented by early 1988 for 1,700 large and medium-sized Shanghai state firms – more than had subscribed to them before. The official who made this announcement implied that leaders had been too slow to switch from planning. He "criticized state-owned enterprises in Shanghai, which form the main source of the city's revenue, for failing to adapt to the planned commodity economy now being developed in China."[56] In the previous year, only 465 companies had adopted contract systems. The reason for factory managers' resistance is not hard to find: Since 1984 at least, managers had been given no reason to be sure contracts would be stable or honored. These agreements were difficult to enforce in courts. Contracts were often just means to localize scapegoats for the collapse of planning.

Reformist policies were supposed to destroy the "mother-in-law/daughter-in-law" relationship (*poxi guanxi*) between supervising corporations and basic-level firms. They did not mean that the managers of factories were under less pressure, but their main problems no longer came from the state. Managers still had to worry about where raw materials were available, where products might be sold, and what the prices would be. Anxiety about "management operations" (*jingying yunxing*) temporarily displaced anxiety about pleasing supervisors. The guarantee system created more flexible factor markets for labor, capital, and other inputs. Because prices were higher than for firms operating with planned allocations, businesspeople often could not make the purchases they expected. Free markets acted like vortex whirlwinds; they pulled in managers who initially did not want to deal on them.[57]

The main incentive that eventually inspired factory managers to accept such responsibility was monetary. State policies promised lower tax extractions over a long period, to allow investment that could make firms more efficient. This was exactly what conservative socialist politicians did not want to offer. Greater management autonomy, which factory directors were given under the contract responsibility system, was not initially worth the expected costs of defaults on contracts. Bargaining for full localization – of money, not just management – was a procedure that extended over several years in the 1980s. Urban Shanghai's economic hinge leaders, the middle managers, gradually had to receive more funds, not just more risk.

The decline of state capacity to supply inputs by either plan or contract, and the increased pressure on factory managers to take this burden, converted to socialist conservatism many local leaders who otherwise might have explored markets energetically by themselves. Shanghai managers were "obedient" in an ambiguous way that is typical of restorations – and sometimes seems comic. A disgruntled columnist said that Shanghai was always overly "law abiding, following the straight and narrow."[58] Shanghai managers came up with many innovations they did not follow, and this was a standing joke in administrative circles. At a national conference, a spokesman from another province listed flexible management procedures that his own units employed with great success. He drew chuckles when he said those ideas "all came from Shanghai."[59]

Enterprises had difficulty in getting repayment of debts owed to them. So researchers at the Shanghai Academy of Social Sciences established a company to specialize in debt collection. Although this sort of firm was entirely legal, municipal officials conveyed the government's opinion that it should not be established. The slow-paying debtors were mainly state corporations. One of the proffered reasons was that lawyers could better handle such work. A second reason was that no such company had been established before. Shanghai was better at coming up with management ideas than at carrying through on them.

Warehoused waste as "production"

Socialist managers often received credit for goods they never sold. State factories got quota credit for profit on all output, whether or not it ever went to consumers. The advent of contracts did not immediately change this situation, because state buyers were still not supposed to refuse their assigned purchases, regardless of whether they needed the goods. Production "for the warehouse" (*na sklad* among Russians, who knew it well) was commonplace in most of China, where it was euphemistically called "surplus saved products" (*chaochu chanpin*). For years, China's amounts of "surplus saved products" were very large. In 1979, for example, godowns contained 60 billion yuan worth of electrical goods and 20 million metric tons of steel.[60] This waste in Shanghai was not as severe as elsewhere, partly because some Shanghai products proved salable at lower-than-planned prices eventually, partly because warehouse space was scarce in the city, and mostly because stringent finances encouraged companies to politick for prices at which the wares could be cleared. But China's institutions did not automatically end the production of goods for which there was no demand. Market competition and booming prosperity, rather than new legalisms, brought this result.

The amount of warehoused waste was usually too embarrassing to publicize, except anecdotally. In 1986, seventy million wrist watches were made in China, but only 40 million were sold. The producers did not get the market message, because in the first three months of 1987, thirty percent more watches were made than in the same period of the previous year. China's bicycle industry reportedly made one-tenth more bicycles in 1986 than in 1985; but sales then were only 53 percent of production. A Ministry of Commerce survey of 650 products concluded that "at least 25 percent are virtually unsalable."[61] Textiles and clothes, non-color TV sets, refrigerators, and bicycles were prominent among the "surplus saved products," made thus for shelves. Unusable goods, sent directly to warehouses, reportedly accounted for 12 percent of China's total GDP by 1991.[62]

Local commerce, local industry, and hesitant urban managers

Trade reformed faster than urban industry. In Mao's time the Party had not prioritized devoting scarce loyal personnel to commerce rather than processing, where taxes and state profits were usually higher. In the 1950s, many small businesspeople had "transitioned to socialism" and put their firms under state corporations. Outlets for consumer goods, foods, pharmaceuticals, hardwares, and apparel had been merged or terminated by 1956. In the Hundred Flowers of 1957, they complained of abandonment by Party cadres (often uneducated former guerrillas) who had promised supplies and capital to them but simply reneged. Pre-1970 ex-bourgeois who had run stores remembered maltreatments by many campaigns, including the Cultural Revolution.[63] Their buildings had often become warehouses or had been converted to factory use. But by the early 1980s, the government realized a need for more stores to spur consumption. It held meetings for retail groups, and some employees were able to restart their old enterprises again, often as "dependent" collectives.[64]

Mercantile firms grew in number. From 1978 to 1988, state commercial enterprises in China tripled (from 103,000 to 327,000). Industrial state enterprises rose far more slowly (from 84,000 to 90,000 in the same period).[65] Many state trading firms were, like the vast majority of collectives, quasi-private in practice. Commercial reform was sharp because resource allocation offices in some ministries and jurisdictions developed retail outlets (*menshi bu*) that increasingly enjoyed market autonomy.

Localization of management within the state sector for both industry and commerce was implemented either by the "contract responsibility system" (*chengbao ziren zhi*) or the "lease system" (*zulin zhi*). The usual difference between these two was that contractors paid a portion of reported profits, whereas lessors paid a fixed remittance. Another difference was that contracts could be made with workers. If part of a factory constantly lost money, and if better-motivated labor would solve the problem, the management could strike a bargain with employees: They could be given permission to take over the shop or part of the production process, nurse it back to profitability, and then share the profits at a prearranged rate with the original firm.[66] In Shanghai by the end of reforms, the criteria for granting contracts became less restrictive than before, especially in retail and service trades that could create new jobs.

This "responsibility system" was not introduced throughout the city – but selected industrial bureaus tried it experimentally, as Table 8.3 suggests, in the early 1980s. The experiment was common in firms for which the state had most difficulty maintaining inputs. The table reports a rise of contracting only in those sectors.

Neoliberal economists might hold their applause despite the very quick rise in these figures – to 100 percent already by 1982 under the selected industrial bureaus. The aim of the reorganization was not just to maximize profits, but to preserve jobs and a lifestyle that had grown up over earlier decades. Legal recategorization of plans as contracts did not end planning. If delivery contracts were not honored in the hectic raw materials markets of the early 1980s, the parties were unlikely to press each other hard. Jobs and habits were at stake. Bankruptcy was normally not yet an option.

By the mid-1980s, there was agreement among top reform leaders to let managers manage, but this remained in many bureaus more a matter of words than actions. The debate climaxed during discussions of an "Enterprise Law." Reformers proposed a "general rule that the organizations of the CCP in enterprises should support factory directors to exercise their powers in accord with laws and regulations." This kind of wording got only as far as the draft of the Enterprise Law. Socialist conservatives objected strongly to such localization.

The result was an ambiguous compromise, assuring that intermediate and local actors rather than any uniform national law would set the primacy of either Party secretaries or manager-technicians. The law held: "The organizations of the CCP in enterprises guarantee and supervise the implementation of Party and state policies in the enterprises."[67] This wording retained Party primacy as a symbol, and the CCP organization was still supposed to have a monitoring, information-gathering role. But the extent to which it would manage firms remained uncertain. What

TABLE 8.3 Quick rise of the production responsibility system, 1979-1982, in Shanghai industries (number and percent of factories with "production responsibility" among firms under eleven of Shanghai's industrial bureaus)

	No. of factories	% of factories	% of output
1979	711	36	58
80	1,242	66	82
81	1,389	75	87
82	1,839	100	100

Source: The "economic responsibility system" means use of the principle that profit should be replaced with taxes and that a factory should be responsible for its own profits and losses. *Dangdai Zhongguo de jingji tizhi gaige* (Reform of the Economic System in Modern China), Zhou Taihe et al., eds. (Beijing: Zhongguo Shehui Kexue Chuban She, 1984), 554.

happened in local companies depended mostly on the personalities and resources of particular leaders there.

Patronist leaders, depending on both their clients and their Party overseers, often became effective local reformers. They had local authoritarian control over people they hired. Leaders who looked like "reformers" from the vantage point of higher administrative levels were often uncivil and unconsultative within their own bailiwicks.

When reforms were attempted at Beijing's mandate alone, the result could be a disaster for mid-level authorities. Selling stock shares to workers in a company, for example, was a major reform. China's first such sales occurred during 1986 at Nanchang, Jiangxi, which was then in the outer periphery of the Shanghai Economic Zone. This reform was first tried in a low-revenue sector, among vegetable shops. Under the plan, 135 state-owned and collective groceries sold shares. In most of the stores, worker-shareholders soon deposed of their old managers and elected new ones. Reportedly the new stockholders did not believe their former leaders reaped sufficient profits.[68] This (quasi-Yugoslav) liberal experiment in worker management was rare, because it took power from bureaucrats. It was not much copied elsewhere.

Usually reform managers ruled their underlings with an authoritarian style of command that even the Chinese state could rarely muster in public until 1989. Examples come from rural enterprises in rich areas of Jiangsu and Zhejiang that employed transients from poorer inland areas to do hard work. Many heads of enterprises also hired managerial talent from elsewhere, because locals found it difficult to make some kinds of economic decisions well. As pressures on firms increased,

> More and more rural enterprises are trying to break away from traditional community interference. They seek independent decision-making power and personnel management. As suppliers of the initial investment, communities frequently tax these enterprises heavily for short-sighted welfare purposes. They claim the right to send more than enough hands to the work force and even managerial staff. These superfluous workers, most of whom are the beneficiaries of nepotism, do not have to work hard but enjoy greater job security than their colleagues [including many contract workers from other areas].[69]

In Zhejiang, the manager of a large rural enterprise said that he "only hired people from outside the community as chief assistants. I've got a system that somewhat resembles the so-called guest official system of the Warring States period. . . . Only the guest officials have the much-needed coldheartedness to turn down a whole batch of products – no locals would do this, because they know the factory is making money for themselves and their parents down in the village." He hired these managerial visitors for short terms and "when the contracts expire and the job is done, I pay them at least five times the amount I pay others and let them go."[70]

The centralized state of Mao's time had only sporadically been able to muster such control by launching political campaigns. Now rural industrialists were commandeering talents more reliably. Reformers sometimes proposed that these methods be imported into the state sector so that it could compete. Wuxi city leaders suggested that "state-owned enterprises above the county level must learn from rural industries."[71] In 1986, Wuxi's industrial output growth in state-owned firms was only 0.6 percent; but in rural industries, it was 26 percent. In Changzhou, city officials claimed that "an important factor for economic development was to adopt rural industrial management in state firms," urging cadres to be more forceful.

On the other hand, the local origins of many township managers – especially heads of collectives – was the main reason why these hinge leaders could not just get by economically but had to succeed. No other place could give them comparable careers. As a news correspondent wrote,[72]

> I once visited a manager in a township factory, and he told me, "It is not easy to be a manager. [We] have several hundred thousand yuan and more than a hundred people, but everybody is a neighbor. Money [for investment] was collected by all of them. If the factory isn't profitable, what can I do? Managers in the state companies can go someplace else to continue their careers after they fail to manage their factories well. They do not have responsibility for their mistakes. But I am a native person here; so where could I go?" This pressure forces them to raise their enterprises' competitive strength in markets.

Also, these local managers' friends, when the local government leaders were reformists or kin, trusted them better than had bureaucrats who were more beholden to higher levels of the state. The same reporter interviewed higher-ranked officials:

> A vice director of the Shaoxing County Rural Industry Bureau told me his unit had only thirteen cadres. They were in charge of 2,680 enterprises. He said, "We cannot be like mothers-in-law (*popo*), like cadres in state-owned enterprises, trying to manage everything. We just do three main jobs: upholding broad policy directions, analyzing markets, and encouraging larger enterprises' development. But as far as production, supply, and marketing go, the enterprises have full freedom."

Even Shanghai, the big tax-paying metropolis, was affected by a fad for rural management styles. This meant even more hiding of financial information relevant to revenues. In early 1987, Shanghai industrial bureaus were supposed to implement "indirect management" over subordinate firms. This was to be realized by "putting" power away from supervising bureaus, "shifting" social services to local governments, "turning" from administrative organs to professional associations, and "reforming" so that economic levers would guide managements (rather than bureaucrats doing so).[73] This rearrangement externalized companies' costs that had been borne by their budgets, but it also externalized from the state most responsibility for materials and sales. The new structure was more "decentralized," and in the long run it empowered local leaders. In the short run, they had to pay heavily for it in new expenses on markets where state budgets no longer had enough money to meet the inflated prices.

Among large and medium-sized Shanghai companies, 19 percent altered their charters in 1987; and three-fifths of these amendments changed the "scope of management," i.e., the products or fields in which they operated.[74] Reportedly, 6 percent of the firms closed in 1987; of these, two-fifths were industrial and over half were suburban.[75] Among rural closures, three-quarters were industrial (almost surely over reported). In urban districts, 82 percent were service firms. Some were shut because of legal violations, including 409 in relatively poor Nanshi District.

A late-reform survey of the autonomy of enterprises in Shanghai claimed that two-thirds had "complete" autonomy to manage production, while the remaining third had "partial" autonomy. In hiring, both of executives and non-managers, 70 percent of the firms surveyed were said to have "partial" autonomy; and another 17 percent to have full powers. Still, only 58 percent had even "partial" autonomy in a matter more relevant to state revenues: the setting of their product prices. Another 29 percent of firms had no say in these prices. About half still had no say in the politically sensitive matter of dismissing workers. Union and CCP bosses tried to keep the authority to hire.[76] The autonomy of state managers in Shanghai was constrained.

Planning or market effects on managerial freedom

Conservative leaders looked broadly for ways to justify planning, which was not just an inheritance from old Soviet models. Old classics, national sources with impeccably Chinese characteristics, arguably validated it. A group of PRC business sages showed a link between ancient intellectualism and modern socialism by hosting a conference to study "How the *Book of Changes* Helps Economic Planning." Planning took help from all quarters. Old military strategists and counselors to princes such as Sun Zi (c. 500 BCE) offered precepts that managers proposed to use. Adherents of these oracles had to admit that the Chinese classics were mostly elitist and often anti-business. An official newspaper held that these scriptures, despite their virtues, also contained "dross to be rejected, such as a general tendency to discard democracy and look down on commerce."[77] Officials held conferences on Sun Zi's principles, but no rural industrialists came – perhaps they were too busy managing all their money.

A purpose of planning was to maintain a relatively stable elite that could distribute resources and jobs. The government's main problem, as the factor crisis grew and a business cycle became obvious, was to maintain productive structures in which loyal cadres had jobs. An example of this problem emerged in hosting travelers. From 1978 to 1980, Shanghai authorities hesitated to approve the construction of new hotels, including the Hongqiao Hotel and the Huating Sheraton.

In the autumn travel season of 1983, the shortage of hotels was so great that some international tourists were shipped off to Suzhou or other nearby cities, because there was no room for them in Shanghai. Their lengths of stay in the city shortened. By the late 1980s and 1990s, however, after construction had begun on big hotels in Beijing, Guangzhou, and Nanjing, Shanghai's planners reversed this policy and approved many projects, trying to keep pace with rising demand.

In an effort to compensate for previous delays, zoning planners approved a great deal of new construction. Policies against overbuilding and inflation led to the cancellation of some projects.[78] A similar pattern (hesitation in the early 1980s, approvals amid shortages in the middle of the decade, and constriction again after 1989) was evident in other decisions by many kinds of units. At Fudan University, a group of alumni in the late 1970s offered loans to build a hotel for the school, which would then have been profitable because guest housing was short in that part of town. The university's authorities urged deliberateness and went forward with the project only after several other hotels in the area had already been started. Profitable enterprises that brought foreign exchange tended to reduce planners' autonomy, and some were resisted by conservatives.

The mid-1980s factor crisis saw an end to effective planning of most commodities – but not an end to the writing of plans. On the contrary, at the beginning of 1985, the State Cabinet ratified an outline for Shanghai's economic development. The city government published a specific, detailed economic strategy document. This was followed by an urban plan for spatial development, a seventh five-year economic plan, a five-year "social development plan," and a "cultural development strategy."[79] Technical committees at various administrative levels, using advice from universities and the Shanghai Social Sciences Academy, drew up local plans for each district and county. The language in these documents overwhelmingly suggested that all serious initiatives for change begin at the top of the governmental system. Then any impetus for serious reform was supposed to work its way down, through the administrative levels. But a look at mid-1980s actual behavior, which was deeply affected by the power of local collectives, offers a sharply different picture. The new plans were indirectly driven by recent activity that had escaped plans, thriving in niches that planners could not control or had not served.

Reform growth did not immediately add a great deal of net value to the state treasury. Conservative efforts to discipline the economy were sporadic both before and after the Tiananmen disaster, but they became more effective in later years. On April 4, 1989, two months before major violence in Beijing, a Shanghai office "for rectifying and readjusting the economy" declared that 22 percent of all firms in the urban area should be closed. Almost three-fourths of the companies slated for termination were commercial, and only a minority had been established by plans. As decrees specified: "Existing companies run by Party and government organs have to separate themselves from these agencies."[80] Like the attempt to close companies, rather than merely force them underground, this may have been largely ineffective preaching. Managers not wishing to close their businesses could turn to local Party leaders for protection against the decrees – which in any case did not last long.

200 Owners manage urban corruption & companies

When state corporations merged, managers seldom lost their jobs.[81] The Chinese Party-state did not plan its withering away. It was weakened by forces it could not control. The Chinese economy of later periods, into the 1990s and beyond, continued to see plan documents. The 1991–1995 Five-Year Plan aimed at "revitalizing existing industrial undertakings, instead of investing in new projects."[82] But the state had lost ownership of many firms during reforms.

Land and leasing

Real estate was property whose ownership by bureaucrats was especially important to planners in a dense city. For more than three decades after 1949, Shanghai in effect had no land market. The reason why the state later gave up control of some land was to raise money for its deficits. For ideological reasons, land was not formally sold. Instead, transferrable "land use rights" were auctioned – and the minimum reserve prices were high. "More land in suburban and urban Shanghai [was] leased out for a maximum term of fifty years," after an "initial experiment" to see what price it could fetch. State banks in Shanghai promised mortgage loans for construction projects on specified categories of land. Payment by foreigners or Overseas Chinese was naturally in hard currency. During reforms, a neoliberal argument for this market became apt: "At present, the efficiency of land use in China is very low, because enterprises can occupy state-owned land for as long as they like and at no cost."[83]

The State Constitution of 1982 provided that "land in cities belongs to the state."[84] Particularism affected city planning and investment in offices at Shanghai. One aim of the late 1984 urban reforms for Shanghai was to bring a "rational distribution of tall buildings in the urban areas."[85] In practice, this "rationality" was just politically distributive; "reason" meant that each district should have some tall buildings. So new buildings were put up in Shanghai on a surprisingly even geographical basis. The pattern of new construction was unlike that of most central cities.

Conservatives tended to hope that all land in the post-Mao era – even most rural land – would be considered merely on loan from the government. This norm grew out of confiscations and enforced "donations" of the early and mid-1950s, but it had never been fully regularized in legal or administrative terms. So by the end of 1987, the state planned a full-scale cadastral survey of the whole country. (Historical precedents for this were many in China.) New "land certificates" (*tudi zheng*) were issued in three kinds: "Certificates for Using State-owned Land," "Certificates for Using Collective-owned Land and Land for Construction," and "Certificates of Collective Land Ownership."[86] The aim was to normalize nationalizations of land from long-past campaigns that had used violence rather than formal law. But for reformers, the same process also codified guarantees to local leaders who managed land.

State land had been treated as a free good. The labor theory of value priced undeveloped land as worthless. Reforms made obvious the need for a radical upward revaluation, and Shanghai's suburbs were affected first. From 1981 to 1985, the social gross output value of Meilong Township, Shanghai County, grew 28 percent annually, and the greatest growth was in construction. Meilong industry grew at 26 percent, transport at 19 percent, agriculture at 14 percent – and construction at 55 percent on average for each of the five years, compounded. The building boom was a major engine of growth, and it required land.

Rural residences have, both traditionally and legally even in the PRC's most centralist eras, been private property. When a farm family built a house on public or collective land, it tended to presume ownership of the footprint on which the new structure stood, along with a surrounding tract. Neighbors might object; and since house-raising was still a matter for neighborhood cooperation (as in many rural societies), local leaders had inherent zoning powers. State administrators usually had scant leverage to prevent farmers from confiscating land by building on it. An official agency reported that 95 percent of the houses constructed by cadres were on land that had been "illegally" occupied.[87] Local officials, many of whom took such land themselves, were hard pressed to prevent other farmers from doing it. This popular means to obtain free acreage spread quickly. Cultivating land did not imply ownership, while residing on it did – notwithstanding law. China's rural construction boom arose not just from farmers' desire to have better houses but also from their desire to lay claims to land.

When peasants became rich, they built houses. This became "a universal phenomenon," as an inland newspaper reported. "Peasants mistake their rights over contracted land for ownership rights and build houses on their responsibility fields."[88] Farmers tore up this aspect of their contracts in such numbers, the state could do little about it. Most local cadres accommodated their fellow locals rather than "higher" levels. There is much evidence that peasants wanted official recognition of long-term rights. They often took the situation into their own hands by squatting on land and using it as they wished.

For larger plots, "contracting" land from collectives was like renting. No matter how tenants used the land (agricultural, industrial, or other) they were ordinarily expected to pay for a state grain procurement quota for that acreage – plus a premium that was the unofficial or local-official rent. This devolution of ownership did not mean, in the reform era, that families necessarily worked their fields separately. Cooperative work had very commonly been arranged among families even before 1949, and the collectivized production teams of the early 1950s (like their successors under communes) had accustomed many tillers to this mode of work. By the 1980s, many still did this, hiring extra hands among migrants when they could. In the Yangzi delta, the number of farm families decreased sharply as a portion of the rural population. Some hired outside labor at exploitive wages, while also cooperating with their friends in busy seasons, either as they had in Mao's time or in other combinations they chose.[89]

Near cities, ex-peasants built new residential space for themselves, leasing their previous housing to renters and to companies for uses such as storage. Warehouses in suburban Shanghai became profitable. Old buildings and barns were converted for transient rental housing or for godowns. Data on residences are less available than on storage, because many renters lacked Shanghai household registrations. "With economic development . . . a lot of goods need to be kept in godowns. . . . So Meilong created storage space by making use of empty houses."[90] The yearly growth of godowns in Meilong over the Sixth Five-Year Plan (1981–1985) was 291 percent, and income from warehousing in this town increased 245 percent annually.

Urban land auctions

Shanghai private real estate was sold for the first time in decades at a fair organized by the Shanghai Real Estate Society in November 1986. For residences, 2,000 suites, averaging 50 m² in size, were sold at 520–550 yuan per m² in the city. Prices in nearby suburbs were more than four-fifths as much.[91] People with state jobs, living in low-rent assigned apartments, had no incentive to pay such high prices. Newly rich industrialists or Overseas Chinese arranging Shanghai residence registrations for relatives could pay such rates.

Commercial and industrial land was also auctioned, at a premium. To eliminate "unpaid utilization of land for unlimited periods," the city at the beginning of 1988 opened public bidding on rights to use land for twenty to fifty years. These not-quite-ownership rights could be inherited, and titles to buildings put on the land could be transferred.[92]

Shanghai's first such auction after 1949 was held as late as 1988. Only two structures were for "sale," but 108 bidders registered, of which 63 were state-owned agencies and 45 were "self-employed people." The more expensive property went for 130,000 yuan, to a company in suburban Nanhui County for a new retail shop. The other, for 89,000 yuan, was sold also to a suburban company that made switch-gears in suburban Chuansha County (soon to be called Pudong, as construction sites and land values boomed there).[93]

Use rights could also be leased for commercial space owned by state enterprises in need of money. State-owned department stores, needing to pay their staffs, rented counters to collective and private firms. This converted many department stores into malls or groups of boutiques (even before Western and Japanese chains bought space in them). Large state stores by the 1990s often garnered more than half their revenues from rents, not from profits on sales. The boutiques might be called "dependent firms" (guahu), but actually their independence was what kept the formerly state staffs of these stores paid. The real dependency ran in an unorthodox direction. These small firms were often more able than state stores to obtain commodities for which Shanghai consumers would pay high prices.

Leasing and renting, though they may allow efficient resource allocation, can also become means for local networks to gain – at the expense of government. Almost anything can be leased. A Shanghai sports shop, for example, "rented" its bank account to a rural construction team from Jiangsu that had no license to make transactions in the city. The state-owned shop wrote receipts, issued checks, and in other ways served as the financial department of the (illicit in the city) construction company. In Baoding, Hebei, a survey of over 100 firms found that at least 15 percent were engaged in various illegal forms of renting.[94] Even in strait-laced Shanghai, many collective "dependent firms" rented legitimacy and facilities from the more august state firms that needed their money.

Brokers for leasing proliferated in Shanghai during the late 1980s.[95] The city had 570 specialized companies for renting (zuling qiye) at the start of 1987 – and just six months later, it reported over 1,400. Many were based in old cooperatives, albeit in Maoist terms they were not "productive." New co-ops and private firms also entered the field, and a few new leasing companies obtained registration as state enterprises. The 1986 average reported income of employees in leasing companies was about 150 yuan (more than state workers generally received). The reforms' uncertainty was nowhere more evident than in the kind of ownership they encouraged: the most temporary kind, which is rental.

Conservatives prefer to conduct reform by leasing state property, while ideological reformers wanted the state to sell its interests. "As long as the system of public ownership remains, politics and production will never be separated," a Chinese economist opined in 1987.[96]

Competition, corruption, and chaotic prices

Sociologist Mark Granovetter writes, "The anonymous market of neoclassical models is virtually nonexistent in economic life, and transactions of all kinds are rife . . . with social connections."[97] These connections often involve transactions among people who see themselves as similar in communal groups, or who conform to norms decreed by group leaders.

Markets require costly attention from both buyers and sellers. When prices change, they require even more attention. An increase of market competition, toward the turn of the decade into the 1990s, meant that retailers of items like grain and oil would "skimp on the pounds and be short in the ounces" (duanjin queliang). Complaints reached police about shortchanging in retail sales of staples: rice, cooking oil, and salt. The portions of whittling on sale weights reportedly ranged up to 18 percent, but they were more usually just 3 or 4 percent.[98] Competition assumes disunity among actors, and efficiency is not its sole result.

The most obvious beneficiaries of communitarian state efforts to restrain prices during the reform era were illegal smugglers and speculators. They bought materials at low state prices, and then sold illegally at higher market prices, making handsome profits from which the state received nothing. A Shanghai brand-name bicycle that could be legally sold for a maximum of 200 yuan in the city fetched between 300 and 400 yuan elsewhere. The price at which Shanghai cigarettes were planned to sell in the city was only half the retail price elsewhere. The metropolis also produced color TV sets, whose distribution was supposed to be limited by ration coupons; but the black market price of the coupons alone (500 to 600 yuan each) was an increment to the official price that reflected high demand.[99] The price of black market ration tickets for consumer durables rose sharply in the late 1980s. If a buyer of any commodity had to pay extra money to get the coupon – but then sold the product to a later buyer – the resale price included the cost of the coupon plus a "rent" for the risk of being caught.[100]

If state companies could have received the difference over the ex-factory planned prices that illegal sales of ration tickets brought, then these firms could have remitted more money to the state in profits and taxes. But the government disallowed this policy. Price hikes would have involved state cadres more obviously in inflation. Such changes would also have made Shanghai actors establish more "horizontal relations" with other areas. Keeping low state-fixed prices aimed to keep such patterns from emerging.

Low state prices were a major cause of corruption in Shanghai; their distortion of retail markets, where the illegal profit on each trade was relatively small, normalized a custom that state decrees were not always serious. This led to larger illegal profits on wholesale trades. Low state prices were supposed to symbolize communist stability. They ideally represented the care of the state for the interests of the people. But reforms gave smaller groups and networks scope to find ways of benefiting themselves, at the expense of a state that was supposed to represent everybody.

Although by 1987–1988 the city had tried to establish revenue guarantees for the central budget, along with a local "right to allocate finances," it still did not have a "right to float prices" or a "right to allocate products" (*caizheng fenpei quan, jiage fudong quan,* or *chanpin fenpei quan*). A local economist suggested that Shanghai ask the central government for these powers.[101] Adoption of that proposal would have led to lower remittances. The conservatives resisted it, acting on their preferences, not intending corruption but nonetheless generating it.

Corruption beyond illegality: define it as benefit to a small community, not a large one

Corruption is risky behavior, and so is entrepreneurship that drives "dynamic efficiency."[102] Because corruption is difficult to observe directly for those not illegally involved, it is often studied through attitude surveys. Unsurprisingly, it is correlated with the extent of "gray" economies, in which business activities are not officially registered.[103] Corruption and non-registration are both common in fast-growing economies. Chinese planners may rue the rambunctiousness of firms that sell 'fake' goods and evade taxes or regulations. Yet such entrepreneurship helped China boom.

Political scientists have tried harder to define corruption than to show how it evolves. They have reached considerable consensus on a definition, albeit a defective one. Scott relies on Nye's words, and Nye relies on Banfield's. In this view, corruption is[104]

> behavior which deviates from the formal duties of a public role because of private-regarding (personal, close family, private clique) pecuniary or status

gains, or violates rules against the exercise of certain types of private-regarding influence.

This definition helps calculate costs or benefits of governmental corruption, and it implies a procedure for research. Public laws can be documented, and normative performance can be imputed from attitude surveys that generate statistics. This standard definition salves the professional itch that social scientists have for numbers. Once rules are set, a researcher can try to show the results of violations and to assess the effects on political stability or economic growth.

This method tells what illegal corruption does – but not how it changes, or how it relates to private corruptions. Realism is lost in two ways: First, the focus is on public politics, as if proper authority were exercised only in government organizations and only by formally higher administrative offices over lower ones. The actual scope of corruption, however, is broader. Much malfeasance is secret, some of it is committed by officials, and private infractions of norms are in practice often linked to police or other state agencies. The government elites of some countries thoroughly dominate sources of data about public norms, which might more realistically be induced from all social networks. The PRC by 2017 established "social credit" ratings and has connected them to facial recognition technologies, public surveillance closed-circuit cameras, and a big database of genetic DNA information on many citizens.[105] Especially in China, any premise that public and private politics should be easy to separate is far-fetched.

Second, the usual definition of corruption refers to duties that are assumed to be stable over time. This may fulfill one purpose of the definition, which is to judge the efficiency of corruption for lubricating or hindering a political economy. But it involves another loss of realism, because it ignores that concepts of corruption can change, sometimes rather quickly. The customary definition has no dynamic aspect. It cannot tell why particular acts (usury is the classic case) are deemed corrupt in some periods and places, but not in others.[106] Political science needs a better definition of corruption than has been standard.

Corruption always implies two identifiable groups. It is a claim that benefits went to one (usually the smaller network of people) that should instead have gone to the other (usually the larger network). Such networks are political; they are led. This is a definition of corruption that allows research on the full topic. Subjective assessments determine whether network leaders are regarded as corrupt or clean. If the heads of enterprises or states are perceived to be successful and kind, most people think their authority is uncorrupt.

Corruption is of several kinds, partly depending on the size of the network that legitimates it. It can be defined as an improper, illegal use of public power – but the effective concept of corruption has changed over time in the PRC, according to the sizes of networks with which people most identified.[107] As China's revolution gained strength, especially by the 1950s, the state with a great deal of patriotic assent tightened criteria of what was supposed to be seen as dirty or clean. But then during a draw-down of centralization in the 1980s, smaller networks more often set criteria for corruption. Research in another Asian country shows that most people,

206 Owners manage urban corruption & companies

especially those with scant education, do not see "petty corruption, gift giving, and favoritism" as corrupt, although they condemn "large-scale bribery."[108] This applies to China, too.

Any claim of corrupt behavior implies networks of two sizes: one which is said to have acted improperly (which is often smaller or individual), and one that sets criteria for the judgment. A straightforward type of corruption is theft by an individual for his or her own sake. Embezzlement for strictly personal gain has often been severely punished in China, with extensive citizen support. A Shanghai newspaperman, who had risen to the deputy directorship of the *Guangming Daily's* Shanghai office, embezzled 43,000 yuan over a period of four years by claiming reimbursements for "labor service fees" under false names, forging receipts, and otherwise pretending expenses that his unit had not paid.[109] The head of the finance office in a chemical fertilizer factory in Changzhou, over the border in Jiangsu, was sentenced to death for listing false construction expenditures, forging receipts for them, and apparently pocketing the money himself.[110]

Police reports do not formally distinguish individual thefts, however, from non-plan and non-contract trades in commodities that state leaders feel they should control. Extractions that benefited local networks often had informal political support. Each jurisdiction has been relatively eager to prosecute criminals from other places. By 1988, more than half of Shanghai's indicted criminals came from other provinces, many of whom traded goods illegally. Some were ordinary workaday robbers, of whom 70 to 80 percent in Shanghai hailed from elsewhere.[111] But collective "gangs" were prominent in indictments, and some of these were procurement agencies for inland places. A "Huaiyin Clique" from North Jiangsu was for many years "robbing materials" from factories and stores in Zhabei District, Shanghai. So the Zhabei Public Security Bureau in 1988 arrested braves of the "Huaiyin Clique" and "Baoying Clique," because they engaged in massive "thefts," i.e., unplanned purchases of metals.[112]

Because Shanghai prices were low, most illegal trades were exports from the city. Police would patrol Shanghai's borders in an effort to prevent leaks, but the hemorrhage was massive. Three quarters of all daily use products (*riyong pin*) bought by Shanghai wholesalers in 1982 were sent out of the city. This comprised about 30 percent of all such products in China.[113] Most of this trade violated laws, and profits on the illegal portion must have been munificent.

Corruption through resales in large and small networks

It would be arbitrary to assume that ethics could be based on one size of human network with no reference to others. The state, which passes laws and helps educate most people, tends to define corruption as violating the norms of the nation, a very large group. Liberal economists, on the other hand, either avoid talking about corruption or point to inefficiencies as the main muddles to be cleaned. Many ordinary people, including most Chinese, stress the importance of mid-size and local groups.

State and collective managers were responsible for most corruption – on behalf of their local firms or clients. Contracts were often "based on blood and locale."[114] Because real prices rose over state-enforced prices during reforms, the golden path to wealth was through illegal reselling (*daomai*). Better profits could be made in commodity speculation than in good management. Government agencies, such as state banks, engaged in this reform practice freely. When the benefited network was large or official, such speculation was not always deemed corrupt. For example, the state for years tried to enforce a monopoly on the purchase of foreign currencies, which in various ways it bought cheaply and sold dearly, taking the profit. When individuals speculated on other markets (for example, by scalping tickets at the Shanghai railroad station), police tried to arrest them.[115] The most important actors on urban markets were state enterprises and large collectives.

One type of "speculation" involved state agencies "selling to big houses" (*mai dahu*), mainly nonstate stores, rather than to state-owned retail agencies that had purchase contracts. The Shanghai Poultry Egg Company in April of 1987, for example, sold 32 percent of its produce to secondary wholesalers, who resold the eggs at a price considerably higher than was fixed for state-owned shops.[116] The official system and its rake-off were bypassed, in this common local form of detour to avoid higher or more enforceable state imposts.

Another type of speculation involved selling low-quality commodities as if they were good. This problem arose especially with bulk items such as fertilizers and chemical products, which can be adulterated with other substances. Cheating raised profits, and many such practices could be justified, as if they were reforms, to establish new horizontal sales relations.[117] Officials or their relatives might serve as middlemen, arranging materials purchases for large state factories and charging an illegal commission. These middlemen, who could pocket large amounts of money in resale transactions, were called "*guan dao ye*" ('official supply grandfathers'). When a Shanghai cable factory could not get enough copper to continue operations, the managers informally consulted with workers to "gather opinions" on whether they should break the law and use an "official supply grandfather." He charged a personal commission of 2,000 yuan for every metric ton of copper for which he could arrange delivery. Consensus emerged in the factory that the deal should be made.[118]

It was often difficult to distinguish where normal business operations ended and corruption began. Managers could always claim they were just making money for their firms. Cotton-purchasing cadres in Jiangsu in 1988, for example, bought at low state prices – and resold at several levels of wholesale trade – until the price paid by the factory that finally did the spinning was two or three times the official price.[119] Such practices violated rules handed down by the State Council. That did not stop them.

More than a thousand small boats leave Shanghai every day carrying industrial goods, according to the Public Security Bureau, and many engaged in illegal trade. From 1979 to 1987, Shanghai's Water Police handled a great number of commercial cases, mostly of people whose household registrations were outside Shanghai.[120]

Corruption was "embedded" in the physical and normative structures where it flourished. The delta's canal system, and the separate communities of boat people who plied its waterways, were facts the state could not quickly change.

Small agriculturalists could be alienated from state officials because of corruption, e.g., when bicycles were resold. The economy of Shanghai's suburbs was prosperous by 1981, and the pancake-flat terrain made bicycles useful for suburban farmers. Demand for them was greater than supply, largely because Shanghai factories were obligated by plans (and encouraged by low official prices in the whole municipality, including the suburbs) to send bicycles for sale elsewhere. Ration coupons, rather than money, were the main means of allocation. Thirty percent of suburban bicycle coupons in the early 1980s were allotted to towns, with the remaining 70 percent going to ex-commune administrations. But town "cadres took some," and "'cooperators' retained some." There was a leakage of 40 percent of the coupons. Less than one-third of them remained for Shanghai individuals.[121] This kind of corruption affected many consumer products. It did not endear state officials to people who earned money but could not buy goods.

Corruption by wholesalers was more lucrative. In May 1989, police cracked "the most serious bribery ever to occur in Zhejiang Province," in which "the criminals used their administrative power or influence to obtain bribes by selling raw silk to Hong Kong businessmen through illegal channels." The scale of this illegal operation was enormous; it reportedly extended throughout the province. The problem arose because the state takes an especially large markup over costs when selling silk. Yet growing mulberry trees and raising worms is a dispersed activity, difficult to monitor all over Zhejiang. Revenues to central state agencies "should have reached about 5 billion Hong Kong dollars for silk exported to Hong Kong [from Zhejiang] in 1988, but the actual income was only 2 billion Hong Kong dollars." The report railed against the sales commissions that forty-seven illegal traders made. A greater sum – this amount plus the HK$3 billion differential that was caused by the high official price – would have been the state's sales commission if the law had been enforceable, as it was not.

The government procurator waxed lyrical about "solving" this case, comparing its complexities to the "silk thread the worms make when spinning cocoons, which is almost endless." But he recovered only 300,000 yuan, plus HK$29,000.[122] Zhejiang is large, and the end of this "almost endless" thread was likelier to be found in scarcity-price markets than in courts. With the market price of silk thread high and production very scattered, the law practically created the corruption.

Correlates and estimates of corruption

Corruption was most feasible and profitable in rural and suburban areas, from which high state cadres were usually absent. Reform China, like other countries after spates of violent centralization (e.g., the US after 1865), reported kinds of corruption that relate to economic growth. Corruption, which is almost always measured as a perceived variable rather than directly from behavior, usually correlates with fast economic development. But the situation is complex, because many nations in their fastest-growth phases rely on foreign capital and export markets. There are plausible arguments that corruption hinders economic growth.[123] Perceptions of corruption, however, are often rife in fast-expanding economies. More empirical research on this link is needed.

Corruption sometimes hinders growth, and research shows that a reason in most developing countries is the desire of foreign (or ethnically distinct) investors to avoid paying bribes.[124] Low corruption, as perceived, can be linked statistically with capital inflows in many countries, and this relationship is robust when controlled for per capita income, domestic savings rates, or raw materials exports. A scatter diagram relating capital inflows to perceived corruption in many countries is revealing. When guesses of corruption are graphed against productivity (the ratio of GDP to capital stock), there is even more scatter than in a diagram that relates corruption to capital inflows.[125] Corrupt rake-offs discourage influxes of foreign capital, lowering that factor of growth. Bribes act like a tax on foreign direct investment.

Foreign investor-entrepreneurs, however, may discount this cost if they expect an economic "rise" to continue and want to establish themselves early in a national market, e.g., China's. On domestic grounds alone, it is possible that corruption helped growth – in part because much "foreign" capital by the 1980s was coming from ethnic compatriots in Hong Kong, Taiwan, and elsewhere, and also because many Overseas Chinese were hired by foreign companies to oversee operations in China. Corruption requires trust among actors, and it may lubricate rather than hinder growth when such confidence is reliable.

The amounts of materials and money involved in PRC illegal exchanges became immense. They were reported especially in periods of conservative Party rule, when high state cadres tried to coordinate businesspeople most forcefully. From January through July 1989, the months surrounding the Tiananmen reaction, police in Jiangsu handled 2.2 times as many corruption cases as in the whole previous year. Most of these involved sales that violated laws. In the first two years of a Jiangsu rural enterprise supply company, it illegally sold "large amounts of iron, wool, and other products." A single oil company in Zhenjiang City illegally sold about 2,000 metric tons of petroleum in these few months.[126] More famous examples of corruption in reform China occurred farther south, notably in Hainan; but Jiangnan contributed to the record.

There was decreasing agreement, as reforms progressed, about the proper definition of corruption. "Some leading cadres resist the fight against corruption and view running a clean government as inconsistent with economic construction and a hindrance to production."[127] The purely economic direct costs of corruption in China became huge during the late 1980s. Partly because of changing definitions and partly because of price changes, these costs may have decreased somewhat during later decades.[128] By 1988, according to economists in the Chinese Academy of Social Sciences who made an heroic attempt to estimate part of corruption costs, endemic shortages meant that total "negotiated" money transfers for capital goods were about 200 or 300 billion yuan more than the theoretical costs at "fixed"

210 Owners manage urban corruption & companies

prices would have been. Of this increment, experts estimated that 20 percent (40 to 60 billion yuan) went for commissions to negotiators, i.e., for corruption.[129] That amount approximates China's total 1988 expenditure on urban housing, for example, or on agricultural price subsidies.

This calculation only counted, however, the cost of corruption in capital goods markets. For other services and commodities, a Chinese estimator has figured the 1988 excess of market over planned costs at 356 billion yuan, of which over 100 billion was "excess interest" that had to be paid to banks over the official rates, before they would make loans. A French analyst, assessing this drain higher and taking all corrupt rents together, estimates that 10 percent of China's national income in 1988 may have gone to graft. These activities led Guilhem Fabre to write about the development of a "casino state."[130]

Localization, marketization, and efficiency

Two major facts about reform China's economy are its quick growth and its inefficient management. How could a regime that largely fostered sinecure jobs, "wrong" prices, chaotic devolution, and uneven taxes enjoy such spectacular prosperity? The answer lies in localization. That pattern aided entrepreneurship, even if it also meant odd allocations. In Shanghai, economic localization finally was a clear trend by the late 1980s. Many Shanghai industries had long been more vertically integrated (performing more processes in-house, rather than going to the market for them) than firms in other large Chinese cities, as Table 8.4 suggests. These figures are an index constructed from two measures of production, one of which is designed to account only the value added by firms (after costs of inputs are deducted), while the other counts the total value when products leave firms. The first is the numerator; the second, the denominator. When the index falls, so approximately does in-house vertical integration. This ratio in Shanghai dropped from 1978 into the 1990s (and from lower bases, it also fell in the comparable cities of Tianjin and Guangzhou), showing an increased use of upstream and downstream markets.

But localization sometimes works against increased allocative efficiency. Local agencies can have as much desire to interfere with markets as do national ones, if they gain from such interference. Entrepreneurial spirit was heightened by competition not just among individuals and small groups, but also among different sizes of collectivity. Small networks responded, after the state's search for rents lost steam. Reform in China's rich coastal deltas occurred in all five categories that Joseph Schumpeter, the main economist of entrepreneurship, listed as engines of fundamental change: China's rural-coastal innovators created new commodities and made old ones of better quality. They introduced new techniques of production. They penetrated new markets. They sourced new factors and semi-finished products. They organized their industries in new ways.[131] Realizing any one of these five criteria would be enough, by Schumpeter's standards, to qualify a reform as a

Owners manage urban corruption & companies **211**

TABLE 8.4 Declining vertical and rising horizontal integration in PRC urban economies (ratio of value added to gross trade, × 100)

	Shanghai	Tianjin	Guangzhou
1978	41	38	37
79	41	38	40
80	40	38	
81	40	37	
82	39	35	
83	39	35	
84	39	35	
85	39	35	38
86	36	35	36
87	35	34	35
88	34	31	35
89	31	28	33
90	30	27	33
91	30	27	33
92	29		

Sources: These figures were calculated by dividing national income (*guomin shouru*) by gross value of social product (*shehui zongchan zhi*). As the value of transactions between companies rises, the denominator rises; so the index goes down. The numerator roughly measures a sum of values added, whereas the denominator double- or multiple-counts the values of trades between units, so that a decline in the ratio correlates with a decline of vertical, and a rise of horizontal, economic integration. (National income is used, rather than the theoretically more appropriate gross domestic product, because of a lack of directly surveyed GDP figures and because it is sufficient to show trends.) See *Shanghai: tongji nianjian, 1983* (Shanghai Statistical Yearbook, 1983), Shanghai Statistical Bureau, ed. (Shanghai: Shanghai Shi Tongji Ju, 1984), 43; ibid., 1988 edition, 20; ibid., 1991 edition, 38 and 43, ibid., 1992 edition, 37 and 42, and ibid., 1993 edition, 44 and 39; also *Tianjin tongji nianjian, 1987* (Tianjin Statistical Yearbook, 1987), Tianjin Statistical Bureau, ed. (Beijing: Zhongguo Tongji Chuban She, 1987), 48 and 50; ibid., 1988 edition, 38–39; ibid., 1991 edition, 148 and 150; and ibid., 1992 edition, 115 and 117; also *Guangzhou tongji nianjian, 1988* (Guangzhou Statistical Yearbook, 1988), Guangzhou Municipal Statistics Bureau, ed. (Beijing: Zhongguo Tongji Chuban She, 1988), 4; ibid., 1991 edition, 15 and 17; and ibid., 1992 edition, 23 and 25. *Quanguo ge sheng zizhi qu zhixia shi lishi tongji ziliao huibian, 1949–1989* (Historical Statistics Collection on Provinces, Autonomous Regions, and Municipalities Throughout the Country, 1949–1989), State Statistical Bureau, ed. (Beijing: Zhongguo Tongji Chuban She, 1990), 93 and 96 has data on Tianjin. The calculations were not made in the sources, and the index is rough but revealing. The extent of continuing vertical integration in Guangzhou (a provincial capital, not fully like other parts of Guangdong) was somewhat unexpected.

seed of change, rather than just a continuation of the previous economic structure. Schumpeter's entrepreneur is like Weber's charismatic leader: a sign of decisiveness and life on an otherwise dull bureaucratic scene.[132]

Urban managers of local state firms (if not of "mother-in-law" corporations) knew that their system was inefficient. To deal with the market, they expressed willingness to shoulder risks if they gained autonomy. Interesting results came from a survey of businesspeople in China during a relatively liberal period of reforms in

212 Owners manage urban corruption & companies

1987, asking the question, "If you had the chance of being either a senior executive of a large [usually state] corporation or the owner-manager of a smaller firm, assuming equal financial rewards, which would you have chosen?" Among government factory managers, not just cooperative and private bosses, there was a clear preference against being a cog in a large state bureaucracy. Most said they would prefer to be owner-managers of smaller firms.[133]

Official use of the term "entrepreneur," which was widespread by the mid-1980s, suggested a manager willing to take risks and make decisions. A group of Chinese economists nonetheless pointed out, very classically, that entrepreneurship means little without free markets in labor and capital.[134] Otherwise, it is difficult to show whether risk-taking has been socially beneficial. According to these analysts, China was burdened by a simplistic psychology, looking down on entrepreneurs and considering them unimportant. These economists stressed cultural rather than policy causes of a decline in entrepreneurial creativity. They blamed age-old Chinese traditions of seeking "moderation," as well as anti-individualist and anti-commercial mores. They described Chinese culture as one that had condoned only egalitarian levels of wealth and thus had discouraged the search for profits.

Neoclassical economic theory holds that if ownership rights of each commodity are clear, so that the owner will not trade a good except at its scarcity price, then factors will be allocated to maximize production. This "Pareto efficiency" among factors at any particular time does not, however, guarantee the fastest rate of economic growth. Progress over an extended period is not necessarily maximized by a static efficient allocation of factors. As Schumpeter wrote, "A system – any system, economic or other – that at every point of time fully utilizes its possibilities to the best advantage may yet in the long run be inferior to a system that does so at no given point of time, because the latter's failure to do so may be a condition for the level or speed of long-run performance."[135] Markets, on which decisions are governed by price competition, distribute goods and money to traders. But price competition alone does not guarantee new technologies, better modes of economic organization, or entrepreneurial zeal finding new kinds of materials, new markets, and new products. Efficient markets do not ensure maximal growth.

In this light, some of the most obvious characteristics of China's reform economy – fuzziness of ownership rights, even diversion of money to corrupt officials – may help rather than hinder long-term growth. These habits do so even if they somewhat reduce the efficiency of factor allocation at any given time, when they are linked to starting firms that make new goods, seeking new places to sell them, finding new finances, and inspiring better managerial and productive techniques.

There is nothing wrong with neoclassical factor efficiency; it may contribute to growth rates. But reform China's experience (or earlier, Taiwan's) suggests it does not refer to the key generators of development. The mainstream models of neoclassical economics have been egregiously unable to predict any long-term economic change. For example in the Far East, the Philippines as late as 1959 had per capita income and apparently factor efficiency higher than Taiwan's; yet as subsequent decades showed, Taiwan had more of something else that the Philippines lacked, i.e., local entrepreneurship.[136] The World Bank in the late 1950s predicted that "the basic economic position of the Philippines is favourable ... it has achieved a position in the Far East second only to Japan, both in respect to its level of literacy and to per capita production capacity."[137] These economists ignored the influence on the economy of local political factors. So their crystal balls were flat wrong. In 1960, the democratic Philippines was still widely seen as the most "advanced" country in the Far East outside Japan. Half a century later, another group of economists remained almost as negligent of local factors in the Philippine economy, especially political factors that are difficult to quantify.[138] Neoclassical economists were also clueless in their failure to predict China's spurt of prosperity from the 1970s onward. The vectors they considered did not explain the economic motion.

Entrepreneurship such as Schumpeter notes, together with local political regimes to support it, was the crucial cause of new prosperity in China. During PRC reforms until the 1990s, the pattern of unclear ownership and rampant corruption did not prevent the economy from growing quickly. Economic theory has not yet sorted these matters, especially for predictions over any time span longer than a few years. The economies of many countries have boomed in periods of "wrong" prices, oligopoly, corruption, and experimentation with mixed forms of ownership. If local managers seek opportunities and take risks, as many did in reform China, the problems that most economists emphasize do not preclude fast growth. An historical overview suggests that some inefficiencies may correlate with quick development.

Notes

1 John Gardner, "The *Wu-fan* Campaign in Shanghai: A Study in the Consolidation of Urban Control," *Chinese Communist Politics in Action*, Doak Barnett, ed. (Seattle: University of Washington Press, 1969), 477–539; Lynn White, "Changing Concepts of Corruption in Communist China: Early 1950s vs. Early 1980s," in *Changes and Continuities in Chinese Communism*, Yuming Shaw, ed. (Boulder: Westview, 1988), 316–53; or on the specific problem of how to be both Chinese and Christian in the 1950s, Philip Wickeri, *Seeking the Common Ground: Protestant Christianity, the Three-Self Movement, and China's United Front* (Maryknoll: Orbis, 1988 [orig. Ph.D. dissertation at Princeton Theological Seminary]).

2 Huan Kuan, *Discourses on Salt and Iron: A Debate on State Control of Commerce and Industry in Ancient China*, tr. Esson Gale (Taipei: Chengwen Publishing, 1967).

3 *Guanzi: Political, Economic and Philosophical Essays from Early China*, tr. Allyn Rickett (Princeton: Princeton University Press, 1985).

4 For historical analysis in light of 1980s Shanghai problems, see Hong Ze and Xu Dingxin, *Shanghai yanjiu luncong: Di yi ji* (Papers on Studies of Shanghai: First Set) (Shanghai: Shanghai Shehui Kexue Yuan Chuban She, 1988), 164–65. In English, also Samuel Chu and Kwangchi Liu, *Li Hung-Chang and China's Early Modernization* (Armonk: Sharpe, 2000).

5 Li Pan, Li Douheng, and Chu Zhongxin, *Gaige yu kaifang xin wenti yanjiu* (Studies of New Questions in Reform and Opening) (Shanghai: Shanghai Shehui Kexue Yuan Chuban She, 1987), 52–53.

6 Much of the military economy is included here, although the exact percentage in the text above is not certain. See Barry Naughton, "Industrial Policy During the Cultural Revolution," op. cit., 166.

7 Peter N. S. Lee, *Industrial Management and Economic Reform in China, 1949–1984* (Hong Kong: Oxford University Press, 1987), 104.

8 Ibid., 51.

9 *SHJJDB*, August 1, 1988.

10 Zhang Shanmin, Li Xin, and Wu Zhangnan, *Zou xiang chenggong* (Marching to Accomplishments) (Shanghai: Shanghai Shehui Kexue Yuan Chuban She, 1988), 107.

11 *SHJJYJ*, September 1985, 23.

12 Ibid.

13 These higher-level units are called *gongxiao bumen* or *shangye bumen*. See *SHJJYJ*, September 1985, 24.

14 In *SHJJYJ*, September 1985, 24.

15 "*Zhe shi guojia tiele chaopiao, rang geti hu facai*," *SHJJYJ*, September 1985, 25.

16 *SHJJYJ*, September 1985, 25.

17 Ibid.

18 *SHJJYJ*, September 1985, 25.

19 Ibid.

20 The factory managers' responsibility system is called the *changzhang fuze zhi*. *SHJJYJ*, September 1985, 26. See Franz Schurmann, *Ideology and Organization in Communist China* (Berkeley: University of California Press, 1965) on the "single manager system" (*yizhang zhi*) of the 1950s, adopted at that time from Soviet models.

21 *SHJJYJ*, September 1985, 25, suggests an analogy between factory Party committees and the Empress Dowager, Ci Xi, a widely detested figure in modern Chinese history.

22 State ownership is not simple, because supply and marketing roles can be transferred among central, provincial, and other administrations. There are ambiguities in the word "collective" too. Audrey Donnithorne, *China's Economic System*, and Barry Richman, *Industrial Society in Communist China* (New York: Random House, 1969).

23 Cheng Xiaonong, "The Structure of Economic Growth in China: An Approach to Measuring the Contribution of the Public and Non-Public Sectors, and Some Estimations," (unpublished paper, Princeton University, 1993), 1–2.

24 Thomas Gold, "Urban Private Business and Social Change," in *Chinese Society on the Eve of Tiananmen*, op. cit., 157–78. Cheng Li discusses "counterfeit goods," in Shanghai dialect called "Daxing" fake goods after a local street where they had long been sold, in *Rediscovering China: Dynamics and Dilemmas of Reform* (Lanham: Rowman and Littlefield, 1997), 35–38.

25 See Liu Gang, Wang Guocheng (Industrial Economics), Xing Yichu Shanghai People's Publishing House, *Shanghai chengshi jiti suoyou zhi gongye yanjiu* (Studies of Shanghai's Urban Collective Industries) (Shanghai: Shanghai Renmin Chuban She, 1980), esp. 97ff.

26 *Shanghai shehui xiankuang he qushi, 1980–1983*, 79–80.

27 Cheng Xiaonong, an economic sociologist who knows much about PRC production, made these calculations. Published PRC data, sometimes cited here in raw form, need further testing for several reasons. First, although GDP figures are reported in Chinese statistical yearbooks, these numbers are not sums based on surveys, most usual method for calculating GDP. Instead, they are figured from social gross output value (*shehui zongchan zhi*) according to a mathematical formula decreed by the State Statistical Bureau. Cheng has attempted to reduce this problem. Second, the quasi-private nature of many collective enterprises makes estimates of state sector size more meaningful than estimates for the collective or private sectors. Third, although relatively straightforward means exist to figure outputs by ownership category in agriculture, industry, and construction, tertiary output in transportation, trade, and services presents difficulties. More is in ibid., pp. 10, 13, and 16. I am grateful to Cheng Xiaonong for sending his unpublished paper on these issues.

28 Interestingly, there was a reported 1990–1991 rise in the portion of Guangdong gross industrial output from state plants from 35 to 37 percent. This is based on sources for Table 8.1 and on 1992 editions of the yearbooks on these pages: Shanghai, 109; Zhejiang, 146; Jiangsu, 135; Guangdong, 184; and China, 408.

29 *Economist*, "When China Wakes: A Survey of China," (November 28–December 4, 1992).

30 Chen Benlin, *Gaige kaifang shenzhou jubian* (Great Change in the Sacred Land [China] During Reform and Opening) (Shanghai: Jiaotong Daxue Chuban She, 1984), 34.

31 In Guangdong, 66 percent was state and 28 percent collective in 1988. In Jiangsu, 59 percent was state and 37 percent collective. Calculated from raw figures in *Zhongguo chengshi tongji nianjian, 1988* (Statistical Yearbook of Chinese Cities, 1988), State Statistical Bureau, ed. (Beijing: Zhongguo Tongji Xinxi Zixun Fuwu Zhongxin, 1988), 158–64 for the state sector figures, 167–73 for collectives, and 176–82 for private firms.

32 An example is in Vivienne Shue, "Beyond the Budget: Finance Organization and Reform in a Chinese County," *Modern China* 10:2 (April 1984), 165.

33 *China News Analysis* 1409, May 1, 1990, 3.

34 National reformers, such as Zhao Ziyang, tended to adopt the coastal viewpoint. Many local conservatives were either Beijing appointees or trade union officials whose clients worked in state plants.

35 This slogan was in the title of a *Red Flag* article by Shanghai's radical Mayor Ke Qingshi, who died shortly before the Cultural Revolution.

36 "*Yousheng, lietai,*" *SHGYJJB*, August 4, 1988.

37 See *SHGYJJB*, August 4, 1988.

38 Other researchers focus on background conditions; William Parish, Xiaoye Zhe, and Fang Li, "Nonfarm Work and Marketization of the Chinese Countryside," 709.

39 Susan L. Shirk, *The Political Logic*, chapter 9.

40 The numerical portions reported above were respectively 61, 72, and 83 percent. This survey, involving large and small state firms in proportion to their outputs, was relatively sophisticated. *SHJJYJ*, September 1985, 23.

41 Chinese romanizations show the official differentiation of acts managers can take: *zizhu tiaozheng quan, zixiao chanpin fanwei er wu chanpin zixiao quan, chao jihua shengchan chanpin wu jiage fudong quan, zixing xuangou quan, zixuan gongzi xingshi zijin shiyong quan, duoyu xianzhi guding zichan chuzhi quan, jigou shezhi quan, renshi laodong guanli quan, bufen zhigong jinji quan, kua bumen kua diqu xuandian lianying quan*. Ibid.

42 *Asian Wall Street Journal*, January 31, 1989.

43 Susan L. Shirk, *The Political Logic*, 281.

44 *FBIS*, November 26, 1986, 4, radio of November 20.

45 Ibid.

46 *FBIS*, November 26, 1986, 3, radio of November 20.

47 *FBIS*, November 26, 1986, 4, radio of November 20.

48 Ibid.

49 Interview with an economist at the Shanghai Academy of Social Sciences.

50 *JFRB*, April 1, 1988.

51 Respectively, *shangjiao lirun jishu baogan/cengzhang fencheng, shangjiao lirun ding'e baogan,* and *shangjiao lirun diceng baogan*.

52 Hu Yanchou, head of Shanghai Cable TV, quoted in *Asian Wall Street Journal*, December 2, 1993, referred by Jan Prybyla.

53 Wang Yu, et al., *Da juanbian shiqi* (The Era of Great Transformation) (Shijiazhuang: Hebei Renmin Chuban She, 1987), 155.

54 Ibid., 156.

55 *JJRB*, January 22, 1988.

56 *CD*, January 30, 1988.

57 *JJRB*, January 22, 1988.

58 This kind of company is called a *taozhai gongsi*. *JFRB*, May 9, 1988.

59 Ibid.

60 Interview with a knowledgeable economist in Shanghai, who had seen these figures in print.

61 Huang Weixin, *Economic Integration as a Development Device*, 127–28.

62 *The Economist*, November 30, 1991; and *FEER*, August 23, 1990.

63 Lynn White, "Leadership in Shanghai, 1955–69," op. cit.

64 *XMWB*, January 5, 1982.

65 Guilhem Fabre, "The Chinese Mirror of Transition," 262.

66 Edward Epstein, "China's Legal Reforms," 9.10.

67 *CD*, March 13, 1988.

68 *FBIS*, November 14, 1986, 3, radio of November 8.

69 *CD*, March 1, 1989.

70 Ibid.

71 Yao Shihuang, *Jin sanjiao de tansuo*, 140–44.

72 Ibid., 145–54.

73 *Jianjie guanli* was summed up in the four characters "fang, yi, zhuan, gai," *JFRB*, March 19, 1987.

74 Charters of some firms already allowed this flexibility. "Scope of management" is jingy-ing fanwei. *SHJJ*, April 1988, 63.

75 These *xieye* firms were, however, 38 percent fewer in 1987 (after planning ended for most inputs) than in 1986. Ibid.

76 Quoted from *JJYJ*, No. 4, 1988, in Huang Weixin, *Economic Integration*, 81.

77 Some businesspeople think Sun Zi offers pointers on how to deal with competitors. A society named for Sun, including both Chinese and Westerners, met in China to dis-cuss his relevance for entrepreneurs. Also *CD*, December 17, 1990.

78 Yan Tingchang, Cai Beihua, and Xu Zhihe, *Shanghai lüyou ye de jintian he mingtian* (Shanghai Tourism Today and Tomorrow) (Shanghai: Shanghai Shehui Kexue Yuan Chu-ban She, 1987), 74.

79 The Cabinet's plan was entitled *Guanyu Shanghai jingji fazhan zhanlue de huibao digang*. Documents mentioned above were the *Shanghai jingji fazhan zhanlue, Shanghai shi cheng-shi zongti guihua*, and *Shanghai shi wenhua fazhan zhanlue*. See a lecture by Shang Yafei, *Yige chengjiao xiangcun de jintian he mingtian: Shanghai shi Shanghai xian Meilong xiang jingji fazhan zongti guihua yanjiu* (A Suburban Village Today and Tomorrow: Comprehensive Plan for the Economic Development of Meilong Town, Shanghai County, Shanghai), Ling Yaochu and Zhang Zhaoan eds. (Shanghai: Shanghai Shehui Kexue Chuban She, 1988), 1–6. For more about Shanghai's urban development plan, approved on Octo-ber 13, 1986, *JFRB*, November 6, 1986. Models of the city's spatial growth are wonder-fully curated at the Shanghai Urban Planning Exhibition Center on People's Square, near the art museum.

80 The total number of such enterprises in Shanghai at that time was reported as 5,288. *XMWB*, April 19, 1989.

81 Nothing in China resembled the Treuhandanstalt, the post-unification German govern-ment office that took over ex-state factories and sold them in a massive liquidation.

82 *CD*, September 18, 1990.

83 *CD*, March 16, 1988.

84 The 1982 PRC Constitution (with some amendments) remains valid in 2017. Article 10 begins with the words "Land in cities is owned by the state."

85 *FBIS*, December 17, 1984, 2, radio of December 15.

86 Tudi zheng is colloquial for *tudi fangchan suoyou zheng*. *FBIS*, December 29, 1987, 40, radio of December 24.

87 Kate Xiao Zhou told me about an article by Ma Gujun in *Dangdai* (The Present Genera-tion), No. 5, 1991, containing this information. The point about village house-raisings is based on my observations in rural Jiangnan during 1994 and 1976 trips.

88 From *Hubei ribao*, October 25, 1981, in Daniel Kelliher, *Peasant Power*, 179.

89 I have been unable to obtain enough data from rural areas of the Shanghai delta about the lineage relations of sibs that continued to cooperate in farming, or about possible demands for part of the land they knew had been tilled by their ancestors.

90 See Shang Yafei, *Yige chengjiao xiangcun*, 9–11. In English, the China Coast term for ware-house is godown (earlier Portuguese, from Tamil).

91 *FBIS*, November 3, 1986, 4, radio of November 3.

92 *FBIS*, December 29, 1987, 50, radio of December 22.

93 *FBIS*, March 9, 1988, 61–62, radio of March 8.

94 Reported by Kate Xiao Zhou, on the basis of a 1985 article by Cai Fuyuan in *Minzhu yu falü* (Democracy and Law).

95 *Tansuo yu zhengming* (Investigation and Debate), March 1988, 51.

96 Zhang Gang is quoted in Edward Epstein, "China's Legal Reforms," 9.4.

97 Victor Nee, "Peasant Entrepreneurship," op. cit., 171.

98 *Shanghai fazhi bao*, January 30, 1989.

99 *JFRB*, May 30, 1988.

100 *Shanghai fazhi bao* carried many articles on illegal trade in ration coupons. Coupons as collectables from many parts of China (including Shanghai) could be bought in Macau in the mid-1990s.

101 *JFRB*, May 30, 1988.

102 Joseph A. Schumpeter, *The Theory of Economic Development* (New York: Oxford University Press, 1934).

103 Simon Johnson, Daniel Kaufmann, and Pablo Loido-Lobaton, "Regulatory Discretion and the Unofficial Economy," *American Economic Review* 88 (1998), 387–92.

104 James C. Scott, *Comparative Political Corruption* (Englewood Cliffs: Prentice-Hall, 1972), 4.

105 Stanley Lubman, "The Unprecedented Reach of China's Surveillance State," *ChinaFile*, www.chinafile.com/reporting-opinion/viewpoint/unprecedented-reach-of-chinas-surveillance-state, September 15, 2017.

106 Benjamin Nelson, *The Idea of Usury: From Tribal Brotherhood to Universal Otherhood*, No. 3, "History of Ideas" Series (Princeton: Princeton University Press, 1953).

107 An ebb and flow in definitions of corruption may be traced in kinds of purported uncleanliness, e.g., physical dirt, political disloyalty, foreign impurity, sharp business, or bribed government. On opposite trends in two PRC eras, 1950s and 1980s, including European historical comparisons on corrupt usury, see Lynn White, "Changing Concepts of Corruption," op. cit.

108 Rory Truex, "Corruption, Attitudes, and Education: Survey Evidence from Nepal," *World Devevelopment* 39:7 (July 2011), 1133–42.

109 *FBIS*, March 16, 1988, 19, radio of March 15.

110 *FBIS*, March 14, 1988, 38, radio of March 14.

111 *XMWB*, December 7, 1988, includes in the crucial sentence the vague qualifier "sometimes" – but this was apparently a matter of courtesy to other jurisdictions, and possibly to N. Jiangsu/'Subei' in particular, rather than a statistical matter.

112 *LDB*, March 19, 1989.

113 *Shanghai jingji, neibu ben: 1949–1982*, 545.

114 Dorothy Solinger, "China's Transients and the State: A Form of Civil Society?" *Politics and Society* 21:1 (March 1993), 91–122.

115 During 1987 and 1988, the author heard much about such arrests in both public media and informal conversations.

116 *Liaowang*, no. 33 (1987), 33.

117 *Liaowang*, no. 5 (1987), 12.

118 Interview with an economist in Shanghai.

119 *RMRB*, August 16, 1988.

120 *LDB*, March 19, 1989.

121 *JFRB*, August 8, 1981.

122 *SF*, May 29, 1989.

123 Gregory C. Chow, "Corruption and China's Economic Reform in the Early 21st Century," *International Journal of Business* 11:3 (2006), 265–82.

124 Susan Rose-Ackerman, *Corruption in Government: Causes, Consequences, and Reform* (Cambridge: Cambridge University Press, 1999), 3.

125 Johann Graf Lambsdorff, "Corruption in Comparative Perception," in *Economics of Corruption*, A.K. Jain, ed. (Boston: Kluwer, 1998), 80–93.

218 Owners manage urban corruption & companies

126 *Xianggang jingji yuekan* (Hong Kong Economic Monthly), August 4, 1989.
127 Margaret Y. K. Woo, "Legal Reforms in the Aftermath of Tiananmen Square," *Review of Socialist Law* (1991), 58.
128 On such definitions, see Lynn White, "Changing Concepts of Corruption,".
129 Guilhem Fabre, "The Chinese Mirror," 262.
130 Ibid., 262–64.
131 PRC economist, Li Shi refers to Schumpeter in "The Growth of Household Industry in Rural Wenzhou," 112.
132 "Politics as a Vocation," in *From Max Weber: Essays in Sociology*, H.H. Gerth and C. Wright Mills, eds. (New York: Oxford University Press, 1958), the gorgeous page 128.
133 Victor Chi-leung Chui, "Chinese Perception of Organization and Authority" (Hong Kong: M.B.A. dissertation, University of Hong Kong Department of Management Sciences, 1987), 34.
134 *Xiandai qiye jia* (Contemporary Entrepreneur), September 1987, 15–16.
135 Quoted from Schumpeter in Cui Zhiyuan, "Epilogue: A Schumpeterian Perspective and Beyond," in *China: A Reformable System?* Gan Yang and Cui Zhiyuan, eds. (New York: Oxford University Press, 1994), manuscript 11; Cui kindly sent me a copy.
136 Shieh Gwo-shyong, *"Boss" Island*; and Lynn White, *Philippine Politics*, 62–99.
137 Michael Pinches, "Entrepreneurship, Consumption, Ethnicity and National Identity in the Making of the Philippines' New Rich," in *Culture and Privilege in Capitalist Asia*, Michael Pinches, ed. (New York: Routledge, 1999), 105, quoted from the World Bank.
138 *Diagnosing the Philippine Economy: Toward Inclusive Growth*, Dante Canlas, Muhammad Ehsan Khan, and Juzhong Zhuang, eds. (Quezon City: Anthem Press, 2011). Development economists have similarly failed to predict major growths (or stagnations) before such events in India, S. Korea, Thailand, and other countries.

9

BANKERS ARRANGE CREDIT, SAVINGS, AND DEPRECIATION

Inefficient allocation of money was, in the view of some Shanghai economists, the central fault that reforms should correct. Investment in the Jinshan Chemical Plant, for example, was said to have been decided by Mao Zedong himself with no regard for economic rationality. Even in the 1980s, reformists thought China's main difficulty was a presumption that high politicos knew what they were doing when they made investment choices. One economist opined that many wasteful "pet projects" could be blamed on particular political leaders, such as "Gang of Four" members Wang Hongwen, Jiang Qing, and Zhang Chunqiao. He then averred, in a mood that was partly jocular, that Shanghai's fifteen largest projects in 1988 could all be identified with Jiang Zemin.[1]

The political habit of allowing high cadres to decide everything, even if they lacked business expertise, could in this economist's view be reformed only if manufacturers made production choices. He called for contract-like relations between different administrative levels.[2] This assessment of Shanghai's problems emphasized not only that the allocation of capital was inefficient, but also that the amount was insufficient because of taxes and that depreciation had been ignored.

Investment in Shanghai was 2 percent of the national total over the first three decades of the PRC.[3] Yet Shanghai was objectively not an indolent place; outlays there were recouped. A comparison of the economic returns from 14 Chinese cities showed that Shanghai in 1987 got better than average results with its working capital, even though many plants were dilapidated. The city's industry overall could reap a full return on cash in 84 days – a result that compares very favorably to the least efficient surveyed city-user of such money, Haerbin (which took 160 days), or Beijing (which took 110 days). The nearby Jiangnan cities of Wuxi and Suzhou, like Shanghai, were quick to return money (taking 97 and 95 days, respectively).[4] Financial credit for Shanghai came mostly through domestic institutions that can

220 Bankers & credit, savings, depreciation

be examined below: the state's budget and quasi-budgets, including depreciation allowances, the banking system, and public sales of stocks and bonds.

Budgetary and extrabudgetary investments

Budgets provide rough indices of comparative political localization or centralization. Budgets also suggest geographical distributions of power. Far from the coast, China's inland capital construction investment peaked about 1970. (Inland capital had risen in the 1950s, and steeply after 1964.) This was followed by a decline of inland investment in 1971–1975. There was a slight rise in the next two years, and then after 1978 a less sharp continuation of the earlier trend into the mid-1980s.[5] This index shows the rise and fall of centralized power created by China's revolution, which was largely but not wholly led by inland politicians. There can be debate about the completeness of data and about the value of heavy inland investments in places that reproduce wealth slowly. But the PRC's political ability to favor inland places until 1971 showed central state capacity before then.

Other sources also provided new capital. Nationally from 1972 to 1977, the growth of "extrabudgetary" investment averaged about 10 percent per year – five times as fast as the growth of the more centrally controlled investment budget. This quick year-to-year rise of nonbudgetary investment was more decisive over time than the slower rise of planned-budget investment.[6] Research by Vivienne Shue and Marc Blecher from a county in Hebei suggests similar trends – and shows the need to look beyond published budgets before claiming an adequate account of local money flows in China.[7]

The portion of total "state" budgets allocated nationally by the central ministries in Beijing decreased from about 70 percent in the 1950s to 60 percent in the 1960s. Then it went further down to an average of about 50 percent in the first seven years of the 1980s. For 1981–1985, the portion of the state budget transferred to individuals, especially as wages and bonuses, exceeded three-fifths.

Also, the portion of national income in the hands of local governments, enterprises, functional agencies, and service units – but outside the state budget – increased sharply, from less than 14 percent in 1979 to 22 percent in 1986.[8] The *reported* extrabudgetary income of these subordinate units was half as large as the state budget, and the increment in these funds by the mid-1980s was similar. Some local credits were reported in neither the budgets nor the extrabudgets.

At Shanghai, the sources of capital for state-sector construction investment changed radically over time. Between 1953 and 1978, almost three quarters (72 percent) of funds for basic construction reportedly came to Shanghai from the state budget. This was almost surely a gross overestimate. Hidden funds from nonstate sources were not included – and later, between 1979 and 1987, the state budget portion reportedly plummeted to 22 percent. It can scarcely have been near 72 percent a year earlier. Other reports offer different numbers, suggesting that the early 1970s state contribution to Shanghai capital was three-tenths at most.[9] As with "the case of the missing money" explored in Chapter 6 above, showing that Shanghai output could not have been produced without far more capital than was admitted in publications, reporting on other credit is also incomplete.

Rural industries' power over factor prices, and the consequent need to use more official money to pay operating expenses, helps account for the drop in state funds for fixed capital. Inflation in factor markets was hidden by planned pricing and appointment systems in the early 1970s, and unreported supplies of credit (as of every other factor) were large at this time. But as an old industrial-commercial center, Shanghai was richly endowed with informal means for supplying nonstate capital. During 1976–1980, the percentage of the city's total investment outside the state budget was reported at 31 percent; but by 1981–1985, this portion rose to 80 percent.[10] In China as a whole, by 1986 a lower portion than in Shanghai (62 percent) of basic construction capital reportedly came from sources outside the state budget.[11] Much is murky about the ways enterprises and governments obtained finances in reform China, because the sources of capital were many and some were concealed by managers intent to avoid rake-offs.

Depreciation

Not all new capital goes into new economic activity; some is needed to offset wear and tear. The capital and infrastructure that Shanghai possessed, to support China's highest rate of tax remittances, had already deteriorated by the 1970s. In 1980, four-fifths of Shanghai's textile factory premises dated from before 1937. One-ninth of the plant space in that industry, the city's largest by employment, was officially classified as too dangerous for work – but was still being used. In the whole three decades after 1949, the state invested a niggardly 500 m. yuan in Shanghai's textile plants (a total, over thirty years, of about one-quarter of the profits of just a single year from this old industry in the city). Facilities for textile workers, who were about 70 percent female, were inadequate. One plant provided a single toilet of 10 m² for 500 women workers. Many textile factories leaked rain. Several of their roofs collapsed in storms.[12]

Shanghai's *budgeted* depreciation rates from 1956 to 1980 overall averaged 4.2 percent per year in industry, but most of the money was not used for the restitution purpose its label implied.[13] Just three-tenths of this designated depreciation money could actually be retained by enterprises in most years. A full 70 percent went directly into general government funds. For city-managed firms, 40 percent was remitted to supervising bureaus of the municipal government; and 30 percent of depreciation allowances from profits went into central coffers. This was another form of tax.

After the late 1960s, however, more depreciation money went into extrabudgetary funds of companies that had equipment whose wear and tear the funds were supposed to recompense. Various depreciation rates were used in different industries and locations, and all the rates were low. In 1970, the central government allowed a 0.5 percent general increase in depreciation allowances. This increment may seem trivial, but since the allowance depended on the value of all fixed assets

222 Bankers & credit, savings, depreciation

in a firm – and since the amount of such assets doubled in China between 1970 and 1978 – this small change alone brought 12 billion yuan more extrabudgetary funds to companies in those early-reform years.[14]

The general rate for depreciation in 1978 was 3.7 percent; but this rose by 1981 to 4.1 percent, in 1983 to 4.2 percent, in 1984 to 4.7 percent, and in 1985 and later to 5.3 percent.[15] These percentage changes may seem small, but they imply large transfers of money because the basis was all fixed capital. With the first of these changes, the central state laid claim to half of the depreciation funds – but decreed that companies (rather than local governments) could retain more of the remainder. The deal for Shanghai may have been different than for most other areas; but the local portion rose in the early 1980s. By the middle of that decade, the central government gave up its share entirely in most areas, and all depreciation funds were supposed to stay in firms.

These depreciation rates had risen by successive decrees of the State Council.[16] But these 1980s plans were slow to be carried out – for an unexpected reason. An outsider might suppose that factory managers would welcome any increase in depreciation allowances. They do not, because depreciation funds were counted as costs of production. So those amounts were not as available for local bosses to use as easily as were bonus, welfare, and production development funds, which were counted as part of profits (not costs). Profit components were subject to less effective higher-level monitoring than were depreciation allowances, whose increase did little for managers' autonomy.[17]

In 1984, the average depreciation rate was allowed to rise slightly, to a level above 5 percent. But the price of goods was rising much faster; so companies could buy less for their wear-and-tear money. For example, a 40,000-yuan automobile that a firm might buy in 1980 cost 3.5 times as much (140,000 yuan) in 1988. Also, depreciation funds at Shanghai often had to be used for purposes other than replacing equipment.

In the early 1980s, two-fifths of the machines used in the city reportedly dated from before 1949. The quality of products suffered because of antique tools. Outdated capital was largely responsible for urban Shanghai's low growth rates from 1981 to 1983. At the start of that decade, Shanghai's Light Industrial Bureau noted that 70 percent of its factory space had been constructed before 1949.[18] From that year until 1978, investment in Shanghai's light industries had been only 4 percent of the city's total industrial investment. Even this small amount could not be freely used by factory managers, because it came in line item funds that were not easily fungible.[19] The Shanghai factories that produced consumer goods had interests in extending their operations. At the start of the 1980s, they called for renovation to improve their "small, old, dispersed" facilities, promising sharp increases of output if the government would give them capital.[20] Beijing responded only in the second half of the decade, and mainly because its urban political and tax bases were threatened by rural industries. To do their jobs, Shanghai managers had long since developed a norm of operating with credit whose flows were not reported in any full or unified way.

Equipment in China as a whole was less old on average than in Shanghai. One-third of all China's machines in large and medium-sized plants in 1985 were less than five years old, and 77 percent had been produced since 1970 (so nearly half were made in the 1970s, including many in suburban factories). Less than one-quarter predated the 1970s.[21] State planners were reluctant to retire old machines or buildings. National depreciation rates remained "so low that much equipment has a standard life expectancy of twenty-five years."[22] In the early 1980s, more than 25 percent of all China's capital was operating beyond its scheduled service life – and the percentage in revenue cities was greater.

High depreciation rates raised managers' nominal costs (*chengben*) and thus lowered their nominal profits. Bonus funds were their most flexible means of establishing links with their workers. Managers' dislike of high depreciation rates resulted from accounting categories. The mid-1980s "contract system" further decreased factory managers' interest in high depreciation allowances, because contracts generally fixed absolute quotas for output and fiscal remittances, leaving bonus funds as a remainder to be reduced on a yuan-for-yuan basis by any increased depreciation.

State investment and profit retention in heavy industry

Fifty-seven percent of Shanghai's total basic construction investment from 1950 to 1985 went into heavy industry, and only 8 percent went into light industry.[23] Nine percent went for public infrastructure. So the pattern remained statist and conservative in built-up Shanghai long after the late 1978 announcement in Beijing, which was actually mixed conservative-cum-reformist, and very long after less hesitant reforms began locally about 1970. Economists wrote countless academic articles showing that relative overinvestment in heavy industry was one of China's biggest problems – yet it continued.

Reformist foxes in Beijing wanted more money for high-tech light industries. In general, they failed to get it (from the state) during the 1970s not just because of central conservatives but also because of local conservative "radicals." The central state for decades had entrenched bureaucrats in urban heavy industries, and that situation did not change overnight. State investment in metropolitan Shanghai was erratic, rising sharply in 1968–1970, 1973–1975, and 1978–1979, with decreases in other years and big rises in 1984 and 1987. Capital-intensive heavy industries, whose technologies and bulk inputs could be controlled centrally, usually followed conservative rather than reformist policies. The zigzag trajectory of change, shown on Table 9.1, suggests tension between different politicians.

The table includes funds from both central and local state organs, but it does not include "self-generated" (*zichou*) and some other investment money. After a spurt of investment in 1987, presumably to pay higher input prices, the rate of change in "investment" was positive but low, to maintain jobs in industries that faced rural competition. By that time, the state budget became less important for Shanghai investment.

224 Bankers & credit, savings, depreciation

TABLE 9.1 State investment in Shanghai

	Yuan (m.)	% Change from previous year		Yuan (m.)	% Change from previous year
1950	16		1970	521	27.4
51	52	233.5	71	507	−2.8
52	141	169.7	72	379	−25.1
53	213	51.6	73	551	45.3
54	177	−17.2	74	919	66.8
55	241	36.6	75	1757	91.1
56	267	10.7	76	1015	−42.2
57	330	23.4	77	594	−41.4
58	851	158.2	78	1139	91.7
59	876	2.9	79	1755	54.1
60	714	−18.4	80	1222	−30.4
61	240	−66.3	81	1008	−17.5
62	169	−29.8	82	733	−27.3
63	260	54.2	83	693	−5.5
64	348	33.6	84	978	41.1
56	283	−18.7	85	1186	10.9
66	169	−40.3	86	1435	3.2
67	91	−46.3	87	1830	87.9
68	196	115.6	88	2179	3.5
69	409	109.1	89	2344	7.6
			90	2441	4.1

Sources: Shanghai tongji nianjian, 1983 (Shanghai Statistical Yearbook, 1983), Shanghai Statistical Bureau, ed. (Shanghai: Shanghai Shi Tongji Ju, 1984), 206; *Shanghai tongji nianjian, 1986* (as above), 243; and *Shanghai tongji nianjian, 1988* (as above), 246, and *Shanghai tongji nianjian, 1989* (as above), 278. Peng Dajin found later data in the same source, but these are hard to compare because of changes in the way state investment was calculated. The figures after 1980 may also not be exactly comparable with earlier ones, because foreign loans and additional domestic borrowing are included. Figures in different yearbooks do not exactly match; but they are close. In cases of discrepancy, later editions have been used.

In China as a whole, the central government was the largest loaner, but not the only creditor. Its budget financed decreasing portions of capital in state enterprises: more than 60 percent before 1980, but only 35 percent by 1984, and 21 percent by 1987.[24] Its firms by 1978 already had unmet depreciation needs, and almost three-fifths (58 percent) of "accumulation funds" outside of operating expenses went for fixed capital. This part of their supposedly non-liquid account rose to 74 percent by 1982.[25] The portion of planned credits dropped from 42 to 27 percent, 1978–1982. Managers were not quite as constrained for money as a cursory glance at these figures may suggest, because the decrease of plan credit was compensated by a sharp increase in the amount of companies' "own capital" (*ziyou zijin*) outside the budget. Supervising bureaucrats, after reforms began, had less extensive control over managers' capital.

Central budget makers let factories keep more of their profits in the country as a whole. Profit retention in state-owned enterprises rose sharply. It had to do so, because of market pressure; many state industries were now competing with nonstate companies earning high profits to reinvest. All Chinese state enterprises retained on average only 4 percent of their profits in 1978, according to one source; but this portion rose in each successive year thereafter to 11, 19, 21, 27, 33, 35, and 39 percent by 1985.[26] By 1986, loan repayments, deducted before profits were calculated, cost 13 percent on average. In 1986, China's national average profit retention in state firms rose to 42 percent (or 58 percent before pre-tax loan repayments).[27]

Even in Shanghai, the rate at which locally run state factories kept their profits rose from 5 percent in 1979, to 16 percent in 1984, and then 34 percent in 1987.[28] The cloud on this silver lining was that they quickly needed far more money to pay new, higher materials prices. Rates of retention outside the state sector, and especially outside Shanghai, were higher. This is just another way of talking about price inflation, because new funds went to pay scarcity prices of inputs that could actually be procured.

Many collectives retained more than state firms. A large Wuxi collective by 1978–1979 was able to keep 71 percent of its after-tax profits. This was more than was admitted for any other collective in a sample of data gathered nation-wide. Other East China collectives in this fairly small sample reportedly kept less, down to about 30 percent; but the high retention rates in some of the collectives represents a sharp change.[29] From collectives, more remitted money remained under local leaders' control. For state companies, especially in Shanghai, new capital for technological improvement was scarce both before and after the onset of contract reforms. By the mid-1980s, the main source of such funds became bank loans.

Banks were various – and borrowers were officially variegated

From 1953 to 1978, twenty-eight percent of new Shanghai capital reportedly came from bank loans and "self-generated" (*zichou*) sources; but by 1979–1987, this figure soared to 74 percent.[30] The earlier number may be an underreport, but the change was substantial in any case. Officially recognized financial reform began about 1979, not because some central politicians had reformist epiphanies, but because the fac-tors crisis became too big to hide then, both in shortages and prices. This also caused liquid and fixed capital to become more fungible, despite plans.

Standard criteria for bank loans suggested that at least 30 percent of funds for renovation in any sizable firm should come out of the company's own money. This might be financed either from the portion of depreciation allowances that the enterprise could keep, or else from the portion of profits that fed its "development fund." Bank loans also required feasibility studies (sometimes including environ-mental studies) by the late 1980s, but negotiations and pulling strings remained the fundamental requirement. Loans were not a whit less political than budget allocations.

226 Bankers & credit, savings, depreciation

A more efficient money market during reforms meant higher interest rates. In 1978, the interest on one-year time deposits was 3.24 percent in China; but by 1985, this had more than doubled to 6.84 percent. For working capital loans, rates of about 5 percent in the late 1970s rose to about 8 percent in 1985.[31]

Rates on loans were different, depending on the identity of the borrower. The economic profitability of a project was in principle a secondary consideration to the borrower's identity. The state, still in planning mode when possible, attempted to encourage specific kinds of development (and to discourage others) by charging different rates of interest on loans to different categories of borrowers. Table 9.2 shows the rates prevailing in Shanghai during 1982. Loans to industrial and commercial firms required relatively high interest. "Agricultural" borrowers were charged slightly higher interest rates than most urban firms – because many of them by 1982 were actually engaged in industry that competed with factories planners could tax better. Except for farm machines and small equipment, the rates they paid were not concessionary. By the mid-1980s, the picture changed because of inflation and because the reported sources of credit became more diverse – but actual sources of credit were still surely underreported because of extensive "back-alley banking."[32]

TABLE 9.2 Interest rates on different Shanghai bank loans (annual percentages, compounded monthly, in 1982)

	Interest rate
INDUSTRIAL/COMMERCIAL BORROWERS	
For liquid cash (esp. nonstate factories?)	6.0
Short- or mid-term construction/repairs	
One year loan or less	4.2
One year to 3 years	4.8
More than 3, up to 5 years maximum	5.4
Surcharge on interest for late repayments	+20 %
Surcharge on interest rate for overdraft	+50 %
AGRICULTURAL BORROWERS	
State farm production loans	4.8
State farm equipment loans	4.2
Township (commune or brigade) production	4.8
Township equipment loans	3.6
Sub-township loans for seeds or agronomy	4.8
Sub-township loans for equipment	3.6
Farm machines, planned item loans	3.6
Loans for downpayment to buy farm equipment	4.8
Loans to individual farmers	4.8 to 5.0

Notes and sources: Administration of these rates was not supposed to discriminate between state-owned, collective, and private clients, except as noted. See *Shanghai jingji, neibu ben: 1949–1982* (Shanghai Economy, Internal Volume: 1949–1982), Shanghai Academy of Social Sciences, ed. (Shanghai: Shanghai Shehui Kexue Yuan Chuban She, 1984), 924.

Deposits and loans

Shanghai bank deposits' nominal value in 1980 were 9.8 times their 1952 value – but bank loans had risen much faster, by 46 times between 1952 and 1980. Industrial loans were up 70 times; and commercial loans, 36 times. Savings deposits were only 22 percent of total deposits, because the bulk of funds (apparently still under enterprise plans) were held in accounts not bearing interest. Shanghai industry was financed by direct allocations more commonly than was commerce, which relied more on loans. The early 1980s ratio of outstanding commercial to industrial loans was 1.27 to 1.[33] Official firms received generous credit for fixed capital investments, as Table 9.3 shows.

The state sector received a reliable supply of loans – especially in Shanghai because state plants there were fiscally important, but also on a nationwide basis. Reported bank loan allocation to the state sector remained surprisingly constant over the reform years. That portion, as compared with the collective and private sectors in Shanghai, was practically identical in 1978 and 1990. It ranged between 80 and 90 percent of all such investment during those dozen years. This continued even while state companies failed to use factors like capital and land productively, so that their contribution to output fell relative to other ownership sectors. Their credit aimed not so much to make goods as to maintain state-sector jobs for workers and local officials. In politically important cities, state firms tried not to fire employees or cause unrest.

TABLE 9.3 Ownership composition of fixed capital investment (percentages of state, collective, and private capital)

	National			Shanghai			Guangdong		
Year	State	Coll.	Priv.	State	Coll.	Priv.	State	Coll.	Priv.
1978				85.4%	11.5%	3.2%	73.6%	3.1%	23.3%
79				90.2%	6.8%	3.0%	70.9%	3.4%	25.7%
80				88.6%	7.9%	3.5%	67.2%	4.4%	28.4%
81	69.5%	12.0%	18.5%	82.4%	9.9%	7.6%	57.3%	10.6%	32.1%
82	68.7%	14.2%	17.1%	86.4%	7.2%	6.5%	61.1%	13.6%	25.3%
83	66.6%	10.9%	22.5%	85.6%	8.2%	6.2%	63.0%	13.4%	23.5%
84	64.7%	13.0%	22.3%	82.1%	9.7%	8.2%	61.9%	14.0%	24.2%
85	66.1%	12.9%	21.0%	80.9%	8.8%	10.3%	71.0%	13.1%	15.9%
86	65.5%	13.0%	21.5%	83.3%	9.5%	7.1%	72.0%	12.5%	15.5%
87	63.1%	15.0%	21.9%	82.9%	10.0%	7.1%	69.3%	14.5%	16.2%
88	61.4%	15.8%	22.7%	81.0%	11.8%	7.2%	70.0%	15.7%	14.3%
89	61.3%	13.8%	24.9%	83.3%	9.8%	7.0%	67.4%	17.7%	15.0%
90	65.6%	11.9%	22.5%	84.7%	8.1%	7.3%	70.5%	15.8%	13.7%
91	65.9%	12.7%	21.5%	80.5%	10.8%	9.5%	71.7%	14.9%	13.4%

Sources: Calculated from *Zhongguo tongji nianjian, 1991*, p. 143, ibid. for 1988, 559, and ibid. for 1992, 145; *Shanghai tongji nianjian, 1991*, p. 260, ibid. for 1989, p. 271, and ibid. for 1992, 280; and *Guangdong tongji nianjian, 1991*, 191, and ibid. for 1992, 230.

228 Bankers & credit, savings, depreciation

Localist credit

Local policies overwhelmed central policies on credit, even when loan criteria seemed to remain stable. Five types of banking reforms were evident, and each can be explained in terms of greater devolution of powers by on-the-spot leaders. First, revenue extraction became a less salient function of banks than it had been. The central People's Bank of China was supplemented by others, often with names denoting sectors, which had fewer fiscal monitoring roles. Banks, like other economic units, were supposed to become more independent of "the government." The 1980s brought them somewhat more autonomy from supervisors – but not necessarily from local officials, whose pet projects needed loans and drove changes in banks as much as did directives from central CCP financiers.

Second, interest rates rose for both deposits and loans. Since China's state firms had previously hoarded credit lines (and other resources) and faced "soft budget constraints,"[34] the higher interest rates often raised their efficiency using funds in companies. This rationalization of the price of money also put the rates slightly closer to what private local lenders charged. State banks were no longer an exclusive source of funds, although the going rates went up, and there was competition among types of banks.

Third, reform banks were supposed to make profits. This meant local bank managers could sometimes claim rights to reallocate credit to potentially performing loans, and to deny money to likely defaulters. But politically sensitive factories still received loans to prevent bankruptcy if they were too big and/or too politically connected to fail. No matter whether these new bank powers were used to make profits – or instead, to make political links – there was a relative rise in the authority of locals. The legitimation of profits in banking also led to new procedures by which banks were supposed to attract more savings from companies and people in their areas. Legitimacy for profits justified bank localization.

Fourth, investment capital had once been centrally planned; but during reforms, this control eroded. Profitable new factories, especially in suburbs and rural areas, meant that some loan recipients could pay high returns. Two-track prices meant that (for reasons unrelated to efficiency) some firms became extremely lucrative, while others, including many pre-reform reliable borrowers, became loss centers. All these changes, some spurred by new technological opportunities and some impelled by uneven norms during the transition from socialism of the mid-1980s, undermined the state's ability to plan capital. In new procedures for finance, local concerns became primary. Either to save jobs or to start projects, the power of local boosters became as important in money management as were any coherent policies from the People's Bank of China and the few other large banks that operated with it (under Party overseers). All these overlapping changes in China's banking system may have raised microeconomic efficiency within some firms and local areas. They more surely helped to finance a suspension of macroeconomic controls. The 1980s inflation spurred restoration of such controls in the 1990s.[35]

The time sequence of these changes in various places was no more uniform than the principles or actors behind them. But the long-term trend before 1990 was clearly localist. Central banking policies had been largely reactive to political and technological changes in needs for loans during reforms, and then to the inflationary results that justified loans because of prosperity. Policies (local, medial, and central) came from situations more than intentions. They bore no resemblance to a coherent macroeconomic plan. There were, however, uncoordinated, diffuse, political plans, run mainly by and for local leaders acting in parallel.

Links of credit with personnel and jobs

The heads of Party groups in Chinese banks are attached to the CCP committees in their localities – and their careers are largely dependent on these, not just on Party leaders in the central bank. Formally, all appointments go through higher-level CCP heads in the same functional system (*xitong*). But in practice, when banks contravene the wishes of local politicos, their managers suffer. At least before 1990, they were not always hurt if they violated national rules. Partly for this reason, China during reforms lacked a central bank that could channel almost all credit allocations.

Managers with political friends have obtained loans fairly easily from bank directors in most years from the Great Leap Forward to 1990. Although the government kept large Shanghai enterprises on a tight rein to ensure delivery of taxes and state profits, it did not gather full information from firms about their loans. Such data were handled through banks, and the amounts of money offered to particular enterprises was a less important issue in practice than was the perennial difficulty of bank managers who were pressed by central authorities to stay within loan quotas, but pressed by local Party politicos to exceed them.

Loans have often been the only means of ensuring remittances, which were the hard constraint for many managers in Shanghai. All else, including output and innovation, was secondary to remittances. When enterprises could not meet their revenue quotas, they took out loans. This was usually a matter of "the state" going in debt to itself. The practice preserved appearances and jobs; and once it was normalized for paying taxes, it extended to other purposes. Bank representatives could seldom stand against advice from local Party officials to give loans. At a nationwide 1988 Beijing meeting of bankers, they asked that local politicians no longer pressure them to exceed authorized loan quotas. But economist interviewees expressed doubts about the efficacy of mere verbal declarations, without means of enforcement against local politicians and financial managers who violated norms against pressuring banks.

"Soft budget constraints" are widespread internationally in many kinds of economy – and they sometimes aid economic growth if easy credit inspires entrepreneurs to make experiments with new techniques, markets, and products. In most capitalist countries, governments allow banks to loan out more funds than they have on

230 Bankers & credit, savings, depreciation

deposit (e.g., through fractional reserve requirements). This policy can bring runs on banks, crises in savings institutions, recessions, or depressions – but it also lowers interest rates and thus provides a countervailing public-political benefit: growth at most times.[36]

So Chinese state companies that needed funds got bank loans – and planners helped them by urging banks to comply, after plans no longer appropriated enough money to keep firms afloat in the context of inflated prices. Total loans for fixed assets soared in the 1980s throughout China, from 8 b. yuan in 1981 to 225 b. in 1990 (on average up 45 percent yearly, compounded). Banks' lending, as a portion of all fixed assets over the same period, rose from 9 percent in 1981 to 50 percent in 1990. In particular, lending by state banks to urban collectives and reporting private firms rose throughout China from 8 b. yuan in 1980 to 83 b. in 1990 (an average rise of 26 percent annually). Between the same years, loans from state banks to rural collectives rose from 18 b. yuan to 104 b. (up 19 percent annually).

Rural credit cooperatives were more effective per loaned yuan than state banks in the enormous 1980s increase of credit. Many of them were unreported. Data from local credit co-ops *which registered their activities* suggest that their loans soared from 8 b. yuan in 1980 to at least 141 b. in 1990 (rising on average by one-third each year over the whole decade).[37] If more local, less formal revolving credit schemes had been fully accounted too, this trend would have been recorded as even sharper. All these statistics were affected by inflation – and were major causes of it. Credit became available to entrepreneurs during reforms in unprecedented amounts, and the sources were by no means restricted to banks that the state could monitor. Having a restricted credit policy would have meant, for many companies, either defaulting on revenue commitments or firing employees. These are precisely the two things that state managers in China by tradition were never supposed to do. Taxes were often paid, except in the periods of "slippage." Above all, money-losing state companies were generally kept from bankruptcy, at least into the early 1990s.

Mid-1980s modifications in banks

These practices met statist norms for a while in inflationary times. The unintended effects were credit expansion and sporadic efforts to control price increases and the money supply. But in 1979, the People's Bank of China received top-level orders to stress its role as a central bank and fight the rising prices. This was a fairly early example of reaction in Beijing to restore control over China's booming economy, but it was definitely not the last such attempt. Exhortations to and by the People's Bank, aiming to control credit, became a hallmark of economic politics into the 1990s.

The People's Bank had previously been an active lender to state firms. It remained so into the 1980s, partly because it had offices all over the country – more branches than any other bank in the world. Economic needs of the time required local lending, but with macroeconomic guidance from this central bank. These functions did not mesh together perfectly. The People's Bank's mandate was increasingly to supervise its branches and other banks. Further loans were supposed to be made by revamped or new banks, to which the People's Bank was gradually supposed to hive off decisions about specific loan contracts. Foreign trade, for example, was the old Bank of China's special area. The People's Bank was complemented in other sectors by China's Agricultural Bank, the Industrial and Commercial Bank, the People's Construction Bank, the People's Insurance Company, the International Trust and Investment Company, the Communications Bank that was headquartered in Shanghai, and others.

The Bank of Industry and Commerce was mainly responsible for short-term loans. The Construction Bank supplied more fixed capital, and the Agricultural Bank worked in suburbs and rural areas. The People's Bank accepted deposits and acted not only as the central bank, but also as the supervising corporation in finance. Reform booms eroded the People's Bank's planning ability, just as they eroded other "mother-in-law" companies.

The idea that major banks were not supposed to compete, because they were theoretically divided by functions, became less enforceable during reforms. Many loans were unplanned and abrupt, as urgent credit became needed to buy scarce materials. In August 1986, several separate big banks were given broader mandates. By October, Shanghai's Communications Bank could conduct almost any transaction. Other banks followed suit in later months; so they began to vie with each other.[38] Among these, the Agricultural Bank became pivotal, because its loans largely went to rural industry, the fastest-growing big sector of the economy.

Shanghai's banking reforms were restrained until the mid-1980s, but the previous financial order buckled in 1986. That year saw the initial rebirth of Shanghai's stock exchange. An interbank short-term credit market was established. The large banks became more autonomous from each other. A "swap" center for trading foreign credit was created; this was supposed to help joint ventures meet their legal obligations not to run hard-currency deficits (and unavoidably, it aided transactions in convertible currency for other purposes too). The Bank of Communications – owned by the state but essentially regional in East China rather than nationwide – was recreated.[39] Each of these five steps was important, and they deserve separate attention.

The Bank of Communications resurrected the name of an institution first established in 1908, but inactive after 1954. In its new form, it was conceived as a joint stock company. Although "the state" at the national level purchased half the stock, the other half was sold to local governments, official and collective enterprises, and individuals (who together were limited to 5 percent of the total shares). Dividends were paid, based on profits. This re-established Bank of Communications in 1986 was accorded wide powers to accept enterprise deposits and make long- and short-term loans. Its interest rates could float within a range set for each term. It could help issue bonds, finance international trade, and loan foreign exchange. This Shanghai institution was then the PRC's closest equivalent to retail "one stop banking."[40]

The interbank market began as a conclave of about forty bank officers, meeting each Thursday morning near the Bund (central Shanghai's waterfront) from

232 Bankers & credit, savings, depreciation

August 1986. Such a market was unusual in the PRC, because it allowed exchanges of short-term credit between different organizations and regions without authorization from any planner. When this interbank market began in 1986, probably one-third of all goods and services in China's economy were already traded at prices that responded strongly to demand. So this new financial institution, which allowed traders in dire need of supplies to get money somewhat easily, had to be inflationary. It supported an economy that was pell-mell producing goods that got higher prices. It also raised the growth and efficiency of other markets. As an official of the People's Bank of China admitted: "The vertical allocation of funds is incompatible with horizontal economic integration. . . . [But] there has been no fundamental change in the actual practice of banks indiscriminately providing funds to enterprises. . . . The economic regulations and control measures have no teeth."[41] The interbank market swept aside many rules. For large firms, credit was no longer the province of planners.

The previous system had dammed parts of the money supply in specific places, so that wealth could not easily flow to spots where it could have the most productive effects. A Shanghai banker complained, "There had been no movement of funds among the specialized banking systems, no flow between Shanghai and other places, nor even within the network of offices and branches of a single system in one place."[42] Each locality and functional system had hoarded credit, just as each unit also hoarded other supplies. Even though new interbank loans pressed prices upward, they created a money supply that might later be controlled.

Banks bailed out many state enterprises that were practically bankrupt by the mid-1980s. Earlier, when strict constraints had been imposed on short-term credit, many firms were unable to roll over or extend their loans – and thus they defaulted. They could not pay their suppliers, many of which then also defaulted. By December 1985, one estimate claimed that state firms' unpaid bills exceeded 10 billion yuan; and two months later, that amount was reported to be "out of control."[43] Horizontal credit markets created this problem long-term and alleviated it temporarily. Financial planning could not be maintained after other plans had eroded.

Along with interbank lending by 1986, Shanghai people also revived local banks that inevitably took loan business from the central bank.[44] Money had to flow more easily in the mid-1980s, because enterprises needed funds to pay for factors. During the first six months of 1986, near the peak of the raw materials inflation, loans to Shanghai firms rose by 15 percent.[45] In these same six months, reported gross output value rose 2 percent. Table 9.4 makes comparisons for this period with other parts of East China.

Loans were harder to procure in Shanghai than in most other areas, despite cadres' needs to buy raw materials and pay taxes. Shanghai's "short-term funds market" opened at the end of August 1986 – and in the next fifty days, 900 million yuan flowed to the city "horizontally" from other Chinese banks. This was, in less than two months, a three-tenths addition to the whole year's planned credit for Shanghai.[46]

TABLE 9.4 Loans and production, East China province units, first half of 1986 only

	Rise of loans (%)	% of output
Shanghai	15	2
Jiangsu	16	9
Zhejiang	36	11
Jiangxi	56	11

Source: *Shanghai jingji* (Shanghai Economy), January 1987, 23.

Independent official banks

Shanghai established early nonstate (*minjian*, "among the people") urban financial institutions during reforms. In August 1986, the local Aijian Credit and Investment Company appeared. That December, two credit cooperatives in downtown Shanghai could be openly registered. In the same month, controls over foreign exchange were relaxed; and the Shanghai branch of the Agricultural Bank and the Shanghai Insurance Investment Company were authorized to act independently of the national corporations that had previously supervised them.

Shanghai's municipal branch of the People's Bank of China by 1986 also made financial decisions separately from the bank's headquarters in Beijing. Previously, all provincial branches of the People's Bank had "allocation and distribution relations" (*diaopo yu fenpei guanxi*) with the headquarters; but in the mid-1980s these were reformed into mere "loan links" (*jiedai guanxi*). The headquarters and Shanghai branch of the bank were enjoined to lend each other money – but in other respects, the central bank could not tell the branch what to do.[47] For administrative and appointment purposes, the People's Bank was still centralized, but the 1985–1987 money crisis forced a transfer of loan decisions to more local actors.

Bankers followed technicians and traders "horizontally" out of Shanghai to other parts of Jiangnan. Shanghai's Bank of Communications in 1988 had eight branches in Jiangsu and Zhejiang (as well as eight main branches in the metropolis, and others in Guangdong, Hubei, Liaoning, Shandong, and Sichuan). It also planned fifteen more branches in further provinces, so as to become "a real commercial bank."[48] All major cities on the Yangzi delta diversified their banking facilities in 1986 and established other credit institutions that tried, with Party approval, to take business from rural cooperatives. Wuxi opened its money market in late 1986, specializing in interbank loans. Within a year, this exchange was handling more than 10 b. yuan and was China's largest money market.[49]

In 1988, the People's Bank of China headquarters in Beijing approved 186 new bank branches in Shanghai – a rise of about 15 percent in one year.[50] The central bank also issued Great Wall credit cards, whose accounts were all in Chinese currency (*renminbi*). By 1987, it joined with MasterCard International, converting these into Great Wall MasterCards.[51] The central bank diversified its services to compete

234 Bankers & credit, savings, depreciation

with other institutions. Facing so much local competition in so many parts of the country, it became more nimble than PRC state enterprises traditionally were.

The new bank offices showed some division of labor. A quarter of the People's Bank new branches were specialized in accepting savings, one-eighth were credit unions, and about three eighths were "business offices" (*yingye suo*) mainly for deposits and loans of companies. Six of the city's main banks, including the local Communications Bank, became independent of control by the Shanghai branch of the People's Bank. These six were designated "nongovernmental" (another translation of *minjian*), supposedly not run by the state.[52] The Party, of course, had cells in them; but they became more autonomous because the Party itself was not perfectly unified despite the formal elegance of its organization chart. Banking requires expertise; and Party technocrats might survive in this field, while Party generalists could not last long in it without losing a great deal of money.

The six banks' new branches in 1988 encouraged savings; new offices of all banks that were "specialized" for savings rose sharply in that year – but they also made loans. Efforts to restrain the money supply were mostly ineffective, as the number of such banks rose. In 1986, fully 26 percent more credit was approved than in 1985. In 1987, the rate of increase decelerated only slightly, to 19 percent.[53] This was inflationary, but urban enterprise managers needed the money to stay in business and in good political odor.

When Moody's Investors' Service in mid-1996 lowered its credit ratings for major PRC banks, it asked in case of bankruptcies "exactly what the government would be responsible for and what would be considered the liabilities of quasi-privatized banks."[54] Credit raters could not tell whether these banks were really state owned or instead should be judged by rules for private firms. Were their debts sovereign? Chinese officials protested hotly that all loans were safe. But they too did not really know the answer to this question.

Deposits and loans in reform markets

Bank loans during the 1980s were supposed to depend on deposits. Relatively poor provinces, which received net subsidies from the central treasury, sometimes had a "gap between deposits and loans" (*cuncha*), a euphemism for a surplus of deposits. They had fewer profitable projects than did richer areas that were said to have a "surplus of loans" (*daicha*). Early in the decade, banks with credit they could not use sent representatives to Shanghai, where they readily found borrowers. Telex was used to transfer such money quickly. Even before an interbank market could open, the need for it was evident in other behavior. The interbank market was partly an unintended result of efforts to maintain fiscal extractions after resourcing plans eroded.

In an attempt to limit credit, the central government allocated to banks an estimated difference between deposits and approvable loans. This was supposed, in 1987, to be the sole quota of loans. From an economic viewpoint, a money market was less inflationary than the previous habit of politicians negotiating a total allowable amount of credit (*xindai zong'e*). But the latter procedure was preferred by conservatives, dominant in parts of China. Planners accused bankers of pressing enterprises to take unneeded loans. These accusations against loan approvers show little more than central inability to control them. The diverse systems used in various jurisdictions made scant difference, because it became generally easier to lend in China. Banks competed to use up their loanable quotas on profit-making projects.

From January to June 1987, Shanghai borrowed one hundred million yuan from banks in Guangdong. Credit during the reform prosperity remained surprisingly inexpensive. "Self-gathered" (*zichou*) funds were monies from any sources except the government and its main banks – from local bonds, foreign investors, other enterprises, or the employees of the borrowing firms with or without their consent. In late 1988, Beijing to scant avail launched efforts to stem the flood of credit and inflation this haphazard pattern had brought.[55]

For attracting deposits, or granting loans, interest rates varied with the identity of the bank's client. Individuals received better rates than "units," apparently to keep entrepreneurs from nonstate banking. Overseas Chinese, even if resident in Shanghai, received more attractive interest on savings than did ordinary citizens – because they might keep their money abroad if the return was higher there. This situation is presented in Table 9.5.

These rates are hardly spectacular, but reform prosperity meant that disposable incomes rose quickly in Jiangnan, as did savings. Bank accounts became larger, and other money went into local nonstate institutions, especially informal loans that bore higher interest. The ratio of consumption to disposable income during reforms probably reflects actual savings better than deposits do. Shanghai consumed less of its disposable income in the mid-1980s than did any other province, as

TABLE 9.5 Interest offered to different Shanghai bank depositors (annual percentages, compounded monthly, 1982)

	Savings	*Time Deposits*					
	Deposits	*6 mo.*	*1 yr.*	*2 yr.*	*3 yr.*	*5 yr.*	*8 yr.*
UNITS							
Firms on plan	1.5						
Extra-plan firms & offices	1.5		3.0	3.6	4.2		
INDIVIDUALS							
PRC citizens	2.4	3.6	4.8		5.7	6.6	7.5
Overseas Chinese	2.4	3.6	6.0	6.9			

Notes and sources: Deposits were apparently seldom made in the categories left blank above. Low interest for planned companies' accounts would have reduced state banks' interest payments, also reducing incentives to deposit. See *Shanghai jingji, neibu ben: 1949-1982* (Shanghai Economy, Internal Volume: 1949–1982), Shanghai Academy of Social Sciences, ed. (Shanghai: Shanghai Shehui Kexue Yuan Chuban She, 1984), 924.

236 Bankers & credit, savings, depreciation

Table 9.6 shows. Savings were relatively high in Shanghai. The specific quantities may mean less than the order of provinces that reported consuming less income than they made. Jiangsu and Zhejiang are not far from Shanghai on the list.

Savings deposits in Shanghai by late 1986 were at an all-time high, averaging 760 yuan per person.[56] At the edge of the city, Meilong Township residents' income in the sixth Five-Year Plan (1981–1985) rose 21 percent each year. They did not report spending such a quick windfall. Throughout these five years, their bank deposits grew *annually* at 39 percent.[57]

The story was similar elsewhere on the delta. Per capita savings in Wuxi County rose almost ten times between 1978 and 1984. This was nearly twice the (reported) output increase of the county's rural industries. Per capita savings in 1978 were 16.6 yuan, and the increase was 9.3 times. The industrial output was 426 m. yuan, and the increase was 5.1 times.[58] Savings from informal service sector activities may have been large, and some industrial output was unreported.

TABLE 9.6 Consumption and disposable income, by province (percentages and million yuan, 1985 reported, for most provinces)

	Consumption/Disp. Income	Disposable Income	Consumption
Shanghai	46%	304.34	139.51
Beijing	49%	212.20	103.70
Tianjin	50%	139.90	69.63
Shanxi	56%	187.20	105.10
Zhejiang	59%	345.48	203.00
Yunnan	59%	196.83	115.45
Jiangsu	62%	507.50	313.48
Shaanxi	62%	192.30	119.64
Shandong	63%	501.65	317.29
Hebei	65%	328.32	214.57
Guangdong	65%	522.40	337.27
Liaoning	66%	370.54	244.91
Hubei	68%	325.22	221.10
Heilongjiang	68%	271.38	184.49
Henan	68%	370.89	251.36
Anhui	69%	276.25	190.87
Inner Mongolia	69%	147.69	101.36
Jilin	70%	187.35	130.23
Fujian	71%	176.39	124.76
Sichuan	72%	511.95	370.65
Jiangxi	73%	190.55	139.64
Hunan	74%	305.50	226.23
Guangxi	74%	179.74	133.39
Guizhou	75%	122.99	92.13

Source: Calculated from *Zhongguo tongji nianjian, 1987* (Statistical Yearbook of China, 1987) (Beijing: Zhongguo Tongji Chuban She, 1987), 40 and 60. A few western provinces are omitted. Rankings of others suggest statistical problems; rich areas may have underreported income.

Shanghai enjoyed quick income growth. A bank economist in 1987 admitted that people were reluctant to deposit money because the interest rate lagged behind inflation.[59] Nonetheless, as Table 9.7 shows, Shanghai bank deposits rose in the 1980s. The areas with the quickest growth, the rural suburbs, had a lower bank deposit rate – but almost surely not a lower total savings or investment rate. The portion of rural deposits peaked in 1982 and was stable after the raw materials inflation hit industrial goods prices. Suburban people were loaning money very profitably to each other, not through state institutions.

High monetized savings became common in many rural areas. From 1981 through 1987, individual deposits skyrocketed, showing a national average *annual* increase of 34 percent. A newspaper noted, "The increase in savings deposits, however, would be bigger if prices were not rising so fast." It pointed out that "when there are no other means to maintain the value of money, such as buying gold and foreign currency, people have to deposit their money in the bank, because more would be lost if they kept cash in hand. In other words, people are somewhat forced to put their money in the bank. Savings were also raised by a shortage of goods that people want to buy, such as color television sets and high-quality bicycles."[60] Economists, concerned about inflationary effects if many creditors withdrew their savings suddenly by the end of reforms, urged the government to encourage gradual withdrawals. The problem was to find new things people could buy. In Shanghai's urban state economy, citizens had some trouble making money; but they also had trouble spending it. High-quality consumer goods were few, and planners wished to limit markets in other fields, notably stocks and land.

TABLE 9.7 Shanghai residents' private deposits in banks (millions of yuan and percentage portions, year-end)

	Shanghai savings	*Shanghai GDP*	*Rural savings*	*% Rural*	*Deposits/GDP %*
1970	1047	15667	53	5	7
75	1466	20412	100	7	7
78	1818	27281	126	7	7
80	3020	31189	256	8	10
82	3794	33707	526	14	11
84	5610	39085	597	11	14
86	9095	49083	1026	11	19
88	14121	64830	1547	11	22
89	19347	69654	2054	11	28
90	22305	74467	2522	11	30
91	32822	85771	3781	12	38
92	41309	106594	4509	11	39

Source: Percentages are calculated from figures in *Shanghai tongji nianjian* (Shanghai Statistical Yearbook), Shanghai Shi Tongji Ju, ed. (Beijing: Zhongguo Tongji Chuban She) 1990 edition, 34 and 403; 1991 edition, 34 and 419; 1992 edition, 33 and 455; and 1993 edition, 37 and 397; and *Shanghai Statistical Yearbook, 1989, Concise Edition*, Municipal Statistical Bureau of Shanghai, ed. (Beijing: China Statistical Publishing House, 1989), 16 and 172.

238 Bankers & credit, savings, depreciation

Zhejiang residents' cash in banks by 1987 was 7 times the 1980 amount of deposits.[61] Zhejiang's total 1987 reported value of output increased to 3.8 times the 1980 amount (in nominal terms, not accounting inflation) – not as quick as the sevenfold increase of deposits. The growth of reported gross industrial output value was 4.2 times over this same period in the 1980s. Because of changed career incentives for local cadre-entrepreneurs, these figures were probable underestimates. "Back alley" loans in Zhejiang apparently grew faster than reported bank deposits.

Deposits in the ordinary state banking system of Jiangsu declined in the late 1980s, although informal loans of credit were "very active." People with spare money used it instead for direct loans to specialized and private enterprises, largely factories run by villages.[62] These private loans garnered higher interest than banks would pay. They were common in developed rural areas of Jiangsu, not just Wenzhou Prefecture. Cadres admitted that "loans among the people" (*minjian daikuan*) had positive economic effects, raising the free circulation of funds, mobilizing idle money, and developing the commodity economy. Private loans also lessened pressures on state banks for credit. But the *Jiangsu Legal System News* noted four major disadvantages from the viewpoint of the state.

First, the supply of savings in state banks declined, and by 1989 the amount of state loans was large. The total amount of loans from all sources was unpublished; nobody knew it reliably. Second, the existence of private loans reduced the possibilities of state control over uses of money. Private creditors reportedly "wasted" funds (although it was not mentioned that the state often did this too). Third, official banks were "affected" because of upward pressure on interest rates and the absorption of personnel into the informal banking system. Illegalities often went unchecked, and especially for "loans based on personal relations" (*renqing daikuan*, a phenomenon that was frequent in state banks too). Fourth, the private financial system was deemed bad for economic stability.[63] Rural industrialization that it financed absorbed raw materials and led to breaches of planned contracts.

A Jiangsu official called for laws restricting the amount private lenders could charge above the interest rates that state banks charged. He called for stricter policing of loan procedures. By 1988, when the North Jiangsu economy began to boom, Xuzhou City had a shortfall of nearly one-third the amount of capital that a standard plan ratio indicated should have been available for its level of production.[64] The area had a "hunger and thirst for capital" (*zijin jike zheng*). Local credit institutions were said to suffer from "bank anemia (*yinhang pinxue zheng*)."[65] Because "state fiscal measures were tight," the local government vowed to raise more money from ordinary citizens. The economy got credit, and the central government got less power.

By late August 1988, Shanghai suffered a run on banks because depositors wanted money to buy goods before the price hikes they expected. A local official said banks throughout the city had been "plagued by long lines" withdrawing funds. Some invested in silver and gold as a hedge against further inflation.[66] People put their wealth in whatever financial instruments they deemed safe or profitable, and these were often local. By early 1989, the People's Bank imposed on its own branches a new rule that set a ceiling on loans, regardless of deposits.[67] But it did not try to impose this rule on other banks, each of which faced the Party's financial monitors separately.

Was inflation the inevitable concomitant of post-revolutionary localization? Perhaps not. Periods of quick economic growth after centralizations in other countries have also sometimes been inflationary. Comparisons show, however, that the main pattern is an increase of savings. In Taiwan during its growth heyday from the 1950s until the oil crisis, inflation was low. Post-revolutionary and post-Napoleonic France did not stoke so much inflation as did China after Mao's centralizations. France in this long period had sharply increasing deposits in savings banks. Although reliable statistics begin only in 1835, they show a quick rise of deposits (16 percent annually, nearly 600 percent total) over the next dozen years to 1847.[68] New savings, mostly uncontrolled by the state, have expanded smartly after spates of violence in other countries. Comparative research on this topic could be attempted for many nations that experienced forceful centralizations followed by localizations, if scholars paid more attention to local-political factors of economic behavior.

Much of China's savings occurred in stores or factories, not banks. Reforms encouraged units to have "small treasuries" (*xiao jinku*) that were often secret – and not small. Materials shortages gave managers both reasons and excuses to stow money wherever they could. The rise of materials prices meant that companies had to keep bigger reserves against insolvency. In a sample of Shanghai light industrial firms, the requirements for cash on hand rose almost one-quarter during the year before mid-1988.[69]

Private saving and lending boomed. They went underground if the central bank tried to stop them. In Zhejiang and elsewhere, formally illegal private banks were established in public and operated openly. When high officials discovered that some private loans carried annual interest rates of more than 40 percent, they decreed guidelines for lower rates. Then they had to admit these policies only meant that "free loan activities have become more hidden."[70]

Bonds

New nonstate enterprises earned a great deal of money that sought a panoply of investment instruments. Bond and stock markets were nothing new in Shanghai, but socialist conservatives professed to be shocked by their reintroduction. The return to financial capitalism in Shanghai took many small steps and changes of rules. Western journalists reported each of them as racy, a kind of socialist striptease.

Aside from pre-1949 equities exchanges, Shanghai's bond markets had also been active in the 1950s. Beginning at low levels during early reforms, and then nationally in 1981, the state issued large tranches of treasury bonds (*guoku zhai*). As budget deficits worsened in the late 1980s, and as opportunities for profitable investments expanded, local governments also issued bonds to raise money. There was practically no regulation of these markets until a 1987 State Council decree, which was supplemented by more rules in 1989 and 1990 – but these superseded each other and were violated.[71]

240 Bankers & credit, savings, depreciation

Good rates of interest on bonds, together with other perks for bondholders, allowed firms to garner significant funds in the mid-1980s. When the Shanghai Petrochemical Works wanted to establish a new ethylene plant in the mid-1980s, it sold bonds. Interest of 12 percent was offered to individual buyers – well above the 7.44 percent for residents' savings accounts at that time. Enterprises that bought the bonds got 8 percent, which was more than the 3.66 percent the government would give them for one-year paper. And corporate buyers could buy bonds that paid only 4.2 percent but included options to purchase the plant's products once it got into operation. On that basis, which was highly attractive in Shanghai at a time of materials shortage, the first tranche of bonds was quickly oversubscribed.[72]

Because of Shanghai's old reputation, the city could attract money from prosperous entrepreneurs, overseas and throughout the country, who wanted to buy bonds. The Construction Bank announced that bonds for a new plant, carrying 12 percent interest, would be sold on November 25, 1986. The queue began forming at midnight on the previous day, and the line was a thousand people long when the bank opened the next morning. Some investors "came especially to Shanghai from other parts of the country to buy the bonds."[73]

Promissory short-term credit, financial regulations, and rural money markets

Commercial paper, under which one company gives to another short-term credit at interest, had been legally phased out after 1949. Such loans "resurfaced in Shanghai after 1981," even without the benefit of laws to enforce repayment. Not until 1988 did the municipal government pass a rule to make this kind of contract binding. "The new law will only apply to those commercial papers signed, issued, negotiated, and paid in Shanghai, including drafts, checks, and cashier's cheques."[74] Party conservatives disdained to give legal recognition to a routine that reduced their ability to control the economy. Practices developed anyway, without rules. Institutions grew without the state's blessing. If they were not hidden but also not politically dissident, the state's monitors could seldom stifle them. Such habits were unofficial and seemed apolitical, peripheral to stately discourse; so how could they be important?

Regulation was delayed for some time after the trading of commercial paper began. By October 1988, Shanghai was only the second mainland city (after Shenzhen) to make systematic rules governing the negotiation of bills, checks, and promissory notes. This was a local law. Its wording relied on the Chinese-language text of a statute from Taiwan, where capitalism was normal. But the advent of rules did not cause a quick acceleration of exchanges in corporate paper.[75] Even before regulation, this market had grown rapidly. It soon expanded into personal checking for people who could convince their bankers.

Previous rules were loosened or ignored at this time. PRC treasury bonds, such as had been sold in the 1950s, could not be freely traded until 1988. Before that year, legal investors were supposed to wait for expiry dates before realizing any money. Shanghai for years had eight official exchange centers – but, as was usual for state agencies, they charged high commissions. "Why should I trade in there?" one bondholder reportedly asked, after the monopoly ended. Unofficial brokers, on the street outside the state agencies, did the same business for lower commissions.[76]

Rural money markets remained mostly illegal. That detail did not keep them from flourishing. Like other unregulated capital markets, they were subject to sharp fluctuations. The Wenzhou money market crashed in early 1989. Local people called it a "second cultural revolution," and more than 100,000 individuals reportedly suffered losses.

> Unregistered financial societies are built on family networks. Members borrow money from each other for working capital and sometimes apparently for speculation. . . . Some of these money societies have grown so large that they have exceeded the boundaries of family and clan relations. Participants have no way to know the credit situation until, all of a sudden, the society goes broke. . . . In the development of township enterprises and the management of rural money, the role of local authorities is minimal.[77]

According to this report, 95 percent of the funds needed by Wenzhou rural and private enterprises came from local sources rather than the state banking system.

New financial schemes proliferated in many rural parts of East China. Wenzhou was extreme mainly because the returns to capital there could be very high. The oddest examples from Wenzhou just tested the limits of what could happen less ostentatiously elsewhere too. The Wenzhou Dongfang Furniture Factory found a bold method to boost immediate sales: It offered a 12 percent rebate on the cost of its products after five years, or the entire money back after 16 years. This raised capital, and inflation was reliably expected to devalue the factory's repayment later. To guarantee its own promise, this furniture factory put 15 percent of its annual profits in a local credit cooperative that offered interest and acted as guarantor. Its furniture sales doubled each month, compounding, during the first ten months of this scheme.[78] The interest given by the co-op was about 20 percent per year.

Another side of the Wenzhou story is that unofficial capital flows could be more safely reported there than elsewhere. They reduced the business of the state banks. As a Chinese economist wrote,[79]

> non-governmental lending has developed, including both direct lending between peasants and indirect forms of credit. There are not only various "associations" (hui), but also a few old-style private banks (qian zhuang). Due to excess demand relative to supply, as well as because of speculation and profiteering by some people, the rate of interest on loans among the people is very high. The volume of deposits taken by the Agricultural Bank and the cooperatives has been affected [the state dialect's standard word for 'reduced'] by the high interest rate on loans among the people.

242 Bankers & credit, savings, depreciation

Stocks

The Shanghai Stock Market is worth a book and many articles – and some have been written.[80] Shares were first sold in Shanghai in 1882, and the local stock exchange grew along with the capitalist economy, until it closed in the early 1950s. Business ownership sales then fell under socialist laws. This rule did not last until 1978, when reforms are often imagined to have started; instead, it lasted until 1984. In the quarter century before that year, no shares of any company were legally bought or sold in Shanghai. By 1984, rules still forbade enterprises from selling more than 15 percent of their worth to any individual, or even to any collective.[81] Supervisory corporations were on official budgets. No matter how dismally their planners performed, they were the effective owners of most stores and factories. Bureaucrats had scant incentive to recommend selling stock that might dilute their supervisory rights.

During China's post-revolution reforms, the "shares system" (*gufen zhi*) was instituted surprisingly late, in January 1985. It expanded slowly.[82] In that year, Shanghai Feile Acoustics was the first PRC company to sell new stock. The Shanghai Stock Market was relegitimated in September 1986. On its board, nearly 15,000 of the city's enterprises soon sold bonds, although only 20 firms sold shares at this stage.[83]

A suitably scientistic-statist justification for stock markets came from an unexpected field: birth planning.[84] Population policy depends on financial markets, because parents have children partly for support in old age. But stock holdings in pension funds also provide old-age security. Bond and equity exchanges are supposed to preserve wealth for old people, and the one-child policy made many aging couples concerned about their futures. A trustworthy mechanism in which savings could earn dividends or interest became crucial. Reforming foxes argued, though conservative lions doubted, that proper planning of population would require stock markets.

Reopening the Shanghai stock market was a media event, on which news was leaked in tantalizing phases. The scope of the market's operation was extended on several occasions in the late 1980s, and each was reported as an ideological revolution. First came a government announcement that this archetypical icon of capitalism, the stock market, might at some future date again raise its ugly head in Shanghai. Bonds were first traded. After a further while, the market slowly listed a few stocks. Each "opening" has been a cause for fanfare in classic striptease style. Party conservatives braved the advent of this most risqué market, but they made sure that nonstate reformers were lured to pay for every step. Here was evidence, from this Chinese city with the most buoyant financial history, to convince capitalist investors throughout the world that the Communist coverings of reform would be no bar to progress.

Investment fever and categories of shares

The State Council decreed in 1987 that no state-owned firm could issue stock on its own. Exceptions soon proliferated. At various times, e.g., February 1992 with Deng Xiaoping's "southern tour," restrictions were temporarily lifted. No enterprises were sold off fully. The state, represented by supervising corporations, retained many shares. Others were sold to "legal persons," which were often other state agencies. Cadres who had run a corporation might muster a controlling majority of shares. A price was imputed for state shares – but later, the People's Bank of China often charged four or five times that much to unofficial buyers. Administrative control often was ensured for Party conservatives on a continuing basis, while outside money was also raised.

Shareholding boomed in Shanghai during 1987, when several large state enterprises, especially the Shanghai Vacuum Electrical Appliance Co., gathered capital by selling stock. About a year later, the city had nine enterprises issuing shares. By late 1988, eleven Shanghai firms sold stocks, and more than 350,000 people in the city owned equities. Shanghai Yanzhong sold its whole first tranche, at a face value of 4.5 m. yuan, in just six hours.

Shanghai Vacuum soon came to dominate Shanghai's nascent stock market, because of the amount it offered to the public. Its manager plainly said the purpose was to separate ownership from management, so as to reduce administrative interference in economic decisions. Shanghai Feile Company sold stock mostly to its own workers, of whom 77 percent purchased shares. The announced aim was to raise enthusiasm in their jobs.[85]

The categories of shares were four: state (*guojia*), legal persons (*faren*), individuals (*geti*), and foreigners. The "legal persons" were collective or state organizations; in practice, they were often companies with which the firm had long enjoyed commercial relations. When companies were "sharized" (*gufen hua*), the manager usually became the new chief executive officer. The Party secretary was often dubbed chair of the board.[86] Capitalist gestures were made, and new money was mobilized – but no further real change was necessary. Shanghai firms that went public in this controlled way were often in financial straits. Some could not pay much in taxes. Even when no other change was made, the managers sometimes did a better job after the ownership change.

This effect was most noticeable among joint ventures that sold shares to "overseas" owners, who were often ethnic Chinese. A striking example was the Shanghai Construction Machinery Factory, into which a Hong Kong company put "cash only" – and enough of that only to buy a "small" percentage of the firm. None of the managers were changed. The "form and functions of the Party organization were left unaltered." The Party secretary still participated in management decisions, especially on personnel. The firm's tax on profits was not reduced at all. Although a consultant's survey showed that 200 of the 900 employees should really be fired to improve the plant's efficiency, only 2 workers were let go. The Hong Kong partners were not represented at the plant on a permanent basis. Their delegate visited just once a year, to ask questions, look at the accounts, and take their share of the profits.

Yet *Liberation Daily*, the local Party newspaper, reported a beneficial "joint venture effect" at this plant where outside participation was very casual. Small nonstate ownership meant that "superior-subordinate relations between the company and the government were weakened, inspections and appraisals were reduced, and the organizational setup was determined independently." Purchases no longer had to be

244 Bankers & credit, savings, depreciation

approved by supervising bureaucrats. Wage bonuses were no longer taxed through the company, but through individual income taxes. Nonstate partners meant the government no longer tried to guarantee the company's materials or markets – but the firm could now seek both upstream purchases and downstream sales on its own, and it could bargain freely on prices. The outside capital was far less important than the firm's ability, for these reasons, to accumulate new money (partly by keeping wages low). The symbolic value of being a joint enterprise ended "ownership by the state" and strengthened local managers at the expense of supervisory cadres. Shares made efficiency, even when nothing else changed.[87]

Firms often sold stock at low, first-issue prices to officials who were important. General "stock market fever" in Shanghai normally ensured that the value would rise after an initial public offering. This was common, and legal, though the stock market fluctuated wildly and many shareholders lost money. After reforms, under more restrictive rules of the early 1990s, no more than one-quarter of the shares of any Chinese company could be offered for public sale. No individual could own more than one-twentieth. State-agent stockholders were always the majority. When state firms were approved by the government for listing on stock markets, many legal conditions had to be met. "A" shares went to mainland entities; "B" or "H" shares, to international buyers. Majority ownership was assured to the state. Also, firms with shares listed overseas had to establish a "surplus reserve fund" to support pensions if the company went bankrupt. An additional "welfare fund" was also legally required. PRC regulators would not approve firms making big losses to be listed abroad, lest Chinese investments acquire a bad reputation. An official holding company would exercise the state's majority vote in any "privatized" firm.[88]

Stock markets after 1989

A new stock market opened in 1990 in renovated rooms of the Pujiang Hotel near the Bund. The main aim was to sell state securities, but a few other stocks (which had already been traded elsewhere less formally) were also listed. The "transaction hall" was equipped with modern computers, several dozen small rooms for bargaining, and electronic transmission of prices "to 47 transaction centers and service spots scattered around the city, to keep a consistent quotation both in and outside the securities exchange."[89]

By December 1990, no securities law had yet attained sufficient political consensus within the government to be passed. Economic reformers continued to conflict with political conservatives. They were eager to recruit foreign investors and to use domestic savings, then estimated at more than US$200 billion. Six weeks after the market reopened in its late-1990 form, still just eight stocks and twenty-two bonds were listed. One of these (Shanghai Vacuum) accounted for 84 percent of the capitalization.[90] After that, the market somewhat diversified.

Socialist conservatives resisted putting large state plants on the auction block. Stock sales could raise funds while also improving management; but these opportunities were taken slowly. In later years, especially for new companies, local money remained important in Shanghai's economy. Shanghai's Jing'an Stock Index fluctuated wildly. It more than doubled, for example, between May and November of 1992, but then fell from a peak of 1,400 to 300 only. It soared back up to 1,500 in March 1993, then down to 1,000 two months later.[91]

Riding this roller-coaster, China had 3,000 joint stock companies nationwide by 1994, although only 400 were listed on the Shanghai Stock Exchange (and 500 in Shenzhen, plus 8 on the less stomach-churning Hong Kong exchange).[92] Regulators abroad wanted many kinds of information before listing a company. These were data that Chinese state managers had long deemed confidential "business secrets." If they were fully revealed, tax extraction would rise. The most solid "red chips" were surveyed by the Hang Seng China Enterprise Index – which nonetheless fell by two-thirds from the fourth quarter of 1993 to the fourth quarter of 1995.[93] Stocks in PRC state enterprises performed abysmally in the mid-1990s, then rose after the turn of the millennium and remained volatile in later years.

Boom and bust cycles

Uncertainties of evaluating enterprises did not dampen many Chinese investors' enthusiasm for informal, unregulated stock offerings. Despite a lack of laws to protect folk transactions, peasants created their own local stock markets. Cooperative finance was a long-standing tradition among rural leaders. The PRC government charged high rents to countenance it in large-scale industry. As a Chinese source reported in English,[94]

> a peasant service agency has been set up for selling shares in Yishan District, Tielong County [Zhejiang] where peasants joined the agency by purchasing shares and electing a board of directors, which takes care of routine matters. In the Pingyang Woolen Mill, workers join the mill by purchasing shares, with each worker investing 500 yuan. . . . The mill has issued 300 shares altogether, and 70 percent of factory profits are shared out. The emergence of a general share market is inevitable, and is wholly necessary, to allow the growth of individual enterprises or large labor-hiring households, at least in the short term.

Fully 29 percent of all PRC shareholders in early 1994 lived in Shanghai, Jiangsu, or Zhejiang.[95] (The portion from Guangdong was 17 percent, but from statist Beijing just 6 percent. Shanghai alone was 16 percent.) Over half the investors were enterprise cadres, technicians, or professionals – and a third were "others," apparently including nonstate entrepreneurs. One-third had more than 30,000 yuan invested in stocks. Jiangnan investors took to securities markets with great gusto, and stocks again became a major means of finance.

These markets wobbled, but business cycles occurred even without stock markets in socialist times. Seven business cycles have been found in China from mid-century to the mid-1990s, with an average length of 4.6 years. The frequency of the

246 Bankers & credit, savings, depreciation

cycle increased during the 1980s, with a trough (by this estimate) of just 4 percent GDP growth in 1981, a high of 15 percent growth in 1984, another relative low of 8 percent in 1986, up to 11 percent in 1988, down again to 4 percent by 1991.[96] In later years, China's growth rate broadly declined despite big fluctuations, converging with other middle-low income economies on single-digit increases.[97]

Government conservatives were interested in the cycle largely because of its effects on inflation, and their post-reform macroeconomic policies were dominated by memories of 1980s politics. China's money supply had risen by about one quarter in 1985, and by a similar portion again in each of the next two years. There were reported inflation rates of 8.8, 6.0, and 7.2 percent nationwide in 1985, 1986, and 1987, but these were underreports. By late 1987, the money supply was out of control. The "social commodity purchasing power" at that time was said to reach 690 billion yuan (one-fifth more than in 1986). Public demand for consumer durables was intense. Officials were aghast at this market expansion. One cadre complained, "Although all this can stimulate industrial development for a short time . . . it cannot sustain development for a long time because of the absence of a solid base."[98] The wide extension of credit was not just an economic phenomenon; it also hurt bureaucrats' power.

As a conservative analyst admitted, "many departments in the national economy are still ill-adapted to such a high industrial growth rate. Thus, there are shortages and strains. For example, as a result of the present heavy pressures on railroad transportation, there is an overstocking of coal and phosphate ores in southwest China, of coal and raw salt in northwest China, and of timber and corn in northeast China." The conservatives' main recommendation was to "check the growth in social demand." Without reversing the reforms' prosperity, it was unclear how this would be done.

By 1988, planners called for a reduction of China's money supply by almost one-third. The lions wanted slower growth, even though that meant less wealth. The Bank of China vowed to "self-supply" its own credit by collecting on loans and by trying to increase citizens' deposits. The Bank had reported 38 percent of the capital it used as "self-supplied" in 1987, compared with 31 percent in 1986. The plan was to raise this portion to 60 percent in 1988.[99] "Self-supply" meant trying to enforce loan repayments. Many local cadres preferred to let loans go unpaid.

By this time, many companies joined unregulated credit cooperatives in extra-plan lending. They flipped old loans by taking out new ones from other institutions, as their costs rose. To get raw materials, managers had to wine and dine anyone who could deliver. Banquets paid by managers of publicly owned firms reportedly contributed between 60 and 70 percent of the total income of large and medium-size restaurants in China. Another cost, typically from managers' funds, was for "company" cars. Yet another went to purchase items for employees, such as luggage, overcoats, and food.[100] There was at that time no effective way to check local managers' uses for such funds; so state leaders were mainly eager to reduce the total amounts. Decrees having this aim were publicized – with uncertain results, because managers for years had developed many methods of hiding money.

On October 1, 1988, new "provisional regulations on cash administration" banned monetary transactions by state firms and agencies, including military units, except through monitored bank accounts.[101] Ceiling amounts were set for cash on hand. "Account transfer certificates" were required to prove that expenditures conformed to plans. Such rules did not relate the profitability of firms more closely to efficiency than to speculation – but they could not easily be enforced anyway. Local state organizations spent 20 percent more in the first seven months of 1988 than in the same period of the previous year, despite central orders to lower their budgets. Bans on new purchases were circumvented. As a government official explained, "They get the garage to write a receipt for car repairs equal to the cost of a new car. A copying machine is billed [vaguely] as 'electrical items.' Who cares? It's the state's money."[102]

By the end of the 1980s, government monitors proposed that credit for "farming" should be more loose than for "industry."[103] The growth of rural factories was supposed to be slowed, and peasants were urged back to fields. But once rural leaders had money, in practice they could usually spend it as they wished. The Agricultural Bank was supposed to support only field (as distinct from rural industrial) production "with all its strength." But countryside factories were, over the previous two decades, a train that had left the socialist station. It was unclear how money, given to or retained by rural units after localization, could be kept from its most profitable uses, which were industrial. Jiangnan provinces continued to prosper. In the first half of 1990, after Tiananmen, Jiangsu registered industrial growth of about 5 percent "while the overall economy just crept along with a 2.3 percent growth."[104]

Fully 40 percent of China's state-sector plants were reported to be running losses by 1991, up from 34 percent in 1990.[105] The 1991 Chinese economy was still accelerating (nominal GDP was 7 percent higher than in 1990, or 5.4 percent in real terms). But the healthiest firms were mostly nonstate. Government economic cadres had enough influence to ensure that banks would keep state firms from collapse. The economic boom led by rural factories kept this system afloat while eroding its foundations. Central Party conservatives and reformers alike had no choice but to let China's new local economic systems prosper out of control, because the demand they generated was crucial for state investments and for preventing recession.

A 1992 economic resurgence made news with Deng Xiaoping's "tour of the South" (*nanxun*). It was linked to political interests that extended far beyond the top leaders of the state. Changes at that time benefited Beijing less than they benefited other parts of China's many-sized polity. Local leaders could speak of Deng's policies in a conventional way, as benefits bestowed by high officials, especially the pre-eminent leader. Tax rates on local enterprises were lowered, municipal bureaucrats referred fewer investment decisions to ministries in Beijing, and restrictions on the Shanghai Stock Exchange and financial institutions were somewhat lessened.

Jiangsu retail inflation at the beginning of 1993 remained near double digits. In cities, the annualized price-hike rate was over 12 percent. This was not Argentinian or Zimbabwean, but it was fast. A reason is that, at the end of 1992, China's

248 Bankers & credit, savings, depreciation

currency in circulation was more than a quarter (27 percent) above the amount one year earlier.[106] In mid-1993, First Deputy Premier Zhu Rongji fired the head of China's central bank, took the job himself, and declared war on the expansion of credit. Many in Shanghai expressed less concern. Especially with Pudong plans afoot, and with some lessening of the extraction rate Shanghai had long paid, the local mood was expansionist. "'No one here is worried at all,' said a Chinese lawyer who was based among the chain-link fences and dusty construction sites that covered Pudong. 'We have 35 office buildings over 20 stories tall expected to come on line in the next three years.'"[107]

Beijing showed predictable concern about overheating. Top leaders' warnings on macroeconomic danger were credible. The size of the problem was difficult to judge, partly because official interests affected reporting about it. Central government conservatives were nostalgic to restore a structure in which they controlled credit, using funds as in the past on pet projects (Premier Li Peng's Three Gorges Dam was then the most obvious example). Conservatives only sometimes weighed carefully the economic value of such investments, as compared with alternative uses of money, or the speed with which they would regenerate capital. Inefficiency was the macroeconomic threat from conservatives.

Many Chinese economic reformers were concerned to limit the quick expansion of the money supply, which the PRC continued to experience in the 1990s. If controls on credit failed, consumer and investor confidence, prices, and output would predictably have gyrations. By 1993, Party cadres at many "levels" had realized that a lack of macroeconomic control (no matter whether it came in the conservative or reform versions) was dangerous for political stability.

The mechanism by which such crises can occur is that businesses using credit, e.g., to expand capacity expecting higher demand, could quickly find their expectations were wrong and lose money. Then they might not pay debts. Their creditors, in turn mostly debtors to other units, would likewise default, furthering the syndrome and lowering demand. The extent to which early-1990s credit expansion in China was justified by future demand was a question on which data were inherently not then available. A common guess among interviewees was that the boom in China's economy could lead to recession. Even if this were later followed by another expansion, the temporary fall-off of performance could hurt the regime's legitimacy. Conservative "lions" were strengthened by such fears in the 1990s.

It was easier to predict this pattern when official controls were weak than to predict the dates when such problems would actually arise. A roller-coaster economy may or may not have been the likeliest way to loosen China's economy so that entrepreneurs could lead its growth. But its influence on the politics of the world's largest authoritarian state was clear: a centralizing reaction. Some business cycle was evident, as reforms deregulated many economic activities. A recession, such as China's economy seemed to be breeding by the 1990s, could create violent politics, not just volatile economic indices. This cloud could also have a silver lining: There may have been no other means except a sharp recession to achieve thorough economic restructuring of inefficient state industries. If the central government found it politically dangerous, because of labor unrest, to close money-losing plants, an economic crisis forcing these closures might be in most Chinese people's eventual interest. But this was not a risk that Party leaders were willing to take.

A second possibility – the actual one, as the new millennium showed – was that the feared recession might not occur even as the economy slowed. Few econometricians claimed to have good tools and data to measure the extent or longevity of pent-up demand in a localizing economy like China's. This was the case in the 1990s, and it remained the case for many years. Massive, uncontrolled credit expansions could eventually prove to have been justified. Markets in the ex-socialist economy might be nearly as rational as some economic theorists liked to claim. It is difficult to prove sustained irrationality, even in a fluctuating market, until a time too late for policy to do much good. If that turned out to be the case in China, the ominous recession could at least be delayed.[108] No really adequate framework for knowing these things had any consensus; so top CCP politicians, always risk-averse about danger, sporadically decreed credit crunches. Local leaders who wanted funds for local projects sporadically but decreasingly got around these restrictions.

By the mid-2010s, it was clear that "China's status quo cannot be sustained forever. Returns on capital are declining. It now takes nearly four yuan of new credit to generate one yuan of additional GDP, up from over one yuan of credit before the global financial crisis. As the population ages and the economy matures, growth is bound to slow further." By 2016, "companies probe for weakness in the mesh of regulations, with the government seemingly always one step behind. In the past year alone [2015], it has spent nearly $200 billion to prop up the stock market; $65 billion of bank loans have gone bad; financial frauds have cost investors at least $20 billion; and $600 billion of capital has left the country."[109] China's stock markets continued to fluctuate wildly, and some gurus predicted popping bubbles in real estate. But while the government owned most of the banks to which non-performing loans were due, it also owned many of the companies that were supposed to repay these dubious debts. Reforms had not brought later prosperity without bumpiness, but they had brought prosperity.

Notes

1 Fudan feng (Fudan Breeze), Shanghai, No. 1 (March 27, 1988), 16–17 (article by Chen Shenshen).
2 See a series of SHJJDB articles by Chen Shenshen on July 18, July 25, August 1, and August 8, 1988.
3 Zhongguo shehui zhuyi chengshi jingji xue, 89.
4 Shanghai was only somewhat above average in produce it could get from each yuan of fixed assets: in 1987, 1.72 yuan. Wuxi and Suzhou did better on this score than any other surveyed places, producing 2.40 and 2.60 yuan respectively. Jiangnan was China's star region in this respect. SHGYJJB, August 19, 1988.
5 See this graphed in Barry Naughton, "Industrial Policy," 162.
6 Nonbudgetary investment rose at an even faster rate from 1977 to 1983. Ibid., 174.
7 Marc Blecher and Vivienne Shue, Tethered Deer: Government and Economy in a Chinese County (Stanford: Stanford University Press, 1995).

250 Bankers & credit, savings, depreciation

8 This statistic is called the "*difang, bumen, qiye he shiye danwei zhangwo de yusuan wai zijin,*" *Caijing yanjiu* (Financial and Economic Research), May 1988, 14, says its average rate of increase from 1979 to 1985 was 22.4 percent; 22.0 percent comes from calculations on other data in ZGTJNJ88, 51 and 764. It is reassuring when different PRC sources offer just trivially different statistics. We are often lucky if in the right decile.

9 In Shanghai from 1950 to 1983, according to another source, about half (54 percent) of the money appropriated for basic construction came from the state budget. But during the last five of these years, from 1979 to 1983, the state's allocation reportedly dropped to less than one-third. Shanghai caizheng yanjiu (Shanghai Finance Research), February 1985, 10. The text is based on *Shanghai: Gaige, kaifang, yu fazhan, 1979–87* (Shanghai: Reforms, Opening, and Development, 1979–87), Shanghai Statistical Bureau, ed. (Shanghai: Sanlian Shudian, 1988), 44.

10 *SHTJNJ87*, 233. This was 81 percent in 1985, and 79 percent in 1986.

11 *ZGTJNJ87*, 474. In the previous year, the national figure was 61 percent. These numbers were authoritatively published, but they are more usable for trends and comparisons rather than measures of absolute levels.

12 By 1982, total profits from Shanghai textiles were 2,303 million yuan (25 percent of national profits in this industry). Shanghai jingji, neibu ben, 151–56. WHB, August 10, 1980.

13 This paragraph is based on information from a Shanghai economist.

14 Michel Oksenberg and James Tong, "The Evolution of Central-Provincial Fiscal Relations in China, 1971–1984: The Formal System," 1–32.

15 Wang Shaoguang, "The Rise of the Second Budget and the Decline of State Capacity in China," unpublished paper, 31.

16 The State Council raised depreciation in various categories by one percentage point on February 6; see Zhonghua Renmin Gonghe Guo jingji guanli dashi ji (Chronicle of PRC Economic Management), Dangdai Zhongguo Jingji Guanli Editorial Dept., ed. (Beijing: Zhongguo Jingji Chuban She, 1986), 494.

17 This was confirmed by completely separate interview sources in Shanghai and Shenzhen.

18 The bureau's total amount of such space was 3.2 m². *WHB*, December 4, 1979.

19 *WHB*, December 4, 1979.

20 *Xiao, jiu, san. WHB*, December 4, 1979.

21 *CD*, February 1, 1988.

22 Richard Conroy, "Technology and Economic Development," in *Reforming the Revolution: China in Transition*, Robert Benewick and Paul Wingrove, eds. (Basingstoke: Palgrave Macmillan, 1988), 130.

23 Seventy-seven percent of all Shanghai investment over this long period was classed as "productive," and the remainder covered all investment in "nonproductive" commercial and service firms, housing, offices, schools, banks, and much else (including transport and all utilities). Another 8 percent went into transport and communications. See *SHTJNJ86*, 250.

24 Zheng Yongnian has compiled this conclusion from several issues of ZGTJNJ.

25 The accumulation fund is called the *jilei jijin. Shanghai caizheng*, 10.

26 *Dangdai Zhongguo de guding zichan guanli*, Zhou Daojiong, ed. (Fixed Asset Investments and Management in Contemporary China) (Beijing: Zhongguo Shehui Kexue Chuban She, 1989). All percentages are rounded from the original.

27 *Caijing yanjiu*, 14, thus implies that pre-tax loan repayments rose from 13 percent in 1985 to 16 percent in 1986.

28 *Shanghai: Gaige*, 44.

29 Kueh, Y.Y., *Economic Planning and Local Mobilization in Post-Mao China*, 16.

30 Increases of "self-sought" *zichou* funds were widespread throughout China – obvious indices of increased localism. *Shanghai: Gaige*, 44.

31 These figures were supplied to the author by Zheng Yongnian.

32 Kellee Tsai, *Back-Alley Banking*.

33 The total of Shanghai deposits at the start of the 1980s was 10.1 b. yuan, and savings deposits were 2.29 b. Savings deposits rose 9.4 times since 1952. The total of end-1979

Bankers & credit, savings, depreciation **251**

credit was 16.45 b. yuan, of which 7.22 were industrial loans and 9.17 were commercial. Shanghai jingji, neibu ben, 921.

34 János Kornai, *The Socialist System* (Princeton: Princeton University Press, 1992).

35 William Byrd, *China's Financial System: The Changing Role of Banks* (Boulder: Westview, 1983); but I note policies of local, not just national, leaders.

36 See Cui Zhiyuan, "Epilogue: A Schumpeterian Perspective,".

37 This is 33.2 percent annually. Zheng Yongnian garnered the raw figures from various issues of ZGTJNJ. The average annual percentage rises are calculated. Bank loan figures are not adjusted for inflation, in this or the previous paragraph.

38 *JFRB*, February 27, 1987.

39 *FEER*, January 10, 1985, 51.

40 *FEER*, December 11, 1986, 94.

41 Ibid., 86.

42 Ibid., 87.

43 Ibid.

44 Vigor Fung, "Peking Loosens the Reins on a Multiservice Bank," *Asian Wall Street Journal Weekly*, November 24, 1986.

45 All of China reported a 15 percent increase then, too. *SHJJ*, January 1987, 23.

46 *SHJJ*, January 1987, 26.

47 *JFRB*, February 1, 1987.

48 The quotation is from the bank's president, in *CD*, March 10, 1988.

49 *NCNA*, November 28, 1987.

50 *Computed from Shanghai Statistical Yearbook, 1989 Concise Edition*, Municipal Statistical Bureau of Shanghai, ed. (Beijing: China Statistical Publishing House, 1989), 25, and *LDB*, January 31, 1989.

51 *CD*, December 21, 1987.

52 *Shiyong Han-Ying cidian* (Practical Chinese-English Dictionary) (Nanjing: Jiangsu Renmin Chuban She, 1983), 708, translates *minjian* as "nongovernmental." This word is like *minban* (run by the people), for institutions that got no state money.

53 *SJJJDB*, February 8, 1988.

54 *FEER*, August 1, 1996.

55 Information from interviewees in Shanghai.

56 *FBIS*, November 13, 1986, 1, radio of November 12.

57 Shang Yafei, *Yige chengjiao xiangcun de jintian he mingtian*, 9–11.

58 Calculated from *China's Rural Industry*, 136.

59 *Post*, August 15, 1988.

60 *CD*, December 17, 1987.

61 Calculated from statistics provided by the author's former student Zheng Yongnian, who proudly hails from Zhejiang.

62 The three kinds of recipients were specified in the article as *geti hu, zhuanye hu*, and *cunzhen ban de xiao gongchang. Jiangsu fazhi bao*, January 24, 1989.

63 Ibid.

64 By the end of the 1980s, a consortium of three organizations in north Jiangsu published a weekly, the *Jingji xinwen bao* (Economic News Report). The consortium members' names show new economic ventures in Subei: the Economic Opening Liaison Group of the Huaihai Economic District (Huaihai Jingji Qu, Jingji Kaifa Lianhe Hui), the Xuzhou City People's Government, and the Jiangsu-Shandong-Jiangxi-Anhui Adjacent Districts News Cooperative (Su-Lu-Gan-Wan Jierang Diqu Xinwen Gongzuo Xiezuo Hui).

65 *Jingji xinwen bao* (Economic News Report), January 26, 1989.

66 *Post*, September 1, 1988.

67 *CD*, January 25, 1989.

68 Calculated from B. R. Mitchell, *European Historical Statistics, 1750–1975*, 2nd revised ed. (London: Palgrave Macmillan, 1980), 507.

69 *SHGYJJB*, July 25, 1988.

70 Daniel Kelliher, *Peasant Power*, 194–95.

252 Bankers & credit, savings, depreciation

71 Solomon Karmel, a graduate student at Princeton, did interviews on "Capitalism with Chinese Characteristics,"
72 *FEER*, December 11, 1986, 83.
73 *FBIS*, November 28, 1986, 2, radio of November 26.
74 *CD*, June 22, 1988.
75 Edward Epstein, "China's Legal Reforms," 9.17.
76 *Post*, May 30, 1988.
77 *CD*, March 1, 1989.
78 *JJRB*, September 26, 1988.
79 Dong Fureng, "The Wenzhou Model," 95.
80 Ellen Hertz, *The Trading Crowd: An Ethnography of the Shanghai Stock Market* (New York: Cambridge University Press, 1998) was an anthropology dissertation at the University of California, Berkeley. Many have worked on this subject, including Bridget Williams and others in Hong Kong. Also Solomon Karmel, "Capitalism with Chinese Characteristics,"
81 Wu Yantao, *Shanghai de gupiao he zhaijuan* (Shanghai Shares and Bonds) (Shanghai: Shanghai Shehui Kexue Yuan Chuban She, 1988), 4, suggests rules for collectives were more stringent than for individuals, of whom some were Overseas Chinese.
82 *RMRB*, September 12, 1988.
83 Charles James in *The China Traveller*, December 1987, 3.
84 Relatedly, *Susan Greenhalgh, Just One Child: Science and Policy in Deng's China* (Berkeley: University of California Press, 2008).
85 *CD*, October 10, 1988.
86 For more, Ellen Hertz, "The Trading Crowd,".
87 Cf. *JFRB*, December 2, 1991, tr. in *Inside Mainland China* 14:2 (February 1992), 55–59.
88 Bridget Williams, untitled MS, Hong Kong, July 1994, 6.
89 *CD*, July 31, 1990.
90 Miron Mushkat and Adrian Faure, *Shanghai – Promise and Performance: Economic and Stock Market Review* (Hong Kong: Baring Securities, 1991), 1.
91 See Solomon M. Karmel, "Capitalism with Chinese Characteristics."
92 Bridget Williams, untitled MS, 1994, 7.
93 See graph in the New York Times business section, 1, December 27, 1995.
94 Li Shi, "The Growth of Household Industry in Rural Wenzhou," 123. In the original, county is xian, district is qu, and township is xiang.
95 *Eastern Express*, March 8, 1994.
96 Hiroyuki Imai, "China's Business Cycles," *China Business Review* (January–February 1994), 14–16.
97 See http://data.stats.gov.cn, for PRC National Statistics Bureau reports.
98 *FBIS*, December 10, 1987, 16, reporting from November 25.
99 This applies to loans affecting the foreign sector, but the same principles were attempted for purely domestic credit at this time also. "Self-supply" is *zichou*. *FBIS*, February 8, 1988, 24–25, radio of February 3.
100 *JFRB*, August 19, 1988.
101 Marlowe Hood, "Crackdown Ordered on Money Abuses," *Post* (September 14), 1988.
102 Reuters, *Post*, September 19, 1988.
103 *Jingji xinwen bao*, January 26, 1989, gives an example from Linyi, Shandong, of this credit situation that was typical of all East China rural areas.
104 *CD*, China's most official English newspaper, August 27, 1990.
105 *Economist*, November 30, 1991, 23, and *FEER*, August 30, 1990, 35.
106 *Social Science Information Monthly* (Sheke xinxi), April 10, 1993.
107 *Reuter*, July 17, 1993.
108 A non-China economist opined to me that there are no adequate models to forecast this kind of situation, irrespective of problems about the accuracy of data that might be used in them.
109 *Economist*, May 7, 2016, "Special Report: Finance in China," 4–5.

10

TECHNICIANS INNOVATE TO SELL QUALITY PRODUCTS

New technologies were not adopted in central Shanghai during reforms as quickly as they would have been if taxes had been lower, but the suburban economy modernized sharply. Overall, the central city lost markets to other Chinese areas that could innovate. In 1980, capital for urban Shanghai's industries had for decades been so scarce that 50 percent of the machines dated from the thirties and forties; 35 percent were from the 1950s and 1960s; and 15 percent had been made in the 1970s.[1] A limited-circulation book was published on the antiquation of Shanghai's industries.[2] Futuristic sectors of the city's economy (electronics, lasers, biological engineering, new materials, optical fibers, and robotics) altogether in 1980 still did not make as much as 5 percent of local product value.[3]

There are ways of measuring the extent to which production is raised by technology, as distinct from material supplies and labor inputs. Shanghai was fourteenth among Chinese provinces (rather than first, as its pre-1949 history might have foreboded) in the portion of its 1964–1982 industrial growth attributable to improvements in technology. During this eighteen-year period, the contribution of technology to Shanghai's development was calculated at only 10 percent. A lack of capital, which could embody new techniques, explains this performance, which improved slowly during reforms. In the 1970s, technology was estimated to contribute 13 percent to industries' growth. Over one-third (35 percent) of Shanghai's economic growth by 1982 was already estimated to depend on new technology.[4]

This situation did not continue to improve so quickly, however. In the mid-1980s urban factories could not put much money into new capital, because they needed it to buy inputs whose prices rural factories had bid upward. Economists reported that much equipment in Shanghai's 1986 light industries still dated back to the 1930s or 1940s.[5] State extractions lowered investment rates.

254 Technicians innovate

High tech or high taxes?

Management specialists Simon and Rehn, despite their "cautious optimism" for Shanghai's potential role in semiconductors after the mid-1980s, reported problems in developing the city's computer industry[6]:

> One can better appreciate the relationship between the central government in Beijing and Shanghai by looking at the competition between the two entities. After the electronics industry in Shanghai had exhibited its technological and economic strengths, the Fourth Ministry of Machine Building (MEI [the new acronym included 'E' for 'Electronic']) . . . tried to acquire control of a number of Shanghai's key electronics enterprises and place them under its administration. The municipality refused to accede to what in reality constituted a grab for resources by the MEI. . . . It was only after Shanghai's computer industry almost collapsed in the early 1980s that measures to reform the system were discussed and introduced. . . . While the importance of electronics was generally recognized, the notion of taking high technology as the core of Shanghai's development was not well received by a large number of influential individuals, many of whom were concerned about the future status of so-called traditional industries in Shanghai.

In this field, Shanghai's main rival was Zhongguan Cun in Haidian District, Beijing.[7] In late 1985, when the government decided to designate one location as "a special site for mainframe computer development," Shanghai was on the short list of places – but Beijing was chosen.[8] Jiang Zemin was Minister of Electronic Industries from 1983 to 1985 (and deputy minister from 1982); but in that post he apparently did not support Shanghai, the city of which he soon thereafter became mayor. As late as 1989, Shanghai's first "Silicon Valley," Caohejing, was still announcing a list of areas in which it hoped for investment (microelectronics, information technology, optical fibers, lasers, bioengineering, aviation, and materials science), without indicating that much money had actually come for any of these.[9]

The Caohejing "*Hui gu*" ('Silicon Valley') began in western Shanghai. In later years, others appeared in Jing'an and Pudong districts. Until the mid-2010s, however, Shanghai was seldom rated as far advanced in IT entrepreneurship as the more politically favored tech-and-capital centers of Beijing and Shenzhen. By that time, some gurus ranked it as better than those centers.[10] Wuxi in Jiangsu also developed similar high-tech industries with scant state support.

Economists in the municipal planning commission during late reforms were already protesting that Shanghai had too many "traditional industries," using old equipment and unimaginative managements to make unstylish products. These economists estimated that 98.6 percent of Shanghai's industrial output came from these "traditional industries" (*chuantong qiye*). To prove this, they offered definitions of international standards for quality in many commodity lines, specified for each decade since the 1950s. They then rated the portion of Shanghai's output that met these criteria. Even in the late 1950s, Shanghai products did reasonably well by such standards. The general decline was not across-the-board; for example, products from plants under the local Electrical Machines Bureau rose sharply in quality between the 1950s and 1960s (prior to declines in later decades). That pattern applied to some other bureaus also; but an overall decline was found for factories under most bureaus between the 1960s and 1980s.[11]

Well into the 1980s, profitable Shanghai companies had to pay high taxes; so they lacked money for innovation. The eleven industrial bureaus of Shanghai in 1982 paid 90 percent of their realized profits and taxes to the state, retaining only 10 percent.[12] Within this tenth, only 4 percent of the total went to "production development funds."[13] In the early 1980s, Beijing planners practically forbade the renovation of Shanghai urban industries.

Some local economists called for a withdrawal of textile weavers and other light industries from the city.[14] These factories' importance as revenue earners for the central government was so great, the state was doing all it could to prevent the city from growing in any manner that might absorb energy from what was officially taken as Shanghai's main task: to send tribute.

"Tributary and petty-capitalist modes came complete with distinctive moral convictions, visions of the cosmos, kinship ideals and practices, contrasting patterns of production and exchange, and a millennial history of conflict and critique between them," as Ellen Hertz writes in her ethnography of the Shanghai Stock Market.[15] Central politicians' actions (despite their avowals) were generally consistent with the following rule: New civilian technologies in Shanghai were discouraged, because they would use capital. Shanghai modernization progressed slowly, especially in the cutting-edge technology, semiconductors. Local plans projected faster development than was financed.

The central government's favoritism to Beijing in research investment was obvious to many in Shanghai. The northern capital in 1983 received 20 percent of all China's investment for research (more than twice as much as the next highest province, Sichuan with 9 percent). Shanghai received 7 percent. The number of engineers in Shanghai during that year was almost exactly the same as in Beijing, but the national allocation for research was far less than half as much.[16]

Shanghai's talent pool for innovation

Technical talent had been drained from Shanghai for decades, just as funds were, although the remaining engineers were still many. By 1983, just 9 percent of the city's state employees (*zhigong*) were technicians or scientists. This compared with 13 percent in Beijing, 12 percent in Nanjing, or 11 percent in Shenyang. Even Lanzhou, a much poorer city, had 8.4 percent, a barely lower density of technicians than Shanghai.[17] Throughout China, especially in industries such as textiles, factories were managed at middle levels by personnel who originally hailed from Shanghai. This brain drain from the metropolis was not new.

The problem was not that the remaining workforce in Shanghai was unskilled, but that the city's supply of educated scientists and technicians had been reduced by send-downs. Levels of schooling among Shanghai's ordinary workers in 1983 were not stellar. Two-thirds of the industrial employees were below thirty-five years of age; and of these, only 1.4 percent had any higher education. Only 20,000 of Shanghai's young workers were deemed "illiterate or semi-literate," but the portion with post-primary educations was inadequate.[18] The portion of Shanghai's whole population that had university degrees was 0.66 percent – as compared with Beijing at 0.95 percent, Wuhan 0.94, Taiyuan 0.94, Nanjing 0.93, Xi'an 0.86, or Lanzhou 0.64 (about the same as Shanghai, which had a more modern economy).[19] The contribution of Shanghai's universities in creating new technical staff for the city's economy largely took place after 1979, because so many previous graduates had been sent elsewhere. From that year until 1986, the city's tertiary institutions graduated 165,000 baccalaureates (43 percent of Shanghai's total since 1949).[20] The number of university students per person in Shanghai doubled from 1978 to 1986.[21]

Schools by the early 1980s were able, at the upper-secondary level, to nurture more local talent that stayed in the city. The return of formerly "rusticated" "educated youths" in 1979 legitimated more education. By 1982 in Shanghai, 24 percent of the population had attended or were in high school (as compared with only 7 percent in the PRC as a whole). Of Shanghai's state employees, 40 percent had attended high school (compared with 20 percent in the country at large).[22] Among Shanghai people of senior high school age, 55 percent in 1982 were actually attending school. Twelve percent of university-age Shanghai-registered people were college students.[23] Primary and junior high schools were important for the city's development, because these schools affected more of the local workforce.

Capital for innovation

From 1949 to 1978, investment in new technology for Shanghai was low, averaging less than 240 m. yuan per year. By 1983, forty percent of local investment came from enterprises' "self-raised funds."[24] The increase of internal investment grew, but in the central city it took off only in the mid-1980s. Until that time at least, high taxes kept Shanghai making old products only, a regime of "closure and guardedness" (*biguan zishou*). The city's marketers were encouraged to rest on their past laurels, because any other policy would have lowered revenues by requiring investment to improve quality. Overconfidence about sales of the city's products was reported as a belief that "[if] foreigners don't want it, the domestic market will; if Shanghai doesn't want it, other places will" ('*Waimao buyao, neixiao yao; Shanghai buyao, waidi yao*').[25]

This attitude might have been sufficient for growth, but new technologies were quickly being developed in other parts of East China that could improve their products. Top-quality refrigerators, for example, had long been a Shanghai specialty. But by 1979, the prosperous Zhejiang city of Jiaxing (on the railroad between Shanghai and Hangzhou) was making refrigerators for the many parts of China where energy supplies were erratic. As Shanghai journalists reported, these Jiaxing coolers could use kerosene, gas, steam, or solar power, and they were free of noise and vibration. These were classy, innovative, adaptable, marketable products such as Shanghai had once sold, when it had money to invest for designing and making them.[26]

Shanghai's loss of inland and international markets

From 1978 to 1983, Shanghai's sales of industrial products to other parts of China were essentially stagnant, rising scarcely at all. The city faced competition from growing industries elsewhere. The values of Shanghai's domestic industrial exports in billions of yuan were flat: in 1978, 11 b.; 1980, 11 b.; 1982, 11 b.; 1983, 12 billion. Because of inflation, this was a decrease in real terms. Between 1981 and 1982, Shanghai's gross domestic sales rose only 2 percent, and only 4 percent during the next year (in nominal terms). Unsold goods in Shanghai's warehouses rose 7 percent in 1982 alone.[27]

These marketing problems became obvious after reforms were hesitantly announced in 1978–1980, but their basis had been cumulating for years. As an official in the Shanghai Clock Company complained,

> It certainly isn't that we don't want to make new styles and products, but we are suffocated by pressure on production amounts and values. In wristwatches, for example, our ability to produce the internal mechanisms is great; but the watch lenses, faces, and pointers have gotten short shrift. The Watch Lens Plant cannot fill its production targets in time. How are we to make our products elegant?[28]

Wenhui News alleged that these "suffocating" pressures in Tianjin were not so great, and the Tianjin watches could be sold at a lower price. Shanghai women's watches were less stylish than Tianjin watches "for little girls."

In textiles, the industry which more than any other had churned out state profits for decades, the city lost most of its market to inland producers. Although Shanghai spun 37 percent of China's cotton yarn in 1952, it spun only 12 percent by 1983.[29] Shanghai in 1985 sold 38 percent of all apparel in China, but by 1986 this portion declined to 28 percent, and by 1988 it plummeted to 17 percent. In household electric appliances, Shanghai still sold 35 percent nationwide in 1986, but only 22 percent in the first half of 1988.[30] These trends were not bad for China. They reflect development inland, especially in Jiangnan, where Shanghai technicians often found second part-time jobs. The problem was that the metropolis could not raise its output of more sophisticated items as it turned over more clothing and household goods production to other places.

Jiujiang, in Anhui, was one of the cities that developed a booming textile industry in successful competition with Shanghai. Jiujiang's total industrial product rose about 18 percent per year in the 1980s. The municipal government there wanted to

258 Technicians innovate

allow factories flexibility to use different raw materials for their products. In textiles, some Jiujiang factories converted from cotton to mixed fibers. Local authorities there planned that rural industries, which by 1988 contributed 27 percent of that prefecture's industrial product, should expand further.[31] This kind of evolution benefited many. The only surprise was that Shanghai, whose products these factories displaced, did not develop to replace its lost markets in textiles.

Yangzi delta factories often made products of superior quality. In 1980, five Wuxi plants making printed fabrics developed a program for "studying Shanghai and raising levels" (*xue Shanghai, shang shuiping*).[32] By 1983, various measures of economic efficiency and product quality showed their output was better than that of factories in the metropolis. By 1984, these Wuxi factories were delivering more profits and taxes per worker, as well as per unit of capital, than were Shanghai printed fabric plants. They enjoyed newer equipment and better access to inputs markets, and their technical staffs were as expert. The reasons for Wuxi's prowess lay not just in better infrastructure, but also in more responsiveness to market demand for new styles – and lower taxes, and links between individuals in Wuxi and Shanghai who cooperated privately.

Demand from other parts of the country for Shanghai brand-name products remained strong. But the city's factories could not raise production of its best products to meet this demand. Many goods were planned to be kept for the city's own consumers – to allay workers' concerns during inflation in the politically sensitive metropolis. Firms in this situation could disperse licenses to use their brand names and technologies in factories that paid lower taxes in other provinces. So "Shanghai" products were decreasingly from Shanghai. In tennis shoes, the city's firms established more than forty joint factories with Jiangsu, Zhejiang, Anhui, Jiangxi, Shandong, Guangdong, and Henan companies. "Shanghai" shoes, not really from that metropolis, were widely sold.

"Forever" bicycles had become famous because a Shanghai company once made them well. But by the mid-1980s, many Forever bikes were produced in Jiangsu. Markets there and in other provinces usually found the Jiangsu Forever bikes cheaper and more available. Many rival inland companies were bettering Shanghai bicycle makers by the mid-1980s and 1990s. Parts for Forever (*Yongjiu*) and Phoenix (*Fenghuang*) bicycles were made in places as close to Shanghai as Jiangsu's Suzhou or Nantong, or as far away as Xinjiang's Urumqi. This kind of cooperation in 1984 increased the number of bicycles with these brand names so much that 30 percent of the bikes and parts with these names were made outside Shanghai. Referring to these two famed Shanghai brands, a reporter quipped, "'Forever' may not stay on the market forever. 'Phoenix' may have to rise from the ashes soon."[33]

Fierce competition came not just from ordinary inland plants, but from inland-foreign joint ventures making bicycles with international brand names. "They have used new materials and have developed new products. Some have turned out world-famous brand bikes. But Shanghai bicycle producers still stick to their old products without making much effort to develop new ones." Shanghai's attempts to set up cooperation with inland plants often led to losses for the city, even if the companies earned profits. Shanghai's bicycle factories set up joint firms with counterparts nearby in the delta (as well as with Hefei, Anhui). Profits in these joint firms were reportedly good. But for these brands, "ordinary customers cannot tell which bike is made in Shanghai and which is not. This has . . . made people reluctant to buy."[34]

So the Shanghai Light Industries Bureau vowed to inspect inland products with Shanghai names randomly. It threatened to "take action against the leading manufacturer as well as the associated factory" if goods were substandard or if they were not marked with the place where they were made. Measures of this sort did little more than to seek a profit from Shanghai's past reputation for product quality. Actual production during the 1980s, for many of these commodities, moved inland.[35]

Such problems were evident not just on the China market, but also on international markets. Shanghai's export prowess fell, because Beijing wanted the money that might instead have allowed the creation of better products. Shanghai had less potential to develop competitive goods; and as Table 10.1 shows, the city's portion of all PRC exports dropped drastically (albeit from a high percentage of the national total). This change was quick throughout the 1970s, and it continued also during later reforms. Inland companies taking Shanghai's domestic and international markets for traditional goods was a predictable and generally beneficial development. It would have been no problem if state leaders' expectations of Shanghai had also left the city free to diversify in modern fields.

Many Jiangsu and Zhejiang county-level administrations by 1990 created joint ventures with Shanghai foreign trade corporations. The aim was to promote exports,

TABLE 10.1 Declining Shanghai share of China's exports (percentage of value)

Year	Shanghai/PRC %	Year	Shanghai/PRC %
1970	38	1986	12
75	31	87	11
78	30	88	10
80	24	89	10
81	17	90	9
82	16	91	8
83	16	92	8
84	14	93	8
85	12	94	7

Sources and note: Calculations are made from raw data quoted in US dollars, since 1970. Only the listed years were reported in *Shanghai tongji nianjian, 1993* (Shanghai Statistical Yearbook, 1993), Shanghai Statistical Bureau, ed. (Beijing: Zhongguo Tongji Chuban She, 1993), 300. These are divided into the national export figures in *Zhongguo tongji nianjian, 1993* (China Statistical Yearbook, 1993), State Statistical Bureau, ed. (Beijing: Zhongguo Tongji Chuban She, 1993), 633. For post-reform years, percentages were calculated from data and exchange rates in the all-China statistical yearbook, 1995, 537, and in the Shanghai yearbook, 1995, 101. A larger portion of China's exports passes from inland factories through Shanghai's docks, but this table covers commodities last processed in Shanghai only.

using Shanghai commercial expertise to sell products from factories elsewhere on the delta. Over four-fifths of all the counties which joined such ventures with Shanghai traders were in the two provinces that border the municipality. Shanghai experts arranged the paperwork – but Shanghai's port did not handle all the shipping (others such as Ningbo and Zhangjiagang were also busy). The municipality's percentage of China's national exports plummeted in the 1980s, and it dropped to single digits after 1990. Even more striking, Shanghai's *re*-exports as a portion of China's outgoing trade fell from 10 percent in 1980 to a mere 3 percent by 1991.[36]

Heavy development: Baoshan and Jinshan

Central investments at Shanghai stressed heavy industries. The "steel eating" pattern persisted in the metropolis, especially in a ring around the old built-up area, until state budget deficits brought its end. This was a classic Stalinist development strategy, and at Shanghai its flagship was the Baoshan Steel Mill. Baoshan was larger than earlier megaprojects in the city, but reforms did not change official pre-reform understandings of how Shanghai's economy should grow. The city's consumption of steel rose seventy-four times in the three decades from 1949 to 1979, and energy consumption rose twenty-four times.[37] By the 1980s, Shanghai could not sustain this pattern for several reasons.

First, Shanghai mines no coal or iron ore. It has neither in its alluvial ground. Leaders of inland provinces that have mines wanted more profits not just from weight-reduction processing, but also from using coal and iron to make goods. Some had political clout in Beijing, obtaining capital for new factories. A second reason was that central reformers, as distinct from revenue collectors, hoped Shanghai could upgrade its technology, rather than relying extensively on old manufacturing know-how, so that China might compete better in world markets. But Shanghai received scant money for this. Third, metals industries were egregious polluters. Less densely populated parts of the country could present valid environmental reasons to take such tasks from Shanghai.

When the central government determined during the mid-1970s that China needed a large new steel mill and that foreign help was necessary to build it, a survey was launched on the suitability of several locations. Shanghai was chosen from a short list of four places (including Dalian in the Northeast, and the prospective foreign capital was from Japan).[38] The central economic politician Chen Yun argued for putting the new plant in Shanghai. Chen, according to one source, "doted on Shanghai" and went there for lunar New Year celebrations – as did Deng Xiaoping sometimes, although the net benefit to the metropolis from these visits is not obvious. Southern journeys of emperors, since the Sui at least, could prove expensive for the places visited. Planning for this vast new steel factory almost surely had to begin years before March 1978, when ground was broken for it. Baoshan, a suburb north of central Shanghai on the Yangzi, was the selected site.

The plant built there has encountered numerous difficulties, partly because its port is shallow. Its profits have been low and sometimes negative. This massive factory's linkages with other aspects of Shanghai have also been problematic: Steel plants tend to be polluting; they absorb vast amounts of capital and land, but they employ relatively few workers per unit of capital. The Baoshan Steel Factory contributes all its profits to the central government, not to Shanghai. It confirms the vertical pattern of economic organization in Maoist Shanghai. It does not allocate local resources by horizontal market contracts but instead by administrative fiats. The Baoshan project also bears a moot relation to the idea (important in plans only since 1983, long after the location decision was made) that Shanghai should develop new Chinese industries, especially in electronics and medicine – and/or that the city should not try to do what inland places could do soon or better.

The Baoshan plant absorbs many Shanghai assets, returning a few benefits for the surrounding area: The plant supplies metal for the Satana cars, made in a joint venture with Volkswagen of Germany, as well as for Shanghai's shipbuilding industry. The second largest project in Shanghai was the Jinshan Chemical Factory. This also fed downstream industries that made bulky products. Metals, chemicals, textiles, and heavy engineering industries, when combined with building materials, food, lumber processing, and energy together in 1984 contributed 95 percent of Shanghai's gross industrial output value.[39]

Heavy industrial investments at Shanghai were rationalized in terms of the idea that modern light industries – especially electronics and robotics – would mesh with them later. The problems of pollution and distance from mines, however, were so cogent that professionals were allowed to publish about the virtues of alternative strategies for the development of more services and light industries instead. But these continued to receive slow funding in the metropolis.

Electronics and bio-tech

Shanghai economists' calculations argued that a program emphasizing the city's development of bio-engineering and other high technology industries, and use of electronics to raise efficiency in more traditional sectors, was superior to either of two alternatives: a plan to raise manufacturing output along traditional lines, or a plan to continue with low-tech light and textile industries. The superiority of the high-tech plan lay in better profit rates, expected competition from inland places in older industrial lines but not these new ones, and less pollution in a crowded city. Economists studied whether Shanghai's main targets should be set in terms of total output, an across-the-board efficiency goal in each sector, or a special emphasis on light industries and services. They figured that the third strategy was best.[40] These academics called on Shanghai to supply more "software" to China – more knowhow, information, and technology – and less "hardware."

Shanghai's electronics industry expanded in the early 1960s, when some textile factories switched to this new field. South Jiangsu's electrical firms also grew from converted Shanghai textile plants, which had been moved to that area by administrative fiats in earlier decades of the PRC. Two-thirds to three-quarters of the workers in these plants were female. After these beginnings until the late 1980s, much discussion about Shanghai's possibilities in electronics was not matched by much investment. Shanghai's relatively dirty water and air were reasons presented against investment to make sensitive electronic equipment, although the alternative of continued heavy industrial investment made water and air dirtier. State money for electronics went to other places, notably Xi'an and Beijing.

The city whose computer industry grew fastest, and with less help from centralists than other places had, was Wuxi. This Sunan city, less than two hours by train from Shanghai, could tap the talents of Shanghai engineers while providing lower taxes and more freedom for electronics managers. As a Shanghai economist put it, the strategy was to "use Shanghai people's heads to develop Wuxi people's wealth."[41] Many in the larger metropolis had kin in Wuxi. The No. 742 Electronics Factory in Wuxi became, by the late 1980s, one of China's foremost producers of desktop computers. As California's Santa Clara Valley became "Silicon Valley," and Cambridgeshire was "Silicon Fen," Wuxi became "Silicon Paddy."

Wuxi has bred new industries, notably electronics, without losing its position in traditional industries such as textiles and silk. By 1987, the gross value of industrial output in Wuxi City exceeded 26 b. yuan. Surrounding Wuxi County in that year had the highest total output value among all of China's 2,000 counties.[42] What accounted for this success? There were lower taxes in Wuxi than in Shanghai; but this does not tell the whole story, because Shanghai's taxes were off the usual scale, and Wuxi like other delta cities paid at higher rates than most places. Inland areas could compete with Wuxi in many commodity lines.

A crucial reason for the quick prosperity in Wuxi seems to be the speed with which local entrepreneurs built industries based on new technologies while keeping profits in their old markets too. Another reason was the ability of the collective sector there to avoid buying or selling on unfavorable terms to the state sector. The Sunan agricultural boom, which meant peasants could purchase more of what Wuxi made, also aided successes for all Yangzi delta cities. Leaders whose local networks could hide most from the central revenue collectors were reportedly among those that did best.

Shanghai's production of computers was for a long time not as notable as Beijing's or even Chengdu's. Instead, Shanghai had been forced to specialize in TV sets, tape recorders, and radios – none of them based on recent technologies. These items, designated for East China production by planners in Beijing, brought revenues to the government but little potential for expansion. They had some prospects for export; but problems of quality and sharp international competition were deterrents in many markets. China's labor costs in electronic industries during the late 1980s remained low: about 1.4 yuan (then US 40 cents) per hour, compared with averages of about $2 in Hong Kong or Taiwan, or $8 in Japan.[43]

By 1989, change was evident. New companies were established at Shanghai in eight key fields: microelectronics, information technology, optical fibers, lasers, biological engineering, robotics, aviation, and new materials. The central government's hope was that financing in Shanghai would come from abroad – as finally it did, by the 1990s, after local networks had in various ways caused the government to reduce taxes.

So Shanghai in the new 1990s era enjoyed several technological success stories – some of which cannot be told well because they were military and secretive. The city's "Space Base" was the major manufacturer of Chinese rockets, especially the Long March 4A type, in the early 1990s. These rockets were used by the Army, but also for commercial launches into orbit of telecommunications and weather satellites. A newspaper could also report that "the improved rocket can shoulder the launching of multiple satellites for foreign clients."[44]

Think tanks

Modern technological improvements often emerge from scientific laboratories. A salient feature of research labs in China and Shanghai was their cellularity, their tendency to isolate themselves from similar institutions. Engineering teams seldom knew what others in the same field were doing. Factories that might have used research findings sometimes failed to do so because much research was secret and unpublished.

According to a survey at the end of the 1970s, more than two-fifths of all new research projects in Shanghai's tertiary institutions and labs duplicated each other. Another third duplicated projects that had been tried as early as 1973–1974.[45] The technical problems these labs addressed may have been important, but multiplication of similar efforts reflected reluctance on the part of decision makers within labs to initiate new projects on their own authority. A national survey of several thousand scientific institutes in 1984 showed that less than 10 percent of their findings were actually being used in production. Research, according to another survey, was not a big budget item: a mere 0.5 percent of total expenditure in metals industries, 1 percent in machines, 1.1 percent in chemicals, and 5.5 percent for electronics – well below international averages.[46] Part of the reason was that intellectuals when they acted as state employees in government think tanks were paid somewhat better salaries than most other educated people. If they left the state sector to act as consultants for collectives, they could both accomplish more and make more money. Nonstate managers were usually more willing both to try new ideas and to support employees who made potentially profitable experiments.

The mid-1980s saw changing links between technology and production in Shanghai. The state's role in this development, as in most reforms, was surprisingly peripheral (especially for a government run by Marxists, who might appreciate the role of technology in progress). High officials were bystanders and commentators, sometimes helping and sometimes hindering basic reform. But most of the effective actors were local.

A Shanghai Industries Technical Development Foundation, for example, was created in early 1985. By 1989, it was described as "half-official and half-civilian."[47] Part of this consortium's funds came from the government, but most came through "horizontal relations" with specialized banks, companies, and investment houses. This consortium-foundation aimed to support a policy of "three changes and one creation" (*san hua, yi chuang*): a shift to more advanced technology in Shanghai laboratories, a shift to better absorption of techniques by factories, a shift to having more components produced within China, plus the creation of more foreign exchange – especially by middle-sized and small Shanghai firms.

Financially, the consortium was a success. In its first four years, it loaned 288 million yuan for 500 projects to about 500 units. (The similarity between the numbers suggests the foundation's criteria for loans may have helped smaller firms more than was usual in China.) For each yuan invested in this way, 5 yuan were produced during the first four years. The average compound annual rate of return from the loaned money over the four years exceeded 50 percent for many projects.[48] The rate of on-time loan repayments by 1989 had been 99 percent. A 1 percent bad debt rate is exceptional anywhere, and in reform China it was spectacularly low, but it applied to this consortium's loans.

Several such organizations were established, often with titles that allowed them to take up almost any scientific or economic role during the mid-1980s. The Shanghai Culture Research Institute was a think tank not founded by the government. It was linked to East China Chemical Engineering University and was classed as a unit "run by the people" (*minban*).[49] Other such organizations were like the "dependent firms" (*guahu*) of large state or collective organizations. These were legally separate from the government. The most famous example in Shanghai was not a think tank but a newspaper, the *World Economic Herald*, dependent on the Shanghai Academy of Social Sciences, whose status as state or nonstate became a matter of sharp controversy before May 1989 (when it was closed). Many consultancies were "dependent" on that Academy or on the Shanghai Science and Technology Association. Of the "suggestion papers" (*jianyi shu*) sent to the municipal government by think tanks in the 1980s, three-tenths were approved and distributed as "important documents."[50]

New technologies were used especially in "joint" ventures. Some combinations were unexpected. Shanghai's Institute of Nuclear Research combined with the Shanghai Vegetable Company, for example, to found a factory in the mid-1980s that bought 35,000 tons of vegetables each year and kept them fresh by extinguishing nascent mold with radiation.[51]

As reform's economic take-off was achieved, first on the delta and then in Shanghai, scientific advice legitimated changes that conservatives often opposed. This pattern began outside the central city first, because the economic boom came earlier in surrounding areas. Technical extension in Jiangsu took the form of a "sparking plan" (*xinghuo jihua*), costing 74 million yuan in 1986, under which scientific research units and factories were supposed to pass modern technology "like sparks" to create new centers of rural industry.[52] Zhejiang also had this kind of program. That province in the mid-1980s had the second highest output value in the country from its rural industries – after Jiangsu.[53] When controls altered in Shanghai, especially in the 1990s, regional exchanges of technology accompanied economic boom. Modes and relations of production were changing. New technologies were situational factors that influenced China's political form in localities. There is little evidence that high Marxists in the government had much interest in promoting these links, but local leaders did.

Notes

1 Rounded from improbably exact percentages in *Shijie xin jishu geming yu Shanghai de duice*, 35, 194–95, 205–206.

2 Mubiao, *zhongdian, duice – Tan Shanghai chuantong gongye de jishu gaizao* (Goals, Keypoints, and Policies – On the Technical Reform of Shanghai's Traditional Industries), Shanghai Municipal Enterprise Management Association, ed. (Shanghai: Shanghai Shi Qiye Guanli Xiehui, 1985) [limited circulation; referred to in *Shanghai qiye* (Shanghai Enterprise) August 1985, 5].

3 *Zhongguo shehui zhuyi chengshi jingji xue*, 89.

4 Technology's contribution to growth in Shanghai averaged 2.34 percent per year in this eighteen-year period, and 1.82 percent in China as a whole, according to Shijie xin jishu, 18.

5 Chen Minzhi and Yao Xitang, "Strategic Target Option for the Economic Development of Shanghai," in *SASS Papers*, Zhang Zhongli et al., eds. (Shanghai: Shanghai Academy of Social Sciences, 1986), 65.

6 Denis Fred Simon and Detlef Rehn, *Technological Innovation in China: The Case of the Shanghai Semiconductor Industry* (Cambridge: Ballinger, 1988), 92–93.

7 For a report on this Beijing electronics area, see *La Chine en construction* 26:8 (August 1988), 14–17.

8 Simon and Rehn, *Technological Innovation*, 74.

9 *XMWB*, January 29, 1989.

10 Rebecca Fannin, "Shanghai Scores as Top New Tech Hub in the World as Silicon Valley Gap Grows," *Forbes*, September 16, 2014, forbes.com/sites/rebeccafannin/2014/09/16/shanghai-scores-as-top-tech-hub-in-the-world-as-silicon-valley-gap-grows/#7574b7c953bd.

11 The main exceptions to the 1960s–1980s decline were under Shanghai's Bureau of Chemical Industries, probably because of investment at Wujing. Even this index fell, precipitously, in the 1980s. *Shanghai qiye* (Shanghai Enterprise) August 1985, 2–8.

12 A complete list of the 1982 municipal bureaus is in Jiang Zemin, *Shanghai dangzheng jigou yange*, 226–30. The next source refers to all the industrial bureaus.

13 Only 3 percent each went into funds for employee benefits and bonuses. *Shanghai jingji, neibu ben: 1949–1982*, 134.

14 Chen Minzhi and Yao Xitang, "Strategic Target," 73–47.

15 Ellen Hertz, *The Trading Crowd*, 24.

16 In 1983, Beijing reportedly had 167,642 engineers, and Shanghai had 166,701. Tony Saich, *China's Science Policy in the 80s* (Atlantic Highlands, NJ: Humanities Press, 1989), compare 90 and 111.

17 *Shanghai shehui xiankuang he qushi, 1980–1983*, 204.

18 *Shijie xin jishu*, 394.

19 Lanzhou at this time was 0.64 percent university educated, about the same portion as Shanghai. *Shanghai shehui xiankuang*, 204.

20 Chen Benlin, *Gaige kaifang shenzhou jubian*, 96.

21 *Shanghai jingji* 1987 (Shanghai's Economy, 1987), Xu Zhihe, Ling Yan, and Gu Renzhang, eds. (Shanghai Academy of Social Sciences) (Shanghai: Shanghai Renmin Chuban She, 1987), 12, indicates that the number of university students per ten thousand of population rose from 46 in 1978 to 67 in 1980, and then to 95 in 1986.

22 *Shanghai jiaoyu fazhan zhanlue yanjiu baogao* (Research Report on the Strategy of Shanghai's Educational Development), Kang Yonghua, Liang Chenglin, and Tan Songhua, eds. (Shanghai: Huadong Shifan Daxue Chuban She, 1989), 3.

23 *Shehui* (Society), Shanghai, June 1985, 11.
24 *SHJJYJ*, April 1985, 32, proposed research on ways of "unifying" the use of "self-generated funds."
25 *WHB*, October 25, 1979.
26 Ibid.
27 *Shanghai jingji, neibu ben*, 553.
28 *WHB*, October 25, 1979.
29 *Zhongguo gongye de fazhan, 1949–1984*, 57.
30 *JFRB*, April 27, 1988.
31 *Huadong xinxi bao*, January 28, 1989.
32 *Shanghai qiye* (Shanghai Enterprise) August 1985, 34–35.
33 *SF*, March 26, 1990, for this and the following quotation. See also Cao Linzhang, Gu Guangqing and Li Jianhua, *Shanghai shengchan ziliao suoyu zhi jiegou yanjiu*, 141.
34 *Hengxiang jingji lianhe de xin fazhan* (The New Development of Horizontal Economic Links), Shanghai Economics Association, ed. (Shanghai: Shanghai Shehui Kexue Yuan Chuban She, 1987), 5–6.
35 This also occurred in Hong Kong, whence many kinds of production have moved into Guangdong.
36 G. Tian, "The Emergence of Shanghai's Role as an Entrepôt Centre Since the Mid-1980s," unpublished MS, esp. 20.
37 Chen Minzhi and Yao Xitang, "Strategic Target," 65–66.
38 Interview with Shanghai economists at the World Economic Herald.
39 Chen Minzhi and Yao Xitang, "Strategic Target," 66.
40 Ibid., 72–82.
41 "Yong Shanghai ren de naodai, fa Wuxi ren de cai,"
42 This amount was over 7 b. yuan. Li Cheng, "The Rise of Technocracy: Elite Transformation and Ideological Change in Post-Mao China" (Princeton University Ph.D. dissertation, Politics Department, 1991).
43 Interview with an economist at the Chinese Academy of Social Sciences, Beijing.
44 This rocket could launch warheads too, as was not mentioned in SF, February 26, 1990.
45 Tony Saich, *China's Science*, 35.
46 Richard Conroy, "Technology and Economic Development," 130.
47 This Shanghai Gongye Jishu Fazhan Jijin Hui was "*ban guan ban min*" – an unusual term, contrasting with traditional verbiage about government that deigned to "attract merchants" (zhao shang). SHGYJJB, February 2, 1989.
48 Calculated from *SHGYJJB*, February 2, 1989.
49 This Shanghai Wenhua Yanjiu Suo, reported in an interview, had an oddly unchemical name considering its sponsor.
50 Tao Yongkuan, *Dali fazhan disan chanye*, 40–41.
51 Tony Saich, *China's Science*, 70.
52 *FBIS*, November 18, 1986, 4, radio of November 15.
53 *FBIS*, November 3, 1986, 5, radio of November 3.

11

LONG-DISTANCE TRADERS AND JIANGNAN REGIONALISTS CREATE NEW MARKETS

Rising domestic trade was a hallmark of China's reforms. The regionalism of this upsurge after 1970 undercut central planning. Self-sufficiency (*zili gengsheng*) – the opposite of trade among localities – had become a Communist ideal during the revolution. All enterprises, according to that norm, were supposed to follow three rules: "go to the local area for getting materials, for processing them, and for selling the products."[1] But local leaders supported self-sufficiency only when they benefited from it. So long as brigade and commune heads openly asserted their formal obeisance to the state, they could often seek new markets nationally or regionally, for either inputs or products.

When supplies were needed, as rural industries on the delta expanded their operations, they sent buyers to other areas. Economic connections of this sort were criticized during the height of the Cultural Revolution in the late 1960s. Liaison offices arranging such trade were sometimes physically attacked. But new commercial links developed strongly in and from Jiangnan during the first few years of the 1970s.

The early part of that decade saw a revival of horizontal (*hengxiang*) relations between rural enterprises and urban experts. Cadres were sent to "May 7 cadre schools" (*wuqi ganxiao*), where most of them stayed for fairly brief periods – and where their reputations and statuses were challenged less than at urban posts where Red Guards confronted them.[2] But country life did not appeal to all cadres. They could get back into cities after a decent interval pretending to be peasants. Leaders at the schools sometimes produced initiatives that were commercial, not just political. Many May 7 schools were in more well-to-do rural areas than were the locations of earlier camps for labor education (*laodong jiaoyu*).

Some May 7 cadres reportedly did little but read newspapers and drink tea during their stints in the countryside. Others on the Yangzi delta helped local peasants run new rural industries. A few May 7 cadres of the early 1970s were the first

268 Traders and Jiangnan regionalists

"Sunday engineers" (*xingqiri gongcheng shi*) in rural factories, except that they stayed for the whole week. These Maoist schools taught more than was official; they had unintended, proto-capitalist results. Radicals criticized technicians and managers who created connections between rural and urban factories. They argued that the cadre schools were supposed to teach city people about agriculture, not to teach peasants about industry and marketing.[3] But if trade prospered, entrepreneurs were too busy to waste time on ideological polemics.

Liaisons of individual technicians and "rusticates" with rural industries

In the thirty years after the mid-fifties, 1,400,000 Shanghai people – *not* counting rusticated youths – were sent to help other places in China.[4] Of these, three-tenths were technicians.[5] Among those seconded from Shanghai jobs to help in other places, a majority were workers. Many had technical skills and went to Jiangsu or Zhejiang, sometimes to places where they had kin. Non-student rusticates accounted for about one-sixth of the total registered emigrants from Shanghai over the three decades after 1949, and this was a larger send-down than that of educated youths. It has received less scholarly attention, because many of the workers and technicians went earlier, often in 1955–1956, and because the program's quasi-coercive aspects involved fewer intellectuals: fewer writers to record what happened. In the second half of the 1950s, Shanghai light industries sent 145 whole factories to other provinces.[6]

Rustication policies inadvertently created rural staffs, connecting nonstate countryside firms with nationwide consumer markets. As a Chinese historian wrote, "Many people sent to rural areas from city offices, research agencies, and universities, as well as young intellectuals, brought science and technology, culture, knowledge, and economic information to the countryside. They linked city and countryside more closely. . . . Rural industry found markets for its products."[7]

This outflow of Shanghai accountants and technicians continued in the two reform decades, almost always on a voluntary basis, as urban workers became aware that suburban and rich rural factories offered good managerial jobs. About 800,000 Shanghai individuals in the 1978–1988 decade went to other provinces for work. Many moved nearby, to Zhejiang or Jiangsu (especially in Suzhou, which is definitely not a hardship post and is just an hour by train from Shanghai). A lesser number of specialists went farther. By July 1980, in China as a whole, 3,400 joint enterprises were registered across provincial jurisdictions, but more had actually begun operations.[8] Many were not organized according to usual "vertical and horizontal" (*tiaotiao, kuaikuai*) frameworks of supervision, but in mixed ways across geographical, functional, and ownership categories.

Old rustication policies and continuing Shanghai residence controls had the unintended effect of strengthening unofficial Shanghai connections with other rich cities in East China.

Jiaxing [in Zhejiang] has attracted many technicians and managers, especially those able to use its proximity to Shanghai. This has caused many technical

Traders and Jiangnan regionalists **269**

personnel, who after 1949 flowed to various parts of the country and now find difficulty returning to Shanghai, to set up [legally registered] households in Jiaxing. Furthermore, their role in the development of Jiaxing's economy, through their personal (*siren*) connections, has caused many Jiaxing enterprises to establish links with relevant units in Shanghai.[9]

Jiaxing, with the rest of the Jiangnan flatland, came into the "Shanghai economic circle," according to some academics. They called for development of this "circle" around Shanghai "as a base" that would later and "gradually" spread its prosperity to farther parts of the country.[10] The city's relations with the delta flourished, although links with areas further inland were varied. Shanghai people for many years had been sent to cities in border provinces such as Xinjiang (where Chinese governments had sponsored military towns before Han times ending 220 CE, and during the Tang, 618–907).[11] The city of Shihezi, Xinjiang, has a population that is 95 percent Han Chinese, and Shanghainese is a language understood in many families there.

Some connections of "Shanghai" firms with other places in East China are simply a matter of the city's businesspeople returning to their *guxiang*, their ancestral homes. The immediate destinations of emigrants from Shanghai, whether departing in a state campaign or voluntarily, were at first either small towns or large cities more often than medium-sized cities. At that stage, the curve on a graph of rates of flow by destination settlement sizes was U-shaped. But permanent emigration from Shanghai, according to a long-term survey, was more than six times more frequent to cities with over a million inhabitants than to smaller cities with more than half a million. More surprisingly, it was also about six times more frequent to smaller settlements of less than 500,000.[12] Some of these were rusticated youths. In locally controlled and less heavily taxed small cities and towns, older professionals and technicians for rural industries could find rewarding jobs.

Many consultants were sardonically called "high-priced old men," when they were not "Sunday engineers" taking weekend jobs away from their weekday posts in Shanghai.[13] The "Sunday" specialists could earn 200 or 300 yuan for only four days of work each month – far more than their ordinary pay rate, if they concurrently held state jobs in the big city. Most worked for rural cooperative factories in small towns. They were employed to solve technical problems, help maintain machines, give lessons, liaise with markets, and help manage. When they still had jobs in the city, they might keep such activities secret from their Shanghai units, partly to avoid others becoming jealous of the extra money they earned or to avoid blame for competition with the city firm. But if such work was known, it might implicitly be approved by Shanghai employers as a means of extending their own connections to rural sources for out-contracting and materials. Alternatively, it might be disapproved because it drained the energies of Shanghai employees. Since the trend could not be stopped, Shanghai factory heads usually just sought profits from it.

Links between specific Shanghai institutions and specific other places on the flatland were nothing new. Before 1977, and continuing steadily thereafter, Shanghai's

Jiaotong University had extensive connections with Shangyu (the largest Zhejiang city between Ningbo and Shaoxing). A group of Jiaotong engineers had family connections in Shangyu. They helped factories there to make glass, metals, refrigeration equipment, and electrical machines. Because of technical help from scientists at Shanghai's premier engineering university, the Shangyu Refrigeration Company was able to produce cooling towers that consumed one-quarter less power than units of this sort normally required. The three largest Shangyu factories, which received help from Jiaotong, reciprocated by giving the university "cooperation fees" (*xiezuo fei*) that totaled 700,000 yuan in the first seven years of the decade.[14]

The Shangyu Refrigeration Company increased its own technical staff (and probably also its less productive tea-drinking staff) so that by 1986 one-fifth of the regular employees were involved in management. In the first two years of the decade, this factory sent forty workers to Jiaotong and to various universities for training.[15] These links began before central planners acknowledged the efficiency of "horizontal relations" in trade. They were publicized not at the time they began, but only later – and they began because of connections that particular people in Shanghai had with particular other East China places.

Conservatives criticize the technology diffusion that rusticates brought

Shanghai individuals made a great deal of money from technical consulting elsewhere. An extensive estimate for 1977–1981 suggests that fifty-six of Shanghai's largest research organizations, operating on commissions mostly for clients outside the city, earned about 20,000,000 yuan for their engineering advice.[16] The pace of such links rose, as the state began to default more regularly on materials deliveries to the metropolis. In 1980, a Shanghai engineer named Han Kun was hired as a consultant by a Fengxian County enterprise in the city's rural suburbs. He received 2,000 yuan for this work. This became a *cause célèbre*, as sharp criticism came from conservatives who felt his compensation was too large. The critics' main purpose was to discourage other Shanghai technicians from offering their services similarly. An explicit part of their complaint was that Shanghai's fiscal importance to China as a whole justified more control of personnel there than elsewhere. With consultancy becoming commonplace in other parts of China during the 1980s, and with a good deal of technical talent in Shanghai, these socialist conservatives fought a losing battle.

"Inopportune resignations" by technical personnel presented a problem for Shanghai state-sector plants. From one company, four scientists left together "to work in a small factory. This withdrawal of expertise caused the key project in which they had been working to collapse. The case was even referred to by Premier Zhao Ziyang. . . . The publicity given to this case gave those who were opposed to reform a weapon with which to counterattack."[17] Some Shanghai managers tried to restrict the employment of technicians and retired people elsewhere, preventing them from taking work in other provinces. They had a well-founded fear that an outflow of technology would create competitors there.[18] The biggest long-term loser from this pattern, however, was the central government budget.

Motives of reform rusticates

The people who left Shanghai voluntarily to live in other places were not very numerous as a portion of migrants at any specific time. But they left in trickles or spurts for various reasons over several decades. Collectively they became important because they provided links for both industrial development and commerce. Many were well schooled; a sample census showed that 80 percent had secondary educations at least. Many were young, although one-fifth to one-third were retired. About half left the city to do business elsewhere, usually in the Shanghai delta. Some freely admitted that they left to escape the city's tough regulatory climate. As a local author said, "Since the open door and reforms, Shanghai has changed a great deal. But occupational mobility, especially in high positions, still is restrained by the personnel system."[19] Many talented people, who had conflicted with monitors in Shanghai work units during earlier political campaigns, found political comfort by moving away.

Other localities in China, some near Shanghai and some distant, generally welcomed the migration of talent. The Yangzi delta's prowess in rural industrialization led to envy in other parts of China – and thus to inland consulting work for Jiangnan people. In 1978, a commune in Shanxi wanted to found an umbrella factory; so it compensated technicians from Zhejiang to help get it started.[20] There was a continuing shortage of educated people in China, even in rural parts of the largest municipality. A miniscule 0.6 percent of employees qualified as college-trained technicians during 1988 in Meilong Township, in suburban Shanghai County. A survey of fourteen enterprises in this town, which is so close to the city that a new rapid transit system runs there, concluded that "skilled" workers made up just 28 percent of Meilong's total workforce. "Among laborers aged 35 or more, the situation is more serious; about 25 percent are illiterate or semi-literate, and 30 percent just had primary educations."[21] This did not render them unable to make money. They were not unintelligent, and in reforms there is much evidence these ex-peasants were not lazy. But they lacked the training necessary for technical management – and for that, the metropolis provided nearby talent.

Retiree technicians and cadres from Shanghai often went to Jiangsu or Zhejiang to live, and others who resided in Shanghai made frequent visits to other delta cities. Inland firms kept records in card files of contacts in Shanghai. These covered lineage ties and information about anyone who might prove useful to the rural business. Such a file would record the address, specialization, telephone, work unit, and other data about any possible consultant.[22] At lunar New Year, or at other times, Shanghai contacts received cordial letters from rural companies, sending respects, sometimes money in "red envelopes," asking specific market information about selling products or obtaining materials, or asking whether the consultant might offer further introductions or perhaps come visit. Few local authorities in Jiangsu or Zhejiang would oppose links of this sort with Shanghai, if they could benefit from trade that developed.

Business or technical people in the metropolis could sometimes establish special connections with their families' old hometowns. Same-place associations (*tongxiang hui*) were an old Chinese tradition that the centralist revolutionary regime generally disliked, but informal groups were hard to repress. Local cadres in the hometowns of Shanghai entrepreneurs had networks that could help make wider linkages. Often it was economically rational to make liaisons with other places without kinship ties but with needed talents or resources. When trade prospered, money might be donated to the towns of chiefs who aided such connections. East China is now sprinkled with schools, clinics, and other institutions that received funds earned through the good offices of local leaders who helped cities with delta commerce near Shanghai.

This kind of high-paid rustication, not organized by the state, could also extend inland. Quick growth in southern Jiangsu and northern Zhejiang by the late 1980s affected adjacent areas, such as Jinhua in the mountains southwest of Hangzhou or nearby parts of Jiangxi and Anhui provinces.[23] Such places supplied factors, notably cheap labor, to the faster-growing flatlands (and less-regulated Wenzhou). Pan'an County, the poorest in Jinhua Prefecture that is Zhejiang's least wealthy, by the mid-1980s still had "no industry and few resources." In 1983, its output per capita was a mere 80 yuan. But the county head and CCP secretary were optimistic, because "in the past thirty years, a lot of university students came out of here. The county is poor, but people here emphasize their children's education. Now, the county has many connections with these university people. Many will come back to contribute to the rise of this poor county. The heads of the county also have university educations."[24]

"Horizontal" economic relationships within East China mutually reinforced old cultural ties. They arose because markets over centuries had created a cultural region – which the Beijing politicians weakened after 1949 for the sake of revenues, but which still in the 1970s and 1980s made sense to many people in Jiangnan. Such liaisons benefited Shanghainese who participated in them; they benefited "governance" less obviously. The expectations of Shanghai and inland firms, when they entered horizontal liaisons, were often high. Inland companies hoped to garner Shanghai capital and technology, while Shanghai businesses often "felt that their own tasks under the state plan were already very heavy" and liaisons would lighten them.[25] Both sides could gain advantages by cooperating among localities, without central oversight.

Joint ventures and personnel retention

The Shanghai Industrial Consulting Service Company was set up in 1979. It soon made good profits and foreign exchange earnings. But this consultancy was under a regime of taxes and controls typical of Shanghai firms; so it ran into problems: "Because this company lacked decision making power in its internal management and in its disposal of its funds, plus the fact that its workers were not able to benefit even when they reaped handsome profits, the consulting company finally encountered difficulties in advancing its business."[26] A sample survey of its transactions, conducted by another organization, determined that "[e]very yuan spent in consulting fees by technology buyers enabled them to create 489 yuan worth of industrial output value per year. There were no specific rules, however, on the remuneration of the technicians who moonlighted and provided consulting services in their spare time." When the company clamped down on moonlighters, "Many of them quit the technological consulting firm." By 1986, the number of this company's new contracts was half that of 1985 – and the company had to "suspend its business, because it could not break even."

Since 1980 especially, there had been a great many domestic "joint venture factories" (*lianying chang*) between Shanghai and other places, especially in Sunan.[27] The means of production – machines, capital, licenses, and the like – were usually supplied by the Shanghai firm and were sometimes moved physically from plants in the metropolis. Some joint ventures reduced the bulk or weight of partially finished products that later were shipped to Shanghai for final processing. Managers in the metropolis generally coordinated the designing, packaging, and selling of the products.[28]

"Mother-in-law" corporations occasionally encouraged such plans. From the beginning of 1981, the Shanghai Light Industrial Machines Company's sixteen factories developed "horizontal relations" with twenty-two plants in Wuxi, Wujin (a suburb of Changzhou), Shazhou (in Suzhou Prefecture near the new foreign-trade harbor of Zhangjiagang), and elsewhere in Jiangsu. Production rose quickly. Between 1979 and 1984, this Shanghai company increased its output by 44 percent. Its joint projects with factories in Suzhou created a 23 percent growth of product value in just one year.[29]

Connections were often made directly between factories. Two printing machine plants in Shanghai and Wuxi combined in 1981. The presses they co-produced were a market success; so another Shanghai plant in the same line soon set up similar arrangements with a factory in Changzhou.[30] Many Shanghai companies moved their activities only to the city's nearby suburbs, which had land for expansions. By 1984, fully 159 companies had been founded on a joint basis between city firms and those in the suburbs. Nine-tenths were producing light industrial consumer products.[31] Among plants of the Garments Company in the city's Handicrafts Bureau by the end of 1985, half of the company's factory space was outside Shanghai's urban districts. Such relocations were also flights from the central city's more intensive bureaucratic monitoring. Supervising companies knew what was happening, of course – and they might approve such arrangements, particularly if their own ability to manage input and product markets had collapsed anyway. When relocated facilities raised remittances and the "mother-in-law" bureaucrats kept their jobs, everything else was negotiable.

The autonomy of municipal governments throughout the delta was reduced by horizontal liaisons; but if joint amalgamation of factories across borders was the best way to make money by the 1980s, local leaders could take a cut rather than objecting. Suzhou cadres reported that 80 percent of all registered firms in their city had Shanghai connections to arrange raw materials or marketing. Three-quarters of the value of Suzhou's total production, by the late 1980s, was made or sold under arrangements with companies in Shanghai.[32]

Companies licensed by higher-level administrative jurisdictions resisted horizontal linking more than did fast-growth firms licensed by townships and especially villages. In small places, the bills for taxes and bribes were local. In 1987 Suzhou, only 27 percent of firms licensed above the township level admitted involvement in horizontal projects with other jurisdictions (mainly Shanghai) – but interviewees make clear that this was a sharp underreport. Non-Suzhou capital that came to these projects was published to be 44 percent of their total assets.[33] More important, presuming this area was like others then on the delta, about half the value of all industrial production came from plants licensed by townships or "lower levels."

In Wuxi, one-third of the township (*xiang*) enterprises were joint with factories, schools, or research units in Shanghai. Others were joint with plants in urban Wuxi or other Jiangnan cities. Competition induced state firms to develop such ties. The number of Shanghai state or large collective firms with registered horizontal relations was reported 37 percent higher in 1987 than in 1986. Joint registrations with other units in Shanghai were up 18 percent; and with other provinces, up 43 percent.[34] If medium-sized Shanghai industrial enterprises are counted along with large ones, more than 90 percent had subsidiaries or special relations with factories in other East China cities.[35]

Wuxi, sometimes called "Little Shanghai" before the Communist era, is the city with the largest production in Jiangsu. Wuxi is in many respects independent of the provincial capital, Nanjing. One-third of all enterprises in Wuxi by 1983 already had "'private' trading links on a voluntary basis" with firms in seven other cities of the Shanghai delta.[36] Local leaders in the delta were creating regional institutions that integrated all of its large settlements.

Not all cooperative links were economic, and many economic ones were small-scale. Two-thirds of all registered connections with Kunshan, for example, reportedly did not require major joint investments. Many joint projects involved exchanges of technology, consultation, or marketing or barter arrangements – rather than money. Joint enterprises might most easily be licensed if new equipment were used, if management styles could be made more efficient, or if new products could be made. Lack of official approval seldom stymied cooperation between firms. Especially for plants licensed at low levels, or by bureaucrats who could be bought, approvals were not hard to obtain, when needed. Rural units in Kunshan by 1987 reported more than 380 projects, of which 65 percent were with Shanghai colleges, labs, or factories.[37] Kunshan also has connections with many other places, including Beijing, Tianjin, Fujian, Sichuan, and Zhejiang; and famous local products such as Kunshan honey are sold internationally. This city, which is close to the official but artificial border with Shanghai, has important cultural resonances for all of Jiangnan and beyond because it is home to the most famous dialectical East Chinese opera (*Kunqu*).[38] In the modern era, Kunshan for decades has been fully part of the Shanghai-Yangzi commercial system.[39]

Local profits or central profits? Localists link similar companies, centralists complain

A socialist-conservative critic said that agreements for horizontal liaisons between companies should be just "short-term activities," joining firms that had merely temporary mutual advantages in technology, materials, or markets. Linkages of that sort tended to be between firms in the same line of work, and they had usually been coordinated earlier under a supervisory state corporation. Each tended to develop capacities in which other partners had similar comparative advantages; so as time went on, this statist argued, the initial benefits from horizontal links beneath the state's radar should lessen. He thought joint firms would become weaker. A more stable, longer-term kind of horizontal connection emerged (according to this critic) when such arrangements were set up between industrial, agricultural, and trade units, i.e., in different sectors supplying each other.[40] This theorist did not explain why so many links were set up between similar plants. Local leaders' aim was what conservatives feared: to reduce state rake-offs and monitoring, and only sometimes to use advantages that could be found in different places.

A minority of links were "arranged marriages," under which firms were "ordered to liaise." A Shanghai vegetable market was mandated to join with an inland trading company in setting up a new hotel, although tourism had not previously been the line of work in either unit. The negotiations were between bureaucrats far above these two firms – and the local Shanghai vegetable sellers were said to disbelieve the connection would be profitable. They were ordered to accept the proposal anyway. Business later proved to be bad, because the joint hotel lost money.[41]

In other cases, marriages were between eager partners whose supervising bureaucrats disapproved. A Shanghai textile plant wanted to extend technical help to a shirt factory elsewhere in East China, and relevant cadres in the city favored the proposal too. But the supervising garment company, whose bureaucratic position was between these two administrative levels, vetoed the proposal.[42] Such links could have been realized quietly through trade and consultation, and this may have occurred, although it was not reported.

So horizontal connections were not publicized when they stirred opposition. Because many different kinds of official units could be involved, none was responsible for taking overall charge of trade development. No comprehensive statistics on Shanghai links with Hangzhou and Jiaxing in Zhejiang were available. No one kept tabs on all the connections in Jiangnan. Many managers in small communities had interests in hiding such ties. At least 800 specific links among Shanghai and Hangzhou firms in that year could nonetheless be documented.[43] Between Shanghai and Jiaxing, another 200 links were registered. Most of these were not with the large Jiaxing prefectural city, but with more local counties or townships in it. One of the reasons for such cooperation was reportedly Jiaxing's "cheap price of land." Normally sales of real estate are difficult to arrange in China; but this attractive Zhejiang city is just 98 kilometers from Shanghai by direct rail, and centrally mandated procedures could be fudged there more easily than in the metropolis.

The Shanghai government in early 1986 classified horizontal links between the municipality and outside provinces into four bureaucratic types: "economic" liaisons, compensation trade (barter), new enterprises, and technical cooperation.[44] These vague categories shaped the gathering of statistics and stately hopes of monitoring links that had long been unofficial. A report was compiled, lamenting that most links were with areas near Shanghai and outreach to more distant regions was less frequent. An attempt to catalogue such activity was most of what remained of planning, but the bureaucrats did not pretend their records were complete.

Different jurisdictions within Shanghai had sharply different degrees of contact outside the municipality – and most did not give full reports of such links. Two of Shanghai's suburban counties (Baoshan and Chuansha) by mid-1987 had invested 9.5 million yuan in other provinces; but four other counties (Fengxian, Jinshan, Qingpu, and Songjiang) together reported their investments at only 2.7 million. Shanghai County, also in the suburbs, had contracted or planned very extensive investments, totaling 11 million. The data from Chongming County, a large Shanghai island in the Yangzi whence boat trade was hard to track, were said to be too insufficient for analysis of "horizontal" activities. Differences in reporting about such links (not just differences in their use) created odd distributions of available information. The total industrial outputs of Jinshan and Qingpu Counties were respectively the highest and lowest in the whole municipality, for example; and it was reasonable to expect some correlation between output and trade or investment – yet these two counties were reported together in the low category for horizontal links. Officials in Jinshan County probably did far more linking than they reported.[45] Entrepreneurs had strong incentives to hide interactions that were unofficial but profitable. The wealth and productivity of various Shanghai counties vary, but not as radically as their reported horizontal investments. The main variance was in the degrees to which local leaders filed reports.

Consortia of enterprises

When Shanghai's supervising industrial bureaus could not deliver materials at low state prices, they decreed the formation of "enterprise groups" (*qiye qunti*, or informally *jituan*, which also suggests 'clan'). These coalitions "worked for the transfer of Shanghai's material-consuming industries to places where the materials are produced." Moving industries out of Shanghai saved the jobs of some executive cadres – but did not provide jobs for most other workers. An official claim was that "[w]hen some materials-consuming industries are shifted out of Shanghai, much space can be made available and much capital funneled back for the development of hi-tech industries in the municipality." That made sense for Shanghai's long-term development. It depended, however, on fiscal and political decisions to set up new industries. These were not guaranteed. Also, the plan to "rusticate" whole industries

Traders and Jiangnan regionalists **277**

neglected the value local foremen placed on relations with their workers. So there was resistance. It was expressed in strikes and complaints. As a Beijing newspaper reported in English:

> The effort has been merely confined to know-how transfer and granting use of [Shanghai] trademarks by local factories. There has been no real merger of capital and assets. As a result, the factories in the interior regions, which are supposed to be members of the Shanghai-based enterprise groups, actually work in the interests of their localities. In this way, Shanghai has only fostered competitors for its industry, much contrary to the original intention of making the best use of raw materials locally.[46]

Such competition was worse for Shanghai workers and tax collectors than for entrepreneurs who had connections with nearby provinces. The economies of Shanghai and the delta were intertwined, and central policies to separate them were overwhelmed by policies from local leaders to link them. In 1952, Shanghai and Jiangsu, if taken as a single unit together, would have ranked only sixth among Chinese "provinces" in *per capita* net value of industrial and agricultural output.[47] But by 1979, Shanghai and Jiangsu together ranked first in per capita output, and Zhejiang had risen to sixth (and by 1984, to fourth). The big change was not in Shanghai, but in adjacent provinces that Shanghai leaders helped. Government economic repression in the metropolis had bred entrepreneurial habits that delivered big profits on the delta outside Shanghai, as China's revolutionary centralization waned.

All major Sunan cities long benefited from Shanghai connections, and together they prospered enormously. Shanghai, Wuxi, and Changzhou had in 1933 contributed 87 percent of the combined output of Jiangsu and Shanghai; and in 1982 they still contributed 62 percent after factories had started in many other parts of the province and municipality.[48] If *all* China's officially designated cities (*shi*) are ranked by their total gross product, counting both industry and agriculture, Suzhou and Wuxi in 1986 were among the top five (after three larger province-level cities Shanghai, Beijing, and Tianjin). An analyst of the growth of these places claimed, "No doubt these results are inseparable from their geographical proximity to Shanghai and their receiving the radiation and diffusion of Shanghai's economy."[49]

Joint ventures and enterprise groups were means for this diffusion. The numbers of such groups were published more frequently than their valuations, which revealed more. The fifty-six Changzhou enterprise groups in the first half of 1986, most of which had members in Shanghai or other places outside Changzhou, accounted for one-third of Changzhou's industrial output. They remitted two-fifths of its profits and taxes.[50] In the first nine months of 1986, Shanghai invested 850 million yuan in sixty-three joint projects, to make a total by that time of 507 such endeavors in "fraternal regions" (*xiongdi diqu*).

Many factories in Shanghai and developed profitable relations with Sunan plants making the same products. The Tangqiao Towel Factory, founded toward the end of 1982 near Suzhou, produced towels in great quantity but had problems selling them. So in 1984, it established liaison (*lianxi*) with the Shanghai No. 15 Towel Factory, which sent technicians to Tangqiao, raising the quality of the towels and helping to market them. In 1983, a village of Tangqiao Township signed a contract with the Shanghai-Wusong Chemical Fiber Factory, under which Shanghai provided equipment and some funds. This rural town put in capital and provided factory space.[51] New Sunan factories could often grow faster if they had friends in Shanghai.

Ningbo and Shanghai: old business relations

Cities along the coast of North Zhejiang, from Ningbo to Hangzhou, have long-standing connections with Shanghai. Zhejiang businesspeople had enormous influence in pre-1949 Shanghai. A 1920 survey of the most famous compradores in Shanghai showed that about half were from Zhejiang.[52] Ningbo and the area around it contain the ancestral homes of many influential Shanghai entrepreneurs – and according to informal reports, perhaps a quarter of the big city's total population had Zhejiang origins. During reforms emigrant Ningbo people overseas numbered 300,000, mostly in Hong Kong or Southeast Asia. Some were extremely wealthy tycoons. Only one-tenth of these had actually visited Ningbo by October 1988 – but their investment in the city was already large. PRC newspapers openly asked them in late 1988 to "help Ningbo."[53] Deng Xiaoping himself urged "mobilizing the whole world's 'Ningbo clique' to construct Ningbo." A Hong Kong shipping magnate, Bao Yugang (Sir Y. K. Pao), financed a new university there in the 1980s. Shanghai similarly benefited from such generosity, but the high-tax and high-regulation climate mandated by Beijing was a deterrent to tycoons' investment. Few of these would put money into a city whose infrastructure had been underfinanced as badly as Shanghai's, especially if alternative Jiangnan sites where they also had personal ties were available.

A Ningbo Association to Promote Economic Construction had its first general meeting in late 1988. A meeting of the "directors" of this association included seven members from Shanghai, of whom the most notable was the group's deputy head, Li Chuwen. This high cadre was originally from Ningbo, and he had extensive experience in Hong Kong. But by late 1988, he was back in Shanghai as the main foreign affairs adviser to the municipal government. In early 1989, nine "Shanghai people with Ningbo origins" set up a Shanghai Association to Promote Ningbo Economic Construction, which was nongovernmental.[54]

Late-1980s entrepreneurs in company groups, or cadres in state corporations

Local notables and state reformers alike found these traditional ties useful, though for different reasons. Just as "administrative cities" were the reformers' recipe for circumventing old conflicts between centralizers and localizers in China's geographical jurisdictions, "enterprise groups" became a way to change the structure of functional bureaucracies that suffered arthritis. A CCP economist claimed[55]:

> The formation of enterprise groups will help remove barriers between different departments and regions, end the situation in which enterprises are "large and complete" or "small and complete," and rationalize enterprise structure. The past practice of "centralizing" and "decentralizing" power . . . failed thoroughly to improve the irrational product mix, [but] enterprise groups will help change the government's functions in economic management and . . . are the principal force for developing China's socialized large-scale production.

Enterprise groups meant a kind of 'local centralization' (a bit like the centralization to middle levels in 1958, but this time among capitalists rather than bureaucrats).[56] They were not a devolution of power by the state. They weakened the autonomy of the central state − and of many very local leaders too. As with "administrative cities" that during reforms centralized locally by annexing nearby geographical areas, "enterprise groups" assumed powers in economic fields that had, during the high tide of socialism, been subject to ministries' plans. Such changes raised revenues, but not for the central state. The coteries behind them were medial leaders who had ties to each other.

Correlates of this reform were changes of status symbols: economic cadres (*ganbu*) gave way to entrepreneurs (*qiye jia*). Shanghai's first major "Entrepreneurs' Club" was founded at a meeting in December 1984, attended but not led by Mayor Wang Daohan.[57] It first included 420 factory directors, managers, and chief engineers. It was followed by many other such clubs (about forty large ones by the mid-1990s). Shanghai managers realized that they could be most effective in pressing for radical change if they combined together, and with businesspeople from other provinces.

The Golden Triangle Entrepreneurs' Club set up a 1988 "round-table conference" in the Shanghai suburb of Jiading. Joint sponsors included the reformist Research Institute for Restructuring the Economic System and several newspapers (including the *Guangming Daily* and the *World Economic Herald*, which after Tiananmen became infamous among conservatives − and was closed). Chief participants from Shanghai included cadres from very large state factories: the secretary of the Party committee at Baoshan Steel, the directors of both the Jiangnan and the Hudong shipyards, the heads of Shanghai Machine Tools, Shanghai Aircraft, Shanghai Bicycle, Shanghai Diesel Engines, Shanghai Solvents, Shanghai Petrochemicals, Shanghai Tunnel Engineering, and several other local power, petrochemical, and iron works. Some were reformers. Other conferees came from Beijing, Shenzhen, Guangzhou, Yantai, Anshan, Shenyang, Dalian, Daqing, Haerbin, and elsewhere, heading fifty-one state-owned corporations.

These socialist taipans showed, in their demands to government, the extent of change by 1988. Acting together, they did less to alter the structure of Shanghai's political economy than "lower level" local entrepreneurs had done; but they were voluble. Partly because of their political stature, they had no need to mince words by the late 1980s in presenting demands to state officials. They wanted to "open a road of genuinely separating two powers," so as to clarify "the administrative subordination of Party and mass organizations [e.g., unions] in enterprises."[58] They demanded the right to "participate in formulating plans." They wanted "to reduce the scope of mandatory planning and gradually to turn mandatory quotas into placement of state orders." They wanted freedom from recurrent checks by supervising monitors in ministries and bureaus, so that they could "make independent decisions on investment." They also demanded that "the time limit on major enterprise contracts be extended" so that they could plan operations more than a few months in advance. They further wanted rights to "establish connections directly with foreign counterparts." They looked forward to more "industrial banking institutions," asking that "major enterprises and enterprise groups be allowed to found industrial banks and group banks." They needed more serious laws, including a "free trade law" and a "corporation law." Just as vehemently, they demanded firmer "social norms to protect creditor rights and property rights" from political interference.

These ex-socialist managers insisted, "Enterprise heads should no longer be put under serialized assessment management, as is the case with government cadres." And businesspeople should be duly compensated, so that "their social and economic position can rise along with the increases of their enterprise asset values and the expansion of their operations." They insisted on the right to set up "entrepreneurial organizations . . . through elections, to voice the demands of enterprises, particularly major ones, and to protect their interests." Finally, they demanded "administrative courts" that could "handle cases of government violations of laws."

These managers were not ideological liberals. Most were almost surely Communists – high ranking ones, unlikely to suffer dissent from their own subordinates. They were not a cowering, unproud lot, and they had every reason for loyalty to the system in which they got posts of power. But to maintain their enterprises, now that their supervisors in ministries and bureaus could no longer deliver materials or ensure markets, they declared independence. Whether or not they should be called an "interest group," they clearly protested acts of the state that threatened their firms' survival. Smaller enterprises, which were effectively outside that system, were among their banes – but because they could not change those, they directed their fire at higher officials instead.

Common-aim networks among entrepreneurs

The Golden Delta Entrepreneurs' Club took as one of its goals the networking of business firms with other kinds of units, especially in government.[59] This club hosted meals for city officials, cadres of local Party Organization Departments that monitored all important appointments, officers of financial institutions, and lawyers. They met regularly on each workday that had a calendar date evenly divisible by five. The Golden Delta Club also tried to link its members with scientists and university people. For example, the club held a seminar about China's development strategy with academic economists.

This club also sponsored links with entrepreneurs from foreign countries and other parts of China. The members wanted legitimation for their activities from state offices, and they needed that particularly when they dealt with foreigners. The Shanghai Entrepreneurs' Club (Shanghai Qiyejia Julebu) was apparently somewhat less active than the Golden Delta Entrepreneurs' Club (Jin Sanjiao Qiyejia Julebu), but its aims were similar. Its main sponsor was the *Economic Daily*, and its membership was more limited to the city. Many such clubs were formed in East China at this time, to foster "networking" among different kinds of local leaders. Bonds between non-officials and officials – especially when nonstate leaders organized the connections – did not show that power flowed from the central government "downward." It flowed, along with funds, largely in the opposite direction. "Follow the money" is good advice for political analysts of any system.

Economic data networks can be analyzed according to the sizes of the geographical units they covered. National exchanges were extensive for commercial and banking data. In all parts of China, there were hundreds of "information liaison stations" (*xinxi lianluo zhan*). In East China, data-exchange activities included sending statistics among six provinces, but also to various think tanks set up by banks, electronic industries, a research center on production materials, and the office of the Shanghai Economic Zone (while this lasted). Shanghai's municipal government in May 1984 established an Industrial Economy Information Exchange Station (Gongye Jingji Jiaoliu Zhan).[60] These were state organizations, but they were different from planning offices. Businesspeople could call on them or not, as they saw fit.

Technicians also founded regional and cross-regional organizations in the late 1980s, albeit with less permanent results because breakneck reform was restrained in the next decade. The Shanghai branch of the Chinese Academy of Sciences established technical cooperation links with 600 inland enterprises. A similar effort to develop cross-regional cooperation was under the aegis of the Shanghai Employees' Technical Association, which was linked to the Federation of Trade Unions.

This Federation was formally not supposed to be a government organization. Its importance in China's Communist movement goes back to the 1920s, long before the PRC government existed. But the Shanghai branch was mandated from Beijing to establish a link in 1986 with its counterpart in Yunnan Province; and in the next year, it expanded such connections to other border regions too.[61] New public groupings of technicians and workers were more frequently reported as having far-flung links to distant Chinese places than did the entrepreneurs' clubs. But the managers' groups were more important – and more concentrated on the Jiangnan flatland. The resurgence of conservatism hindered such links, especially after Tiananmen in mid-1989 when the Party especially feared connections between workers and intellectuals.

282 Traders and Jiangnan regionalists

Commercial embassies and traveling salespeople

The main effect of economic reform was that state planners could no longer ensure companies of raw materials and product markets. Before 1979, Shanghai's pharmaceutical factories already had increasing difficulty maintaining sales volumes inland, because new factories in other provinces made drugs from raw materials that the state had previously been able to requisition for the city's higher-tax firms. In an attempt to restore production, Shanghai established a Pharmaceutical Management Bureau, whose head made trips to Zhejiang, Jiangsu, Fujian, and farther places for "market research."[62]

Permanent and temporary offices were set up by many Jiangnan agencies to seek markets and materials inland and abroad. In 1985, the Jiangsu provincial government set up a representative office in Hong Kong.[63] Zhejiang established a Hong Kong trade office in 1988 (partly because the British colony was Zhejiang's largest overseas investor).[64] Commercial embassies flowed in many directions. By March 1985, offices from practically all of China's other provinces had "come to Shanghai to open stores and run factories."[65] Of the 307 such offices that the metropolis registered by that time, 46 percent came from within the Shanghai Economic Zone, including 36 percent from Jiangsu and Zhejiang, and 10 percent from Anhui and Jiangxi. When Shanghai agencies approved these offices, usually when the aim was to avoid reducing Shanghai's inputs supplies, units of the city provided about half the capital for them; they were joint ventures.

Before 1986, there was a formal rule that allowed each jurisdiction outside the city to establish just one representative office in Shanghai. Under this restriction, seventy-six provinces and ministries had established commercial embassies in the municipality by that year; but their subordinate units were not supposed to do so. When the restriction was abolished in 1987 – apparently because it failed to ensure the registration of most visiting traders – 106 subprovincial agencies established their own bureaus to deal directly with counterparts in Shanghai. Over a thousand branches of non-Shanghai factories and stores were registered in the city, and most of these opened (or admitted having) offices almost immediately. Their total revenues exceeded 1.8 billion yuan, and their profits and tax remittances were worth 62 million yuan.[66]

"Embassies" of Shanghai Municipality, as distinguished from those sent from companies within the city, were limited in number. During the 1950s, the city had run only one such office – in Beijing. Not until the 1980s was this number higher, although city offices made many interprovincial connections. By 1987, Shanghai Municipality had quasi-consulates in five other PRC cities (Chongqing, Guangzhou, Haerbin, Wuhan, and Xi'an). These dealt with groups of provinces larger than the cities in which they were located, but there was an interesting discrepancy between the city government's relatively few offices elsewhere and the full-coverage representation in Shanghai of nearly every other province.

In 1987, Shanghai signed agreements "to protect the legal rights and interests of enterprises in horizontal economic relations." Such treaties were made with relatively distant places: Heilongjiang, Hunan, Jiangxi, Jilin, Sichuan (including a separate agreement with Chongqing before that city acquired province status in 1997), and Xinjiang.[67] Most sales teams, both to and from the city, came and went from smaller units and administrative levels. High layers of bureaucracy, in which appointments or promotions were influenced by Beijing, only supported horizontal relations they could monitor. Administratively lower layers supported other kinds, which could function freely under more local tax regimes.

A 1987 survey of over 4,000 PRC travelers to Shanghai, which claimed to be random, showed that a majority (69 percent) came to the city for "connections." Most of these were surely with families, but some were for trade. Only 12 percent came for tourism, 6 percent for study, and 5 percent each to see friends and to get medical treatment in Shanghai hospitals.[68] By 1988, fifteen percent of the 1.1 million visitors in Shanghai came either to purchase materials or sell products.[69] These were traveling salespeople. Since their activities were outside government coordination, they received scant high-level official help. But if banks would not finance their trade, they might barter in kind. As one conservative writer put it, "the state plan is flouted by barter arrangements which have very far-reaching administrative implications. They also have far-reaching implications for some of the familiar commonsense arguments for the encouragement of local industry, such as fortifying local self-sufficiency."[70]

The economic boom led by locally cooperating companies overwhelmed planners. Rural spending on consumer goods rose from 1978 to 1981 throughout China by 122 percent (a 30 percent annual growth rate). By 1987, three-fifths of all retail sales were in rural areas, and one-fifth of China's money supply was in the hands of peasants.[71] This exuberant new demand would be met. Since the state did not foster commercial channels that could fill it, nonstate and nominally "low" state institutions did so.

Planners and buttons

The most notoriously uncontrolled market in all China was in south Zhejiang, and its commodity was one that planners had scarcely considered making. A Wenzhou township, Jiaotou, became the country's biggest market for buttons. One-fourth of all buttons sold in China by the late 1980s came through or from that single town. As people doffed their "Mao suits" for clothes they deemed more fashionable, the reform era saw a booming demand for buttons.

Planning commissions had not thought much about buttons. Newly rich urban and rural Chinese, however, suddenly wanted many million fasteners. So 300 Jiaotou households supplied them: "Every family opened a small factory to make buttons. Within less than one year, there were a lot of three-story buildings, and a street was formed. In each building, the first floor is the store, the second is the factory, and the third is the living room. . . . About 100,000 Wenzhou people now are scattered over the whole country. They form an information circuit, a business network," not just selling buttons.[72]

The south Zhejiang economy filled many niches the state sector had missed. Wenzhou's buttons became famous, but they contributed less than 5 percent of national trade from that prefecture in 1984. More important were appliances (28 percent), acrylic fiber clothes (23 percent), and plastic bags (19 percent). Wenzhou became, and still is, the planet's dominant producer of cigarette lighters. Prereform planners had failed to find wide markets for any of these commodities. Wenzhou traders, with their centuries-long tradition of migration, seafaring, piracy, geographic isolation, and gross evasion of inconvenient state policies, were well placed to fill demands that the state plan missed. They got into markets early, and they made a great deal of money.

The exceptionally free traders of Wenzhou flourished nationally in localities where there had been traditional trading fairs. They increasingly sold nontraditional goods, ranging from plastic utensils to computer chips. Buyers of Wenzhou goods were spread as far as Xinjiang and foreign countries.[73] Purchasers bought from Wenzhou salespeople because the commodities were diverse and the prices lower than in their own places. Shanghai sales representatives in Wenzhou were surprisingly few; a compendium of offices in Wenzhou recorded just one from Shanghai, a cooperative – but that firm advertised it could arrange buying or selling any product.[74]

"Materials loans" and barter in commerce

Salespeople often traded without money. Barter was common in horizontal links. Officially, such exchanges had to be documented in terms of "compensation trade," even if they were ordinary sales based on under-the-table money.[75] Rather than being a hindrance to reform, official support for barter was often a lubricant of change; the reform process evinced many such ironies. As new industries grew up, barter was a useful means to obtain raw materials. Inland suppliers often would not sell to burgeoning rural industries at the state's fixed low prices; so transactions had to be called "compensation trade" rather than purchases – even when the buyers actually compensated the sellers in money.

Terms of trade for Shanghai Municipality's suburban industries deteriorated in the mid-1980s, mostly because other rural industries in Jiangsu and Zhejiang would not send materials except at high prices. Terminology about this trade was obscurantist because much of it skirted laws; the inputs were "materials loans" (*wuzi daikuan*). Four counties in Shanghai "compensated" places outside the municipality with a vast amount of cash (53 million yuan) from early 1985 to June 1986, but in return they had received only 22 percent as much by value in "materials loans."[76] Baoshan County alone, from 1983 to 1986, had thirty compensation trade agreements from which it claimed to receive only 38 percent of the value it supplied. This was intended "horizontal trade," led by managers after the state left them in the lurch by abandoning delivery plans it could not fulfill. When inland suppliers found higher prices elsewhere, they delayed filling their sales contracts indefinitely.

Raw materials shortages gave Shanghai state cadres incentives to get "horizontal liaison" contracts that could be reported in the bureaucracy – whether or not these actually delivered inputs. Firms under the Light Industrial Bureau, from 1979 to 1984, set up 48 "liaison enterprises." In the second half of 1984 and in 1985, that Bureau allowed a tripling of the number of accounting units under its jurisdiction – mostly liaison firms – of which it registered the establishment of 241.[77] In some cases, the Bureau may have done this under pressure from formally subordinate factory managers who needed supplies it had promised. Not all liaison agreements benefited the partners, although many did so. Formal liaising and contracting was easier than producing results.

By the mid-1980s, managers could get permission from embarrassed procurement officials to sign almost any deal with inland places that promised materials – whether or not these would be delivered. When such bargains worked to the advantage only of inland places where the urban managers had personal ties, these businessmen more willingly bore consequent problems for their plants back in the city. Success in production usually led to higher taxes and remittances anyway. For years, supervising bureaucracies had made abundantly clear that they did not care about Shanghai firms except as sources of revenue; and Jiangnan managers in Shanghai with interests elsewhere could be similarly nonchalant. The disruption of Shanghai supplies provided a chance for managers with interests elsewhere to serve these. In this "tense" market, unintended industrial reforms could easily overwhelm planned ones.

As commerce boomed, merchants still did not escape traditional ex-Confucian opprobrium simply for being traders. Their markets were engines of reform – but unreliable ones. Many merchants broke laws to get their business done. They did this often, but they did not like the illegality as such. Their norms and situations were in conflict. Salespeople often had multiple personality disorder of a political kind. A surprising number of theater producers during reforms chose Arthur Miller's tragedy *Death of a Salesman*, which the playwright himself visited China to direct.[78] Its description of impersonal market pressures passed muster with conservatives as a critique of capitalism, and reformers liked it as a critique of alienation. The play solved nothing, but it was a means to explore a common Chinese problem at that time.

Commercial people were a very large group. *Wenhui News* reported that by 1988 Shanghai had more than 100,000 traders in its 10,000 enterprises, although it is unclear how many of these were wholesalers. About an eighth of all visitors to Shanghai came as merchants. A radio broadcast reported,[79]

> Some stay in luxury hotels and travel by taxi, while others wait for customers to come begging for the rare raw materials they can supply. But the majority are out all the time, trying their luck and getting their business done with popular brands of cigarettes and other small "bribes." It is a recognized fact that most salespeople enjoy low social status, even though some have helped their businesses achieve big profits. Some try to establish "connections" with those playing key roles in their companies by offering small bribes, small benefits, and other sorts of gifts. Others, especially those who look for

state-controlled raw materials such as chemicals and iron, go door to door, from one department to another, begging for what their factories need. Still others, people who work in small township factories and have little access to the urban administrative network, have to buy their way into each layer of the city's bureaucracy. They are willing to do whatever is necessary to make deals, occasionally at the cost of personal dignity and funds.

"More channels and fewer links" (*duo qudao, shao huanjie*) was a reform slogan calling for more horizontal trade and fewer vertical allocations. The economic advantages of letting producers sell directly to consumers, without going through state agencies, were clear. Laws to protect such trade, however, are anathema to conservatives. They have been easier to draft than to pass. This was like political reform – easier to discuss than to achieve. Yet horizontal trade was an endemic, unauthorized, structural kind of political reform among localities. The rise of diverse trade lessened the power of "high" Party officials. Forty years of planning tradition militated against direct trade, but shortages meant these habits no longer prevented it.

The rise of the Shanghai Economic Zone

China's largest plan for horizontal trade went through many forms and had predecessors. In the 1950s, the East China Economic Coordination Zone (*Huadong jingji xiezuo qu*) was one of several organizations that Chen Yi's field army bequeathed to the region. In July 1957, the Shanghai Party called a conference on "economic coordination" among the six provinces of Jiangsu, Zhejiang, Anhui, Fujian, Jiangxi, and Shanghai.[80] Many non-Shanghai enterprises that attended were either primary extractors (e.g., in mining) or producers of intermediate goods. "This coordination is expected to stimulate Shanghai's industry."[81]

A basis for regional cooperation and conflict was the East China electric grid (*Huadong dianwang*).[82] This network, which later came under the purview of the Shanghai Economic Zone, aimed to ensure coal production in Anhui so that cities on the Yangzi delta could generate energy. In return for capital and talent sent to other parts of East China, the metropolis got something as valuable as credit: more electric power and markets for its industries. But the quid pro quo, from the viewpoint of Beijing planners, was that Shanghai could retain very few profits from these industries. This arrangement was stable so long as state planning remained strong.

Already by 1970, however, national distribution was localized, so that the national state plan merely collated separate prospectuses for "cooperation regions" (*xiezuo qu*), which worked rather independently of each other.[83] The economy in 1970 was already regionalized. Interprovincial cooperation flourished in many fields during the first part of that decade, even though radicals often opposed it.

An early example came in the field of public health. Eight counties around Shanghai, Jiangsu, and Zhejiang cooperated during the early 1970s in a local campaign against schistosomiasis, a disease called "liver fluke" or "snail fever." This debilitating and potentially fatal ailment is caused by parasites that infect snails and workers in rice paddies. It remained a major medical problem in rural parts of East China, even after communitarian campaigns in Mao's time made progress against many contagious diseases. Interprovincial cooperation organized by local authorities had previously been rare; but by the spring of 1970, two medical organizations linked Shanghai with Jiangsu and Zhejiang to combat schistosomiasis. They established thirteen "joint prevention areas" near their borders.[84] Cultural Revolution radicals at this time were running their own campaigns against "four pests," and they resented this competition by local governments for medical resources. They reportedly "struggled against" the interprovincial anti-schistosomiasis campaign – but without much effect. Regional cadres called meetings; and when higher authorities issued orders to quash these activities, the meetings simply continued their work anyway.[85]

Jiashan, Zhejiang, experimented with anti-snail "firebreaks." Other counties reportedly contributed various kinds of scientific research. Such cooperation among eight Shanghai, Jiangsu, and Zhejiang counties extended from schistosomiasis to other fields. Local authorities in Wujiang, Jiangsu, promoted a particular kind of garbage-fermentation chamber for producing methane gas, which could be used for cooking. Leaders in all eight nearby counties adopted this as an agricultural extension project. Kunshan, Jiangsu, reportedly treated its "barefoot" doctors in a way that made them particularly effective; so other localities copied these best practices too. Early reforms in the late 1960s and early 1970s saw across-the-board improvements in nationwide medical indicators. The World Bank estimates that the average life expectancy of a Chinese citizen increased from forty-nine years in 1964 to sixty-six years in 1979.[86]

Connections among localities developed because of actual similarities of problems and opportunities. Markets between counties and communes, convened at fairs in the early 1970s, involved traders from different sides of provincial borders also. They were condoned by some central leaders and opposed by others.

At the end of 1978, an official fad emerged for foreign trade zones and "special economic zones" (SEZ). Three of these were authorized in Guangdong, and one in Fujian. But in Shanghai, the premier tax-paying city, such plans were delayed. Taiwan's "export processing zones" at Kaohsiung, Nantse, and Taichung had been highly successful in the 1970s, as had similar zones in other countries.[87] These were sharply focused on external markets, with a limited list of enterprises and fenced borders that were easy to patrol. The zones in Taiwan together took less than three square kilometers.[88] China's Shenzhen SEZ alone was over one hundred times that size, it relied mostly on Overseas Chinese rather than ethnically foreign capital, and its domestic interactions were as important as its effects on markets abroad. Shenzhen later became a flagship of change, a place where entrepreneurs made money.

Such a development in Shanghai might have promoted a lower tax regime. The idea thus was locally welcomed. As two economists pointed out, the Shanghai delta covers one of the richest and most densely populated parts of China. They called

288 Traders and Jiangnan regionalists

for something better than the old 1950s "cooperation zones" (*xiezuo qu*).[89] As late as the 1976–1980 Five-Year Plan, the power of provincial jurisdictions had been formally retained. But reformers called for "breaking through provincial boundaries" so that large areas could "both join together and compete."[90] From 1980, Shanghai Mayor Wang Daohan began to hold regular joint meetings with the governors of Jiangsu and Zhejiang provinces and the mayors of Changzhou, Hangzhou, Jiaxing, Nantong, Ningbo, Shaoxing, Suzhou, and Wuxi cities. The office of the Shanghai Economic Zone emerged from these sessions, but it never had the authority to countermand provincial or municipal cadres. It existed only to coordinate them after they already agreed.

In 1981, "more than one hundred experts" convened at Wuxi to confer about the economic future of the Yangzi delta. A report concluded that "Zhejiang, Jiangsu and Shanghai should cooperate to study the delta's agrarian areas, industrial network, and distribution of cities, and to make new plan from a 'natural and economic' perspective." After this conference, the Shanghai Social Sciences Academy established a research group to make a more detailed report. On May 19, 1982, *Wenhui News* summarized proposals for founding an office to reconcile the economic plans of Jiangsu, Zhejiang, and Shanghai – not over their whole extents, but only "in the Yangzi delta, mainly in the Shanghai-Nanjing and Hangzhou areas." (North Jiangsu and South Zhejiang were omitted.)

This initiative came from people in the region, although of course any plan over such a prosperous region would require bargaining for central allowances. Zhao Ziyang apparently began looking at maps centered on Shanghai, because he referred in several speeches to a "200 kilometer circle" that covers this natural market area. A Japanese economist, brought in by central reformers to analyze the proposal, specified that the Shanghai zone should "not be like the Guangzhou economic area, which mainly absorbs foreign money, but an economic zone given special powers to extend itself through cooperation within itself . . . not a closed but an open economy . . . a relatively independent part of the country as a big system."[91]

On October 7, 1982, Zhao Ziyang proposed a Shanghai Economic Zone to overcome the "separation of horizontal from vertical management" (*tiaokuai fenge*). Zhao continued to be a patron of the zone into the mid-1980s, sending "instructions" (*pishi*) for many years to encourage conferences among local leaders. The upshot, however, was that regional and local jurisdictions became more important. On December 22, 1982, the State Council in principle approved the zone involving Shanghai and eight other cities: Suzhou, Changzhou, Nantong, Wuxi, Hangzhou, Ningbo, Huzhou, and Jiaxing. Shaoxing was included later.[92] This allowance from Beijing was belated. Economic liaisons within the delta had actually been booming for years. The Shanghai Economic Zone was like other reforms: Central recognition of them came after local leaders had started them, as an attempt to monitor and tax them.

The Shanghai Economic Zone mandate remained vague, perhaps because central conservatives saw disadvantages. Tax rates throughout the delta remained higher than for most of China. Province-level governments on the delta did not have identical interests. Some inland jurisdictions were unsure they could benefit from the new arrangement. Only some leaders in less prosperous areas agreed with Shanghai politicians and economists that the city should specialize in high technology and let other places produce goods that had previously been Shanghai's strengths. A deputy mayor of Nanchang, Jiangxi, argued that if more technology and investment came to his province, transport costs for products could be lowered, and Shanghai's own economic structure could be freed to develop in new fields.[93] This Jiangxi leader called for a shift of processing industries inland. A problem was that this strategy required money for technical renovation in Jiangnan. No one knew whence such funds would come unless delta taxes fell. If that happened, the defense, hydraulic, and heavy industrial ministries in Beijing would somehow have to fund their budgets with less help from Shanghai.

In January 1983, the Planning Office of the Shanghai Economic Region started its work. From the beginning, its independent authority was small. Most of its early efforts stressed construction projects that would help multiple jurisdictions, e.g., more ports on the lower Yangzi and better flood control for Lake Tai (whose shores are in two provinces).[94] The zone's office mainly convened conferences of autonomous local leaders in various functional areas, ranging from dike construction to data collection. On some stated goals (e.g., Lake Tai flood control) progress was slow or absent.

The Shanghai Economic Zone in this early, compact form consisted of ten cities (the original nine plus Shaoxing), along with fifty-five rich counties covering the whole delta. These counties were all formally put under the administrations of cities.[95] Although this zone comprises a tiny 0.7 percent of China's total area and has only 2.7 percent of the country's arable land, its population (50 million then) was about 5 percent of the nation. These are small percentages. But the compact zone in 1984 produced about one-third of China's textiles, one-forth of all machines, and one-fifth of chemicals. Rural industries already accounted for 16 percent (perhaps underreported) of the zone's total output value and a higher portion of the nation's products from rural factories.[96] In terms of culture, or at least language, this zone coincided almost exactly with the Shanghainese-speaking flatland.

This version of the Shanghai Economic Zone was grandly hailed as involving two "great breakthroughs in the thinking of the [central] leadership." These two new insights were that Shanghai should pioneer a drive for the four modernizations (agriculture, industry, defense, technical science) and that it should develop more foreign trade.[97] Both ideas were in fact old, much mooted – but for two earlier decades scarcely implemented. Continued high taxation in Shanghai suggested that the central leadership was not united behind the zone, and local leaders had envisioned these "breakthroughs" long before. Yet when investment was finally in prospect, there seemed no reason to quibble with pomp.

Interests in the Shanghai Economic Zone were far from identical, as held by central leaders, provincial politicians, and individual managers. Jiangsu's assent to the zone was closely related to that province's hopes for more foreign trade. Most leaders in the provincial capital, Nanjing, came from poor parts of North Jiangsu or neighboring Shandong. But the richest large parts of East China are on the delta, especially in South Jiangsu. Some competition for resources and markets was inevitable between the provincial authorities of Jiangsu, Zhejiang, and Shanghai – even when indigenous leaders tended to see this situation as less zero-sum.

In 1983, Wuxi City wanted closer connections with Shanghai than Jiangsu planners in Nanjing had allowed. By 1984, the Jiangsu government cut Wuxi's investment (in favor of parts of North Jiangsu); but the reason was not merely a political dispute. Instead, it arose because Shanghai's and Jiangsu's economies soon became more similar and less complementary. Both had relatively advanced industries. As the open policy became more important, Shanghai's ability to market products abroad became a potential advantage for Jiangsu. This was sometimes an argument to include North Jiangsu in the Shanghai Economic Zone, so that Shanghai might help export its products.[98] That strategy did not work well, however, for various reasons. Technically sophisticated Jiangsu enterprises (mostly in the south) soon found they could export directly, perhaps paying consultants in Shanghai but not necessarily engaging Shanghai officials. Also, North Jiangsu industries still produced little that could compete internationally. Shanghai exports many products from Jiangsu – but the city was mainly connected (except in the part of the province nearest the metropolis) with relatively small Jiangsu firms, which were not strongly linked to the provincial government.

Added peripheries for the Shanghai zone

Announcement of the Shanghai Economic Zone's "readjustment" (expansion) came at a late 1984 symposium to discuss strategy for the development of agriculture. North Jiangsu and south Zhejiang were now included – as well as all of Anhui and Jiangxi. The zone was thus divided into first and second "layers" (*cengci*). The "first layer" was the delta (*sanjiao zhou* was a commonly used term), identical with the earlier compact zone. The "second layer" comprised all the rest of Jiangsu and Zhejiang, plus Anhui and Jiangxi.[99] This second layer in 1985 had a population of almost 150 million people, while the first layer had a population of more than 50 million.

Local Jiangnan silence, after much central commotion about the zone's enlargement, was deafening. Not a peep was heard, and not a thing was done. Perhaps delta leaders knew that such an expansion would render the zone almost meaningless. They could make their own connections anyway. So for the sake of symbolic compliance, regional leaders did not object to the change. In the mid-1980s materials crisis, when diverse leaders were constructing other institutions that replaced plans with localized arrangements, there was no political reason to object to a zone idea simply because it would be mostly a fiction. Local leaders want to be formal loyalists so long as their interests are not hurt, and it was evident that Shanghai Economic Zone enlargement was harmless.

This was not, however, the conservatives' view – and they expressed themselves in public. A member of the Central Advisory Committee, Zhang Pinghua, said that

Shanghai should "set an example in modernizing agriculture....This is its bounden duty and is expected by the people."[100] One analysis distinguished Shanghai's relations to nearby areas, which involved extensive professional cooperation, and its links to more distant areas, which tended to involve extraction of raw materials.[101] Two subzones within the whole expanded zone were clear, and the delta was the most industrialized part. (Guangdong near the Pearl River was similarly divided.)[102] In 1985, the industrial portions of income in Jiangsu and Zhejiang were respectively 51 and 47 percent; but from Anhui or Jiangxi, about 35 percent.[103] In Shanghai, which is smaller and not fully comparable on this index, the industrial portion was 73 percent.

The dominance of the Yangzi delta area – the "first layer" of the economic zone – is evident in Table 11.1. Jiangsu and Zhejiang were far richer than Jiangxi or Anhui, despite the relative poverty of northern Jiangsu and southwestern Zhejiang. Jiangxi and Anhui had per capita incomes below the national average. They ranked in the upper half of provinces by wealth; but the national average was raised by a few coastal provinces – of which Shanghai, Jiangsu, and Zhejiang were among the most obvious.

Rough comparisons of gross and net output figures (even though they do not cover identical sets of activities) suggest that degrees of vertical economic integration in these provinces correlated with reported per capita incomes. This variable also links to the rates at which all sizes of government extracted fiscal remittances

TABLE 11.1 1983 Economic indices for provinces in the expanded Shanghai Economic Zone

	Sh'ai★	J'su★	Zhe★	J'gxi	Anhui	Sh.Ec. Zone	All China
"nat'l income"	2553	621	556	369	357	612	481
g.v. output	6025	1344	1033	578	570	1235	898
g.v. industry	5838	1028	762	337	332	969	594
g.v. agri'ture	342	416	357	264	252	332	305
retail sales	912	338	316	216	203	312	278
(sales/output	.15	.25	.31	.37	.36	.25	.31)

Notes and source: The abbreviation "g.v." means gross value. Three zone provinces are asterisked; their flatlands were the zone's "first layer." In order of per capita wealth, the ranking of provinces in the Shanghai Economic Zone is Shanghai, Jiangsu, Zhejiang, Jiangxi, Anhui. That is also (with an interesting reversal of Anhui and Jiangxi) the order of the rate of fiscal remittances to government, or also the degree of vertical economic integration. (To estimate this last: The national income figure approximates a sum of values added, but the gross output figures involve extensive double-counting of values added. Their ratio roughly estimates vertical integration.) The retail sales figure is the *shehui shangpin lingshou zong'e*. The last line of the table, a portion of retail sales in gross output, has been computed from the source and shows an inverse relation between provincial productivity and the rate at which value can be retained there. *Shanghai jingji qu fazhan zhanlue chutan* (Preliminary Research on the Development Strategy of the Shanghai Economic Zone), World Economic Herald and Shanghai Economic Zone Research Society, co-eds. (Shanghai: Wuxi Branch of Shanghai Eighth People's Printers, 1986), 50, a book that was "distributed" (*faxing*) not on a "confidential" limited-circulation (*neibu*) basis but also without public sale.

and taxes. Shanghai's expanded 1984 economic zone was larger than the previous version, but also less coherent. It had a population of 200 million, 19 percent of China's people; and at mid-decade, this area's industrial and agricultural output value was 29 percent of China's total.[104] In comparison with the earlier and smaller zone, Shanghai was now being asked by the central government to ensure development for four times the number of people – but to do that with an increase of resources less than twice as much. This was not, at first face, a very good deal; so in practice, it did not last. Horizontal mutual advantages, not central decrees, determined fast or slow cooperation among areas. Regional plans were duly trumpeted, although they were implemented only insofar as they met local interests.

Especially in fields involving modern technology, competition among delta cities for investment was sharp. In the new and important optical fiber business, for example the Shanghai Economic Zone generally had China's best facilities. But each major city wanted to develop this field independently, and officials (as distinct from entrepreneurs) did not coordinate with each other; on the contrary, they reportedly "fought" each other.[105]

As conflicts among jurisdictions became evident, individual businesspeople could maneuver around obstacles that any of them presented. Conflicts between central politicians on the delta and inland provinces were among "high" leaders. Inland cadres often doubted that more industrialized areas paid enough for the materials their places sold.

Shanghai has for decades made major investments outside the city. In Anhui, up the Yangzi from Nanjing, the Ma'anshan Iron Mine was a major Shanghai project. So were several mines at the Huainan colliery, as well as other Anhui extractive projects. The municipality owned factories making semi-finished products for later work in Shanghai; but the usual purpose was to supply the metropolis with raw materials. Operating in low-cost areas brought advantages. Factories owned by the city but located outside it together in 1980 sold as much output as each of six Shanghai counties did.[106] But by 1985, partly because of inland localizations of ownership, only three counties produced less than Shanghai's investments outside the municipality.[107] This localization came from political pressure by resurgent low-tax provinces to process their own resources during reforms.

Complaints against Shanghai imperialism

Anhui was a leading supplier of industrial raw materials. From 1952 to 1983, sixty percent of its coal production and one-third of its pig iron left the province.[108] During the 1970s, Shanghai invested in several PLA-related industries there; but these proved unprofitable because even the Army did not want their products. These plants were disbanded, but the employees were not all dismissed; some found new jobs in Shanghai. Relations between Shanghai and Anhui – both official and individual – were complex. Some concerns between Anhui and Shanghai were complementary, but the metropolis was usually dominant. Provincial leaders elsewhere understandably feared becoming dependent.

This kind of tension was not new. A governor of Zhejiang during the Cultural Revolution was irate about the "unified management and distribution" of hydroelectric power from Zhejiang's Xin'an Dam to Shanghai, where the main East China electric authority was located. In 1969 he reportedly said, "If I get mad enough, I can destroy it [the dam] with an atom bomb." He summed up his complaint by declaring, "Zhejiang is not a colony of Shanghai."[109]

A professor from Anhui grumbled in the mid-1980s that his province produced raw materials that were processed elsewhere (notably Shanghai), and then sold as finished goods back to Anhui at high prices. He demanded that "Shanghai, Jiangsu, and other developed provinces" give Anhui more technical support in return.[110] He particularly suggested that Shanghai move its old equipment inland; so these places could develop and the metropolis could start new lines of business. A great many bridges, railways, and canals had been constructed in his province – as he put it, "built in Anhui, located in Anhui, but by no means just for the benefit of Anhui."[111] On the contrary, these facilities were mostly designed to take his province's minerals elsewhere.

A deputy mayor of Huaibei, Anhui, complained that his city's mining bureau sold in 1983 almost a million tons of coal to Shanghai. But because of high production and transport costs – and a low state-fixed price for coal – Anhui lost 0.57 yuan on each ton. In the next year, Huaibei sold ten percent more to Shanghai; so it lost more money. As this Anhui local leader complained, the price of Shanghai products was high.[112] In fact, the metropolis did not profit much from such transactions because of its tax rate; the central government was making the money. But from the viewpoint of Huaibei as an inland East China city, Shanghai looked like a colonial metropole. At a 1988 meeting of 10,000 Anhui cadres, a provincial Party secretary said that Anhui would "study" Guangdong and Fujian far away, and Jiangsu and Zhejiang nearby – pointedly leaving out Shanghai.[113] In an article about Anhui's relation to the Shanghai Economic Zone, the provincial governor in 1985 slyly averred that Anhui was only a "Third World" place, without much technical capacity. But, as he said, it had many resources that coastal areas lacked.[114]

Technical cooperation between Shanghai and Jiangxi, though subject to some of the same pressures, seems to have progressed more smoothly during reforms. The oddly named "Sincere Discussion Society to Vitalize Jiangxi" and the "Shanghai Research Association to Vitalize Jiangxi" got together in the metropolis for a meeting, which was attended by notables from both places.[115] Technical cooperation projects were at the center of these discussions. The meeting was held among units that had not been created by central fiat from Beijing, and its explicit goal was to spur "horizontal liaisons" (*hengxiang lianhe*) between Shanghai and Jiangxi. For Shanghai, the payoff was raw materials supplies; and for Jiangxi, new technologies.

The viability of each connection depended on two traits of any particular proposal: whether local leaders or large bureaucracies would run the management, and the extent to which benefits would go to contributing participants. Governments in provinces, but also in smaller localities, did not always cooperate with each other easily. "In terms of ecology, artificial boundaries within the delta led to bad results, and these lines made it impossible to have a unified plan. An example was water. A program to control the level of Lake Tai was on the agenda for several years, but because it involved many offices and local governments, a unified plan was not agreed."[116] The Jiangsu-Zhejiang border follows the lake's shore, and provincial and local authorities could not easily agree on procedures for controlling the water level. Lacking a consensus, each jurisdiction did as it pleased.

There is evidence that provincial authorities in Nanjing were less eager for close cooperation with Shanghai than were many entrepreneurs nearer to the metropolis within Jiangsu. The campaign for industrial reforms led to a multi-province meeting, held at Zhenjiang, which resolved "to energetically improve southern Jiangsu and speedily develop northern Jiangsu." The southern (Sunan) area was the site of most past economic successes and current potentials. Its bureaucrats were urged to "break free from the limits of administrative divisions" within the province, especially to "step up port construction."[117]

Yangzi River cities could and did develop deep-sea maritime facilities, and they sought international help in these projects. The Nanjing International Container Shipping Company, established in late 1987, was a joint enterprise of the Nanjing Harbor Administration and the International Corporation of Alameda, California, which leased a container pier equipped with big cranes and the latest Wang computers.[118] Because of its decades-old role as a tax farm, the port of Shanghai had trouble competing with such improvements elsewhere.

Nanjing bureaucrats wanted to unify their province, roughly split by the Yangzi. In 1988, Jiangsu authorities developed a plan to improve Wuxi communications with northern parts of the province by means of a bridge across the Yangzi at Jiangyang.[119] Realization of this concept was delayed, however. By the early 1990s, a "Sunan development area" was defined by Nanjing/Jiangsu authorities as excluding Shanghai.[120] Official boundaries did not, however, allow links that Jiangnan people had. Local ties span the Shanghai-Jiangsu border – whose current location is an administrative whim no more ancient than 1959. This line has no cultural meaning. Shanghai was, in imperial times, part of Jiangsu. Provincial officials on both sides pretended the border was important, but people living near it have no such notion. The delta, the flat part of the Yangzi floodplain where people speak Shanghainese, is for them the natural unit.

Local cities' concerns and the zone

Zhejiang provincial authorities were more eager than those of Jiangsu in 1988 to make liaisons with Shanghai. The mayor of Hangzhou made a speech calling for closer links, praising the large metropolis as "head of the dragon" in the Yangzi, and proposing Hangzhou-Ningbo-Shanghai cooperation to create an export zone with fewer regulations. He also suggested that joint ventures, materials trades, and technical and personnel exchanges be "intensified," as had happened in newly prosperous areas of Guangdong that are near Hong Kong.[121]

Officials in the province-level municipality (as in the central government) made less definite statements on what and where the Shanghai Economic Zone should be. What actually happened showed that these ranking leaders were largely irrelevant. After 1984, especially in 1986, Shanghai's trade with both Jiangsu and Zhejiang accelerated very quickly – at 40 to 60 percent per year according to one economist's estimate. Businesspeople could interpret mandates from on high in whatever ways best served themselves. They could find like-minded government officials to support them. By 1985, the Shanghai Economic Association (Shanghai Shih Jingji Xuehui) sponsored the publication of a series of glossy books covering the whole economic zone, with detailed maps of counties, full lists of products and factories whence they could be obtained, complete with pictures and company telephone numbers.[122]

Subprovincial units, whose leaders obtained their jobs locally, cooperated readily with each other. Members of the Changzhou City Planning Commission in mid-1984 expressed pleasure at deals done among their city, eight others, and Shanghai firms. They expressed confidence that Changzhou would be able to develop its own specialties within the region, especially in specific kinds of cloth and machines. Shanghai was expected to contribute technical expertise. But the Changzhou planners did not speak of major new investments to come from Shanghai, presumably because the metropolis's publicly solicitable money was still limited by demands from Beijing – and Changzhou had resources of its own. Some money as well as designs and personnel came from Shanghai. These Changzhou officials did not mention that Nanjing (their provincial capital) also has more centralist economic planners.[123]

Shanghai's urban districts established "brotherly" relationships with twenty-nine subprovincial cities and at least five counties in the economic zone during the mid-1980s; and Shanghai's rural counties set up links with twenty "fraternal counties" inland. It is interesting that associated counties were fraternal (*xiongdi*), while universities were always sisterly (*jiemei*). It was unmentioned which were elder (*xiong* or *jie*), and which younger (*di* or *mei*) – though perhaps Shanghai negotiators were suave enough to keep their viewpoint on that to themselves.[124] Family links, in any case, were deemed politically strong. Families are the polities that have most "Chinese characteristics." The municipal government, part of the state-family (*guojia*) was supposed to approve such connections; it claimed the parental role. But Shanghai individuals with particular interests in other places were the actual initiators. Nongovernmental organizations established most such ties.

The Yangpu District Science and Technology Association, for example, organized nearly 10,000 engineers and technicians to help other places in East China. This association set up twenty-eight work groups in functional fields like chemical engineering, food processing, machinery, electronics, and bicycles.[125] A primary kind of cooperation between Shanghai and hinterland places was technical cooperation run by local leaders.

A second kind aimed at getting materials for the city's factories. Shanghai enterprises organized "compensation trade"; firms in the city exchanged money and

296 Traders and Jiangnan regionalists

expertise for factors or out-processing. By 1985, the metropolis had financed 304 projects in the Shanghai Economic Zone to exploit raw materials or labor sources. More than fifty kinds of inputs were involved, including coal, cement, iron, pig iron, nonferrous metals, and inputs for light and chemical industries.[126] Investments flowed in various directions. By 1987, units from other provinces ran more than 800 factories and shops in Shanghai with gross revenues of 1,130 million yuan. Shanghai, for its part, financed 579 projects in other provinces that got raw materials for the city at a cost of more than 800 million yuan. The value of materials obtained from these plants during that single year was, at quickly rising prices, fully half as much as the city's investment.[127]

A third kind of cooperation with subprovincial localities was based on the market value of Shanghai brands. Inland places provided factories and inputs to make Shanghai-labeled products – and reap more money for Shanghai companies that franchised them. Capital seeks low labor costs in socialist economies, as it does in capitalist ones. In the first nine months of 1985, joint ventures between Shanghai and all of China's other provinces were estimated to have raised the total market value of their products by about two billion yuan.[128]

A fourth kind of local cooperation involves professional liaisons. For example, 120 enterprises under the Shanghai First Electronics Bureau by 1985 established "mid- or long-term fixed cooperation links" with 300 units outside the city. A fifth kind of cooperation emerged when enterprises were financed by different jurisdictions together, either to avoid high taxes in Shanghai or to raise more capital. Sixth, scientific research institutes in the metropolis established profitable relations with inland companies; and by the mid-1980s, over 1,000 links existed between specific Shanghai academic institutions and factories elsewhere. A seventh kind of cooperation involved the opening, by outside jurisdictions, of stores inside Shanghai. By the end of 1985, almost 700 such companies had been registered, of which 25 percent were retail outlets designed to sell local specialties of their areas (which presumably did not compete with Shanghai products), 5 percent were service firms largely in consulting, 11 percent sold machines and building materials, 28 percent were in tourism or transport, and 31 percent sold garments and general goods that almost surely competed with Shanghai firms. Possibly because of resistance from retailers in the big city, only 326 of the approved companies actually opened. Among these, 59 percent were financed entirely from elsewhere, and the remaining 41 percent got some of their capital from the metropolis. Local investment in them was possible, despite their competition with Shanghai firms. Many of the managers were Shanghai residents with personal ties to the outside places that owned these firms.[129]

Companies that stood to benefit established such arrangements. The Shanghai Light Industrial Machines Corporation spurred horizontal links with three particular counties of Jiangsu. Its "one city, three counties" committee in the mid-1980s involved the Shanghai corporation with counterparts in Wuxi, Shazhou, and Wujin.[130] This form of organization was novel as a publicized model, because it was coordinated at the administrative levels of corporations and counties. Each such unit was under a different mid-level jurisdiction.

Local officials increasingly acted like commercial boosters, as reforms made Shanghai's border with south Jiangsu less hermetic. The head of Kunshan County in Jiangsu Province, Wu Kequan, called in July 1988 for more economic cooperation with Shanghai – and no fence could have effectively separated these contiguous places anyway. He pointed out that Jiading and Qingpu counties, by then in Shanghai Municipality, used to be subordinate to Kunshan – a city just forty minutes from Shanghai by train. One-third of the 1,500 nonprivate enterprises in Kunshan by 1988 were "horizontal liaison projects" (*hengxiang lianhe xiangmu*). Sixty percent of these "liaised" with Shanghai. Kunshan cooperated with the Shanghai Textile Bureau, establishing export firms that sent cloth to twenty foreign countries. The Kunshan branch of the Shanghai First Television Plant regenerated its full capital within thirty months. A Kunshan politician expressed a hope that his county would become the "supporting actor" in the "backyard" (*houyuan*) of Shanghai's outward development.[131] Such terms suggest a strong sense in Kunshan of reliance on the metropolis. There was scant conflict between this Jiangsu place and its big neighbor.

Links flourished throughout China in the mid-1980s, although the flatland of the Shanghai Economic Zone was arguably the densest regional concentration. In the whole country during late 1986, there were 65,000 registered "economic liaison organizations" (*jingji lianhe zuzhi*). In addition, China at this time had seventy-five "economic cooperation zones" (*jingji hezuo qu*), of which the Shanghai Economic Zone in its large form, while it lasted, was the most populous. The aims of cooperation included raising productivity and gathering similar enterprises into groups, as well as technical help and investments.[132]

Such extensive regionalism and localism entailed problems too. First, central and provincial governments that oversaw firms creating new "horizontal" entities generally remained reluctant to commit their scarcest resources (raw materials, capital, foreign exchange, or land) to cross-jurisdiction enterprises if their own companies needed these resources. Second, traditions of appointing cadres who promised high central remittances, especially from Shanghai, reduced incentives for some governments to approve horizontal ventures outside their borders – unless that was necessary to obtain inputs – since taxes on production elsewhere seldom went to local coffers. Third, cross-provincial enterprises suffered from a lack of laws to protect them. These problems were counterbalanced by the benefits of less bureaucratic interference and less tax-or-profit extraction. The inadequate legal regime was, to some extent, replaced by networks of personal relationships between local leaders.[133]

Kinds of zones

Economic zones were a national trend by 1984, and all large regions pressed or were pressed to create them. The list of new zones in the mid-1980s is impressive on paper:

> Some zones came out of various equal negotiations, from the regions below upward; an example is the Southwest Economic Coordinating Association....

Some are second- or third-rank economic zones. By June 1986, there were 30 such economic associations. . . . Ten first-level economic areas can be identified: the Shanghai Economic Zone, including Shanghai, Jiangsu, Zhejiang, Anhui, and Jiangxi; the Northeast Economic Zone, including Liaoning, Heilongjiang, Jilin, and a part of Inner Mongolia; the North China Economic Zone, including Beijing, Tianjin, and Hebei; the Shandong Economic Zone; the Southeast Economic Zone, including Guangdong, Fujian and Guangxi; the Central China Economic Zone, including Hubei, Hunan and Henan; the Shanxi-centered energy base area; the Northwest Economic Zone, including Shaanxi, Gansu, Qinghai and Ningxia; the Xinjiang Economic Zone; and the Southwest Economic Zone, including Sichuan, Yunnan, Guizhou, Tibet and Chongqing.[134]

What the new economic administrations meant, however, differed enormously from zone to zone. Each was subject to flexible interpretation, not just by the central government but also by local networks and their leaders.

The notion of extended and empowered "zones" was by no means restricted to coastal areas. The same concept was instituted in many different sections of China. Sichuan's Chongqing was supposed to coordinate an economic zone extending into Yunnan. (Chongqing was Sichuan's largest city until it became a province-level municipality like Shanghai. The provincial capital is Chengdu, where reformer Zhao Ziyang ruled from 1975 for four years.) Wuhan in Hubei was to be the industrial center of a "Central China Economic Zone." Shanghai was to be the dynamo of the zone that bore its name.[135] These regional zones were encouraged from Beijing, although few finally had strong permanent effects in their areas.

The zones were not identical, and they were classified in somewhat different official categories. Each was centered on a large metropolis and was conceived as a "comprehensive economic zone" (*zonghe jingji qu*), supposed to develop all kinds of goods and services. The Shanghai Economic Zone was of this type, in centralist imaginings of it. But the Guangdong and Fujian special areas were officially supposed to be only "sectoral economic zones" (*bumen jingji qu*), specializing in external finance (partly because of Fujian's ancestral connections to Taiwan, and Guangdong's to Hong Kong). Other zones could be devoted to other sectors. The economic zone Northeast China specialized in coal and electricity, already fortes there.[136] Shaanxi's comparative advantage was in energy and heavy industry. Even impoverished Guizhou was dubbed a "sectoral economic zone" to develop coal mining. Zones were a publicized fad during China's reforms, but not all zones were created equal even when they were centrally approved.

"Comprehensive" economic zones, such as Shanghai's, shared a strength that reflected the importance of informal networks in their regions. They contrasted with sectoral economic zones, whose head offices acquired powers to plan production in definitive, legal, mandatory ways. But the head offices of comprehensive economic zones were only supposed to "harmonize (*xietiao*) relations between other agencies," including geographical jurisdictions.[137] If one of these preferred not to cooperate on any issue, a comprehensive zone's leaders could do little to bring it into line. This difference was clear in documents, and it emerged from the actual potentials of different areas owing to their geographical locations and pre-existing resources.

The Shanghai Economic Zone was comprehensive; but unlike comprehensive zones centered on Wuhan or Chongqing, it was also coastal. It was supposed to have a major role in attracting foreign capital, but it continued to pay higher taxes than zones in Guangdong or Fujian that were specialized for different aims and had much lower imposts. This difference was not lost on external investors. For the Shanghai zone, something more than "comprehensiveness" was needed to bring in serious amounts of capital. Eventually, in the 1990s, Pudong (former Chuan-sha County) received benefits that made development more profitable there. Such change came only after central conservatives realized, after 1989, that China's new industrial structure would not allow Shanghai to perform as much of its previous role for the central budget.

The Shanghai Economic Zone was never dubbed "special" (*tebie*, like Shenz-hen), despite hopes among local entrepreneurs it might become so. Zhang Jingfu, an important central economic bureaucrat, visited Guangdong in 1983, shortly after Shanghai had been given more autonomy to approve larger foreign invest-ments. As he explained to his Cantonese audience, "This autonomy has a special meaning." He likened Chen Yun's "bird-in-a-cage" image of a semi-constrained socialist market economy to a situation that he idealized for Shanghai: "Within this 'cage,' we would loosen the 'strings.' However, the 'cage' has limits. We are not loosening the 'strings' in an abstract way. . . . In special economic zones, you [in Guangdong] have definitely more power than Shanghai."[138]

Shanghai firms received no import or export tariff preferences, few national subsidies to start new industries, and tax breaks only when such benefits could be arranged on a project-by-project basis. If there had been anything "special" about the Shanghai Economic Zone, it might have lasted as a more powerful organiza-tion. The name was a fishing license, but the pool was not stocked. After 1989, the Shanghai Economic Zone existed mainly on paper. It had no permanent status. When it became a central project, it never got off the ground. The zone did not die with fanfare, but it faded away.

Other zones dissipated similarly. Regional-functional groupings lasted, the most famous of which were in aviation. Shanghai-based China Eastern Airlines, like regional counterparts elsewhere, began after bad publicity about accidents of the national carrier, CAAC, brought its demise. Few developing countries have more than one international carrier, but China became an exception. By the spring of 1990, China Eastern Airlines flew not just domestically, but also to Hong Kong and four cities in Japan. It had thirty new aircraft on order, and it advertised that its maintenance engineers were reliable and "most of the fleet's captains were trained in foreign countries."[139]

300 Traders and Jiangnan regionalists

The practical demise of the Shanghai Economic Zone

Most reforms arose separately from the state's efforts to regulate it in zones. The plan for the Shanghai Economic Zone, as finally reformulated in 1987, remained long-term and vague. Shanghai was designated in State Council documents as the center of the region, and closer cooperation among its participating units was mandated "by 1990."[140] Central politicians wanted to protect their most important fiscal base, but they had insufficient wealth or power to ensure this by either contracts or plans. "Harmonization" in East China – when centrally organized – did not work harmoniously because in the end it meant taxes. Local harmonization, outside the central system, worked well because it was based on pre-existing or new connections between individual local elites in Shanghai and other parts of Jiangnan.

High agencies of the state gradually turned over their interests in regional trade to local officials and entrepreneurs, whether they wished to do so or not. An odd announcement proclaimed that official "industry cooperation networks" around Shanghai were already "basically established" by early 1988.[141] These were mainly calls for periodic meetings between economic leaders in East China provinces that were supposed to cooperate. They conferred, but it is unclear whether they had sufficient consensus to bring economic results that would not have occurred on the basis of local interests anyway. Shanghai top officials agreed to these meetings when the city's tax contribution was declining. Because more local Shanghai and other interests prevailed to determine which interprovincial economic links flourished, centralist politics in this era had limited effects. After 1989, China changed. Localism was then reversed, and centralism gained.

The Shanghai Economic Zone still survived formally, but its name was mainly used for junkets and conferences. The idea of the zone was somewhat useful in luring external capital. Already in April 1988, a Shanghai zone delegation visited Hong Kong, trying to strengthen cooperation in electronics, computers, textiles, toys, microwave ovens, and sound equipment. By this time, Hong Kong had infused US$440,000 into Shanghai – a total that was second only to the American investment there.[142] So one purpose of the zone was to garner external investment. But different – and conflicting – ideas came into different Party leaders' statements about the Shanghai Economic Zone, as it declined. The hope of using Shanghai's industrial base to raise hard currency from foreign investment, imports, and exports was similar to that in the newer "special economic zones" of Shenzhen, Zhuhai, and Xiamen.

Shanghai–Hong Kong links grew faster than Shanghai-Shenzhen economic connections. There was some flow of Shanghai people to Shenzhen, but there was scant flow of information or projects. Compared with other provinces' agencies in Shenzhen, the ones from Shanghai were relatively constrained by administrative rules, and they lacked "management autonomy." Shanghai representatives were said to be bound by "old attitudes" that made them unfit for competition. In Shenzhen, "a majority of Shanghai firms lacked rights" to import and export as freely as other companies there did, and they "were run only like administrative offices."

They tended to be there less for business than as "travel reception stations" (*lüyou jiedai zhan*). Although offices in Shenzhen from most provinces operated under Shenzhen laws, the supervising agencies in Shanghai restricted branches more than did those from other areas. Shanghai's businesses had deficient "management autonomy" (*jingying zizhu quan*).[143]

A concurrent and basically different concept of the zone, however, was that the metropolitan industrial center of Shanghai might generate entrepreneurial energy to make the economies of China's hinterlands more efficient. Economic advisers to Zhao Ziyang hoped that market centers might break the habit of backward-looking provincial cadres running their own administrative "kingdoms." Less regulation might weaken companies' links to vertical networks of planners that stifled trade. Large areas might be made more efficient, if they were more accountable to advanced cities. Naturally enough, powerful local cadres in recently rural places did not like that suggestion. Many localists were conservative.

Regional market efficiency and regional specialization throughout the reform years

Jiangsu and Zhejiang had faster growth than China's other provinces during the first decade of reforms, even as early as 1972–1973. These provinces, together with Shanghai help, maintained this record into the 1990s – but not thereafter. This change mainly reflected wonderful growth for places further inland, and it is a credit to China as a whole. The rightmost column in Table 11.2 roughly shows

TABLE 11.2 Yangzi delta growth rates, in national perspective (billions of yuan of gross reported output value, and percentage changes) (PRC, Shanghai-Jiangsu-Zhejiang, all other provinces, and a ratio)

Year	National	Change	3 Prov.	Change	Oth. Prov.	Change	3P/Oth
1970	380.0	19.35%	72.2	13.17%	307.8	20.90%	0.63
71	420.3	10.61%	79.8	10.53%	340.5	10.62%	0.99
72	439.6	4.59%	86.0	7.77%	353.6	3.85%	2.02
73	477.6	8.64%	93.5	8.72%	384.1	8.63%	1.01
74	485.9	1.74%	94.6	1.14%	391.3	1.88%	0.61
75	537.9	10.70%	100.8	6.59%	437.1	11.70%	0.56
76	543.3	1.00%	104.6	3.77%	438.7	0.37%	–
77	600.3	10.49%	115.9	10.80%	484.4	10.42%	1.04
78	684.6	14.04%	134.6	16.13%	550.0	13.54%	1.19
79	764.2	11.63%	155.2	15.30%	609.0	10.73%	1.43
80	853.4	11.67%	174.7	12.56%	678.7	11.44%	1.10
81	907.5	6.34%	187.8	7.50%	719.7	6.04%	1.24
82	996.6	9.82%	202.5	7.82%	794.1	10.34%	0.76
83	1113.1	11.69%	222.6	9.93%	890.5	12.14%	0.82
84	1317.1	18.33%	267.1	19.99%	1050.0	17.91%	1.12

(*Continued*)

302 Traders and Jiangnan regionalists

TABLE 11.2 Continued

Year	National	Change	3 Prov.	Change	Oth. Prov.	Change	3P/Oth
85	1658.2	25.90%	345.2	29.24%	1313.0	25.05%	1.17
86	1904.5	14.85%	404.8	17.26%	1499.7	14.22%	1.21
87	2303.4	20.95%	497.7	22.96%	1805.7	20.40%	1.13
88	2980.7	29.40%	644.3	29.46%	2336.4	29.39%	1.00
89	3460.4	16.09%	698.6	8.43%	2761.8	18.21%	0.46
90	3799.6	9.80%	791.3	13.27%	3008.3	8.92%	1.49
91	4380.3	15.28%	920.8	16.37%	3459.5	15.00%	1.09

Notes and sources: Growth in Shanghai Municipality was usually lower than in Jiangsu and Zhejiang. Outputs are at current prices. Data come or are calculated from *Zhongguo tongji nianjian, 1991* 47, and 1992 edition, 47; *Shanghai tongji nianjian, 1991*, 39, and 1992 edition, 38; *Zhejiang tongji nianjian, 1991*, 27, and 1992 edition, 21; and *Jiangsu tongji nianjian, 1991*, 27, and 1992 edition, 27.

the ratio of Shanghai delta output growth over other provinces' rates. From 1970, this ratio jumped sharply. The relatively high rate of Shanghai growth as early as 1972 – the highest figure in the right-hand column – reflects the early-1970s start of reforms in coastal growth.[144] Reliable figures are more difficult to obtain for 1965–1970 industrial production. In 1974–1975 the index comparing the three East China provinces with all others was again low; but by 1978–1990, it converged to somewhat more stable rates between 1.0 and 1.5, dipping below this range in only three years.

A reason for these three provinces' good performance is that they traded with each other. Even during the early 1980s, when Shanghai's total retail sales of manufactures scarcely changed, the city participated in more interprovincial trade than most parts of China. The number of contracts for a wide variety of consumer goods that Shanghai enterprises signed in the second half of 1982 with other PRC companies was 48 percent of the national total.[145] Maoist policies had not uniformly discouraged trade. On the contrary, they had encouraged inter-jurisdiction trade that could be controlled and taxed. When inputs to a production process could not be monitored, for example because of factors' dispersed sources, non-bulkiness, or low costs of extraction capital, then planning reduced trade when it was enforced. Such commodities were many, and their increased production was a major aspect of reforms.

"Large and complete" (*da er quan*) self-sufficiency was not a reform ideal, but it was built into Shanghai's economic institutions because of high taxes and low funding to finance new investment. Among 164 kinds of industries that were categorized for all of China in the mid-1980s, Shanghai had 90 percent of those types. This was a low degree of specialization.[146] Shanghai made everything from steel to buttons – though other places clearly could make some things better. Mineral industries were practically the sole ones that Shanghai lacked, because of its sandy sedimentary ground. Shanghai reform economists argued against the tradition of comprehensiveness. Not everything, they thought, should be "crammed into" their city. Because this had been attempted, the "special characteristics" of the local economy and its comparative advantages were reduced. Furthermore, this tradition in Shanghai had given a bad example to other places, which also wanted to engage in all kinds of production, so that they would "not need to ask people for anything" ('*wanshi bu qiu ren*').[147] But that policy loses efficiencies of comparative advantage.

Reforms were most productive when they specialized production locally. An economist quantified this by calculating a ratio, e.g., for any commodity, of the per capita output in any province divided by the per capita output in the rest of China. If this quotient is exactly 1, there is no local specialization; if it is greater than 1, the place specializes; and if it is less, then other places specialize in that product. Over time, if the ratio increases and is greater than 1 (or decreases and is less than 1), then specialization is rising. These tests have been made for Jiangsu. It is no surprise that specialization continues in commodities for which Jiangsu has been traditionally famous. For silk, the ratio was 4.4 in 1988 – very high for this statistic. But anti-specialist policies of encouraging "self-reliance" (*zili gengsheng*) for many years affected Jiangsu. In practically all commodities for which the ratio could be calculated in both 1957 and 1970, it moved closer to 1.0 between those years, showing that the province became less specialized in Mao's time.[148] But the start of reforms brought a new story.

Comparing 1970 with 1978, the movement of about half the commodity ratios showed increased specialization – showing that reforms in the early 1970s moved toward specialized production, reversing the previous trend. In the next decade, between 1978 and 1988, this kind of comparison showed continuation of the 1970–1978 movement; about half the goods evinced higher specialization over both these reform periods.[149] None had shown this between 1957 and 1970. Of about fifteen products, paper was the sole exception in which Jiangsu "specialized" between 1957 and 1970 by producing less and importing more; Jiangsu had few exploitable forests. In 1978–1988, the number of commodities for which the ratio indicated more specialization was roughly the same as in 1970–1978; but for some commodities, the degree of Jiangsu's specialized production became great: radios, 9.9; woolens, 5.2; synthetic fibers, 5.0; pesticides, 4.0; and small tractors, 3.0. For small tractors, the 1988 ratio implied less specialization, relative to other provinces, than Jiangsu had in 1978 (although the 1978 figure implied more than in 1970).[150] All provinces needed tractors. The reform decades from 1970 spurred provincial specialization.

Trade, too, increased sharply. For example by 1984, Shanghai exported 25 percent more industrial products to other Chinese provinces than it had in 1978.[151] Comparative advantages increasingly structured this trade. Shanghai's contribution of products for daily use (*riyong gongye pin*) had been 19 percent in 1957; but because many places later found they had the resources to make these simple commodities, and the metropolis had comparative advantages in other fields, Shanghai's contribution of these utensils decreased to 10 percent by 1983.[152]

It would be too easy to interpret a rise of horizontal trade in terms of increased market or production efficiency alone. Not all of it was a matter of economic rationality, based on comparative advantages among different places. On the contrary, horizontal trade also arose in search of speculative profits based on artificial price differences, as central officials continued to resist scarcity prices so that they could maintain remittances from state factories. Economic change does not occur without agents, leaders.

Horizontal trade's contribution to efficiency nonetheless accounts for part of China's economic growth during reforms. As Audrey Donnithorne wrote in 1972, "China forms a Customs Union but not a Common Market. That is to say, the whole country has common trade barriers against the outside world, but it [also] does not have free trade within its national boundaries."[153] Reformers somewhat reduced the internal barriers. If factors, technology, labor, capital, and retail goods all flow more easily between different places, the result over time is greater production and consumption. The ultimate reasons for such growth involve both greater economies of scale and greater competition in marketing. It is hard to compute the increment of Yangzi delta growth that can be attributed to horizontal trade among the three provinces.[154] But that amount is very large, and regional integration raised it.

Very local transport and trade

The benefits of trade, during reforms, went increasingly to local leaders rather than to state bureaucrats. "Whereas Europe is pursuing an integrated and supra-national market, China still has its 'kingdom economy' (*wangguo jingji*)," according to Shanghai's *World Economic Herald* in 1988. "Recently, while we are having our economy decentralized [localized], such 'kingdom segments' or 'feudal segments' have become more serious. . . . Local authorities try to have dominant influence and put up protective fences."[155]

In some rural areas of East China, counties charged "fees for road upkeep" (*yan-glu fei*) that truck drivers paid. In one Anhui region, an official regulation specified that only one such impost could be made on any vehicle – but in practice, that rule did not effectively prevent counties and cities from charging more than once.[156] A Chinese interviewee reported taking a short pleasure trip in 1988 on back roads from Shanghai to Suzhou, through one of China's richest areas, and he was stopped four times for "tolls." Such impositions on trucks, especially in inland provinces such as Anhui, were reportedly frequent.

Regional disintegration of trade and investment created an "economy of dukes" (*zhuhou jingji*). This troll-at-the-bridge school of management, as in the 'billy goat gruff' story, advocated collecting what economists less colorfully call rents. It was localist and not market-efficient, but in many places during reforms it was common. Central and provincial bureaucrats espoused a more modern school of economics, but this mainly meant they wanted rents collected by larger jurisdictions instead. Their tolls were high too. Local reformers' commitment was to local profits, not to national market efficiency. They did, at least, support a good deal of labor and enterprise.

Trade requires conveyances. Water transport remained crucial to growth on the delta, as it had been for centuries. Aside from the Yangzi, the main inland/westward waterway from Shanghai was toward Suzhou, and the Party newspaper overenthusiastically claimed Suzhou 'Creek' had a history of "more than 6000 years."[157] A 1930s survey already reported "28,000 native cargo boats" in Shanghai's harbor. Other boat censuses by Chinese and Japanese researchers before 1949 indicated well over 100,000 junks in the Yangzi delta – then about two-thirds of the nation's total.[158] With reforms and more rural production, this system had a resurgence of use. Shanghai's canal network carried a large portion of total trade, though not all was reported. Local newspapers praised the modern cost-efficiency of the ancient waterways. At least two major routes, through lakes west of Shanghai, had very heavy use. From 1980 to 1988, the traffic on these arteries rose at least 6 percent annually (an increase of about three-fifths in those years alone, for reported tonnage). In the middle of the decade, the average daily number of barge ships on nearby waterways was more than 4,000, carrying 46 million metric tons. Canals brought more weight to and from Shanghai than railroads did.

Lines of boats, pulled by a tug, were called "waterborne trains" (*shuishang lieche*). They had dominated Yangzi delta shipping since official moves to collectivize local boat people in the 1950s. Monitoring the transport of raw materials to the metropolis was, from the government's viewpoint, a prerequisite to planning. Pressure on "boat" families to take up shore residence (and educate their children in schools on land) had therefore been intense – and probably was effective only because state-subsidized tugboats put individually powered vessels at a cost disadvantage until boat people bought more motors.[159] This 'subethnic' community was proletarian, and the Cultural Revolution had taught them not to respect cadres too much.

The volume of reported boat transport in Shanghai Municipality rose between 1976 and 1982 by 17 percent, although this report almost surely understates the increase. The average distance of haulage became longer, so that the weekly number of ton-kilometers rose 55 percent in this period (according to a source that was officially supposed to remain confidential).[160] The beginning of this rise in regional trade preceded the 1978 announcement of reforms. Private transport firms (*geti yunshu hu*) continued to grow quickly in the 1980s, using trucks as well as boats.[161] These companies crossed provincial borders; and by the late 1980s, boats from Jiangsu, Zhejiang, and Anhui accounted for 37 percent of the tonnage on Shanghai's inland rivers. They carried mainly construction materials, coal, nonferrous ores, and other industrial and agricultural inputs.

The economic efficiency of water transport was its decisive advantage. Capital costs for railroads or highways were far higher. Many of the canals had been dug long ago, with conscripted labor, and they required scant new investment because their depreciation was slow, even though many were widened or dredged. Cost-efficiency was also impressive for the main operating expense, i.e., fuel. On a per-ton basis, water transport took 60 percent less energy than trains and 88 percent less than trucks. Land-use efficiency in waterways was also great, because the canals on

306 Traders and Jiangnan regionalists

the flatland doubled as sources of irrigation and fertilizer. Algae grow on still canal water (as on wet paddies), and they use solar energy to fix nitrogen from the air, then sinking; dredged mud is therefore fertilizer.[162] Each kilometer of railway, on the other hand, was estimated to remove more than 30 *mu* of land from any other use.

Finally, the size of loads on canals could be huge; a single barge could handle a larger weight than several railroad cars or many highway trucks. A standard large barge could, by one enthusiastic report, take more weight than a thousand of the small trucks most usual in rural Jiangnan.[163] The canals were a public good, initiated long ago. But when officials in the 1980s could not stop the re-emergence of collective and private boat transport, they lost a crucial means of planning Shanghai's economy.

A letter to the editor in the *Jiangsu Legal System News* in January 1989 complained that boat people asked for bribes, above the fixed transport prices, before they would agree to carry goods. For example, the price of hauling a ton from Xuzhou to Yancheng had been illegally raised in this way from 13 to 35 yuan. There were four basic problems, according to this analysis. First, the lawyer-writer alleged unfair competition. "Individual transport households," i.e., families on boats, used gifts to establish relationships with companies that needed to have goods hauled. These households were called *geti yunshu hu*, but apparently some were not legal individual-private enterprises (as *geti* implies), but were informally independent parts of state firms, collectives, larger private firms, or unregistered. The ambiguity of such a term actually adds clarity to what is being described; sharp lines among categories of ownership were not realistic in reform China, and differences within official categories were as important as differences among them. Since the state-fixed price for barge haulage was too low to inspire that service, boat people were able to arrange higher fees. The transporters had to pay tolls at the watergates of nine locks on the Xuzhou-Yancheng route. The amount of these payments inflated sharply during reforms. In 1982, a cheap pack of cigarettes was enough to get a boat through; but by the end of the decade, a 10-yuan bribe ('great solidarity', *da tuanjie*) was needed. A police newspaper had no need to define the phrase, since everybody knew it.[164] One side of the PRC 10-yuan note depicts a Han cadre, peasant worker, and soldier, standing before a crowd including costumed minority people, all in warm solidarity. But solidarity comes in local, not just national, forms. The state's slogan served small networks, as laws fell to humor and 10 yuan became the market's standard petty bribe price.

A second reason for inflation in haulage was that many land-based heads of transport companies let valued boat households receive gifts. These guarantors (*baocheng ren*) in transport companies "turned a blind eye" (*moxu*) on boat people accepting bribes.[165] A third cause was that the waiting time to open locks became longer, as local watchmen delayed service until fees were paid. In sum, boat transport became slower. Before the reforms, it was possible for a boat to ply this whole route twice in a month – but by the end of the 1980s, a hauler had to press for service at each lock, in order to make the trip just once a month. A fourth problem was that the boat people tended to "make chaos of the costs" (*luantan chengben*), refusing to haul unless they were offered much more than the state-fixed price. They demanded a "business fee" (*yewu fei*, which sounded valid despite its illegality). All these surcharges raised costs as local powers overwhelmed official ones. In 1990, the government announced a "Movement against Three Arbitraries," namely, capricious impositions of fees, fines, and contributions.[166] But a campaign was not enough to stop such habits.

"Horizontal liaisons" against the law

From nearby provinces, boats came to transport goods both legally and illegally. Shanghai firms needed inputs. In 1988, Shanghai waters were visited by 120,000 boats – more than during the previous year. Police tried to stop the smuggling, but "some parts of the harbor were very disorderly."[167] In 1987, seventy-two percent of all "crimes" on rivers were committed by boatmen from outside the city. More local smugglers may have known which police to pay.

At the end of 1988, "free-market" rice in Shanghai's island county of Chongming was supposed to be sold for only 0.7 or 0.8 yuan per catty; but in Qidong, Jiangsu, a short boat trip away, it could be sold for 1.3 yuan. So a traveler, who might transport 100 catties and who paid 0.8 yuan for the ferry ticket, could make a handsome profit of more than 50 yuan for taking this brief voyage.[168] In a temporary 1988 crackdown against such traffic, over 200 peasants, private entrepreneurs, state employees, and teachers were arrested for trading rice regularly out of Chongming. In the period of about a week, police confiscated some 360,000 catties of smuggled rice. The profits on this rice, moving out of a single Shanghai county during just a few days, would have exceeded 200,000 yuan. The total extent of Shanghai's unpublished boat trade is unknown, but it was large.

The government's "price basin" policies in Shanghai unintentionally financed wholesale smuggling:

> In 1988, the city's entire retail commodity value was 312 billion yuan, but 55 percent was purchased by non-Shanghai people in Shanghai. As a result, the contradiction between demand and supply rose. The government had to issue ration tickets for [local] people to get goods. So the Shanghai government spent several billion yuan to supply grain to outside people.[169]

Illegal transfers of industrial raw materials soared in Jiangnan as the 1990s approached. In the last month of 1988, there was a campaign to arrest illegal materials traders in Suzhou. One-third more unauthorized industrial traders were found than in a similar crackdown one year earlier. The rate of arrests for illegal transfers of bulk materials in Suzhou during the second half of 1988 rose five times over the previous year. The value of these black market inputs increased 2.5 times in 1988 alone.[170] Many arrested criminals had worked in the organizations from which they hijacked materials, so they were familiar with the ways to obtain these. Some were

308 Traders and Jiangnan regionalists

buyers from Zhejiang industries, and their business boomed: "The more they steal, the more bold they become" ('*yue tou, yue dan da*').[171]

Water transport remained crucial to Shanghai's expansion well into the 1990s at least, because the Ministry of Railways had bureaucratic arthritis. It was unable to handle the bulk haulage that East China's booming economy demanded. Public roads, when bureaucracies were responsible for them, were also insufficient until well after the reform years. So in 1992, less than 19 percent of the total tonnage of Shanghai trade came or left by railroad, and less than 32 percent by highway, but 49 percent by water.[172] Over the previous several years, the relative portion of tonnage by boat had risen. Railways and roads depended on medium and high-level officials. Canals, rivers, and the sea were available to anyone who had a boat.

Readers should not be surprised that a chapter centered on discussions of linkages among large areas should end with data on relatively short-haul canal traffic. Local nonstate commerce enabled China's reform prosperity at least as much as large-scale monitored commerce did.

Notes

1 "Three go to the place" (*san jiu di*) norms were: *jiudi qucai, jiudi jiagong, jiudi xiaoshou*.
2 These schools were named for the date of an essay by Mao, May 7, 1966.
3 This comes from interviews in Shanghai.
4 The term "rusticated youth" is standard for xiaxiang qingnian. Most were "educated youth" (*zhishi qingnian*).
5 The number of technicians was specified as 410,000 in SHJJNJ88, 11.
6 *Shijie xin jishu*, 195.
7 *Xin Zhongguo gongye jingji shi*, 361–63.
8 *Zhonghua Renmin Gonghe Guo jingji dashi ji*, 657.
9 *Chengshi wenti* (Urban Problems), January 1988, 25.
10 "Shanghai economic authority," called Shanghai jingji quan.
11 Lynn White, "The Road to Urumqi," op. cit.
12 The survey year was specified, but not the migration years. *Zhongguo 1986 nian 74 chengzhen*, 24.
13 *Gaojia laotou* is a term sardonically based on *gaojia guniang* (high-priced girls). I interviewed a researcher at the Shanghai Academy of Social Sciences.
14 *Hengxiang jingji*, 168–70.
15 Ibid., 174.
16 Tony Saich, *China's Science*, 41.
17 Ibid., 133.
18 Hanson C. K. Leung and Kam Wing Chan, "Chinese Regional Development Policies: A Comparative Reassessment," *Canadian Asian Studies Association*, Winnipeg, June 6, 1986, 41, quoting *Hong Kong Dagong bao*, June 29, 1984.
19 *Shanghai liudong renkou* (Shanghai's Floating Population), Shanghai Statistics Bureau, ed. (Shanghai: Zhongguo Tongji Chuban She, 1989), 187–197.
20 *RMRB*, October 7, 1978, quoted in Frank Leeming, *Rural China Today*, 116.
21 *Yige chengjiao xiangcun de jintian he mingtian*, 19–21.
22 A Shanghai interviewee, originally from Zhejiang, had seen his name in such a file, with data on other Shanghai contacts.
23 Dong Fureng, "The Wenzhou Model," 78.
24 Yao Shihuang, *Jin sanjiao de tansuo*, 35–68.
25 *Hengxiang jingji*, 22.

26 *FBIS*, November 20, 1984, 3, radio of November 20, for this and the next quotation.

27 Interviewees reported many "Shanghai-Suzhou XX [product] Lianying Chang,"

28 Interview with a Shanghai Social Sciences Academy economist.

29 *Fazhan zhong de hengxiang jingji lianhe* (Horizontal Economic Links in Development), Bureau for Economic System Reform, State Economic Commission, ed. (Beijing: Qiye Guanli Chuban She, 1986), 191.

30 *Shanghai qiye* (Shanghai Enterprise), February 1985, 12.

31 Cao Linzhang, *Shanghai shengchan*, 146.

32 Interview with a Shanghai economist who had personal experience with Suzhou leaders and Shanghai-Suzhou links.

33 *Hengxiang jingji*, 96, carries the story only to 1986.

34 *SHJJ*, April 1988, 63.

35 Interview with an economist, 1989.

36 Huang Weixin, *Economic Integration*, 83.

37 *Hengxiang jingji*, 143–45.

38 UNESCO in 2008 declared Kunqu (Kunshan melodies/arias/opera) an "intangible cultural heritage of humanity," www.unesco.org/culture/ich/en/RL/kun-qu-opera-00004.

39 For more on Kunshan, Andrew Marton, *China's Spatial Economic Development: Restless Landscapes in the Lower Yangzi Delta* (London: Routledge, 2000). Shanghai, a younger city than either Kunshan or Suzhou, was historically in Jiangsu.

40 Ibid., 22.

41 "*Baoban hunyin*," "*fengming lianhe.*" *Hengxiang jingji*, 243.

42 Ibid.

43 *Chengshi wenti*, 25.

44 *Jingji lianhe, buchang maoyi, kaidian banchang*, and *jishu xiezuo*, including unclear distinctions. *Hengxiang jingji*, 206.

45 *Hengxiang jingji*, 207.

46 *CD*, March 9, 1988, quoting World Economic Herald, for this and the previous quotation.

47 Zhejiang at this time ranked twelfth. Combining "directly ruled cities" with adjacent provinces renders a list of 26 jurisdictions. In the 1950s, after revolutionary centralization, the most productive per capita of these were less dense or previously Japanese-run places, in order: Heilongjiang, Liaoning, Inner Mongolia, Jilin, and the Hebei-Beijing-Tianjin combination. Hanson Leung and Kam Wing Chan, "Chinese Regional Development Policies," table 2.

48 Thomas Rawski, "The Economy of the Lower Yangtse Region, 1850–1980," 1985 essay sent by the author, 40.

49 *Chengshi wenti*, 24. The surprisingly high ranks, in total productivity, of Suzhou and Wuxi are confirmed by tables in *China: Urban Statistics, 1986, State Statistical Bureau, PRC, compiler* (Hong Kong: Longman, 1987). The crucial difference between Suzhou and Wuxi, on one hand, and the next-most-productive group (Guangzhou, Shenyang, and Wuhan) was the boom of Sunan rural industries. The population national ranks of Suzhou and Wuxi in 1986 were much lower. This information is relegated here to a footnote because the geographical areas from which such numbers are collected are based on official administrative borders. Some "cities" include larger portions of farmers than others. On that basis, within Jiangsu alone, many 1986 cities (Huaiyin, Yangzhou, Nantong, Yancheng, and Xuzhou in that order) were more populous than Suzhou, and another (Nanjing) was larger than Wuxi. Shanghai's official separation from Jiangsu is equally arbitrary. The fourth and fifth total production national ranks of Suzhou and Wuxi are high. In the next year or so, Wuxi's total production overtook Suzhou's. Compare James Scott, *Seeing Like a State: How Certain Schemes to Improve the Human Condition Have Failed* (New Haven: Yale University Press, 1998).

50 *Liaowang*, no. 5 (1987), 12.

51 Xu Yuanming and Ye Ding, *Tangqiao gongye hua zhi lu*, 40–41.

52 The number was forty-three out of ninety. *Shehui kexue zhanxian* (Social Science Front) 4 (1984).

53 In a pun, this *Ningbo bang* was urged to *bang Ningbo*; *JFRB*, October 20, 1988.

54 Shanghai de Ningbo ji renshi set up the Shanghai Shi Ningbo Jingji Jianshe Zujin Xie-hui, which was a *qunzhong tuanti*, not a branch of the state. *XMWB*, February 25, 1989.

55 *FBIS*, February 8, 1988, 28–29, reporting *JJRB*, January 14.

56 Compare Franz Schurmann, *Ideology and Organization in Communist China*.

57 *FBIS*, December 19, 1984, 4, radio of December 17.

58 *FBIS*, March 9, 1988, 33–36, reporting a journal of February 11.

59 *SHJJNJ88*, 160. The "overpass function" was called a *lijiao qiao*.

60 Tao Yongkuan, *Dali fazhan*, 27.

61 The Association was called the Zhigong Jixie for short. *SHJJNJ88*, 148.

62 *WHB*, October 27, 1979.

63 *Post*, August 29, 1988.

64 *CD*, October 10, 1988.

65 "*Lai Hu kaidian banchang*," *Shanghai jingji qu*, 316.

66 *SHJJNJ88*, 130, with slightly different figures on 144. These statistics report offices that had been officially acknowledged by the Shanghai Municipal Government; but others existed on informal bases.

67 *SHJJNJ88*, 32, 144–45. It is unclear whether such agreements had previously been signed with Jiangsu or Zhejiang.

68 "Connections work" is *lianxi gongzuo. Shanghai jingji nianjian, 1988*, 54.

69 *FBIS*, March 11, 1988, 30–31, radio of March 11.

70 Frank Leeming, *Rural China Today*, 116, citing a 1979 Jingji guanli article by Wang Gengjin and future Shanghai Mayor Zhu Rongji about flouting the plan – and Dwight Perkins about self-sufficiency.

71 Jean C. Oi, *State and Peasant*, 160.

72 This three-storey (commercial, industrial, residential) arrangement appears in Taiwan too. Family altars are often on the first floor. Fei Xiaotong and Luo Yanxian, *Xiangzhen jingji*, 5–9.

73 Zhang Lin, "Developing the Commodity Economy in the Rural Areas," *Market Forces in China*, 95. The classic on market areas is G. William Skinner, "Marketing and Social Structure."

74 *Wenzhou qiye dachuan*, 1986, op. cit., 385.

75 *Hengxiang jingji*, 207.

76 The counties were Baoshan, Fengxian, Jinshan, and Songjiang. Ibid.

77 *Hengxiang jingji*, 236–37.

78 Miller published memoirs: *Salesman in Beijing* (New York: Viking, 1984). See www.amazon.com/Salesman-Beijing-Arthur-Miller/dp/067061601X. "Norms" and "situations" exhaust motivations for Talcott Parsons, The Structure of Social Action, op. cit.

79 *FBIS*, March 11, 1988, 30–31, radio of March 11.

80 The conference met July 19–25; *NCNA*, July 30, 1957.

81 *NCNA*, March 12, 1958.

82 *Shanghai jingji qu*, 11.

83 Jiang Zemin, *Shanghai dangzheng*, 132.

84 *Lian fang pian*. The last word, *pian*, is informal as an official designation for an administrative area; but these small areas crossing provincial boundaries were unusual.

85 The *sihai* campaign, against mosquitos, flies, sparrows, and rats, began during the Great Leap. In 1960, bedbugs replaced sparrows. Radicals revived this movement in the early 1970s. But Jiading, Qingpu, and Jinshan in Shanghai; Taicang, Kunshan, and Wujiang in Jiangsu; Jiashan and Pinghu in Zhejiang were counties that led localist medical cooperation. *WHB*, December 12, 1977.

86 Quoted in Eisenman, *Red China's Green*, 4.

87 Based on a paper by George Fitting in my seminar at Princeton.

88 Ezra Vogel, *One Step Ahead* (Cambridge: Harvard University Press, 1989), ch. 4.

89 *Shanghai jingji qu*, 213–14.

90 "*Dapo shengshi jiexian*," and "*you lian you jing*."

91 Yao Shihuang, *Jin sanjiao*, 82–88.

92 *Shanghai jingji qu*, 8–20.

93 Ibid., 285.

94 Ibid., 5. Geologists have guessed Lake Tai is an ancient impact crater.

95 The number of counties is in parentheses after each city name: Shanghai (10), Suzhou (6), Wuxi (3), Changzhou (3), Nantong (6), Hangzhou (7), Jiaxing (5), Huzhou (3), Ningbo (7), and Shaoxing (5). Note that Nanjing (and Yangzhou and Zhenjiang) were not included.

96 *Shanghai jingji qu*, 1–2.

97 Ibid., 65.

98 Interview with a Shanghai economist.

99 *Shanghai jingji qu*, 32.

100 *FBIS*, December 7, 1984, 4, radio of December 5.

101 *SHJJNJ88*, 139.

102 In Guangdong, the Pearl River's "small delta" (xiao sanjiao zhou) was contrasted with the "large delta" (da sanjiao zhou). Ezra Vogel, *One Step*, ch. 5.

103 This difference would be greater, if north Jiangsu and southwest Zhejiang prefectures off the delta were excluded. Huang Weixin, *Economic Integration*, 119, from 67–69 of the 1986 zone statistical yearbook.

104 Chen Dongsheng and Chen Jiyuan, *Zhongguo diqu jingji*, 82–86.

105 *Zhongguo shehui zhuyi chengshi*, 155.

106 Baoshan, Chongming, Fengxian, Nanhui, Qingpu and Songjiang, and the Shanghai factories outside, are covered in *Shanghai shi 1985 nian gongye pucha ziliao*, 514.

107 These three were Baoshan (because the steel mill was run by a ministry, it did not count as a Shanghai firm), Fengxian, and Qingpu.

108 *Shanghai jingji qu*, 149.

109 Zhejiang Radio, Hangzhou, January 13, 1969, text of a Zhejiang ribao editorial, Far Eastern Broadcasts 2983, 11–14.

110 *Shanghai jingji qu*, 174–76.

111 "*Jian zai Anhui, jia zai Anhui, liyi bing bu dou zai Anhui,*" ibid., 177.

112 *Shanghai jingji qu*, 147–48.

113 *JFRB*, February 7, 1988.

114 This article, by Anhui Governor Wang Yushao, is in *Shanghai jingji qu*, 138–47.

115 *JFRB*, June 28, 1988.

116 Yao Shihuang, *Jin sanjiao*, 67–74.

117 *FBIS*, December 13, 1984, 2, radio of December 11.

118 *FBIS*, December 9, 1987, 26, radio of December 5.

119 *JFRB*, February 7, 1988.

120 *Sunan fada diqu jiaoyu fazhan zhanlue huanjing yanjiu baogao* (Research Report on the Environment for Educational Development Strategy in the Developed Region of Southern Jiangsu), Task Force on the Environment for Educational Development Strategy in the Developed Region of Southern Jiangsu, ed. and pub. Mimeographed "discussion draft" (taolun gao), n.p., 1991, 3.

121 *JFRB*, May 12, 1988.

122 *Shanghai jingji qu gongye gaimao* (General Description of Industry in the Shanghai Economic Zone), thirty volumes, Shanghai Economic Association, ed. (Shanghai: Jiaotong Daxue Chuban She, 1985).

123 *Shanghai jingji kexue* (Shanghai Economic Science), May 1984, 3.

124 Chinese from other places have long thought Shanghailanders all too smooth; Wolfram Eberhard, "Chinese Regional Stereotypes," *Asian Survey* 5:12 (December 1965), 596–608, shows long-term constancy in such images. On the 1980s, Cao Linzhang, *Shanghai shengchan*, 141.

125 Ibid., 141. The Association was the Yangpu Qu Kexue Jishu Xiehui.

126 Ibid., 142.

127 *Shanghai jingji nianjian, 1988*, 6.

128 Ibid., 143, which used the term *zhongchang qi dingdian xiezuo guanxi*.

129 Ibid., 144.

130 Wuxi County is administratively subordinate to Wuxi City; Shazhou County is under Suzhou; and Wujin is under Changzhou. *Shanghai qiye* (Shanghai Enterprise), February 1985, 13.

131 *Shanghai tan* (Shanghai Shore), No. 7, July 1988, 1.

132 *Liaowang*, no. 5 (1987), 12.

133 Guanxi networks substituting for laws also explains massive Overseas Chinese investments, despite deficient legal protection for property. Wang Hongying, "Transnational Networks and Foreign Direct Investment in China" (Ph.D. dissertation, Politics Department, Princeton University, 1996).

134 *Chen Dongsheng and Chen Jiyuan, Zhongguo diqu jingji jiegou yanjiu* (Studies on the Structure of China's Spatial Economy) (Taiyuan: Shanxi Renmin Chuban She, 1988), 19–20.

135 The "*Xinan Jingji Qu*" and "*Huazhong Jingji Qu*" are mooted in Shanghai jingji qu, 79.

136 This "Dongbei de jingji qu" was not an official name, though it appears in *Shanghai jingji qu*, 94.

137 The Shanghai Jingji Qu Guihua Bangong Shi only had powers to "coordinate" such relations. Ibid., 94.

138 Quoted by Linda Li, 5, from Zhang Jingfu's speech to the Shenzhen Party Committee, May 26, 1983.

139 *Shanghai Focus*, May 21, 1990. By the mid-2010s, China Eastern provided direct service from Shanghai to 14 Japanese, 6 South Korean, 6 European, 4 American, 9 Southeast Asian, 2 Australian, and 2 Canadian cities, plus many within China.

140 *Shanghai jingji qu*, 26.

141 The networks were *hangye xiezuo wangluo*. *JFRB*, April 18, 1988.

142 *JFRB*, April 19, 1988.

143 *JFRB*, April 27, 1988.

144 The year 1976, is a clear outlier – best omitted from calculations about this subject. The ratios before 1970 are also erratic, in part because of reporting issues. These quantities, like others here, should not be taken as exact but should be read in qualitative terms, for trends that might overwhelm reporting problems. Thanks to Peng Dajin for aiding me with this table.

145 These statistics cover contracts for department store goods, cultural commodities, clothing, metals, and transport and electrical goods. Shanghai jingji, neibu ben, 562.

146 Tao Yongkuan, *Dali fazhan*, 21.

147 *Shijie xin jishu*, 9.

148 Penelope Prime, "Industry's Response to Market Liberalization in China: Evidence from Jiangsu Province," esp. 33.

149 Based on ibid., 33, comparing the second, third, and fifth columns of its Table 1. A potential concern, as Prime also suggests on 34, is that Sunan became better integrated with Shanghai and Zhejiang during reforms, and markets can become efficient, just as production can. Repeating the exercise with groups of provinces and parts of them might reveal the trends more strongly. There is evidence, based on a similar analysis covering Jiangsu's eleven administrative regions, that specialization also occurred among localities within Jiangsu.

150 Ibid., 33, comparison of Table 1, columns 1 and 2.

151 Tao Yongkuan, *Dali fazhan*, 8–9.

152 Ibid., 9.

153 Audrey Donnithorne, "China's Cellular Economy," 605.

154 Huang Weixin, *Economic Integration*, approaches this calculation but honestly admits not being close enough to offer a figure.

155 Quotation from SJJJDB, November 21, 1988, in Huang Weixin, *Economic Integration*, 5.

156 "Likin" (*lijin*) toll-taxes were common in imperial times. For moden examples, *Gaige mianlin zhidu chuangxin*, 308.

157 The site of urban Shanghai had not yet emerged from the East China Sea 6,000 years ago (although tidal 'creeks' reached Suzhou then). *JFRB*, February 1, 1988, for gusto, not geology.

158 Thomas G. Rawski, "The Economy of the Lower Yangtse Region, 1850–1980," 21.

159 For more, see Lynn White, *Policies of Chaos*, 62 and 78.

160 *Shanghai jingji, neibu ben*, 498.

161 Interview in Hong Kong. In some areas of East China, such as the Zhoushan Archipelago, larger private boats for shipping and fishing became numerous in the 1980s.

162 Lynn White, "Agricultural and Industrial Values in China," 141–54.

163 *JFRB*, February 1, 1988.

164 *Jiangsu fazhi bao*, January 28, 1989.

165 Ibid.

166 *Fan san luan* is mentioned in Wang Hongying, "Transnational Networks and Foreign Direct Investment in China" (Ph.D. dissertation, Politics Department, Princeton University, 1996), chap. 3, 7.

167 *XMWB*, March 22, 1989.

168 Calculated from *XMWB*, December 26, 1988 – whose figuring from raw data slightly underestimated the profit, perhaps because of embarrassment about its size. Publication of this information could have spurred illegal traders to clear markets in Qidong and Chongming. Shanghai's borders were especially difficult to monitor along the wide river.

169 *XMWB*, March 24, 1989.

170 *Jiangsu fazhi bao*, January 21, 1989.

171 Ibid.

172 Calculated from *Shanghai shih duiwai jingji tongji nianjian, 1993* (Foreign Economic Statistical Yearbook of Shanghai, 1993), Shanghai Municipal Statistics Bureau, ed. "neibu ziliao" [internal materials] (Shanghai: Shanghai Tongji Ju, 1993), 11; but these figures include domestic as well as foreign trade.

12

SERVICE PROVIDERS RULE
COLLECTIVE AND PRIVATE
ENTERPRISES

Statist and Marxist theories place high value on one service: government. Other services receive scant support. Whatever rational justifications might be offered for brokerage, insurance, restaurants, tourism, entertainment, commerce, or advertising, radicals in Mao's time deemed these tertiary-sector activities "nonproductive," frivolous at best and exploitative at worst. A crucial aspect of China's reforms has been a revival of commerce, after fulsomely theorized official discrimination against it that lasted for about fifteen years from the mid-1950s. Collective and private service firms began to grow again, after a hiatus for them that lasted from that time into the 1970s.

Service sector productivity had by 1970 already recovered from a sharp recession that has been calculated from 1957. Pricing and capital allocation restraints against services still remained in the early 1970s, but demand for commerce was growing. By 1975, service productivity regained its 1957 level, although it had been growing from a low base since 1970, as Table 12.1 shows for Shanghai. Then it rose quickly – especially in 1980 and 1985, during periods of inflation and pressures to register service firms so that they could be taxed. Service companies in the city numbered about 140,000 during the early 1950s, but only 10,000 by the mid-1970s. This reduction of 93 percent was largely a result of business mergers, lumping earlier stores into large state corporations with many branches. But also, despite the city's population growth over these years, the absolute number of service employees had gone down.[1]

Shanghai's industrial sector, which was largely state-owned but increasingly collective, showed some labor productivity increases during the early 1970s. Industrial productivity rose during 1978 – but then suffered a five-year decline from 1979 to 1983. State workers received lower incentives, and their salaries did not keep up with inflation. The total supply of registered labor expanded, as sent-down Shanghai youths and ex-peasants came from rural places into the metropolis throughout

TABLE 12.1 Labor productivity in Shanghai services and manufacturing (reported gross output per worker in yuan, and annual percentage change over previous report)

	Tertiary (services)	% ch.	Secondary (manufactures)	% ch.
1957	2600		3070	
62	2185	−4	3960	5
65	2174	0	5150	9
70	2538	3	5244	0
75	2884	3	5687	2
78	3407	6	6900	7
79	3518	3	6724	−3
80	4106	17	6669	−1
81	4157	1	6533	−2
82	4206	1	6442	−1
83	4559	8	6320	−2
84	5197	14	6541	3
85	6235	20	7367	13
86	6690	7	7418	1
87	7594	14	7930	7
88	8682	14	9375	18
89	9252	7	10174	9
90	10516	14	10458	3
91	12030	14	11861	13

Notes and sources: Primary extraction and agriculture, which decreased in Shanghai during this period, is omitted to emphasize services; manufacturing was in both urban and suburban places. Reporting problems and inflation affect these data strongly, but finding appropriate factors with which to adjust them would not be easy; so the table reports them unadjusted. When the data are comparable, they are not available for some years. Calculated from *Shanghai tongji nianjian, 1988* (Shanghai Statistical Yearbook, 1988), Li Mouhuan et al., eds. (Shanghai: Shanghai Shi Tongji Ju, 1988), 41 for gross national product (*guomin shengchan zongzhi*) and 97 for laborers (*shehui laodong zhe*); and for later years, calculated from ibid., 1990, 71 and 34; 1991, 72, and 34; 1992, 86 and 35 (each book reports the previous year). The denominator is supposed to include not only regular, unionized laborers but also others. For more on the numerator, see *Tongji cidian* (Statistical Dictionary), Jia Hongyu, ed. (Shanghai: Shanghai Renmin Chuban She, 1986), 293–1995.

the 1970s, especially in 1979 under the *dingti* program. The advance of industrial productivity after 1984 was slower than inflation. Both output and workers were almost surely underreported in Shanghai's most dynamic sector, suburban collectives. At some times (such as 1985 and 1988) higher incentives to report output probably affected the apparent results. The situation is further complicated because many employees straddled different sectors, working sometimes in manufacturing and sometimes in services. Fields were increasingly tilled by immigrants during busy seasons, in the declining primary sector that of Shanghai suburbs was mostly in fields or fisheries.

The revival of services was bumpy. In some of the most obvious fields, it related to changes of lifestyles. Services were resuscitated partly by overseas trade, even

316 Service providers

from the early 1970s, but then more powerfully by domestic demand. The Shanghai government did not set up a bureau for tourism until 1978, although many visitors came under various auspices before then. From that year to 1982, the number of foreign tourists increased by 30 percent yearly. Many travelers within China found Shanghai, with its low consumer prices, to be very attractive for shopping. By 1982, more than half the city's revenues from tourism came through retail commodity purchases, especially from domestic travelers.[2]

Changes of fads and tastes affect services. As early as 1975, Shanghai clothing began to diversify away from baggy "Mao-suit" styles. Miniskirts (*chaoduan qun*) were seen in parks; their appearance was officially condemned by radicals, and women wearing them were few but noted at this time. Collars were deemed by conservative arbiters of taste to have become unnecessarily large. Fabrics of distinctive colors came in for puritanical criticism; these were deemed capitalist styles. But the Cultural Revolution had subsided by the mid-1970s (it had practically ended for non-intellectuals), and some people wore such clothes without suffering struggles. New styles were popular among many Shanghainese, and a bit of chic was a symbol of cultural opening.[3] Some people wearing "strange clothes" were "individual peddlers" – who later might increase their businesses and found private firms. Others were ethnic minorities, whose styles were officially supposed to be less constrained.

Youths employed in services

The slowness of new employment before 1970 in China's large cities correlated with send-downs, as well as with "steel eating" investments that absorbed much money but little labor. State stores in early 1970s cities were apparently urged not to hire young people, whom radicals wanted to stay in rural "rustication." But many found urban jobs at collective service firms, or individually as hawkers, especially in mid-size cities. By 1976, Shanghai's urban districts contained nearly a million youths aged 21 to 30. Because many returned from the countryside in the next few years, this number by 1983 was up by 86 percent, to 1.7 million youths.[4] This near-doubling of the 21-to-30 age cohort was much faster than the rise in Shanghai's total population during the same years (16 percent).[5] At the end of 1982, all of Shanghai had 11,000 collectives hiring 1,030,000 people, 22 percent of the city's labor force. They made a reported (or underreported) 8 percent of industrial product value then. But service collectives, then comprising 28 percent of Shanghai's registered firms, were more important. Their fiscal payments were only 4 percent of the city's revenues, but they employed between a quarter and a fifth of all workers.[6]

The *dingti* program of 1979–1980 implicitly legitimated rusticates' return to cities. The government wanted to make sure that ex-rusticate youths who did not take their parents' jobs got off the streets and into employment. In all of China, the portion of service workers rose from 12 percent in 1980 to 16 percent in 1985.[7] Shanghai and other cities could support many small service firms in the 1980s. They absorbed most new urban labor.

Reported employment growth in some crucial services was nonetheless slow until the mid-1980s watershed of reforms. In historical perspective, among all of Shanghai's financial institutions from 1952 to 1984, the annual average number of reported new employees had been almost nil: only ten persons annually![8] That rate was not just low; it was grotesque in such a large city. By 1983, the registered finance and insurance industries still contributed only 3 percent of Shanghai's gross product – though Shanghai was still a major financial center.

Local nonstate leaders attempted to make jobs available to people they favored while avoiding state firms' normal responsibility for housing, health, rations, pensions, and benefits. The main parts of the tertiary sector, as defined in Chinese accounts, were commerce, finance, technology, consulting, and hotels and restaurants. The government and the military – along with education – were not included.[9] Hawking and illegal services were also not included because not accounted or taxed; so the available data were surely underreports.

For years, as Table 12.2 shows on a long-term basis, state policies had discouraged growth in Shanghai services.

The tertiary sector of the economy had employed 28 percent of the city's workers in 1952, but the mid-1950s "Transition to Socialism" and the post-Leap depression reduced this to about 21 percent. It stayed at that level for more than two

TABLE 12.2 The fall and rise of Shanghai's service sector, 1952-1992 (percentages of reported product, and of registered employees, in the primary, secondary, and tertiary sectors)

	1952	1957	1975	1978	1983	
Services	42, 28	37, 27	19, 21	18, 21	22, 24	
Industry	54, 30	59, 36	77, 42	76, 44	72, 52	
Agricul.+	4, 42	4, 37	5	5	6, 24	

	1986	1987	1989	1990	1991	1992
Services	28, 26	29, 27	29, 28	31, 28	32, 29	33, 30
Industry	69, 59	67, 60	67, 60	65, 60	64, 60	64, 60
Agricul.+	3, 15	4, 13	4, 12	4, 11	4, 11	3, 11

Notes and sources: In each pair of percentages, the first refers to sectoral product, and the second to employment. Good data were not found for the 1960s or early 1970s. Figures for agricultural employment in some years are misleading (and reports for industry are too low) because persons registered as tillers were actually working in factories established by rural leaders. The tertiary sector comprises services, including trade (but not the government, education, or military). The secondary sector is manufacturing industry, and the primary sector is agriculture and fishing (mining is negligible from sedimentary Shanghai ground). Compiled from separate but consistent accounts in Cao Linzhang, Gu Guangqing, and Li Jianhua, *Shanghai shengchan ziliao suoyu zhi jiegou yanjiu* (Studies of Materials about Shanghai Production and of the Structure of Ownership) (Shanghai: Shanghai Shehui Kexue Yuan Chuban She, 1987), 127; *Shanghai tongji nianjian, 1988*, 44; and *Shanghai jingji yanjiu* (Shanghai Economic Research), May 1985, 46. For 1988 and 1990, see *Shanghai tongji nianjian, 1990* (Shanghai Statistical Yearbook, 1990), Shanghai Shi Tongji Ju, ed. (Beijing: Zhongguo Tongji Chuban she, 1990), 34 for product data and 71 for number of workers by sector; and ibid., 1991 edition, respectively 34 and 72. For 1991 and 1992, see the same yearbook, 1993 edition, 37 and 74.

318 Service providers

decades. Its rise in the 1980s (perhaps also in the 1970s, if reporting were complete) was steady; and by 1989 services employed the same portion of Shanghai workers as in 1952. The service sector rose from two-tenths to three-tenths of all registered employment from the mid-1970s into the early 1990s, and nonreported workers in services may have been an even greater portion than in industries. The rise would be more if unregistered illegal migrants were recorded. PRC definitions of the three sectors do not exactly match Western ones, with differences that are unimportant here. The increase in the primary sector in Table 12.2 is mainly caused by an addition of more rural areas to the municipality in 1958–1959. But the decline of agricultural employment, the rise of manufactures, and the decline and then revival of service employment are all valid stories, despite reporting problems.

The portion of laborers in the service sectors of other international cities was higher than in Shanghai, in the mid-1980s for example. This was true for a wide variety of cities in both developed and developing countries, both socialist and capitalist: Tokyo, 69 percent; Singapore 66; Chicago, 64; Mexico City, 60; Warsaw, 57; Cairo, 49 – but in Shanghai, just 24 percent to the extent service workers were reported.[10]

Service subsectors

Commerce was the most important absorber of labor, but nonstate stores in Shanghai for years had difficulty obtaining physical space in which to show their wares. Despite that problem, collective trade developed at a quick rate because quasi-private collective firms often offered better goods for lower prices than state stores did. By 1984, collectives and movable market stalls sold about 40 percent of all products (while in Shanghai's manufacturing sector, collectives still produced only 14 percent of commodity value).[11] State stores seldom searched the whole country for the best items to sell in view of actual consumer demands, but some collectives were nimble at this crucial function.

In many service trades, such as insurance, Shanghai firms could establish agencies beyond the city's boundaries. Shanghai's insurance companies were particularly active on the Yangzi flatland in Changzhou, Hangzhou, Ningbo, Suzhou, and Wuxi.[12] Proliferation of local companies competing with each other, especially new collectives, provided by the late 1980s a greater choice of insurance providers than China had seen for decades.

The travel business also illustrates this mid-1980s intensification of local reforms, especially for small companies. Only thirteen travel agencies were officially registered in all of Shanghai as late as 1983 (when most travel brokers were surely unregistered). But by the end of 1984, the number was sixty, and it rose to eighty in the next year. Many at first had difficulty getting ticket reservations inland, because transport infrastructure was capital intensive and still run by state bureaucracies. In 1986, the number of registered travel agencies fell again, to sixty-seven – but this was probably an accounting phenomenon. With the mid-1980s general collapse of planning, official registration became unnecessary in this business. Tourists coming in or out of Shanghai in 1985 averaged almost 100,000 daily. Half of them stayed for several days.[13] Tourism is an archetypical "nonproductive" sector from the viewpoint of Party conservatives, but that view no longer stopped Shanghai agencies from booking tours.

Suzhou and Hangzhou were, for the expansion of tourism services, two of Shanghai's biggest attractions.[14] These two historic centers of Jiangnan culture and gardens are easy train rides from Shanghai. So the metropolis's economic interests in this field, as in others, overlapped strongly with the interests of Jiangsu and Zhejiang. Economic cooperation in such areas was speedy; by 1980, agents in Shanghai, Jiangsu, and Zhejiang established the "regional tourism coordination small group" (Quyu Lüyou Xiezuo Xiaozu). This organization was later expanded to cover all of East China and was said to "escape the administrative cage" ('*baituo xingzheng kuangkuang*'; this word *kuangkuang*, meaning frame or coffin, has a history of use in Shanghai by authors as varied as Ba Jin and Yao Wenyuan; it was the incubus in which conservatives wanted bourgeois kept, and the frame reformers wanted to see broken).[15] Actually, local agents did not need official advice; they were already arranging trips wherever they could.

Shanghai's tourism was expected to develop first by providing expeditions to close scenic cities on the delta, and later to farther sites such as Huangshan and Lushan.[16] Tourism development was not mainly organized by either city or central authorities; it followed efforts of collective and private travel agencies, and it grew especially because of China's new wealth. Agencies established "horizontal" links with private and collective counterparts in other Jiangnan places. The reforms were a boom time in this and other service sectors.

Hawkers

In many developing cities, the most obvious "individual enterprises" are street peddlers. Hawkers have never mixed well with statism. During the Cultural Revolution, when police efforts to ban them were effective because of support from activists against "petty capitalism," hawkers were seldom seen in Shanghai. They reappeared gradually during the early 1970s, closing their stands and packing their wares quickly whenever police enforcers of the ban against them came near. This was an ancient ritual.

Licenses for hawking were implicit in earlier allowances for "specialized agricultural households" to sell freely their over-quota goods. Not until February 1983, however, did the Shanghai city government formally declare that tillers, after making their deliveries to the state for fixed sums, could peddle any agricultural products (except cotton) at whatever prices the market would bear. In fact, they had been doing so for years. But a consequence of official admission of the practice was that profits from such individual trading were legal – and were supposed to be taxed. Officially announced policies about hawking were reactive and variable.

Prices for staple goods, in regular Shanghai state stores and large collectives, were more heavily subsidized and lower in the city than inland. Low state prices reduced hawking of these goods more effectively than police could. But this system broke

320 Service providers

down in the 1980s, because the government ran out of subsidy money. Shanghai officials ruled that the city's suburban farmers could sell their over-quota grain "freely" – but only so long as they did so in Shanghai, where the prices were still supposed to be low. By mid-July 1983, just a few months after legalizing individual trade, the government held a campaign trying to punish Shanghai farmers who sold surplus crops elsewhere to make more profit.[17] The reform-era state wanted to maximize incentives to produce, but it also wanted an official monopoly of profitable commerce. This was a contradiction. Suburban households went easily into trade. Private commerce became increasingly difficult for cadres to prohibit during the pre-1990 reforms.

By the 1990s, there were at least 100,000 hawkers in Shanghai who lacked legal licenses – and this figure was about the same as the number of licenses the local government had issued.[18] So at least half of hawking was illegal. Unregistered salespeople were officially counted among the unemployed (*daiye*, 'waiting for vocations'), including youths who had returned from the countryside. Others were retired. Newspapers castigated people for being "lazy" when they refused to take temporary non-union jobs at low wages in large firms. But many hawkers were moonlighters; they also had regular jobs. Some were quoted complaining against inadequate salaries in their day jobs. According to one, hawking was "better than going to work."

Policies for dealing with illegal hawkers, like those for dealing with migrants, threatened the public benefits their activities brought. Officials admitted in print that many of the unemployed needed their hawking jobs for livelihood – and the citizens who used their services did so willingly. Local governments therefore began to issue such people "temporary business licenses" (*linshi jingying xuke zheng*). Retirees, however, were encouraged to get out of trade, live on pensions, and participate in unpaid "social charity" (*shehui gongyi*).[19] Younger people who had returned to Shanghai from rural assignments often applied for temporary business licenses – and when they did this, they would be given a hard time if they lacked Shanghai household registrations, which they might acquire if they were well connected.

Food vendors were common among hawkers, but the post-socialist context bred new sectors. At least 10,000 Shanghai women were estimated by 1989 to be professional traders of surplus ration tickets. This activity was illegal; so they used the standard cover of peddling tea-boiled eggs (which I found delicious and convenient in Shanghai in 1988). A newspaper guessed tea-egg sellers made at least ten yuan a day on average – a respectable income, and profit from clandestine trade in ration coupons was often additional.[20] Shanghai had an influx of hawkers from Anhui, Henan, and north Jiangsu. Plainclothes police could easily stop some trade; but officials knew that it would reemerge soon on any particular street, if they moved against the tea egg-and-surplus-coupons industry that employed many people.

It was not hard for police to find worse illegalities in both manufacturing and commerce. Child laborers as young as fifteen years reportedly knew they could clear 200 yuan a month working in Shanghai. They came to Shanghai from poorer provinces, often slept outside small hotels, and worked in order to eat. Some joined gangs or became pickpockets. Teenagers reportedly made railroad stations and docks somewhat dangerous. Sixty percent of all injuries near railways, according to a 1989 estimate, were caused by people who had "blindly flowed" into Shanghai.[21] Considering the amounts some of them earned, especially in comparison with the low wages of many state employees, they were actually not blind. The workaday illegality of part-time hawkers did not predispose them to obey any other laws.

June 1989 reactionaries led a quick campaign against unlicensed street hawkers, who were then reported to number "about 40,000" in Shanghai. The report admitted this statistic was "incomplete," without giving the reason: Tiananmen-era conservatism dissociated authorities from economic realities. As cadres occasionally confessed, legally licensed vendors did a great deal of trade that was never accounted for taxation. Common commodities in Shanghai's grey economy ranged widely from tea eggs, cigarettes, and transport tickets to bulk industrial goods. More than 800 scalpers were caught selling train tickets illegally at the new Shanghai station in a July 1989 campaign. The Railroad Ministry would neither raise its prices to finance better service nor keep up with the booming demand for transport that the nonstate economy generated.[22] Both in the state sector and outside it, 1989 was a climax of urban unrest.

The Shanghai Public Security Bureau led a campaign at this time in which it arrested 236 entrepreneurs. Illegal transactions had exceeded 10,000 yuan during the first half of 1989 in each of 134 reported cases. Gold ingots, cultural relics, calligraphic scrolls, and many kinds of Chinese and foreign currency were involved, for a total value above 4 million yuan.[23] This was just the tip of the iceberg of illegal commerce. Police did not catch most traders who broke laws. Bureaucrats found hawkers unbecoming in China's largest city, but illegal private traders were hard to stop. Their threat to the regime was political; but it was indirect and cumulative, not specific or immediate. Many citizens found the hawkers convenient.

The 1991–1995 Five-Year Plan scheduled an increase of only 10 percent in the number of officially recognized free markets in China, over the 1990 total.[24] The state tried seriously to enforce this low limit on the growth of the economy's most dynamic service sector. This was a change after the 1970s–1990s reforms. Fewer markets in fewer locations were easier to monitor than many. The limit on planned growth, however, was mainly an admission that state cadres were stretched thin trying to keep track of commerce they were supposed to oversee. Conservatives wanted to stop the growth of unmonitored markets. Small traders just wanted to keep on making money.

Not just hawkers: commercial companies in history and during reforms

The 1980s renaissance of the service sector meant mainly a rise of collectives. Formally legal private stores in Shanghai revived slowly. The story of Shanghai's early capitalist development need not be retold here; but after 1949, private ownership in this largest Chinese city was severely discouraged by Party hardliners.[25] The

322 Service providers

Transition to Socialism of 1956 almost eliminated private firms in both manufacturing and commerce, and the Great Leap Forward extended this result beyond policy to behavior. During 1958 alone, the number of Shanghai private firms shrank from 22,000 to 6,000. The number of employees in these shops reportedly fell in that year from 31,100 to 14,500; but this just counted legally registered employees, and many workers and firms were unregistered until the post-Leap depression dried up their supplies and markets.[26] Less than 1 percent of retail products in the city were sold by private firms. In manufacturing, less than one-tenth of 1 percent of the legally priced industrial products' value came from private firms by 1959.

In the early 1960s, private firms reappeared in Shanghai; about 10,000 existed by 1965. The Cultural Revolution, despite its ideological socialism, was not sufficiently organized to nationalize all the remaining private firms. Red Guards criticized them and scared the owners – but did or could not take over their operations. Hawkers, with no fixed abode, were never totally eliminated. By the mid-1970s, the number of employees in very local firms was reportedly 13,000, about the same as during the early sixties, although such figures are probably underestimates.[27]

The history of quasi-private urban companies, legitimated by local lane and street committees, is not well known. "Street industries" emerged in post-Leap Shanghai; many were startups by individual entrepreneurs. In 1963, after the post-Leap economic depression, they came nominally under district or street administrations. Their productivity was reported as rising quickly when they were legalized by street offices (rather than by smaller neighborhood committees), and they had more success in some urban districts than in others. In relatively poor and crowded Nanshi District, for example, the product value from enterprises under street committees by 1976 was seven times that of 1963 – but in richer Hongkou or Putuo districts, the rise was over forty times. On average over all the urban districts, it was over twenty times. These firms responded to newly available technologies more flexibly than did state-owned companies. Fully 43 percent of the total value of "street-level enterprises" by 1977 (and 28 percent of the workforce employed in these shops) was for making, selling, and repairing electronic devices. Parallel portions for street factories in other sectors are summarized on Table 12.3.

TABLE 12.3 Street factories in Shanghai, 1977, by product

	% of value	*% of workers*	*% of firms*
Electronics	43	27	23
Handicrafts	22	28	31
Machines	21	26	24
Arts co-ops	11	13	15
Technical support	3	7	7

Source: Shanghai jingji, neibu ben, 255–58. This report of percentages within street units' totals was published as officially confidential but became available anyway. It covers both "street factories" (*jiedao gongchang*) and smaller "lane production groups" or "street industries" (*lilong shengchan zu* or *jiedao gongye*).

Firms legitimated by relatively local neighborhood committees hired more than twice as many workers as those under larger street companies by the mid-1970s. These were 250,000 regular permanent employees, and probably many more on temporary (and non-unionized) bases. These neighborhood bodies, more local than street committees, were not formal offices of the government. The reported product value from their lane industries expanded more slowly than the number of workers they employed, at least after 1963 policies that attempted to put such plants under materials supply plans. But they may well have left part of their output off the official books. In lane factories, the increase of gross product from 1965 to 1978 reportedly rose five times; and from 1978 to 1982, it rose again more than three times.[28] A portion of output in the early period was surely hidden to avoid taxes and criticisms. The productivity of labor in street-committee-run enterprises was reportedly ten times that in lane-run plants[29] – on the unlikely premise that the latter reported all their production. The purpose of the small plants, for people who worked there and for neighborhood cadres who got them jobs, was not just wages and profits, but the possibility of living in the big city.

Individual enterprises in the 1970s and 1980s: quasi-privatist economic legitimacy

"Individual" (geti) and especially "private" (siying) are somewhat pejorative terms in Chinese. Firms in these categories existed on a small scale at Shanghai during the early 1970s, although the political shadow over them affected journalistic and academic coverage of them. One source, for example, indicated that 8,000 Shanghai private entrepreneurs were registered in 1976.[30] Another reported that private enterprises, in the form of small "individual households," were not legally revived in Shanghai until 1979.[31] There is extensive evidence that private vendors and small factories never completely vanished. The history of these firms has been distorted, because some writers have taken state pronouncements about their non-existence at face value. Private enterprises were often small, nominally collective, legally chancy, and sometimes underground – but they did exist.

Most such firms were officially supposed, by the late 1970s, to be ex-peasant households that had signed contracts to specialize in non-agricultural work. In fact, they were small private entrepreneurs who could usually operate with or without a license. Traders from whom they were nearly indistinguishable had been legalized. Open markets for sellers of handicrafts, farm produce, and increasingly other goods became common. These expanded sharply in the late 1970s and early 1980s. By 1983, Shanghai registered 34,000 households on such markets. Unlicensed vendors made the total higher.

Wenzhou was the PRC's most brazen experiment with free markets. Mountains cut off this Zhejiang port from the Yangzi flatland, but Wenzhou people speak a "Wu" language related to Shanghainese. Wenzhou's economic institutions by the late 1970s echoed the unbridled capitalism, exploitation, ambition, and economic tumult of pre-1949 Shanghai. Many observers reported this – causing others, who

324 Service providers

liked it, to publish apologies claiming practically the opposite: that Wenzhou was a "socialist market experiment." Conservatives had more doubts about this pattern than did reformers. Many of the latter hoped that patterns in the "Wenzhou experimental zone" might flow northward onto the delta.

Shanghai's *Liberation Daily*, a CCP newspaper, was early to publicize the Wenzhou "model."[32] Wenzhou firms were economically successful, and aspects of their management experience are treated in chapters above. Shanghai exponents of the "Wenzhou model" were many. The fly in the ointment, from conservatives' viewpoint, was the prominence of private commercial enterprises in Wenzhou. Private ownership was not adopted widely in reform Shanghai, but publicity about Wenzhou nonetheless lent political legitimacy to collective companies that paid managers high salaries. Street collectives in Shanghai were praised during the early 1980s when they made profits, but they seemed less capitalist than the much-publicized firms of Wenzhou. Four Shanghai street collectives, which each sent more than 100 million yuan of their profits to the government, were honored in a lead article of *Xinmin Evening News* on New Year's Day, 1982. They dealt in electrical supplies, plastics, instruments, and semiconductors.[33] Before reforms, firms that came in for public praise had practically always been in the state sector.

Nonstate workers also received more official respect during reforms. Almost a thousand "labor models" (*laodong mofan*) and 360 "model collectives" (*mofan jiti*) were chosen by an office of the municipal government in 1987. Less prestigious awards, especially for "civilized units" (*wenming danwei*), were given to agencies that did public services such as planting trees on streets, offering good service, or keeping premises clean. Plaques boasting this title were displayed in neighborhood offices, factories, and schools. Titles for individuals could justify bonuses; so the inclusion of nonstate workers involved material incentives, not just symbols. Still, of all the people selected for such honors, 81 percent were CCP members (and 36 percent had university-level educations). Entrepreneurs were supposed to be favored, although conservatives resisted that criterion for public praise. Holding a large rally to fête model workers and units had become a tradition; and in 1987, an audience of 1,700 attended Shanghai's celebrations.[34]

The nonstate sector, which was still overwhelmingly collective in Shanghai, involved less uniform salaries and fewer communal benefits than the state sector. A high Gini coefficient indicates income inequality. This statistic among households of state employees in Shanghai, by the second quarter of 1984, was 0.0755, an extremely low Gini if it really covered all income – as apparently it did not. But for "non-employees" (i.e., mostly workers or farmers in collectives), the coefficient was 0.2149, showing greater income inequality in the nonstate workforce. Independence from the official system also meant higher absolute earnings. People working for state firms or offices got an average of only 78 yuan per month in 1984; but "non-employees," those who were independent or under nongovernmental managers, averaged 94 yuan.[35] Inequality rose quickly in later years.

Shanghai's unemployed during reforms flocked to quasi-private collectives, because they made money and could offer jobs. But small commercial operations cut into the profits of state shops. So government policies encouraged laid-off and unemployed workers to join established firms rather than found their own. Official employment agencies would help locals who had legal registrations to seek jobs and get "waiting for work certificates" (*daiye zheng*). But any unemployed person who wanted to start a private firm had to turn in that certificate first, before applying for a business license.[36] The reaction of many was simply to ignore the bureaucrats, start enterprises, and make money without benediction from the state.

The mid-1980s watershed saw the start of serious expansion beyond the collective sector. Private "individual households" (which were small companies) numbered 85,000 in Shanghai by the end of 1986, and they employed about 120,000 people – or many more, presuming reports were incomplete. Fifty-three percent of these workers, and 47 percent of the firms, were in the officially "agricultural" suburbs. These companies were restricted, because they were not supposed to hire more than 5 people on a regular basis. Not until 1987 did the government restore legal status to "private enterprises" (*siying qiye*) that could employ more than 5 people. The average reported monthly income of these licensed individual enterprises was 312 yuan per month, and the average income of those that paid taxes was over 400 yuan. This rate was 2.7 times the average reported income of Shanghai cooperative workers, as well as more than twice the average in state factories, stores, and offices.[37] Private entrepreneurs made more money than employees of collectives, who made more than employees of state enterprises.

A survey found that 7 percent of Shanghai private companies were "ten-thousand yuan households," making that much yearly. (A separate survey estimated that one-tenth got that much. For comparison, the highest-paid state employee, the Premier of China, each month was supposed to receive just 530 yuan.[38]) The scale of private firms was kept small. By 1988, Shanghai still registered just 1,000 private enterprises employing eight or more people. Amounts of fixed and operating capital were surprisingly large, considering the reported incomes. Those who worked in urban markets were especially prosperous. At the Fumin Street Market, 19 percent of the firms surveyed in the mid-1980s were 10,000-yuan households ('*wanyuan hu*'), and another 42 percent made at least half as much. At the Liuling Road Clothes Market, a 1985 survey showed that one-third (34 percent) of the firms had net incomes greater than 10,000 yuan. By 1986 this portion had *reportedly* decreased to less than 30 percent. But the Municipal Tax Bureau estimated that more than 85 percent of Shanghai's private firms presented false accounts to evade taxes.[39]

In the mid-1980s, Shanghai had 86,000 "individual" firms, employing 134,000 people (already more, by half, than similar companies had hired immediately after Liberation in 1949).[40] The reported number of such firms had risen ten times from 1979 to 1985, and the number of employees was up by sixteen times. Of these companies in 1985, more than 98 percent were apparently registered under the names of single owners, although some were run by more than one person. Multi-entrepreneur businesses were less than 2 percent by number, but they employed 15 percent of the sector's workers. The private economy's total revenues in Shanghai were reported as 700 million yuan, of which 61 percent were in retail sales. This

326 Service providers

was surely an underreport; it represented only 2.4 percent of the city's total retail revenues. The private sector was expanding.

Laws slowly catch up with private enterprise

Private property is not among the topics on which the *Communist Manifesto* leaves much room for interpretation. It says that "the theory of the Communists may be summed up in the single sentence: abolition of private property . . . i.e., that kind of property which exploits wage labor."[41] China's reform communists increasingly violated this tenet. They arguably chose good policies for the nation; but formally, they were no longer communists while remaining Leninists. Their country prospered. It postponed solutions to the problems created by making labor a market commodity. The communal costs of pell-mell development were less obvious than the great wealth achieved by individuals and families.

A nearly official PRC sequence for legitimation of any public activity is that it should be first approved in principle through national decrees, then registered with regional governments, and only afterward begin in local institutions. The actual sequence for private firms (and other activities in the reform era) was the inverse: local establishment first, municipal registration second, and national legislation last. A law was drafted in 1988 to set the rights and duties of private firms that hired more than eight employees – even though many such enterprises had actually begun earlier, often in the form of collectives that were *de facto* private under their managers. For ideological reasons, the formally private sector was still small. There were a hundred times as many small family businesses that employed fewer than eight workers, and many used temporary and contract workers without legal urban residences.[42]

Economists and lawyers discussed whether large private firms should have the status of legal persons.[43] Sizable private enterprises seemed more threatening to socialist conservatives than the cumulative effect of many individuals' businesses, although both types competed with the state sector. Situational reforms and local models helped private firms. These factors were more important for their expansion than were laws.

Individuals could apply to establish new companies in Shanghai, but only if certain requirements were met. The entrepreneur needed permanent residence in the city. Cadres or state employees were legally disqualified from receiving business licenses – although suburban farmers, retired cadres, and the unemployed could apply to start private firms. The types of businesses they could legally found were specified in long lists, and different criteria and procedures were published for each trade.[44] The regulations contained vague wording that the state might prohibit some kinds of enterprise. This proviso gave local bureaucrats power to stop the legal establishment of enterprises they did not like. But more of the rules became public in the reform era.

An aspiring entrepreneur would first apply to the local trade and commerce administrative office (*gongshang xingzheng guanli suo*). The prospective businessperson would show an ID card and proof of not being a current cadre or state employee.

The office was supposed to decide on each application within ten days, forwarding the file to the city's Industry and Commerce Administrative Management Bureau, which was then mandated to make a further ruling within twenty days. These procedures were relatively clear, although the criteria for approval were less so. For each kind of trade, many additional documents were required from specific city offices. Obtaining space for businesses was particularly problematic in Shanghai. The procedure involved so many red-seal chops on so many papers, many entrepreneurs began their operations first as "dependent households" (*guahu*) under large state or collective enterprises, using the latter's facilities or bank accounts, waiting for later rules that might legitimate them.

"Dependent households" as camouflaged privatizations

The distinction between public and private organizations in China became blurred during reforms, because advantages given to collective nonstate firms discouraged the formally private category. Laws on these "individual" businesses were formalized in the 1980s, and courts and cadres alike gave private businesspeople incentives to vanish or hide. So they registered as collectives "for reasons of protective coloration."[45] The legal title of a collective enterprise, especially if it could become a "dependent firm," allowed it to prosper. Larger legitimating companies could charge rents for this local-political service, but they did not have to manage or take economic risks. Collectives or small state firms gave entrepreneurs "red caps" (*hong maozi*). They were thus legal and sometimes enjoyed low taxes. Their local patrons might demand kickbacks, but this kind of clientelism weakened rather than strengthened state control. As a saying put it, "Li wears Zhang's crown" (*Zhang guan Li dai*).[46] Local state cadres could retain fulsome official symbolism while substantially abandoning the state's interests.

Throughout China, private firms near the end of the 1980s employed more than 200,000 CCP members, as well as many model workers and delegates to people's congresses and political consultative committees.[47] The Tiananmen disaster had a temporary effect, slowing the replacement of state companies by assorted flavors of nonstate companies. The number of registered private businesses in China by the end of 1990 climbed 7 percent over the end of 1989, and the number of workers reported in private firms rose 8 percent. But such companies did not provide guaranteed job security for their employees. These firms were not line items on any large budget. They were founded in a time of tumultuous economic change, and they could fail financially. Officials complained in the early 1990s that 3 million private firms had gone bankrupt nationwide since a late-1988 austerity program against inflation. But China's total registered number of such companies at the start of 1990 was 13 million and rising.[48] There were high birth and death rates among these firms. Small companies had incentives to register publicly during reforms when they could best prosper (raising the number of foundings), but then to deregister, declare bankruptcy, or go underground (or become collectives) during conservative spells when they would more likely founder on economic grounds too.

Taxes in private firms

The central state's main incentive to register a private enterprise was to tax it. According to a temporary national law on private businesses, such firms had to pay 60 percent of their earnings in taxes on the first 30,000 yuan of profits, and 84 percent on profits above that.[49] Small firms could try to avoid these high tax rates by not filing registration papers, which might classify their income as personal earnings (to the extent the state could monitor it). The extraction was very heavy, however, and it did not include other additional enterprise taxes and management fees. Such steep corporate taxes meant that private firms remained small for many years, and they registered as collectives whenever possible. They could practically never make money if all the laws were strictly enforced. This tax code was written so that the state and its collectors could use it as a hunting license. It was not a coherent instrument of fiscal policy. Nobody, apparently, expected these laws would be followed to the letter. Local cadres might be induced not to enforce them.

Deregistration became a standard way for private Shanghai businesses to keep working. Fully 110,000 private entrepreneurs were on the city's official rosters at the start of 1988 – but by August of that year, as government constraints against such firms grew; so "nearly 10,000 of them returned their registration certificates to the government." This trend served municipal cadres' interests, because they could report on their prowess enforcing the policy to reduce companies that were not nationalized. It also served the interests of entrepreneurs, who welcomed their removal from tax and inspection lists. But it was a shell game. As a Chinese paper reported in the spring of 1989, "While the number of registered self-employed people is decreasing, the number of those without licenses is on the increase. According to a survey, certified self-employed people account for less than one-third [sic] of the total self-employed people in more than 400 markets in Shanghai."[50]

The tax law was revised later. The rates remained near the extortionate range for private enterprises, and the government clearly expected illegal underreporting. These firms had to pay a high "accumulation tax" on capital they could be seen as keeping, which changed over time if they boomed and could not hide it. The rate schedule was sharply progressive. For firms making over 50,000 yuan a year, the basic profit tax rate became 60 percent, with surcharges of 10 to 40 percent of that portion for additional profits.[51] It was reported that some Shanghai firms actually paid the maximal 84 percent of their profits in taxes. This impost was not out of line for state plants, counting both their remittances and taxes; but it inspired truly creative initiatives in private accounting.

Other places on the Shanghai delta generally enjoyed lower tax rates. Jiangsu in the late 1980s reported only a 20 percent income tax (*suode shui*) and another 5 percent business tax (*yingye shui*) for many enterprises. Shanghai rural private-sector managers, seeing this, were reported to complain that the taxation they faced was "heavy and diverse." The manager of a metal-punching factory in Shanghai's Jiading County figured that if he moved his plant a few kilometers into Jiangsu Province, his profits would rise by 50,000 to 60,000 yuan each year because of lower official extractions. Prohibitive levies in the metropolis were the main reason why – until the 1990s at least – large private enterprises remained scarce.

The Shanghai Coral Knitting Factory in the first quarter of 1988 had a gross revenue of 317,000 yuan, on which it reported profits of 36,000 yuan. This private firm, after taxes, could retain only 4,000 yuan – so the effective tax rate on the (reported) profits was 89 percent. Private entrepreneurs demanded by 1988 that the Shanghai municipal government should pass a law to protect them. The *Wenhui News* reported, "Some self-employed people complain that after registration they are asked for more than 20 kinds of taxes by different government departments. Another reason cited for the increase in market chaos is the lack of a sound legal system and the lack of professional ethics on the part of individual businesspeople and government officials." The entrepreneurs did not stop work, however. "They take advantage of the technology and transportation in Shanghai, producing along with factories elsewhere, and selling outside Shanghai. Lenient economic policies and loopholes of management in other places make life easy for these self-employed businessmen. . . . They get commissions and bonuses from factories outside Shanghai. In order to make a sale, they sometimes bribe shop managers and assistants."[52] Imposts and rules against private businesses in the metropolis were so strict, it is hardly surprising that entrepreneurs went elsewhere.

New personal income tax rules were used in Shanghai from early 1987, and eighteen months later a survey showed that the portion of households that had earnings over the minimum threshold was just one of every forty. Nonetheless,

> There are still a lot of people who fail to pay their income taxes according to the tax law, including some well-known personalities, leading cadres, and ordinary citizens. Some don't know about the tax law, while some know about it but fail to abide by it. In literary and art circles in Shanghai, for example, only 250 people paid their income taxes last year, just 0.02 percent of the total number of people in those circles. Some who intentionally evaded their taxes said they did so because the tax law was grossly unfair.[53]

Rates were high, and implementation was uneven. If the whole of Shanghai's population had a tax compliance rate like that of the group mentioned in this quotation, then just 1 out of each 5,000 taxpayers complied with the law. Actual compliance was probably higher than that, but it was still very low.

Surtaxes on private profits depended on the kind of trade. The tax scheme was published in tabular form, but it was complex enough to be subject to a good deal of administrative interpretation.[54] Official policy swung like a pendulum – even though it did not always affect the practical operations of private firms. Crucial reasons for high taxes were political, not economic or fiscal.

Enterprise and politics: two environments interact

Private entrepreneurs were criticized after Tiananmen, but the most prominent dissidents were student intellectuals. Comparisons with business politics in other countries, such as Iran or the Philippines, show that most bourgeois people are more interested in economic benefits for themselves than in political change.[55] There is a

330 Service providers

long-term correlation between per capita wealth and the liberal democratic regime type, which the CCP rejects. But over no short period of time do entrepreneurs become democrats, according to most evidence from comparative politics. Various factors are useful for explaining the democratization process – either its operation or stoppage. These include elite decisions, the level of modernization or wealth, fears of asset redistribution, historical legacies in politics, recurrent protest repertoires, and international norms. But these causes or hindrances work over different spans of time.[56]

The *Economic Daily* argued, "It is true that in a private enterprise, employees' pursuit of personal interests may bring about high efficiency. [But] in a country like China, with short supplies of resources, the creation of too many private enterprises would lead to an unbalanced economic structure." In this conservative view, "government policies" had "put the public economy in a disadvantaged position, losing ground to the private sector. That is what we are going to reform."[57] But such "reform" was really a post-reform effort to restore an older order.

The state affected the legal ownership types of nonstate enterprises, but it had less effect on their presence, absence, or overall growth. This political phenomenon was evident also in other countries that underwent a deflation of socialism. For example, János Kenedi describes three kinds of house contractors in Hungary: the state firms that have low prices but low reliability, the licensed private builders who do their jobs well at high prices, and illegal ones who do their jobs well at low prices (partly because those builders steal materials from the state).[58] The private and illegal economies in China, as in Hungary, depend on the state sector and would be structured differently if it did not exist. They are deeply affected by tax laws, bureaucrats, and the existence of state companies. But they do not always react to this environment as conservative officials intend they should, or as outside observers think they will.

The same point is true in inverse form: In a context of more enterprise and hard work, socialist politics slowly change. Markets among communist traders, connected to each other through the CCP, did not work well to spur growth; nor were Chinese planners in the reform era able to inspire much hard work within the state sector. But traders and managers who were really independent actors, i.e., capitalists, did this – and their obvious prosperity tended to delegitimate planning. Richard Smith sees this phenomenon from a Marxist viewpoint: "It was precisely the failure of market reform to transform the 'socialist' state sector that forced the reform leadership . . . to tolerate the growth of an initially small but rapidly growing private capitalist sector." He adds with regret: "Today, this dynamic and increasingly powerful capitalist 'economy within the economy' is threatening to bring down the entire bureaucratic social order and restore capitalism in China."[59] Smith's evaluation of the educated bureaucrats' order may be mooted, but his analysis of a political danger to state socialism as an economic system calls a spade a spade. If high PRC leaders could not deliver goods, many Chinese sought other leaders who could.

Notes

1 *SHJJYJ*, May 1985, 46.
2 *Shanghai jingji, neibu ben*, 869–71.
3 *WHB*, September 12, 1975.
4 The 1976 figure was 908,000, and the 1983 number was 1,690,000. *Shanghai shehui xiankuang he qushi, 1980–1983*, 21.
5 Calculated from *SHTJNJ86*, 52.
6 *Shanghai jingji, neibu ben*, 96.
7 *Zhongguo shehui tongji ziliao, 1987* (Chinese Social Statistics, 1987), Social Statistics Office, State Statistical Bureau, ed. (Beijing: Zhongguo Tongji Chuban She, 1987), 1.
8 Tao Yongkuan, *Dali fazhan disan chanye*, 13.
9 Zhang Zhongli, Zhu Qingzha, *Disan chanye de lilun yu shixian: Jianlun Shanghai disan chanye fazhan zhanlue* (Theory and Practice of the Tertiary Sector: On the Development Strategy of Shanghai's Tertiary Sector) (Shanghai: Shanghai Shehui Kexue Yuan Chuban She, 1986), 16.
10 *Shanghai shehui xiankuang*, 31 and 36.
11 Cao Linzhang, Gu Guangqing, and Li Jianhua, *Shanghai shengchan ziliao suoyu zhi jiegou yanjiu*, 217.
12 *SHJJNJ88*, 84.
13 Yan Tingchang, Cai Beihua, and Xu Zhihe, *Shanghai lüyou ye de jintian he mingtian*, 98 and 103.
14 As an old poetic ad says, "Above is paradise, below are Suzhou and Hangzhou" (*shang you tiantang, xia you SuHang*).
15 *Hengxiang jingji lianhe de xin fazhan* (New Development of Horizontal Economic Links), Shanghai Economics Association, ed. (Shanghai: Shanghai Shehui Kexue Yuan Chuban She, 1987), 182–85.
16 Yan Tingchang, Cai Beihua, and Xu Zhihe, *Shanghai lüyou*, 2–3.
17 Also, Dorothy Solinger, *China's Transition from Socialism*, 76.
18 *XWB*, February 2, 1989.
19 Ibid.
20 *LDB*, March 19, 1989.
21 Ibid.
22 *Xianggang jingji bao* (Hong Kong Economic Journal), July 21, 1989.
23 Ibid.
24 China's legally registered free markets at the end of 1990 numbered 72,130, but trading occurred elsewhere too. *CD*, December 14, 1990.
25 Lynn White, *Policies of Chaos*, Chapter 2, e.g., Table 1 on 76, and other works cited there, e.g., by Robert Loh and by John Gardner.
26 Cao Linzhang, Gu Guangqing, and Li Jianhua, *Shanghai shengchan*, 193.
27 Ibid.
28 *Shanghai jingji, neibu ben*, 260. Labor productivity in lane factories from 1963 to 1965 might be calculated on a district-by-district basis from ibid., 259.
29 Mid-1970s raw data are ibid., 258 and 260.
30 *Dangdai Zhongguo de jingji tizhi gaige*, 564.
31 Interview with a Shanghai economist, November 1988.
32 Alan Liu, "The 'Wenzhou Model' of Development and China's Modernization," *Asian Survey* 22:8 (August 1992), 704.
33 *XMWB*, January 1, 1982.
34 *JFRB*, May 11, 1988.
35 *Shanghai shehui xiankuang*, 100 and 106, does not give time series Gini coefficients, and its reporting of evenness in state employees' incomes is so extreme that it may omit some emoluments. Nonstate incomes varied more.
36 *Shanghai shimin banshi zhinan*, 82.
37 *Tansuo yu zhengming* (Investigation and Debate), March 1988, 50.

332 Service providers

38 The Premier's expense accounts and perks were extras. Report from an interviewee.
39 *Tansuo yu zhengming* (Investigation and Debate), March 1988, 51.
40 Cao Linzhang, Gu Guangqing, and Li Jianhua, *Shanghai shengchan*, 194.
41 Karl Marx and Frederick Engels, *Manifesto of the Communist Party* (Beijing: Foreign Languages Press, 1965), 48–49.
42 Calculated from raw figures in *FBIS*, March 11, 1988, 26, radio of March 10. Partly based on interviews.
43 This has also been an issue in the United States. The city council of Berkeley, California, asked voters to evaluate a "Measure P" referendum on general election day 2014: "Should the United States Constitution be amended to abolish the legal concept that corporations are persons entitled to constitutional rights, and the doctrine that the expenditure of money may be treated as speech?" The 'yes' vote was 84 percent
44 *Shanghai shimin banshi zhinan*, 105–06.
45 See Alison W. Conner, "To Get Rich is Precarious: Regulation of Private Enterprise in the People's Republic of China," *Journal of Chinese Law* 5:1 (Spring 1991), esp. 3.
46 This phrase was reported by Kate Xiao Zhou. For more on "dependent firms" see an article that Zhou and I co-authored, "Quiet Politics and Rural Enterprise in Reform China," 461–90.
47 *CD*, March 11, 1989.
48 *CD*, April 16, 1991.
49 This law was passed before the 1988 announcement that such businesses were legal in Shanghai. A table of rates (from 7 percent on incomes less than 1,000 yuan; but 25 percent on twice that) is in "Temporary Income Tax Regulations for Urban and Rural Private Businesses in the PRC (Jan. 7, 1986)," in *Chinese Private Enterprises*, State Council Investigation Team, ed. (Beijing: Reform Press, 1990).
50 *CD*, April 18, 1989, based on a WHB report.
51 *Zhongguo shuiwu baike chuanshu* (Encyclopedia of Chinese Taxation), Encyclopedia of Chinese Taxation Editorial Group, ed. (Beijing: Jingji Guanli Chuban She, 1991), 286.
52 *CD*, April 18, 1989, based on a WHB report.
53 *CD*, August 5, 1988.
54 *Shanghai shimin banshi zhinan*, 120–22. The complex tables of tax rates would be reproduced here, if other documents did not show that private Shanghai businesspeople widely ignored them.
55 Misagh Parsa, "Entrepreneurs and Democratization: Iran and the Philippines," *Comparative Studies in Society and History* 37:4 (October 1995), 803–30.
56 These six factors organize the central chapters of Lynn White, *Democratization in Hong Kong – and China?* (Boulder: Lynne Rienner Publishers, 2016).
57 *CD*, July 14, 1989.
58 Barrett L. McCormick, *Political Reform in Post-Mao China: Democracy and Bureaucracy in a Leninist State* (Berkeley: University of California Press, 1990), 86, quoting Janos Kenedi, *Do It Yourself* (London: Pluto Press, 1981).
59 Richard Smith, "The Chinese Road to Capitalism," *New Left Review* 199 (May–June 1993), 60–61.

13

MIGRANTS STAFF CHINA'S REFORM ECONOMY

The reform boom brought millions of Chinese to new jobs and homes. Urbanization and migration are salient aspects of development anywhere. Finding ways to capture the value of labor in modern places is a basis for capital accumulation. Arthur Lewis has explained the mechanism by which the capital-gathering sector grows for a long period before its prosperity begins to help most workers.[1] Output gains, at an early stage of modern growth, involve the migration of ex-agricultural laborers into industry or commerce – and usually toward cities. These workers earn wages not far above traditional subsistence pay, as long as the supply of them lasts. The value of what they make is greater than what they receive, and capital-accumulating networks sell far and wide to take the difference. Following Lewis, Michael Todaro shows how this syndrome brings ex-peasant workers to towns, where they can get wages higher than they earned in farming.[2]

China's population surviving near subsistence was, before the 1970–1990 reforms, most of the people. Mao's state developed political constituencies of workers, for whom the wage markup that Lewis noted was guaranteed but low. The government enforced – and less effectively still tries to enforce – residence controls in cities. Urban wage costs were partly restrained because police "paid" high-productivity manufacturing workers partly with rights to city residence. This policy maximized state revenues, with Maoist cadres in effect serving the role of Lewis' "capitalist sector." The success of this system began to decline in the 1970s, and it buckled in the mid-1980s for reasons shown earlier in this book. But it delayed the migration of labor that Lewis and Todaro describe in general for early modern growth.

Extent of migration

China's largest metropolis and the "green city" surrounding it provide extensive evidence of these trends.[3] Shanghai has long been a settlement of "sojourners."[4]

334 Migrants staff China's reform economy

This place was already a transshipment center before the arrival of European settlers in the early 1840s. Landowning elites came especially in three political waves: Refugees fled the Taiping Rebellion during the late 1850s. A second influx flowed to Shanghai's International Settlement because of the 1930s Japanese invasion. China's civil war of the late 1940s saw a further deluge of about 2 million.[5] Former farmers came for economic reasons during all these periods.

Table 13.1 offers a survey of registered migration in and out of Shanghai, and it shows the strength of state efforts to move people away during Mao's time.

TABLE 13.1 Registered migration to and from Shanghai (migrants in, out, and net; and percentages of total population in the municipality)

	Sh. pop.	pop. in	in %	out	% out	net in	% net
1950	4978213	566951	11.4	623342	12.5	−56391	−1.1
51	5224621	1004032	19.2	566208	10.8	437824	8.4
52	5624141	430039	7.6	352117	6.3	77922	1.4
53	5939367	487806	8.2	255492	4.3	232314	3.9
54	6339740	457576	7.2	296712	4.7	160864	2.5
55	6429039	260430	4.1	847293	13.2	−586863	−9.1
56	6290196	382551	6.1	443326	7.0	−60775	−1.0
57	6623157	418474	6.3	134833	2.0	283641	4.3
58	7202492	193728	2.7	513432	7.1	−319704	−4.4
59	8895972	323163	3.6	322050	3.6	1113	0.0
60	10423439	237697	2.3	265903	2.6	−28206	−0.3
61	10576449	192723	1.8	335522	3.2	−142799	−1.4
62	10584286	213809	2.0	375867	3.6	−162058	−1.5
63	10657542	152565	1.4	238262	2.2	−85697	−0.8
64	10799301	154140	1.4	200999	1.9	−46859	−0.4
65	10900050	161679	1.5	206458	1.9	−44779	−0.4
66	10948123	101005	0.9	178724	1.6	−77719	−0.7
67	11007744	39983	0.4	73385	0.7	−33402	−0.3
68	11073463	94274	0.9	172413	1.6	−78139	−0.7
69	11014847	77488	0.7	352535	3.2	−275047	−2.5
70	10832725	58527	0.5	370955	3.4	−312428	−2.9
71	10698848	126392	1.2	253829	2.4	−127437	−1.2
72	10654624	128718	1.2	188503	1.8	−59785	−0.6
73	10670592	171298	1.6	158909	1.5	12389	0.1
74	10718962	166509	1.6	161670	1.5	4839	0.0
75	10752502	212096	2.0	217199	2.0	−5103	0.0
76	10790117	200180	1.9	202068	1.9	−1888	0.0
77	10838868	196291	1.8	188350	1.7	7941	0.1
78	10923759	248335	2.3	181288	1.7	67047	0.6
79	11152094	598260	5.4	333390	3.0	264870	2.4
80	11465200	287559	2.5	210834	1.8	76725	0.7
81	11628400	236223	2.0	192127	1.7	44096	0.4
82	11805100	234601	2.0	196557	1.7	38044	0.3
83	11940100	226773	1.9	190821	1.6	35952	0.3

	Sh. pop.	pop. in	in %	out	% out	net in	% net
84	12047800	196551	1.6	174842	1.5	21079	0.2
85	12166900	182904	1.5	129873	1.1	53031	0.4
86	12323300	197700	1.6	135000	1.1	62700	0.5
87	12495100	221700	1.8	154000	1.2	67700	0.5
88	12624200	221100	1.8	170200	1.3	50900	0.4
89	12764500	210900	1.7	169500	1.3	41400	0.3
90	12833500	188700	1.5	174100	1.4	14600	0.1
91	12872000	167000	1.3	145400	1.1	21600	0.2
92	12893700	175300	1.4	149200	1.2	26100	0.2
93	12947400	185500	1.5	118600	0.9	66900	0.5
94	12988100	199600	1.5	125400	1.0	74200	0.6

Notes and sources: Percentages are calculated. Note the change from negative to positive net immigration in 1972–1973. Most figures after 1979 are rounded in the sources, as prior ones surely should have been. The basis for data collection has changed somewhat in certain years, as noted below. Migrants to and from Shanghai have often been registered; but increasingly after the mid-1980s, arrivals who were not counted became numerous. Many migrants have gone into urban districts, although this also became less pronounced after the mid-1980s when more lived in suburban counties.

Administrative changes compromise the comparability of figures among periods. The population of places incorporated into Shanghai from Jiangsu in the late 1950s (by decrees with different dates) was a noticeable fraction of the municipality's total at that time. This boundary change, which mainly affects the first column, means that 1950–1959 figures are not quite comparable to later ones. The reliability of reporting also varied over political periods: The 1958 and 1967–1970 migration figures may be wrong by especially notable margins, overstating the net outflow; they are republished here from the source mainly to encourage in the reader a sense of critical humor about such things. Also, the first-column figures through 1987 are average populations during those years; but the best source found for 1988–1990 does not specify this. None of these problems affect the most important trends the table shows.

Raw data begin in Zhongguo renkou: Shanghai fence (China's Population: Shanghai Volume), Hu Huanyong, ed. (Beijing: Zhongguo Caizheng Jingji Chuban She, 1987), 77. Slightly different figures are in *Shanghai tongji nianjian, 1988* (Shanghai Statistical Yearbook, 1988), Li Mouhuan, ed. (Shanghai: Shanghai Shi Tongji Ju, 1988), 92 and 76. The last years' data are on 60 and 67 of the 1990 Shanghai yearbook, 60 and 68 of the 1991 edition, 60 and 82 of the 1992 edition, 64 and 70 of the 1993 edition, 41 and 44 of the 1994 edition, and 47 and 50 of the 1995 edition. Some figures are separately confirmed (with slight differences) in Lin You Su, "Urban Migration in China: A Case Study of Three Urban Areas" (Ph.D. dissertation, Department of Geography, Australian National University, 1992), 72. The first source makes clear that these numbers come from police records on legal permanent and temporary residents. Illegal migrants are not counted; and their number was sometimes substantial even before the last years reported above.

In the next four decades, especially after 1954, the tide of people into Shanghai ebbed. Quasi-forced emigration from the city was at an all-time high in 1955. This topic deserves more research than it has received; the 1955 change was greater than that in 1969–1971. From 1950 to 1992, a cumulative total of 11.2 million people had their household registrations removed from Shanghai. Fewer, 10.8 million, came legally into the city. During the years of greatest emigration, from 1955 to 1972, the net outflow was 2.2 million people (see Table 13.1). Immigrants who did not obtain police permission to live in Shanghai increased after 1971; but they had

336 Migrants staff China's reform economy

to hide, and their number is unknown. Low net rates in the early 1990s show that the state tried to control registrations – and because urban residence is a major issue in family and local politics, that was a change.

The demographic table displays a great deal of political-economic history. The huge 1950–1951 round-ups of "vagabonds" were almost completely balanced by an influx of Communist ex-guerrillas and others to the metropolis then. Third Field Army Marshal Chen Yi, the first PRC mayor of Shanghai, whose former soldiers liked to live there, declared: "We must evacuate the population of the city systematically and transfer factories to the interior whenever possible."[6] But he and many of his ex-guerrilla troops stayed there. The 1955 food shortages, along with pressure on urban people to move inland before the 1956 Transition to Socialism, caused the highest rate of net emigration Shanghai has had since the 1940s. The sham-liberal Hundred Flowers of early 1957 allowed more immigration than the Anti-Rightist campaign of late 1957 forced in emigration. The Great Leap Forward of 1958–1959, with its sequel depression, spurred high rates of emigration – but immigration was also fairly high at that turbulent time. The period of revolutionary China's most intensive state influence, in the early 1960s, saw many years with only slight net emigrations. The Cultural Revolution of 1969–1970 brought the most famous "rustication" campaign, though in comparison to 1955 or 1958 it was not the most massive tide of policy-generated emigration.[7] Rusticated intellectuals have received most scholarly attention. The 1955 campaign was proportionately larger than the 1969–1970 rustications, and it was quicker. But the portion of writers in the early send-downs was lower; so their history is less recorded. The small and underreported reversal after 1970 is also missed, because intellectual writers still fared badly then.

During reforms, a new pattern of net migration emerged by the early 1970s. In 1973, for the first time in many years, the net inflow percentage was positive. The reform pattern began then, and it showed a positive but low influx of legally legitimated immigrants. Full data on migration are unavailable because of nonregistered settlers; but when temporary residence (*linshi hukou*) status became easier to obtain in Shanghai during the 1980s, many people came. On this topic, as on others, behavioral data raise doubts about the oft-repeated notion that 1966–1976 should be conceived as an homogeneous period of Chinese history.

A greater influx came in 1979, when rusticated ex-youths could return to Shanghai under the '*dingti*' program allowing them to take their parents' jobs. Actually, children returned even though most of the parents did not retire – despite policy pronouncements that they should. This laxness was caused by temporary political allowances to families that had suffered during the Cultural Revolution, at a time when the current state elite blamed for many injustices an earlier state elite (the Gang of Four). After 1972, no year except 1979 showed a major net influx of registered residents. Those who came without registrations tell the main new story below.

Suburban managers and ex-peasant workers, especially in mid-sized cities

Pressures attracting people to modern settlements had been matched in Mao's time by state counterpressures to maintain the government's fiscal and political bases in large cities. Beyond the rural/urban division, workers in cities were split into two tiers: permanent and transient. The first post-revolution government in Shanghai, which was mostly ex-military after the Third Field Army arrived, already stipulated that "directly employed temporary workers" (*zhijie guyong linshi gong*) should not exceed in each company 20 percent of the authorized number of "regular workers" (*zhengshi gong*).[8] When firms hired permanent employees, they were supposed to report to the city's Labor Bureau, which kept files on names and numbers. Soon the rules allowed that "according to the needs of production" temporary workers might receive regular status; but this was supposed to occur only when the result was an increase of state profits. Statistics during the First Five-Year Plan suggest there were on average 160,000 temporary laborers then in Shanghai – or about 10 percent of the regular workforce. During the depression after the Great Leap, "when there were no production tasks," many contract workers were fired. The government ordered that they not be regular workers. This limitation was not, however, strictly enforced.

As the post-Leap depression eased, construction teams could again come to Shanghai, under a "both worker and peasant" (*yigong yinong*) norm. Rural production brigades acted as labor contractors, receiving money directly from urban companies that needed help. The builders were supposed to get only 40 percent of their work points from construction, and the remaining 60 percent from farming – so they were also called "four, six workers," but this ratio was not applied uniformly.[9]

Immigration to Shanghai and to other cities on the delta cannot be understood separately from two major factors that structured it: flows back from quasi-coercive rustications in 1955–1958 and 1968–1971, and the boom of rural industries around the metropolis. After 1967 throughout China, the army was ordered to dampen the Cultural Revolution's urban chaos. More than 16 million young people were sent "up to the mountains and down to the villages" (*shangshan xiaxiang*).[10] With these "rusticates" went many older cadres who had been attacked during the movement, although their number has been estimated with so much variance that it is hard to know. During the 1970s, about half of these came back; and by the 1980s, the cumulative portion was two-thirds.[11]

New building projects were, by the early 1970s, more common in small Yangzi delta cities than in the big metropolis. For ex-peasants, as for ex-rusticates, the story of Shanghai immigration cannot be separated from the tale of migrations to smaller places. Medium-sized settlements on the Yangzi delta were affected, as was the central city, by official efforts to limit urban population size – but in an unexpected way. Mid-size cities were harder for central bureaucrats to monitor, and economic growth in them expanded the total number of adjacent industrial and agricultural

338 Migrants staff China's reform economy

TABLE 13.2 Migration to and from Yangzi delta cities: Shaoxing and Xiashi (percentages of population)

Shaoxing	1949–1960	1961–1970	1971–1980	1981–1985
Immigration	3.3	1.5	1.3	2.7
Emigration	2.1	2.4	1.4	1.6
Net migration	1.2	−0.9	−0.1	1.1
Xiashi				
Immigration	2.5	2.0	3.5	4.4
Emigration	1.4	2.5	2.4	1.8
Net migration	1.1	−0.5	1.1	2.6

Source: Registration data of the Shaoxing and Xiashi public security bureaus, 1986, in Lin You Su, "Urban Migration in China: A Case Study of Three Urban Areas" (Ph.D. dissertation, Department of Geography, Australian National University, 1992), 75.

jobs. Details are available from two Zhejiang places. The larger is Shaoxing, a very famous cultural center and prefectural capital with a 1986 population just over 250,000. The smaller is Xiashi, a county seat containing about 40,000 people, inland from Hangzhou Bay's north shore in Zhejiang. As Table 13.2 shows, both these places showed some net outmigration between 1961 and 1970. The county seat in particular had net immigration at other times, especially during the 1980s – when Xiashi had lower emigration than in either of the earlier periods for which data are available. Jobs were available in small Jiangnan cities throughout reforms.

Comparative migration: genders, ages, settlement sizes, and schooling for migrants' kids

If migration means movement between any settlements, probably most migrants in the reform period (56 percent, according to a 1987 study) have been women. Leslie Chang has written a riveting book about migrant girls' experiences in factories.[12] Young women could change their residences in Chinese society, which was traditionally patrilocal; but in many low-income countries, most migrants have been men. Women from poor areas during the 1970s could apparently begin to move more frequently than at earlier times, because they could obtain permissions from team or village leaders to take jobs in industries that were developing rapidly. By the 1980s, many Chinese girls worked in suburban factories that traded internationally. Young women, having a lower status than men in boondock areas, were more readily allowed to move elsewhere if they remitted money to their families.[13] As light-industrial factories expanded exports, their number grew.

Most people who moved during reforms from Chinese rural areas to *large* cities, however, were men.[14] The influx to coastal places was greatest; and most provinces, which are inland, showed net outflows of population.[15] From 1983 to 1987, over 30 million people moved long distances between different cities, towns, or counties in China. That was about 3 percent of the national population, moving in just a few years. Such a figure would not be high in an industrialized nation, but it is high for a developing country – and is underreported because of unregistered people.

Migration volumes correlated inversely with the distance the migrants moved. Comparative data from Shanghai, Shaoxing, and the smaller Zhejiang city of Xiashi show this for the reform years. (Only the Shanghai data do not show it for earlier periods, because of the government's long-distance send-down programs, which in many cases sent Shanghai people far west, e.g., to Gansu or Xinjiang.) Also, young people tended to move farther than older people. Retirees often moved within the same county. Migrants who came from larger settlements tended to go farther to their new residences; those from small places typically traveled within regions. Especially after 1970, most migration to Shanghai delta cities was toward medium-large settlements there, but an increasing majority of migrations were short-distance.[16] These patterns became more pronounced in China during reforms, as pre-1990 state efforts to limit urbanization became less effective.

The sources of immigration to Shanghai have been mostly nearby, but previous send-downs to provinces far away brought some people back from a distance. A 1986 survey showed that 70 percent of interprovincial migration to Shanghai came from five other provinces: Jiangsu, 31 percent; Zhejiang, 14; Anhui, 11; Jiangxi, 8; and distant Heilongjiang, 7.[17] But later, by 1986–1990, because of very fast economic growth in southern Jiangsu that reduced "push factors" for emigration from there more than from provinces further inland, only one-fifth of Shanghai registered immigrants hailed from Jiangsu. Jiangnan migrants to Shanghai reportedly tended to have somewhat less difficulty being registered than migrants from elsewhere – but because of proximity, they also could make repeated trips between the city and their previous homes.[18] Booming Jiangnan industries kept many potential migrants out of Shanghai.

Construction teams (*jianzhu dui*) became busy in the metropolis from 1986 to 1990, when roughly two-thirds of the registered immigrants were men. From Jiangsu, 213 male migrants came to Shanghai then for each 100 women. Men were nearly as high a proportion from Zhejiang and Anhui (199 and 181 men per 100 women, respectively).[19] This was typical of what comparativists call the "construction phase" of migration. Women, more liable to take jobs hawking in Shanghai and less likely to have work units register their residences, may well be underrepresented in these figures; but most migration to Shanghai urban districts was male. When these men were recorded, most had legal residency that was just temporary, though many "overstayed their visas."

To see what the overall pattern means politically – for the people who moved, for established residents, and for national and local leaders – it is useful to look not just at broad trends but also at the motives of individuals and families. Former "educated youths" wanted their places in Shanghai back, ex-agricultural workers wanted higher incomes, old city residents wanted domestic helpers and low-paid subalterns to justify better jobs for themselves, local managers and police could find clients by arranging urban household registrations, and state leaders wanted fiscal revenues and political support.

340 Migrants staff China's reform economy

Early 1970s reverse rustication

The return of sent-down people to Shanghai began well before Mao's death. "Educated youths" did not all wait for state permission before reappearing at Shanghai. To discourage their return, the Chairman himself had ordered rural communes to treat urban rusticates well in terms of housing and ration allowances; but interviewees report that peasant leaders generally ignored such calls, even from the "Great Helmsman." Urban youths were often unwelcome in the countryside. Unless they started factories or taught school, many local farmers saw the city youths as drains on resources, languid contributors, and inept field workers. The main exceptions were nubile ex-urban women who, if willing to remain in rural areas, were excellent marriage prospects for peasant men because city families did not ask the high bride prices that rural clans demanded. These family politics had almost nothing to do with state politics.

Many city youths had been reluctant to leave Shanghai, at least in the last two years of the 1960s. Not all of their volunteerism was insincere; some had a will to learn from peasants who were still the majority of their compatriots. (In Hong Kong, whose government never sponsored rustication, some university and school students in the middle of the twentieth century went on stints to work with farmers in the New Territories, hoping to discover how most Chinese lived.) Most Shanghai parents strongly wanted to keep their children in the city, and family politics is powerful politics. Radical administrators in schools had earlier run the rustication program, and Army soldiers also aided this campaign. After the Cultural Revolution disrupted schools, municipal leaders transferred the hard job of trying to persuade families to rusticate their children instead to the work units of the parents.

In the early 1970s, the rate of rustications plummeted, but cadres did not publicize this until later years. "In major cities like Shanghai, the policy of sending youths to the frontiers was sharply cut back."[20] The rustication program, by stirring the residential pot, quickened migration then *and later* between all sizes of cities – and from rural to urban places.

If all of China's officially designated "cities" (about 300 '*shi*') are ranked by size, the fall-off by population for mid-size settlements is less steep than in most countries. The number of China's middle-sized cities is large. Young rusticates, if they absconded from rural posts, often tried to enter metropolises such as Shanghai rather than going back to the rural places where authorities had rusticated them. They saw little to lose, trying the big-city chance – but police hounded them there far more than in medium-sized cities.

For these "rusticates," the effect of policy was opposite to what the state had intended. In effect, rustication sent many, at least temporarily, from big cities via stints in boondocks to medium-sized cities in the early 1970s, before they could return to their birth cities in 1979. Send-down campaigns made migration seem a live option. By 1975, return tides to medium and then large cities had already risen, despite radicals' efforts to stem these counter-flows. Many parents held their state employers responsible for having enforced rustication – and thus responsible for making amends after it ended.

In Shanghai urban districts, the second most common entry on police forms validating permanent residents, accounting for 21 percent of the approved household registrations from 1968 to 1977, was "educated youth returning to the city" (*zhiqing fancheng*). This predated 1978 and the 1979 *dingti* program. Youths who had been sent from huge metropolitan centers to villages often first returned to medium-large cities in the early 1970s. Settlements having less than a million but more than 500,000 people were affected initially; and to these places, the early-1970s reflux was heavy. From approximately 1969 to 1972, gross immigration *trebled* to cities in this large but not gigantic category. Such high rates were not matched for these cities even a decade later. A graph showing these changes clearly for the early 1970s was published in China – but with an accompanying text that studiously avoids interpreting them.[21] The immigration line for "large-sized [500,000–1,000,000] cities" soars in an unmistakable way for 1970–1972. This change in the early 1970s is stunning, and the sample contains no provincial capitals (which tend to have relatively high taxes and strong residence controls). The Chinese text below the graph merely speaks of "re-education in rural [*sic*] areas" and "transfer to a lower level" during the "ten years of upheaval" (1966–1976). The graphed findings about actual behavior are conspicuous, but they are not really 'found' or admitted by the demographers who did the research. It boggles the mind to witness careful PRC scholars doing arduous survey work, coming up with very interesting results, graphing them so that they strike any viewer between the eyes, then blithely ignoring them because 1966–1976 was officially supposed to be a homogeneous period. Everyone was thought to know that nothing really new could possibly have happened in the early 1970s, because these years were part of the Cultural Revolution.

Various "J-curve" forms of migration have been evident in other countries, too.[22] The rate of immigration to China's cities of more than a million climbed after 1970, rising from that year to 1972 – and achieving levels that had not been seen since the Great Leap Forward. After a slight reported dip in 1975–1976 (during the last gasp of the Gang of Four), this rate rose to a new high in 1979, when many rusticates returned. Then it stabilized at a medium level. The influx to very large cities had begun somewhat earlier, but 1979 showed a quantum leap in it, as the available percentages within periods of the total 1949–1986 inflow show: 1969–1970, 3.4; 1971–1972, 4.4; 1973–1974, 3.7; 1975–1976, 5.5; 1977–1978, 7.1; 1979–1980, 12.3; 1981–1982, 7.8; 1983–1984, 8.3; and 1985–1986, 8.1. Figures for later reform years are difficult to confirm, because unregistered immigration to big cities soared.

A survey for a sample of cities whose populations were over 500,000 but less than a million – where residence restrictions were less severe – show percentages of total 1949–1986 immigration more heavily weighted toward the early 1970s: 1969–1970, 10.5; 1971–1972, 10.5; 1973–1974, 5.7; 1975–1976, 6.5; 1977–1978, 5.4; 1979–1980, 7.2; 1981–1982, 6.9; 1983–1984, 7.3; and 1985–1986, 8.9.[23] For these cities, the early reform rate to 1972 was never topped (at least through the next decade and a half on a reported basis). Many youths and cadres sent to rural areas from very large cities found they could return to somewhat smaller cities then.

An unusually frank Chinese source explains the reasons (while concentrating on later dates): "From 1973 on, more and more youths returned to cities. From 1976,

342 Migrants staff China's reform economy

the government carried out new policies toward these people and toward cadres who came back to cities."[24] An even larger influx occurred in 1978–1979, when 13 million people crowded into urban places all over the country. In Shanghai, police still tried to enforce the household control system. But also, high state remittances and factor costs left urban companies with little money to increase wage budgets. This somewhat discouraged legal regular employment for many years after reforms began. So not all hires were legal. Many migrants came, but their reasons can be more easily attributed to their own interests than to state policies, which both abetted and obstructed migration.

Returns in 1979: with or without jobs

By 1979, public pressure in Shanghai to allow more returns of rusticates was greater than the state could either contain or admit. In that same year, many cadres still tried to urge youths flowing toward Shanghai to return to their inland assignments; but 1979 was also the year of the *dingti* program, allowing ex-rusticates to take their parents' Shanghai jobs if the latter retired. It was entirely typical of the 1978–1981 era (and to a lesser extent the late 1980s) that conservative and reformist cadres were still both strongly represented in the state and at odds with each other. The official 1978 start of reforms showed government divisions in all policy fields, including rustication. Shanghai's Nanshi District Office for Educated Youth called a meeting at which a "consolation team" (*weiwen tuan*) from Heilongjiang tried to propagandize youths, who had returned from that northeast province, to go back.[25] By the time this Heilongjiang team's visit to Shanghai was finished, it had held meetings in Nanshi, Nanpu, Putuo, Jing'an, Hongkou, and Changning districts, as well as Shanghai County. The names of youths who re-volunteered to return north were published with fanfare in newspapers.[26] Whether they actually went is less certain.[27] These procedures were practically identical to the rustication campaigns of the late 1960s – but the reform context was different. Few of the potential re-rusticates were under severe pressure to comply.

A similar problem for state policy existed among graduating university students, who were reluctant to leave the metropolis but in 1979–1980 were often still told "unconditionally to obey the state's requirements."[28] They were supposed to take job assignments that were announced through Party organizations in their schools. Cultural Revolution excesses had made the enforcement of such mandates difficult. The Party was blaming previous leaders, the Gang of Four, for past problems; and it could not at the same time effectively enforce Maoist migration policies. Anger not just against the old policies, but also against the bureaucrats who had implemented them, was intense within families. Everyone, including the potential young recruits, knew this. Occasionally in the early 1980s, "educated youths" back from rural areas went to their old schools in Shanghai and physically attacked their previous "teachers" (often administrators), who had assigned them to permanent lives outside Shanghai that they refused to live.[29]

In late May 1979, there seems to have been a battle in Shanghai, unreported in newspapers but apparently between returned youths and cadres at a police office that had arranged their deportation. A *Shanghai Public Security Yearbook* reached a Hong Kong bookstore despite its "internal circulation" status. It offers a list indicating that, of all the forty-six Shanghai officers killed in line of duty from 1949 to 1980, more than one-quarter (thirteen) died on a single day: May 30, 1979.[30] Of those killed, eight were members of the Communist Youth League, and five were in the Party. Information about collective political violence in China has generally been treated as a state secret. The exact motives of this 1979 case are unclear, but it was lethal for government agents at Shanghai, and rusticates' resentment was apparently the cause.

Returnees to the city peaked in that year. More than 90,000 educated youths were re-registered at Shanghai in 1979. About 20,000 of these received jobs in state units, but 70,000 – the vast majority – reportedly found work in collectives.[31] This was the first year in which state factories were authorized to hold open recruitments (*gongkai zhaogong*), but most of the youths returned from inland were not hired in this way. The collective sector, which then employed 21 percent of Shanghai's total registered labor force, was able to absorb almost four-fifths (78 percent) of the new job seekers. The state sector, which in 1979 still had four-fifths of the city's workers, absorbed only one-fifth of the new influx.[32]

State officials had multiple reasons to oppose "educated youths" returning to Shanghai, but they could do nothing effective to stop the flow tide. To cap wage budgets in state firms (whose materials costs were rising very quickly), they announced a policy that youths could come back to take their parents' jobs if the older generation would retire; this was "substitution" (*dingti*). But most youths came back and found jobs outside the state sector, and not all their parents retired. Established norms that women retire at age 55 and men at 60 meant that some did.

Managers of state-owned enterprises could set up "attached" (*guahu*) collective firms where ex-rusticated children could get jobs. Their personnel rosters required only local approvals. Other nonstate enterprises were linked to "collective offices" (*jiti bangong shi*) at the city, district, or street levels.[33] Leaders at "low" levels could induce local police to re-register the returnees in Shanghai. The problem of finding more permanent jobs was often left until later.

A major criterion for employment was based on an applicant's "character." State managers may well have doubted the rectitude of some ex–Red Guards who were now still angry about their years in the bush. Only a small minority of the 600,000 educated youths who filtered back to Shanghai received high level jobs in state-owned institutions.[34] Ex-youths could not be prevented from returning, but they did not always receive desirable work. In Shanghai alone, roughly half a million (413,000 by 1985) were officially "returned" from rustication – out of the approximately one million who had been sent down.[35] Many returnees retrieved or received legal household registrations and jobs, often in collectives. Others came back to find work in unregistered firms.

Former "educated youth" rusticates and their children

In a sample of people whose registrations had been moved out of Shanghai urban districts, fully 62 percent had returned by the mid-1980s. Among those whose original reasons for leaving had been politically correct, the portion of returnees was particularly large. For example, 91 percent of those who left to join the Army were back in the metropolis. So were 69 percent of those who had gone for "adjusted" work assignments elsewhere. And 66 percent had returned among those who had left to "go up to the mountains and down to the villages."[36]

Other immigrants to Shanghai were the children of rusticated parents who remained outside the metropolis. They came to live with their urban grandparents. Evidence for this major phenomenon (three-generation families, in which the middle generation is absent) can be compiled from various sources. Although national primary school enrollments fell sharply, by 16 percent in the decade beginning 1978 because of lower birth rates in China, for example, Shanghai primary school enrollments in the same period rose by 3 percent.[37] The reason for this stark difference was not that Shanghai families went against the national trends to reduce births or enroll school-age children. Data show that primary enrollment in Shanghai had already been nearly universal by the early 1970s and remained so thereafter; and birth rates in Shanghai were unsurprisingly lower than the national average. Both these factors pushed against the rise of enrollments in Shanghai that nonetheless occurred. Other data indicate that two-thirds of permanently registered immigrants to Shanghai were, at the time of their arrival, in young age cohorts, fifteen to twenty-nine; very many were even younger. Police had not been able to expel from Shanghai young children living with their grandparents, even if the kids had no legal registrations in the city and the inland residences of their parents were known. Three-quarters of all newly registered people were unmarried.[38]

Over three-fifths of all migrants who were listed as "temporary" at Shanghai in the mid-1980s were either the children or in more cases the grandchildren of the household head.[39] Grandchildren were more frequent than children, especially among grandsons (family decisions kept granddaughters more often inland). Most of the parents were "educated youths," sent down in previous years. Some of these people remained away from Shanghai, having established their lives elsewhere. Among Shanghainese who had married elsewhere, only one-quarter returned. But by the 1980s they wanted to send the youngest generation, especially sons, to attend schools in the metropolis.

The state long ago had forced these parents (one or both) out of their city. Because monitors had sent batches of rusticates from particular schools to particular inland places, the chance that both parents came from the same urban districts was considerable. In many cases, they became accustomed to their new places – marrying there, sometimes becoming "big fish in little ponds." They wanted more future choice for their offspring, and education in Shanghai was a way to obtain that. They had done their bit for the state, and they now made decisions according to the interests of their families. The revival of the effective power of families to resist official pressures was real politics, and it made real policy outside official institutions, even though it did so quietly. Evidence for family politics is practically ignored in official documents and political science. It is circumstantial but considerable. Anyone who theorizes that families are not powerful polities, especially in China, should look for more behavioral data. This whole book argues that scholars will learn more if they look locally, and migration politics provides major examples of the approach.

The employment pull: inland workers to village collectives

Half the migrants to Shanghai suburban towns in the 1980s admitted they came "to change jobs."[40] People left inland China in droves to seek employment in cities as large as Shanghai. The rate of absconding was astounding from some boondocks. From one county in Henan, 190,000 people departed; if that county was of typical size, this outmigration was about two-fifths of its population.[41] Women especially sought jobs in housekeeping; and men, in building. As a survey showed: "After all expenditures are excluded, each person can have an average income of 500 yuan per year," far more than could be earned in most inland places. A popular saying put it in rhyme, "If you want to get rich, run to Shanghai!" ('*Yao facai, pao Shanghai*'). A rap specified the city's newest and fastest-growing district: "East, west, south, north, center; to find a job, go to Pudong!" ('*Dong xi nan bei zhong, dagong dao Pudong*').

Most ex-agriculturalists "come to cities because they can make more money and because they are surplus in the countryside. Recently, the development of services and municipal engineering projects provide a lot of employment opportunities. These jobs generally are manual; and urban people, especially youths, are unwilling to do such work. So cities have to absorb skillful people from the countryside, towns, and small cities." Many transients also became domestic maids – and this trend was approved in publications: "In big cities, the family structure is being transformed . . . so family service workers are popular. . . . It is not an exaggeration to say that without them cities, especially big cities, would not operate well. . . . Another stable source of services is contract workers. They organize themselves voluntarily and contract with the units or companies that need them."[42]

The organization of these labor hiring systems was "voluntary" only in the sense that the state could no longer control it. Autonomous labor bosses flourished, of a sort known in many developing capitalist countries, including China before 1949.[43] Booming rural industries absorbed great amounts of labor on the Shanghai delta. Different parts of the flatland varied in their rates of change. In Zhejiang by 1984, rural industry accounted for 46 percent of all product value. Zhejiang factories then used (at least) 23 percent of the rural workforce. Ex-peasants had been displaced from field labor by new technologies and by "responsibility" contracting

346 Migrants staff China's reform economy

in agriculture. Many rural people, not working in either fields or local factories, "floated" to cities like Ningbo and Hangzhou. From Zhejiang, some also left the province for Sunan or moved from poor to rich areas within the province. So by the mid-1980s,

> Over 1.3 million [Zhejiang] laborers are working in other provinces. . . . Jinhua Prefecture [the province's poorest] 'exports' about 200,000 workers, which is about 25 percent of the total agricultural labor power in that prefecture. . . . The local government of Yongjia County allowed [or could not prevent?] 30,000 peasants to work at other places in 1983; this figure was about 15 percent of the county's total labor power. These [absentee] peasants had a total income of 56 million yuan that year, which was about 49 percent of the county's total agricultural [i.e., rural] income.[44]

Half of this non-coastal county's income was coming from the sixth of its workers who had migrated to factory jobs in the Jiangnan flatlands (or in nearby Lishui or Wenzhou).

Long-distance migration to rich cities like Shanghai occurred because the supply of cheap rural labor near the metropolis became depleted. A Chinese economist has calculated the demand for labor in agriculture, in rural industries, and in other local activities. He charted these kinds of employment throughout rural Wuxi between 1975 and 1985, for each year deducting the county's demand for workers from its total supply, calling the residual a surplus. He showed that "rural surplus labor" that had legal Wuxi registration was already down to 55 percent of the work force by 1975, and just 4 percent by 1985.[45] Inland migrants arrived to take jobs on the delta, as local subsistence-wage labor began to disappear in the mid-1980s. So local lineages, reorganized in more presentable modern ways (such as rural CCP committees), could take high "rents" from arranging production they hired migrants to make.

Although the PRC government has traditionally attempted to prevent the formation of a national labor market, rising prosperity meant jobs and migrants. Entrepreneurs in collectives promoted locals into desirable jobs or administrative posts – and imported inlanders to work in factories or fields near subsistence wages. During 1985, Wuxi's permanent work force in rural factories was still more than nine-tenths local (on the brave assumption that migrant workers were reported). With an expansion of contract labor, this portion went down in later years – but the managers of nonstate rural enterprises in Wuxi remained overwhelmingly local.[46] A sample showed that 93 percent of the managers were born in the township where their firms operated. Most well-paid workers were also local. Most ill-paid workers were not.

There was variation according to the administrative level that licensed a factory. Township (or higher) collective factories in the 1980s largely employed local labor. A survey near Jiading, Shanghai, indicated that district- and town-run enterprises seldom hired temporary laborers who came from a distance even as late as

1989. But the pattern was strikingly different for the increasingly important and nominally collective – *de facto* private – factories licensed more locally. Village-run (*cunban*) Jiading firms by 1989 so often hired outside workers that 90 percent of the labor force in some of their factories came from Anhui or Jiangxi.[47]

Two-thirds of Shanghai's "agricultural" farmers (over 3 million people) by the late 1980s were actually working in suburban industries and services. Municipal officials publicly reckoned that the city then had "several hundred thousand" contract workers.[48] The vagueness of the estimate suggests that nobody was able to make a reliable count. Village factory managers, protected by village leaders against any effective state controls, had reasons not to divulge their full lists of workers.

Labor bosses and urban life

It was relatively easy during reforms to justify labor exploitation. As a demographer wrote in 1987, "Some peasants have contracts with urban units. . . . Generally, the income of those doing temporary work in cities is much higher than of those working in rural areas. When peasants go to cities, they widen their vision, increase their knowledge, and become familiar with life in cities. Especially, they learn what urban people need. Peasants see a lot of new products, which they produce following the city models. . . . Because of growing unofficial markets in cities, many surplus workers get jobs."[49]

The reasons "floaters" came to Shanghai, according to a 1988 survey, was occupational for 68 percent and "social" for 23 percent. (Actually, there is no need to distinguish these categories, because 'city air makes freedom' – *Stadtluft macht frei*, as an old phrase said – although cities also had some jobs.) Over seven-tenths of the incoming workers were men in 1988, and at least a quarter of the total came explicitly to work in construction projects. Nearly half (48 percent) of this influx had previously been farmers, and only 15 percent said they had earlier been workers. Only 8 percent of the registered floaters were of school age, and 16 percent were retirees.[50]

A separate report indicated that seven-tenths of legal transients came to Shanghai seeking jobs, and they generally lived in accommodations provided by their employers, with relatives, "or in houses they made by themselves on areas just outside the city or on the streets."[51] These workers would often stay in Shanghai for a several-month job, then go elsewhere, and later perhaps return for further work. A second, more affluent group of transients consisted of cadres and businesspeople, who generally lived in small hotels or reception stations (*zhaodai suo*), staying for relatively short periods but returning often to Shanghai. This group comprised one-fifth of the transients.

Labor seekers who came to the metropolis did not remain second-class citizens forever. Three-fifths of permanent Shanghai immigrants since the regime's early years had, by the mid-1980s, acquired regular blue-collar jobs. More than a quarter had achieved managerial or professional posts. More long-term immigrants held white-collar jobs than previous Shanghai citizens did. Some of these were political

348 Migrants staff China's reform economy

appointees (sometimes kin of ex-rural former guerrillas), but most were ordinary migrants who worked hard and did well.

Many newcomers with temporary household registrations took menial tasks. But people who had been in the city for a number of years made more money, on average, than nonmigrants (those born in Shanghai or living there before 1950). They put up with harsh conditions to establish urban households – and in time, they were successful. This was true not just in the metropolis, but also in smaller cities.[52] Economic pull is not just a demographic abstraction. From the viewpoint of the individual or the family, statistics show that migration to Shanghai, followed by years of work there, was in the long term a highly rational action.

Managers and police: the erosion of household controls, more temporary registrations

Managers try to hire cheap labor, and they have some interests that parallel migrants' hopes. In Shanghai, each large firm includes public security liaison officers, who generally must approve residence registrations for any new employee, either permanent or temporary. So long as the firm does not incur excessive costs for housing, and so long as the total number of (reported) new employees passes muster with higher officials, this system ties legal migration to economic work. What it also did, especially if local managers' reporting was not closely checked, was to keep a power of managers in state enterprises to recruit new personal clients. The result was extensive registered "temporary" migration of workers, who often stayed in Shanghai on a permanent basis.

This was not supposed to happen, according to official rules. All temporary household approvals were, at least by the mid-1980s, formally subject to police review for renewal or termination after three months. "Numerous officials have indicated, however, that these requirements for temporary registration are not always rigorously enforced, nor is careful attention given to the length of time that an individual has remained at a destination, provided that the individual does not become a burden on the community."[53] Such approvals are local. Even after "temporary" residence expires in one company or construction project or urban district, a worker may be able to find another.

Any rural migrant into a city is also supposed to have a letter from police in the town whence he or she comes. Urban police are supposed to require that document (among others) when the migrant applies for temporary or permanent registration. By no means, however, does every farmer leave a rural area with such a letter. Nor does every urban immigrant apply for the benefits of registration.

A merely apparent incentive to comply – since food rationing and job allocation were less effectively regulated than before reforms – was the possibility of having an employer find housing. Little new space was available for the state to distribute, because low urban rents and high taxes had for years discouraged residential construction. Housing reform largely became a matter of building at the edge of the city, so that the government could evict old downtown residents to build more centrally located structures that brought high official rents.[54] At first, reforms did not much raise real rents for residents who stayed in their assigned housing. State enterprises had scant new money to build homes for staff. Cheap housing still created a strong tie between state sector employees and their employers into the 1990s, because for most ordinary people in Shanghai, space is the scarcest resource. Immigrants got little housing anyway. For registering, most migrants did not even receive temporary quarters. They had to find shelter on their own – and they did so.

They could apply for permanent (*changzhu*) registration, and well-connected immigrants received this. If the police did not issue this document, the effect on the newcomer's behavior was usually not immediate. Since most facilities other than housing had become available for money, many who preferred permanent registration in Shanghai nonetheless stayed there with lesser or no licenses. Manager-patrons, following their own interests that could differ from those of the state, kept better control both of their budgets and of their worker-clients by arranging less permanent documents.

Nonpermanent household registrations were of two kinds: Temporary (*linshi* or *zhanzhu*) documents were legally required, in theory, for any citizen staying in Shanghai for more than three days – though this rule was seldom enforceable, especially if the person moved from place to place within the city. Seconded (*jizhu*) registration was for officially sanctioned activities, e.g., in the economy or in government. Application for either kind of license was supposed to be made within three days of arrival in the city.

These urban immigration forms usually went through either of two agencies: the city's Personnel Department (Renshi Ju) for cadres, or the Labor Bureau (Laodong Ju) for most people. The ordinary sufficient criterion for approval was backing from a Shanghai employer. Professional cadres could move to Shanghai if they were sent by state units (including most companies). Returned youths were often helped by their parents' employers, whether or not they took jobs at those firms. There was also a procedure by which unmarried rusticates from Shanghai families could be brought back to the city without jobs, but the conditions were written restrictively: A single member applies to return home, but the application is approved only if older relatives in Shanghai are "severely sick" and have no able-bodied family members to care for them (especially if the offspring outside Shanghai is an only child).[55] Actual practice was less restrictive than the fearsome law. Many rural migrants arrived either under the auspices of a labor contractor, or else without papers.

The procedures became easier in the 1980s, because of the demonstration effect on other groups of insistent pressure from sent-down youths by 1979. People who attained permanent registrations usually reached Shanghai because a company gave a job and arranged some kind of household registration at the same time. A survey comparing large samples of 1958–1976 immigrants with those of 1977–1986 found that registered hiring was the main reason for moves to Shanghai of only 7 percent of immigrants in the Maoist years – but of 31 percent after that.[56] Leaders of established urban firms could populate their patronage networks during reforms by arranging Shanghai household registrations for new followers. This practice was traditionalist in an old (not new) Chinese sense, adding to "relationship networks" (*guanxi wang*); but it weakened Communist organization in favor of small networks. It was not a neotraditionalism that strengthened the state.

Greater freedom of movement for citizens within the country was an aspect of reforms that many writers have neglected.[57] Urban intellectuals generally doubted that freedom of movement is an unalloyed good. Internal migration accompanied the 1979 removal of bad labels (such as 'rightist,' 'bourgeois,' or others), and norms in other fields were loosened too. Most Chinese could then buy a train or bus ticket between cities without having to show as many official documents as had been required in earlier eras (except the late 1960s).[58] Already by the early 1980s, the arthritic Ministry of Railroads was far behind the demand for passenger transport from newly rich entrepreneurs and ex-farmers, foreign tourists, Taiwanese, migrants, and other travelers. Getting tickets was sometimes difficult, and getting seats was a matter of luck; but people could travel.

Ordinary trains from Anhui to Shanghai were chock-full. Anhui stations would sell tickets to would-be migrants, who might wait for days trying to get inside the slow trains (often climbing through windows when the doors were blocked by other passengers). Train 311, on one day, reportedly was so packed that eight people could find standing room only in a car's small toilet. Claustrophobic migrants were reported sometimes to have died as they jumped out of moving trains on the Anhui-Shanghai line. A survey of one such train found a high frequency of "mental disorders" because of crowding. On this route from Hefei to Shanghai, 86 percent of the passengers were migrants.[59]

"The large majority did not have official permission to change their registrations from rural to urban."[60] As a late 1980s source said, "The portion of the people who are 'temporarily resident' is getting higher and higher. Although the government has not recognized their urban citizenship, they are playing important roles in economic and social life."[61] But obtaining food and shelter depended less on state documents than in Mao's years.

The declining effectiveness of household registers and ration controls

During the 1980s, the registration and ration systems remained in force but lost their previous power over citizens' lives. Households with legal registry books (*hukou bu*) were entitled to grain certificates (*guliang zheng*) and supplementary food certificates (*fushi pin zheng*). Grain and food stores would mark the ration cards when selling specified amounts of provisions in set time periods. But during reforms, the same products could also be bought at slightly higher prices, with better quality, on free markets. So the ration system lost its effectiveness as a means of residence control.[62]

Identification cards (*shenfen zheng*) for urban residents were issued by the PRC government in 1987, and these became the main documents police might require. After Tiananmen, the Ministry of Public Security on September 15, 1989, decreed an "interim provision" that urban citizens should carry these cards at all times.[63] This revived an individual registration system like that used by Chiang Kai-shek's Kuomintang before 1949 (bitterly criticized then by the CCP). The identity cards ordinarily included a name, photo, home address, and ID number – but without information on employment or on "class origin," as had earlier been used in the household registries.

The ID cards were issued to individuals, not families. They did not much raise state control over persons. They were more common, and thus permissive, replacements for previous cards issued by employers for purposes such as buying travel tickets. Household registration books for a while still had to be presented for obtaining rations, school admissions, jobs, housing, moving vans, marriage licenses, or birth or death certificates (sometime occasions to edit the books). But household registration also ceased to be an effective system of complete control.

Police legally could fine citizens for failure to show their ID cards, but officers unless annoyed seldom held people to this rule. The number of unregistered people in Shanghai was high, but police asked to see ID cards mainly during temporary campaigns.

By 1994, however, the municipal police tightened rules during a rise of conservative change. They required work certificates (*wugong zheng*) in hopes of limiting migrants, approving only those who had backing from regular companies. This plan aimed at legalizing work permits in the city for employees who were "needed" – but only with expiry dates. When work projects were finished, the workers were supposed to leave. "Floaters" or "vagabonds" understood the temporary certificates differently: At long last, they thought, the police had legitimated them in Shanghai. Because the documents were blue, they were popularly called "blue cards" (*lan ka*, or *lan hukou*, on analogy to the famous American "green cards"). That was not the official notion of them, but the state lacked either the will or personnel to keep all the illegal migrants out of Shanghai.

It was usually possible for people from outside in the city to remain without any permission.[64] As a PRC scholar wrote ruefully,

> With dramatic changes in Chinese society, the function of the household registration system actually no longer exists. In the early stages of the PRC, the system's main role was to control the mobility of population, in order to implement the growth of urban populations. But now, because of reforms, we can no longer check the population's mobility. In Chinese cities, and especially in big cities, non-urban citizens have increased dramatically. They are an important part of the stable urban population and have had – and will have – a great impact on economic and social life.[65]

Migrants affected the views even of some who represented the state. Despite official efforts to reverse this trend, state power over residents declined over the two decades after 1970.

352 Migrants staff China's reform economy

Permanent residents: against criminals but for housemaids (*amahs*)

Urban immigrants called themselves "free people" (*ziyou ren*; the English term was 'freemen'). They broke bonds cadres had previously placed on them.[66] Established residents in Shanghai, while benefiting from migrants in many ways, at the same time often looked down on them – and tended to think them libertines or even thieves. As Dorothy Solinger writes, migration created "contested citizenship" in urban China.[67] Open disdain between subethnic groups in Shanghai, especially toward people from Subei (North Jiangsu), is an old story.[68] During reforms, immigrants became convenient social scapegoats. They often lived in flimsy housing, were said to compete with long-term residents for jobs, and were actually numerous among criminals.

Three-tenths of migrant workers in the Shanghai suburbs during the mid-1980s had no fixed dwellings – and half had no fixed jobs.[69] Nonregistered residents, to the extent they could be sampled in urban areas during late 1988, lived approximately as follows: 6 percent literally "floated" on boats in the Huangpu River, Suzhou Creek, or canals; 16 percent were in "temporary work shacks [*linshi gongpeng*], agricultural markets, terminuses, and docks"; 17 percent resided in hospices or hotels – and most, 61 percent, had beds with permanently registered collectives or families. Fully 85 percent of these "floaters" in the urban districts hailed from outside Shanghai, not from nearby counties.[70]

Another survey of the flow to Shanghai showed that in 1984, more than 700,000 people were immigrants without permanent registrations. In the next year, the number rose to 1,110,000, and the flood of arrivals continued at about the same level in 1986. Only 3 percent were boat people (some of whom may have obtained legal Shanghai residence during earlier campaigns to settle them on land). Just 1 percent came officially as rural traders or representatives of rural market fairs. Over 30 percent stayed in hotels or reception houses (*zhaodai suo*), and many came to do business. Over 20 percent were classed as "transport workers," and this apparently included construction carriers. Slightly less than half in that Fudan University survey came into individual or collective households.[71]

The total registered and unregistered floating population of Shanghai has been difficult to estimate, but the municipal police (who knew their records were incomplete) periodically enlisted the support of academics to conduct censuses. Police were aided by the Statistics Bureau, Fudan University, East China Normal University, and the Population Institute of the Social Sciences Academy. In 1988, one such survey tried to cover people without fixed abodes: in hotels, markets, boats, and transport stations. This survey reached the conclusion that on October 20, 1988, only 2 percent of Shanghai's population was floating – which was surely a sharp underestimate. Unregistered persons in Shanghai had scant incentive to make themselves available when the surveyors arrived. Of the illegal respondents, three-fifths alleged they had applied for legal temporary or permanent registration in Shanghai.[72] Many surveyors had long questionnaires, but the respondents were

TABLE 13.3 Reported transient populations of PRC cities during reforms (thousands of persons)

	Shanghai	Beijing	Tianjin	Wuhan	Guangzhou	24 cities
1978		300				
85		900			600	
86	1,340				880	
87	2,000	1,150	860	800	1,000	10,000

Sources: *Chengshi wenti* (Urban Problems), March 1988, 64, and (for 1987) *Shanghai jingji* (Shanghai Economy), June 1988, 6. The twenty-four cities were all those with total populations in excess of one million. *Zhongguo chengshi tongji nianjian* editions have further figures, but reporting on this topic is spotty because many actual "transients" lack legal household registrations. Police in cities smaller than the largest five reporting here may have tried less assiduously to register transients.

few. The pollsters asked each adult's name, sex, age, education level, former job, and reason for coming to Shanghai. In 1988, they added questions about number of children, method of birth control, and (of women) whether pregnant. For some queries, as for the census as a whole, it would have been too hopeful to expect complete coverage. Round figures (probable underestimates) from another source are in Table 13.3.

One writer claimed credibly that by 1988 Shanghai had "the country's biggest floating population."[73] Another confirms that the portion of floaters in the urban districts rose in the mid-1980s.[74] At least up to 1987, as the table suggests, Shanghai had more unauthorized immigrants than any other Chinese city. By about this time, migrants already comprised one-fifth of the population in China's twenty-four largest cities – and probably more than that in the built-up parts of Shanghai. In those urban districts, according to an early 1989 estimate, one of every four persons lacked permanent household registration.[75] Toward the beginning of the 1990s, further diverse reports suggest that one-fifth of the people were migrants; but these guesses may be low. Comprehensive, credible, and comparable figures from many cities have not yet been found, but Shanghai sources indicate that by 1994 the portion of recent arrivals in the population was still rising. One mid-1990s report estimated that Shanghai's "floating population" was 3.3 million.[76] More than one-quarter of Shanghai's whole population was migrant by that time.

Immigrants' occupations and incomes

The portion of floaters who were unregistered – i.e., who had no employers to arrange documents – rose quickly in most Jiangnan cities after the mid-1980s.[77] In Hangzhou, for example, migrants were 11 percent of the population in 1985 and had earlier been 9 percent in 1975, but only 4 percent in both 1965 and 1955. In a 1988 census of migrants, working-age persons (ages 15 to 59) made up 81 percent. Males were 62 percent. Only 52 percent were in urban districts. Almost half (practically all from Jiangsu or Zhejiang) lived in the suburbs. Illiterates and semi-illiterates comprised 15 percent of the total, but those with middle school educations were 45 percent (and with university educations, 2 percent – higher than among the legally resident population at that time). These immigrants, self-reporting their former occupations, were 48 percent farmers, 15 percent workers, 8 percent technicians, 4 percent businesspeople, 3 percent cadres, and 20 percent unemployed. Many worked in construction and transport. Of the women (38 percent of the total), 51 percent were married, many earning incomes. Fully 68 percent were of child-bearing age; 24 percent had actually given birth to babies in Shanghai, and 5 percent were pregnant during this census. At least 14 percent of all the floating population worked as domestics, apparently full-time. One-third of the floaters came from Jiangsu, and a strong majority hailed from either Jiangsu or Zhejiang.[78]

Many who were unregistered, or who were supposed to be only temporary in the city, could nonetheless make satisfactory livings. Some did so illegally. A man from Xinghua in northern Jiangsu, for example, came to Shanghai and "stole" materials from factory rubbish bins. He could in this way make a then-high income of 70 or 80 yuan per day. Legal activities were less profitable, but they still paid far more than migrants had previously received as peasants. A twenty-five-year-old legal migrant from Henan to Suzhou explained in 1994 why he was so much more productive on the delta: "We used to spend three months doing farm work, one month celebrating the Spring Festival, and eight months in idle time every year." Now he was a restaurant waiter, working fourteen hours each day, seven days a week – but receiving 400 yuan (about US$50 per month, which was four times his previous Henan wage).

When asked whether he thought he was working too hard, he replied with great eloquence, showing the human motives that complement economic theory about subsistence wage labor. He explained not so much why he migrated, but what his work meant for change in his life. Heating, television, food, and showers were important to him:

> No, it is better than sitting idly by watching people in cities getting rich. The conditions here are not bad at all. Color TV, electric heating, free meals – these are great. What I like most here is that I can take a shower every day. I was not able to take a bath during the entire winter at home. It would be too cold to do so in the river.[79]

The end of most residence controls, as exploitation rates normalized

A report from the mid-1990s indicated that one of every six people in Shanghai had "recently arrived" from rural areas. This immigrant labor force was said to number 2.5 million, but only three-fifths had reliable jobs. One million had to forgo money or else look for work each day. Most immigrants with steady employment came from other places in Jiangnan, and many had relatives already in the metropolis. As one construction team chief from Jiangsu said, "We hire workers from our home town and from neighboring towns, so that we can be sure of their credibility."[80] These were fairly fortunate migrants.

Others, who came disproportionately from Anhui, Henan, Jiangxi and Sichuan, often took Shanghai jobs without residence permits and thus broke the law. So they lacked any medical or injury benefits, despite the dangerous work that many of them did. They also lacked recourse to police, if their labor contractors did not pay them. Many lived on the edge of the city near green suburbs. Their shacks looked like storage sheds, made of corrugated metal, with asphalted canvas for roofs, bamboo for pillars to hold the structures up, and cardboard or woven straw mats to separate the "rooms." The Pengpu New Town area north of the central city became one of several major centers for the "tide of workers" (*min gong chao*).[81] When they were not hired by construction or stevedore teams, they took up individual work selling food on the streets, repairing shoes or bicycles, or picking rubbish.

Further places just on the edge of Shanghai city, such as Zhenru, which has a train stop, or the suburbs of Wujiaochang or Wanshanbang, also became abodes for ex-peasant migrants without urban registrations. These newcomers wanted to make money; but as illegal residents, they could not obtain business licenses. So they set up factories and shops without official blessing. Police, during a 1990 raid in Wanshanbang, found thirty "underground" food processing factories, which baked and catered mainly for people living in Shanghai's central districts.[82]

Women domestic workers came especially from Anhui to Shanghai. Already in the 1970s, they had organized a housemaids' union informally called the "Anhui group." Authorities of the inland province were perturbed by this exodus, which reduced both economic production and political control in their area; so they prevailed on the Shanghai government to ship some migrants back to Anhui by train.[83] Domestic helpers were both welcomed and exploited by Shanghai residents, and most bureaucrats gave up hope of monitoring all their goings and comings. About three-fifths of Shanghai's theoretically temporary migrants, according to a mid-1980s study, lived in households of permanent residents. When they were not members of the same family, they were usually in Shanghai to work. When they were relatives, they frankly told pollsters they were there to visit or live.[84] Neither of those activities has any status in state planning documents.

Many immigrants stayed for long periods. Contract work for building projects usually justified six months or more. Of Shanghai's "floating population" without permanent residence, at least one fifth were in building trades. They formed more than 400 construction teams, a larger force than the city's legally registered population in that industry. Two steady facts about these near-subsistence wage laborers were that they were cheap and they worked hard.

Local Shanghai construction teams were less profitable, when they did jobs in the city, than were those brought whole from other provinces. The outside teams also in practice paid lower taxes; so the state's uneven fiscal structure was for this group an unintended spur to urban immigration. In the late 1980s, *Labor News* reported that half the construction teams working in Shanghai had been recruited within the municipality. In Pudong, formerly Chuansha County, the sharp objections of local peasants to confiscation of their land were partly allayed by giving their construction teams a great deal of lucrative work. But in the city as a whole, fewer teams were staffed by locals than those brought from a distance. The 346 registered Shanghai local teams at the start of 1989 employed 358,000 workers. The 300 teams from elsewhere used more, 370,000. It is certain that unregistered contractors were also building in the city. Although the skills of Shanghai builders were deemed better, local contractors' costs were higher; so they tended to lose money. As a newspaper politely put it, the "competitive opportunities" of non-Shanghai teams were better.[85] Their tax and state remittance expenses were also lower – even for work on the same project.

Migrants did a great variety of other jobs, too. By 1988, "Almost all the tea-egg salesgirls . . . are from northern Jiangsu. . . . Many of them earn 15 to 20 yuan a day, about six times a government employee's daily pay."[86] Other trades in which illegal and impermanent residents predominated were furniture repair, quiltmaking, and knife grinding. These functions, and the services of housemaids, were appreciated by permanent Shanghai residents even when performed by illegals.

Interests of immigrant criminals, long-term residents, police, and civilian officials

Young rural immigrants to Shanghai often failed to obtain living space in the crowded central city. But peasants on the outskirts offered them space – at high rents, and without blessings from any official authority. The life styles of these young people were often unstable, and some migrants became criminals. When they were already violating registration laws, it was a short step to break others. Largely because of their influx, suburban economic crime soared in 1984, rising by 60 percent above the 1983 rate.[87] Non-registered people committed only 7 percent of Shanghai crime in 1983, but this portion rose to 11 percent in 1984 and 1985, 18 percent in 1986, 20 percent in 1987, 30 percent in 1988, and 31 percent in 1989 – and this was just the floaters' portion. The total crime rate also rose rapidly over these years.[88]

At the end of the decade, an estimated 3 percent of all temporary residents had been arrested for crimes. The portion among the permanently registered citizens was 1 percent. Shanghai had 7 million bicycles in 1993, of which 150,000 were stolen in that year alone (despite locks, police, and professional bicycle-watchers at bike parks). Four-fifths of the bicycle thieves who were caught in 1993 turned out to be immigrants to Shanghai.[89] The victims of such crimes, not just the perpetrators, tended also to be in the city unofficially. Migrants were sometimes dunned for "taxes," payable to violent protection gangs, often from their own home provinces. One such group was called the "Vegetable Knife Gang" (Caidao Bang), indicating its members' favored weapon.[90]

Permanent residents could disdain such behavior while at the same time benefiting from migrants. The attitudes of established families to the influx were often negative but complex. Even beyond the useful maids and construction workers, there was grudging acceptance of migrants. As one writer put it by 1989, the "floaters . . . do not live in Shanghai temporarily; they are 'actual' Shanghai residents." Locals also had a new (illegal) source of income from the migrants: "Now, because a lot of peasants came, Shanghai [registered] citizens could sell surplus grain [from ration coupons] to them. . . . Some outsiders are working for Shanghai residents. They did not want to be paid in cash but in rice." The price of rationed rice in April 1989 at Shanghai (.55 yuan per *jin*) was 27 percent less than on the free market. So the state subsidy was still heavy – and costly. Unrationed foods were available, but legitimated residents could get rice cheaply.[91]

The monthly legal grain quota per Shanghai resident had not been lowered since the 1950s (despite nondeliveries in bad times, and despite much greater availability of meat and vegetables since the early 1970s). But because many foods could during reforms be bought "for ready money," Shanghai legal residents could easily forgo some of their grain. A newspaper suggested: "If we reformed this policy [by decreasing ration amounts], the problem [for official budgets] would be solved."[92] But nothing happened. The matter was politically sensitive. Top conservative administrators thought a reduction of Shanghai legal residents' traditional food entitlement could stir resentment among workers in state factories. PRC leaders occasionally reminded themselves that proletarians in cities like Shanghai actually have revolutionary histories, although cadres wanted to keep all that in the past.

Leaders and residents

A Shanghai author concluded: "We should have a positive attitude toward the current floating population." He admitted that migrants brought big problems. Among Shanghai crimes "in the water area, 72 percent were perpetrated by the transient population [most of whom there were the subethnicity of truly floating 'boat people']." Other migrants "were also responsible for 32 percent of the burglaries, 34 percent of frauds, and 22 percent of rapes and homicides. . . . Many women in the floating population gave birth illegally. Among those who did so in Shanghai, 13 percent had two children, and 4 percent had three or more." Some of these floaters had been in or near Shanghai for generations, but officially permanent old Shanghailanders vaguely distinguished useful groups from those they liked to disdain. Subaltern migrants helped to construct a modern metropolis. "Without them, it would be difficult to imagine so many new buildings in today's Shanghai. A quarter million laborers from other places work in the textile industry and in environmental sanitation."[93] Such a sanguine attitude was not shared by all, but established citizens and state leaders had mixed interests in immigration, even the illegal kinds.

Managers and cadres rightly supposed the influx of cheap labor would not bring much unrest among permanent workers, if the worst jobs could be turned over to outsiders. Migrant proletarians, even if they lived under cramped conditions, were often in their own "communities outside the system" (*tizhi wai qunluo*). One young unmarried man had arrived in early 1994 at a "Sichuan village" in Pengpu New

358 Migrants staff China's reform economy

Town of Shanghai. He lived with five hundred other Sichuan migrants in a 300 m² asphalt-roofed shack – but he expressed some contentment: "I like to stay with my fellow Sichuan people. We take care of each other like brothers. We shoulder our hardships together, just as we share our dreams."[94]

It is unclear whether strong traditional organizations among temporary laborers in China – which correlated with past unrest among contract laborers – will provide forums through which immigrants make political demands. Comparative research from other cultures, especially on the politics of migrants to Mexico City, Lima, Rio de Janeiro, and other developing cities, has suggested that ex-peasant urban villages do not become hotbeds of political unrest – at least not for the first generation of "urban villagers." Latin Americanists reporting on slums in São Paolo, Lima, and Mexico City provide the earliest and best material.[95] New arrivals to big cities from rural areas, reproducing their traditional communities separate from the surrounding metropolitan environments, have in general been politically quiescent. Even when sanitation, water supply, and other urban services have been minimal – as is still the case for many in Shanghai – they are not a direct threat to the political order.[96]

The migration to cities of millions of unlicensed migratory workers in the 1980s and 1990s remained unpopular with some long-term Shanghai residents, who feared their jobs were endangered by immigrants' cheap labor. Such fears have become politically important in wealthy economies (including those of the US and UK). The state's public policy regularly calls for migrants' expulsion back to the countryside, and China has not yet abandoned the household registration system – but a test of that possibility has been made in the Zhejiang city of Huzhou.[97] Official sermons on the need for "vagabonds" to leave cities please most state-sector workers. Long-term residents readily tend to believe that official coercion has a rightful role keeping vagrants in line. Migrants provide occasions for police to prove their constabulary worth. Officials can publicize the expulsion of relatively few unregistered migrants – while actually allowing most to stay.[98] Effective enforcement, except in random campaigns, is another matter. So long as migrants provide low-cost help to many state enterprises with tightly constrained budgets, they will not be leaving Shanghai.

Urban intellectuals in China have long fulminated against "blindly flowing population" (*mangliu renkou*). When a book on *The History of Chinese Hooliganism* was published in 1993, it traced in loving detail the state's efforts to control migrants from before the First Emperor (r. 246–221 BCE) until 1911.[99] Planners, who want to tell citizens where to live, suggest that intellectuals linked to the state know how ordinary people should conduct their lives better than people themselves do. This is not a silly opinion, because there is no sure invariant way of knowing the general conditions under which benefits to groups (or individuals) come from collective arrangements – or the general conditions under which they do not. There is a chance that planners may plan sagely and fairly; the state promotes any discourse suggesting this possibility. But urban intellectuals with good state jobs tend to live in choice spots already. Even if would-be migrants fully obeyed whatever China's leaders decreed, it would be hard for an outside observer to believe that such officials give much weight to the interests of people so different from themselves.

Links of migration to green revolution and income changes

Agricultural modernization was, until recently, imagined by some planners to be a potential disaster for most peasants. Labor-saving machines might free farmers from back-breaking field work, but it also separated them from their surest resources for survival. These portents of disaster were not realized. Green revolution has brought many migrants from impoverished areas to richer ones. They fare better economically in new urban places than they did in the villages they left, which still grow a great deal of food.

Inland poverty pushes young people away from the places they leave, as much as coastal wealth pulls them toward prosperity. Recurrent temporary floods or droughts combine with the steady growth of demand for industrial labor to bring people into cities like Shanghai. Severe summer flooding struck the middle Yangzi in several years of the mid-1990s – for example 1996. Much of the water came from rain that hit ground east of the Three Gorges (downstream on the Yangzi), in the watersheds of the Xiang, Gan, and Huai Rivers. Many people therefore began to doubt that the new dam could solve China's flooding problems. The delta was swamped, especially in Jiangsu. The deluge was almost as bad there as in poorer Hunan, Jiangxi, and Anhui, where millions of farmers saw their crops, factories, and houses ruined by water. Many were washed out in more than one year during the 1990s. These events gave them compelling occasions to migrate elsewhere, trying to find a better life.

Urban immigrants' expectations that their incomes would later rise have, in past years, actually been realized. Inland places suffer drains of talent, but average farm sizes there increase, as China follows the pattern of other countries after green revolutions.[100] The chief buffering factor against social disaster, after a seminal reform of farm techniques such as China experienced from 1970, is migration. Arthur Lewis, writing in the early 1950s, could not have predicted the effects of then-future agronomy. Yet the green revolution achieved, in fields, changes somewhat like those the capital-accumulating sector using new technologies accomplished in factories: At first it raised the supply of cheap workers, but eventually it speeded the decline of subsistence-wage labor.

So workers moved, because opportunities in their situations changed. Migration has the effect of a political decision that is taken in parallel by many actors. The real liberation of China, which occurred from the 1970s as millions of peasants became workers, threatened both the patronist state and intellectuals' ideals of legitimate power. But migration is a concomitant of development, and increased income has been a strong interest of many. The state no longer effectively controls where most Chinese people live.

360 Migrants staff China's reform economy

Notes

1 Arthur Lewis, "Economic Development with Unlimited Supplies of Labour," 139–99 (also, Indianapolis: Bobbs-Merrill Reprint E-189).
2 Michael Todaro, *Economic Development* (New York: Longman, 1994).
3 The "green city" description of Shanghai's suburbs is detailed in the present author's "Shanghai-Suburb Relations," op. cit.
4 *Shanghai Sojourners*, Frederic Wakeman, Jr., and Wen-hsin Yeh, eds. (Berkeley: University of California Institute of Asian Studies, 1992).
5 Lin You Su, "Urban Migration in China: A Case Study of Three Urban Areas" (Ph.D. dissertation, Department of Geography, Australian National University, 1992), 71.
6 Rhoads Murphey, *Shanghai: Key to Modern China*, 27.
7 For more on the 1950s, Lynn White, *Careers in Shanghai* (Berkeley: University of California Press, 1978), 148+.
8 *Shanghai jingji, neibu ben*, 965.
9 *Yigong yinong* were thus also called *siliu gong*. Ibid.
10 Chen Benlin, *Gaige kaifang shenzhou jubian*, 65–66. For background, Thomas Bernstein, *Up to the Mountains and Down to the Villages: The Transfer of Youth from Urban to Rural China* (New Haven: Yale University Press, 1977).
11 *Shanghai jingji, neibu ben: 1949–1982*, 961.
12 Leslie T. Chang, *Factory Girls: From Village to City in a Changing China* (New York: Spiegel and Grau, 2009).
13 My former student Solomon Karmel reports interviewees about "bachelor villages" in destitute parts of inland provinces, whence many young women had left.
14 Li Wen-Lang, "Migration, Urbanization and Regional Development," in *Forces for Change in Contemporary China*, Lin Bih-jaw and James T. Myers, eds. (Taipei: Institute for International Relations, 1992), 153.
15 *JFRB*, Shanghai, March 16, 1988.
16 Except as noted, these relationships tend to hold regardless of the size of destination settlement. Lin You Su, "Urban Migration," 81–84 and 184.
17 Beijing supplied 3 percent of immigrants; Xinjiang, 2; Yunnan, 2; Fujian, 3; and Shandong, 4; all other provinces were less. *Zhongguo 1986 nian 74 chengzhen*, 14.
18 Many data, and the sex ratios on immigrants reported later, come through the generosity of Ronald Skeldon. The base for the estimated portions comes from figures in Table 13.1.
19 These data were provided by Ronald Skeldon, who has nationwide statistics on migration in the PRC.
20 See Jonathan Unger, "China's Troubled 'Down to the Countryside' Campaign," *Contemporary China* (1979), 88.
21 *Zhongguo 1986 nian 74 chengzhen*, 340.
22 In Japan, individuals often moved from villages to very large cities (e.g., Tokyo, Osaka) for most of their careers, but then retired to medium-sized places near but not identical to places whence they originated. The text above describes migration from metropolis to village to medium city.
23 *Zhongguo 1986 nian 74 chengzhen*, 334.
24 Zhe Xiaoye, *Chengshi zai zhuanzhe dianshang* (Cities at a Turning Point) (Beijing: Zhongguo Funü Chuban She, 1989, 30–31.
25 Nanshi District had this *zhishi qingnian bangong shi*. *Weiwen tuan* had been common in 1964–65 also. *WHB*, May 20, 1979.
26 *WHB*, May 29, 1979.
27 See a 1976 photo by Lynn White, published in Thomas Bernstein, *Up to the Mountains*, showing a bulletin board in a Wuxi silk factory that differentiated young migrants (children of the factory's workers) who had volunteered from those whose household registrations had been changed – as well as from those who had actually gone, rather than just saying they would go.

28 *WHB*, May 24, 1979.
29 *Post*, October 12, 1981, or *Xingdao ribao* (HK), October 14, 1981. Reports about this topic (and other subjects such as strikes) could not readily be printed in mainland newspapers, but they appeared in Hong Kong. Interviewees also give insights.
30 The police martyrs are listed by name, with birth dates and other particulars to honor them, in *Shanghai gongan nianjian, 1988* (Shanghai Public Security Yearbook, 1988) (neibu, photocopy reprint sold in Hong Kong, 515 pages), "Shanghai Gongan Nianjian," Editorial Department, ed. (Shanghai: Shanghai Shehui Kexue Chuban She, 1988), 99–101. Thanks go to a British friend for showing this source.
31 *WHB*, October 30, 1979.
32 These portions are calculated from raw data in *SHTJNJ86*, 70. Interviewees report that from the mid-1950s to 1979, new hires to Shanghai state factories were "distributed" there by organizations above or outside the factories.
33 Interview with a student at Fudan University.
34 *JFRB*, December 20, 1979.
35 This is based on a rough calculation from figures in *Shanghai jingji, neibu ben: 1949–1982*, 961.
36 The sample covered rustications between 1950 and 1985. *Zhongguo renkou qianyi yu chengshi hua yanjiu* (Studies on Chinese Migration and Urbanization), Editorial Group for Studies on Chinese Migration and Urbanization, ed. (Beijing: Zhongguo Shehui Kexue Yuan Renkou Yanjiu Suo, 1988), 296.
37 *SHTJNJ88*, 327, and *Zhongguo tongji zhaiyao, 1988* (A Statistical Survey of China, 1988), State Statistical Bureau, ed. (Beijing: Zhongguo Tongji Chuban She, 1988), 105.
38 The first datum is based on a survey of long-term immigrants by the Population Research Institute of the Chinese Academy of Social Sciences, and the second reports 1977–1986 migrations. More (above half) of the 1977–1986 immigrants to the smaller Shanghai delta city of Xiashi were married. See Lin You Su, "Urban Migration," 111 and 115.
39 Alice Goldstein, Sidney Goldstein, and Guo Shenyang, "Temporary Migrants in Shanghai Households, 1986," *Demography* 28 (1991), 275.
40 Zhuanhuan gongzuo, *Zhongguo yanhai diqu xiao chengzhen*, 195. Interesting in this respect is Sidney Goldstein, "Forms of Mobility and their Policy Implications: Thailand and China Compared," *Social Forces* 65:4 (1987), 915.
41 The county was, unfortunately, not identified in the source. *FBIS*, December 17, 1987, 30, radio of December 16, for the quotation below and the number of departing ex-peasants.
42 Zhe Xiaoye, *Chengshi zai zhuanzhe dianshang*, 23–9. The disdain of registered residents for immigrants – and the formers' need of the latter – are discussed in Dorothy Solinger, *Contesting Citizenship in Urban China* (Berkeley and Los Angeles: University of California Press, 1999). Also Lynn White, *Careers in Shanghai*, chapter 4 on residential legitimacy.
43 On labor contractors in "old Shanghai," Jean Chesneaux, *The Chinese Labor Movement, 1919–1927* (Stanford: Stanford University Press, 1968).
44 Rural migrants' income is classed as "agricultural" even if it comes from industries. *Zhongguo renkou qianyi* (Population Shifts in China), Tian Fang and Ling Fatong, eds. (Beijing: Zhishi Chuban She, 1987), 248–259.
45 Graphs based on work by Meng Xin, in *China's Rural Industry*, 300. Wuxi's portion of permanent workers was higher than a comparable county in Anhui, and much higher than one in Guangdong for which data have been gathered – but this does not report contract labor.
46 *China's Rural Industry*, 326–27.
47 Interview with Lu Feiyun, who did field work in Jiangnan. Also Hua Daming, "*Xiangban chang dui nonggong de guofen bodu ying yinqi zhuyi*," Shanghai, 12–13. Wang Juan, Sinews, explains weakening county and township controls over village leaders.
48 The exact figure is probably unknown to anyone. *FBIS*, December 21, 1987, 42, radio of December 18.

49 Of the remaining tenth, half came for adult training and half for other reasons. *Zhongguo renkou qianyi*, 19–21.

50 *Liudong renkou dui da chengshi fazhan de yinxiang ji duice* (Policies on the Influence of Transient Population for the Development of Large Cities), Li Mengbai, ed. (Beijing: Jingji ribao Chuban She, 1991), 153, and for following data to 156. *Stadtluft macht frei* was a medieval European legal norm that ex–feudal serfs became free after living more than a year in a city.

51 Zhe Xiaoye, *Chengshi zai zhuanzhe dianshang*, 23–29.

52 The main survey, a 1986 effort by the Chinese Academy of Social Sciences, oddly omits to report temporarily registered migrants or illegal migrants. Lin You Su, "Urban Migration," 96, 98, and 103.

53 Ibid., 930.

54 Qin Shao, *Shanghai Gone: Domicide and Defiance in a Chinese Megacity* (Lanham: Rowman & Littlefield, 2013).

55 *Shanghai shimin banshi zhinan* (Shanghai Citizen's Practical Guide), Shanghai Municipal Government, ed. (Shanghai: Shanghai Renmin Chuban She, 1989), 2, 91–92.

56 These hires were supposedly from administrative seconding or transfers of jobs. Lin You Su, "Urban Migration," 173.

57 An exception is Guilhem Fabre, "The Chinese Mirror of Transition," 263.

58 Red Guards, revolutionary tourist-pilgrims, hopped on trains without tickets. Gordon Bennett and Ronald Montaperto, *Red Guard: The Political Biography of Dai Hsiao-ai* (Garden City: Doubleday, 1972).

59 *Liaowang*, no. 36, 1993, 18, and XMWB, April 21, 1994; I owe thanks also to Cheng Li.

60 Alice Goldstein and Guo Shenyang, "Temporary Migration in Shanghai and Beijing," *Studies in Comparative International Development* 27:2 (Summer 1992), 42.

61 Zhe Xiaoye, *Chengshi zai zhuanzhe dianshang*, 23–29.

62 This was predicted in my *Careers in Shanghai* (1978), last chapter.

63 Margaret Woo, "Legal Reforms in the Aftermath of Tiananmen Square," 59.

64 Interviews and *Shanghai shimin banshi zhinan*.

65 Zhe Xiaoye, *Chengshi zai zhuanzhe dianshang*, 23–24.

66 Edward Friedman, "Deng vs. the Peasantry: Recollectivization in the Countryside," *Problems of Communism* (September–October 1991), 30–49.

67 Dorothy Solinger, *Contesting Citizenship*, develops this and shows its political importance.

68 Emily Honig, *Creating Chinese Ethnicity*.

69 *Zhongguo yanhai diqu*, 205.

70 Portions are calculated from raw data surveys in *Laodong renkou*, 152.

71 *SHJJNJ88*, 25.

72 *Zhu Ci in Shanghai liudong renkou* (Shanghai's Floating Population), Shanghai Statistics Bureau, ed. (Shanghai: Zhongguo Tongji Chuban She, 1989), 11–16.

73 Ibid., 11.

74 The 1982 census found only 246,000 transients in Shanghai's urban districts, about 4 percent of their population then – but later reports are much higher. Beijing claimed a 3 percent rate as late as 1988, and this may well be an underreport. The portion for Guangzhou was very high, and different census methods may make such rates incomparable. Zhe Xiaoye, *Chengshi zai zhuanzhe dianshang*, 23–4.

75 LDB, March 19, 1989.

76 *Shanghai Star*, March 22 and April 15, 1994, suggested that about one-quarter of the migrants were in construction, and another quarter were not working. Found by Cheng Li.

77 *Laodong renkou*, 281.

78 Zhu Ci, in *Shanghai liudong renkou*, 11–16.

79 An interview by Cheng Li in 1994 offers the perspectives of individuals and families that most China studies often lack.

80 T. S. Rousseau in *Eastern Express* (Hong Kong), February 23, 1994.

81 Pengpu Xincun in the 2000s became a stop on Shanghai Metro Line 1, whose extension into northern suburbs is long.

82 Kate Xiao Zhou reports this from Huang Wanwei, *Zhongguo de yinxing jingji* (China's Hidden Economy), a 1993 Hebei source.

83 Kate Xiao Zhou mentioned a Shanghai 1991 book, "Food is the Basis of People: Report from Rural China."

84 Alice Goldstein, Sidney Goldstein, and Guo Shenyang, "Temporary Migration," 275, gives details on methods in the 1984 Shanghai Temporary Migration Survey.

85 *Laodong bao*, January 31, 1989, reports data from Shanghai's Construction Bank. This lead article particularly mentioned projects to build new hotels, and it amounted to a complaint against high extraction from Shanghai.

86 *CD*, November 25, 1988.

87 *FBIS*, December 14, 1984, 3, radio of December 13.

88 *Laodong renkou*, 160. A similar and compatible report is *XMWB*, March 24, 1989.

89 *Eastern Express* (Hong Kong), February 23, 1994.

90 Solomon Karmel, "The Neo-Authoritarian Contradiction," 142, uses work by Zhou Daming, especially on Hunan and Sichuan gangs in Guangzhou. This pattern is old and is recorded in various books by Jean Chesneaux, especially *The Chinese Labor Movement, 1919–1927* (Stanford: Stanford University Press, 1968).

91 Sheng Li and Fu Qiping in *XMWB*, April 18, 1989.

92 Ibid.

93 The number of such laborers was 240,000. Mao Zhongwei and Zhou Zigeng in *Shanghai laodong renkou*, 47–57.

94 Cheng Li mentioned the phrase and provided this interview quotation about community.

95 Wayne Cornelius, "Urbanization and Political Demand Making," *American Political Science Review* IX:74, 1125–46, has data from Mexican barrios, as does Oscar Lewis; François Borricauld writes similarly on Lima. Also Albert Hirschmann, "Changing Tolerance for Income Inequality," op. cit.

96 The best student of labor unrest in China, Elizabeth Perry, has orally suggested that Latin American and African experiences might not be replicated there. Chinese organizational traditions, especially in same-place associations, seem strong. I suppose the main threat migrants pose to the state is indirect, rather than direct through their own political capacities.

97 Ran Ran, "Reforming the Household Registration System in Huzhou Municipality, Zhejiang Province: An Overview and Detailed Analysis" (Singapore: Lee Kwan Yew School of Public Policy) lkyspp.nus.edu.sg/cag/publication/reforming-the-household-registration-system-in-huzhou-municipality-zhejiang-province.

98 Similar arguments appear in Dorothy Solinger, "China's Transients and the State," 91–122.

99 Chen Baoliang, *Zhongguo liumang shi* (The History of Chinese Hooliganism) (Beijing: Zhongguo Shehui Kexue Chuban She, 1993).

100 See *Modern Rice Technology and Income Distribution in Asia*, Cristina C. David and Keijiro Otsuka, eds. (Boulder: Lynne Rienner, 1994).

EPILOGUE

Local and medial powers, not just central powers; situations, not just ideas

What does the PRC's experience with reform tell us about the structure of Chinese politics? One thing it suggests is that "reform" was so different before and after 1990 that use of the same word to describe two periods, c. 1970–1990 and 1990+, obscures crucial differences between them. Evidence presented here also suggests further problems with conventional accounts of China after the late 1960s.

First, most writers recognize that 'politics with Chinese characteristics' is led by strong authoritarians, and they are generally right about that. But they neglect that such dictators are common in local and medial units, not just in the government at Beijing. Chinese central, provincial, county, town, village, and family patrons all tend to be strong vis-à-vis their clients. All sizes of polity have decisive *policy*making leaders. They often vie with each other while praising autocratic leadership as a principle.

This situation is not unique to China, though it is salient there. Tip O'Neill's thesis that "all politics is local" applies as well in a coterie of national leaders as it does within families – and to all the degrees of zoom between these sizes. E. E. Schattschneider wrote, "We have had difficulty perceiving change because we have looked for the wrong kind of conflict (conflict *within* the government) and have underestimated the extent to which *the government itself as a whole* has been in conflict with other power systems."[1] Influence over behavior anywhere is naturally dispersed in diverse kinds of collective entities: kin groups, corporations, businesses, unions, churches, parties, universities, schools, clubs, and other associations, as well as states, their parts, and nonstate villages and neighborhoods. Few of these are ever "democratic" in any thorough sense. Governments claim to be sovereign, and their agents try to monopolize violence. Behavioral evidence shows that they often overrate their effectiveness. They have obvious interests in doing so.

Chinese regimes for millennia have understandably propagated traditions of following central state leaders, and the heads of both large and small sizes of collectivity tend to be strong. Confucius put great responsibility on the shoulders of the imperial leader: "The moral character of the ruler is the wind; the moral character of those beneath him is the grass. When the wind blows, the grass bends."[2] Mencius expanded and refined this notion in a reservedly populist way: "Heaven sees as the people see; heaven hears as the people hear."[3] These are prescriptive norms of legitimacy, although they are not "modern." There is nothing distinctively democratic about finding empirical evidence that many kinds of leaders have power in polities of different sizes. The comparative politics of democratization strongly suggests that different vectors for or against that regime type interact (these include elite decisions, historical traditions, fears of asset redistribution, modern socio-economics, recurrent protests, and international fads for regime types). They operate over different spans of time.[4]

A second trait of usual discourse about Chinese politics, different from this emphasis on leadership in diverse groups, is a hope that leaders should have brains in their heads. Both Chinese and Western intellectuals tend to stress the political legitimacy of their own status. Societies and associations benefit from having leaders who are bright rather than stupid; so people who claim competent "merit" tend also to claim power. Because mandarins, qualified by imperial examinations, helped to hold China together as a large polity for centuries, this assertion remains especially prominent in that country.[5]

Ideas are important in shaping political action. But information about unintended facts (inflations, geographies, unexpected technologies, many more) shows that China's reforms for prosperity were also affected by factors beyond intentions. Instances of influence from circumstances, rather than ideas, are many: These include the new seeds and agronomies after 1965 that let local leaders expand triple cropping, raw materials shortages and price rises of the 1980s that made planners unable to allocate most commodities, and other examples. Ideologies, understandable though they may be, often become relevant or irrelevant to human purposes depending on situations that were unpremeditated. Concrete accidents and understood ideas together determine what happens. Neither kind of factor alone is adequate to explain behavior.

In practical politics, the extent of actors' knowledge of each other is also important. Jae Ho Chung argues that local implementers of central Chinese policies may, to serve their own interests, "bandwagon" with leaders who try to control their careers, or they may "pioneer" policies in their own interests, or "resist" measures that hurt them. Chung's cases are in northern Chinese provinces, and his question is asked from a mostly centralist viewpoint: How best can the government "decentralize," how can it derogate power that it assumes it has? That is a legitimate query, usual in Beijing. This book tries to ask a different question: How do most leaders serve their clients' interests while also getting along sufficiently well with state bureaucrats at the center and in provinces? How do they localize politics? Both viewpoints are valid. The main issue becomes informational: How much do leaders at various sizes of collectivity (analytical degrees of 'zoom') know about each others' perceptions and situations? As Chung admits, "local leadership matters."[6]

This book is mainly about the first roots of reform and their results for about two decades thereafter, until 1990. It does not claim fully to cover later times, when Chinese economic growth rates began to "converge" to somewhat lower international norms, as per capita wealth increased further. That pattern in China echoed previous development in other countries. One aspect of this normalcy is that growth fluctuated up and down. After China's total GDP increase rose to a reported peak of 14.3 percent in 1992, it remained in double digits from that year through 1995, then fell below 10 percent until 2002, trending up again until 2007 when it was claimed to be 14.2 percent, then down again to single digits in 2008 and later years (except for 2010, when the reported rate was 10.6 percent). China's rates of modernization, including changes in all fields ranging from higher pollution to higher education, have been fast. But the country's economic growth has converged downward toward 6 or 7 percent after 2010, as China's per capita income rose.[7] The nation is much richer than it was before reforms, but its growth rate has slowed while many inland Chinese are still fairly poor.

Economist Charles Jones offers a scatter diagram that relates actual past income growth rates (on the vertical) to income per worker (on the horizontal) for many countries.[8] The modal shape of the curve amid the scatter is a hump with a quick rise on the left (low-income) side and a very gradual slope on the right as growth rates "converge" lower in richer nations. The degree of scatter on the left side among poorer countries is impressive. Income growth rises until a certain output-per-worker level is reached (about $7,000 in 1960 dollars), albeit with some places strewn off a loose central curve on the left. Growth slows after countries pass that middling threshold of wealth – and it varies less. It "converges" downward. China's early reforms brought the planet's most populous country near the top of the hump very quickly; and now the economy is starting to reach lower, normal middle-developing, single-digit overall growth rates. This change is political as well as economic, and it relies on entrepreneurship as well as order.

Mid-level wealth, which reforms brought to China, created modern problems and potential solutions to them, which the country's politicians have had to face over recent decades. Boy Lüthje and Christopher McNally write that Chinese "plans identify paths to economic rebalancing through intensive growth, driven by rising investment in new technologies and manufacturing processes, improved wages and skills, and improved worker and environmental protections." Industries such as autos and information technology "offer improved employment conditions with better wages, but continue to incorporate large swaths of low-wage employment with little protection for workers' health and the environment." Many of these industries, when prosperous, are largely local-run. For example, "IT production rests on low wages, cheap land and infrastructure, and violations of labor and environmental laws."[9] The car industry, for instance, has made China the largest producer and consumer of automobiles. This and other sectors have fared best where companies have been able to combine high-quality components made locally.[10] The most obvious results of such prowess do not all come from careful planning. Despite increased government spending on roads, every large city in China is now a traffic jam. Even on major intercity highways for which the state has recently paid immense sums, slowdowns and blockages are not restricted to rush hours. Prosperity has brought practical and environmental costs, as well as great happiness, to hundreds of millions of Chinese.

The nation's development has become social and attitudinal, not just economic. Evan Osnos writes about a turn toward "ambition," adducing anecdotes that are mostly local.[11] Changes have also been political and institutional; Xi Jinping advertises the "China dream." Leadership succession to China's top posts was normalized during the 1990s into "generations," each of which was expected to have ten years at the helm. Party leaders below the supremo were given distinct portfolios in functional fields: the economy, public security, the military, and others – although a quasi-emperor "core" leader has usually been respected. Some balance between political coalitions has emerged nationally and regionally.[12] Provincial membership in the Party Congress has become more equal. Institutions have tried to give central leaders somewhat better information about public grievances, although local leaders coalesce to stymie these.[13] Local elections, surveys, and petitions have not always aggregated interests effectively but have given post-1990 government leaders somewhat more sense of the places they purport to govern. Administrative laws have proliferated and have sometimes been enforced. Much of this institutionalization began in the 1990s under President Jiang Zemin and continued under President Hu Jintao.

President Xi Jinping has led centralist, anti-localist campaigns whose intensity reflects the strength of the post-1970 reforms they were designed to weaken. These structures were not democratic, but Xi has been mainly a conservative trying to undo their long-term effects, which weakened Party autocracy.[14] Nobody claims to be sure whether other politicians will moderate Xi's quasi-imperial power, although Cheng Li provides evidence of a balance of conservative and reformist forces, lions and foxes.[15] The post-1990 trend to political centralization could accelerate under the leadership of a demagogue, but nobody knows (at the time of this writing) whether that will occur. It is a national issue, though smaller polities still exist in China.

A 2013 document, sent confidentially and internally to all major divisions of the Party, listed five top "false ideological trends," as follows in order: The first and worst was "promoting Western constitutional democracy [including] the separation of powers, the multi-party system, general elections, independent judiciaries." The second worst sin was espousal of "universal values," although this CCP tirade against them specified that they are all "Western," while some Confucianists such as Lee Kwan-yew famously argued that Asians also contribute to universal values. The third worst was "promoting civil society." Fourth was "neoliberalism." Fifth was "the West's idea of journalism, challenging China's principle that the media and publishing should be subject to Party discipline."[16] Perhaps the most revealing aspect of this document was that it was supposed to be kept confidential – an apparent admission it was so blunt it would be politically counter-effective to present in public (in Taiwan and Hong Kong or internationally – or even on the mainland).

368 Epilogue

Xi's era has seen many arrests of Chinese lawyers who sued to enforce Chinese laws in Chinese courts.

Reactionary conservatism is currently dominant but is contested in China. For example, Peking University law professor Shen Kui sharply criticized the Minister of Education for claiming that liberal principles should never be studied.[17] Party conservatives may rule China at particular moments and at particular degrees of zoom, but they have reformist opponents. Xi has revived imagery from Mao's time; but unlike Mao, he has not led mass campaigns that scare people into compliance with the wishes of the state.[18] Xi may preserve some balance, as may smaller polities within China. Current Party rhetoric is partly about Confucius and China's past glories, without movements to "destroy the old" such as Mao led. Xi's "China dream" is both futuristic and nostalgic. The Party claims its leadership to prosperity gives legitimacy to its rule. Officials, journalists, and academics in many countries have ignored facts showing that the roots of reform growth were actually diverse.

The CCP also claims patriotism as another reason why Chinese must revere its leaders. Yet if the Party-state is to remain "resilient," its "governance" has actually not followed a consistent "model." The Party is not all of China, and its elite will continue to need both conservative lions for internal coordination and also reformist foxes for external adaptation.[19] No coherent ideological group can permanently be sure of controlling everything political in China. Most of the realm is not in Beijing – or any other single place. Intellectuals who write about this nation's politics tend to be centralist in their ideals. What actually happens is affected by such thinking, but also by leaders of smaller places. Future discourse about politics, in China as in other countries, will become more accurate if writers avoid limiting their concept of leadership to large collectivities, and if they admit that both intentions and unintended circumstances actually shape what people do.

Notes

1 E. E. Schattschneider, *The Semi-Sovereign People*, 124; italics in original.
2 Confucius, *The Analects*, Din Cheuk Lau, trans. (New York: Penguin, 1979), A:1.
3 Mencius, here using the translation of S. K. Lao, *Zhongguo zhixue* (Chinese Political Philosophy) (Taipei: Sanmin, 1988), Chapter 18:8, translated similarly (sometimes with 'my people' rather than 'the people') by James Legge, Wm. Theodore deBary, and others. See deBary's book reconciling *Asian Values and Human Rights: A Confucian Communitarian Perspective* (Cambridge: Harvard University Press, 1998).
4 The title of my recent book includes a question mark: *Democratization in Hong Kong – and China?* (Boulder: Lynne Rienner Publishers, 2016). Other accounts are for the most part more admirably impatient, in order by the authors' surnames: Kerry Brown, *Ballot Box China: Grassroots Democracy in the Final Major One-Party State* (New York: Palgrave Macmillan, 2011); Bruce Gilley, *China's Democratic Future: How It Will Happen and Where It Will Lead* (New York: Columbia University Press, 2004); Merle Goldman, *Sowing the Seeds of Democracy in China Political Reform in the Deng Xiaoping Era* (Cambridge: Harvard University Press, 1994); Baogang He, *The Democratization of China* (London: Routledge, 1996); Suzanne Ogden, *Inklings of Democracy in China* (Cambridge: Harvard University Press, 2002); and Keping Yu, *Democracy Is a Good Thing: Essays on Politics, Society, and Culture in Contemporary China* (Washington, DC: Brookings Institution Press, 2008). Chinese

Epilogue **369**

leaders could eventually establish some kind of pluralist democracy, although they are unlikely to do this soon.

5 A controversial recent work is by a Canadian professor at Qinghua University, with whom his liberal friends such as myself enjoy debate: Daniel A. Bell, *The China Model*. Bell's earlier books from the same press, *China's New Confucianism* (2008) and *East Meets West* (2000) are relevant. Contrary discourses are in *Confucianism and Human Rights*, Wm. Theodore de Bary and Tu Weiming, eds. (New York: Columbia University Press, 1998); de Bary, *The Liberal Tradition in China* (New York: Columbia University Press, 1983); R. Randle Edwards, Louis Henkin, and Andrew Nathan, *Human Rights in Contemporary China* (New York: Columbia University Press, 1986); and Vitaly Rubin, *Individual and State in Ancient China* (New York: Columbia University Press, 1976).

6 Jae Ho Chung, *Central Control and Local Discretion in China: Leadership and Implementation during Post-Mao Decollectivization* (Oxford: Oxford University Press, 2000), 10.

7 See http://data.stats.gov.cn, for PRC National Statistics Bureau reports.

8 Charles I. Jones, *Introduction to Economic Growth* (New York: W.W. Norton, 2002), 60, Fig. 3.8. An interesting aspect of this diagram is that the horizontal wealth axis is not logged. Variance off a notional main curve is wild for poor countries, although some middle-rich ones are also below the curve. The premises chosen, especially the 1960 starting date, inevitably affect results (for example, Japan and S. Korea are on a finial off the top of the curve's apex, and they would be located differently if different timings to calculate product or different starting and ending dates had been selected). But Jones shows with solid empirical data the scatter of growth rates among poor places, and the convergence of growth as wealth increases.

9 Boy Lüthje and Christopher McNally, "China's Hidden Obstacles to Socioeconomic Reblancing," *Asia Pacific Issues*, 120 (October 2015), 1.

10 On local SMEs that make quality automobile components, Eric Thun, *Changing Lanes in China: Foreign Direct Investment, Local Governments, and Auto Sector Development* (New York: Cambridge University Press, 2008).

11 Evan Osnos, *Age of Ambition*.

12 Cheng Li, *China's Leaders: The New Generation* (Lanham: Rowman and Littlefield, 2001) is the pioneering study.

13 Wang Juan, *Sinews*, passim.

14 Recent books about Xi's rise include Bruce Dickson, *The Dictator's Dilemma* and Willy Wo-Lap Lam, *Chinese Politics in the Era of Xi Jinping: Renaissance, Reform, or Retrogression?* (Abingdon: Routledge, 2015).

15 Splendid documentation on Xi's and others' coalitions is Cheng Li, *Chinese Politics in the Xi Jinping Era*.

16 "Communiqué on the Current State of the Ideological Sphere: A Notice from the Central Committee of the CCP's General Office," April 22, 2013, Document No. 9, chinafile.com/document-9-chinafile-translation, November 8, 2013, tr. Mingjing Magazine, authenticated by Asia Society's China File editors. Also Hongyi Lai, *China's Governance Model*, 60.

17 Donald Clarke, "Shen Kui and his Three Questions," lawprofessors.typepad.com/china_law_prof_blog/2015/01/shen-kui-and-his-three-questions.html, January 31, 2015.

18 Jeremy Wallace, "Is China's Reform Era Over?" For a different view, "Carl Minzner on the Shift to Personalized Rule in China," www.nytimes.com/2016/05/ . . . /china-carl-minzner-xi-jinping.html. Minzner, "China After the Reform Era," *Journal of Democracy* 26 (July 15, 2015), 129–43 says reforms were "born" in 1978 – a thesis which which I differ – but Minzner's later periodizations are interesting. He claims reforms were "constrained" in 1989–2003, "stagnated" in 2003–12, and now are "unwinding" since 2012. Anyway, changes have not been homogeneous over time, and "reform" is no longer the word to describe them.

19 Vilfredo Pareto, *The Rise and Fall of Elites*, or *The Other Pareto*, Placido and Gillian Bucolo, tr. and eds. (New York: St. Martin's, 1980), shows these two opposite functional needs of

370 Epilogue

a resilient elite, saying "lions" and "foxes" will coexist and circulate in any healthy polity. Pareto takes animal metaphors from Niccolò Machiavelli; see *The Prince* (New York: Mentor, 1952), chapter 18. Machiavelli took them from Cicero, who was mainly interested in their bestiality. Neither conservatives nor reformers will disappear from politics. Policies of constricting (*shou*) have alternated with policies of liberating (*fang*) for many years. Even if there is a very strong swing to conservatism, as is possible in coming years, this creative country may later revert to liberation for many people.

INDEX

Note: Page numbers in bold indicate a table on the corresponding page.

accumulation tax (*leijin shui*) 137, 224
adjustment meetings (*tiaoji hui*) 106
Agricultural Bank of China 76
agricultural workers 345–347
agricultural-industrial contracts 25–27
agricultural involution 9
agricultural machinery 4–5
agricultural technology 17, 359
"Agriculture is the root" slogan 2
allocation and distribution relations
(*diaopo yu fenpei guanxi*) 233
autocracies 27, 367
autonomy: countryside leaders 3–7;
enterprises 198; labor bosses 345;
local management of collectives 43;
management autonomy 300; municipal
governments 273–274; practical
managers 83–84; supervisors 228

back alley loans 238
bank anemia (*yinhang pinxue zheng*) 238
bankers, credit, savings and depreciation:
bonds 239–240; boom and bust fever
245–249; budgetary/extrabudgetary
investments 220–221; credit links with
jobs/personnel 229–230; deposits and
loans 227, **227**, 234–239, **235**, **236**, **237**;
depreciation 221–223; independent
official banks 233–234; introduction to
219–220; investment fever 242–244;

localist credit 228–229; modifications
in banks 230–232, **233**; regulations
240–241; rural money markets 241;
short-term credit 240; state investment
and profit retention 223–225, **224**;
stocks/stock market 242, 244–245;
variegated borrowers 225–226, **226**
bank loans 225–227, **226**, 234–239, **235**,
236, **237**
bankruptcy 116–120, 195
Baoshan Steel Plant 150, 165
Bao Yugang 278
Bates, Robert 2
behavioral turning points 64–66
bigotry 144
biotech innovation 261–263
black market 307–308
Blecher, Marc 220
blindly flowing population (*mangliu renkou*)
358–359
boat people 51
bonds 239–240
boom and bust fever 245–249, 283
Bramall, Chris 12
bribery 206
brigade-run enterprises 40–41, 44
brigade sizes and centralism 23–25, **24**
Bright Daily 104
budgetary/extra-budgetary investments
220–221

372 Index

budgetary revenues *vs.* expenditures **135**
budget deficit: control of funds and
taxes 168–169; debates about imposts
169–170; economic growth and fairness
170–171; effects of inland competition
159–160; high-tax regimes 167–168;
introduction to 158–159; slippage 147,
164–166, **165**; state profits 160–164, **161**,
163; taxes/taxation and 166–167
business fee (*yewu fei*) 307
business tax (*yingye shui*) 137, 328
Butler, Steven 47

cadres (*ganbu*): cotton-purchasing cadres
207; economic cadres 278–280;
introduction to 2, 3–4; state cadres 72,
181–183, 278–280; in state corporations
278–280
Cangnan County 71
Cao Diqiu 50
Caohejing "*Hui gu*" ('Silicon Valley') 254
capital (*zijin*) 162, 256–257
capitalism 23–24
capital-output ratio 129–131
Catholics 51
cellular bargaining *vs.* overall planning
152–153
census data 67
Central China Economic Zone 298
Central Committee 65
centralism (centralist revolution):
agricultural-industrial contracts 25–27;
autonomy of countryside leaders 3–7;
brigade or village sizes 23–25, **24**;
decollectivization 11–15; efforts to
revive state agriculture 27–30; ex-field
hands and 7–8; fields to factories **20**,
20–23, **22**; introduction to 1–3; local
industrialization 30–31; opposition to
15–20, **17–18**
central stores (*zhongxin dian*) 175
Changjiao village, Changshu 25–26
Changzhou City Planning
Commission 295
cheap prices 94
chemical fertilizers 10
Cheng Li 367
Chen Peixian 50
Chen Yi 132, 139, 143, 336
Chenyuan Chemical Factory 118
Chen Yun 120, 299
Chiang Kai-shek 75, 351
child laborers 320–321
China Daily 28
China's Agricultural Bank 231
Chinese Academy of Sciences 281

Chinese Academy of Social Sciences 209
Chinese Communist Party (CCP):
collective/private enterprises 330;
corruption by 175; demographic changes
to 63–64; endorsements by 73; Enterprise
Law 195; introduction to 20, 21;
legitimization of 50; *Liberation Daily* 170,
243, 324; patriotism and 368; role of 114
Chongming County Agricultural Machines
Research Institute 5
Chuansha County **20**, 20–21, 50–51, 202
civilian business associations (*minjian hangye
xiehui*) 175
civilized units (*wenming danwei*) 324
Cleaning Class Ranks Campaign
(1968–1970) 65
closure and guardedness (*biguan zishou*) 256
closures 116–120
clothing styles 316
collective firms/industries 48, 49, 70,
183–186, **184**, **185**; *see also* service
providers and collective/private
enterprises
collective localization 26
collective offices (*jiti bangong shi*) 343
commerce administrative office (*gongshang
xingzheng guanli suo*) 326–327
commercial companies during reforms
321–323, **322**
commercial embassies and salespeople
282–283
common-aim networks 280–281
communalist ideology 15
Communications Bank 231, 233
Communist Manifesto 326
communists/communism 144, 175
Communist Youth League 57, 343
communities outside the system (*tizhi wai
qunluo*) 357–358
comparative migration 338–339
compartmentalized economy 129
compensation trade (*buchang maoyi*) 105
comprehensive economic zones 298
comprehensive sales team 41
confidential (*neibu*) 94
Confucius 365
Conservative Party 183
consolation team (*weiwen tuan*) 342
consortia of enterprises 276–278
construction teams (*jianzhu dui*) 28, 339
consumer goods 110
consumption-oriented industries 138–139
contract responsibility system (*chengbao
ziren zhi*) 194
contract systems 188–190, 192
control of funds and taxes 168–169

Index

cooperative links 274
cooperative processing points 102
cooperative work 201
Coral Knitting Factory 137
corruption *see* urban industrial corruption
cotton-purchasing cadres 207
countryside leader autonomy 3–7
county-level bureaucrats 82
credit in rural industry 71–75
credit links with jobs/personnel 229–230
crop innovation 14
Cultural Revolution: clothing styles
    after 316; economic connections 267;
    educated youths and 342; effects on
    governance 64, 65; hydroelectric power
    293; introduction to 2, 4, 7; localization
    and 176; official investment policies
    66; peak of violence during 94; policy
    violations during 14; private firms and
    322; resentment of Shanghai's role
    in 139–143, **140**, **141**; revolutionary
    regime 67; rural industries 39, 44, 46,
    49; rustication campaign 336; 'subethnic'
    community and 305; supervisory
    agencies 175; weakened monitoring
    offices in 24–25

daily use products (*riyong pin*) 206
Death of a Salesman (Miller) 285
decentralization 148, 188
decollectivization 11–19
democratization politics 365
Deng Xiaoping: decollectivization 16;
    economic development 128; Ningbo
    mobilization 278; reforms by 6, 65;
    "Sixty Articles" 15; southern tour
    restrictions 242–243; tour of the
    South 247
Dengyi brigade 23–24
dependent firms (*guahu*) 45, 58, 202
dependent households (*guahu*) and Kate
    Zhou Xiao 327
deposits and loans 234–239, **235**, **236**, **237**
depreciation 221–223
deregistration 328
dingti program 315, 336, 341
directive (*zhidao xing*) plans 178
discrimination 144
diseconomies of scale 6
Dongfang Township 25
Donnithorne, Audrey 129, 304

East China Chemical Engineering
    University 264
East China electric grid (*Huadong
    dianwang*) 286

economic cadres 278–280
economic cooperation zones (*jingji
    hezuo qu*) 297
Economic Daily 119, 170, 281, 330
economic depression 39
economic development 128
economic expansion 45
economic growth and fairness 170–171
economic liaison organizations (*jingji lianhe
    zuzhi*) 297
economic modernization 4, 13
economic planning 93–94
economism 17
economy of dukes (*zhuhou jingji*) 304
educated youths 342, 344–345
efficiency in urban industrial corruption
    210–213
eldest brothers in Chinese tradition 169
Electrical Machines Bureau 255
electricity usage 4–5
electronics innovation 261–263
Eleventh Party Congress 12
emigration growth 48
employment growth 317
energy-consuming factories 118
enforceable plans (*zhiling xing jihua*) 178
Enterprise Bankruptcy Law 116
enterprise freedom 189–190
enterprise groups (*qiye qunti*) 276–278
Enterprise Law 114
enterprise mergers (*qiye jianping*) 187
entrepreneurs 48, 70, 175, 176–178,
    278–281
ex-agriculturalists 30
ex-field hands 7–8
ex-peasant workers 337–338, **338**
exploitation of workers 67–71
external economies 131

Fabre, Guilhem 210
factory leadership 60–63, **61**, **62**
fake statistics 74
family-run shops 186
Federation of Trade Unions 281
fees for road upkeep (*yanglu fei*) 304
Fei Xiaotong 26, 44, 63, 69, 74, 87, 100
Fengxian County 44
feudal segments 304
field mechanization 3
First Ministry of Machine Building 101
fiscal slippage (*caizheng huapo*) 158–159
fish-farming brigades 14
five small industries (*wu xiao gongye*) 45
Five-Year Plan (1981–1985) 202, 236
Five-Year Plan (1986–1990) 151
Five-Year Plan (1991–1995) 200, 321

374 Index

fixed (*dingjia*) prices 94
floating (*fujia*) prices 94
floating population 352–353, **353**, 355
"Forever" bicycles 258
freed labor 5
free-market rice 307
free traders of Wenzhou 284
Fudan University 199
Fujian Province 104
functional system (*xitong*) 229

Gang of Four 6, 41, 47, 94, 139–140, 152
Ge Hongsheng 84
Gerwitz, Julian 101
Gini coefficient 171, 324
Golden Delta Entrepreneurs' Club 280–281
Golden Triangle Entrepreneurs' Club 279
government business management
    departments (*zhengfu hangye guanli
    bumen*) 175
grain ration certificates (*guliang zheng*) 350
grain storage 11
Granovetter, Mark 203
Great Leap Forward 15, 18, 38–42, 95,
    139, 229
Great Third Front (*da san xian*) 66, 101
Greenhalgh, Susan 75
green revolution 3, 38, 88, 359
gross domestic product (GDP) 131, 183,
    185, 366
gross value of industrial output (GVIO) 130
Guangming Daily 206, 279
Guanzi 175
guaranteed delivery contracts 97
guaranteed management contracts (*chengbao
    jingying hetong*) 191
guarantee system (*chengbao zhi*) 14, 192
guarantors (*baocheng ren*) 306

Haiyan Shirt Factory 73
Han Chinese 175, 269
Hangzhou-Ningbo-Shanghai cooperation
    294–297
Hangzhou Planning Commission 164
hawkers 319–321
heavy industry growth 64
heavy-industry/light-industry gap 139
heavy taxes 149–152
hepatitis and reforms 114–116, 148
Hertz, Ellen 255
hidden funds 220
higher level (*shangji*) offices 115
high-tax regimes 167–168
high-tech industries 159–160
Hirschman, Albert 170

horizontal (*hengxiang*) relations 267
horizontal liaison projects (*hengxiang lianhe
    xiangmu*) 297
horizontal liaisons (*hengxiang lianhe*) 293,
    307–308
hot commodities (*rexiao shangpin*) 179
household contracting 15, 26
household registers and ration controls
    350–351
housing reforms 109
Hua Guofeng 65
Huang, Philip 29–30
Huan Kuan 174–175
Huayang Commune/Township 50
Hu Jintao 128, 152, 367
Hundred Flowers (1957) 194, 336
hydroelectric power 293

identification cards (*shenfen zheng*) 350
illegal factories 44–50
illegal private traders 179
illegal reselling (*daomai*) 207
imperialism 292–294
implicit subsidies to cities 127–128
imposts debates 169–170
incentives of managers/owners 191–193
income tax (*suode shui*) 328
independent official banks 233–234
indicative planning (*zhidao xing jihua*) 115
individual enterprises 319, 323–326
individual transport households 306
Industrial and Commercial Bank 231
Industrial Economy Information Exchange
    Station 281
industrial energy shortages 111–112
industrial sector productivity 314–315
industry-agriculture terms of trade 106
inflation effects 153
information liaison stations (*xinxi lianluo
    zhan*) 281
inland competition 159–160
inland/international markets 257–260, **259**
inland poverty 359
inland workers to village collectives
    345–347
input factor crisis 93–96
International Corporation of Alameda 294
International Trust and Investment
    Company 231
investment fever 242–244

Jae Ho Chung 365
"J-curve" forms of migration 341
Jiangnan's disdain of Subei politicians
    143–145

Jiang Qing 219
Jiangsu Legal System News 238, 306
Jiangsu Party 46, 86–87, 144
Jiangsu rural industries 38–39, 66
Jiang Zemin 133, 144, 152, 167, 168, 219, 367
Jiaotong University 270
Jinshan Chemical Factory 165
Jinshan County 43
joint ventures 272–275
Jones, Charles 366
junked assets (*dai chuli liudong zichan sunshi*) 162

Kelliher, Daniel 13, 30
Ke Qingshi 50, 139
kingdom segments 304
Kunshan County 73

labor bosses 347–348
labor education camps (*laodong jiaoyu*) 267
labor exploitation 67–71
labor models (*laodong mofan*) 324
Labor News 355
labor sector productivity **315**
land and leasing 200–202
Langfang model 82–85
Lardy, Nicholas 129
large-scale bribery 206
Law on Agriculture (1993) 51
leaders and residents 357–359
lease system (*zulin zhi*) 194
Lee, Charlotte 21
Leeming, Frank 10
legal registry books (*hukou bu*) 350
Leninist appointment system 21
Leninist organization 64
Leninist promotion norms 127
Lewis, Arthur 130
liaison (*lianxi*) 278
Liberation Daily 103, 104, 107, 170, 243, 324
Li Chuwen 278
Light Industrial Bureau 285
literal power 116–117
loan links (*jiedai guanxi*) 233
local commerce/industry managers 194–198, **195**
local industrialization 30–31
localist credit 228–229
localization 176, 181, 210–213
local-political entrepreneurialism 88
local-run state factories 163
local/countryside talents (*xiangcun tiancai*) 10
local transport and trade 304–307

local *vs.* central profits 275–276
Lüthje, Boy 366

macroeconomic management 179–181
management autonomy 300
management operations (*jingying yunxing*) anxiety 192
managers: freedom of 198–200; incentives to desist from managing 178–179; migration and 348–350; responsibility system 177
managers' reform of rural industry: factory inefficiencies 66–67; factory leadership 60–63, **61, 62**; introduction to 57–60; labor exploitation 67–71; periodization and behavioral turning points 64–66; rural youths 63–64; self-capitalization by autonomous localists 75–76; technology, taxes, and credit 71–75
mandatory payroll deduction schemes 148
Maoists 6
Mao Zedong: centralizations by 239; criticism of 65; decollectivization 15, 19; economic rationality 219; grain storage 11; introduction to 2, 15; poverty strategy of 31; rural arrangements 26; socialist tax base 125; "Ten Great Relationships." speech 132
market broker 120
market economists 84
marketization in urban industrial corruption 210–213
Marxism 31, 49
MasterCard International 233
materials loans (*wuzi daikuan*) 284–286
materials shortages 102
McNally, Christopher 366
meeting shortages 105–107
Meilong Township 271
merger mania 186–188
migration and reform boom: comparative migration 338–339; educated youths 342, 344–345; end of residence controls 354–356; extent of 333–336, **334–335**; green revolution and 359; household registers and ration controls 350–351; immigrant lawless 356; immigrants' occupations and incomes 353–354; inland workers to village collectives 345–347; introduction to 333; labor bosses 347–348; leaders and residents 357–359; managers and police 348–350; permanent residents 352–353, **353**, 356–357; returns of rusticates 342–343; reverse rustication 340–342; suburban managers and ex-peasant workers 337–338, **338**

376 Index

migration data 67
Miller, Arthur 285
Ministry of Agriculture 86–87
Ministry of Electronics Industries 187
Ministry of Materials and Equipment 120
"Miracle" rice 3
model collectives (*mofan jiti*) 324
monopolistic structure 186
Moody's Investors' Service 234
mortality in China 4
"mother-in-law" supervising corporations
174–176, 189, 273
multi-faceted interventions (*duofang chashou*) 60
multi-village enterprise (*duozhen qiye*) 60

Nanchang County 46
Nanhui County 202
Nanjing Harbor Administration 294
Nanjing International Container Shipping
Company 294
Nantong County 70
national guarantee (*baogan*) system 168–169
national income (*guomin shouru*) 94
nationalism 1, 174
Naughton, Barry 129
negotiated (*yijia*) prices 94
neoclassical economic theory 212–213
neoliberal economists 195
new sales channels 107–111
Ningbo Association to Promote Economic
Construction 278
Ningbo mobilization 278
nominal costs (*chengben*) 223
nonfarm jobs 30
non-educated rural entrepreneurs 119–120
non-monetary coercion 127, 136
nonpermanent registration of
immigrants 349
non-Shanghai interests 111
nonstate agriculture 29
nonstate plant closures 119
non-use of budgeting **134**
North China Agricultural Conference 44
Northern Districts Agricultural Conference
(1970) 12
NPC Standing Committee 114

official investment policies 66
Oi, Jean 59
one crop producers (*danyi shengchan zhe*) 11
open recruitments (*gongkai zhaogong*) 343
Osnos, Evan 76, 367
out-contracting (*waibao*) 102
own capital (*ziyou zijin*) 224

ownership norms 175, 176–178
ownership rights in land 28
ownership systems 181–183

patriotism 107, 174, 368
peasant households 14
People's Bank of China 85, 228, 230–234
People's Construction Bank 231
People's Daily 104
People's Insurance Company 231
People's Liberation Army 132
periodization and behavioral turning points
64–66
permanent (*changzhu*) registration of
immigrants 349
permanent residents 352–353, **353**,
356–357
personnel retention 272–275
Petition Regulations and Budget Law
(1995) 51
Pharmaceutical Management Bureau 282
physical materials costs 108
planned market economy 120
planned prices (*jihua jia*) 100
plant epidemics 11
police and migration 348–350
police enforcement 127
policy violations during Cultural
Revolution 14
political links (*guanxi*) 182
political risks in industries 41
politics and collective/private enterprises
329–330
post-entrepreneurialism 136–137
post-Leap depression 18, 66, 317, 337
post-Leap famine 50, 88
prefectural (*di*) leaders 73
price-adjusted costs 99
private enterprises (*siying qiye*) 137, 325,
326–327; *see also* service providers and
collective/private enterprises
production capital (*shengchan zijin*) 162
production team enterprises (*shedui qiye*) 45
profit retention 223–225, **224**
promotion norms 127
property rights (*chanquan*) 177
protectionism 107
provincial (*di*) leaders 73
Pudong Chemical Factory 118

Qingcun Commune 40
Qingpu Catholic Patriotic Association 51
Qingpu County 24–25, 50–51, 81
Qingpu County Party Congress 81
quasi-capitalism 16, 67

Index 377

quasi-forced emigration 335
quasi-privatist economic legitimacy 323–326
quota management (*ding'e guanli*) 12

radicals 7–8, 175, 176–178
Railroad Ministry 321
ration controls 350–351
raw materials 96–100, **98**, 109
real wages, declines 112
reform deficits 158–159
reform politics: commercial companies during reforms 321–323, **322**; deficits 158–159; Deng Xiaoping 65; hepatitis and 114–116, 148; housing reforms 109; introduction to 2–3; rates of reform 50–53, **51**; rusticates and 271–272; standardization reforms 188; summary of 364–368; *see also* managers reform in rural industry; migration and reform boom
regionalism and trade: business relations 278; commercial embassies and salespeople 282–283; common-aim networks 280–281; consortia of enterprises 276–278; criticism by socialist conservatives 270–271; economic zones 297–299; entrepreneurs in company groups 278–280; horizontal liaisons against the law 307–308; imperialism 292–294; individual technicians 268–270; introduction to 267–268; joint ventures 272–275; local transport and trade 304–307; local *vs.* central profits 275–276; materials loans 284–286; personnel retention 272–275; planners and buttons 283–284; reform rusticates 271–272; regional market efficiency/ specialization **301–302**, 301–304; Shanghai Economic Zone 286–292, **291**, 299–301; state cadres 278–280
regional market efficiency/specialization **301–302**, 301–304
resales in large and small networks 206–208
Research Institute for Restructuring the Economic System 279
reserve capital (*chubei zijin*) 162
residential construction 82
responsibility system 16, 99, 177, **195**, 195–196
retail outlets (*menshi bu*) 194
reverse rustication 340–342
revolutionary regime 67
Roman Catholics 20
rural competition 2

Rural Enterprise Bureau 85
rural incomes 20
rural industrialization: illegal factories 44–50; introduction to 38–39; rates of reform 50–53, **51**; reforms 88; types of workers and industries 39–44, **40**, **42**; *see also* managers reform in rural industry
rural land contracting 15
rural leaders *vs.* urban planners: closures, subsidies, and bankruptcies 116–120; growth and exports 85–87; hepatitis and reforms 114–116; hiring, wages, grain 92–93; imports and new sales channels 107–111; input factor crisis 93–96; introduction to 81–82; meeting shortages 105–107; non-Shanghai interests 111; raw materials 96–100, **98**; rural industrial market 88; Shanghai investment inland 101–103; shortages 111–114
rural production brigades 23
rural residences 201
rural subsidiary products 127–128
rural youths 63–64
rustication campaign 336, 340–342

Schmalzer, Sigrid, and Joshua Eisenman 10
Schumpeter, Joseph 210, 212
scissors gaps 138
Seagull Foreign Trade Industry United Corporation 86
seasonal employment 70
secret file (*dang'an*) 70
seed changes 10
self-capitalization by autonomous localists 75–76
self-generated (*zichou*) funds 225, 235
self-sufficiency (*zili gengsheng*) 267
sent-down people 340
service providers and collective/private enterprises: commercial companies during reforms 321–323, **322**; dependent households 327; hawkers 319–321; individual enterprises 319, 323–326; introduction to 314–316, **315**; politics and 329–330; private enterprises 137, 325, 326–327; service subsectors 318–319; taxes in 328–329; youth employment 316–318, **317**
service sector productivity 314
service subsectors 318–319
Seventh Five-Year Plan 74, 187
Shanghai Academy of Social Sciences 159
Shanghai Association to Promote Ningbo Economic Construction 278
Shanghai Blanket Factory 179

378 Index

Shanghai Cigarette Factory 103, 149
Shanghai Clock Company 257
Shanghai Collective Enterprises Administration 116
Shanghai Construction Machinery Factory 243
Shanghai Coral Knitting Factory 329
Shanghai Cotton Textile Corporation 190–191
Shanghai Culture Research Institute 264
Shanghai Dalei Clothing Factory 188
Shanghai disease (*Shanghai bing*) 99, 114
Shanghai Dyeing Factory 112
Shanghai Economic Zone 196, 286–292, **291**, 299–301
Shanghai Electric Cable Factory 108–109
Shanghai Entrepreneurs' Club 281
Shanghai First Commerce Bureau 119
Shanghai First Electronics Bureau 296
Shanghai First Television Plant 297
Shanghai Flour Factory 149
Shanghai Handicrafts Bureau 95, 99
Shanghai Industrial Consulting Service Company 272–273
Shanghai industrialists 93
Shanghai Industries Technical Development Foundation 263–264
Shanghai Insurance Investment Company 233
Shanghai investment inland 101–103
Shanghai Joint Development Corporation 102
Shanghai Light Industrial Machines Corporation 296
Shanghai Light Industries Bureau 259
Shanghai Materials Bureau 108
Shanghai Municipality 102–103, 119, 305
Shanghainese language 269
Shanghai No. 10 Iron and Steel Corporation 190
Shanghai Paper Company 104
Shanghai Planning Commission 151
Shanghai Poultry Egg Company 207
Shanghai Production Materials Service Company 95
Shanghai Public Security Bureau 321
Shanghai Public Security Yearbook 343
Shanghai Real Estate Society 202
Shanghai Revolutionary Committee 6, 142
Shanghai Chemical Industries Bureau 118
Shanghai Science and Technology Association 264
Shanghai sickness 99, 114
Shanghai's Nanshi District Office for Educated Youth 342

Shanghai Solvents Factory 118–119
Shanghai Stock Market 242, 247, 255
Shanghai's Water Police 50, 207–208
Shanghai Third Steel Mill 178
Shanghai Vacuum Electrical Appliance Co. 243
Shanghai-Wusong Chemical Fiber Factory 278
Shangyu Refrigeration Company 270
Shanhuang brigade 23–24
Shaoxing County 46
Shen Kui 368
Shenzhuang Commune 43
shortages 111–114
short-term credit 131, 240
single crops 11
Sixty Articles (1961) 4
slippage (*huapo*) 114, 147, 164–166, **165**
slogans for rural industries 48
small treasuries (*xiao jinku*) 239
Smith, Richard 330
social charity (*shehui gongyi*) 320
socialist tax base erosion 125
social responsibility (*shehui fudan*) 180
social youths 49
soft budget constraints 116
Songjiang County 21–22, **22**
Southwest Economic Coordinating Association 297
sparking plan (*xinghuo jihua*) 264
specialized agricultural households 319
specialized companies for renting (*zuling qiye*) 203
sprouts of capitalism 23–24
standardization reforms 188
Star Brigade in Chengbei Commune 47
state agriculture revival 27–30
state cadres (*guojia ganbu*) 72, 181–183, 278–280
State Constitution (1982) 200
state extraction unevenness 143–145
state-fixed price differences 109
state-guided price (*guojia zhidao jia*) 100
state investment and profit retention 223–225, **224**
State Planning Commission 20, 153
state profits 160–164, **161**, **163**
stocks/stock market 242, 244–245
street-level enterprises 322, **322**
'subethnic' community 305
subsidies 116–120
substitution (*dingti*) program 49
"substructural" technology 31
suburban managers 337–338, **338**
Sunan model 85–87, 182

Sunday engineers (*xingqiri gongcheng shi*)
 268, 269
Sun Zi 198
supervising agencies 113
Suppression of Counterrevolutionaries
 campaign 174
Suqian County 72
surtaxes 329
Suzhou Prefecture 9

Taiping Rebellion 3, 334
Taiwan as formerly autocratic 75
Taixian woman 10
Takeuchi, Hiroki 158
talent pool for technical innovation
 255–256
Tangjiacun industrial growth 40, **40**
Tangqiao factories 41–42, **42**, 277–278
tax-and-profit extractions 67
tax collectors/collection in Shanghai:
 capital-output ratio 129–131; cellular
 bargaining *vs.* overall planning
 152–153; city comparisons **135**,
 135–136; city competition 137–138;
 consumption-oriented industries
 138–139; heavy taxes 149–152; implicit
 subsidies to cities 127–128; introduction
 to 125, **126**; justification of high tax
 131–133, **134**; post-entrepreneurialism
 136–137; state extraction unevenness
 143–145; state-owned industries 128; tax
 negotiations **145–146**, 145–149
taxes/taxation: accumulation tax 137, 224;
 budget deficit and 166–167; business tax
 137, 328; high-tax regimes 167–168; in
 high tech industry 254–255; negotiations
 over **145–146**, 145–149; in rural industry
 71–75; service providers and collective/
 private enterprises 328–329
Technical Recruiting Team 136
technological innovation for quality
 products: capital for 256–257;
 electronics and biotech 261–263; heavy
 development 260–261; high taxes and
 254–255; introduction to 253; loss of
 inland/international markets 257–260,
 259; talent pool for 255–256; think tanks
 263–265
technology in rural industry 71–75
temporary business licenses (*linshi jingying
 xuke zheng*) 320
temporary migrants 344, 348
"Ten Great Relationships" speech 132
ten Sunan Townships 27
think tanks 263–265

"Third Front" projects 129
three breakouts (*sange tupo*) 92
Three Gorges Dam scheme 66
Tian Jiaying 15
Tianjin Daily 104
Tobin, James 101
Tongxiang County 29
top-down politics 27
total factor productivity 66
tourism industry 318–319
tour of the South (*nanxun*) 247
town industries (*xiangzhen gongye*) 45
township and village enterprises (TVEs) 60,
 63, 100–101
Township Enterprise Administration 86
trade: compensation trade 105; illegal
 private traders 179; industry-agriculture
 terms of 106; local transport and
 304–307; *see also* regionalism and trade
traditional industries (*chuantong qiye*) 254
Transition to Socialism 186, 194, 317, 336
traveling salespeople 282–283
travel reception stations (*lüyou jiedai
 zhan*) 301
Tsai, Kellee 76
"turnpike" metaphor 131–132

unemployed (*daiye*) 319
Unger, Danny 76
unified receipts, unified expenditures
 (*tongshou, tongzhi*) system 180
unregistered floating population 352–353,
 353, 355
urban district corporations (*qu gongsi*) 175
urban industrial corruption: beyond
 illegality 204–206; collective industries
 183–186, **184**, **185**; competition,
 corruption, chaotic prices 203–204;
 contract system for state-owned industries
 188–190; correlates and estimates of
 208–210; freedom of managers 198–200;
 incentives of managers/owners 191–193;
 introduction to 174; land and leasing
 200–202; local commerce/industry
 managers 194–198, **195**; localization,
 marketization, efficiency 210–213,
 211; macroeconomic management
 179–181; managers' incentives to desist
 from managing 178–179; merger mania
 186–188; "mother-in-law" supervising
 corporations 174–176, 189; ownership
 norms 175, 176–178, 181–183; through
 resales in large and small networks
 206–208; urban land auctions 202–203;
 warehouse waste as production 193–194

380 Index

urban inflation 105
urban intellectuals 358
urban land auctions 202–203
urban planners *see* rural leaders *vs.* urban
  planners
urban/rural gap 139

variegated borrowers 225–226, **226**
vertical (*tiaotiao*) hierarchies 13
vetos (*foujue quan*) 181
village sizes and centralism 23–25, **24**

wage-based bonds 148
Wang Bingqian 170
Wang Hongwen 219
warehouse waste as production 193–194
Warring States period 196
waterborne trains (*shuishang lieche*) 305
water police (*shuijing*) 50, 207–208
Wenhui News 105, 257, 285, 329
Wenzhou Dongfang Furniture
  Factory 241
Wenzhou model 82–85, 323–324
Wenzhou money market crash 241
white slips (*baitiaozi*) 60
wholesaler corruption 208
women domestic workers 355
women factory workers 42
World Economic Herald 144, 169, 264,
  279, 304
World War II 4
Wujing Chemical Factory 118, 119

Wutang Township 72
Wuxi collective 225, 258
Wuxi County 43, 44, 45, 63, 72

Xianjiang Township 84, 85
Xi Jinping 128, 152
Xinmin Evening News 324
Xu Jiatun 46

Yangpu District Science and Technology
  Association 295
Yang Shangkun 151–152
Yangzi delta town construction 74
Yangzi Lumber Mill 180
Yantie lun (Discourses on Salt and Iron)
  174–175
Yao Wenyuan 50
Yao Yilin 166
year-end bonuses (*nianzhong jiang*) 112
Yuqi Township 25

Zhang Chunqiao 6, 11, 39, 40, 41, 47,
  49–50, 140, 142, 219
Zhao Ziyang 5, 12, 166–167, 298
Zhejiang CCP Committee 73
Zhejiang Township 27, 28
Zhenjiang Prefecture Building Materials
  Bureau 95
Zhongguo, defined 1
Zhou Enlai 6, 46, 92
Zhu Rongji 91, 128, 133, 138, 153, 248
Zweig, David 15